everybody's guide to the law

everybody's guide to the law

Fully Updated & Revised 2nd Edition

All the Legal Information You Need
In One Comprehensive Volume

MELVIN M. BELLI, SR. & ALLEN P. WILKINSON

Quill
A HarperResource Book
An Imprint of HarperCollinsPublishers

HarperCollins books may be purchased for educational, business, or sales promotional use. For information, please write to: Special Markets Department, HarperCollins Publishers Inc., 10 East 53rd Street, New York, New York 10022.

Designed by Oksana Kushnir

Author photo © 2003 by Steve Burns

Library of Congress Cataloging-in-Publication Data
Belli, Melvin M., 1907–1996
    Everybody's guide to the law / by Melvin Belli & Allen P. Wilkinson.— Fully updated and rev.
       p.   cm.
    Includes index.
    ISBN 0-06-055433-9 (alk. paper)
    1. Law—United States—Popular works.   I. Wilkinson, Allen P.   II. Title.
KF387.B38   2003
349.73—dc21
                                     2003047893

03 04 05 06 07 WBC/RRD 10 9 8 7 6 5 4 3 2 1

CONTENTS

ACKNOWLEDGMENTS

I would first and foremost like to thank John Radziewicz, whose belief in this book and my writing abilities has sustained me through the dark times as well as the sunny ones. I am proud to call him my friend; prouder still that he calls me his.

Special thanks are due Susan Agronick-Roth for her assistance with the manuscript. Thanks, too, to my agent, Daniel Bial, and to everyone at HarperCollins, especially my editor, Edwin Tan. David Bradlow's graciousness and cooperation was greatly appreciated.

Finally, a word of thanks to my parents for their loving support.

—A.P.W.

MELVIN BELLI
1907–1996

Melvin Belli was the last of a now bygone era of lawyers whose ranks included such luminaries as Clarence Darrow, Louis Nizer, and the fictional Atticus Finch and Perry Mason. In September 1979, approximately five weeks after taking the California Bar exam, I had the great fortune of going to work for Mr. Belli, whom *Life* magazine had crowned the "King of Torts" in 1954, a year before I was born. I was hired to help Mr. Belli revise *Modern Trials*, his landmark work on tort law, trial techniques, and demonstrative evidence. My office was in the basement, directly beneath Mr. Belli's. A spiral staircase connected our two offices, and I heard everything that was said in his office; that in itself was quite a learning experience.

During the first months of working for Mr. Belli, I kept a low profile, just doing my research and writing the best I could. After six months Mr. Belli took me into his confidence. Our relationship slowly developed into one of which I have often described as "father-son," but it went much deeper than that. Whenever he was bored or feeling a little low, Mr. Belli would struggle down the narrow, winding, wrought-iron staircase to my office, pull up a chair, and talk to me for an hour or two just to pass the time.

One of the best things about my relationship with Melvin Belli was that at least once or twice a week when he was in town he and I would go out for a two- or three-hour lunch by ourselves. Our lunches consisted of nonstop talk, discussions of the latest developments in the law, throwing out idea after idea; some would stick, others wouldn't. The best times, though, were when he had had a bit too much of the grape, and fondly and longingly reminisced about long ago cases and colleagues. He regaled me with stories of such famous and infamous clients as Jack Ruby, the killer of President John F. Kennedy's assassin, Lee Harvey Oswald; notorious "red light" murderer Caryl Chessman, who became a best-selling author while on Death Row; Muhammad Ali, who demonstrated the sincere depth of his Islamic faith and convictions when he refused Uncle Sam's call to duty, even though it meant losing his heavyweight title belt for several years while he was in his prime; tennis great and three-time Wimbledon champion Maureen "Little Mo" Connolly, whose promising career was halted prematurely at age 21 when she was hit by a truck; the controversial, brash, profane, brilliant comedian Lenny Bruce; the topless dancers on Broadway who were being harassed and arrested by the police for the simple act of baring their breasts; the outspoken Martha Mitchell; and mobster Mickey Cohen, among innumerable others.

Mel loved to talk about the early days, when awards were minuscule, and how he slowly got them raised. He told me about how he got a jury to award $5,000 to a client who had lost an arm when the highest verdict before that for a lost arm was $3,000. Then, in his next case, he won $7,500, then $10,000, for the same type of injury. Slowly but surely he managed to raise the amount juries were awarding so that his clients were adequately compensated for their injuries. I remember being at one seminar and the speaker said that every victim's lawyer should send 10 percent of their earnings to Melvin Belli, because if it weren't for his groundbreaking work throughout the years, they wouldn't be earning half of what they were.

The publicity in the last ten years of Melvin Belli's life was more often than not on the negative side, focusing on Mel's personal and professional turmoil and his deteriorating skills. What got lost is the tremendous contribution he made to the law over more than sixty years of practicing. For the many years he was at or near his peak, he was without a doubt the best trial lawyer in the country. He was the father of demonstrative evidence, the master of trial techniques, the dean of medical malpractice. During his lifetime Melvin Belli did more to help the underdog and raise public awareness than anyone else. He was the original consumer protectionist. Consumer advocates such as Ralph Nader owe Mel a great debt, as he was a lone voice taking on corporate America, trying to hold it liable for making faulty or dangerous products that killed and maimed innocent citizens.

Melvin Belli died on July 9, 1996, nineteen days short of his eighty-ninth birthday. He had practiced law for sixty-four years. One sad note is that Mel did not live long enough to see the tobacco industry finally brought to justice. He started battling the cigarette companies in the 1960s, claiming back then that nicotine was addictive and smoking causes lung cancer.

In the 1980s, after a particularly horrendous natural disaster had resulted in the loss of thousands of lives, one political cartoon depicted Melvin Belli, briefcase in hand, standing on the top of a mountain, with the words, "It's Melvin Belli to see you, Lord," booming across the sky. That's the kind of person Melvin Belli was. He didn't care who he had to sue or whose feet he had to step on to get justice for the little guy.

WHEN MELVIN BELLI and I were having lunch one afternoon in 1985 talking about projects we could do together, I came up with the idea for doing a consumer's guide to the law, much like a home medical reference guide; something the average layperson with a legal problem could consult to determine how serious it might be and whether he or she should try to take care of it himself or herself or whether a lawyer's assistance was necessary. Mel immediately liked the idea.

I did some research to see whether there were any similar books on the market and found several, but none of them did what I considered a good job; some weren't very comprehensive, while others were written in "legalese" rather than plain English. I reported back to Mel with about four or five books in hand and explained the deficiencies of each. Mel said, "Do you honestly think we can come up with a better book that will help people?" Without hesitating, I said, "Without a doubt," and went into a half-hour-long argument of why we could put together a book that would outshine everything on the market and be an invaluable legal resource to the average layperson. By the end of my presentation, Mel was leaning back in his chair, saying, "Okay, okay, you've convinced me. Now, do you think you can convince a publisher?" "I'm positive of it," I replied.

So I prepared a thorough proposal and three sample chapters and blindly submitted them to ten of the leading publishers. One publisher was interested immediately; the editor who would be handling the book and the head of the sales department flew in within two weeks to seal the deal. Little did I realize that that meeting would result in my forming a fast and lifelong friendship with the editor, a writing schedule that put me in the hospital briefly for sheer exhaustion, and a book that could still be found on bookstore shelves in paperback sixteen years after its original release date. (The enormity of this accomplishment can be appreciated only when you realize that the shelf life of the average book is only six weeks.) And what was extremely satisfying to me was that all of the book reviews were positive. "Well-written and clearly organized," "surprisingly readable, information packed," "an excellent piece of work" were just a few of the accolades the book received. One reviewer gushed that the book should be on everyone's bookshelf between Dr. Spock and *The Joy of Cooking*. I had done a tremendous amount of writing for the legal profession before this book, but the praise is muted.

We received letters from people who said they had had a problem with their landlord and showed them the page in the book that supported their view, and their landlord had backed down. That's what I wanted to hear. People all over the United States were contacting us saying they had a legal problem, it was addressed in the book, and they were able to use the information in the book to their advantage to settle the dispute favorably. I hope that you will have the same experience with this fully revised, updated, and expanded edition of the book.

Although the first edition of this book was praised as being comprehensive, I have added five chapters in this new edition, four of which were in their legal infancy when the first edition was written back in 1986. These chapters are: The Elderly (chapter 5); Gays, Lesbians, Bisexuals, and Transgenders (chapter 8); The Physically and Mentally Disabled (chapter 14); Computers and the Internet (chapter 15); and Visas, Immigration, and Naturalization (chapter 21).

USING THIS BOOK EFFECTIVELY

When you reach for this book, the chances are that you've got a specific legal question. You want an answer, and you want it now. With this in mind, we designed each chapter to be as self-contained as possible, with appropriate cross-references when useful. If you're interested in only one subject—automobiles, for instance—you can turn to that specific chapter and learn what you need to know about buying and selling a car, insurance, fighting traffic tickets, drunk driving, accidents, and other topics.

I recommend that you read the entire chapter pertaining to your inquiry, because it may point you in the right direction concerning other questions or problems you haven't considered but that may be lurking in the background. You should also consult the index at the back of the book, which will guide you to related subjects that may affect your situation.

You'll notice that we omitted the glossary of legal terms usually found at the back of a law book written for the layperson. This was not due to any oversight on our part, but because experience told us the reader refers only infrequently to such glossaries. More important, we felt that glossaries rarely provide adequate, understandable definitions and examples of legal terms and concepts. We opted instead to reduce the amount of "legalese" throughout this book in favor of plain English. And when we use a legal word or concept, we define it then and there, so you don't need to look it up in a glossary.

CAN YOU DO WITHOUT A LAWYER?

THE THRESHOLD QUESTION in a situation involving the law is whether you can "do it yourself" or whether you need a lawyer to advise you on your rights or to handle the matter for you completely.

With the help of this book, you may be able to take care of many relatively minor problems yourself by reading the appropriate chapter or chapters, then negotiating with the other person or filing your own lawsuit in small claims court (chapter 19). But if you find that it's more than you can handle, or if your case involves a large amount of money, possible imprisonment, or serious injury or death, then a lawyer is certainly required. (In chapter 24 you'll find practical advice on finding the right lawyer for your situation.)

Having this book in your home library is much like having a consumer's guide to medicine. Even with the medical guide, you wouldn't consider treating yourself for potentially serious problems. For some minor illnesses you may be able to treat yourself with over-the-counter drugs, rest, fluids, and the like. But there's always the danger that your illness is more serious than you think or that it may worsen. In that case you need a doctor to diagnose your condition and prescribe appropriate treatment.

The same applies to law. Only a lawyer can assess your complete "legal health," by investigating the facts, researching the latest developments in the law, applying his or her legal training and experience, and then advising you of your alternatives. A good lawyer can spot the jagged rocks that may lie below the waters of a seemingly simple dispute and can help you plan a course of action to avoid them.

Just as you have a family doctor whom you visit not only when you have a medical condition that needs attention but also for routine checkups to prevent medical problems, you should have a family lawyer to consult both therapeutically and preventively. You'd be surprised how inexpensive many legal "vaccines" are, especially compared to the costs of a legal problem that goes untreated too long.

This book can't take the place of a lawyer. One reason is that the law differs from state to state—often significantly—and your rights vary accordingly. For example, in one state you may have six years to file a lawsuit after you've been hurt, in another you may have three years, while in yet another you may have only one year. (And if the government is at fault, you may have to file a claim with the appropriate agency within as few as sixty days or six months of the incident.) Even adjoining states may have fundamental differences in their laws concerning divorces, wills, real estate law, and small claims court procedures. There simply isn't enough space in this book to provide a state-by-state rundown of every law discussed in the following pages.

Remember, too, that the law is in a continuous state of change. Every day judges are making new decisions and legislatures are passing new laws that affect your life. The advice a lawyer gives a client today may not be the same as the advice he or she might give a month or a year from now. A lawyer must always research the latest developments in the law to make sure the advice he or she gives today is sound and correct. And each case is different from every other case. To you, the layperson, a certain fact may seem unimportant. To a lawyer, however, that particular fact may make or break the whole case.

If you do find the need for legal counsel, read over the applicable material in this book before seeing the lawyer. This will make you more aware of the nature of the problem and your rights, enabling you to ask the lawyer the right questions and to better understand your alternatives. In short, a review of your rights will make you an "informed consumer" in selecting the right lawyer and getting your money's worth for any legal services rendered.

—ALLEN P. WILKINSON

Marriage, Divorce, and the Family

fAMILY LAW—sometimes called the law of domestic relations—deals with all aspects of your legal rights and obligations as they apply to the family unit. It covers a vast field: marriages, annulments, divorces, separations, domestic violence, premarital agreements, child support and custody, visitation rights, property division and alimony, adoption, name changes, child discipline, establishing paternity, living together, responsibility for damages done by other members of the family, and more. Just by reading this list you begin to see how broad and complex this area really is.

Family disputes involve strong emotions—emotions that can get in the way of rational thinking and reasonable settlements. When feelings of anger and revenge take over, we lose sight of reality, so it is important to keep our emotions in check as much as possible. If you find your emotions getting out of control, particularly where a divorce or children are concerned, do yourself a favor and see a family counselor or other professional immediately. The advice of a good family law lawyer is also recommended for most domestic problems.

GETTING MARRIED

Age Limits

All states have limitations on how old you must be before you can marry. In most states, both the man and the woman must be at least 18 years old to marry without parental consent. The exceptions: in Arkansas, the man must be at least 17, the woman 16; in Georgia, each must be at least 16; in Louisiana the man must be at least 18, the woman at least 16; in Mississippi, the man must be at least 17 and the woman at least 15; and in Nebraska, each must be at least 17. If you are under the prescribed age, you'll need the consent of your parents or court approval to get married. Parental consent is not required if you can prove that you are emancipated; that is, that you are living apart from your parents and are self-supporting. You may first have to obtain a court order declaring you emancipated, however.

There is no upper age limitation on marriage. Persons over 90, even 100 years old have entered into legally binding marriages, some to mates their own age, others to mates decades younger. Specific information concerning age and other requirements for a valid marriage, as discussed below, usually can be obtained simply by calling your local county clerk's office.

Whom You Can't Marry

You can't marry just anybody. First of all, except in Vermont (see chapter 14), your spouse-to-be must be a member of the opposite sex. Except for Vermont, "marriages" involving persons of the same sex are not legally valid, even if performed by a religious authority.

You can't marry certain close relatives. All states prohibit marriages between a parent and a child, grandparent and grandchild, great-grandparent and great-grandchild, brother and sister (including half-brothers and half-sisters), uncle and niece, and aunt and nephew. Many states also ban marriages between first cousins, and some bar marriages between a former stepparent and stepchild, a former father-in-law and daughter-in-law, and a former mother-in-law and son-in-law.

Suppose that first cousins wish to tie the knot, but the state they live in won't let them get married. So they go to a state that allows marriages between first cousins, get married there, and then come back to their home state to live. Will their home state recognize the marriage? Maybe not. Ordinarily, if a marriage is valid in the state in which it is made, all other states must recognize its legality. Some states, however, refuse to recognize a marriage if the couple's only reason for going to the other state was to get around the law. If you are thinking about going to another state to marry a first cousin (or other prohibited relative) and coming back to your home state to live, first consult a family law lawyer in your home state to see whether your home state will likely recognize the marriage as valid.

A person who is insane at the time of the ceremony is legally incapable of entering into the state of matrimony. The fact that a person is somewhat mentally retarded, however, does not necessarily mean that he or she cannot marry, but such a person must understand the nature of marriage, its rights and responsibilities.

At one time many states had miscegenation laws prohibiting marriages between persons of different races. The United States Supreme Court long ago ruled those laws unconstitutional, and marriages between persons of different races cannot be banned.

Formal Procedures before Marrying

Before you can get married, you must comply with certain legal requirements. You must complete an application to marry (available at the county clerk's office or marriage bureau) and pay a fee. All but four states—Maryland, Minnesota, Nevada, and South Carolina—require a blood test showing that you are free from venereal disease (usually only syphilis). Washington requires an affidavit that the applicant is not afflicted with any sexually transmitted disease. Many states have a waiting period of two to seven days between the time the marriage license is applied for and issued. In most states, you can marry immediately after receiving your marriage license. The license is usually good for only a prescribed time period, such as thirty days or six months. A marriage that takes place after the license expires is not legally valid.

The person who performs the ceremony must be authorized by law to do so—either a recognized religious authority, such as a minister, priest, or rabbi, or an authorized civil servant, such as a judge, justice of the peace, or authorized clerk. (Contrary to popular belief, the captain of a ship can't perform marriages.) The marriage ceremony normally must be witnessed by a set number of people (usually two). After the ceremony, the person who conducted it will fill in and sign the marriage license, then have the bride, groom, and witnesses also sign it. The newlywed couple is given the license. The person who performed the ceremony is ordinarily responsible for reporting the marriage to the county clerk's office or marriage bureau.

A few states have a procedure available to qualified couples that does away with many of the formalities, such as the blood test and the license. The couple must have been living together for a specified length of time and holding themselves out to the community as husband and wife. The couple can apply to the county clerk or clerk of the court for an "authorization for the performance of a marriage." After this is issued, the couple can be married by any person authorized to perform a marriage.

Common Law Marriages

Eight states—Alabama, Colorado, Iowa, Montana, Pennsylvania, Rhode Island, South Carolina, and Texas—and the District of Columbia permit a common law marriage to be made within their boundaries, which does away with many formalities, such as the license and blood test. (Another seventeen states recognize common law marriages but only if they were entered into before a certain date. For example, Georgia recognizes common law marriages made there if made before January 1, 1997. Idaho recognizes common law marriages made in that state prior to January 1, 1996. Common law marriages attempted after that date are not valid.)

How is a common law marriage made? A man and a woman who live together must agree to be married and thereafter present themselves to the community as husband and wife. The fact that a couple has lived together for a long time does not by itself mean that they have a common law marriage. They must intend to be married—both of them—and they must conduct themselves in public as being married. Referring to the other as "my husband" or "my wife," using a common last name, buying a house together and taking title as husband and wife, and sharing each other's earnings are all evidence of a common law marriage.

Suppose that a couple enters into a valid common law marriage in Pennsylvania, then later moves to Kentucky, which requires a formal marriage ceremony in front of an authorized religious or civil authority, a license and blood test, and such. Will Kentucky recognize the validity of the couple's common law marriage? Yes. So long as the common law marriage was valid in the state in which it was made, the other state must recognize its legality, even though it does not permit that type of marriage to be made within its borders.

On the other hand, suppose that a man and a woman attempt to enter into a common law marriage in Oregon, which doesn't recognize such a marriage, then move to Colorado, which does. Does the fact of moving to Colorado make the invalid marriage valid? No. The validity of the marriage hinges on the date and the place it was attempted or made. Since it was attempted in Oregon, which doesn't permit common law marriages, it is invalid from the start. However, although the move to Colorado does not validate the purported common law marriage, the couple can enter into a common law marriage in Colorado. Generally, though, the marriage is valid only from the date when it is made in Colorado and is not retroactive to when the couple lived in Oregon.

Bigamy

You can only have one spouse at a time. If you remarry before divorcing your current spouse or obtaining an annulment of the earlier marriage, you are guilty of bigamy. The second marriage is void from the beginning and is not made legal if you later legally terminate the first marriage.

Can you defend a criminal bigamy charge on the ground that your religious beliefs permit multiple spouses? No. Although the first amendment to the United States Constitution guarantees the free exercise of religion (see chapter 20), the courts have consistently held that while this gives you the absolute right to *believe* in any religious doctrines, the right to *practice* those beliefs can be restricted when there is an overriding social concern. For example, a person cannot defend a murder charge on the ground that his or her religion requires human sacrifice. The government cannot prevent a religion from teaching that you have a right to have as many spouses as you want. In the interests of society, however, the government can prevent you from practicing that aspect of your religion. Accordingly, the law ordains the rule of one man, one wife, and one woman, one husband, at one time.

PREMARITAL AGREEMENTS

A PREMARITAL AGREEMENT, also called an "antenuptial" agreement, is a contract a man and a woman enter into before marriage, a contract that governs their rights and obligations in the event of death or divorce. At one time, courts enforced only premarital agreements that covered the rights of the couple in the event one of them died. Premarital agreements that purported to set the couple's rights if they got divorced had no legal force or effect because of the belief that such agreements promoted marital disharmony and divorce. Today most, if not all, states will uphold a premarital agreement in either situation (i.e., death or divorce) if it meets some fairly rigorous guidelines.

Not everyone has to be concerned about premarital agreements, and some people need to be more concerned about them than others. For example, a young couple with no children from prior relationships, no assets to speak of, and no business interests, generally would rarely need a premarital agreement. But a middle-aged person with several children from a prior marriage, his or her own house, an established business, and other assets should seriously consider a premarital agreement.

What can be covered by a premarital contract? Anything you like. It can be as exhaustive or as short as you like. The typical premarital contract, however, does not cover such things as who takes out the trash and who does the dishes. Rather, it usually speaks to the end of the marriage, when the time comes to divide the property and determine the amount of alimony payments or even whether alimony should be paid at all. Sometimes there is a paragraph or two relating to the custody and support of any children that are born of the marriage. However, any provisions regarding children are not binding upon the court; the best interests and the needs and welfare of the child (discussed later in this chapter) are the deciding factors.

A court will enforce a premarital contract only if, before the agreement was made, both parties made a *fair and full disclosure* of all of his or her assets and other relevant information. If one party misrepresented the nature or extent of his or her property, the court most likely will refuse to enforce the agreement.

The agreement should by all means be in writing. State law usually requires this, and it also is the only way of ensuring that there is no dispute as to the terms of the agreement. The premarital agreement should be written in as simple English as possible, to prevent either spouse from coming back at a later date and saying that he or she didn't really understand the agreement and signed it only because everyone was pressuring him or her to do so.

It had generally been assumed by family law lawyers that a couple about to be married who were entering into a premarital agreement should each be represented by their own attorney, otherwise the party that was not represented by legal counsel could claim that the agreement was unfair. However, in a high profile case involving baseball star Barry Bonds, the California Supreme Court ruled that whether a party to a premarital agreement was represented by his or her own independent lawyer was only one of several factors to consider in determining whether the premarital agreement was valid.

Then budding baseball player Barry Bonds met his wife Susan (Sun) in Montreal in the summer of 1987. In November of that year, Sun moved into Barry's house in Phoenix, Arizona. In January 1988, the couple decided to get married, and to do so before the start of the baseball spring training season. On February 5, 1988, Barry presented Sun with a premarital agreement his lawyer had drawn up for him. The agreement provided that each party waived any interest in the earnings and acquisitions of the other party during the marriage. After the two signed the agreement, they flew to Las Vegas and got married the next day.

At the time the premarital agreement was signed, Barry had been in baseball only two years and was earning $106,000 annually with the Pittsburgh Pirates. Sun had worked as a waitress and bartender, and had expressed interest in going to cosmetology school and becoming a makeup artist for celebrities. However, she was unemployed at the time she signed the premarital agreement and did not work during the marriage.

On May 27, 1994, Barry filed a petition for a legal separation and later amended his petition to ask for a dissolution of their marriage (a divorce). The Superior Court judge awarded Sun $10,000 in monthly support for each of the couple's two children, and $10,000 in spousal support (alimony) ending on December 30, 1998. Sun also sought a division of the property the couple had acquired during the couple's six-and-a-half-year marriage.

As for the premarital agreement, Sun claimed among other things that she was Swedish and did not understand English very well at the time she signed the premarital agreement, and therefore did not comprehend its importance. She also asserted that she felt pressured and coerced into signing the agreement, as Barry had told her he would not marry her if she did not sign it.

The case went all the way up to the California Supreme Court, which, on August 21, 2000, held that the agreement was valid and freely and voluntarily entered into by Sun. The court held that Sun's lack of legal representation was only one factor to be considered in determining the validity of the premarital agreement. The court also held that Sun could have had the agreement reviewed by her own lawyer and also that she understood the nature of the agreement and therefore was bound by it. Consequently, the court concluded that Sun was not entitled to any of Barry's now quite substantial property.

This case is the law only in California. However, because many states look to California as a trendsetter, other states may reach a similar conclusion when faced with a premarital agreement in which only one party had an attorney. It is our recommendation, however, that if you are asked to sign a premarital agreement, you have the agreement reviewed by an experienced family law lawyer so you will know exactly what you are getting or giving up.

Many courts have refused to enforce premarital agreements in which either party waives his or her right to spousal support in the event of a divorce. It had always been assumed that the waiver of spousal support violated public policy, and therefore would not be upheld. In a ruling made the same day it handed down its decision in the Barry Bonds case, the California Supreme Court upheld a premarital agreement that waived spousal support in the event of a divorce. Both parties were well educated and each was successful in his or her own field. During the divorce proceedings, the wife challenged the premarital agreement on the basis that it violated public policy by waiving her right to spousal support. The California Supreme Court held that no public policy is violated by permitting the enforcement of a waiver of spousal support signed by two intelligent, well-educated persons, each of whom is self-sufficient in property and earning ability, and each of whom had been represented by an attorney when negotiating the premarital agreement.

ANNULMENTS

AN ANNULMENT IS A LEGAL declaration that a marriage never existed, that it was null and void from the beginning, that something at the start prevented the marriage from being valid. The difference between a divorce and an annulment is this: In a divorce a valid marriage is legally ended, while an annulment means that the "marriage" never existed in the first place.

At one time, courts could not make an award of alimony if an annulment was granted. Today many states permit the courts to award alimony and divide the property much the same as if a divorce were involved. A person has never been allowed to use an annulment to avoid his or her responsibilities toward a child born of the "marriage."

Grounds for an Annulment

We already have discussed four things that are grounds for annulment in most states: an under-age party; an incestuous marriage; bigamy; and lack of mental competency. Sexual impotency or physical inability to have sexual intercourse is reason for an annulment in most states, at least where the other person was not aware of it before marriage. Some states permit an annulment if one of the parties is a drug addict, a habitual criminal, or a prostitute. An annulment is available in some states if the woman was pregnant with another man's child at the time of the marriage. Failure to comply with all of the formalities of marriage (such as getting the blood test or marriage license) or remarrying before a previous divorce becomes final is also grounds for annulment.

Fraud is sometimes a sufficient ground for an annulment. Suppose a woman falsely tells her boyfriend that he has gotten her pregnant, and he marries her primarily out of a feeling of duty toward the nonexistent child. A court can annul the marriage because of the woman's deception. (If she honestly but mistakenly believed she was pregnant, a court usually won't grant an annulment when the truth becomes evident.) An example of deception that isn't enough to annul a marriage: A man tells a woman that he is a multimillionaire, has a villa in Spain, a château on the French Riviera, and so on. They get married and she soon learns that he is in fact an assistant French-fry cook at a local fast-food restaurant and has no money. In the eyes of the law, she married the man for the love of him, not for the love of his money, so it shouldn't make any difference how rich or poor he is. (Of course, she can file for a dissolution of marriage.)

In some cases, coercion or duress can be the basis for a court to grant an annulment. For example, if the bride's father threatens to physically harm the groom if he doesn't marry his daughter (a "shotgun" wedding), this is probably enough to get the marriage nullified.

Void and Voidable Marriages

Some marriages are void from the start; others are merely voidable. The distinction between the two can be critical. A void marriage can never be recognized as legal. A voidable marriage, on the other hand, can be annulled within the time limit set by law, but if not so annulled, it becomes valid.

A marriage between close relatives, such as first cousins in states that forbid such marriages, is void and can never be made legal. Similarly, if a person is married at one time to two people (bigamy), the second marriage is void and nothing can be done to validate it.

Marriages based on fraud or coercion are generally voidable. If you fail to take steps to annul the marriage within the prescribed time after learning that you were deceived or after the coercion ends, the marriage is recognized as valid. If you wait too long, the only way you can then get out of the marriage is through a divorce. The period of time in which you must file to annul a voidable marriage varies from state to state: anywhere from ninety days to four years after you learn of the ground for annulment. However, we strongly advise that once you discover facts that would give you grounds for an annulment of your marriage and you want out of your marriage, you contact a competent family law lawyer as soon as possible.

A marriage involving an underage person is voidable. The underage party must file for an annulment within the set period—before reaching the age of consent to four years after coming of age, depending upon your state's law—or this ground for annulment is lost. Likewise, a person who was mentally incompetent at the time the marriage took place has to file for an annulment within the time set by law once he or she regains mental capacity.

Who Can File for an Annulment?

Usually only a party to the marriage (that is, the husband or wife) can file for an annulment. Sometimes just one party can ask that the marriage be annulled. For example, if the marriage is between an uncle and niece, either could seek an annulment. But if an underage person gets married, only he or she can assert lack of age as a ground for an annulment. (If both were underage, then either can file.) If fraud or duress was the basis for the marriage, only the person deceived or coerced can ask for an annulment. If one person was impotent or physically unable to have sexual relations at the time of the marriage, usually only the other person can get the annulment. The one exception to this last example is the rare instance when the person did not know of the problem before marriage; either party can file for an annulment in such a case.

Occasionally, someone not a party to the marriage can ask that it be annulled. For instance, the parents of an underage bride or groom can ask the court to annul the marriage. If a mentally incompetent person got married, his or her legal guardian or closest relative can file for an annulment.

SEPARATION

You MAY WANT TO SEPARATE from your spouse for several reasons. Maybe you can't go on living with him or her, yet aren't emotionally ready to get a divorce. Or you may want to use the separation as a "trial divorce" to see whether you really do want a divorce. It is a sad fact that over eighty percent of couples who separate eventually gets divorced.

You can (but generally don't need to) obtain a court order granting a separation. A court usually can grant a separation only for the same grounds as those upon which a divorce is granted (discussed below). You can, however, separate from your spouse by mutual agreement for any reason, or no reason at all. A written agreement regarding spousal support (alimony), child support, custody, and visitation rights is always advisable and may even be required by state law to make the separation a "legal" one.

DIVORCE

A DIVORCE, OR "DISSOLUTION OF MARRIAGE," is a legal declaration that a valid marriage is now terminated. Except for the obligations ordered by the court—such as the payment of alimony or child support and child custody and visitation rights—the parties are no longer obligated to each other in any way. Once a divorce is final, a person is free to marry again without being guilty of bigamy.

Originally, divorces were allowed only if there was sufficient "fault" by one spouse—he or she did something so wrong that it essentially destroyed the marriage. Most states today permit divorces that are based not on any particular fault of the parties but rather on general incompatibility ("irreconcilable differences")—the parties simply can't go on living together. These are called no-fault divorces, or divorces by consent.

Some states with a no-fault system of divorce no longer call a divorce a divorce but rather refer to it as a "dissolution of marriage." (These states also have some other changes in terminology: alimony, for instance, is "spousal support.") The effect of a dissolution is the same as that of a divorce; it ends the marriage, divides the property, orders financial support for an ex-spouse and any children, and provides for custody of the children and visiting rights.

Divorces Based on Fault

The types of fault most commonly recognized as grounds for divorce are adultery, mental or physical cruelty, desertion or abandonment (usually for at least one year), nonsupport, gross neglect, alcoholism or drug addiction, impotence, insanity, and conviction of a felony (a prison sentence of at least one to three years may be required). One important ground rule: To obtain a divorce based on fault, the innocent spouse must be the one who initiates the legal proceedings; a person cannot go out and commit adultery, then file for divorce on the ground that he or she has been unfaithful. In some states, a divorce is available if the parties have been separated under a court order or written agreement for a specified length of time, ordinarily six months to two years, depending on the state.

Before no-fault divorces, adultery and extreme mental cruelty were the two most common types of fault alleged in divorce actions. The adultery often was staged or committed with the other spouse's approval. The "guilty" spouse usually would be caught in the act by the "innocent" spouse's private investigator, who always had just enough time to take several incriminating pictures for evidence.

Divorces based on mental cruelty frequently included testimony from friends, neighbors, and relatives, stating that they had heard one spouse verbally abuse or humiliate the other incessantly. The children might even be called to testify about general living conditions—the house was unsanitary, a parent was drunk every night—or about constant and heated arguments they overheard between their parents. Not infrequently, except for the children's testimony, much of the testimony was exaggerated, even completely fabricated, to ensure that the divorce would be granted.

No-Fault Divorces

In a no-fault divorce, you don't have to prove that your spouse has committed some sin or physically or mentally abused you. You need only to show that such disharmony has developed that the two of you are no longer able to live together, and the marriage is beyond repair. The buzzwords usually found in no-fault divorces are that "irreconcilable differences leading to the irremediable breakdown of the marriage" have developed. (Some states refer to it as an "irretrievable breakdown" of the marriage.)

The concept of no-fault divorce evolved for two primary reasons. The first was the realization that the courts should not force two people to live together if they could no longer get along. The second was the recognition of the emotional effect that "fault" divorces have on children. Children would, for example, be subjected to the trauma of being put on the witness stand to testify that they saw Mommy in the company of several men while Daddy was at work, or that Daddy started drinking the moment he got home and soon began slapping Mommy all over the house. A no-fault divorce is difficult enough for children to go through.

Does the development of no-fault divorces mean that fault is completely obsolete in states where no-fault laws are in effect? Not at all. Fault can still play an important part in determining the rights and obligations of the parties after the divorce. If, for example, the breakup resulted from one spouse's frequent belligerent conduct after drinking, that would be considered in deciding which spouse should get custody of the children.

Defenses to Divorce

Suppose that your spouse sues you for divorce, but you don't want one. Is there anything you can legally do to "defend," or prevent, the divorce? Defenses to divorce actions aren't nearly as important today as they were forty or more years ago, when divorces were harder to obtain. Defenses are only relevant in divorces based on fault. No-fault divorces are essentially undefendable: If one spouse wants a divorce, there isn't much the other can do to stop it.

In a fault divorce proceeding, if an innocent spouse forgives the adulterous spouse, the defense of "condonation" stops the divorce. Another defense is the assertion that the other spouse provoked the conduct complained of. The provocation must be sufficient to justify the wrongful act, however. For instance, a husband cannot justify an adulterous relationship because his wife refused to have intercourse with him one night.

At one time, a frequent defense was recrimination: The spouse who filed for the divorce was accused of being equally guilty of immoral or other wrongful conduct. If the wife asked for a divorce on the ground that, say, her husband committed adultery, the husband could defend the divorce on the basis that the wife herself had also committed adultery. Even if the husband agreed to get a divorce, some courts would not give the couple a divorce, since they were equally culpable. Holy wedlock became unholy deadlock. This made absolutely no sense, as the two people obviously no longer wanted to be married, and the marriage was beyond salvage. Today most courts simply would grant the divorce, end the couple's suffering, and let them get on with their separate lives.

When divorces were permitted only because of one spouse's fault, a couple who could no longer live together occasionally would agree that one of them should commit adultery so they could get the divorce. Unfortunately, if the judge found out about it, he or she would deny the divorce because of the parties' collusion.

Residency Requirements and "Quickie" Divorces

Before you can file an action for divorce, most states require that you live in the state for a certain amount of time, usually six months or one year. This type of law is designed to prevent a state from becoming a "divorce mill," a term applied to states that routinely grant divorces even though the person has lived there for only a few weeks.

As long as it was properly obtained and issued, a divorce obtained in one state is valid in all other states. Thus, a divorce obtained in Las Vegas, which has a short residency requirement before getting a divorce, is valid in all other forty-nine states and the District of Columbia. But if you get a divorce on an overnight trip to Mexico or some faraway exotic island, don't expect it to hold up in the United States, particularly if your spouse wishes to contest it. Before you go to another state or another country to obtain a divorce, you should talk to two lawyers—one in your home state, another in the other state or foreign country where you will be getting the divorce—to see whether the divorce will in fact be recognized as valid when you return home. If you think this is too expensive, rest assured that the expense will pale in comparison to the costs if your home state doesn't recognize your divorce. Also, the "quickie" divorce in a foreign country doesn't divide the property, settle issues of child custody, visitation, and support, or spousal support.

The Divorce Proceedings

The first step in obtaining a divorce is the filing of a complaint (or petition) for dissolution of marriage in the proper court, usually called the family court or domestic court. When the complaint is filed, the clerk of the court issues a summons for your spouse to answer the complaint. The summons is an official court document informing your spouse that a complaint has been filed against him or her and that some legal action must be taken by your spouse within a certain time (usually thirty days) or the court may decide the case against him or her. Your spouse must be served with the summons and complaint, which lawyers call "process" or "papers." Depending on the state, service of the summons and complaint generally may be made by a marshal or sheriff, a registered process server, an employee of the attorney's firm, or anyone 18 and over (19 and over in some states) who is not a party to the lawsuit. If your spouse cannot be found after a diligent search, you can ask the court to permit service by publishing the summons in a newspaper of general circulation.

Between the time you first file the complaint for divorce and the time the divorce becomes final (the procedure for which is discussed later), a number of things may require temporary or interim orders. For example, if children are involved, there should be a provisional order not only stating who gets custody of the children and how much child support the other spouse must pay, but also laying out exactly what rights the other spouse has to visit the children. An interim order should also be obtained regarding how much money one spouse is to pay the other spouse for support. All of these provisions should be part of the interlocutory (temporary) decree of divorce that determines the rights of each party until the judge enters the final decree of divorce.

If your spouse is bothering or threatening you, you should obtain a court order prohibiting harassment. This prohibits your spouse from calling you on the telephone, coming to your house, coming within, say, one hundred yards of you, or otherwise speaking with or annoying you. It also can prevent friends of your spouse from harassing you. If your spouse threatens to take all of the money out of your joint bank accounts or to give all of your property away, a court order can and should be obtained to prevent this.

Most divorces are uncontested. Usually your spouse will not file an answer or objection to the complaint because you—through your lawyers—will already have worked out a complete settlement concerning the division of property, spousal support, child support, and child custody and visitation rights. You will need to show only that your spouse was properly served with the summons and complaint and that there are irreconcilable differences that have led to the irremediable breakdown of the marriage. In a fault state, you may be required to briefly present the testimony of one or two witnesses to corroborate your claims of your spouse's fault.

If the divorce is contested, your spouse must file an answer denying the charges of the complaint and stating the reasons why the divorce should not be granted. Sometimes your spouse really does want to try to work things out; other times he or she is just trying to make things as difficult—and costly—as possible for you. The answer must be filed within the time limit specified in the summons (usually thirty days), or a default can be entered against your spouse. If you don't settle the dispute, a trial eventually will be held, and each of you will present testimony to support your contentions. Such cases usually are heard by a judge sitting without a jury. At the end of the trial, the judge will either grant or deny the divorce. If the divorce is granted, the judge will divide the property, decide who gets custody of the children, and rule on the issues of spousal support, child support, and visitation rights.

Even in no-fault states, there are frequently trials based not upon whether there should be a divorce or not, but rather upon the division of the property or who should get custody of the children.

Many states impose a waiting period between the time the complaint for divorce is filed and the time the divorce decree becomes final. This generally varies from twenty days to six months. A handful of states have a waiting period between the time the interlocutory decree is issued and the final decree is granted, and some states have restrictions on how soon a person can remarry after the final decree of divorce has been entered. (Remember that in any state, you cannot remarry until your divorce is final.)

Should You Be Your Own Lawyer

Because of the emotions involved, a lawyer is more important in divorces than in most other areas of law. Usually you are better off hiring a lawyer to handle your divorce rather than trying to do it yourself. One thing many people overlook is the fact that a lawyer will always first try to save the marriage if that is a real possibility. If the divorce is inevitable, however, and involves minor children, substantial assets, or disputes as to who gets what, by all means you should have an attorney on your side. (Your spouse should hire his or her own attorney, too.)

What about the low prices you see some lawyers advertising for a divorce? These prices are generally good only if you don't have any children or many assets and your spouse isn't going to contest anything. If your divorce involves more than merely filling out and filing a few forms, be prepared to pay more. Before you hire a lawyer—any lawyer—get a written estimate of the expected fees based on your individual situation.

Many people today are doing their own divorces, with the help of a do-it-yourself kit or a divorce assistance group usually made up of paralegals. The problem with most prepared kits is that they speak only in generalities and may not adequately address your particular circumstances. By law, divorce assistance groups made up of nonlawyers such as paralegals can only type out the forms and file them for you; they can't tell you what boxes to check or what words to use to fill in the blanks, as that would be the unauthorized practice of law. Many of these companies have an attorney available to assist you, but your cost likely will go up if you use his or her services. About the only time to use a divorce assistance company is if you don't have any children, spousal support is agreed upon, and you know how you're going to divide your assets. If you do decide to go with a divorce assistance company, make sure you get a written estimate that includes an hour or two of an attorney's time, as you may need to consult with the attorney or you may need the attorney to make a court appearance for you. This estimate will give you a more realistic appraisal of your ultimate cost.

One danger of a do-it-yourself divorce is that one party may come back to court a year or two later, asking that the settlement be modified or declared void because he or she didn't understand the agreement, and that it is unfair. Courts are more likely to accept this argument if the parties did not have separate attorneys advising them when the settlement agreement was made. Tax considerations are another important reason to stay away from do-it-yourself divorces when more than a nominal amount of property is involved.

If your spouse agrees to an amicable divorce, and you therefore plan on doing it yourself, try to sit down with your spouse before you file for divorce and work out your settlement agreement—every bit of it—put it in writing, and have your spouse sign it. If you can't do this now, forget about doing it yourself and hire a good family law attorney. Never do your own divorce if your spouse is going to contest anything—the amount of spousal support, the division of the property, custody of the children, or visitation rights.

Sometimes, to save money, a couple will agree to have just one lawyer handle the divorce. This should be done only if there are no children, no substantial assets, and no disputes as to the division of property or the amount of alimony or how long it is paid. If you do decide to use just one attorney, that attorney probably will tell you that he or she can really be the attorney for only one of you. A divorce is an adversarial situation, and an attorney can look out for the best interests of only one party. Before signing the settlement agreement, the other spouse should have an independent attorney review it.

DIVIDING THE PROPERTY

THERE ARE TWO PARTS to every divorce. The first part is the termination of the marital relation itself by court decree. The second part consists of dividing the house, cars, furniture, bank accounts, and other assets; providing for the payment of spousal support; and settling issues of child support, custody, and visitation rights. The division of marital assets is referred to as the "property settlement." The divorce and the property settlement do not have to take place at the same time. When the division of the property is disputed, the divorce is often obtained first and the property settlement worked out later, especially when one of the spouses wishes to remarry.

If the parties can't agree on how to divide the property, then a judge will do it for them. The manner in which the assets acquired during a marriage are distributed can differ greatly from state to state. Forty-one states and the District of Columbia are so-called "separate property" states, while the other nine states are "community property" states.

Separate Property States

Years ago, when a married couple divorced, who got what depended on where the money to buy each asset came from. Everything a spouse earned or received (such as gifts and inheritances) during marriage was his or her own separate property, and anything bought with those earnings was that spouse's separate property. It was that simple. If the family home was purchased with the husband's earnings, for example, it was his and his alone, and the wife had no claim to it.

Strict separate property laws frequently led to unfair results, so a new rule—equitable distribution—was developed to remedy this imbalance. Under the equitable distribution rule, the judge looks at the assets of the couple, the length of the marriage, and the contributions each party made during the marriage, and then divides the property in a fair and just manner.

If the divorce is granted because one spouse was at fault, the judge may adjust the division of the marital assets. For example, if one spouse was guilty of frequent extramarital affairs, the other spouse may get as much as 75 percent of the marital property and a hefty sum of alimony to boot.

Community Property Laws

Nine states—Arizona, California, Idaho, Louisiana, New Mexico, Nevada, Texas, Washington, and Wisconsin—have community property laws. In Alaska, a married couple can elect to have their property treated as community property by written agreement. Community property is split right down the middle, with each spouse receiving an equal share. Community property generally consists of everything owned or acquired by a couple during marriage. For example, the wages earned by one spouse during marriage are community property. If a house is bought with those wages, the house is also community property, and each spouse has equal ownership of that house, even if only one spouse worked during the marriage. Under community property laws, anything you own before you get married is your separate property, as are any gifts or inheritances you receive during the marriage.

The judge can divide only the community property; separate property remains the property of the spouse who owns it. In dividing the community property and awarding alimony and child support, the court can, however, consider the amount of separate property either of the parties owns.

Problems often arise when separate property is mixed with community property. In some cases, it is necessary for the parties' lawyers to hire accountants to track the history of an asset claimed to be separate property. For instance, a racehorse that one spouse claims to be a community asset may have been purchased by the other spouse with the rental monies from a house he or she inherited from a parent. By going through the financial records of the parties, an accountant may be able to discover (trace) just where the money came from.

ALIMONY

ALIMONY (OR "SPOUSAL SUPPORT") is money one spouse pays to the other to help support him or her after the divorce. If you don't agree with your spouse on whether spousal support has to be paid, how much should be paid, and for how long, a judge will decide for you. At one time, it was invariably the husband who wound up paying spousal support. Today, however, when both spouses have a working history the judge is less likely to award spousal support, or if it is awarded, it is less than if the wife had stayed home taking care of the kids for twenty-five years. Today, some men take on the role of primary caregiver for the couple's children, and they are entitled to collect spousal support until they are retrained and can enter the modern marketplace.

We normally think of spousal support in terms of monthly payments. But any other means of payment that the parties agree to or the court orders—such as quarterly or annual payments—is possible. Sometimes a spouse will accept a single, lump sum payment of spousal support and the bulk of the community property in place of future monthly support payments. When this happens, the other spouse should make sure that he or she is not giving away too much too fast in order to get out of an unpleasant situation.

How much spousal support will you get? There is no set formula for determining how much spousal support, if indeed any, must be paid in a particular case. The alimony may range from nothing at all to half of what the other spouse makes. The judge will look at all of the circumstances of each case before making a decision. Some of the factors the judge considers are how long the parties were married, how much money each earns, the number of children and their ages, whether one spouse stayed at home raising the children, the health of the parties, and how self-supporting each spouse is. Obviously, a forty-five-year-old woman who never graduated from high school and who has stayed home taking care of the kids for the last twenty years is not as readily employable and self-supporting as a twenty-five-year-old woman who has a master's degree in computer science with no children who has been working throughout a three-year marriage. A higher amount of spousal support often is awarded for the time a spouse is being trained for the current job market.

Another factor taken into consideration is the overall standard of living the couple enjoyed during the marriage. While most people have heard that the wife (or husband, if he was the primary caregiver) is entitled to be supported "in the manner to which she has become accustomed," it is rarely possible for either party to continue living in the same style after a divorce. Earnings that previously supported only one household must now be stretched to two. To allow either spouse to continue living in his or her accustomed manner could mean that as much as *70 percent or more* of the other's paycheck might have to be turned over. Except in cases of the very wealthy, a divorce will reduce both parties' standard of living for a while.

The judge may also consider the fault of the parties in determining spousal support. In some states, when a divorce is granted because of one spouse's adultery, that spouse cannot receive any alimony. And if an unfaithful spouse is required to pay alimony to the innocent spouse, the judge may take that misconduct into consideration and order larger payments.

The amount of the spousal support payments can be changed by agreement of the parties, or by the judge upon the request of either party, but only if he or she can demonstrate sufficiently changed circumstances. (Only court-ordered spousal support payments can be changed by the judge. If a property settlement agreement spells out the terms of spousal support, the court generally cannot modify it.) The spouse who is paying the spousal support frequently will ask for a reduction if he or she is out of work or disabled for a time, is demoted to a job that pays less, or retires, especially if the retirement is related to his or her health. A reduction in the amount of spousal support often is requested if the spouse receiving it begins earning substantially more money than before. The spouse receiving the spousal support usually has a harder time getting the payments increased. That the other spouse who is paying the spousal support received a raise or suddenly came into a great deal of money ordinarily is not a good enough reason for the court to increase spousal support. The spouse receiving the spousal support must show that his or her own situation has changed sufficiently to justify an increase in spousal support.

How long must spousal support be paid? For as long as the court orders (unless modified) or the parties have agreed that it should as part of their property settlement. Spousal support stops when the spouse receiving it dies or, usually, when he or she remarries. If the new marriage is terminated by an annulment, however, spousal support can be reinstated in some cases. This usually happens only if the marriage was void, not merely voidable, as discussed above.

Say, for example, that Tom and Jane get divorced, and Tom is ordered to pay Jane $1,200 a month for five years in spousal support. Two years later, Jane moves in with her boyfriend (but does not marry him). Does this affect Tom's obligation to pay spousal support? Spousal support payments end in some states if the spouse receiving the payments has been living with a person of the opposite sex for a certain period of time, such as thirty days. Other states apply the rule that if a man and woman present themselves to others as husband and wife, the ex-spouse's obligation to pay spousal support ends. One court ruled that signing a hotel register as "Mr. and Mrs." was sufficient to show that the couple presented themselves to the public as married, and accordingly cut off spousal support payments. In any event, if Jane is receiving financial assistance from her live-in companion, Tom's attorney may be able to persuade a judge to reduce the spousal support payments in light of this new support.

Suppose that your spouse has been ordered to pay you $800 a month in spousal support for ten years. What happens to the remaining payments if the spouse dies after, say, only five years? In many states, the obligation to pay spousal support ends with the death of the person who is obligated to make the payments. In some states, however, the obligation to pay future spousal support can be enforced against the deceased ex-spouse's estate. But if the person doesn't leave much of an estate, a judgment against it isn't worth the paper it's written on. If you will be receiving spousal support (and child support as well), you should insist that the settlement agreement require your spouse to maintain a life insurance policy insuring his or her life, with the proceeds payable to you. This way, if your spouse does die before fulfilling the entire obligation to you, you are protected. (This type of protection is usually available only if you and your spouse agree to it as part of your property settlement. A judge generally does not have the power to order a spouse to insure his or her life to guarantee alimony payments.) But this protection is worthless, of course, if your spouse lets the policy lapse. An experienced family law lawyer can prepare an agreement to prevent this from happening to you, such as by making you the owner of the policy and the one to make the payments on the policy, which expense is added to your monthly spousal support.

If your ex-spouse falls behind in making spousal support payments, your lawyer can obtain a court order requiring that the payments be made current. If the person has moved out of state, it is still relatively easy to enforce the delinquent support obligations through the Uniform Reciprocal Enforcement of Support Act. At a court hearing, the person will be given an opportunity to explain his or her failure to pay. If the court orders the payments brought up to date, and the person fails to do so, he or she can then be found in contempt of court and jailed. Although it is said that there is no "debtors' prison" in America, the fact is that many ex-husbands (and a few ex-wives) currently are spending time in jail for failing to make spousal support payments. The law relies on the technicality that the person is in jail not for failing to pay the debt, but rather for failing to comply with a court order. It's really just a matter of semantics, made necessary by the fact that it is unconstitutional to incarcerate a person for failing to pay a monetary debt.

Spousal support paid to an ex-spouse (or support payments made as part of a written separation agreement) can be deducted from the payor's federal income taxes if certain requirements are met, and the spouse who receives the spousal support generally must include the payments in his or her taxable income in the year received. Spousal support payments may also be deductible or includable on state income tax returns. The rules regarding the tax treatment of spousal support payments are too extensive to go into in any detail here. If you are paying or receiving spousal support, get a copy of I.R.S. Publication 504, "Tax Information for Divorced or Separated Individuals," from the Internal Revenue Service or visit a library for the latest rules regarding spousal support and other tax questions involving divorce. Note that while spousal support may be deductible from the payor's taxes and includable in the recipient's taxes, it is not this way with child support payments: Child support is neither deductible from the taxes of the spouse paying it nor includable in the taxes of the spouse receiving it.

CHILD CUSTODY, VISITATION, AND SUPPORT

BEFORE WE DISCUSS legal questions involving children and divorce, a few observations are in order: Too often, children become the pawns in a divorce, with one parent using them to hurt the other parent. One parent may try to convince a child that the other parent does not love the child or that the other parent is evil and wants nothing to do with the child.

The question of who gets custody of the children can turn into the fiercest battle during the divorce, even if one parent doesn't really want custody; that parent may just want to make sure the other parent doesn't get custody. Sometimes the parent who receives custody refuses to let the other parent visit the child, even though a judge has ordered visitation rights. All these tactics have a devastating emotional effect on the child.

It is vital to the welfare of the children that the parents put aside any hostile feelings toward one another and cooperate with each other as far as the children are concerned. Parents who find themselves using the children as weapons should obtain family counseling or other professional help.

Who Gets Custody of the Children?

Child custody is an issue only if both parents want custody of the children. If the parents can agree on who gets custody, the judge will almost always accept their decision without second-guessing it. Any understanding regarding custody of the child(ren) should be incorporated into the written settlement agreement. (However, any provisions concerning children are generally subject to court modification.)

Custody of the children used to be routinely awarded to the mother. The law presumed that the mother was in a better position to take care of the children. The father could get custody only if he could prove serious charges of immorality, child abuse, or neglect against the mother. Today the judge focuses on the welfare of the child: Is it in the best interests of the child to award custody to the mother or to the father?

A stable home environment is at the top of the judge's list in deciding what is in the child's best interests. A divorce is a major disruption in the child's life, and the judge will do everything possible to minimize that disruption. The parent who keeps the family house usually gets custody of the children, especially if the children have lived there for several years and attend school in the area. If no house is involved, or if the house will be sold, the judge will take into consideration how far from the area either parent plans on moving.

If more than one child is involved, the judge usually will want to keep the children together and therefore will award custody of all children to one parent. But if one child is considerably older than the other, the judge may give each parent custody of one child. If there is a boy fifteen years old and a girl only three, for example, the judge may well award custody of the boy to the father and the girl to the mother.

Will the parent be home enough to take care of the child? If the parent works long hours or at night, who will be home looking after the child? Will a young child be left alone for much of the day? Does a parent frequently come home drunk? The answers to these and other questions tell the judge which parent has the time and interest to properly care for the child.

The judge also will consider what types of people the child will be around. If the parent's friends are drug addicts or known criminals, the judge will think twice before awarding custody to that parent. Sexual preference of the parent may be considered by the judge but often is not the deciding factor itself. Judges have awarded custody to a homosexual father rather than a heterosexual mother where other factors dictated against giving the mother custody (see chapter 14).

Depending on the age and maturity of the child, the judge may ask the child which parent he or she wants to live with. The child's preference, however, is only one factor the judge considers; it alone is not controlling. The judge gives more weight to an older (14 and above) child's wishes than a younger child's desires.

If one parent left home one day, abandoning the other parent and the children, the judge will rarely award that parent custody, even if he or she admits to having made a mistake. Seldom is there sufficient assurance that that parent will not abruptly walk away from the children again.

When one spouse entered the marriage with children from a previous relationship, the stepparent does not have any claim to custody of those children. If, however, the stepparent has adopted the child, then the judge could award the adoptive stepparent custody of that child.

Sometimes neither parent is fit to take care of the child. This situation may arise where the parents are minors in high school or both are totally irresponsible. In such a case, the judge may award custody to the grandparents or to an aunt and uncle who are willing to provide the child with a stable, loving home. If no suitable relative can be found to take care of the child, and the parents are declared unfit, the child becomes a ward of the court and is placed in a public institution or foster home.

Once the judge has awarded custody to one parent, the other parent can return to court at a later date and present new evidence showing that the parent having custody is no longer fit to care for the children. Testimony of neighbors may establish, for instance, that young children are frequently left unwashed and unfed, and that their house is unlivable. The judge can then take custody away from one parent and award it to the other.

Custody orders frequently prevent the custodial parent from moving out of the county or state unless the court's permission is first obtained. A parent who violates such a court order is in contempt of court, subject to a possible fine or jail sentence, and even loss of custody. If the custodial parent's reason for moving out of state is legitimate, such as his employer has promoted him or her and the job requires a move out of state, the judge generally will allow it. But if the move to a new and faraway state is solely to keep the noncustodial parent from seeing the children, the request to move the children to a new state will be denied.

Many times the child custody battle will be resolved by awarding both parents "joint legal custody." Joint legal custody generally relates to decisions involving the child, such as those affecting which school the child goes to or medical and dental treatment the child receives. In joint legal custody, each parent has an equal say in these matters. Even so, one parent will have physical custody of the child most of the time. True joint *physical* custody, where each parent has physical custody of the child for six months of the year or alternate weeks, is rare indeed.

Visitation Rights

If you don't get custody of your children, the judge usually will give you reasonable visitation rights. Again, a judge makes the decision only if you and your spouse can't decide for yourselves about visitation. Visitation rights may consist of one night a week, every other weekend, one month during summers, and alternating major holidays (one parent gets the kids for Thanksgiving one year, say, and for Christmas the next year).

If your ex-spouse refuses to let you visit your children, have your lawyer call his or her lawyer, if he or she still has one; otherwise, your lawyer should call your ex-spouse directly. If that doesn't change your ex-spouse's behavior, you'll have to return to court to enforce the visitation order. This can be a costly procedure, emotionally as well as financially. To punish a parent for refusing to allow the other parent to visit the children, the judge might suspend all support payments until visitation is permitted. And if the custodial parent continues to refuse the other parent his or her visitation rights, the judge could well give custody of the children to the other parent.

If you feel that there is good reason to refuse your ex-spouse his or her visitation rights—you fear your ex-spouse will abduct the children, for instance—talk to your lawyer immediately. If your fears are justified, your lawyer can go back to court and ask the judge to terminate your ex-spouse's visitation rights or permit visits only if he or she is accompanied by a marshal or other law enforcement officer.

Grandparents' Rights

To many people, being a grandparent is an even greater joy than being a parent. Do grandparents have any rights to a continued relationship with their grandchildren after a divorce intervenes? Prior to June 5, 2000, the answer would have been a resounding "Yes." All fifty states have laws on the books recognizing and protecting a grandparent's right to visit his or her grandchildren in the event of a divorce.

All of these laws have been put into uncertainty with the United States Supreme Court's decision in *Troxel v. Granville*. In that case, an unmarried couple had two children. While the father was still alive, his parents (the paternal grandparents) had no problems visiting their grandchildren. However, after the father committed suicide, the children's mother wanted to restrict the visitation rights of the paternal grandparents to one day of visitation a month, with no overnight stays. The paternal grandparents wanted visitation rights of two full weekends a month, with overnight stays, and two weeks in summer.

The state of Washington had a law that permitted *any person* to petition a superior court for visitation rights *at any time* and authorized such visitation rights whenever visitation was in the child's best interests. The United States Supreme Court held that Washington's law was unconstitutional in that it was overly broad. The nation's highest court emphasized that the due process clause of the Constitution's fourteenth amendment protects the "fundamental right of parents to make decisions concerning the care, custody, and control of their children."

The Supreme Court held that the United States Constitution permits a state to interfere with a parent's right to raise a child only to prevent harm or potential harm to the child. The Supreme Court further held that the parent's decision must be given substantial weight. There was no allegation, the court noted, that the mother was an unfit parent.

Does the *Troxel* case mean an end to grandparents' visitation rights when a parent objects? The fallout from the *Troxel* decision will have to be sorted out in the next five to ten years. First, the decision was only by a plurality (four) of the Supreme Court's nine justices. A majority decision requires five of the judges to agree with the decision.

Second, the Washington statute was written very broadly, as it allowed "any person" to petition for visitation rights at "any time." Some of the justices who disagreed with the Supreme Court's decision contended that the plurality decision went too far in essentially abolishing grandparents' rights when it could have limited its holding to the ground that the statute was unconstitutionally overbroad.

Are grandparents' rights a thing of the past now? It appears that way, although we will only know by watching how the lower courts interpret the *Troxel* decision. Certainly we will hear more from the Supreme Court on this issue.

Child Support

The parties usually agree to the amount of monthly child support the parent not having custody of the children must pay as part of the settlement agreement. The settlement agreement should also spell out who pays for such things as medical and dental expenses, college, and automobile or health insurance for the children.

If the parents can't agree on how much should be paid for child support, the judge will order that a certain amount be paid for each child. Two factors determine the amount of the child support: the needs of the child and the parent's ability to pay. The needs of the child are defined as the necessities of life—food, clothing, medical care, and shelter. The amount of child support, whether agreed to by the parties or ordered by a judge, can be modified as the child's needs or parent's ability to pay change.

Unlike spousal support, which usually stops when the spouse receiving it remarries, the duty to support one's children usually isn't affected by either party's remarriage. The obligation to support a child ends only when the child reaches the age of majority—18 in most states, 19 in a few—or becomes emancipated (gets married or moves out on his or her own and becomes self-supporting). Another difference between spousal support and child support payments is how they are treated for tax purposes. As we have seen, spousal support payments ordinarily can be deducted from the taxable income of the spouse paying it and must be included as taxable income by the spouse receiving it. The paying spouse, however, cannot deduct child support payments, nor does the spouse who receives them on the child's behalf have to include them as income on his or her return.

LEGITIMACY AND PATERNITY

Legitimate and Illegitimate Children

A child born to a married couple is legitimate. One born out of wedlock or from a void marriage (such as an incestuous one) is illegitimate.

For years, the law cast a stigma on illegitimate children by treating them as second- or third-class citizens who had fewer rights than legitimate children enjoyed. Fortunately, as of today the courts and legislatures have realized that an illegitimate child is generally entitled to the same treatment as a legitimate child (although a few vestiges of the distinction still remain). For example, an illegitimate minor child now has a right to financial support from his or her biological father. If the father dies because of another person's negligence, the illegitimate child can bring a civil lawsuit against that person for causing the death of the father, something illegitimate children could not have done before. If workers' compensation benefits are given for the father's death, an illegitimate child gets to share in them. An illegitimate child generally shares in his or her father's estate when the father dies, provided the child can prove the fact of paternity.

An illegitimate child becomes legitimate when the child's parents marry. An illegitimate child also becomes legitimate if the biological father acknowledges the child as his in writing and accepts the child into his family. Once legitimized, the child has the same rights as other legitimate children.

Because of the stigma society once cast on illegitimate children, the law presumes that a child is legitimate if the parents were married at or near the time of conception or birth. For example, if the parents are married and living together up to ten months before the child is born, the law usually presumes that the child is born of that marital relationship and is therefore legitimate. This is true even if at the time of the child's birth the parents are divorced or the father is dead. In a few states, the presumption that a child born of a husband and wife who live together is legitimate is a conclusive presumption, one that cannot be rebutted by any evidence. The husband is the legal father of the child, even if the child's appearance clearly indicates otherwise. Some states let the husband prove that he could not possibly be the child's father by, for example, presenting DNA evidence that conclusively proves that he is not the father.

Proving Paternity

Why is the question of who is a minor child's father so important? Primarily because the mother and minor child can compel the father to assist in the child's financial support. It also goes to whether or not the child has any rights to inherit from his or her alleged father when the father dies. If the father openly admits that the child is his, then establishing paternity generally is not an issue. If you are the mother, you should have the father sign a statement saying that he is in fact the child's father, so if you ever need to go to court to get child support payments, the hardest task—that of proving paternity—will be taken care of already.

If the man disputes paternity, then a paternity lawsuit must be filed to prove that he is indeed the child's father. Sometimes the child's mother files the paternity suit of her own accord. In other cases, when the mother applies for public assistance, such as Temporary Assistance for Needy Families (TANF), the successor to Aid to Families with Dependent Children (AFDC), the agency usually will initiate the paternity suit in an effort to get reimbursed by the father for money advanced to support the child.

How is paternity proved in court? Until the recent development of new techniques, paternity was established through circumstantial evidence, such as proof that the couple had engaged in sexual intercourse—even if only once—near the time of conception. The child (or photographs) would be brought to court so the jury could compare the physical appearance of the child and the suspected father. Blood grouping tests would be performed also, but such tests could only rule out a certain class of blood types, such as men having type A or type B blood.

Other evidence that was considered: Did the man ever acknowledge that he was the child's father? Witnesses might have testified that they heard the suspected father refer to the child as "my son" or "my daughter." Letters and birthday and other cards from the father to the child would be used as evidence, particularly if the letter or card was signed "Dad." The father may also have acknowledged the child as his tacitly by letting the child live with his family and treating him or her as a legitimate child.

When blood typing was the standard and the test did not exclude the man suspected of being the father, the suspected father could try to defend the paternity action by proving that the mother had had sexual intercourse with other men around the same time as with him, and any one of them could just as well be the father. Since it was up to the mother to prove which particular man was the father, the judge usually would dismiss the case if she could not prove just which of the men was the true father. However, in one unusual case, the judge ruled that it was up to each of three men in such a situation to prove that he could not possibly be the father. If he couldn't, he had to pay a proportionate share of the child's support. So if there were three suspected fathers, none of whom could adequately establish that he was not the father, each "father" would then have to pay one-third of the child support payments.

Today, the most important tool in establishing paternity beyond doubt is DNA testing, which compares genetic markers between the alleged father and the child. Unlike older tests such as blood typing, which could serve only to exclude a man as the child's father, DNA testing is used affirmatively to prove that the man is in fact the child's father. If the DNA matches, the man is established conclusively as the child's father and has all the responsibilities (and rights) that go with fatherhood. DNA matching replaces the Human Leucocyte Antigen (HLA) test, which matched not only blood type but also tissue type and other genetic factors. Experts claimed that the HLA test was at least 98 percent accurate. A man whom the HLA test results pointed to as the father could succeed in his defense that he was not the father only by proving beyond any doubt that he was out of the state or was impotent (this was pre-Viagra) or sterile at the time the child was conceived.

Custody and Visitation Rights of an Unwed Parent

Unwed mothers generally are entitled to sole custody of their minor children. This is true even if the unwed mother is a minor living at home with her parents. Unless the father wants custody of the child, the mother usually doesn't need to go to court to get an order awarding her custody. If there is a custody battle, the unwed mother usually will get custody. But if she is physically or emotionally unable to care for the child, is a drug addict or a prostitute, the court ordinarily will award custody to the biological father, unless doing so would be detrimental to the child's welfare. In such a case, the judge may order the child turned over to children's services and put in a foster home or other setting.

If the mother refuses to let the biological father see the child, the father can get a court order granting him reasonable visiting rights. A judge might deny visitation rights if the father's interests in seeing the child are not sincere—if, for example, the purpose of the visits is to harass the mother rather than spend any time with the child—or if the visits are particularly disruptive and emotionally trying for the child.

ABORTION

IN THE 1973 CASE *Roe v. Wade*, the United States Supreme Court made one of its most controversial rulings: that a woman has a right to an abortion. In its decision, the Supreme Court broke the nine-month pregnancy term into separate periods of three months each. During the first three months (the first trimester) of pregnancy, the government—federal, state, or local—has no say in whether a woman can have an abortion. That decision is left entirely up to the woman, and the procedure left to the judgment of her physician and her. A state can, however, pass laws regulating the medical procedures under which an abortion must be performed during the second trimester. During the final three months, the third trimester, a state can prohibit most abortions. The Supreme Court found that at this point of development, the fetus is "viable"—capable of surviving on its own outside of the womb—and the government therefore has a recognizable interest in protecting its potential life. But if the pregnancy threatens the woman's life, a state cannot stop the woman from getting an abortion, even at this stage.

Roe v. Wade involved a number of complex issues—legal, medical, and moral—but the Supreme Court focused on whether a fetus is a "person" within the meaning of the United States Constitution. The Supreme Court concluded that the Constitution applies only to persons who have been born. (This conclusion is in accord with long-standing common law principles that distinguish between an unborn fetus and a child that is born alive.)

Roe v. Wade is probably the most contentious case ever decided by the United States Supreme Court. It brings out a strong emotional response, both for and against it. In 1992, the Supreme Court revisited the question of whether abortion is still legal and concluded that it is. Although the U.S. Supreme Court rejected the trimester approach of *Roe v. Wade* as "too rigid," the Supreme Court affirmed the principles behind *Roe v. Wade* and declared that a state law regulating a woman's right to an abortion is unconstitutional if it places an "undue burden" on the woman. The Supreme Court defined an undue burden as one that has the purpose or effect of placing a substantial obstacle in the woman's path to getting an abortion of a nonviable fetus.

In June 2000, the United States Supreme Court struck down a Nebraska law that prohibited late stage abortions. The Supreme Court held that the Nebraska law prohibiting abortions in which part of the fetus is pulled outside of the womb did not make any exception for the preservation of the mother's health. The high court also ruled that the law imposed an undue burden on a woman's right to choose a "D&E" (dilation and evacuation) abortion, thereby unduly burdening the woman's right to choose abortion itself.

Can the father of the fetus sue to prevent the woman from having an abortion? No. The choice to terminate the pregnancy is the woman's, and hers alone. Laws that require a married woman to tell her husband that she is going to have an abortion have been held unconstitutional. Laws that require the woman to wait twenty-four hours before having an abortion and to be given "truthful, non-misleading information about the procedure, the attendant health risks and those of childbirth, and the probable gestational age of the fetus," have been held constitutional.

Does a minor (a girl under 18 in most states, under 19 in a few) need the permission of her parents to get an abortion? In *Roe v. Wade*, the Supreme Court ruled that parental consent is not needed if the girl is old enough to understand the consequences of the abortion and can weigh the issues reasonably well. But if the girl is too immature, parental consent or court approval may be required. A law that requires a pregnant minor to obtain the consent of one or both of her parents to get an abortion but has no provision for judicial permission is unconstitutional. A minor has the right to seek judicial consent if her parents refuse to permit the abortion. Or the girl may bypass her parents altogether and go straight to a judge for permission to get an abortion.

The Abortion Pill

In late September 2000, the Food and Drug Administration (FDA) approved the use of the controversial abortion pill RU486, which gives women the option of ending early stage pregnancies with drugs instead of through surgery. The FDA approved use of the drug, marketed under the name Mifeprex (or mifepristone, its scientific name), through the first seven weeks of pregnancy. However, some doctors have stated that they will use the drug through the ninth week of pregnancy.

Mifeprex works by blocking the uterus from receiving the hormone progesterone, which prepares the uterine lining so that an embryo can implant itself and grow. The lining nourishes and maintains the development of the fertilized egg. Without the progesterone, the uterine lining breaks down and bleeds away. A second drug, misoprostol (already available as an anti-ulcer medication) is given two days later, which causes the uterus to contract and flush out the fertilized egg.

Use of the abortion pill is not a simple "take one time with a glass of water" procedure. The woman will have to make at least three trips to a doctor's office or clinic over two weeks. At the first visit, the doctor will offer counseling and a guide that explains how the drugs work and who is medically eligible, that is, is still in the early stages of pregnancy. If the woman is eligible, she then takes an oral dose of Mifeprex, consisting of swallowing three of the pills.

The woman returns to the doctor's office or clinic two days later to take the second drug, misoprostol, which takes hours to cause uterine contractions to expel the embryo. The woman may stay in the doctor's office or clinic during this period, or she may return home. The woman must then return for a third visit twelve days later so the doctor can make sure that the procedure is complete and there is no fetal tissue remaining in the uterus. Many women using the drugs will experience some side effects, such as cramping and bleeding. The bleeding may last from nine to sixteen days.

Using the two drugs—Mifeprex and misoprostol—together is effective in ending pregnancy in 92 to 95 percent of the women who take them. For those women for whom the drugs do not work, a traditional abortion is required. If the woman then decides not to have an abortion and decides to carry the fetus to term, there is a risk of birth defects.

ARTIFICIAL INSEMINATION, EGG DONORS, AND SURROGATE MOTHERS

Artificial Insemination

When a husband is sterile or otherwise incapable of fathering a child, the couple may opt for the medical procedure of artificial insemination, in which a woman is impregnated with the semen of a donor. If the husband consents to the procedure in writing prior to the artificial insemination, he is treated as the legal and natural father of the child. In some states, the written consent must be filed with the court or the Bureau of Vital Statistics. In the rest of the states, the couple keeps the written consent themselves.

About half the time the sperm donor is an anonymous stranger whose sperm is obtained through a facility commonly known as a sperm bank, or from a physician. (Some states have rather strict guidelines regarding the operation of sperm banks, while others are quite lax about it.) The other half of the time, the donor is somebody the couple knows, such as a relative or a close friend who agrees to provide the semen for artificial insemination. Many sperm banks and physicians perform artificial insemination on married women only. Single women, including lesbians (see chapter 8), may have a harder time finding a physician who will perform the procedure on them and often may attempt to do the artificial insemination themselves, using a male friend's sperm. In some states, however, it is unlawful for anyone other than a doctor—or someone working for a doctor—to perform artificial insemination. When sperm is donated through a sperm bank or physician, many states require that it be screened for sexually transmitted diseases, including HIV, the AIDS virus.

Be aware that there is a greater, more stable body of law when it comes to sperm donors who donate their sperm anonymously through sperm banks and physicians. Regardless of whether or not the woman is married, where the donor of the sperm is anonymous and a physician or someone working under his or her direction performed the artificial insemination, the donor generally is *not* considered to be the legal father of the child. The anonymous sperm donor cannot be compelled to provide any financial or emotional support for the child, nor does the child have a right to any of the sperm donor's estate when the donor dies. On the other hand, the donor usually has no right to visit the child, nor can he gain custody of the child. Indeed, most of the time the mother does not know the identity of the semen donor, nor does the donor know if a child was ever conceived from his semen. In the case of a married couple where the husband has consented to the artificial insemination procedure in writing, the husband normally is considered the child's natural father. If the couple should divorce at a later time, he cannot get out of paying child support by claiming the child isn't biologically his.

Sperm donors traditionally have been anonymous, and the sperm bank has kept their identities sealed. Some courts, however, have permitted certain discovery about the donor, especially his medical history. One case involved an 11-year-old girl afflicted with kidney disease. The girl's parents sued the sperm bank, claiming that the anonymous donor was allowed to give sperm even though there was a history of kidney disease in his family. The court held that the anonymous donor had to testify in the case as to his family's health history, but that his identity was to remain concealed to the fullest possible extent.

When a woman is artificially inseminated with the sperm of someone she knows, she is treading in murky waters. Even if she is married and her husband has signed a written consent to be the child's father, this is no guarantee that the sperm donor will not attempt to gain visitation rights to the child. In cases involving a minor child, the judge is more likely to ignore the written consent and look at the whole picture. There is very little law in this area to guide the judge. And if the mother is single, or gets a divorce, the biological father may sue for custody of the child or, conversely, may be required to pay child support. We cannot stress too much how important it is to hire a lawyer who specializes in this area to assist and counsel you. It may cost you a few dollars now, but that is preferable to losing the child to the donor in the future.

Egg Donors

When a couple (we'll assume they're married) is unable to have a baby because of a problem with the wife's eggs, they may wish to consider in vitro fertilization, in which another woman's healthy egg is fertilized by the husband's sperm, then implanted in the wife's uterus. The wife carries the fetus to term and gives birth to a healthy baby boy or girl.

One major question is, where do the healthy eggs come from? Some come from women who are already trying in vitro fertilization and have extra eggs. Others come from women who are donating the eggs out of the goodness of their hearts so an infertile couple can have a child. But a growing and disturbing trend is that some women, particularly college students and recent college graduates, are advertising their eggs for sale, and not at bargain prices. A five-foot-ten-inch blonde with a dazzling figure who is both a star athlete and a top scholar at a prestigious university may advertise her eggs as high as $80,000 to $100,000. Women with less spectacular qualifications may offer their eggs for $10,000 to $20,000.

Unlike the law as it pertains to anonymous sperm donors, there is very little law in the area of egg donors. For instance, who would be considered the child's "mother"? The wife in whom the fertilized egg was implanted? Or does the donor remain the mother? And by charging for her eggs, is she violating any laws prohibiting the sale of body parts? Further, is she making any warranty that a child born with her egg will inherit her stellar qualities, and can the buyers "return" the child to the seller if it is only average or has a "defect"? State legislatures will be looking into whether this practice should be regulated, or even prohibited. It goes without saying that before embarking on this alternative, you should seek the advice of a lawyer with expertise in this specific field.

Surrogate Motherhood

When the wife is unable to bear children, a couple may decide to have another woman impregnated with the husband's semen through in vitro fertilization and artificial insemination. Sometimes it is possible to impregnate the other woman (the "surrogate mother") with the fertilized egg of the married couple. You should consult an attorney who is experienced in this area to help arrange everything and prepare a written contract spelling out the agreement between the couple and the surrogate mother saying, most importantly, that after the baby is born, the surrogate mother must turn it over to the couple.

Suppose, however, that after the baby is born the surrogate mother decides that she wants to keep the child. Can the couple go to court and sue to force her to give up the baby? In this situation, courts do not apply the strict rules governing contract law. This is because although the written agreement to bear the child and give it up when it is born is a contract, the subject matter of the contract—a child—obviously involves more weighty considerations than, say, a car or refrigerator. The judge will look at all factors, including what is in the best interests of the child, before making a decision. If the judge does award custody to the surrogate mother, the married couple will most likely be awarded rights to visit the child. The judge may also order the surrogate mother to reimburse the couple for all medical and living expenses they paid in connection with the pregnancy and birth. And if the judge awards custody to the parents, he or she may well grant visitation rights to the biological mother.

Suppose that a woman is impregnated with the fertilized egg of the married couple, yet wants to keep the baby after birth? In such a case, the judge will usually rule that the surrogate has no right of custody to the child since there is no biological connection between the baby and her. Rather, the couple are the child's biological parents; it was *their* embryo that was implanted in the surrogate mother.

A number of states have laws making it illegal to pay the surrogate mother to be a surrogate mother. In those states, the couple may pay only her medical and living expenses and the like. Any excess paid to the woman for her services as a surrogate are unlawful. If you are thinking about surrogate parenting, you should seek the advice and counsel of a lawyer who specializes in this area.

ADOPTIONS

ADOPTION CREATES THE LEGAL relationship of parent-child where a person is not a child's biological parent. Three separate parties are usually involved in the adoption process: the child, the adoptive parents, and the child's biological parents or a public agency such as the department of social services. A lawyer may also be involved in many adoptions, especially private adoptions arranged by the lawyer or another person, such as a physician. Adoptions by single persons make up about 10 percent of all private adoptions and 20 percent of all agency adoptions. Homosexuals are prohibited in some states from adopting children (see chapter 8).

Someone who marries a person who already has a child may want to legally adopt that child as his or her own. If not, he or she becomes the child's stepparent for the duration of the marriage with considerably different legal obligations from those of an adoptive parent. In some states, a stepparent is not required to provide any type of support for a minor stepchild. In other states, the stepparent must support the minor stepchild while married to the child's biological parent. However, should the stepparent divorce the child's biological parent, the stepparent usually will not be ordered to pay any child support to an unadopted minor stepchild.

When a child is legally adopted, the adoptive parent takes on the same legal obligations toward the child as if he or she were the child's biological parent. The adoptive parent is not only responsible for the financial support of the minor child—food, clothing, shelter, education, and so forth—but also for the emotional rearing of the child: providing a safe and happy household with warm and loving support. If an adopted child is injured or sick, the adoptive parents are responsible for seeing that the adopted child receives proper medical care, and they are financially responsible for that care.

When they give up a child for adoption, the biological parents forfeit all rights concerning the child, including the right to visit the child. Conversely, the child generally loses all rights involving the biological parent, including the right to compel them to support him or her financially and the right to inherit from a biological parent who dies without a will. (A few states still let an adopted child inherit from its biological parents.) Instead, the adopted child acquires rights in and to the estate of the adoptive parents upon their deaths. Of course, the biological parents still could provide for the child in their wills or living trust (see chapters 3 and 4), just as the adoptive parents could expressly disinherit the adopted child in their wills.

How Adoptions Are Arranged

Traditionally, adoptions are arranged through an adoption agency operating under the auspices of the state or county. The public entity (if the parents are both dead or have been judicially declared as unfit to be parents because of abuse, neglect, or abandonment) or the biological parents of the child place the child with the department of social services or other appropriate state or county agency, which then takes over. The agency reviews its list of prospective parents, interviews likely candidates, does a home inspection, and otherwise conducts an inquiry to determine who is most suitable to be adoptive parents for the child.

Many states permit a lawyer to arrange for a private adoption directly between the biological parents and the adoptive parents, without the intervention of a governmental or other public adoption agency. The lawyer will make an investigation similar to the one the department of social services or other adoption agency would make to ensure that the prospective parents are well suited to care for the minor child. The biological parents sometimes desire to meet with the prospective parents before approving the adoption or at least to see some photographs of them and learn about their backgrounds.

In many states, licensed private adoption agencies can arrange adoptions also. Before using such an agency, always know with whom you are dealing. Check out the agency with your county social services department to see whether it is properly licensed, does not have a history of complaints against it and the like, to ensure that it is legitimate and aboveboard. There are a few disreputable agencies (and lawyers) that arrange adoptions for outrageous fees or make promises and don't deliver, then abscond with your hefty deposit. A private adoption agency can charge only those fees allowed by state law. If you suspect an adoption agency or a lawyer is charging an exorbitant fee (bearing in mind that adoptions can be costly in the first place), keeps stringing you along by repeatedly telling you a baby will soon be forthcoming when one isn't, or otherwise is engaging in questionable practices, you should consider contacting your local district attorney's office immediately.

The Adoption Process

Once the matchup is made (and this can take a long time, especially if you are trying to adopt through a public adoption agency), the parents who wish to adopt the child must file a petition with the court. This filing is done by your lawyer, whom you should be working with closely from the time you decide to adopt, whether it be through a public agency or through the lawyer himself or herself. The court that has jurisdiction over adoptions differs from state to state: In some states it's the probate court; in others, the surrogate court; in a few, the juvenile court; and in still others, the superior or district court. The court will set a hearing on the petition at which the judge will terminate the parental rights of the biological parents and approve or deny the adoption. The child's biological parents or legal guardian must be given notice of this hearing so they can oppose the adoption if they want. If a parent is unknown or can't be found, notice of the adoption proceedings usually will be published in a local newspaper of general circulation.

At the hearing, the judge, who should have a plethora of information before him regarding the biological parents, the adoptive parents (or single parent), and reports of the home studies, will question the prospective parents and other witnesses to determine the fitness and suitability of the prospective parents to take on the responsibilities of parents. In deciding whether a couple is fit to adopt a particular child, the judge takes into account their ages, health, marital status, religion, race, sexual orientation, and ability to provide the child with a stable environment. The adoptive parents do not have to be rich; they need only be able to provide the child with a loving and secure home, even if that home is a rented apartment.

Placement based upon race is one of the most controversial issues in adoption law. In the 1980s, there was a movement by the National Association of Black Social Workers to block transracial adoptions, believing such adoptions would ultimately prove harmful to the adopted child. As a result, several states enacted laws, and some public agencies adopted policies, requiring racial matching. However, because there is a disparate amount of African-American children available for adoption, these policies left many children bouncing from one foster home to another. Accordingly, in 1996, Congress passed a law that prohibits discrimination based on race in adoption placement.

Like race, placing children on the basis of religious compatibility can be a touchy subject. For instance, if the mother of the child is Jewish, she may wish to have her child raised in that religion rather than, say, a Catholic home. Some states permit religion matching when requested by the biological parent or where the prospective adoptive parents are of the same religion. However, courts usually find that religion is but only one factor to consider when placing a child with an adoptive couple, and looks at the whole picture and what is in the best interests of the child. The biological parent(s) are more likely to have a say what faith the child is reared in when the adoption is made through private channels, that is, through a lawyer, than one that is made through the public sector.

After the judge approves the adoption, in most states the child then lives with the adoptive parents for a probationary period, usually from six months to a year. At the end of this time, if no problems or objections arise, the adoption is permanent, the files are sealed, and a new birth certificate listing the adoptive parents as the natural parents of the child is issued.

If a Biological Parent Opposes the Adoption

What happens if a biological parent puts his or her child up for adoption, then has a change of mind? If the change of mind occurs within a specified time (for example, ten or thirty days to six months), generally the biological parent can get the child back. But if the biological parent(s) don't act quickly after being notified of a pending adoption and the adoption is approved, they probably won't be able to do anything about it.

An adoption generally cannot take place over the timely objections of either biological parent, even if the biological parents are unmarried. About the only way to proceed with an adoption in such a case is to bring a court action to have the biological parent who opposes the adoption declared totally unfit as a parent, so that any rights he or she has as a parent are legally terminated. For example, if the child's mother marries a man who wants to adopt the stepchild as his own natural child, but the biological father objects, the adoption cannot go through unless and until a judge terminates the biological father's rights after a court hearing. A judge will normally terminate a biological father's rights only if he has demonstrated absolutely no interest in the child and is objecting to the adoption in order to harass the child's mother and her new husband; if the biological father abuses the child; or if the child was the product of a casual relationship and the biological father never had custody of the child. The mere fact that the man who wants to adopt the child will make a better father than the biological father is not an adequate reason for taking away a biological father's rights concerning his child.

For further information on adoption, contact:

National Adoption Information Clearinghouse
10530 Rosehaven Street, Suite 400
Fairfax, VA 22030
(703) 246-9095
http://www.calib.com/naic

Adoptive Families of America, Inc.
2309 Como Avenue
St. Paul, MN 55108
(800) 372-3300
(612) 645-9955
http://www.adoptivefamilies.com

Council on Adoptive Children
589 Eighth Avenue, 15th Floor
New York, NY 10018
(212) 475-0222
http://www.coac.org
(An organization devoted to finding parents for hard to place children in New York; click on "Links to other sites" for a number of helpful nationwide resources.)

Finding Out the Names of the Biological Parents

In the typical "closed" adoption, the adoption agency, lawyers, and others involved in the adoption must treat the names of the biological parents with the highest confidentiality, and all documents, including the child's original birth certificate and all court records concerning the adoption are kept private ("sealed"). Even the adopted child frequently is thwarted in a search to find out who his or her biological parents are. A court order must be obtained to open the file, and this will be granted only if there is a good reason. A judge may order the file unsealed where there is an issue relating to the child's health, such as a medical emergency requiring a bone transplant from a biological relative. Today the trend is to permit adoption agencies and attorneys to release the biological parents' medical information and history, but no identifying information. Some states have passed laws that give the adopted child access to his or her adoption file when the child turns 18.

Several groups exist to help adopted children in their search for their biological parents, and sometimes they have success where the child alone has failed. Some reunions are happy; others are extremely unpleasant. An adopted child should seriously consider all of the possible consequences before beginning a search for his or her biological parents. One group that provides information on how to search and has a registry of names is the Adoptees' Liberty Movement Association, P.O. Box 85, Denville, New Jersey, 07834; http://www.almasociety.org. The National Adoptive Clearinghouse Information listed above also has information regarding searches for one's biological parent(s).

There are more "open" adoptions today than there were twenty years ago. In an open adoption, the identity of the adopted child's biological mother or father, or both, is not concealed from the child. Contact is permitted between the biological parent(s) and the adopted child. This contact may be limited to allowing the biological parent(s) to send Christmas and birthday cards and to receive periodic pictures of the child as he or she grows up. Or it may be more intensive, such as a written agreement giving the birth mother full-blown visitation rights of two weekends a month. Granting a biological parent visitation rights might invalidate an adoption, as the judge may conclude that the biological parent(s) never intended to relinquish all of his or her parental rights regarding the child. If you are planning on including the biological mother or father in the adopted child's life, you should do so only upon the advice of an attorney skilled in this area to avoid nullifying the adoption.

Does a Parent Have to Pay for Damage Caused by a Minor Child?

Must a parent pay for the personal injuries or property damage caused by his or her minor child? That depends on the circumstances surrounding the incident. Generally speaking, the extent of a parent's financial responsibility for damages or injuries resulting from a child's conduct is largely regulated by state law. Most states hold a person liable only for harm resulting from the child's willful misconduct; a parent is not liable for a child's mere carelessness or negligence (see chapter 10). Some states require the parent to pay for the personal injuries or property damage caused by the intentional, or deliberate, conduct of the child, but not for injuries or damages that are the result of the child's mere negligence. A number of states limit the parents' liability to property damage only and does not include personal injuries. Even when a parent is liable, there is usually a ceiling on the amount he or she must pay, generally ranging from $500 to $10,000.

Suppose a teenage driver is driving the family car and causes an accident. Are the parents/owners of the car liable for the damages? In states that have a "permissive user" statute (see chapter 2), the parents ordinarily are liable for all injuries resulting from the child's use of the family car. But in states without a permissive user law, the parents are liable for the minor's careless driving only if the child was running an errand for a family purpose, such as going to the grocery store at the request of a parent. In those states, the parents would not be liable if, say, the child caused an accident while on a date. (In any event, if you have a teenage driver in the house, he or she should be listed on your automobile insurance policy).

The discussion above relates only to the parents' liability when they themselves have done nothing wrong, when the injury or damage was completely the fault of their minor child. Sometimes when a child hurts someone else or damages another's property, the parents can be held liable for the damages if they were not supervising their child adequately. In this situation, the parents' fault is separate and distinct from the child's act. Let's say that Debbie takes her son Peter to a playground, where Peter picks up a branch and starts swinging it while Debbie looks on silently. Eventually Peter swings the branch such that it pokes another child in the eye, blinding that child in one eye. Debbie can be held liable for the medical and other costs incurred in treating the injured child, since she should have realized what could happen and therefore should have taken the branch away from Peter.

Can a Minor Child Sue a Parent?

At one time, a minor could not sue his or her parents for injuries the parent inflicted upon the child, even if the parent had acted with a deliberate intent to harm (for example, by throwing boiling water over the child). Today, in most states, a minor can sue a parent for injuries resulting from the parent's intentional wrongful acts. Many states also permit the child to sue if he or she is harmed by the parent's negligence (such as a failure to pay attention while driving, which results in a traffic accident). Adult children generally are permitted to sue their parents without any restrictions.

Why would anyone worry about whether a minor child can sue his or her own parent? Mainly because the cost of medical and other treatment is so expensive. The question of a minor's right to sue the parents is important because it determines who has to pay for these and other damages suffered by the minor child. If a minor child has no right to sue the parents, the parents must pay the bills resulting from their negligence—which can run into thousands of dollars—out of their own pocket. But if the law allows the minor to sue the parents, the parents' automobile liability insurance or homeowner's insurance usually covers the costs. If the insurance company refuses to pay the damages (by claiming that the injury wasn't the parent's fault, for example), the parent can be placed in the unusual situation of encouraging the child to sue him or her for purely economic reasons.

For a minor to file a lawsuit, a *guardian ad litem* must be appointed by the court to bring the action on behalf of the child. *Guardian ad litem* means guardian "for the suit." Usually a parent (but not the one the child is suing) or the legal guardian of the child is the *guardian ad litem*.

Can a minor sue a parent for not supervising him or her adequately—in effect, for not protecting the child from himself or herself? Usually not. For example, suppose that Hal let his five-year-old daughter Vera play unsupervised on the front lawn. Vera wanders into the middle of a busy street and is struck by a passing car. Vera cannot sue her father for failing to supervise her and keep her out of the street.

Now suppose that Jerry and his brother Jeff were playing cowboys and Indians. Using a bow and arrow his mother, Alice, had bought him for his birthday, Jerry shoots Jeff with an arrow, hitting him in the eye. *Jeff can sue* his mother for failing to supervise Jerry. Had a neighbor's child been injured rather than one of her own, Alice would have been liable for negligent supervision, so the law usually makes no distinction between Alice's own child and a neighbor's child in this situation. But if Jerry had shot himself with the arrow instead of his brother Jeff, many states would not permit him to sue his mother for failing to supervise him.

If a parent punishes a child and in so doing injures the child, can the child sue the parent? That depends on whether the punishment was "reasonable." Parents have the right to discipline their children reasonably. Spanking a child for misbehaving or sending him or her to bed without dinner one night is considered reasonable punishment. But hitting a child so hard that an arm is broken, or depriving a child of food and water for several days, are unreasonable. Holding a child's hand in scalding water is obviously child abuse. Vigorously shaking a child is a form of child abuse that can cause brain damage. When a parent exceeds the bounds of reasonable punishment, not only can the child sue him or her, but the offending parent may be criminally charged as well.

Suits Between a Husband and Wife

A while ago in the development of our law, you could not sue your spouse for injuries he or she inflicted on you, even if he or she acted intentionally to hurt you. For example, if a wife deliberately shot her husband and injured him, the husband could not bring a civil suit against her. (But it was different if the wife shot and *killed* her husband. Besides being criminally responsible for murder or manslaughter, she would forfeit all rights to inherit her husband's estate. This remains the law today.)

Most states have abolished the old doctrine of "interspousal tort immunity" and now hold that you can sue your spouse both for intentional acts and ordinary negligence, such as carelessness in the operation of an automobile resulting in your spouse's injury or death. A number of states, however, let you sue your spouse for intentional wrongful acts but not for injuries resulting from his or her mere negligence. As with suits by children against their parents, the question of whether one spouse can sue the other frequently determines who has to foot the bills for hospital, doctor, and other expenses—you or your insurance company.

Suing a Third Person for Injuries to a Family Member

If a third party (someone who is not a member of the immediate family) either deliberately or negligently injures a family member, the injured person can sue that person to recover damages. If the injured person is a minor child, the parents can bring an action for medical and other expenses they paid to have the child treated. If a member of the family is killed by a third person's intentional or negligent conduct, the surviving family members can sue that third person for the death. (In some states, the estate of the deceased person must bring the lawsuit.) The types of damages recoverable in a "wrongful death" action are governed by state law and usually include such things as lost wages, medical and hospital costs, funeral expenses, and loss of companionship.

If someone else injures your spouse, your spouse can sue for his or her own injuries, and if you witnessed the accident, you can sue in many states for your own emotional or psychological injuries, as discussed below. In many states, when your spouse has been injured by a third person's wrongful conduct, you are entitled to sue that third person for "loss of consortium," which consists of such things as comfort, companionship, society, affection, solace, and sexual relations. When a child is seriously injured, a few states permit the parents to bring an action for loss of "filial" consortium, but limits the recoverable damages to lost wages the child otherwise would have earned and other monetary losses. For instance, if a boy worked on his parents' farm, and they had to hire someone else to do the boy's work after he was injured by the carelessness of a third person, the parents could recover the wages paid to the hired hand who took his place.

Only a few states permit a child to bring an action for loss of consortium when a parent is severely injured. But if the parent dies, many states allow damages for loss of consortium as part of a lawsuit for the parent's death. For example, suppose that Victor is drunk and runs into Helen's car. Helen suffers extensive brain damage and is left a vegetable. In all but a handful of states, Helen's children cannot sue Victor for loss of consortium even though Victor's conduct has effectively deprived them of their mother. Had Victor's conduct resulted in Helen's death, many states would have permitted the children to recover damages for loss of consortium as an element of their wrongful death action.

Witnessing Injuries to or Death of a Parent, Spouse, or Child

A mother is watching her child play on the front lawn, when a car suddenly jumps the curb and runs over and kills the child. Although she herself was in no danger of being hit by the car, the mother suffers severe emotional shock from witnessing the accident. Without question, a suit can be brought against the driver of the car for the child's wrongful death. But can the mother bring a lawsuit against the car's driver for her *own* injuries resulting from the emotional trauma?

Many states allow the mother to recover damages from the driver under the doctrine of "bystander recovery." To recover pursuant to this doctrine, three items must be satisfied: (1) there must be a close familial relationship (usually limited to husband-wife, parent-child, and siblings) between the victim and the person who witnessed the incident; (2) the person who witnessed the event must have been located near the scene; and (3) the person must have witnessed the actual incident, not merely the results or learned about the accident sometime after it happened.

This last requirement has presented the greatest problem for persons seeking to recover damages for their emotional injuries when a loved one is hurt. Minutes, even seconds, become crucial in determining many of these cases. Clearly the mother in the example above who saw her child being struck by the automobile was a witness to the accident. But in one case, the parents and their daughter were leaving church services, and the daughter decided to ride home with a friend and the friend's parents. On the way home, her parents followed closely behind. As they rounded a curve, the car with their daughter in it went out of sight for a brief moment. Seconds later the parents found the car off the road, crashed into a tree. Although the parents arrived at the scene *before the dust had settled*, they could not recover damages for their suffering because they had witnessed only the result of the accident that seriously injured their daughter, and not the accident itself.

Witnessing an accident does not necessarily mean you have to *see* it. Hearing an accident or otherwise perceiving what is happening can be sufficient. In one case, a husband who was sitting in the car while his wife was taking groceries out of the trunk was allowed to recover damages for the emotional distress he suffered when another car ran into the back of his. Although he did not actually see the accident, he knew where his wife was in relation to the other car and realized what was happening to her.

Injuries to or Death of an Unborn Fetus

A fetus injured in the womb by a third party's wrongful act can bring a lawsuit against the wrongdoer for those injuries, but only if the fetus is born alive. For example, Mary is seven months pregnant when she is involved in an automobile accident caused by Rick's negligence. When the baby is born two months later, it is discovered that the child has suffered head injuries and brain damage in the accident. The baby, through its *guardian ad litem*, can sue Rick for these injuries.

But suppose that the accident causes Mary to miscarry, and the fetus is stillborn. Can Mary (and her husband, Chuck) sue Rick for the wrongful death of the fetus? Not in all states. Some states hold that a fetus, even a *viable* one—one capable of surviving outside the womb (usually starting around the seventh month of pregnancy)—is not yet a "person" under the state's wrongful death statute. If the child is born alive and lives only a few seconds, however, the child is considered a person, and the parents can thus sue the third person for the child's wrongful death. Of course, in cases where the accident causes death to the fetus, although an action for wrongful death of the fetus cannot be brought, the jury can consider the death of the fetus as part of the mother's damages.

Birth of a Defective Child

A forty-two-year-old woman becomes pregnant. Her physician does not inform her of the baby's risk of being born with Down's syndrome, nor does he suggest any diagnostic tests, such as amniocentesis, to see whether the fetus is normal and healthy. The child is born afflicted with Down's syndrome and the mother claims that if she had been informed of the defective fetus she would have had it aborted. Or, a Jewish couple of Eastern European descent consult a physician to see whether they are carriers of Tay-Sachs disease. The physician erroneously tells them they are not, and the couple decides to have a baby. The baby is born with Tay-Sachs disease, and the couple claim they would never have conceived a baby if they had known they were carriers. In each case, tremendous hospital bills and doctors' fees are incurred in treating the child, and other large expenses are paid for special care throughout the child's lifetime.

Do the parents have any recourse against the physicians? What recourse does the *child* itself have? These are difficult legal—and moral—questions, as they ask a judge or jury ultimately to weigh the difference in value between being born in a defective condition and not being born at all. Traditionally, the courts would not permit a lawsuit against a doctor, hospital, or laboratory in this situation; the reasoning was that the child suffered no damage, since life, even in a seriously defective condition, is better than no life at all.

However, some courts permit the parents and child to recover some damages in these situations. Only the extraordinary medical expenses and other costs incurred in caring for the child throughout his or her lifetime are usually recoverable. "Extraordinary" expenses are those over and above the costs of raising a normal, healthy baby. A few courts also permit the parents to recover damages for their own emotional distress from the birth of the defective child.

Unsuccessful Sterilization Resulting in the Birth of a Healthy Baby

Vivian has given birth to three children already and decides that that is enough. After the birth of her third child, she has her tubes tied. Eight months later, however, she discovers she is again pregnant and later gives birth to a healthy baby boy. Can Vivian sue the doctor for malpractice in performing the sterilization procedure, even though the baby was born healthy and normal?

A number of states permit the parents (or single woman) to bring a suit in such a situation. But the damages the woman can get usually are limited to the costs of the unsuccessful sterilization operation, the mother's pain and suffering during the pregnancy and birth, any medical complications she suffered, and the mother's lost wages. Recovery of the costs and expenses of raising the child usually are not allowed. In the few states that do allow the costs of rearing the child, the damages are offset by any benefits the parents receive from the child's aid, companionship, and comfort. In those states that allow this type of action, a lawsuit can be filed on behalf of the child to recover extraordinary medical expenses. Care must be taken to ensure that both the child and the parents do not each receive compensation for the same expenses.

Unlike a child who is born in a defective or impaired condition, a child who is born healthy generally cannot bring a suit against a physician based on the physician's negligence (medical malpractice; see chapter 11) in the performance of a sterilization procedure.

LIVING TOGETHER

Hundreds of thousands, if not millions, of couples are choosing to live together without benefit of marriage. Before the famous *Marvin* case, the law generally took a hands-off approach to those who "lived in sin." A woman could live with a man for twenty-five years, bear him two children, raise them, and keep house during that entire time, but if one day he told her to leave, there wasn't a thing she could do about it if she knew they had never been married. If title to the house, the car, and other assets were in the man's name, the woman generally would have no claim to any part of it.

Things were better if the woman had an honest belief that they were legally married, but for some reason the marriage wasn't valid. For instance, the woman may not have known that the man was married before and the final decree of divorce was never entered. Or the person who performed the marriage ceremony may not have had the legal authority to do so. In such situations, the law has always protected the innocent "wife."

The Marvin Case

In 1976, a new era in the treatment of unmarried couples was ushered in with the decision in the case of *Marvin v. Marvin*. In that case, Michelle Triola Marvin claimed that she had given up her career as an entertainer and singer to live with actor Lee Marvin for some seven years. Michelle asserted that in return for this, Lee orally promised that they would combine their efforts and earnings, and they would share equally in all property they accumulated. Michelle also claimed that Lee had agreed to provide for all of her financial support and needs for the rest of her life if she gave up her promising career to devote herself to him as a companion and homemaker.

In the *Marvin* case, the Supreme Court of California ruled that an express contract—one in writing and signed by both parties—between an unmarried couple is enforceable, except to the extent that it is based on the performance of sexual services. (To allow a person to collect on a contract essentially for the performance of sexual acts would be tantamount to endorsing prostitution.) If there were no express written contract, the court held that an oral agreement or tacit understanding regarding the property could be demonstrated by the parties' conduct. Even if no such understanding could be shown, one partner could still sue the other for the reasonable value of household services he or she had rendered—minus the value of any support received—if he or she performed those services in the expectation of a monetary reward.

Following the *Marvin* decision, a rash of so-called "palimony" suits were filed, some by the rich and famous, more by the anonymous of average means. These cases, mind you, are not being tried under traditional family law principles of marriage and divorce, but rather upon contract theories (see chapter 17). Sometimes there is an express written contract that sets forth the rights and obligations of each partner. More frequently, though, one partner alleges that the other partner orally stated that all money earned and property acquired during the relationship would belong equally to both partners, or that one would take care of the other for life in return for taking care of him or her now. Some of these cases based on an implied contract have been successful. More have been unsuccessful because of the difficulty of proving the existence of the oral agreement and its terms. And not all states have agreed with the *Marvin* decision.

Get It in Writing

If you are planning on getting into (or staying in) a relationship based upon your partner's verbal assurances that he or she will "take care of you" or will split everything he or she makes while with you, get it in writing and signed by your partner. Proving an oral contract of this sort is difficult, to say the least. Although Michelle Triola Marvin won her case before the California Supreme Court, it was sent back to trial to see whether she could prove the existence of an implied oral contract. She could not. The courts are aware of the potential for fraudulent claims and want some hard proof that there was in fact an agreement. Without a written document, the chances that you will win your case diminish greatly.

What should you do if your partner refuses to put the agreement in writing, perhaps telling you that there's nothing to worry about, that he or she won't go back on what was agreed? Think seriously about getting out of the relationship now. Putting a signature on a piece of paper is not an arduous task. If your partner refuses to do it, consider yourself on notice that, should disharmony develop and the two of you split, he or she will likely assert that no agreement to share money or property ever existed.

The agreement should be prepared by an attorney experienced in family law, one who can anticipate the types of problems likely to arise and who can protect you accordingly in the agreement. As with premarital contracts, you and your partner should be represented by separate attorneys. This will reduce the chances that either person will succeed later in claiming that the other partner took an unfair advantage or that he or she did not really understand what the agreement said.

Buying a House Together

An unmarried couple (or even friends) who are living together may decide to buy a house together for tax or investment purposes. Before you buy the house, both of you should sign a written agreement that spells out the amount of the down payment, how much of it each of you is paying, what percentage each of you will pay of the monthly mortgage payment, the property taxes, insurance, and utilities. The agreement also should provide for how the net proceeds from the sale of the house will be divided between you. (It's not a bad idea to have a lawyer prepare the agreement.) If you each plan to live in the house, the agreement should specify what rights each of you has if the other moves out. What happens, for instance, if you are transferred out of state or find it impossible to continue living with the other person? Some provision should be made to give one person the right to buy out the other at the fair market value, rent his or her share, or sell the house and divide the proceeds.

If you are buying a house, condo, or town home with someone else, it is important to consider how you should hold title to the property. Title to real estate is discussed in detail in chapter 6; however, briefly: if title is in only one person's name, that person can usually sell it whenever he or she pleases. If that person dies, the house goes to the person(s) designated in his will or living trust, and if there is none, to the next of kin (see chapter 3). If the property is in the names of both of you as joint tenants, the house automatically goes to whoever of you is the survivor. A provision in a will or living trust has no effect on property held in joint tenancy. If title is taken as tenants in common, then upon the death of either owner, only his or her share of the house is distributed according to the terms of his will or living trust or, if there is none, to his or her next of kin.

CHANGING YOUR NAME

Some people change their names because they have been the butt of tasteless jokes or ridicule. Others change their names because of marriage, divorce, or fallings-out with family. Many immigrants change their names because of the difficulty Americans have pronouncing or spelling foreign names. At one time in our history, immigration officials arbitrarily changed the names of many immigrants upon their arrival at Ellis Island or other ports of entry. Applications for United States naturalization still provide a space for a name change if the applicant so desires.

You are free to use any name you want, as long as you don't use the name for a fraudulent purpose, to confuse people, or to invade someone's privacy. When one man applied to change his name to "Peter Lorre," the judge found that he only intended to cash in on the reputation of the famous movie star and therefore denied the application. Another man tried for several years to have his name changed to "God," but was repeatedly turned down because of the confusion it might cause. He eventually was successful when he applied to change his name to "Ubiquitous Perpetuity God."

Although a person's name usually consists of a given name and a surname or family name, in some states there is not steadfast legal requirement that you have both a first and a last name. A number of people have legally changed their names to just one name.

A "name" is legally defined as "the distinctive characterization in *words* by which a person is known and distinguished from others." Several courts have refused to approve a change to a name consisting solely of numbers. For example, the Supreme Court of North Dakota refused to grant one man's petition to change his name to "1069." Undaunted, the man then applied to a Minnesota court to so change his name, but the Supreme Court of Minnesota also denied his request on the basis that the number was not a "name." A similar result was reached in California in the case of Thomas Boyd Ritchie III, who wished to change his name to the Roman numeral "III," pronounced "three." If Mr. Ritchie had decided to change his name to "Three," the judge quite possibly would have granted his petition.

How to Change Your Name

Most people believe that a legal proceeding is necessary to change your name, but this is not theoretically true. The law has long recognized the right to change your name without legal proceedings, so long as it is not done for an improper purpose or to confuse or mislead others, such as creditors. For example, Marsha Bonnet can change her name to Alice Jackson simply by referring to herself by that name, changing her name with the Social Security Administration and on her driver's license, credit cards, bank accounts, and the like. As a practical matter, though, many financial institutions and other agencies will not recognize the new name unless she has a court order changing her name signed by a judge.

To have a judge change your name, you will need to file a petition with the court. The petition must state your current name, age, and address, the name you wish to change it to, and the reason for the change. Ordinarily, after you have filed your petition for a name change, you must publish your request in a newspaper of general circulation for a specified period of time, such as once a week for four weeks. (The court clerk can instruct you how to go about this. Indeed, the local newspaper may be able to assist you in this matter.) A court hearing will follow at which the judge will review your file to make sure the request for a name change was published in the newspaper as required by law. The judge then will ask whether anyone in the courtroom has any objections to your name change. If there are none—and there usually aren't—the judge routinely grants the name change. About the only time a judge will refuse a name change in the absence of any objection is if the new name is obscene or utterly absurd. But a somewhat bizarre or humorous choice of name ordinarily will not prevent a judge from approving the change.

Changing Your Name after Marriage or Divorce

When a woman marries, her last name does not immediately and automatically become that of her husband. Rather, the woman voluntarily chooses to assume the last name of her husband, and continued usage of that name brings about the change. She changes her driver's license and notifies the Social Security Administration and her credit card companies of the name change. Of course, it is not necessary for a married woman to assume the last name of her husband, and many women—especially those who have careers—are choosing to keep their own last names for professional purposes. Other women use a combination of the two last names, linking them with a hyphen. Thus, when Thelma Howard marries Benjamin Jackson, she may refer to herself as Thelma Howard-Jackson. All of this is perfectly legal and doesn't require court approval.

When a married woman gets divorced, she often wants to reassume her maiden name. This can be accomplished several ways. One is simply to insert a provision in the settlement agreement or divorce decree that the wife shall henceforth be known by her maiden name. Another way is to go through a formal name change procedure. Or the woman can change back to her maiden name the same way she changed to her married name: simply by using it and changing her driver's license, Social Security card, credit cards, and so forth back to her old name.

Changing the Names of Children

By custom, children born of a marriage take their father's last name. Some parents hyphenate the child's surname with both parents' last names. On the other hand, children born out of wedlock often have taken on the surname of their mother, especially where the father is unknown or disputes paternity. Where the identity of the father is known and he acknowledges the fact of paternity, the mother may choose to use the biological father's last name as the child's surname.

In the case of a divorced couple, the children ordinarily keep the father's last name (providing they have been using that name until then), even if the mother has legal custody. The mother cannot change the last name of the children without court approval, which is usually granted only if the father has essentially abandoned the children or otherwise demonstrated absolutely no interest in maintaining contact with them.

Other reasons may compel a child's name change. For example, if the father is convicted of murder in a highly publicized trial, a judge will approve a name change to protect the child from the stigma its last name may carry. Names of children can be changed only if the father is notified of the requested change so he can appear at the court hearing if he wishes to challenge it. If the father is nowhere to be found, the judge will permit the mother to notify him by publishing the petition for name change and hearing date in a local newspaper.

TWO

Automobiles

*n*O SINGLE PRODUCT HAS had more impact on the law than the automobile. Millions of cars, trucks, Jeeps, sport utility vehicles, minivans, and other vehicles are purchased each year and driven billions of miles. Hundreds of thousands of Americans are killed or injured each year in automobile accidents, and many more are charged with various traffic offenses ranging from illegal parking to drunk driving to vehicular manslaughter. These and other automobile-related topics are the subjects of this chapter.

Some of the advice in this chapter may not be what you might technically call legal advice. There are consumer tips about getting the best price on a new or used car, for instance, or on avoiding being ripped off by an auto repair shop. We have chosen to include this material because it relates so closely to the best type of counsel: preventive legal advice. By following the suggestions in this chapter, you'll have a much better chance of later avoiding a messy—and costly—legal dispute.

BUYING A NEW CAR

NEXT TO BUYING A HOUSE, purchasing an automobile is the largest expense in the lives of most Americans. The average price of a new vehicle today is about $25,000. Several things besides the price should be considered in the purchase of every automobile. Probably the single most important factor is safety. The safer the construction of the car, the better your chances of surviving an accident, and with fewer serious injuries. Before buying a particular make and model of car, find out how safe it is by consulting car magazines or publications of consumer interest groups, which can be found in your local library or bookstore. Your insurance agent can also give you valuable information about which cars generally are safer than others.

Many safety defects have been found in popular makes of cars. Because of the gas tank placement and the designs of some cars, for example, the fuel tank may explode when the vehicle is rear-ended by another car. Some cars and trucks had automatic transmissions that could slip from park into reverse, resulting in the death of or injuries to persons passing behind the car or working under it. Other vehicles have a higher center of gravity, which makes them more likely to roll over, and some lack the strength to protect the occupants if the car lands upside down. The most recent widespread automobile-related defect is the alleged problem with hundreds of thousands of tires manufactured by Firestone and installed as original equipment on the Ford Explorer. The alleged defect caused the tread to separate from the tire and, with the popular sports utility vehicle's high center of gravity, resulted in a rollover of the Explorer. At least 101 deaths and thousands of injuries are claimed to have resulted from this occurrence.

Besides the safety factors of the car, you also will want to find out the costs of operating and maintaining it. The insurance rates for cars can vary drastically for vehicles costing about the same price. A two-seat convertible sports car, for instance, will have a much higher insurance premium than a four-door family sedan. The gas mileage you can expect from the car also affects operating costs. Don't rely too heavily on the EPA test results, as these are based on driving conditions in the 1970s and generally are higher than the mileage your car actually will get. Also consider routine maintenance in figuring your ultimate costs.

Getting the Best Price

Federal law requires the dealer to place on all new automobiles and light trucks offered for sale a schedule (the "Monroney sticker") showing the make and model of the vehicle; the manufacturer's suggested retail price (MSRP) for the base model; every item of optional equipment and its price; and the dealer's charge for transportation. The options may be part of a package or special model of the car. The Monroney sticker must also show the manufacturer's transportation charge, and the fuel economy for both city and highway driving. By law, the Monroney sticker must be affixed to the window of the vehicle and can be removed only by the consumer once the car or light truck is sold.

In addition to the Monroney sticker, many dealers will add an additional amount on top of the MSRP, especially if the model of car is popular. This is the Monroney sticker price plus the suggested retail prices of such dealer services or products as dealer preparation or undercoating. The dealer may also list such things as ADM (additional dealer markup) or ADP (additional dealer profit). Keep in mind that, except for Saturn dealers—who sell cars only at the sticker price—the sticker price on the car is ordinarily the starting point for negotiations. It is up to you to take it from there and get the lowest price you can. (And remember that, in addition to what you pay for the car, you will have to pay sales tax and license and documentation fees.)

Advice about getting the lowest price from a car dealer abounds, but the most important point to remember is always to shop around. Some say the best time to buy is when business is slow, such as on a rainy day, during Christmas time, or at the end of the month or quarter, when the sales force is trying to meet their quotas. Others suggest that you take care of the financing *before* you buy the car. Although car manufacturers may offer interest rates that are lower than those offered by banks, you'll usually make up the difference by paying more for the car. Many banks will preapprove a loan up to a certain amount, so you can negotiate the best cash price from the dealer. Especially attractive financing rates offered by dealers often require a larger down payment and a shorter time for repayment—with a corresponding increase in the amount of the monthly payments—than a bank loan. Compare bank and dealer loans to see which one your budget can handle better.

Does this sound familiar: A salesperson entices you by quoting a good price for the car you have fallen in love with. You are then taken to the sales manager's office, where you are told that the salesperson had no authority to make such an offer. (Car dealers generally do not give their salespeople the legal authority to enter into any contracts on behalf of the dealership; usually only the sales manager and his or her assistants can commit the dealer to selling a certain car at a specific price.) The sales manager then raises the price hundreds of dollars over what the salesperson quoted. Sales managers prey on people who have fallen in love with a particular car, people who let their emotions take charge and already see themselves driving home in their dream car. If this happens to you, offer to pay the sales manager the price the salesperson quoted you earlier. Tell the sales manager to "take it or leave it." If your offer is refused, show them that you can live without the car—leave the office. You will be surprised at how quickly the sales manager will follow you out and come down in price. If they let you go, they'll probably give you a call a day or two later, offering to split the difference. If they don't come after you, don't worry about it. Don't fall for the old "you'll never find another one like it" ploy. Chances are you will find a car that is just as good for a better price somewhere else.

Remember that in either a new or used car sale you have the ultimate power—the power to walk away. One thing not to do is to fall in love with a particular car, as hard as that may be. If the sales manager detects a glint in your eye or enthusiasm about buying that specific vehicle, you will be at the mercy of the dealership. Also, if you will be trading in your old car, experts say don't let the dealer know that until you have settled on a price for the new car. If the salesman asks you about trading in your used car, just say that you're not sure yet. Remember, though, that the better the deal they give you on the new car, the less money they will offer for your trade-in to make up for any lost profit.

Beware of Illegal Practices

Here are some illegal practices to watch out for: A dealer cannot advertise a car for sale if he or she doesn't have it, unless it is a new car and the ad states that delivery of the advertised vehicle has been promised by the manufacturer on or before a certain date. An automobile dealer cannot advertise one car, then attempt to substitute another. This is the old "bait and switch" game: You are lured to the lot by a newspaper ad or television commercial with an extraordinarily good buy, but when you get there the dealer switches to an older vehicle or one with fewer options than advertised (for the same price, of course) or substitutes another car at a higher price. The dealer must also tell you if a new car has been damaged, repaired, or repainted before you buy it. If you suspect any illegal or fraudulent practices, contact the fraud division of your local police department or district attorney, your state's consumer affairs department, and the Better Business Bureau. You may also want to contact a lawyer to take action on your behalf against the car dealer.

The Purchase Contract

An agreement to purchase an automobile is a contract (see chapter 16) and therefore must meet certain requirements to be enforceable. There must be an offer to purchase the vehicle, a timely acceptance of that offer, and the giving of something of value by each side ("consideration")—usually money in exchange for a car.

Thoroughly inspect and test drive the car before you sign on the dotted line and give the dealer your money. If there are any problems with the vehicle, have them fixed before you sign the contract. Unless the defect is minor, don't be talked into paying now and bringing the car back later. You have a lot more leverage before you hand over your check, so use it to your utmost advantage.

You usually make an offer to buy the car when you sign a purchase order or similar document. Sometimes the purchase contract is disguised and given a seemingly innocuous title. Read all papers carefully, and don't sign anything that refers to you as the buyer or says "My offer is $_____" unless you are prepared to buy the car then and there. If you're not ready to buy the car at the stated price, the best advice is not to sign anything. If the salesperson tells you that the paper he or she wants you to sign isn't a binding contract, respond that if it's not binding, then there's no need to sign it. Don't fall for the line that your signature is just a show of "good faith."

The purchase order normally contains words to the effect that your offer is not accepted and a binding contract not made until it is signed by the dealer or the dealer's authorized representative (usually the sales manager). The Statute of Frauds requires that if the price for the car is over a certain amount, typically $500, the agreement must be in writing and signed to be enforceable. This means that if the sales manager orally agrees to sell you a car over the telephone for a certain price to get you down to the dealership, you cannot hold him or her to it if you don't get the deal in writing. You can, however, report him to the Federal Trade Commission, state board of consumer affairs, the fraud division of your local district attorney, and others. (The Statute of Frauds is discussed in more detail in chapter 16.)

The purchase order should specify clearly the make, model, and year of the car, as well as the engine type, mileage, and the vehicle identification number (the VIN number). All options should be listed: air conditioning, power windows, tinted windows, AM-FM stereo with a CD or cassette player, special wheels or tires, and so forth. A complete description of the car and optional equipment is necessary to prevent the dealer from getting away with a fraudulent or deceptive practice, such as telling you that certain optional equipment has been added after the car left the factory when in fact it hasn't; that a used car is a new car or an older model is a newer model, or that a certain engine is in the car when a different engine is actually there.

If the dealer has made any oral representations, such as stating that he or she will install a certain accessory after the sale without charging you for it, this too should be included in the purchase order. *Do not sign the purchase order until you are sure that everything—repeat, everything—has been put in writing and is included in the purchase order.* If the dealer refuses to put something in writing or tells you not to worry, that is precisely the time to start worrying.

The purchase order should, of course, state the price of the vehicle, the names of the parties involved in the transaction, and whether the car is to be financed by the dealer or manufacturer's credit division, such as General Motors Automobile Credit (GMAC). If the dealer or manufacturer's credit company will be financing the car, then the purchase order must comply with the Truth in Lending laws concerning disclosure of the amount financed, the annual percentage rate, the length of the loan, and the total amount of interest to be paid. (Truth in Lending laws and financing in general are discussed in more detail in chapter 18.)

Sometimes, to convince you that you are getting a "great deal" on a car, the salesman or sales manager will show you the invoice from the factory with the car's price to the dealership on it and tell you that you are getting the car for only a couple of hundred of dollars more than it cost the dealer. Don't believe a word of what he or she is saying. The invoice price is not necessarily the dealer's true cost of the automobile. It does not include such things as factory rebates to the dealer, allowances, discounts, and incentive awards. The dealer's true cost could be hundreds, even thousands, of dollars lower than the invoice price.

ORDERING A NEW CAR

SOMETIMES YOU FIND THAT the cars on the dealers' lots are not exactly what you had in mind. You like the car as equipped, but you want it in another color. Or you want it with air conditioning or cruise control. If you can't find the car with just the right equipment and in the right color, and the dealer can't find one on another dealer's lot, you may wish to order a "custom-built" car from the factory through the dealer. (Factory orders are usually available only for American-made vehicles.) As with buying a new car off the lot, the order form should specify the make, model, year, and color of the vehicle, engine type, a complete list of options, the color and type of interior you want (black leather as opposed to blue cloth, for instance), the estimated delivery date, and other pertinent information. The VIN number cannot be included on the purchase order since it isn't known until the car is built.

The dealer usually reserves the right to adjust the price you have agreed upon to cover any additional costs in manufacturing or transporting the car. You should insist upon a reciprocal right to cancel the contract if there is an increase in the final price. You don't want to pay $22,000 for the car you thought was only going to cost you $19,500 when you ordered it. If the dealer raises his price because of alleged increases in his or her cost, ask for cold, hard proof of exactly what those increases were. The dealer should merely be passing on its additional costs, not making a higher profit off you. You might also include a provision in the purchase contract stating that if the dealer's cost for the car does come down (because of, say, a new rebate program or other factory incentive), this savings should be passed on to you.

If you are planning to trade in your old car, have the dealer appraise it and include in the purchase order the amount they are willing to give you for it at that time. The dealer will ordinarily reserve the right to reappraise your trade-in when you take delivery of the new car. Your car could be damaged between the time you order your new car and the time you pick it up, and you, not the dealer, assume this risk. If you have driven your car only a few more miles, and no damage has occurred or mechanical problems have arisen, the dealer should give you the same amount quoted earlier. If there is no appreciable difference in the condition of the car since the dealer first appraised it, but he or she tries to reduce the price of your trade-in, the dealer may be guilty of a deceptive or fraudulent practice. You may wish to discuss the matter with an attorney or report your suspicions to the police or district attorney fraud division, Federal Trade Commission, state board of consumer affairs, or the Better Business Bureau.

When you order a new car, expect to pay a certain percentage of the purchase price as a down payment if you're not trading in your old car. When the new car is delivered, you are required to pay the remainder of the purchase price in cash or by cashier's check, unless you have informed the dealer that you will be financing the purchase through the dealer's lender. If the dealer agrees, you can use a personal or business check to pay off the balance due. The purchase is contingent upon the bank honoring the check, however. If the bank refuses to honor the check (if, for example, you are overdrawn), and you are unable to make good on it or obtain financing quickly, the dealer can repossess the car and recover damages from you for the decreased value of the car, as well as other costs, including the costs of repossessing the car and reasonable attorney's fees incurred by the dealer if the contract calls for it, which such contracts usually do.

When you are ordering a car, the purchase order should include the approximate delivery date. If the car is not delivered within a reasonable time after it is due, you may have the right to cancel the order and recover any damages from the dealer. If the dealer can't give you a reasonable estimate as to when the car will be ready, have him or her call the factory and find out. If the dealer knowingly misrepresents the amount of time it will take to deliver the car (telling you it will be two weeks when he or she knows it will take at least four months, or vice versa), not only will you be able to cancel the deal, you may be able to sue the dealer for fraud.

If the dealer doesn't deliver the car on the agreed date or within a reasonable time after that, he or she is in breach of the contract. Most form contracts used by dealers contain an escape clause that excuses the dealer if the manufacturer fails to build or ship the car as ordered. If the order form contains such a clause, you usually are limited to the recovery of your down payment. In determining what your rights are, study the contract carefully or consult an attorney.

Suppose that the car you ordered arrives on time, but it is not quite what you wanted or there is a defect. Are you obligated to accept it? No. If the car does not comply exactly with the specifications contained in the order form or is defective in any way, you can reject it. But you ordinarily must reject the car at the time it is delivered (that is, when you go to pick it up). If, for example, the car is light brown instead of medium blue, you must reject it on the spot. If you take it home, you have waived the discrepancy and accepted the car, since the difference in color was obvious.

If the radio, air conditioning, or another feature doesn't work, you are free to reject the car. The dealer, however, usually has a corresponding right to "cure" the defect (repair it) within a reasonable time—say, seven days. If the defect is minor and promptly repaired by the dealer, and the car is sound in all other respects, then you must take the vehicle.

NEW CAR WARRANTIES

WHEN YOU BUY A NEW CAR, you get a standard manufacturer's warranty of some kind. Examples of a manufacturer's warranty are a three-year, 36,000-mile guarantee against defects in products or workmanship for most items; a five-year or 50,000-mile rust protection guarantee; and a ten-year or 100,000 power train warranty. This type of guarantee is called an express warranty and usually is found in the purchase contract or the owner's manual. Except for warranties imposed by law (discussed below), the manufacturer's and dealer's obligations are limited by the wording of this warranty.

There are other ways express warranties are created. For instance, the manufacturer or dealer may tell you that a certain model of the vehicle comes with a powerful V-8 engine. If it turns out that within a reasonable time you find out that the engine is only a V-6, the manufacturer or dealer has breached an express warranty. A common way an express warranty is created is through the manufacturer's or dealer's advertising. For instance, an ad may boast that the car can go from 0 to 60 miles per hour in 8.5 seconds or is capable of pulling a heavy boat.

What are your rights when you discover that it takes 15 seconds for your new car to get to 60 mph, or the only way your vehicle can pull your boat is by going downhill? If you saw the ad before you bought the vehicle, and the ad's depiction of what the vehicle could do was a major factor in your decision to buy it, you've got a good chance of getting your money back. But note well: Just as soon as you discover the car isn't as advertised, contact the dealer and manufacturer, inform them of the problem, and demand your money back. Always send a letter to both the manufacturer's customer service department and the dealer describing the warranty made, by whom and when it was made, and how the car differs from the express warranty. If you don't get immediate satisfaction, seriously consider hiring an attorney to assist you. If you fail to notify the dealer and manufacturer promptly and continue using the car, you may lose your right to enforce the warranty.

If the dealer makes a specific warranty about the vehicle, its equipment, its condition, or its performance, get it in writing and see that it is incorporated into the purchase contract before you sign on the dotted line. If the dealer is unwilling to put this in writing and sign it, think twice about buying the vehicle. Failure to include the warranty in the purchase contract could result in its loss.

In addition to the manufacturer's express warranty, the law imposes certain warranties in the sale of a new car, even if the purchase contract or manufacturer's warranty doesn't mention them. All states except Louisiana imply a warranty that a new car is of "good and average quality" and that it can be operated on the streets and highways in its intended manner with reasonable safety. This is called the implied warranty of merchantability. "Lemon" laws (discussed below) are another type of warranty imposed by law. Frequently the manufacturer's express warranty states that it supersedes any and all other warranties, including those implied by law. Many states limit the manufacturer's or dealer's right to restrict or "disclaim" warranties that are implied by law. Lemon laws in particular usually cannot be disclaimed or limited by the manufacturer, nor can the consumer waive them.

IF YOUR DREAM CAR TURNS OUT TO BE A "LEMON"

NOT TOO LONG AGO, if you bought a new car that turned out to be a "lemon," your rights against the automobile dealer were quite limited. The dealer was given an almost infinite number of chances to repair the vehicle. Your only recourse was to retain a lawyer and file a lawsuit against the dealer. This was a costly and frequently lengthy procedure, and your chances for success were not very good. And even if you did win, you usually could not recover your attorney's fees from the dealer unless the purchase contract permitted it. Many people were discouraged from pursuing their legal rights against the dealer for fear that it would cost more to hire the lawyer than it did to buy the car.

Today, most states and the District of Columbia have passed so-called lemon laws. Also important is the federal Magnuson-Moss Act, which lets you sue in state court for the breach of an express or implied warranty involving a consumer product. Although initially consumers were not winning many cases under lemon laws, that trend has changed. Today more and more consumers are succeeding with their lawsuits against manufacturers and dealers when their cars turn out to be lemons.

Under a typical lemon law, the manufacturer is required either to replace the car or light truck or refund your money if a major defect in the car has not been repaired after four attempts, or if the car has spent a cumulative total of thirty days in the shop being repaired for the same defect during the first eighteen months or eighteen thousand miles, whichever comes first. In some states, the lemon law covers the earlier of two years or eighteen thousand miles. Some states have slightly different requirements concerning the number of days the car must be in the shop or the number of tries the dealer has at repairing it. Some states use business days to determine how long your car was in the shop, while others base it on calendar days. Note that in some states you must notify the manufacturer at least one time of the problems you are having with the car to be protected by the lemon law.

The legal requirements for attempts made to fix the problem or how many days the car must be in the shop vary from state to state. If you feel that you bought a lemon, it is best to consult a lawyer versed in this area to find out what the exact requirements are in your state to deem a car a lemon. Plus, if your car does meet your state's standards for being a lemon, you will still need to hire a lawyer to write letters to the dealership and manufacturer on your behalf, and even possibly sue them if the dealership will not take the car back even though it meets your state's definition of a "lemon." Be sure to keep all of your receipts and invoices, as well as a log of dates you took the car into the dealer and the number of days the car was in the shop. Also keep copies of any letters you send to the dealer or manufacturer concerning the attempts to fix your vehicle.

In addition to the price you paid for the car, you can generally also seek reimbursement for other expenses, such as the costs of registering the car, sales tax, license fees, and dealer preparation. Several states also let you recover additional expenses, such as towing the vehicle and renting a replacement while your car is in the shop. On the other hand, the manufacturer or dealer usually can deduct from the refund a reasonable charge for your use of the car—for example, so many cents a mile. If, for instance, you drove the car 8,500 miles, and the dealer is allowed to deduct 15 cents a mile, your refund would be reduced by $1,275.

If the defect occurs during the warranty period, and you give the manufacturer or dealer written notice before the time limit expires, the manufacturer must repair or replace the defective part, even if, for any reason, the repair itself is made after the warranty expires. For example, if something goes wrong during the last week of the warranty period, and you immediately notify the manufacturer in writing, the manufacturer must make the repair even though the car is not brought into the dealership until several days after the warranty has expired.

Your chances of winning a lemon law lawsuit improve significantly with the amount of documentation that you have to back up your claims of what the problem is, your efforts to resolve it with the dealer or manufacturer, and the number and length of times your car was in the dealership for repairs. Each time you take the vehicle in, get a copy of the work order showing the date the vehicle was brought in and the problem complained of. When you pick up the vehicle, get another copy of the finished work order showing the work done and the date you got your car back. All conversations with the service manager or employees of the dealership should be summarized in letters to the manufacturer and dealership if the problem persists.

Before the warranty period is over and the problem(s) are still not satisfactorily repaired, send a letter to both the manufacturer and the dealer detailing the problem(s) and the attempts to fix it. This letter should contain such basic information as the make, model, and year of the car, the vehicle identification number, and the date purchased, as well as a complete description of the defect(s), the number of times and days (including the specific dates) the car has been in the shop, and copies of any repair invoices, along with a statement that the defect has not been corrected. Send the letters to the manufacturer and dealership by certified mail, return receipt requested.

Most states require you to arbitrate the dispute before you can sue the manufacturer. Section 703 of the Magnuson-Moss Act requires the arbitrator to make a decision within forty days after you file for arbitration.

When it becomes evident that your car probably will never be fixed properly, you should hire a lawyer experienced in lemon law disputes to represent you. You can find a lawyer who specializes in such cases by calling your local trial lawyers association or consumer attorneys association or by checking the yellow pages. Some lawyers require you to pay by the hour as the case goes along. Others will agree to a small up-front retainer, then prosecute the case and try to collect attorney's fees from the manufacturer if and when the case is won. Some state lemon laws permit the judge to award attorney's fees if you win, and the federal Magnuson-Moss Act also gives the judge this discretion.

If a manufacturer buys back a lemon car, purports to fix the problem(s), and then puts it back up for sale, the dealer usually is required to attach a notice to the vehicle stating that the vehicle was repurchased pursuant to consumer laws, and the vehicle has been permanently branded as a lemon law buyback vehicle. Additionally, the manufacturer must give the buyer at least a one-year warranty that the vehicle is free of the designated problems that made it a lemon.

LEASING A VEHICLE

MANY PEOPLE WHO CANNOT AFFORD to buy their dream cars are leasing them instead, mainly because the monthly payments are lower than buying. Also, people can qualify for a lease where they would not qualify to purchase the vehicle. The most common type of car lease is the "closed-end" lease. That means that at the end of the lease period, you simply bring the vehicle back to the dealership, drop off the keys, and walk away. Unfortunately, it's not that easy. The federal Consumer Leasing Act (see chapter 18) governs automobile leases to ensure you know exactly what you are getting into. There are three types of expenses you are going to incur in leasing a car: the up-front expenses; the expenses during the lease term; and the expenses at the end of the lease.

Up-front lease expenses can vary greatly depending upon the promotion being offered by the dealer. Generally, you can expect to pay the first month's payment, a refundable security deposit or your last month's payment (sometimes both), and fees for state and local taxes, license, registration, title, and documentation. Additionally, you may be required to pay a "capitalized cost reduction," which is somewhat similar to a down payment, an acquisition fee, and freight or destination charges.

Before you sign your lease, make sure you are getting the lowest possible price on the vehicle. The cost of a car is not set in concrete just because it is a lease rather than a sale. Plus, the lower the cost of the car, the lower your monthly lease payments will be. Also, at the end of the lease, the cost to purchase the car (if you should choose to do so) will be less. Occasionally you will see a dealer offering to lease a vehicle for only the first month's lease payment, license fees, documentation fees, and taxes. They make up the additional fee by charging a higher lease payment.

During the term of the lease, you are responsible not only for the monthly lease payments, but for keeping the car in good repair and insured. You are also liable for any taxes that may be assessed on the car, as well as for the annual registration. Lease terms generally vary from thirty-six months to sixty months. If you wish to cancel your lease before the term expires, you will have to pay an additional—and often substantial—early termination fee.

At the end of the lease, you have the option of buying the car at the price you agreed to when you first leased the vehicle, or of turning it in and walking away. However, if you do not purchase the vehicle, you may have to pay a disposition fee and charges for excess miles and wear and tear on the car. Most leases limit the amount of miles you can drive each year before you have to start paying additional per mile fees. For instance, if you are permitted 10,000 miles a year free, over a period of five years that would total 50,000. You would then be charged a fee set forth in the lease agreement—usually 10 to 12 cents a mile—for every mile driven over 50,000. So if you drove 60,000 miles but were allowed only 50,000, you could end up paying $1,200 if your lease charges you 12 cents a mile for every mile over 50,000.

Additionally, you must return the car in good repair and maintenance. If you had to replace the vehicle's transmission, that is a fee that you are going to have to foot. If you return the car to the dealer dented, with bald tires, and the paint scratched all over and needing a new paint job, the dealer is going to add all of these to the end-of-lease payment as excessive wear and tear.

Leases are easier to get into than a traditional purchase, but they are harder to get out of. And at the end of the lease period, unless you purchase the car you have nothing to show for it but memories. Had you purchased the car, after you paid off the loan, you would own the car free and clear.

BUYING AND SELLING USED CARS

BUYING OR SELLING A USED CAR generally involves a whole different set of rules from those involved in buying or selling a new car. As far as used vehicles go, the law is still pretty much caveat emptor—buyer beware.

While a rose is a rose is a rose, the same is not true of a used car. What is considered a used car in one state can be a new car in another. Some states define a used car as one that has been driven farther than is reasonably necessary to road test or deliver a new car to the buyer. Cars used for demonstration, rental, or the transportation of automobile executives, dealers, salesmen, and other employees are considered used cars under this standard. Other states define a new car as one whose title has never been transferred to the ultimate purchaser. By this definition, a dealer's demonstrator would be a new car, despite its considerable mileage. Still other states define a used car as one that "has been so used as to have become what is commonly known as 'secondhand' within the ordinary meaning thereof." The difference between a new and a used car becomes significant in determining what warranties apply. For instance, a consumer in one state who buys a demonstrator car is protected by the more stringent new-car warranties, while a consumer in another state who purchases a demonstrator is protected only by used-car warranties.

Used-Car Warranties

As with a new car, the seller of a used car can make an express warranty as to the condition of the car or the optional equipment included with the vehicle. This express warranty can be either oral or written, but it is always best to get it in writing. An oral warranty is always harder to prove than a written one, so don't take any chances.

When a dealer sells a used car, most states impose the implied warranty that the car is "merchantable"—that it is reasonably safe for ordinary driving. For example, the steering wheel must turn the tires, and the brakes must stop the car. No such warranty is imposed upon a private party who sells his or her car. When a private party sells a used car, the buyer generally takes the car in its current condition and has no recourse against the seller if the car falls apart a block down the road.

This brings up the question of how a "dealer" in used cars is defined. A dealer is one who is regularly engaged in the business of selling used cars. Obvious examples of used-car dealers are the dealerships that sell new and "preowned" vehicles and "Honest Bob's Used Car Lot." In some states, "used-car dealers" include banks or insurance companies that sell repossessed or damaged cars, rental agencies that sell their used cars, and auctioneers. Some states define a dealer as one who has an established place of business and sells a certain number of cars each year.

Federal law requires used-car dealers to place a window sticker on every used car indicating whether any warranties come with the car. If the car is sold "as is"—without a warranty of any kind—that fact must be shown clearly on the sticker. If a warranty is given, the dealer must state whether it is a full or a limited warranty, the system(s) covered, the length of the warranty, and what percent of the costs of labor and parts the dealer will pay. Before buying a used car with a limited warranty, carefully read all of the warranty information on the window sticker to see just how limited the warranty really is. Some warranties are so limited they really don't cover a thing.

New York has a used-car "lemon law" that applies to dealers. The dealer cannot disclaim this law, nor can the consumer waive his or her rights under it. This warranty covers certain parts: the engine, transmission, drive axle, brakes, radiator, steering, alternator, generator, and starter or ignition system (excluding the battery). The warranty applies only to cars that are sold for more than $1,500, or leases where the dealer and lessee (the person leasing the car) agree that the car's value is more than $1,500.

If the car has 18,000 miles or fewer on it, the buyer may be protected by New York's new-car lemon law. If the used car has more than 18,000 miles and up to 36,000 miles on it, the warranty must be provided for at least 90 days or 4,000 miles, whichever comes first. If the used car has more than 36,000 miles but fewer than 80,000 miles, the warranty must be for the first of 60 days or 3,000 miles. For used cars having at least 80,000 miles but fewer than 100,000 miles, the warranty protects the buyer for the earlier of 30 days or 1,000 miles. Cars having over 100,000 miles are not covered by the used-car lemon law.

Under New York's used-car lemon law, if the dealer cannot fix the same problem after three or more attempts, or if the car is out of service for a total of fifteen days during the warranty period, the dealer must refund the purchase price, sales tax, and fees, less a reasonable allowance for any damages not attributable to normal wear and tear. If you leased the car, the dealer must refund all of the payments you have made on the car and cancel all future payments. If the contract calls for arbitration in the case of disputes, the dealer may refuse to refund the purchase price (or lease payments) until after you have won the arbitration. Of course, if you lose the arbitration, you are stuck with the car and paying the balance of the purchase price or lease payments.

Many dealers offer an optional used-car warranty. Before buying such a warranty, read it carefully to see what it covers and for how long. You may find that only a few things are covered— the things least likely to fail. Some dealers charge exorbitant amounts of money for extremely limited warranties. Before buying the car and the extended warranty, you should go to another dealership that handles used cars and ask to see the used-car warranties it offers and find out what they cover and how much they cost. When buying a used car from an independent used-car lot, consider whether the place will be in business next week or next year. An extended warranty is worthless if no one's going to be there to honor it when you have a problem.

Protecting Yourself When Buying a Used Car

Before buying a used car, first check out the consumer magazines to see what they have to say about the car's safety, reliability, and longevity. Then find out whether the car is being offered at a fair price. One way of doing this is simply by looking through the classified ads in your local paper to see what comparably equipped vehicles for the same year, with the same equipment, and in a similar condition are going for. Another way is to find out the *Kelley Blue Book* price. One way to get the *Blue Book* price on a used car is to call or visit your automobile insurance agent's office and have him or her look it up for you; you also can find out the *Blue Book* price by going online at the *Kelley Blue Book*'s website, http://www.kelleybluebook.com, to get the price for a new or used car. Many libraries also have the *Kelley Blue Book*, or have Internet access where you can log on to its website. In comparing the *Kelley Blue Book*'s price to the price of the car you are considering buying, take into account the overall condition of the car, the mileage, and the optional equipment. Such factors can add or subtract hundreds of dollars from the average selling price.

In addition to satisfying yourself that the price is fair, have the vehicle thoroughly checked out by a competent mechanic not affiliated with the dealer who is selling the car. Remember that the burden is on you to check out the car thoroughly before purchasing it. Ask your mechanic if there are any known problems with this particular make, model, and year of car, such as a propensity for the engine block to crack or the transmission to fall apart after so many miles. Ask the mechanic or check with another dealer or in consumer publications to learn whether the year, make, and model of car in question has ever been recalled for the repair of any defects. If there has been a recall, find out whether the car you are interested in buying was in fact repaired.

If the seller tells you that certain repairs have been made to the car, such as the installation of a new clutch or a new transmission, ask to see the receipts and get copies of them. In reviewing the receipts, make sure they apply to the car in question and not to some other car. Get the receipts before you have your mechanic check the car out, so that your mechanic can verify that the repairs were in fact done. (Perhaps the seller was ripped off by an unscrupulous repair shop!) If the seller doesn't have any receipts or work orders to show you, ask that the information be included in the written purchase contract, and have your mechanic do a visual inspection, if possible, of the repaired or replaced part(s).

When buying a used car, keep an eye open for the possibility that the odometer has been turned back, disconnected, or broken for a while. Another twist on older cars: The seller may state that the car has only 50,000 miles on it when in fact it has 150,000 on it. In both cases, older odometers would show only 50,000 miles. (Today, however, most if not all cars have an extra digit to let you know there are over 100,000—or even 200,000—miles on it.) In cases of older cars, always check the car out to see if the wear and tear on the car is consistent with the mileage reading on the odometer, and have your mechanic do the same. If there is any doubt, you should assume the worst—that the car has extremely high mileage.

If the seller misrepresents the mileage on the car, the damages the buyer can recover are the costs of any repairs made because of the higher mileage, or the difference in value between the car as represented—say, as having only 50,000 miles—and the value of the car as it really is—say, 150,000 miles. Under federal law, any person who alters or disconnects the odometer with intent to defraud is liable for $1,500 or triple the buyer's damage, whichever is greater, as well as reasonable attorney's fees incurred by the buyer. A person who deliberately tampers with an odometer also may be guilty of a federal or state crime.

When looking for a used car in the classified ads, you will probably see some ads seeking someone to "assume monthly payments." If the seller of the car is a bank, other financial company, or leasing outfit, the car probably was repossessed, and there's no problem with assuming the payments. But if the seller is a private party, there are a few things to think about. Does the bank know about the intended transfer, and if so, does it agree to have you assume the payments? Usually banks will not permit car loans to be assumed. Rather, they will refinance the whole thing, and only if you meet their usual credit requirements. A lease normally cannot be assumed until the leasing company checks out your credit history and driving record and approves the transfer.

If the seller doesn't want the bank to know about the transfer, look out. You're headed for trouble if you're supposed to pay the seller directly, who in turn must make the monthly payments to the bank. If the title remains in the seller's name, and the seller fails to make the payments, the bank will repossess the car. Your only recourse then is to try to get your money back from the seller.

Protecting Yourself When Selling a Used Car

If you are a private party selling your car, you usually don't have to disclose defects you know about if the buyer doesn't ask. But if the buyer does ask specific questions, you must either answer truthfully and completely, or tell the buyer you are not going to say anything about the car's condition. If you give the buyer only half an answer, the buyer can sue you when the whole truth is discovered.

Never knowingly make any misrepresentations concerning the condition, equipment, or mileage of your car. If you don't know enough to answer the buyer's question, tell him or her so. Offer to let the buyer have the vehicle checked out by a mechanic if he or she has any doubts.

Before letting a potential buyer test drive your car, check that his or her driver's license is up-to-date and not suspended. If the buyer refuses to show you the license or tells you that it's at home, do not let him or her drive the car. Instead, offer to let the buyer test drive the car when he or she returns with a valid license. A buyer's failure to show a license could mean that he or she intends to steal the car, to simply drive away and not come back. Or the buyer could be a careless driver whose license has been revoked because of too many accidents. Remember, you can be held liable for any injuries caused by a person who is driving your car with your permission. (For this reason, you should maintain insurance on your car until you transfer title to the buyer and send notice of the sale to the department of motor vehicles.)

One way of protecting yourself from having your car stolen is to accompany the buyer on the test drive. If you don't want to go with the buyer, have the buyer leave the keys and registration to his or her own car as security. First check the registration to make sure it is in fact the buyer's car. If there is any discrepancy, exercise common sense in deciding whether to allow the buyer to test drive your car alone.

Salvage Titles

When a vehicle has been in an accident and the cost of repairing it exceeds the vehicle's fair market value, the insurance company will declare the vehicle a total loss and pay its fair market value (less any deductible) on the date of the accident to the owner. If you wish to do so, you can keep the vehicle by paying the insurance company its fair market value after the accident. Otherwise, the car will most likely be sold at an insurance auction. The individual who purchases the vehicle may sell it for parts or fix it into running condition and then sell it.

The title to such a vehicle is known as a "salvage title." The person who buys the car and fixes it up must disclose to the buyer that the car has a salvage title. In many states, the fact that it is a salvage title is listed prominently on the certificate of ownership. Be especially careful if you are considering buying a car with a salvage title. Serious damage may have been done to the car that has not, nor cannot, be properly repaired. For instance, the frame may be bent beyond repair.

Your best bet is to avoid buying a used car with a salvage title altogether. However, if you are absolutely set on buying such a car, before you purchase it, take it to a good mechanic and have him or her go over it with a fine-toothed comb. Be sure to tell the mechanic that the insurance company declared the car a total loss and that the car has a salvage title. The car may look fine to a superficial visual inspection by the untrained eye. But a thorough check and test drive by an experienced mechanic may reveal a number of defects that will be costly—or impossible—to repair.

Paying the Money and Transferring Ownership

If you are buying a used car from a reputable dealer, then there usually isn't much to worry about in paying your money and getting the title. But transactions between private parties should be structured carefully to protect both sides from getting ripped off.

If you are selling your car, always insist that the buyer pay the full price in cash, or better yet, by cashier's check. If you agree to accept a personal check, don't give the buyer the car until the check clears. If you let the buyer take the car and the check bounces, you might have to go through a lot of trouble and expense to get the car back. Don't agree to finance the purchase price unless you're prepared for the headaches that go along with it; if the buyer defaults, you will have to go through the time, expense, and trouble of repossessing the car.

If you are the buyer, before giving your hard-earned cash to the seller, ask to see the owner's certificate of title to make sure the seller owns the car. If the title is in someone else's name, ask for written proof authorizing the person to sell the car on behalf of the owner. (To be on the safe side, it's a good idea to get the license plate number and the vehicle identification number from the certificate of title and check with police or department of motor vehicles to make sure the car isn't stolen.)

If a bank holds the legal title, arrange a meeting at the bank between yourself, the seller, and the bank's representative. At this meeting, pay the outstanding balance of the loan directly to the bank, which will release the certificate of title to the seller. Then give the seller the rest of the purchase price, and have him or her sign the title over to you. In no event should you give the seller your money upon the seller's assurance that he or she will pay the bank off and get the title to you in the near future. What happens if the seller doesn't pay off the bank? The bank may repossess the car, the seller may spend all of your money, and you could be left holding the bag—an empty bag at that.

After the sale of the car is consummated, both the seller and the buyer must promptly notify the department of motor vehicles. The buyer needs to record the new ownership and change the title and registration accordingly. Most states require the seller to send in a form giving certain information, such as the date of the sale, the seller's name and address, the buyer's name and address, a description of the car, the VIN number, the license plate number, the odometer reading, and the purchase price. In many states, the seller remains liable for parking tickets and even personal injuries caused by the new owner until the proper governmental agency (usually the department of motor vehicles) is notified. To be on the safe side, if you are the seller, keep your insurance in force on the vehicle for a couple of weeks to make sure there are no problems with the sale and that the title transfers over to the new owner.

In some states, before the ownership of a car can be transferred, it must be tested to see whether it complies with applicable emissions (smog) regulations. Unless there is an agreement to the contrary, it is the buyer's responsibility to bring the car up to standard if it doesn't pass the inspection. Before completing the transaction, a prudent buyer will have the car checked out at an authorized station, to see whether any work has to be done. If some work is necessary, the buyer should ask for a corresponding reduction in the purchase price.

TITLE TO THE CAR

WHEN A CAR IS SOLD either by a dealer or a private party—even on an "as is" basis—the law implies that the seller has title to the car (legal ownership, usually in the form of a certificate issued by the department of motor vehicles) and the legal authority to transfer it. The law also implies that, unless otherwise expressly stated, the title to the car is free from all security interests, liens, or other encumbrances, such as a bank's lien if the car is collateral ("security") for a loan. If the seller attempts to disclaim these "warranties of title" or "warranties against encumbrances," this is your cue that something is amiss.

Once in a while, a person who has bought a used car discovers that another person claims that the car was stolen from him or her. If the car was indeed stolen, the person who owned it at the time it was stolen is legally entitled to the car—a thief does not acquire title to the stolen car and neither does anyone who buys the car from the thief or subsequent purchasers, no matter how innocent they may be. If the car you bought turns out to be stolen, you have a right to recover the full price you paid from the person who sold you the car, even if that person didn't know the car was stolen. That person in turn has the right to recover his or her purchase price from the person from whom the car was bought. Of course, the person who unknowingly purchased the car from the thief usually will be left out in the cold.

When more than one person owns the car, how title is held is worth considering. For example, if the title states "John Doe *and* Mary Doe" (or "John and Mary Doe"), this means that both John and Mary Doe must sign the certificate of ownership to transfer title of the car. However, if the title reads "John Doe *or* Mary Doe" or "John *and/or* Mary Doe," either John or Mary can transfer ownership of the car without the other's signature. If the title to the car is held as "John and Mary Doe" and one of them dies, the survivor may have to get a court order approving the transfer prior to a sale. In many states, though, the surviving co-owner need only show the department of motor vehicles a certified copy of the death certificate of the co-owner's death and fill out the necessary paperwork in order to sell the vehicle.

If you have obtained a loan to purchase the car, the bank's security interest in the car will be noted on the certificate of title. This prevents you from transferring title without disclosing the bank's security interest. As another means to prevent an unauthorized transfer, the bank will keep the original owner's certificate of title until it receives the last loan payment. Meanwhile, you will have use of the car and are the registered owner. You cannot sell the car without the bank's permission.

AUTOMOBILE REPAIRS

As THE OWNER OF A MOTOR VEHICLE, you are ultimately responsible for keeping it in good repair and safe for driving on the streets and highways. If the car is not kept in proper working condition, with all lights operable, brakes, tires, and steering in good shape, and so forth, you can be cited for a traffic offense. Should the car be involved in an accident, your failure to maintain the vehicle in good shape can make you liable for the injuries sustained by the other person.

Consider this example: Donald knows that the brake lights and turn signals on his car do not work and has been planning on getting them repaired for some time. So far, he has avoided getting a ticket, although one police officer did stop him and let him off with a warning on Donald's promise to get them fixed immediately. While driving down a busy street one day, Donald suddenly decides to make a left turn to go into the parking lot of a department store. He hits his brakes, but since the lights don't work, the driver behind Donald has no forewarning that Donald is stopping. Donald has not bothered to signal the turn with his arm, even though he knows his turn signal and brake lights are out. The other driver doesn't realize until too late that Donald is making a turn and runs into him. In this case, Donald is liable for the injuries sustained by the other driver and the damage to the other car, as the cause of the accident was Donald's failure to have the brake lights and turn signals in proper working order. Since the car behind Donald had no warning that Donald was making an abrupt stop to make a turn, the driver is not liable for the accident unless he or she was following too closely or speeding.

Maintaining your car in a safe operating condition is what the law calls a "nondelegable duty." You and you alone are responsible for seeing that the car doesn't pose an unreasonable risk of harm to other people on the road. This is true even if you don't know the first thing about car repair or maintenance and have entrusted your vehicle to the best mechanic in town. The mechanic, however, has a duty to perform the repairs in a skillful, or "workmanlike," manner, and is liable for any damages resulting from his or her faulty work.

Suppose that you have just had your brakes relined at Joe's Tire and Brake Service, a reputable repair shop. You pull out of Joe's driveway and drive down the street about two hundred yards. As you come to a red light at a crowded intersection, you push the brake pedal. Unfortunately, nothing happens and you crash into the car in front of you. The owner and occupants of that car sue you for not having your brakes in working condition. Can you defend the lawsuit on the basis that you just had the brakes "repaired" at Joe's Tire and Brake Service and they should be held liable, not you? No. This is an example of a "nondelegable" duty. However, you are not out of luck. You can turn around and sue Joe's for the cost of your lawyer and the amount of the judgment you must pay because of Joe's faulty work.

How to Avoid Getting Ripped Off

The fraudulent practices of a relatively small percentage of automobile repair shops have given the whole car repair industry a tarnished reputation. Some repair companies have been accused of charging for work not done; using used or reconditioned parts but charging for new parts; doing repairs the customer did not authorize and threatening not to release the car until all charges are paid; stating certain repairs are necessary when in fact they are not; and failing to return old parts or to make them available for inspection, despite the customer's request they do so (which can mean that the customer was charged for a part that wasn't replaced or didn't need replacing and was billed for unnecessary or undone labor as well). Many states now have comprehensive laws for licensing automotive repair shops, certifying mechanics, and regulating estimates and repair work. California has one of the best acts in the nation, with the Bureau of Automotive Repair as a watchdog agency to investigate consumer complaints. In California, the repair shop is required to give the customer a written estimate and get the customer's express authorization before any work is done. Should the repair shop fail to give the customer a written estimate, the customer may not have to pay for the repairs.

Here are some things you can do to ensure that you don't get ripped off when your car needs repairs:

1. Investigate the repair shop. Contact the local Better Business Bureau and ask whether any complaints have been lodged against the shop. Even if the shop isn't a member, the BBB may still have a file of complaints on it. Ask your friends and neighbors if they are familiar with the repair shop and would recommend it. The local chapter of the American Automobile Association may be able to give you information about the reputation of repair shops in the area.

2. Get an estimate in writing. Tell the repair shop that you want only an estimate at this time and that you are not authorizing the shop to do any work. Most repair shops will give a free estimate. About the only time a shop won't do this is when it has to disassemble part of the car to see what the problem is.

   If your car is under warranty, you should check the warranty and contact an authorized dealer to determine whether the warranty covers both the diagnosis and repair of the problem. Don't let the dealer try to charge you a fee for opening the hood to see what the problem is if the warranty includes the cost of diagnosis, which it often does. If necessary, pull out the warranty information that came with your car and show the dealer everything the warranty covers.

3. Request that the estimate itemize the parts needed, their individual costs, and the labor charge to install each part. Ask whether the parts to be installed will be new, used, or reconditioned. If all parts will be new, that fact should be stated on the estimate sheet.

4. Make sure that the shop is competent to handle the work on your particular type of car. If you have an imported car, for instance, you usually would not want to take it to a shop that deals exclusively in domestic cars. And if your problem is covered by a warranty, you must take the car to a dealer that accepts the warranty.

5. *Get at least two estimates*, and get them in writing. This cannot be overemphasized. The first repair shop may be trying to charge you for work that doesn't need to be done or may be grossly overestimating the amount of time the job will take. If the repair work to be done is extensive and expensive, it may be wise to get three or four estimates. In addition to price and quality of work, you also should find out how long it is going to take. It may not be worth saving $100 if your car is going to be tied up in the shop an extra week or two.

6. Find out whether the repair shop will guarantee its work for any period of time. If the shop doesn't give some kind of warranty, forget the place. If it doesn't have enough confidence in its own work to give any kind of guarantee, that only spells trouble—including possible legal trouble—in the long run.

7. Once you have decided on a particular repair shop, and once the work order contains the notations made on the estimate sheet (itemization of parts and labor, whether new, used, or reconditioned parts will be installed, and so forth), be sure to have the following provisions added to the work order: (a) If the price is going to exceed the estimate by a stated amount (say, $50), the repair shop is to call you and get your consent before proceeding further; (b) All old parts must be returned to you or at least retained for your inspection, so you can determine that the part needed replacing and was in fact replaced.

If the Shop Refuses to Return Your Car Until You Pay

Most states give the repair shop a "lien" on your car when it works on the vehicle to ensure that it will be paid. If you unjustifiably refuse to pay for the repairs, the repair shop can hold your car for a reasonable time and charge you a reasonable storage fee. Should you not pay within a certain time, say two weeks or thirty days, the repair shop may be entitled to sell the car to pay the repair bill. If, after the vehicle is sold and the bill paid off, there is any money left over, this must be given to the owner of the car. Before selling the car, the repair shop ordinarily must notify both the owner and any lien holder (such as the bank) that it intends to sell the car on a certain date and at a specified place.

All too often, people find that they are being charged for work they did not order or the charges are considerably more than they agreed to in advance. They complain to the shop's manager, who tells them that if they don't pay the bill in full, the shop will enforce the lien on their car and sell it. The manager also tells them that if they do not pick the car up by the next day, they will be charged a daily storage fee of $10 or $20. What can a person do in this situation?

In most cases, the easiest thing to do is simply to pay the bill in full, and then file a small claims action (see chapter 19) to recover the charges you believe were unwarranted. If you present your case well and show the judge just what the repair shop did wrong, there's a good chance that the judge will agree with you. Before filing the small claims action, send a letter to the repair shop stating exactly why you believe the charges were excessive or detailing the exact work that was done without your authorization. Your letter should also include a demand that the repair shop refund you the disputed amount. Make it clear that if it doesn't, you will seek reimbursement through the legal system. Sometimes the repair shop will offer to refund part of the difference prior to the hearing. You may also want to report your complaint about the shop to your local Better Business Bureau or American Automobile Association. If you suspect fraud or similar illegal conduct, you should contact the fraud department of your local district attorney's office. But you generally can't threaten the shop that you will go to the police or district attorney if it refuses to give you your money back. The law does not permit you to threaten criminal prosecution to coerce a settlement in a civil matter.

Some people will write out a check for the full amount, give it to the repair shop, take their car home, and then call the bank to put a "stop payment" on the check. (For this very reason, repair shops have started insisting that you pay in cash or use an ATM debit card.) We advise against this practice, since writing a check with the intent to stop payment on it may subject you to criminal penalties.

If possible, pay with a credit card such as a MasterCard or Visa. Then get your car, drive home, and call the credit card company and say you dispute the charges of the repair shop. It may take a couple of days for the repair shop's charge to show up on the credit card company's files.

What to Do If Your Car Wasn't Repaired Properly

Say that you take your car to the repair shop, leave it there for several days, then get it back, only to discover that the problem has not been corrected or returns in a week or so. When this happens, the first thing you should do is take the car back to the repair shop as soon as possible. If; for some reason, you can't get the car back to the shop for, say, a few weeks because you are going out of town on business or a long-planned family vacation, call the repair shop, inform the owner or manager that the problem has not been corrected, and say that you will bring the car in as soon as you get back. You should follow up this telephone call with a letter to the repair shop.

Do not drive the car, unless it is safe to do so and will not aggravate the condition. For instance, if the problem is with the radio or power windows, you can drive the car but just not play the radio or use the windows. But if the problem is with something as vital as the brakes, the car should only be driven to the repair shop and then only if that is safe. (If the car needs to be towed back to the repair shop because a repair wasn't done right the first time, make the repair shop tow the car in or reimburse you for the cost.) If you do any driving other than back to the repair shop, the repair shop may claim that your continued driving of the car made the problem worse, which relieves the shop of any responsibility for correcting the condition.

All this points up the importance of discussing the guarantee with the repair shop before any work is authorized. Should the shop now claim that no guarantee of any kind was made, you may be up a creek if you don't have a written warranty to back you up. Even if the repair shop insists that there is no warranty, don't take it lying down. The law generally imposes the warranty that all repairs be made in a skillful manner. If the repair wasn't done correctly, then the repair shop must either do it right or return your money.

After giving the repair shop a second chance, you have several options if you're still not satisfied. You can give the shop a third chance at correcting the problem (at no expense to you, of course). Since it hasn't been able to get it right in two tries, however, a third attempt might not be worth your time. If you are fed up with the repair shop, speak to the shop's owner or manager and demand a full refund. If they refuse to give you a full refund, inform them that you are going to have another repair shop fix the problem and that you will seek reimbursement from them for this cost. You should back up this statement with a letter to the shop's owner or manager. Remember to always keep a copy of any letter you send so you can show it to the judge in small claims court if necessary.

Then take your car to another repair shop for an estimate. If you think this new repair shop can do the job, let it do the work, then pay the bill and send a copy to the original repair shop, repeating your demand that it reimburse you for this cost. If the shop owner or manager refuses to do so, or if you get no response to your letter, you should file a small claims action or have a lawyer contact the repair shop on your behalf. The mechanic at the second shop will frequently be willing to testify that the first shop did not repair the problem correctly. This is usually enough to convince a judge that justice is on your side.

AUTOMOBILE INSURANCE

Most states require that you maintain certain minimum liability insurance coverage if your vehicle is driven on a public street or highway. (Technically speaking, these are "financial responsibility" laws that often permit the owner of the car, in lieu of purchasing insurance, to deposit an equivalent amount of money in cash or bond with the department of motor vehicles.)

If you don't have insurance as required by your state's law and get into an accident, you face loss of your license for a year or more, plus a fine. To cut down on the number of uninsured drivers, many states now require you to show proof of insurance coverage when stopped for a traffic violation by a police officer or when renewing your car's registration each year.

Apart from the consequences to your driver's license, getting into an accident without insurance can be very expensive. If you do not have insurance and cause an accident, you will be required to pay out of your own pocket all the property damage, medical expenses, lost wages, and other damages suffered by the injured person(s). If you believe you didn't cause the accident and decide to contest liability, you will have to pay for your own lawyer. An insurance company takes care of all these costs (up to the applicable policy limits) for insured drivers.

Who and What Is Covered

An insurance policy is a contract between the insurance company and the person who is insured. The terms of the policy specify who is covered, the extent of the coverage, and any limitations. If your claim falls within the provisions of the insurance policy, the insurance company must pay that claim, up to the maximum amount of the policy. On the other hand, if the particular claim isn't covered by the policy, the insurance company does not have to pay you anything. If the policy is vague or a dispute arises about whether a claim is covered, either party—you or the insurance company—can file a lawsuit to have the controversy decided in court or by arbitration, depending upon the terms of the policy.

Suppose you lend your car to someone else and that person causes an accident. Or you're driving a friend's car and *you* cause an accident. Does your personal automobile insurance policy cover the damages and injuries in those situations? Perhaps. The typical personal automobile insurance policy will pay for all of the injuries and property damages—to the limits of your policy—someone else causes while driving your car, if that person is driving with your permission and for pleasure and does not regularly drive your car. (Your personal automobile insurance policy normally doesn't cover any damages if someone is driving your car for business purposes or if you are driving someone else's car for business.) Similarly, your friend's insurance, if he or she has any, ordinarily covers you while you are driving his or her car with permission and for pleasure.

Your own policy also covers any injuries and property damages you cause others while driving another person's car for pleasure. This is especially important if the car you borrow isn't insured, or it is insured, but only for a minimal amount of coverage. Your policy probably doesn't cover the damage to the car you're driving (the borrowed car) unless you have additional coverage. If the owner of the car you borrowed doesn't have collision insurance (see below), the cost of repairing or replacing the borrowed car may have to come out of your own pocket. If he or she does have collision insurance on the car, his or her insurance company will pay for the damage to it; you are responsible for reimbursing the car's owner for any deductible he or she is required to pay, however. To determine the extent of your coverage while you are driving someone else's car or while another person is driving your car for pleasure, read your policy carefully or check with your insurance agent. If your car will be used in a business and driven by employees or others on business errands, you will need to get special insurance to cover the business usage of your vehicle.

If members of your family (such as your spouse and children) will be driving your car, you will want your insurance policy to cover each family member who will be driving the car. Having a teenage driver in the house may mean that your insurance premium will be at least several hundred dollars more each year, as they are considered high-risk drivers. If you're thinking of saving money by not telling your insurance company that your teenager drives the car, think twice. If the teenager gets into an accident while driving your car, the insurance company will refuse to pay because the teenager wasn't covered by the policy.

HOW YOUR INSURANCE RATES ARE DETERMINED

AUTOMOBILE INSURANCE RATES are based on such factors as your age, marital status, and driving record; the ages and driving records of other people who will regularly be driving the car; the make, model, and year of your vehicle, plus any equipment on the vehicle, such as a deluxe sound system; whether you will use the car to commute to and from work; whether the car will be used for business; and where you live (your "zone"). Two people with everything else identical may find that their insurance premiums with the same company are hundreds of dollars different just because they live in different zones. The zones usually are determined by the insurance company on the basis of the number of claims made by and the amounts paid to people living in that zone. Frequently it seems unfair that a person living across the street or two blocks away should be paying less for insurance, but insurance companies base their rates on statistical risks, not necessarily on fairness.

The cost of an insurance policy is not uniform throughout the insurance industry. By shopping around, you may be able to save as much as several hundred dollars a year. But when comparing the price of policies offered by competing insurance companies, make sure you are comparing the same amount of coverage in terms of monetary limits, what is covered, and exclusions. Also consider the reputation of the company for paying claims. It might not be worth saving $100 or $200 every six months or a year if you'll have to fight tooth and nail with the claims adjuster to get fair and fast action on your claim.

Personal Injury and Property Damage Insurance

States with financial responsibility laws require that you have certain minimum limits of coverage to pay for the personal injuries or property damage your carelessness causes. Most minimum limits were set decades ago, when the costs of medical care, auto repairs, and other expenses were much less than they are today. A typical minimum requirement is that you have insurance coverage (or other means) to pay up to $15,000 for each person injured in an accident, up to a total of $30,000 for each accident, plus $5,000 in coverage for property damage. (This is the standard "15/30/5" insurance policy found in many states.) Once the insurance company pays its limits under the policy, its obligation stops, and you are personally liable for the remaining amount. Because hospital costs and car values have risen so much over the years, we recommend that your personal automobile insurance policy provide at least $100,000 coverage per person, $300,000 per accident, plus $25,000 to $50,000 in property damage. You should also purchase an "umbrella" policy that starts where your automobile (and homeowner's) insurance ends. The typical umbrella policy provides for up to $1,000,000 worth of protection, and kicks in only when the limits of your automobile (or homeowner's policy, in case of a claim under it) are exhausted. Umbrella policies are generally very reasonably priced, especially for the amount of coverage they provide. Businesses should, of course, have considerably higher limits than this and should discuss their needs with their insurance agents.

Medical Payments Insurance

Medical payments insurance pays medical expenses and funeral costs if you, a member of your immediate family who lives with you, or a passenger is injured or killed while riding in your car or getting in or out of it. You are also covered if you are walking on the sidewalk and are struck by a car, motorcycle, or other vehicle, or if you're riding as a passenger in someone else's car. Medical payments insurance coverage does not cost much, and we suggest that you have coverage of at least $5,000 per person.

Collision and Comprehensive Coverage

Collision insurance covers damage to your car caused when the car runs into something (such as a telephone pole), is run into by another vehicle, or flips over. Damage to car windows, whether in a collision or not, is usually covered by comprehensive insurance.

Comprehensive insurance protects you against damage to the car caused by something other than a collision. For example, if your car is stolen, damaged by someone trying to break in, or hit by a falling object, comprehensive covers it. Comprehensive insurance also covers damage to your car caused by fire or natural disaster—for instance, a flood, an earthquake, a tornado, or a hurricane.

Collision and comprehensive coverage is not usually required by law but is generally a good thing to have, unless your car isn't worth much. Your insurance agent will probably offer collision and comprehensive insurance with different amounts that are designated "deductibles," such as $250 or $500. The deductible is the amount that first comes out of your own pocket; your insurance company pays the rest. The higher the amount of the deductible, the lower the premium will be. But if your car is ever damaged, you'll have to pay more money out of your own pocket to fix it if you opted for the policy with the higher deductible.

The deductible applies to each claim you make. Say that you purchased comprehensive and collision damage with a $250 deductible. One day your car is hit by a falling branch that does $500 worth of damage. The next day your car is struck by a hit-and-run driver who does an additional $1,500 worth of damage. You will wind up paying a total of $500 (the $250 deductible for the tree damage and the $250 deductible for the hit-and-run damage), and the insurance company will pay the rest.

Radio Equipment and Personal Property

Electronic equipment, such as stereos, CD and cassette players, DVD players, and the like, that was installed by the factory usually is covered by your automobile insurance policy, but generally only up to a certain amount, such as $500. If your equipment is more expensive or if it was installed after you bought the car (so-called "aftermarket" equipment), talk to your insurance agent about getting it covered.

The typical personal automobile liability insurance policy does not cover loss of or damage to personal property of any value. For example, if you have some jewelry stolen from the car, or if a painting is injured in a car fire, your automobile policy usually won't cover this. You should, however, be able to collect under your homeowner's or renter's policy if you have one.

Uninsured and Underinsured Coverage

Uninsured motorist coverage is designed to protect you in the event that a person who causes an accident and injures you is not insured or a hit-and-run driver injures you. Underinsured motorist coverage begins where the other driver's insurance ends. In some states, uninsured motorist coverage is mandatory. Uninsured and underinsured motorist coverage are both good investments and are readily available at reasonable cost.

No-Fault Insurance

About half the states have enacted some type of no-fault insurance system. No-fault insurance is designed to cut down the amount of time and the administrative costs involved in processing relatively minor claims. Some groups, particularly the insurance industry, greatly favor no-fault insurance, as it avoids litigation and cuts down on the time it takes for claims to be processed. Other groups, notably lawyers who represent the victims of automobile accidents, feel that too frequently the damages awarded in no-fault systems are inadequate for the injuries suffered, and that the system sacrifices justice and fair compensation for expediency.

Under a typical no-fault plan, a driver who is injured in an automobile accident is entitled to collect up to a certain amount (for example, $5,000) from his or her own insurance company. The liability—that is, fault—of the parties is not at issue. Even if one driver was negligent and caused the accident, he or she can still collect up to the maximum amount from his or her own insurance company. After the innocent driver has collected from his or her own insurance company, if it was not enough to fully compensate him or her for the damages suffered, he or she may then sue the party who caused the accident. Thus, if the innocent driver sustained damages of $10,000 in the accident under the no-fault policy and was paid $5,000 by his or her own insurance company, he or she can sue the other driver for the remaining $5,000.

If the injuries you suffer are not covered under the no-fault plan, many states let you sue the at-fault driver for those injuries. For instance, a typical no-fault plan does not pay you damages for pain and suffering. In many states, you can sue the other driver for pain and suffering only if your other medical expenses (hospital bills, doctors' fees, and related costs) exceed a specified amount.

Insurance When You Are Financing a Car

If you are financing the purchase of your vehicle, the bank will require that a certain minimum insurance be kept on the car at all times. If you fail to maintain the required insurance, the bank may either repossess your car or purchase the insurance itself and charge it to your account. But keep in mind that the insurance the bank puts on the car relates only to the damage to or theft of the car, that is, collision and comprehensive coverage. The bank just wants to be assured that the security for the loan—in other words, the vehicle—is properly insured against any damage or theft. The bank generally will not get liability insurance for you, even if your liability insurance lapses or is canceled. You should also be aware that the insurance obtained by the bank for damage to or theft of the vehicle is generally much more expensive than what you could obtain yourself through an insurance agent.

Filing Your Insurance Claim

If you are involved in an accident or if your car has been damaged, promptly notify your insurance agent of the claim, regardless of whose fault the accident was. If you fail to let the insurance company know of the accident within a reasonable time, you may unwittingly be letting it off the hook to defend you or pay any judgment against you. Your insurance agent can advise you on the necessary forms to file with the insurance company so it can start processing the claim.

Your insurance company has a duty to deal with you fairly and in good faith. This means that if you submit a legitimate claim to your insurance company and the claim is covered by the policy, the insurance company must pay it. If your insurance company refuses to pay on a valid claim, and you are forced to hire a lawyer to defend you and you ultimately settle the case or the other party gets a judgment against you, you can sue your insurance company for any damages you suffer. You may also be able to sue your insurance company for punitive damages to punish the insurance company for failing to defend you and pay the settlement or verdict against you.

Suppose that you cause an accident because you weren't paying attention, and the passenger in the other car is seriously injured. Your automobile insurance policy covers you to the extent of $100,000 per person, $300,000 per incident. The injured person offers to settle the case with your insurance company for your policy limit of $100,000, but your insurance company refuses. A trial follows and a jury awards the injured passenger $500,000. You don't have $400,000 to pay the excess over the insurance policy limits, and paying what you can will lead to your financial ruin. Do you have any rights against your insurance company in this situation? Yes. If an insurance company receives an offer to settle a case for the limits of your insurance policy, and there is good reason to believe that a jury will probably award more than the policy's limits, generally the insurance company has a duty to settle the case. If it doesn't, the insurance company must pay any sums awarded over the limits.

If a lawsuit is filed against you, you have a duty to cooperate with your insurance company and assist in the legal defense of your case. If you don't, your insurance company may not have to defend you or pay off on your policy.

AUTOMOBILE ACCIDENTS

Your Liability If Someone Else Uses Your Car

If you let another person drive your car and that person causes an accident, are you liable for the damages? That depends on the state. Some states have a "permissive user" statute, which makes you liable for injuries and damages caused by the carelessness of anyone driving your car with your permission. However, such laws may limit the amount of your financial responsibility. In other states, you aren't liable unless you yourself did something wrong, such as failing to maintain the vehicle in a safe condition and that dangerous condition caused the accident. In all states, you can be held liable for injuries and damages if you lend your car to someone you know is an unsafe driver. An example: Stacy lets her cousin Jim drive her car, even though she knows Jim has caused several accidents and has accumulated a number of traffic citations for speeding and other offenses. Jim gets into an accident with Stacy's car, caused by his speeding. Is Stacy liable to the injured person for his or her bodily injuries and the damage to his or her car? Yes. In this case, Stacy exercised bad judgment when she handed the keys to her car to a known poor driver, Jim, and is therefore liable for "negligent entrustment."

Is a parent liable if a child causes an accident while driving the family car? A number of states have a rule called the "family purpose" doctrine, which makes the owner of a vehicle liable for the injuries and damage caused by a spouse or child while driving the car on a family errand. If, for example, a daughter is on her way to the supermarket at her mother's request and gets into an accident, her parents are liable for the injuries and damages she causes (assuming both parents' names are on the title). However, if their son, a high school senior, gets into an accident on the way to the school's Friday night football game, the parents would not be liable, since the boy was not running an errand for the family, but was on a purely personal outing. In states with permissive use statutes, the owner of the vehicle is liable regardless of why the child was using the car, as long as the child was using the car with permission, which can be either express or implied. Hence, in both of the examples used above, in a state with a permissive user law the parents would be liable in both situations. The only way they would not be liable for the injuries and damages done by the son is if they had "grounded" the son and took away his driving privileges for the weekend, and the son was acting in defiance of their orders.

Suppose a thief steals your car and gets into an accident. Can you be held liable for the damages? Clearly you're not liable if you locked your car with the windows rolled up and the thief broke in and hot-wired it. But what if you parked the car outside a store with the door open, the keys in the ignition, and the engine running—in short, an invitation to a thief. Surprisingly, many states do *not* hold you liable should someone steal your car in this case and cause injuries to someone else or damage to another's property. These states hold that the acts of the thief are an "independent superseding cause" of the injuries and damage to others and their property, and therefore relieve the owner or driver from any responsibility for the car thief's actions.

The Driver's Liability to Passengers

In all but a few states, if your careless driving results in an injury to a passenger in your car, you are responsible for that person's injuries. Sounds simple enough. But the law has not always been so easy. Earlier in our legal history, whether you were liable to a passenger depended on who the passenger was and the extent of your fault. For example, a married person was prohibited from suing a spouse for careless (negligent) driving. The reason for this rule was to promote marital harmony, as it was thought that by pitting one spouse against the other would result in marital discord and phony claims. In fact, this rule was a windfall for the insurance companies.

Similarly, in many states, at one time a nonpaying passenger (in legalese, a "social guest") could not sue the driver of the car for injuries resulting from the driver's negligence. The rationale behind the rule was that a person doing a favor for a friend should not be penalized because he causes an accident, that it would cause friends not to ask other friends to go along on motor outings. Suppose that Bill and his friend Debbie are on their way to see a movie; Bill runs into the car in front of him because he didn't see that the light had turned red, and Debbie is injured. In a state having a so-called "guest statute," Debbie could not sue Bill because Debbie was merely a nonpaying passenger (a social guest) who did not pay for the ride. It was a different story, however, if she had contributed money toward gas. Then she became a paying passenger to whom Bill owed a duty not to act in a careless (negligent) manner.

In states that prohibited nonpaying passengers from suing the driver, the prohibition usually applied only to injuries resulting from the driver's "ordinary negligence" (see chapter 10). Ordinary negligence can be defined simply as carelessness: making an unsafe turn or lane change without looking; speeding (but not excessively); or not paying attention to the traffic around and in front of you. But if the driver deliberately tried to harm the passenger or was "grossly negligent" (such as speeding excessively, weaving in and out of traffic, or going around a railroad crossing barrier when a train was approaching rapidly), the passenger usually was able to sue the driver for his or her injuries.

Most states permitted a passenger (even one who was a social guest, that is, a nonpaying passenger) to sue the driver if the driver was intoxicated, since this is considered at least gross negligence. (In some states, when a person driving under the influence of alcohol or drugs gets into an accident, the injured party or parties may be able to sue him or her for punitive damages as well as traditional damages for personal injuries, pain and suffering, lost wages, etc.) A few courts would not let you sue the drunk driver if you were a passenger, on the theory that by accepting a ride with a person you knew to be intoxicated, you "assumed the risk" that an accident would probably result. As a matter of common sense, always think twice about accepting a ride from someone who has been drinking.

What to Do If You Get In an Accident

If you are involved in an accident, there are certain things you should do. The first thing is to stop. If you hit another car (or a pedestrian) and take off, you may be guilty of "hit and run," which is usually considered a felony—even if you were not at fault in hitting the other car or the pedestrian. It is best to remain on the scene and take it from there, rather than complicate your predicament by fleeing.

If you hit an unattended parked car, you must first make a reasonable effort to find the owner, and if he or she is nowhere to be found, you must leave a note with your name, address, telephone number, and license plate number on the windshield of the damaged car. Include a brief description of the damage you believe you caused. Some people will place a note only when they think someone is watching them. Others will place a blank note on the windshield, or false information. However, if you get caught doing this (a bystander may have taken down your license plate number), you may find yourself in serious trouble.

After an accident, if possible, move your car to a safe spot at the side of the road. If your car cannot be moved because of the damage to it, at least get yourself to a position of safety. Warning signals such as flares, reflective triangles, or traffic cones should be placed to let approaching traffic know of the danger ahead.

If you have been injured, try to assess the seriousness of your injuries. Unless you absolutely have to, try not to move if your back or head has been injured. If you aren't seriously hurt, check to see whether the occupants of your car and the other vehicle are injured. The paramedics should be called immediately if anyone has been seriously hurt or suffered a head wound. Qualified personnel should administer first aid. If the injuries are severe or the impact was strong and you hit your head, you should be taken to the emergency room of the nearest trauma hospital, so you can be checked out for possible fractures, concussion, or bleeding in the brain.

Anytime someone is injured or killed or a car is damaged beyond a scratch or small dent, the police should be called. If for some reason they don't arrive, go down to the police station and make a report. If you fail to report an accident in which someone has been injured or killed or has resulted in property damage over a specified dollar amount (such as $500), you may face a criminal penalty, even if you didn't cause the accident. If your car was substantially damaged or if you suffered any personal injuries, do not let the other driver talk you into not reporting the accident. Many times one driver will say, "Don't worry about it; I'll take care of it. I just don't want my insurance company to know about it." The truth of the matter may well be that the driver doesn't have an insurance company to worry about. Your legal obligation is to report the accident.

Write down the license number and a description of the other vehicle or vehicles involved in the accident. Ask to see the other driver's license, vehicle registration, and insurance information. Get the name, address, and telephone number of the other driver. If there were any passengers in the other car, get their names, addresses, and telephone numbers as well.

Get the names, addresses, and telephone numbers of all witnesses. Do not wait for the police to arrive and do this, since some of the witnesses may leave before the police get there. Ask each witness if he or she noticed any other person who saw the accident but who left the scene before you could talk to him or her. As soon as you can, get a written statement from each witness describing in detail what he or she saw, and have the witness date and sign it.

If someone has a camera, take pictures of the accident scene—as many pictures as you can, from every angle you can think of. If you can, get to the roof of a nearby building and take some "aerial" photographs of the scene. When the police arrive on the scene, ask them to take pictures and measurements of skid marks, the distance from the point of impact to where the vehicles ended up, and so on. This information can be used to estimate the speed of the vehicles at the time of the collision and help to determine who caused the accident.

Avoid taking responsibility for the accident, as this can come back to haunt you. Liability is a legal question to be settled only after *all* the facts have been gathered and studied. Many times a person will think that he or she was the sole cause of the accident when in fact the other driver was at least partially to blame. And even if you were partially at fault, in most states you may still be able to recover compensation for some of your injuries and damage to your vehicle.

As soon as possible after the accident, write a thorough account of the facts and events leading up to the accident. Note such things as the time of day, where you were going, whether you were late and in a hurry to get somewhere or had all the time in the world to get to your destination, weather conditions (was it cloudy or sunny, perhaps raining), road conditions (dry or wet, slick with oil, etc.), whether traffic was heavy or light, and how fast you were going. Draw diagrams indicating your movement and speed prior to the accident and the movement and speed of the other car. One diagram should show the final resting positions of the cars immediately after the collision.

Notify your automobile insurance agent of the accident right away. Your agent will be able to get a copy of the police report and start processing your claim immediately. If you are solely or partially responsible for the accident, your insurance company should provide you with an attorney to defend you in case of a civil lawsuit based on the accident. (If the insurance company refuses to provide you with a lawyer, consult your family attorney immediately to see what your rights are.)

If the other driver was at fault, and his or her insurance company accepts responsibility, it normally will pay you for the damages to your car before settling your claims of personal injuries. You should have the mechanic check your car out thoroughly to see that there is no hidden damage from the accident. You can't, however, expect the other party's insurance company to pay for damages to your car that were there before the accident.

Always be careful not to sign any papers sent you from the other driver's insurance company until you have read them carefully. Discuss them with a lawyer if you have any questions or don't understand how the document will affect your rights. Never sign a release form relating to your personal injuries until you have been thoroughly examined by your own physician. Many injuries do not show up for weeks or months after the traumatic event. Since you usually have at least one year to bring suit against the other driver (if a public entity is involved, you may have to file a claim within six months or less from the date of injury), don't feel pressured by the other driver's insurance company to settle immediately. Particularly if you suffered any injuries to your head, neck, back, or knees, you should be evaluated several times over the course of six months or more to determine whether there are any permanent injuries.

If you suffer more than minor injuries in the accident, contact an experienced personal injury lawyer as soon as possible. (See chapter 24 for information about finding a competent attorney and the fee structure involved.) Depending on the state, you have from one to six years to bring a lawsuit for your injuries. However, if you were hit by a government-owned vehicle (such as a police car or fire truck, department of transportation truck, or city bus), you usually have to file a written claim with the appropriate government agency within a much shorter period of time, such as not more than sixty days or six months after the accident. Your failure to do so may cause you to lose your right to sue the government.

If the other driver was cited for violating a traffic regulation, you may be asked to testify at any criminal proceedings. You may wish to have your attorney accompany you, as what you say at the criminal trial may have a bearing on the later civil trial. If you were the driver cited, you'll definitely want to be represented by your own lawyer at the hearing, certainly if it's a serious charge, such as driving under the influence. (Your insurance company normally does not have to provide you with a lawyer in a criminal case against you, only in a civil action based on a claim covered by your insurance policy.)

Preventing Accidents

Lawyers are in a special position to see not only the results, but also the causes of automobile-related accidents. Many accidents could be prevented if every driver realized that driving is a full-time job, one that requires considerable care, skill, and patience. Here are a few things every driver should do to minimize the risk of getting into an automobile accident and to minimize the risk of injury in the case of an accident. Most of them are required by law, as well as by common sense.

* Do not mix alcohol with driving. Even a couple of drinks affects the perception, slows physical response time, and clouds judgment. The majority of traffic accidents involve alcohol to one extent or another. So if you're going out for a night on the town, be sure to have a designated driver, call a cab, or sleep it off on your host's couch.
* Keep your car in good working condition. Tires should be checked regularly for signs of wear and to ensure that they are properly inflated and aligned. Headlights, brake lights, and turn signals should all be checked periodically to see that they are working correctly. Make sure your brakes are in good working order and will stop the vehicle abruptly, if need be.
* Anytime you go driving, whether it's just to the neighborhood supermarket or on a cross-country trip, wear your seat belt, even if your car is equipped with air bags. Infants and younger children should be secured in the backseat in safety seats facing backward, which in turn are held in place by seat belts. Due to the powerful force with which an airbag deploys, a number of infants secured in their car seats properly buckled in the front seat have been seriously injured or killed by the force of rapidly deploying airbags. Most, if not all, states have laws requiring infants under forty pounds or four years of age to be placed in a rear-facing infant seat properly secured in the backseat of the vehicle. Children up to six years old or sixty pounds often are required by law to be fastened in a booster seat in the backseat.
* Do not drive while talking on a cellular telephone, unless you are using a hands-free set that lets you keep both of your hands free. Don't forget that you are driving a vehicle capable of causing tremendous damage and death if not operated in a safe manner. A Harvard study released in December 2002 revealed that using cell phones while driving contributed to 2,000 to 3,000 deaths and 300,000 injuries in one year alone.
* If you ride a motorcycle, wear a helmet at all times. A number of states have laws that make it mandatory for motorcyclists and their passengers to wear helmets. In some states,

a motorcyclist who was not wearing a helmet at the time of the accident cannot recover damages from a negligent driver for injuries a helmet would have prevented.

* Always practice defensive driving. If you can anticipate the accident possibilities of various situations, your chances of having an accident- and injury-free driving record will increase.

DRIVING UNDER THE INFLUENCE

THE CRIMINAL OFFENSE OF DRIVING in an alcohol-impaired condition is known in various parts of the country as driving under the influence (DUI), driving while intoxicated (DWI), or simply "drunk driving." Driving under the influence includes not only driving while intoxicated, but also driving while under the effects of drugs—both illegal drugs, such as marijuana, cocaine, or PCP, and prescription drugs that severely limit a person's ability to operate a motor vehicle safely. When alcohol is combined with many prescription drugs—or even many non-prescription drugs, such as those taken for colds or hay fever—the impairment may be much worse.

At one time, drunk driving was virtually a "socially acceptable" crime, since it seemed that almost everyone did it at one time or another. That time is long since past. Largely through the efforts of Mothers Against Drunk Driving (MADD), a national group originally formed by mothers of children killed by drunk drivers, the penalties for driving while intoxicated have become much more severe. Previously a person charged with drunk driving for the first time often avoided any time in jail by pleading guilty to the lesser charge of reckless driving in exchange for a dismissal of the drunk driving charge. (This is an example of a plea bargain; see chapter 23.) A number of states now have laws severely restricting—even prohibiting—a first-time offender's plea to a lesser offense and mandating that a convicted driver spend at least forty-eight hours in jail for the first offense.

The new laws also have been made tougher by lowering the blood alcohol content level at which a person is legally deemed too impaired to drive. This means that under the new laws it takes less alcohol for you to be considered drunk. Only a few drinks within an hour or two can significantly impair your driving ability, especially if you are tired, haven't eaten much that day, or are taking medication, prescription or over-the-counter.

Today, in a majority of states you are considered intoxicated if your blood alcohol content (BAC) is .08 or higher. Some states do not consider you to be impaired until your BAC is at least .10. This is a far cry from the days when you were not considered intoxicated unless your BAC was .15. As a result of lower blood alcohol levels, combined with aggressive law enforcement, there have been fewer alcohol-related deaths and injuries, although alcohol still plays a role in over 50 percent of all traffic accidents.

Stopping and Testing the Suspected Drunk Driver

A police officer may detect a drunk driver by his or her erratic driving: weaving from side to side; being unable to stay in one lane; speeding up and slowing down without reason; or making unsafe turns; for example. Or the police officer may stop a driver for a routine traffic violation—such as a taillight being out—and then smell alcohol when questioning the driver. Some police departments have taken to setting up sobriety checkpoints on Friday and Saturday nights and holidays to catch drunk drivers.

If a police officer suspects that you may be driving under the influence of alcohol (or drugs), you will normally be put through a variety of field sobriety tests. These tests are designed to assess your awareness and coordination. The police officer may ask you to walk a straight line by placing the heel of one foot in front of the toe of the other foot, proceed several yards, then turn around and return in the same fashion. You also may be requested to close your eyes, tilt your head back, and spread your arms. If you can't maintain your balance and start to fall back, the police officer will suspect intoxication.

You may also be asked to touch the tip of your nose with the first finger of your left hand, then with the first finger of your right hand. If you are unable to touch your nose, the police officer will suspect that you are under the influence. The officer may ask you to stand on one leg for a bit, then on the other to see if you can maintain your balance. You also may be requested to recite the alphabet or perform simple additions or subtractions. Or the police officer may ask you to repeat a tongue twister, such as, "Peter Piper picked a peck of pickled peppers." The officer may shine a flashlight in your eyes to see how quickly your pupils contract.

If you ever find yourself being asked to perform field sobriety tests, make sure that all conditions are as much to your advantage as possible. For example, at night, ask that the tests be performed in a well-lighted area. The ground should be firm, level, and clean, preferably concrete. Tell the officer of any physical disabilities you have that may affect your performance on the tests. Ask the officer to repeat the directions if you don't understand them. If they are still unclear, have the officer demonstrate what he or she wants you to do. When possible, it may be a good idea to have a third person watch the field tests to ensure that the officer conducts them properly.

If you fail the field sobriety test, the officer will take you back to the police station, where you usually will have a choice between having a breath test or blood test. Previously you also had the choice of giving a urine sample. Most states have abolished the urine test because of its inherent unreliability. Before a urine test could be administered, you first had to empty your bladder completely, and then wait until your body produced enough urine for a second sample.

What You Should Do If You Are Stopped for Drunk Driving

Suppose you are driving home from a nice dinner or from a bar where you had a few drinks and a police officer pulls you over on the pretext that your back light is out or that the officer saw you weaving from side to side. The officer smells alcohol on your breath and asks you to step out of the car. The officer asks you whether you have been drinking that evening, and you apply in the affirmative. The officer then asks you how much you had to drink and you reply "two or three beers." (Everyone stopped for suspicion of drunk driving tells the officer they had only two or three drinks.) The officer says that he or she suspects that you are driving under the influence and then tells you that he or she is going to conduct a field sobriety test on you. Should you comply with the officer's request? Many lawyers who specialize in defending motorists accused of drunk driving advise that you do *not* comply, because the field sobriety tests are difficult to do even if you are sober. And if you fail the field sobriety test, this will not look good in the eyes of the jury if you end up fighting the case.

Rather, these expert lawyers advise, calmly and politely tell the officer that you refuse to perform the tests. The officer tells you that if you refuse to take the field sobriety tests, he or she will arrest you immediately on suspicion of drunk driving and take you down to the station for a breath or blood test. The officer may have a portable breath test device he or she wants you to breathe into. Again, experienced drunk-driving defense lawyers advise drivers against doing this type of breath test, as it is not reliable.

Instead, seasoned drunk-driving defense lawyers advise that you only submit to a breath test administered down at the police station. By the time you get there, your blood alcohol level is likely to be higher than when you were stopped by the police officer, as the alcohol has had more time to be absorbed into your bloodstream. A good drunk-driving defense lawyer may be able to convince the jury that when the police officer originally stopped you, your blood alcohol level was well within the .08 level (or .10 level in some states). This is the time that counts to determine your guilt for drunk driving—your blood alcohol content at the time you were stopped, not at the time the breath test was administered.

Drunk-driving defense lawyers generally advise you to take the breath test rather than the blood test; it is generally harder to challenge the results of a blood test than a breath test. Note that if you refuse to take either the breath or blood test at the police station, your license in many states is automatically suspended for a year. To get it back before then, you must file for a hearing with the department of motor vehicles within a specified time, such as ten days, and there is no guarantee that you will get your license back, even if the results of the breath or blood test showed that your blood alcohol content was within the legal limit. Note that refusing the police officer's handheld breath test generally will not result in an automatic suspension of your license.

Even if you refuse to take the breath or blood test at the police station, that does not mean you will escape punishment for drunk driving if you were indeed intoxicated while behind the wheel. The police officer can still testify as to what he or she observed, such as your car weaving all over the road, the smell of alcohol on your breath, any belligerence you demonstrated when you were requested and refused to do the field sobriety test (which is why it is important to conduct yourself reasonably, respectfully, and politely at all times while dealing with the officer), slurred speech, and the like.

If the breath test reveals that you are over the limit, or if you choose the blood test, you will be booked. Many jails and police stations do not fingerprint or photograph people arrested for drunk driving due to the sheer volume of drunk-driving suspects. You will be given the chance to call your spouse, a lawyer, a friend, or anyone else to come down and get you. The police usually will release you to anyone who has a valid driver's license and is not intoxicated.

The police forward all evidence, including the results of the blood alcohol content test, to the district attorney's office, where a decision about whether to prosecute you will be made. If the district attorney's office decides to prosecute you for drunk driving, be advised that because of the stricter laws and more severe penalties these days, you should obtain a good drunk-driving defense attorney with considerable experience in this field to represent you. Ask the lawyer how many trials he or she has defended drunk drivers in, and with what rate of success. Since many states now require that even first-time offenders spend two days in jail, many defendants find they have nothing to lose by going to trial. You certainly don't want a lawyer who simply tells you to plead guilty and take the consequences. You could do that by yourself, and it wouldn't cost you a nickel!

Liability for Injuries Caused by a Drunk Driver

When a drunk driver gets behind the wheel of a car and causes an accident, the drunk driver must pay for all of the injuries to and damages suffered by the injured victim. But can the injured person sue a bar, restaurant, liquor store, or other business that sold or served the alcohol to the driver? Some states allow the injured person to recover damages if the commercial establishment knew that the patron was intoxicated already but nonetheless served or sold additional alcohol to him or her. Many states also impose liability if a liquor store, bar, or other business sells alcoholic beverages to a sober minor who then goes elsewhere, drinks the alcohol, and causes an accident because of his or her impaired condition.

Suppose you give a party at home one night. One of your friends gets drunk and causes an accident while driving home. Are you liable to the person injured by your drunken friend? Today the answer is no. Courts hold that it is the act of drinking the alcohol rather than the mere furnishing of it that is the cause of the intoxication. Nevertheless, if you are having a party where alcohol will be furnished, you should monitor your guests to ensure that they do not become intoxicated. The "designated driver" program whereby one member of a group does not drink while the others do is a sane, reasonable way of reducing the number of drunk drivers on the road. If you notice that one of your guests has become inebriated, you should not let him or her leave until he or she has sobered up sufficiently to handle a car safely. Better to call a cab or let the intoxicated person sleep it off on your couch than to put a ticking time bomb on the road.

Employers who give office parties should likewise exercise caution and common sense to keep an intoxicated employee off the streets and highways. In some cases, the employer can be held liable if an employee gets drunk at an office party, then drives home in an intoxicated condition and injures someone on the way.

FIGHTING TRAFFIC TICKETS

BEFORE MAKING THE DECISION to fight a traffic ticket, first consider the evidence you have to support your version of the facts. If it's simply a case of your word against the word of the police officer, you can be sure that the judge will believe the officer 99.99 percent of the time. For example, if you received a citation for failing to stop because the police officer claims you only came to a "rolling stop," the judge will believe the officer's version over your word that you came to a complete stop. You will need some solid evidence to back up your side of the story.

The testimony of a witness can swing the scales of justice in your favor; however, the judge will consider the reliability of the witness's testimony based on who the witness is. If the witness is your best friend or your spouse, the judge probably won't put much faith in his or her story. But if the witness is a complete stranger to you, his or her testimony is more likely to persuade the judge that your story has merit.

Another thing to consider before fighting a ticket is whether you have a valid legal defense or merely some excuse the law doesn't recognize as sufficient. For instance, a handicap parking space is for use by persons who have applied for and received a special permit to park in such areas. You can't park there because your back is sore that day. Likewise, trying to defend a speeding ticket on the basis that you were late for work is no defense. If, however, a true emergency existed—for instance, you were taking a person who had just severed a limb to the hospital—this may act as a valid defense. Towing a car with a rope instead of a tow bar cannot be justified on the basis that you were only towing it to the repair shop; on the other hand, using a rope to tow the disabled vehicle from the middle of a busy intersection to the side of the road might be justified if the car posed a clear danger to passing motorists.

In some cases, you might get out of the ticket by using a photograph. For example, suppose that you are given a ticket for speeding on an unfamiliar road. You were traveling at 45 miles per hour, which to you seemed reasonable, but the posted speed limit was 35 miles per hour. If a tree hid the sign, go back and take a picture of it to support your contention. Should the city maintenance crew have trimmed the tree before you got a picture of it, obtain work orders from the appropriate city department showing that landscaping and tree trimming work was done in the area after you received your ticket.

Here is another example of how a picture may be helpful: Suppose you were cited for parking in a handicap zone—something you did unknowingly because the space was not properly marked. You should take a picture of the space when no vehicle is parked there to show the lack of an adequate warning. Some states require that a handicap parking space be marked clearly by a blue-and-white sign and blue painting on the ground. If there was no sign and the painting was faded, you should be able to beat the ticket with a photograph.

Several weeks before the trial, you will be "arraigned" (see chapter 23). At this time you will be brought before a traffic commissioner, told of the charges against you, and asked how you plead: guilty or not guilty. If you plead guilty, the judge will impose the sentence then and there, usually a monetary fine. You may be offered the chance to plead guilty "with an explanation." This has the same effect as pleading guilty, but if you have a legitimate excuse, the judge may suspend your fine. At this time, you may also be given the option of going to traffic school. Traffic school usually is offered as an alternative only if the offense was routine and not serious, and you have not had another moving violation or attended traffic school in the last year or two. Traffic school—once renowned for its gory pictures of blood-spattered highways— now generally consists of a six- to eight-hour classroom refresher course on traffic rules and safety. Upon your successful completion of traffic school, the ticket is expunged from your record. This usually means that your automobile insurance company doesn't hear about the ticket, so it won't be used against you in determining your insurance rates. If you plead not guilty at the arraignment, the judge will set a date for the trial.

Sometimes it is worth fighting a ticket simply in the sheer hope that the police officer will not appear. (This is more apt to occur if you've received a parking ticket rather than a moving violation.) If the officer doesn't show up, oppose any request for a continuance that the prosecution may make, and ask the judge for an immediate dismissal of all the charges.

The Trial

Trials for traffic tickets are usually informal hearings presided over by a traffic commissioner who acts as judge. You can have a lawyer represent you, but this is usually unnecessary because the cost of the lawyer ordinarily will exceed the maximum fine. If, however, you are facing more serious ramifications than a $50 or $100 fine—such as the suspension of your license or a greatly increased insurance premium—you may wish to have a lawyer represent you.

An attorney from the district attorney's office will prosecute the case against you. He or she will question the police officer and attempt to establish that you violated the traffic code. In the typical trial, the prosecutor will spend five to six minutes questioning the police officer. They have done this hundreds of times and know the routine pat. When the prosecutor is finished questioning the police officer, you are free to cross-examine him or her. After your cross-examination, the prosecution may have a couple of questions of the officer to rebut any new issues you brought up, and will then rest its case, unless there was another officer present at the time the ticket was given. Once the prosecution rests, you present your version of the facts. When you are done telling your version of the facts, the prosecution has the right to cross-examine you. If you have any other witnesses to present, now is the time to do it.

If you received a traffic citation in connection with a traffic accident, the driver of the other car and any witnesses who saw the accident happen usually will be called to testify against you. Where the police officer did not see the accident, the officer can testify only to the physical evidence he or she witnessed at the scene of the crime, such as the length of skid marks and the final resting positions of the vehicles.

After you have presented your testimony and rested your case, the prosecution has the right to put on any "rebuttal" witnesses to discredit or contradict any of the witnesses you called. When that is over, you get to make a closing argument to the judge, telling him or her why you shouldn't be convicted of the traffic violation. The prosecutor also gets to make a closing argument. The traffic commissioner then renders a verdict, usually on the spot. Occasionally, the commissioner will take a case under advisement ("submission") and mail the decision to you in a day or two.

Why will the judge believe the police officer over you? Because the police officer has no incentive to lie, nothing to lose if he or she wins or loses the case. You, on the other hand, have a lot to lose if you are found guilty of the offense: You will face a monetary fine and an increase in your insurance premiums. When a judge is faced with two witnesses, one of whom has nothing to gain or lose from his or her testimony, and the other who has a lot to lose, the judge will invariably believe the witness who has nothing to win or lose from the case, in this case the police officer.

The Winning Edge

Two things will greatly improve your chances for success in traffic court: your appearance and your presentation. Going in neatly groomed and nicely dressed will make a better impression on the judge than arriving unshaven and with uncombed hair and wearing sloppy or overly casual clothes. Practicing a few times beforehand what you plan to say will not only help to make your testimony flow better, but also give you more confidence at the trial. You may want to prepare a few notes several days in advance to make sure you cover everything, but the judge will not let you read a prepared statement.

Be calm, cool, and methodical during the presentation of your case. Know where you're going, and then thoughtfully and thoroughly plan how you're going to get there. Never show any anger toward or frustration with the police officer, the prosecutor, or the judge. Rather, show the judge the logic of your defense and you'll have a good chance of "beating the rap."

Example of Testimony in a Speeding Case

In the following case, the defendant was cited for speeding while she and a friend were on their way home from work. The police officer who cited her has testified that as he was coming onto the freeway, he noticed a dark blue sedan going at a high rate of speed and weaving in and out of traffic. He gave chase and found the defendant proceeding along in the number three lane at 65 miles per hour (the legal speed limit) in a dark blue sedan. The defendant contends that she had been traveling in the number three lane at this speed the entire time and that it was another car that the police officer observed speeding. Here is an example of some questions the defendant might ask of the police officer on cross-examination to support her theory that the officer saw another car speeding:

Q: How many lanes away from you was the dark blue car when you first spotted it?

A: Four.

Q: How would you describe the traffic at this time: light, moderate, or heavy?

A: Moderate.

Q: Were there any cars between yours and the dark blue car when you first observed it?

A: Yes.

Q: Approximately how many cars were there between your car and the dark blue car when you first saw it?

A: I would say four or five.

Q: What made you notice the dark blue car?

A: I noticed it because it was weaving in and out of traffic, traveling at a high rate of speed.

Q: Did you get a good look at the driver when you first saw the car, or were you just looking at the car itself?

A: I was just looking at the car itself.

Q: So you didn't see the driver at that time?

A: That's correct.

Q: Could you tell at that time whether the driver was a man or a woman?

A: No, I could not.

Q: Did you see any passengers in the car at this time?

A: No, I did not.

Q: Did you see the license plate on the car at this time?

A: No.

Q: Did you notice anything on the back of the dark blue sedan when you first saw it, such as bumper stickers or dents?

A: No.

Q: Were you able to move in immediately behind the dark blue sedan and give chase when you first saw it?

A: No.

Q: Isn't it true that you actually lost sight of the dark blue sedan before you could get behind it?

A: That's correct.

Q: And you never saw a passenger?

A: That's correct.

Q: So it's possible that the car you first saw was only occupied by the driver, with no passengers?

A: That's possible.

Q: And it's possible that the car you first saw was driven by a man and not a woman?

A: That's possible.

Q: How long did you chase the dark blue sedan?

A: About a mile . . . a little more than a mile, I'd say.

Q: And during this time you did not have it in sight, correct?

A: That's correct.

Q: How fast were you going during this pursuit?

A: Seventy-five, eighty miles an hour.

Q: Isn't it true that you had already passed the car I was driving before you noticed it?

A: Yes, that's true.

Q: So up to that point, you believed the car you were chasing was somewhere in front of you, perhaps far ahead of you?

A: Yes.

Q: What did you do after you spotted my car?

A: I applied my brakes, slowed down, moved in behind you, and put on the flashing lights.

Q: Did you notice anything on the back of my car?

A: Not that I remember, no.

Q: I have here a picture of the back end of my car as it appeared on the date and at the time in question, your honor. I would like to show it to the officer to refresh his memory. [First show the picture to the prosecuting attorney, then hand the picture to the bailiff to take to the witness.] Now can you tell me whether you noticed anything about the back end of my car?

A: Yes, I noticed that the right rear end appeared to have been damaged in an accident.

Q: And didn't you wonder why you hadn't observed that damage when you first spotted the dark blue sedan when you got onto the freeway?

A: I guess it may have struck me as a little strange that I didn't see it originally.

Q: Thank you. I have no more questions of this witness, Your Honor.

At this point, the defendant will testify that she had been proceeding in the number three lane at sixty-five miles per hour the entire time and that she observed a similar car, but newer and not damaged, speeding along and weaving through traffic. The defendant will also testify that there was only one person in the other car and that the police officer had passed her own car before slowing down. The defendant will also present the testimony of her passenger, who will corroborate the defendant's testimony.

This example demonstrates how being prepared and presenting your defense methodically will help you win your case. If you take the time to plan your presentation, you'll greatly increase your chances of walking out of the courtroom with a smile on your face.

RESPONSIBILITIES OF PAY PARKING LOT OPERATORS

If your car is stolen from or damaged in a pay parking lot, your ability to recover damages from the operator of the lot depends on exactly what the parking lot operator provides. If the operator merely gives you a space to park your car in and you are responsible for parking it, locking it, and taking the keys with you, generally you assume the risk that the car may be broken into. If, however, there is a history of frequent break-ins into cars parked in the lot, the operator can be held liable if a sign informing you of that risk has not been posted in a conspicuous place. And if you can prove that it was the operator or an employee who broke into your car, you can recover damages from the operator, regardless of what any sign says.

If there is no attendant, or if each driver is responsible for parking his or her own car, the parking lot operator usually is not liable for damages to your car caused by another driver trying to park his or her own car. Liability might be imposed, however, if the parking spaces are small and not marked "Compact Cars Only" or the like, or if there is not enough room to maneuver a car into or out of a space without hitting another vehicle parked in a marked space. Likewise, if the driver who hits your car was following the instructions or directions of the lot attendant, the parking lot operator is liable for the damages, and the driver of the car that hit you is probably liable as well.

When a parking lot attendant damages your car while trying to park it or another car, the operator is generally liable for the damages to your car. If the attendant fails to lock your car after parking it, the operator is also usually liable for any items stolen from the car. If it is likely that even locked cars in the lot may be broken into, the attendant has a duty to maintain a reasonable lookout to prevent break-ins.

Suppose that your car is stolen from an attended parking lot. Does the parking lot operator have to pay for it? If the attendant locked the car, the lot is not in a high-crime area, and no cars had ever been stolen from this lot or other lots in the area before, then the operator probably isn't liable. But if the employee left the keys in the unlocked car or the car was locked but the keys were left unguarded, then the operator may be liable.

When you park in a pay parking lot, invariably there will be a "disclaimer of liability" or "waiver of damages." If you receive a ticket stub, the disclaimer ordinarily will be printed on the back. If ticket stubs are not issued, or in addition to ticket stubs, the parking lot operator will usually post signs disclaiming responsibility for damage to the vehicle or for theft of the car or its contents. The courts do not recognize these disclaimers if the parking lot operator or an employee is in any way responsible for the damages or theft.

THREE

Estate Planning

*e*STATE PLANNING HAS traditionally been thought of as a luxury reserved only for the wealthy. Today, as we will see, estate planning has become necessary for nearly everybody. Few estates are so small that they will not receive any of the benefits of estate planning.

For most of us, estate planning means planning for death. Who gets the property? How much will be due in taxes? Who will take care of our minor children? Will the estate be tied up in probate court for years? These are some of the considerations that motivate us to put our affairs in order. Estate planning also can involve complex strategies to reduce taxes during a person's lifetime, but this is generally a concern only of the very wealthy.

This chapter focuses upon what the average American needs to know about estate planning: How to determine the size of your estate; what happens to your property if you fail to plan; the impact of taxes imposed after your death; and ways to avoid probate. The following chapter discusses wills—an integral part of any estate plan—and includes instructions for making your own simple will.

People set up an estate plan to achieve a number of goals. For many the main goal is to avoid or minimize estate and gift taxes, so more of the estate goes to loved ones instead of to the government. Others are primarily motivated by a wish to avoid the expenses and delays of probate. Ensuring that there are enough liquid assets or ready cash to pay any federal estate or state inheritance taxes and to provide for the surviving spouse and minor children while the estate goes through probate are other important concerns.

DETERMINING THE SIZE OF YOUR ESTATE

Before doing any estate planning, you need to determine the size of your estate—what you own and how much it's worth. When lawyers talk about estates, they speak of property: "real property" and "personal property." Real property is legalese for real estate. Personal property, or personalty, is everything else: cars, boats, airplanes, cash, stocks and bonds, clothing, furniture, jewelry, coin and stamp collections, dishes, antiques, and so on. This is an important distinction to make because the average person often thinks of "property" as only real estate. When a lawyer uses the word "property," it usually includes every type of possession—real estate and personal assets—that a person has.

If you're like most Americans, the major assets of your estate are your home, perhaps a second piece of real estate (such as a vacation home or investment property), life insurance proceeds, retirement benefits, stocks and bonds, bank accounts, automobiles, furniture, and jewelry. The easiest way to get a handle on the size of your estate is to buy a thorough financial statement form at your local stationery store that carries legal forms, and complete it or use a computer software program. Be sure to include all retirement plans and death benefits, such as life insurance benefits (including term insurance if you plan on keeping it in force), Individual Retirement Accounts (IRAs), certificates of deposits, treasury bills, and pension plans. If your jewelry is worth a good deal of money or you have a valuable stamp or coin collection, consider getting an expert appraisal. (It's also a good idea to have an appraisal in case you ever have to file an insurance claim.) Note that if a business is an important part of your estate, it requires special planning. What will happen to the business after you die: Will it be shut down and its assets liquidated; sold to a third party; or kept going by your children or someone else, such as a valuable employee with whom you have entered into a buy-sell agreement in the event of your death?

Title to Property

To determine the size of your estate, you need to find out how title to your various belongings is held. Title is also important in determining what right you have to dispose of an individual asset. Obviously, you can't give something away if you don't own it. When you own property with someone else, the manner in which title is held can affect the type of planning you can do with it. The various forms of ownership and their distinguishing features are discussed below. To find out how title to something is held, you will have to see the document of ownership, such as the deed to a house; the certificate of ownership for a car, airplane, or boat; stock certificates, bankbooks, and the like.

Separate Property

When title to anything is in your name alone, it is generally presumed to be your separate property, to do with as you see fit. You can sell it, you can give it away during your life, or you can even give it to someone in your will or living trust. But if you own the property with someone else and title was taken in your name alone—say, for convenience—your right to sell or give the property away may be affected. Also, if you are married, your spouse may have some rights in the property even though title is in your name alone.

Joint Tenancy

Two (or more) people can hold title to property as joint tenants. Each joint tenant owns an equal share of the property and can dispose of only that share. The most important thing to know about joint tenancies for estate planning is that a joint tenancy carries with it the automatic right of survivorship. This means that when one joint tenant dies, the remaining joint tenant(s) automatically receives the other's share. The property does not go through probate (although its value is still subject to federal estate and state inheritance taxes, which is discussed later in this chapter), and any provision in the deceased person's will or living trust relating to the distribution of property held in joint tenancy is ignored by the court. If you own property in joint tenancy with someone else, be sure you want that person to get your share of the property when you die. If not, then you should change the title to tenants in common (see below).

Tenancy by the Entireties

Approximately twenty states recognize a tenancy by the entirety, which is basically a joint tenancy that can exist only between a husband and wife. As with a joint tenancy, there is the right of survivorship, and the deceased spouse's interest automatically passes to the surviving spouse, without the need for probate. One way a tenancy by the entirety differs from a joint tenancy is that some states have special rules limiting the ability of a creditor to satisfy one spouse's debt from property held in tenancy by the entireties.

Tenants in Common

A tenancy in common is another form of joint ownership that can exist between any two or more people. Each tenant in common owns an equal share of the property (unless they agree otherwise), and can sell or give away only his or her share. The major difference between a tenancy in common and a joint tenancy is that in the former, there is no right of survivorship. When a tenant in common dies, his or her share of the property is distributed according to the wishes expressed in his or her will or living trust. If there is no will or living trust, the share goes to his or her heirs—the next of kin—entitled to it by state law.

Community Property

Nine states—Arizona, California, Idaho, Louisiana, New Mexico, Nevada, Texas, Washington, and Wisconsin—recognize a form of joint ownership between a husband and wife called community property. Married couples in Alaska can elect to have their property treated as community property if they sign a document to that effect. If you live in Alaska and wish to have your property treated as community property, you should do so with the advice of an experienced family law attorney or estate planning lawyer.

Holding title as community property for the most part gives a husband and wife the same rights as joint tenants. Each spouse owns one-half of the community property and can generally dispose of only his or her share. There is one major difference from a joint tenancy, however: The owner of a share of community property can distribute his or her share of the community property according to the terms of his or her will or living trust. Remember that with property held as joint tenants, the property automatically goes to the surviving joint tenant(s), regardless of what the deceased joint tenant's will or living trust provides.

In community property states, for a married couple it is almost always better to hold title to property as community property rather than as joint tenants. Like property owned in joint tenancy, property owned as community property generally doesn't have to go through probate if there is no will and it goes outright to the surviving spouse. There may also be important tax advantages in determining the "basis" of the property as to how much taxable capital gain is due at the death of one of the owners of community property.

WHAT HAPPENS IF YOU DON'T PLAN

IF YOU DIE WITHOUT A WILL or living trust (or other estate planning tool), your property will be distributed according to the laws of "intestate succession" of the state where you were living at the time of your death. In this event, it is the state—not you, the owner of the property—that determines who gets what and how much. This may or may not be the way in which you would like to have your property distributed.

The laws of intestate succession vary greatly from state to state. The following examples show just a few of the ways in which property may be divided if a person dies without a will. Keep in mind that if you own property with someone else, the title can affect who gets it. For example, if the property is held by you and another person as joint tenants, that person gets your share if you die first, regardless of what your will or living trust provides.

When There Is a Surviving Spouse

It is a common misconception that when a married person dies without a will, his or her surviving spouse automatically gets all the property. In fact, the amount the surviving spouse receives depends upon the ownership of the property (e.g., community property versus separate property), whether there are any children or grandchildren, and whether the parents or brothers and sisters of the deceased spouse are living.

In many states, when a married person dies without a will or living trust and leaves a spouse and one child, the surviving spouse gets half of the property and the child gets the other half. (If the child is a minor, someone will have to be appointed guardian of the property until the child reaches the age of majority, 18 in most states, 19 in a few.) If there are two or more children, the surviving spouse receives only one-third of the estate, and the children receive the other two-thirds equally. Other states give the surviving spouse one-half or one-third of the estate regardless of the number of children. In some states, the surviving spouse receives cash up to a certain amount and then a percentage (typically one-half) of the rest of the estate.

In most community property states, the surviving spouse receives all of the community property, but shares the deceased spouse's separate property (property the deceased spouse owned before marriage or acquired during marriage as a gift or inheritance during the marriage) with the children, and if there are none, the parents or siblings of the deceased spouse.

In a few states, the surviving spouse gets a percentage of the personal assets and a life estate in anywhere from one-third to all of the deceased spouse's real estate. A life estate gives a person the right to live on the property and use it for the rest of his or her life (see chapter 6). This is a remnant of old English law, when women had "dower" rights and men had "curtesy" rights.

If a child dies before a parent but leaves a child of his or her own (in other words, a grandchild), when the grandparent dies the grandchild is entitled to the share of the estate that his or her parent would have otherwise received. Consider the following illustration: John Jones had two children, Jimmy and David. When John died, only David was still living; Jimmy had died several years earlier. However, Jimmy left a daughter, Kristen, who was living at the time of John's death. David and Kristen each get one-half of John's estate. (We'll assume for this example that John did not leave a surviving spouse.) If Jimmy had left two children, they would have divided equally the one-half share he would have received had he been living at the time of John's death. If Jimmy left no children or other issue, David gets his entire share.

If a person dies leaving a spouse but no children or other issue, some states give the surviving spouse everything. Other states split the estate between the surviving spouse and the deceased person's parents (or brothers and sisters, if the parents are no longer living). In community property states, the surviving spouse usually gets all of the community property but must share the separate property with the deceased spouse's parents, if living, and if not, his or her brothers and sisters. If there are no surviving children, parents, or brothers and sisters, the surviving spouse generally gets all of the deceased spouse's separate property in addition to all of the community property.

When There Is No Surviving Spouse

If a person dies without leaving a surviving spouse, then the property goes to the children (or grandchildren if a child has died). An adopted child is entitled to share in an estate to the same extent as a child born to the deceased person. (In some states, the adopted child shares in the estate of his or her biological parents as well.) Unadopted stepchildren ordinarily do not share in the estate of a stepparent who has died without a will or living trust. As for children born out of wedlock, the rule used to be that the child was entitled to inherit from his or her mother, but could inherit from his or her father only if the father had admitted in writing that the child was his. Today, a child born out of wedlock is entitled to inherit from both mother and father. Of course, the child still has to prove that a particular man is its father. Advances in DNA testing have made this much easier and certain than the old days when the father would be brought into court and the jury would compare the features of the alleged father and child in making their decision. (More on proving paternity is found in chapter 1.)

When there are no children, grandchildren, great-grandchildren, and so on (in law, "issue" or "lineal descendants"), the deceased person's parents usually each get one-half of the property. In many states, if only one parent survives, he or she gets all of the property. Some states divide the property among the deceased person's parents and his or her brothers and sisters. If the parents are not living, the brothers and sisters usually split the estate. When a person dies without a close relative, then the closest next of kin, such as a niece or nephew, aunt or uncle, or cousin, share the estate. What happens when no heir can be found? The state steps in and sells all of the property. The net proceeds are then deposited in a special state bank account. If the money is not claimed within a certain period of time, the state gets it. If a distant relative of yours has died without leaving a will or living trust or close relatives, it may be to your benefit to consult a probate attorney to investigate whether you have any rights to the estate.

Other Considerations

If you have any minor children, by failing to plan your estate you throw away the chance to nominate a guardian for them should the worst happen to you. Who will raise them if you're not around? You also lose the right to name the executor or executrix of your will (or successor trustee, if you use a living trust)—the person you wish to oversee the management and distribution of your estate. The judge will appoint a guardian for your children and an executor or executrix of your estate without your having a say about it. And if your estate is larger, your failure to plan may make the government tens, even hundreds, of thousands of dollars richer—money your loved ones could have received.

What Probate Is and How It Works

Probate is the legal process in which the probate court (called "surrogate court" in some states) authenticates a written document as the will of the deceased person and directs the distribution of the estate to the persons entitled to it according to the will. If there is no will (or living trust) or if the will is declared invalid, the probate court distributes the property to the heirs entitled to it under the state laws of intestate succession (discussed above).

Within a certain time after a person dies, usually thirty days, the person named as the executor or executrix of the will must file the will, a certified copy of the death certificate, and a petition to probate the will with the court clerk and begin probate proceedings. (Usually the executor or executrix will hire a probate attorney who will take care of these things for him or her. The attorney's fees are paid from the deceased person's estate.) These papers are filed in the probate court in the county where the deceased person had his or her principal residence, his or her "domicile." If the person died without a will, the next of kin can file the same documents—except the will, of course—with the probate court.

The close relatives of the deceased person usually must be notified of the probate proceedings. Later, a court hearing is held at which the executor or executrix must prove that the document in question is in fact the deceased person's will, that the person was of sound mind when he or she signed the will, and that the will satisfies all legal requirements. Most states permit a person who witnessed the will to sign an affidavit stating that he or she was present at the signing of the will, saw the testator (or testatrix) sign the will, and that the witnesses then signed the will. In some states, at least one witness may have to appear in court and testify that he or she witnessed the signing of the will. If none of the witnesses can be found and the will is proper on its face, the law presumes that the will is valid and places the burden to prove otherwise on any person objecting to it. Some states now allow a will to be "self-proving," which requires the witnesses to sign the will under penalty of perjury that they witnessed the testator or testatrix sign the will, that he or she appeared over the age of 18 (19 in a few states), seemed mentally competent, and did not appear to be acting under the influence of anyone.

If a holographic (handwritten) will is involved, someone familiar with the deceased person's handwriting can testify as to whether the handwriting is indeed that of the deceased person. If a forgery is suspected, known writing samples of the deceased person can be used for comparison, and professional handwriting experts and document examiners may be called upon to assist the court.

After the will has been proved to be that of the deceased person, the court will give an order accepting the will for probate, and the court usually confirms the executor or executrix. If the executor or executrix named in the will refuses or cannot accept the position, the court will confirm the testator's or testatrix's second choice if there is one and, if not, will appoint another person. If the person died without a will, the court will appoint an administrator (or administratrix) of the estate, whose functions are the same as the executor. The administrator is usually the deceased person's next of kin—the person who will inherit all or the largest portion of the estate. Like the executor, the administrator generally hires an attorney to probate the estate; the fees, like those of the executor's attorney, are paid by the deceased person's estate.

The executor (or administrator, as the case may be) collects all of the deceased person's assets, inventories them, and then has them appraised. Creditors of the deceased person are notified so they can file their claims with the probate court. If a creditor fails to file a claim within the specified time—say, four months after being notified—that claim is lost forever. If a creditor's claim is disputed, an amount sufficient to satisfy that claim may be put in a separate fund pending the outcome of the litigation, and the rest of the estate may be distributed. A large creditor's claim can hold up distribution of the entire estate until the dispute is settled.

After any challenges to the will and disputed creditor's claims have been resolved, the taxes, costs of administration (including fees to the executor or administrator and attorney), funeral expenses, creditors, and the like are paid. Finally, the remaining property is transferred to the persons named in the will or entitled to it by law.

Why Avoid Probate?

There are some rather serious disadvantages to probate that prompt many people to seek ways to avoid the probate process. In his classic novel *Bleak House*, Charles Dickens painted a grim picture in which it took several generations to probate an estate. By the time the estate was finally ready for distribution, however, lawyers' fees and court costs had devoured the entire estate, leaving the heirs with nothing but heartache for their years of anguished waiting and suffering.

Although probate isn't quite that bad these days, even with modern procedures probate can be interminably long, unduly expensive, and unbearably insufferable, especially to a grieving family that is trying to get on with their lives as best as possible after the death of a loved one. It still takes anywhere from six months to three years to probate an estate depending upon its size and complexity, with the average probate taking one to one-and-a-half years.

During the probate process, restrictions are generally placed on dealing with and selling the estate's assets. If the surviving spouse or other beneficiary wishes to sell a piece of property, for example, the executor or administrator may first have to seek permission to do so from the probate court. The proceeds from the sale of an asset usually are placed in the estate's bank account until the judge orders the distribution of the account.

During the time an estate is in the probate court, the surviving spouse and minor children are given a reasonable allowance for living expenses. What amount is "reasonable" depends on the size of the estate, the circumstances of the survivors, the standard of living to which they are accustomed, and the solvency and liquidity of the estate.

Another reason many people want to avoid probate is the cost involved. The ordinary costs involved in probating an estate are the executor's (or administrator's) fee, the fee of the executor's (or administrator's) attorney, court filing fees, and advertising fees (to publish notice of the person's death to allow creditors and others to file their claims or challenges). On top of these expenses, there could be additional fees to the executor or administrator and the attorney to compensate for "extraordinary" services, such as defending the estate in a will contest or against a disputed creditor's claim.

A final reason some people want to avoid probate is to reduce the emotional effect on the survivors, so they can get on with their lives. This can be very hard to do when the survivors are constantly being reminded of the death of a loved one while the estate is tied up in the courts. A bitter will contest among relatives can certainly leave deep emotional scars. A living trust or other estate planning tools that avoid probate can provide for the quick distribution of the estate and let everyone start making a new life as soon as possible.

Avoiding Probate May Not Mean Avoiding Taxes

Many people believe that avoiding probate means avoiding death taxes (federal estate taxes and state inheritance taxes). This is not necessarily true. It is possible to avoid probate and reduce or even eliminate death taxes in many cases through proper planning. But just because some assets don't go through probate does not mean they aren't counted for tax purposes.

An example: Juan, an elderly man in poor health, owns a piece of real estate that he wants his niece, Cory, to get when he dies. Juan knows that if the land passes through probate with the rest of his assets, it will be subject to estate taxes. Thinking to avoid such taxes, Juan deeds the land to himself and his niece Cory as joint tenants and dies the next week. At the moment of Juan's death, the land automatically belongs to Cory; it does not go through probate. But the land is subject to the same amount of taxes as if it had gone through the probate process. Its value is included in Juan's estate, and the federal estate taxes and state inheritance taxes, if any, are based on the total amount of Juan's estate, including the land. In short, Juan didn't save a penny in taxes by avoiding probate. (Juan did, however, manage to speed up the transfer of the property to Cory and did reduce the fees his executor or administrator and the attorney received. However, by making the gift during his life rather than at his death, Juan lost important benefits regarding the "basis" of the property.)

Ways to Avoid Probate

Here are some of the common methods for avoiding probate:

Joint Tenancy

As we discussed earlier, when two or more people own property as joint tenants, title automatically transfers to the surviving owner(s) upon the death of a joint tenant. A provision in a will or living trust that attempts to dispose of the joint tenant's interest in the property in any other manner will not be enforced by the court. If your estate is large enough for you to think about reducing estate and inheritance taxes, holding property in joint tenancy may defeat the plan, since that property will not be available for a trust to take full advantage of the marital deduction, discussed later in this chapter. (Proper estate planning with a living trust, discussed below, that includes a marital deduction trust, lets you avoid probate *and* save estate taxes.)

Contrary to popular belief, in most cases *joint tenancy does not avoid probate; it merely delays it.* When a husband and wife own property as joint tenants, it is true that when the first spouse dies, the property automatically goes to the surviving spouse. However, when the surviving spouse dies, the property will then have to go through probate.

As observed earlier, holding title as joint tenants does not necessarily mean avoiding death taxes. The net value of the deceased joint tenant's share of the joint tenancy is still included in his or her estate for tax purposes.

Suppose that Tom and Pam are married and hold title to their house as joint tenants. Assuming Tom dies first, his share automatically goes outright to Pam. Jeff, Tom and Pam's only child, convinces Pam to put his name on the deed as a joint tenant so the property will avoid probate when Pam dies. By doing so, Pam may have some immediate gift tax implications. By adding Jeff's name as a joint tenant, Pam may be deemed to have made a gift of one-half of the property to the new joint tenant (Jeff) and may be required to file a gift tax return.

Also, suppose that a few years down the road Pam and Jeff have a falling out. Jeff could go to court and bring an action to partition (divide) the property, which invariably means the property would have to be sold. And once Jeff's name is on the deed, his creditors—including an ex-wife seeking back alimony or child support—could force a sale of the property to get up to one-half of the sale proceeds. And what happens if Jeff dies in a car accident while Pam is still living? These are just a few of the possible scenarios that illustrate why putting a child's name on a deed (or bank account or investment account) should be done only with the greatest caution and with the advice of a knowledgeable estate planning attorney.

Giving Gifts during Your Lifetime

Many people today are not waiting until they die to make a gift to their loved ones, but rather are making gifts during their lifetimes so they can share in the beneficiary's enjoyment of the gift. But making a gift during your lifetime may have an effect on your estate taxes.

Every year, you are entitled to give a gift of up to $11,000 per person to as many people as you want without having any gift or estate tax consequences. A married couple can make combined gifts up to $22,000 to as many people as they want each year without any tax ramifications. If you are single and wish to give your grandchildren $11,000 apiece for graduating from college, you can do so and you won't even have to file a gift tax return.

But if you are single and give more than $11,000 to any one individual, then you will have to file a gift tax return. For instance, if you are a widow and you give your daughter $50,000 to keep her struggling business afloat, you will have to file a gift tax return for that year for $39,000 (remember, the first $11,000 is not counted). Whether you will have to pay taxes on that gifts depends on whether you had made any previous gifts that counted against your gift tax exemption.

An important caution: Do not start making substantial gifts without first discussing it with a good estate planning lawyer, who can advise you on all of the implications, tax and otherwise. Remember that even if gift giving might benefit you taxwise, you have to be in the position to afford to give the gift. This depends in large part on your financial liquidity (ready cash or liquid assets that can be sold quickly), your age, and your health. If you give away too much of your estate, and some of your major cash-producing assets (such as stocks and bonds) decline in value, your income—and standard of living—may drop dramatically. You could well find yourself having to ask for your property back. Be aware, though, that once you make a gift, you cannot revoke it, and you can't compel the person you gave the gift to (the donee) to return it—assuming he or she hasn't already spent it.

Totten Trusts and Pay-On-Death Accounts

So-called "Totten Trusts" and pay-on-death accounts are bank accounts that let you direct funds to be paid to a designated person upon your death. An example of the wording of a pay-on-death account could be something like: "Peggy Smith as Trustee for Stephen Smith and Katie Smith." During Peggy's lifetime, there are no restrictions on her use of the funds in the account, and she may even close the account completely at any time, in effect revoking the gifts to Stephen and Katie. During Peggy's lifetime, neither Stephen nor Katie could access the money in this account. However, if the account is still in existence upon Peggy's death, then all Stephen and Katie need to do would be to bring a certified copy of Peggy's death certificate and their own identification (valid driver's licenses or passports, for example) and they could claim the balance of the account.

Many people also use "as Trustee for" (ATF) accounts for stock certificates. As with ATF bank accounts, you can sell these stocks at any time during your life without having to give the proceeds to the beneficiaries. If at your death the ATF stocks still exist, the beneficiary or beneficiaries are entitled to them upon proper proof.

ATF accounts should be used only for relatively small amounts of money or stock, since at death all of the money or stock is paid to the beneficiary in one lump sum, assuming he or she is at least 18 (19 in a few states). And even though ATF accounts do not pass through probate, they are still counted as assets belonging to your estate for estate tax purposes.

LIFE INSURANCE

Life insurance is an essential part of estate planning. Indeed, the proceeds from a life insurance policy frequently constitute the largest or second largest asset (after the house) of many estates. Life insurance provides ready cash to support the surviving spouse and children, pay any debts and taxes that may be due, keep a business running, and more. When there isn't sufficient cash on hand to pay these expenses, other assets must be liquidated, often in a hurry and at bargain basement prices.

In a family where one spouse works and the other stays at home taking care of the kids, life insurance is needed on *both* lives. It is clear to see why life insurance is necessary on the bread-winner's life: If he or she dies, the family will have no source of income. But if the spouse who cares for the children dies, many people overlook the fact that outside help will probably have to be hired to assist with the household management.

How much insurance coverage you need depends upon a number of factors, including how much tax, if any, will be due upon your death, how many people you support and their standard of living, and your age and health. Several different types of life insurance policies are available, the most popular of which are whole life and term insurance.

With a whole life insurance policy, you pay a set premium every year for the rest of your life (or a specified number of years). The amount of the premium is based upon your age and health at the time you buy the policy and the amount of coverage you get. A $100,000 policy is going to cost less than a $200,000 policy, and a younger person will pay a smaller premium than an older one will.

After a couple of years, your whole life policy will have a "cash value." If you want, you can terminate the policy and take the cash value instead. (The amount of the cash value depends on how much you've paid on the policy over the years. The longer you've had the policy and the more you've paid, the higher the cash value will be.) Or you can borrow against the cash value. This means that the insurance company lends you part or all of the policy's current cash value, at an interest rate usually lower than a bank's. You can pay this loan back but generally don't have to. If you don't pay it back, when you die the amount of the loan and all outstanding interest charges are deducted from the policy's face value, and whatever is left over is paid to the policy's designated beneficiary.

As people get older and retire, they sometimes find it is difficult to keep up the insurance premiums. It is usually possible to modify the original policy so that you can stop paying the premiums in exchange for reduced coverage.

Term life insurance pays out only if you die within a certain period of time—for instance, ten years from the date you take out the policy. Unlike whole life insurance, you do not build up any cash value with a term policy. You can't trade your policy in for cash, and the insurance company won't lend you money against a term policy. So why are term life insurance policies so popular? Because they cost so much less than whole life policies for the same coverage, and by wisely investing the money you save on the premiums, you can build up an even greater "cash value" than you would get with a whole life policy.

Who gets the money is usually the most important consideration, apart from what type and how much insurance you should buy. The "primary beneficiary" of the policy is the person who gets the money when you die. If the primary beneficiary dies before you, and you don't get around to changing the policy to name a new primary beneficiary, the "secondary beneficiary" gets the money. If you haven't listed a secondary beneficiary, the proceeds from your life insurance policy may have to go through probate.

We already have seen that by naming someone other than your estate as the beneficiary of your life insurance proceeds, you can avoid probate and its attendant delays and costs. You can even make a trust the beneficiary of the policy, which is something to consider if the policy is fairly large and the beneficiary is young. By using certain subtrusts, such as a marital deduction trust, you also can take advantage of tax savings. If you're worried about giving someone the entire amount of the insurance money in a single cash payment but don't want to go to the trouble of setting up a trust, many insurance companies offer you the option of spreading out the payment over a period of years.

Another thing to consider is who owns the policy. If you own an insurance policy on your life, the proceeds are considered part of your estate when you die and are included in your estate for tax purposes. If, however, someone else, such as your spouse or child, owns the policy, the money is not included in your estate, nor is it taxed. Even if you have a policy in force right now, you can transfer ownership to someone else to avoid estate taxes when you die. Consult an estate planning lawyer to help you to determine whether this would be a good strategy for you.

RETIREMENT PLANS

LIKE LIFE INSURANCE POLICIES, many retirement plans, pension plans, 401(k)s, and the like provide for the designation of beneficiaries if the employee dies before receiving all of his or her benefits. The same considerations as to life insurance proceeds generally apply here. There may, however, be some special considerations as to whom you should—or shouldn't—name as the beneficiary of certain retirement plans. Ordinarily you want to avoid naming your own estate as a beneficiary, as the proceeds would then have to go through probate. Many pension plans pay the retired worker a fixed sum each month, and after his or her death, pays the surviving spouse the same or a lesser amount. Such plans generally stop paying out after the death of the surviving spouse.

REVOCABLE LIVING TRUSTS

A REVOCABLE LIVING TRUST IS a trust set up during the lifetime of the trustor (or settlor), the person who makes the trust. A testamentary trust, on the other hand, is found in a person's will and takes effect only upon the person's death. Lawyers refer to a "living" trust as an *inter vivos* trust, *inter vivos* meaning "between living persons." A living trust may be either revocable or irrevocable. An "irrevocable" trust is ordinarily a device only the very rich take advantage of, primarily to minimize income tax liability. The person with an average-size estate is more interested in the "revocable living trust," in which the trustor retains control over the property, including the right to change or revoke the trust at any time.

Unlike revocable living trusts, the settlor of an irrevocable trust generally must give up complete control over the trust property from the moment the trust is created. If the settlor doesn't relinquish all control, the trust assets will be considered a part of his or her estate, thereby subjecting that property to income and/or estate taxes, the avoidance of which is usually the primary goal in using irrevocable trusts.

For most people, the funded revocable living trust (RLT) is the most flexible estate planning tool available today. There are three main goals of a revocable living trust: (1) avoid probate and its costs and delays; (2) eliminate or substantially reduce estate taxes; and (3) distribute your property the way you want it distributed. Even though it may avoid probate and completely eliminate estate taxes, the best living trust is utterly worthless if the property does not go to the people you want it to go to. That should be foremost in the estate planner's mind in preparing an estate plan for you.

Advantages of a Living Trust

A properly drafted and funded revocable living trust avoids probate and its high financial and emotional costs, as well as long delays. With an RLT, settling an estate usually can be accomplished quickly and smoothly, at a much lower cost. A lawyer's assistance in winding up an RLT is advised, but the lawyer's overall fee should be considerably less than his or her fee would have been had the property gone through probate.

You will have the same amount of control over your property when you place it in a revocable living trust as you have right now. You will be able to use your property or give it away or sell it as you see fit.

In community property states, revocable living trusts take full advantage of the increased, or "stepped-up," basis rules used to determine taxable gain when community property is sold. Upon the death of the trustor, the basis of the entire property is stepped-up to its fair market value on the date of death.

Unlike probate proceedings, which are open to the public, revocable living trusts are for the most part completely private documents and not available for public inspection. However, if you are selling real estate owned by the trust, it may be necessary to record the trust along with the grant deed, warranty deed, or quitclaim deed that you are using to transfer title.

If you become so ill or injured that you are unable to manage your financial affairs or make health care decisions, ordinarily proceedings in the probate court will be necessary to have you declared incompetent and a conservator appointed to make decisions on your behalf. This is a costly, public, and often humiliating process. By using an RLT, combined with a durable power of attorney for property management and an advance health care directive, conservatorship proceedings usually can be avoided, and the person that you—not a judge—select can take over the management of your estate and health care concerns with minimal interruption.

As to your principal residence, transferring it to your RLT ordinarily will not trigger a due-on-sale clause (which permits the lender to accelerate and call in the loan in full upon its sale or transfer). As for other real estate, however, such as rental property and commercial real estate, the lender's consent to the transfer into trust may need to be obtained before transferring the property to an RLT.

If a resident of one state dies and owns real estate in another state, it is usually necessary to have a separate probate (an "ancillary probate") in the county where the land is situated. Probate is not necessary, however, if the property is owned by a revocable living trust. However, when it comes time to sell the property, you probably will need to record the trust along with the deed at the county recorder's office.

The burdens of administering a revocable living trust are relatively minimal for most small- and medium-sized estates, especially when balanced against all of the benefits of an RLT.

DEATH AND TAXES

BENJAMIN FRANKLIN ONCE WROTE, "In this world nothing is certain but death and taxes." Could anything be more certain than a combination of the two, with taxes being imposed upon your property when you die? And so it is that the federal government imposes an estate tax. (Many states also impose their own inheritance tax, but because these vary greatly from state to state, the following discussion is limited to federal estate taxes.)

Fortunately, taxes upon a person's property when he or she dies are not quite as certain as old Ben Franklin would lead us to believe. Only 2 percent of all estates are subject to federal estate taxation. And through proper estate planning, all or much of the bite can be taken out of the taxes due upon a person's death. And the passage of the federal Economic Growth and Tax Reconciliation Act of 2001 has reduced the burden of death taxes considerably.

Federal estate taxes are imposed only if the *net* value of the deceased person's estate exceeds a certain amount (the "estate exemption equivalent"). In 2003, estates having a net value of $1,000,000 or less are free from federal estate taxation. Figure 3.1 shows the size of an estate that will be exempt from estate taxes in the coming years. Note that, unlike probate fees, which are based on the *gross* value (fair market value) of the estate, estate taxes are based on the *net* value (fair market value minus all outstanding loans and other debts against the property) of all property owned by the decedent at the time of his or her death. As the law is currently written, there will be no estate taxes in 2010 on any size estate regardless of how large it is. Then, in 2011, the estate exemption equivalent reverts to $1,000,000. It is doubtful that Congress will let the current law stand and will most likely change it before 2010.

FEDERAL ESTATE TAX EXEMPTION EQUIVALENT	
Year	Exempted Size of Estate
2003	$1,000,000
2004–5	$1,500,000
2006–8	$2,000,000
2009	$3,500,000
2010	No Limit
2011 and thereafter	$1,000,000

Fig. 3.1: Size of Estates Exempt from Federal Estate Tax

Table 3.2 shows the highest tax rates for estates based on the current law, which took effect in 2002.

HIGHEST ESTATE TAX RATES	
Year	Highest Tax Rate
2003	49%
2004	48%
2005	47%
2006	46%
2007–2009	45%
2010	0%
2011 and thereafter	55%

Fig. 3.2: Highest Estate Tax Rates Beginning in 2003

As has been mentioned, all property owned by a person at the time of his or her death is subject to estate taxes, regardless of whether or not it goes through probate. This includes any property held in joint tenancy, the proceeds from life insurance policies (unless the decedent was not the owner of the policy), and retirement benefits. Property does not escape estate taxes simply because it was put into a basic revocable living trust.

THE UNLIMITED MARITAL DEDUCTION

MARRIED COUPLES WHO are citizens of the United States enjoy an "unlimited marital deduction" for gifts between them. This permits either spouse to give any amount of money or property to the other spouse without incurring any estate or gift tax liability. (This applies to gifts made during a couple's joint lifetimes as well as to gifts made at death.) Thus, if upon the death of the husband in 2003 he directs that his share ($1,500,000) of the couple's $3,000,000 estate goes to his wife, no estate taxes would be due upon the husband's death, even though the amount passing to his wife is $500,000 more than the 2003 $1,000,000 estate exemption equivalent.

PLANNING FOR INCAPACITY

TRADITIONALLY, WHEN A PERSON, because of illness, disease, advancing years, or injury, becomes incapable of managing his or her financial affairs and making health care decisions, it is necessary to institute legal proceedings to have the person declared incompetent and a conservator appointed to act on his or her behalf. Conservatorship proceedings can be costly, lengthy, and emotionally traumatic for all persons involved. Conservatorship proceedings are especially traumatic to the incapacitated person, who suffers the humiliation of being publicly branded incompetent.

Two documents—the durable power of attorney for property management and the advance health care directive—signed by the person while he or she is still mentally competent usually can avoid conservatorship proceedings altogether. Also, these documents let *you* decide who will make decisions on your behalf when you're not capable of doing so, rather than putting the decision in the hands of a judge, who is a stranger and doesn't know whom you trust with these decisions.

The Durable Power of Attorney for Property Management

Traditionally, when a person, because of illness, disease, injury, or advancing years, becomes incapable of managing his or her financial affairs, it has been necessary to go to court to get a conservator of his or her estate appointed. As we have already noted, conservatorship proceedings can be expensive, lengthy, and emotionally trying for all persons involved. A durable power of attorney for property management made when the person was still mentally competent will avoid the costs and hassles of going to court and proving that the person is mentally incapacitated and getting a conservator appointed.

An "ordinary" power of attorney is a document giving another person the right to act on your behalf, in your stead and place. Some powers of attorney can be oral, but all powers of attorney should be in writing, signed by the "principal"—the person giving the authority—and notarized, especially if the power of attorney involves real estate. There are several types of powers of attorney.

There is also the "limited" power of attorney, which permits the person you designate your "attorney-in-fact" to handle a specific situation for you. For instance, suppose your company transfers you to another state and you need to sell your home. You may give your attorney-in-fact the specific right to act in your place and on your behalf in all transactions dealing with the sale of your house. Once the sale of the house is consummated, the power of attorney is extinguished. You can, of course, revoke the power of attorney at any time, but you need to notify your attorney-in-fact and all third parties with whom he or she has been dealing of this fact.

An ordinary power of attorney ends at the time specified in it, if any, when—in the case of a limited power of attorney—the purpose of the power of attorney has been fulfilled (such as when your house is sold, in the example used above), or when you revoke (withdraw or cancel) it. If you are married and name your wife as your attorney-in-fact in a power of attorney, the power of attorney generally is terminated by divorce or the annulment of your marriage.

The problem with the ordinary general power of attorney is that it is automatically revoked by operation of the law if you become mentally incapacitated and unable to act on your own behalf. This is where a durable power of attorney comes in. Pursuant to a durable power of attorney, your attorney-in-fact can act on your behalf in doing basically anything you could do, even though you are no longer mentally competent to act on your own behalf, without the cost and hassle of having to go to court to be formally appointed your legal conservator.

A durable power of attorney is good for as long as the principal lives, even if he or she becomes mentally incompetent after making it. Two events cancel a durable power of attorney: (1) the principal's death; and (2) the revocation of the durable power of attorney by the principal while he or she is living and is mentally competent. The agent, or attorney-in-fact, may be removed by a court only for abusing his or her fiduciary duties owed to the principal.

As noted above, a power of attorney, both general and durable, automatically terminates upon the principal's death. Suppose, however, that the attorney-in-fact has not been notified of the principal's death and in good faith enters into a transaction on the principal's behalf. Who bears the cost of fulfilling that transaction, the principal's estate or the attorney-in-fact? So long as the attorney-in-fact was acting in good faith—that is, without knowledge of the principal's death or reasonable grounds to believe that the principal may have died—the principal's estate is bound by the transaction.

It is of utmost importance that you sign the durable power of attorney for property management and get it notarized while you are still mentally competent. If you wait too long to get one drawn up and become mentally incompetent before you sign it, it will be null and void. In such a case, court proceedings will have to be instituted to get a conservator appointed for your estate to handle your financial affairs for you. This may or may not be the same person you would have chosen had you made the choice yourself. This is one of the main reasons for completing a durable power of attorney for property management while you are still mentally competent to do so.

We recommend that, except in the case of the very elderly or infirm, that you use a "springing" durable power of attorney for property management. A springing durable power of attorney comes into effect only when you become mentally incapacitated. Usually the durable power of attorney provides that the determination that you are no longer mentally competent to handle your financial affairs must be certified by two independent physicians, neither of whom are related to you, your relatives, or the proposed conservator. While you are still mentally competent, you may wish to let the person whom you have named as your attorney-in-fact take over the management of your financial affairs to see how well he or she performs his or her duties. If the attorney-in-fact does not live up to your expectations, you may wish to change your attorney-in-fact.

Advance Health Care Directives

In addition to the durable power of attorney for property management, a complete estate plan includes an advance health care directive, also known as a directive to physicians, a medical directive, or a health care proxy. The advance health care directive names the person you choose to make medical decisions on your behalf in case you are unable to make them for yourself because of injury, disease, advancing years, Alzheimer's disease, or other debilitating condition. The person you name as agent on your advance health care directive need not be the same person you name on your durable power of attorney for property management. Naming a person as your agent to make medical decisions for you when you are not able to do so yourself should be discussed thoroughly with that person.

Make your wishes known as to what procedures you want and don't want and make sure that the person will fulfill his or her duties faithfully when the time comes. For instance, if for religious reasons you do not believe in blood transfusions, you want to make sure the person you appoint as your agent for health care decisions will respect your right. On the other hand, if you have no religious or other objections to blood transfusions but the person you are contemplating as your health care proxy does, you probably wouldn't want to name that person as your attorney-in-fact.

So long as you are mentally competent to make your own medical decisions, then you—and not your agent—will make the necessary choices. The advance directive for health care comes into play only when your medical or mental condition renders you unable to exercise the degree of understanding necessary to understand the proposed method of treatment, its inherent risks, any alternative procedures and their risks, and the risk of doing nothing at all. This is known as "informed consent" and is discussed in more detail in chapter 11.

Suppose that you have irreversible kidney failure and the doctor has given you a couple of months at most to live. You have decided to accept your death sentence and do not want your doctors taking heroic measures that would simply prolong your death by at most a few months, months in which you would be in severe pain, completely dependent upon others for your care.

Or you have been injured in an automobile accident and are left in a persistent vegetative state, dependent upon machines to make you breathe and tubes to provide you nourishment and hydration. Is there anything you can do legally to prevent your doctors from taking extraordinary measures to keep you alive when you prefer to die with dignity? Yes. You can fill out the "living will" provisions of your advance health care directive. The living will provisions permit you to state your wishes regarding the provision of medical care, hydration, nutrition, and the use of life-support equipment if you are unable to make those decisions yourself, and without which you will die.

Living wills first made their appearance in the mid-1970s. Two things happened in 1976 that had a profound impact on the difficult question of dying with dignity: the New Jersey Supreme Court recognized the parents' right to disconnect life-sustaining equipment in the famous Karen Ann Quinlan case, and California became the first state in the nation to enact a right-to-die law. Today, all states have a right-to-die law.

The provisions of the laws and the form of the advance health care directive may vary greatly from state to state. You should follow precisely the form for your state, as any deviation could result in a doctor, hospital, or court refusing to recognize the living will provisions of your advance health care directive. You may be able to obtain an advance health care directive (or directive to physicians, medical directive, living will, or health care proxy) from the legal forms section of a good business stationery store. Alternatively, you can obtain a state-specific advance directive with instructions on filling it out for five dollars from the Partnership for Caring Distribution Center, 325 East Oliver Street, Baltimore, Maryland, 21202; telephone: (800) 989-9455. They also have a website at http://www.partnershipforcaring.org.

ORGAN DONATIONS AND FUNERAL INSTRUCTIONS

IN ADDITION TO THE DOCUMENTS discussed above, as part of a comprehensive estate plan you may wish to prepare other documents relating to your death, including organ donation cards and funeral instructions.

Organ and Body Donations

All fifty states have enacted the Uniform Anatomical Gift Act, which makes it easy for a person to donate all of his or her body or specific organs upon death. Generally you need only fill out a donor card and keep it with your driver's license. If you wish to donate your body to a medical school for teaching purposes, you should contact the school in advance and make the necessary arrangements with the school.

Advances in medical techniques and antirejection drugs have made organ transplants more successful than ever. Now the problem is that there are more people needing organs than there are organs to be harvested. Many states have therefore passed laws that require physicians to ask the families of persons who die whether they wish to donate the deceased person's healthy organs for transplant.

Funeral Instructions

Funeral instructions should specify whether you wish to be buried or cremated, by which mortuary, where you wish your ashes to be scattered, kept, or buried in the case of cremation or where (cemetery and plot, if known) you wish to be buried, along with any special arrangements regarding any special songs you'd like played or prayers said at the funeral service. If you already have made preburial or precremation arrangements with a particular mortuary or association, you should include this information in your funeral instructions.

Some people plan to cheat death by having themselves frozen after they die, hoping to be brought back to life when, for example, the disease that killed them is curable. Rumors persisted for years that Walt Disney had himself frozen, but that was all they were—rumors. A legal battle ensued following the death of baseball legend Ted Williams, with one child wishing to bury him and another child wanting to preserve him using cryogenics according to his handwritten instructions made shortly before his death.

Often, the cryogenics company freezes only the head of the deceased person. This naturally leads to the question of where will they ever find the healthy bodies to attach the frozen dead heads to when medical science can cure the disease that killed them and can make the reanimation of dead tissue and reattachment of a head to a body possible?

Where to Keep Funeral Directions

If you have made funeral instructions, purchased a burial plot, made arrangements with a crematorium, etc., it is important that you make these arrangements known to your executor, successor trustee, or others who likely will be among the first to hear about your death. These documents generally should be kept in a separate packet or envelope from your other estate planning documents and should be readily available to your survivors. Do not keep these documents in your safe deposit box. Let your loved ones know where in the house these documents are kept. In fact, you may wish to make a copy of the instructions and give them to the person who will be in charge of making your funeral arrangements.

Why not include funeral directions in your will? Because wills and trusts often are not found or read until after the person has been buried or cremated. When the will or trust is finally opened and read, it is belatedly discovered that the decedent wished to be cremated rather than buried, or that he or she had a prepaid burial plan with another mortuary than the one that was used.

Similarly, if you have a disabling stroke that robs you of the ability to communicate without telling those closest to you that you have executed an advance health care directive, you don't want it read after you die. You want people to know about the existence and location of these documents when they are needed. And your signed organ donation card won't do much good if it's found with your will after you've been buried or cremated.

The following are samples of funeral instructions. The first are instructions for a person who wishes to be cremated; the second are instructions for a person who has already made pre-burial arrangements with a specific mortuary.

CREMATION INSTRUCTIONS

I, _____, hereby direct the disposition of my remains upon my death as follows:

1. It is my wish to be cremated and that the cremation and all other arrangements be handled by the _____ Society [or Mortuary], located at _____.

2. It is my wish that after cremation, my remains be disposed of as follows: _e.g. scattered in the ocean]_ _____.

The original of my Last Will and Testament [or Revocable Living Trust] is located in: [_my safe deposit box #555 at Hometown Bank, Main Street Branch, Hometown, USA; the top right drawer of my living room desk]_ _____.

DATED: _____ , 20___

_____[signed]_____
Type Name Here

BURIAL INSTRUCTIONS

I, _____, hereby direct the disposition of my remains upon my death as follows:

1. I have made preburial arrangements with _____ Mortuary, located at _____[address]_____.

2. The original documents for my burial arrangements are in the top left drawer of my bedroom dresser.

The original of my Last Will and Testament [or Revocable Living Trust] is located in: _____ [my safe deposit box #555 at Hometown Bank, Main Street Branch, Hometown, U.S.A; the top right drawer of my living room desk] _____ .

DATED: _____ , 20___

_____ [signed] _____
Type Name Here

Your Rights under the Funeral Rule

When a loved one dies, it is a very trying time for the survivors. Emotions may get in the way of rational decision making about funeral arrangements (if the deceased person didn't take care of this beforehand). More than two million funerals are arranged each year in the United States, at an average cost of $6,000. To protect consumers from abuses by the funeral industry, the Federal Trade Commission instituted a regulation known as the Funeral Rule.

According to the Funeral Rule, if you call a mortuary (or funeral home) for information over the telephone, the mortuary must tell you the prices and give you any information about services. It cannot refuse to give out such information over the telephone.

If you visit the mortuary in person, you must be given a list that specifies the price of each funeral item and service offered. The list must also disclose certain legal rights and requirements regarding funeral arrangements, including information on embalming and caskets for cremation. Generally, you have the right to choose which items you want and do not have to buy services you don't want, unless state law requires it. In the event that the law does require the purchase of certain goods or services, the mortuary must give you a written statement informing you of the specific law that mandates the purchase. If the mortuary adds a fee to its cost (or gets a refund, discount, or rebate) for items it buys for cash in advance, such as flowers, obituary notices, pallbearers, or clergy honoraria, this must be disclosed to you in writing. The mortuary must give you an itemized statement showing the total cost of the funeral goods and services you have selected.

The law generally does not require embalming, and the mortuary cannot falsely tell you that it is required by law. If the mortuary does embalm the body without your consent, it usually cannot charge you for this. The mortuary must inform you that if you want certain arrangements, such as a viewing of the body, embalming is a practical necessity and therefore a required purchase. If you do not want embalming, then you should opt for a direct cremation or immediate burial. If you select a direct cremation, one without a viewing or ceremony at which the body is present, the mortuary must offer you either an inexpensive alternative container (one made of pressboard, cardboard, or canvas) or an unfinished wood box.

If you have a question or seek further information about your rights, or if you have a complaint about a mortuary or funeral home, contact your state's office of consumer affairs or consumer protection. You can also contact the Conference of Funeral Service Examining Boards, 520 East Van Trees Street, P.O. Box 497, Washington, Indiana, 47501; telephone:

(812) 254-7887; ThanaCAP, 135 West Wells Street, Suite 600, Milwaukee, Wisconsin, 53203; telephone: (414) 276-9788 (which arbitrates consumer complaints regarding funeral directors); or your regional office of the Federal Trade Commission.

THE DANGERS OF DO-IT-YOURSELF ESTATE PLANNING

THERE IS AN ABUNDANCE OF "do-it-yourself" books and computer software programs in bookstores and computer stores today touting that you can make your own will or revocable living trust with their book or computer program and save hundreds of dollars in attorney's fees. Many of these books and programs claim to have hundreds of forms and clauses to custom tailor your will or RLT to your individual needs.

How good are these books and programs? From a lawyer's perspective, not very good. Four software programs were tested in the preparation of this chapter, and all used a general question-answer format to fill in a boilerplate trust form. All had serious flaws and were difficult, if not impossible, to custom tailor to specific situations.

The problem with these do-it-yourself books and computer programs is that they are written in a generic format. Every estate and every person's desires are deemed to be the same within the limits of the book's forms or computer program's clauses. But the fact is that every estate is unique and every person's goals are different. Tax avoidance may be the objective of one person; ensuring that property is given to the correct persons the desire of another; setting up educational trusts for minor children or grandchildren the desire of another; creating a "special needs" trust for a disabled child so the child will not lose his or her government benefits the goal of another; and making sure a drug-addicted child not get anything the plan of still another. None of the books and computer programs tested by the author addressed all of these questions adequately.

There is a lot more to estate planning than just filling out a few forms, filing them away, and forgetting about them. By doing it yourself, without the advice of a competent estate planning lawyer, you risk blowing the whole thing. There are just too many pitfalls for the untrained layperson to do his or her own estate planning.

We recommend that you not try to do anything more complicated than preparing your own simple will, according to the directions in the next chapter. If from reading this chapter you think that your estate can benefit from some estate planning—and most people's estates can—or if you want to avoid probate, discuss your needs and goals with a lawyer experienced in estate planning. While there are nonlawyers who advertise their services as estate planners—such as financial consultants and paralegal typing services—the first person to contact is an experienced estate-planning lawyer. Depending upon the size of your estate and your objectives, your lawyer may work with other professionals, such as an accountant, a life insurance agent, a financial planner (or even all three in larger estates) to design a complete estate plan tailored to your particular needs and desires. This really is the only way you can get the assurance—the peace of mind—that everything is in order and will hold up after you pass away.

If despite the above warning you are bound and determined to create your own estate plan with a computer software program, we highly recommend that before you sign it, you have a lawyer review it to make sure it is in order and carries out your wishes the way you want them to. And remember that there's more to an estate plan than just the will or revocable living trust. As we have seen, there are the durable powers of attorney for property management and advance health care directives. Plus, if you make a revocable living trust, will the software program give you instructions on which assets should be transferred to the trust—as well as which assets should *not* be transferred to the trust—and how it is done? For instance, to transfer your home into a trust you will need to draw up a new deed transferring the property from yourselves individually to yourselves as trustees of your family trust and record it with the county recorder. Does the software program tell you how to go about doing that?

MERCY KILLINGS—EUTHANASIA

A TERMINALLY ILL CANCER PATIENT is in the final stages of the disease. The pain is insufferable. Even the most powerful painkilling drugs do little to alleviate the suffering, and their side effects add to the patient's discomfort. The patient has accepted the inevitability of death and wishes to hasten it because the pain is just too much to bear. Does the patient have the right to take his or her own life? Or can the patient ask his or her doctor to end the suffering with an injection that would provide a quick, painless death? The answer, in all but one state, is no. The law does not permit the practice of euthanasia, or "mercy killing."

In the United States today, it is still a crime to aid or abet a potential suicide. If a dying man asks his wife to supply him with some poison or drugs so he can take his own life and she does so, she risks being prosecuted for abetting a suicide. If she administers the poison or drugs to her husband, she could be tried and convicted of first-degree murder, even if her husband would have died of natural causes the very next day. Since the woman deliberately shortened her husband's life, even though it was at his request, she has committed the crime of murder (see chapter 23).

In one widely publicized example, Roswell Gilbert, a 75-year-old Florida man, was charged with murder after shooting his 73-year-old wife twice in the head. Mrs. Gilbert suffered from Alzheimer's disease and advanced osteoporosis, two diseases that had caused brain degeneration and painful bone disintegration. On the day of her death, Mrs. Gilbert was in extreme pain and crying and allegedly pleading for death. The jury convicted Mr. Gilbert of first-degree murder, on the basis that his actions were deliberate and premeditated. He was sentenced to life in prison.

Dr. Jack Kevorkian and his suicide machine helped a number of people commit suicide by inhaling a lethal dose of carbon monoxide or taking a fatal amount of drugs. Kevorkian would set the machine up, but the patient had to operate it by lowering his or her chin on a lever to release the gas or drugs. Kevorkian was tried for murder several times but was found not guilty each time. Finally, to emphasize his strong beliefs in favor of euthanasia, Dr. Kevorkian actively assisted a patient to commit suicide and was convicted of murder.

In 1994, Oregon voters approved a law that legalizes assisted suicide by permitting doctors to prescribe lethal doses of drugs in certain cases to patients who have six months or less to live, and who have repeatedly expressed their intention to die.

In *Washington v. Glucksberg*, a 1997 decision of the United States Supreme Court, three gravely ill patients (who died before the case got to the Supreme Court), four doctors who occasionally dealt with terminally ill and suffering patients, and a nonprofit organization brought suit to declare unconstitutional a Washington state law that made it a felony to cause or aid another person to attempt suicide. The doctors asserted that they would assist terminally ill patients in ending their lives if not for Washington's assisted-suicide ban.

The plaintiffs alleged that the law prohibiting assisted suicide was unconstitutional because it infringed upon a person's fundamental liberty interest under the due process clause of the fourteenth amendment to the Constitution in ending their death when they were terminally ill and suffering. The nation's highest court disagreed, ruling that a person's right to assistance in committing suicide is not a fundamental liberty interest protected by the due process clause.

The Supreme Court reviewed the history of punishment for suicide and attempted suicide and noted that for seven hundred years of Anglo-American law, suicide was not looked upon favorably. Indeed, the Court noted, at one time suicide—once known as self-murder—was punished by forfeiting all of the suicide's real estate and personal property to the king, leaving the suicide's innocent family impoverished.

The Supreme Court observed that while the state of Oregon had enacted through a ballot initiative an assisted-suicide law, no other state had passed a similar law, and had in fact defeated legislation that would have permitted so-called mercy killings. The high court also noted that the Federal Assisted Suicide Funding Restriction Act of 1997 expressly prohibits the use of federal funds in support of physician-assisted suicide.

The Supreme Court distinguished Washington's Natural Death Act, which provided that "withholding or withdrawal of life-sustaining treatment at a patient's direction shall not, for any purpose, constitute a suicide." Washington's Natural Death Act also stated that nothing in that act "shall be construed to condone, authorize, or approve mercy killing."

What does the *Glucksberg* decision mean? It means that you do not have a legal right—except in Oregon—to have your death hastened by a physician by, for example, administering an overdose of morphine or other drug, even if you are a mentally competent adult who is terminally ill and in considerable pain and discomfort despite morphine and other pain medications. The Supreme Court did not rule that laws such as Oregon's authorizing physician-assisted suicide are illegal. Rather, it ruled only that there is no "fundamental liberty interest" in such instances, and that assisted-suicide laws are not unconstitutional. Thus, except for Oregon, a physician who assists a terminally ill patient in hastening his or her death can be prosecuted under a state's criminal law prohibiting assisted suicide.

The issue of mercy killings is a difficult one—legally, medically, and morally. There is the danger that some killings may be done not so much to relieve the victim's suffering as to remove a burden from a loved one's life. Alzheimer's disease, for example, may place a tremendous strain on the afflicted person's spouse or children, and the spouse or children could be motivated more by their own considerations in making the decision to end the life of the ill person. Some people fear that a terminally ill person may persuade a healthy spouse to join in a double suicide. And persons who are only temporarily ill, or whose conditions are not that serious, may be encouraged to end their lives when appropriate treatment could save them or lessen their pain.

Rather than turning their backs on this sensitive issue, legislators, lawyers, physicians, and representatives of various advocacy groups for senior citizens and terminally ill patients should get together and form strict guidelines for permitting the practice of euthanasia in appropriate cases. The decision on whether to allow a person to end his or her life should involve the terminally ill person, the family physician, and a family lawyer, plus an independent review board. This decision should not be in the hands of one person alone, particularly someone who is so close to the ill person that he or she is unable to look at the matter objectively.

FOUR

Wills

*I*N THIS CHAPTER, we discuss everything most people need to know about wills. Many of you will even be able to write your own simple will with the directions and examples listed here. But before going any further, if you haven't already done so, read the preceding chapter on estate planning and probate avoidance. That chapter contains explanations and definitions that are necessary to understand fully the following material. It also has valuable information to help you decide whether you should write your own will or whether something else, such as a revocable living trust, might be better for you.

WHY YOU NEED A WILL

A WILL IS A DOCUMENT that takes effect upon the death of the person who made it—the "testator" if a man, "testatrix" if a woman. It directs who gets your real estate, automobiles, money, furniture, stocks and bonds, jewelry, and anything else you own. A will also carries out other final instructions, such as naming a guardian to care for your minor children. (It shouldn't, though, as discussed in the previous chapter, include funeral arrangements.) In effect, a will allows you to speak "from beyond the grave" to ensure that things are done according to your wishes.

But a will is much more than a cold legal document. It is truly an expression of love. You make a will because you care enough about someone to share the things that you treasure most during life. Which brings us to the main reason people make wills: peace of mind. Why take a chance on what will be done with your property? Dying without a will is one risk that just isn't worth it.

Who needs a will? Just about every adult. Of course, the reasons can be very different. Here are a few examples: A young couple who don't have much in the way of money and belongings need a will to appoint a guardian for their minor children if they die. A middle-aged couple with substantial assets can use a will to eliminate or minimize the taxes that may be due upon their deaths. Older persons prepare wills to ensure that their estates go to their children, grandchildren, or a favorite nephew or niece, or to make gifts to a hospital, religious institution, or disease research foundation. Another person might make a will to give a gift to someone who has been kind to him or her, especially in a time of illness.

Sixty to 70 percent of American adults do not have wills (or living trusts). If you talk to them, you'll find that most have been meaning to make a will for quite some time but keep putting it off. Ask them why and they'll give you the same answers: "It costs too much to have a lawyer draw a will," or "I don't have enough property to go to the trouble." Many, particularly older, people have more money and assets than they think. For example, a couple who bought their house for $20,000 years ago may not realize that it could easily be worth $200,000 or more today. And some of the "junk" they have collected over the years may prove to be of considerable value.

But the main reasons so many people don't have wills are psychological: People don't want to think about their own deaths. Or they believe that by making a will, it will somehow hasten their death. Picasso, for instance, refused to make a will for this very reason. Granted, he did live to the venerable age of 91. But it took four-and-a-half years of bitter fighting before his estate—worth about $300 million—was settled. This wasn't unexpected. Picasso himself once predicted that "the settling of my estate, I am sure, is going to be worse than anything you can imagine." Had he made a will, the estate no doubt would have been resolved sooner, with less of a toll on his family and loved ones—and he probably would have lived just as long.

One final observation: Of the 30 to 40 percent or so who do have wills, many have wills that are at least ten years old. If the person died today, the old will might not now dispose of the property in the way he or she would like. An old, outdated will often is as bad as, and sometimes is even worse than, no will at all. Occasionally, the old will will be so outdated that the lawyer will have the testator or testatrix rip it up (revoke it) on the spot, even before the lawyer can prepare a new one.

TYPES OF WILLS

THERE ARE THREE TYPES of wills: the formal witnessed will, the "holographic" (handwritten) will, and the "nuncupative" (oral) will. A number of states do not recognize holographic wills, and oral wills are permitted only in very unusual circumstances. We will therefore concentrate on formal wills, particularly with regard to making your own will.

The Formal Witnessed Will

A formal witnessed will is one that is typed up (or printed from a word processor) and signed by the testator or testatrix and by two witnesses (except in Maine, New Hampshire, South Carolina, and Vermont, which require three witnesses). In Louisiana, the witnesses must sign in front of a notary public, who then attaches his or her seal and signature.

We usually associate formal wills with those drawn up by a lawyer, but there's no reason you can't make a simple one yourself following the step-by-step instructions found later in this chapter. But only you or your lawyer can prepare your will. A person who is not a lawyer cannot prepare a will for you, since drafting a will involves the practice of law, for which a proper license and admission to the state bar is required. If a nonlawyer, such as a paralegal service, prepares a will for you, you're taking a big chance that the court will throw it out or that the will will be poorly drafted and won't dispose of your assets in the way that you'd like.

Holographic (Handwritten) Wills

A holographic (also called "olographic") will is one that is entirely in your own handwriting and that you have signed and dated. Holographic wills can be made in the following states: Alaska, Arizona, California, Colorado, Idaho, Kentucky, Louisiana, Michigan, Mississippi, Montana, Nebraska, Nevada, New Jersey, North Carolina, North Dakota, Oklahoma, Pennsylvania, South Dakota, Tennessee, Texas, Utah, Virginia, West Virginia, and Wyoming. Four other states—Maryland, New York, Rhode Island, and South Carolina—permit only servicemen to make holographic wills, and even then only under certain circumstances. If made according to the state's requirements, a holographic will is just as good as a formal witnessed will. This usually remains true even if you later move to a state that doesn't recognize holographic wills made in that state.

Because holographic wills are more the exception than the rule, courts traditionally have been very strict in accepting them for probate. Since a holographic will must be *entirely* in the handwriting of the testator, courts have ruled holographic wills invalid where the testator used a rubber stamp to sign his name, where the date was typed in rather than written, where an address identifying a piece of property was inserted by rubber stamp, or where other provisions were not in the testator's own handwriting. A holographic will written by someone else other than the testator is not valid.

What about buying a preprinted will form at your local stationery store, filling in the blanks, and dating and signing it; will that stand up as a holographic will? Many courts will not accept this as a holographic will, since it is not entirely in your own handwriting. Some courts, however, will allow a holographic will to be admitted for probate, notwithstanding the fact that it is on a preprinted form, so long as all of the substantive provisions—such as who gets what, the appointment of the executor, the date, the testator's signature, and other key provisions—are in the testator's own handwriting.

If you decide to prepare your own will, however, we recommend that you type it up (or compose it on your word processor and print it out) and then sign it and have it witnessed in the manner described below (in other words, make a formal witnessed will).

Nuncupative (Oral) Wills

When a person doesn't have enough time to prepare a written will before he or she dies, many states recognize an oral, or "nuncupative," will. Oral wills, which are very rare, are valid only if made during the person's last sickness. In some states, for an oral will to be valid, the person must expect immediate death from an injury received the same day. Depending upon the laws of the particular state, the person must state the oral will in front of two or three witnesses. The oral will usually must be put into writing by one of the witnesses within a certain number of days and signed by the witnesses. Finally, the will must be offered for probate within a specified period, such as six months.

There are usually strict limits on the amount of money or types of assets that can be passed down through an oral will. For example, real estate cannot be disposed of by an oral will. And there may be a limit of, say, $5,000 on the money or assets a person can give away through an oral will.

Joint and Mutual Wills

Joint and mutual wills aren't really a separate category of wills, but rather are special types of formal wills. Although these kinds of wills can be made by any two (or more) people, they usually are made by a husband and wife. Many gay and lesbian couples are also using these kinds of wills. For purposes of this discussion, we will assume that it is a husband and wife who are making the joint or mutual wills.

A joint will is a single will signed by two people (the husband and the wife) in which each gives his or her share to the survivor; when both have passed away, the property goes to their children or other designated beneficiaries. Mutual wills contain the same provisions a joint will would, but instead of just a single will, each spouse has his or her own will. For instance, the husband's will might provide that all of his assets go to his wife, and if she is not living, to their children; the wife's will in return would give her assets to her husband, and to their children if he has died. (Examples of mutual wills are found near the end of this chapter.)

It is usually preferable to make mutual wills rather than a joint will. One reason is that the single joint will may become tattered going through probate on the death of the first spouse. Another reason is that problems may arise if one spouse wants to change the joint will but the other doesn't. A mutual will, on the other hand, ordinarily can be changed without the other spouse's consent or even knowledge.

WHAT YOU SHOULD KNOW ABOUT WILLS

Age Requirements

In most states you must be at least 18 years old to make a will. In Georgia, you only need to be 14, in Louisiana 16, and in Alabama, Alaska, and Wyoming, you must be 19 years old. There is no upper age limit; as long as a person has the necessary mental capacity, he or she can make a will. A person under the required age usually must go to court and get a guardian appointed to make a will.

Sound Mind and Body

Almost every reading of a will in a movie or television show begins, "I, John Doe, being of sound mind and sound body, hereby declare that this is my Last Will and Testament." The fact is that there simply is no such thing as a "sound body" requirement. Physical condition is not important, except to the extent it affects a person's mind and mental capacity. A paraplegic, amputee, or person suffering from multiple sclerosis or other physical disability is certainly not precluded from making a will.

When lawyers talk about "sound mind," they mean that a person has the "mental capacity" or "mental competency" to make a will. Being of sound mind to make a will does not mean that you must be perfectly sane (if there is such a thing!), have a clear and unfailing memory, and otherwise have the mental sharpness you had when you were 18. You only need a general understanding of how much property you own and who the natural objects of your affection are—your children and grandchildren, for instance, or a favorite nephew or niece. And you must be able to put these two factors together and form an orderly plan as to who gets what.

Your competency to make a will is determined by your mental state at the time you sign your will. A person who is insane may become sufficiently lucid to make a will and then again lose touch with reality. As long as the will was made during a period of mental lucidity, it is valid. Suppose a person is in the early stages of Alzheimer's disease and makes a will. There is no question that the person had the requisite mental capacity to make the will at the time she signed it. But suppose her condition deteriorates and she loses all of her mental faculties. Is the will still good? Yes. That a person loses mental capacity at some time after the will was made and signed is of no consequence. It becomes important only if the person tries to revoke or amend the will after becoming mentally incompetent.

The person who indulges in alcohol or drugs, even to excess, the eccentric who exhibits bizarre behavior, the older person who has occasional lapses of memory—all may at times have sufficient capacity to make a will. For example, an alcoholic or drug abuser can make a valid will when sober.

Another example: Ruth, an 89-year-old widow, has been in ill health for several years. She is occasionally forgetful but is aware of the fact that she owns the house she lives in; that she owns some stocks and bonds (although she is not quite sure of what exactly she owns); and that she has some jewelry, furniture, and the like. Her only living relatives are a cousin she hasn't seen in fifty years and a nephew who visits her once a month. She makes a will, giving her house, furniture, jewelry, and the like to her nephew, and her stocks and bonds to her favorite charity. Her will is valid because, under the legal test, she was "of sound mind."

Is a will made on a deathbed good? Again the real question is whether the person was of sound mind. The fact that a person is on the verge of death does not alone invalidate a will. If a disease has resulted in brain deterioration, however, then that person may not be of sound mind. What if the person was medicated when the will was made and signed? If the person didn't know who or where he or she was and didn't know he or she was signing a will, then the will is no good. But if the medication only made the person tired or weak, and he or she fully realized what was going on, the will is valid. If a will is to be made on a deathbed, the lawyer should prepare the will after meeting privately with the testator. A videotape recording of the signing of the will is highly recommended in this situation—particularly if you foresee the possibility of a will contest—as it will give the judge a better picture of just how sound of mind the person was when he or she signed the will.

What You Can and Can't Give Away

Before sitting down to make your will, you have to figure out what you own and how you want to distribute it. Use the guidelines in the previous chapter to do an inventory of your assets. If something is your own separate property, you have the right to dispose of it any way you want. If you own the property jointly with someone else, you can give away only your share. Remember that if you own something with someone else as joint tenants (or tenants in the entirety), your share automatically goes to the surviving joint tenant upon your death; consequently any provision you may have in your will concerning the disposition of such property is invalid. If you want someone other than the joint tenant to get your share of the property, you will have to change the title during your lifetime to tenants in common.

You cannot give away property that is subject to a contract. Say, for example, that you want to give the proceeds of your life insurance policy to someone other than the policy's named beneficiary. Even if your will gives the life insurance proceeds to someone else, the beneficiary named in the policy gets the money. Why? Because the terms of the policy—a contract—control the distribution of the money. If you want the proceeds to go to someone other than your currently named beneficiary, you'll have to contact your insurance agent and fill out the necessary change of beneficiary forms. This same advice applies to retirement benefits, IRAs, deferred compensation plans, and similar accounts or employee benefits.

Here is another example of how a contract can affect your right to dispose of your property: Donald, an ailing octogenarian, tells his niece, Linda, that if she will move in and take care of him for the rest of his life, he'll give her the house in his will. Linda moves in and takes care of Donald until he dies six years later. But when Donald's will is read, Linda learns that he has given the house to someone else. Can she do anything? Yes. If Linda can prove there was in fact an agreement between Donald and her, a court will enforce it against Donald's estate, and Linda will get the house. For your own protection, if you ever find yourself in the position of making a deal to perform services in exchange for a gift by will, put that agreement in writing and have the other party sign it. If the agreement involves real estate, get the document signed and notarized and record the signed agreement in the county recorder's office in the county where the land is situated.

RESTRICTIONS ON GIFTS

Generally speaking, you have the right to give your money to anyone you want. If you give property to a minor, however, a guardian will have to be appointed to manage the property until the minor turns 18 (19 in a few states). Some restrictions may be placed on gifts to charities or religious institutions and gifts to animals, and these are discussed below.

What happens when a person gets impatient for his inheritance and kills the testator to speed things up? A murderer forfeits any gift that he or she would have received from the victim. But if the death is accidental or the result of negligence, such as carelessness while driving a car, the gift usually is not forfeited, even though the recipient was the direct cause of the testator's death.

Gifts to Charities and Religious Institutions

Some states do not allow gifts to religious or charitable institutions if the will was made less than a certain period of time (such as thirty days or six months) before the person died. What happens to the gift in that case? It goes to the person named in the residuary clause (see below) of your will or to your next of kin if there is no residuary clause. The state you live in may also have a law limiting the amount of your estate that the charity or religious institution can receive—for instance, one-fourth or one-third of the estate.

One usual restriction imposed on all gifts to charities or religious institutions is the requirement that the recipient be a bona fide, legitimate organization. A gift of $50,000 to, say, Sister Mary's Religious Sect for the Divine Rutabaga probably would be void in all states.

Gifts to Animals

Every now and then you read in the paper or hear on the television news of the eccentric millionaire who left all of his or her estate to a cat, dog, bird, or other pet in his or her will. (Imagine the surprise of the children or other heirs when they learn of this!) Is such a gift valid? No. A gift of money or property to a pet does not hold up legally, for the simple reason that a pet is legally incapable of holding title to property. A cat cannot own a house, a dog cannot own a car, a bird cannot open a bank account, and a hamster cannot get a Social Security card. To get around this, some people will nominate a human as "guardian" of the pet, and occasionally a court upholds this. Instead of attempting to give your money to your pet, you should discuss the matter with the person you would like to take care of your pet in case anything happens to you, and leave them a gift to cover food, veterinarian bills, and the like. You may also want to consider making a gift of part of your estate to your local humane society.

Directing That Your Pet Be Put to Sleep

Many people put in their wills that when they die their pets should be be put to sleep. At one time these provisions were enforced without question. Animal protection groups successfully challenged this practice as cruel and inhumane, especially when applied to younger, healthy pets. As discussed above, make arrangements with someone who is fond of your pet(s) to take care of them after your death.

PROVIDING FOR YOUR MINOR CHILDREN

PARENTS WITH MINOR CHILDREN should have a provision in their wills naming a guardian to care for those children if both parents should die before the children reach the age of majority. What should you look for in a guardian? Some important factors are the age and health of the guardian and the child(ren), the guardian's standard of living, whether the guardian has other children, the religious beliefs of the guardian, whether the child(ren) will have to change schools or move a long distance from their present home, and other considerations. Many young parents name their own parents as guardians, without realizing that when their children reach their mid-teens the grandparents may be a little too old to handle the natural energy and rebelliousness of teenagers.

Before you name a guardian for your children, first discuss it with the person to make sure he or she is willing to be the guardian. You should also name an alternate guardian in case your first choice refuses or is unable to accept the position at the appropriate time because of, for instance, poor health. The probate judge is not legally bound by your choice, but will give your choice for guardian great weight and will usually follow it. The "best interests" of the child—the same guideline used to resolve family law issues involving child custody (see chapter 1)—is the determining factor.

If your estate is large enough, it might be wise to set up a trust in your will for your children. Even though your estate is not large enough to worry about planning for estate taxes (see the preceding chapter), it can be large enough to think about a trust for your kids. Suppose your estate is worth $100,000. If you take that and invest that amount at 5 percent interest per year, in ten years you'll have over $160,000. In fifteen years, it will have grown to more than $205,000!

If there is no trust, and you die when your child is three, that means when your child turns 18, he or she will be getting a lump sum of over $200,000. Unfortunately, many 18-year-olds who suddenly come into a large sum of money aren't as financially responsible as we'd like them to be.

To protect the child from himself or herself, a trust typically provides that the child is entitled to all of the interest of the trust while he or she is in school, and the guardian can use the trust money for college tuition, books, living expenses, and the like for the child. When the child graduates from college or turns 25, whichever occurs first, the child receives half of the remaining principal of the trust. When the child turns 30, he or she receives the remainder of the trust estate. Trusts for children can get very complex, and each situation is unique. If you are thinking of setting up a trust for your children, we advise you to do so with the advice of a good estate planning attorney rather than trying to do it yourself.

DISINHERITING SOMEONE

THE FIRST THING YOU NEED to know about cutting someone out of your will is that the courts as a rule don't like it. They'll usually do anything possible to get around disinheritances. For example, suppose you wish to disinherit one of your children, so you just don't mention that child anywhere in your will. It's as if that child doesn't exist. Is that child disinherited? Generally not. The law presumes that you simply forgot or overlooked the child and didn't intend to leave him or her out of you will. That child then receives the share of your estate that he or she would have received had you died without a will. You must therefore make it clear in your will that you are deliberately disinheriting the child or other person.

The only sure way to disinherit someone is to state expressly in the will something like: "It is my desire that _[name of person]_ take nothing under this will," and then give all of your property to another person or other people. This leaves no doubt as to your intention. In one case, a bitter father's entire will (which he had prepared himself) read: "It is my greatest wish that my only child, my son Fred, get nothing, as he has turned out to be a worthless, good-for-nothing bum who squanders all of his money on women and gambling." Guess who wound up with all of the property? That's right: Fred. Why? Because the testator did not give his property away to others. If not to Fred, then to whom? The court couldn't guess who should receive the property, so it gave it all to the man's next of kin—Fred. You don't even have to give the disinherited person a dollar or other token gift. In fact, we strongly advise against leaving the disinherited person anything, as you have now made him or her a beneficiary of your estate, and he or she could become a major nuisance.

What happens if a married person's will expressly disinherits his or her spouse and gives all of the property to others? Is the surviving spouse left with nothing? No. Most states give the surviving spouse a "right of election." The spouse gets to choose between what the will gives and an amount or percentage of the estate that the law provides to protect a married person in this very situation.

A final word about disinheritances: You only have to disinherit a person if he or she would get any of your estate if you didn't leave a will. (Who gets your property if you die without a will or living trust is discussed in the previous chapter.) If someone isn't entitled to any of your property upon your death, then you don't have to worry about disinheriting that person. But if you're intent on cutting someone out of your will, be on the safe side and have a lawyer prepare the will.

APPOINTING AN EXECUTOR OR EXECUTRIX

THE EXECUTOR (executrix if a woman) of a will has a demanding job: He or she must take possession of the deceased person's personal property; make an inventory of all the property and get it appraised; probate the will; arrange for the interim support of the surviving spouse and minor children, if any; pay funeral bills; file insurance claims; give notices of the decedent's death; file all tax forms; see that creditors are paid; and ensure that the beneficiaries get what is rightfully coming to them. Depending upon the size of the estate, the job of executor can be one requiring great business sense and expertise. The executor won't be alone in these burdensome tasks, however. The executor's lawyer will be guiding and helping him with much of the work.

A married person usually names his or her spouse as executor or executrix. But if your estate is large and complex, and your spouse does not have much business experience, consider appointing someone with more business acumen. Some people with larger estates prefer to name a bank as the executor or to name their spouse and a bank as coexecutors. Others like to name an adult child or a trusted friend. Whomever you decide to name as executor, talk it over with that person before making your will. Ideally, the person you select as the executor should live in or near the same county as you, since your will will be probated in the county where you resided at the time of your death.

Unless your will states otherwise, the person you name as executor will have to post a bond to ensure proper, professional, and faithful fulfillment of the duties and obligations required by the position of executor. (The cost of this bond is paid by the estate, not out of the executor's own pocket.) If you're selecting your spouse, a close relative, or a trusted friend as your executor, you will probably want to consider putting a clause in your will that the executor doesn't have to post a bond.

The executor of the will receives a fee, which is usually a percentage based on the size of the estate. The lawyer who probates the will on behalf of the executor also receives a fee, often equal to the executor's fee. If the estate is small and there are no problems, the fees of the executor and attorney will be relatively small. But if the estate is large, and there is a fierce will contest and several disputed creditor claims that have to be litigated, the fees will be considerably greater.

HOW TO WRITE YOUR OWN WILL

IN THIS SECTION, we show you various clauses you can adapt and use to draw up your own will. Later in this chapter several complete wills are provided to assist you. You may want to take a moment to look at them now, if only because they will give you the complete picture. It's frequently easier to understand things when you see the assembled product before taking a look at the nuts and bolts.

When Not to Do It Yourself

Be forewarned that not everyone can or should make his or her own will. A lawyer is absolutely necessary in certain situations. Have a lawyer prepare your will if any of the following apply:

* You are unsure about anything or have a question that isn't answered here. By necessity, we address only the most common situations in this chapter. More complex matters have not been included. If your question is relatively simple, you might get the answer by visiting your local law library or calling the clerk at the probate court. Otherwise, consult a lawyer.
* Your estate is large enough to benefit from some estate planning to eliminate or reduce estate taxes. This requires the expertise of a competent estate planning lawyer. (Whether your estate will be subject to federal estate taxes is discussed in the previous chapter.)
* You own a business. What happens to a business when the owner dies? Is it kept running, and if so, by whom? Or is it shut down and the machines, office furniture, and the like sold off? There is a big difference in the value between selling a business as a going enterprise and shutting it down and liquidating its assets. Proper planning with the help of a good

lawyer can mean the difference of tens, even hundreds of thousands of dollars between closing the doors and liquidating the assets for next to nothing and selling it as a going enterprise at a fair price.

* You want to disinherit your spouse or a child, or your will is going to leave somebody terribly unhappy. In fact, if there's a chance that someone might challenge your will for any reason at all, a lawyer should draw up the will.

The Title of Your Will

The first thing your will needs is a title. Use:

Last Will and Testament of

_____

or simply:

Will of

_____

The Declaration

Immediately after the title, state who you are, where you live, and what you are doing (that is, making your will).

I, _____, a resident of the City of _____, County of _____, State of _____, hereby make, declare, and publish this, my Last Will and Testament.

This paragraph does several things: First, it identifies who is making the will. Second, it indicates where you are living (your "domicile") at the time you make the will. Finally, it clearly states that the document is in fact your will.

Lawyers usually insert a clause stating that the person making the will is of sound mind and is acting free from the influence of others. If you don't include this language, it does not raise a presumption that you were not of sound mind or that someone was pressuring you to make a gift. If you want to include something along this line, use this clause:

I, _____, a resident of the City of _____, County of _____, State of _____, being of sound and disposing mind, and acting of my own free will, hereby make, declare, and publish this, my Last Will and Testament.

Recital of Marital Status and Children

In this paragraph, state whether you are single or married, and if married, state the name of your spouse. If you have any children, biological or adopted, give their names and birth dates. If you have any children from a previous marriage or out of wedlock, be sure to include their names and birth dates as well. Here are some examples:

1. Married, Have Children

I am married to _____, and all references to my [husband/wife] are to [him/her]. I have _____ children now living. Their names and dates of birth are:

_____[name]_____   Date of Birth: _____
_____[name]_____   Date of Birth: _____

I have no deceased children.

2. Married, No Children

I am married to _____, and all references to my [husband/wife] are to [him/her]. I have no children or other issue, living or deceased.

3. Single (Including Widowed or Divorced), Have Children

I am not married. I have _____ children now living. Their names and dates of birth are:

_____[name]_____   Date of Birth: _____
_____[name]_____   Date of Birth: _____

I have one deceased child, _____, who died without leaving any living issue.

Revoking Prior Wills

If you have an earlier will, then you should expressly revoke it with a sentence such as: "I hereby expressly revoke all wills and codicils that I have previously made."

Disposing of All Property

Somewhere in a will a lawyer usually puts in a sentence saying that you are disposing of all of your property. (Remember that in legalese, real property is real estate, and personal property is everything else—cars, clothing, jewelry, cash, stocks and bonds, and so on. "Mixed property" is a combination of the two, such as a house—real property—with easily removable fixtures—personal property.) This isn't really necessary, particularly if other provisions in your will make this clear. Still, if you want to include such a clause, here's one you can use: "It is my intention to dispose of all property, whether real, personal, or mixed, and wherever situated, I own or have an interest in, or which I have the right to dispose of by will."

Who Gets What

Now we've come to the heart of the will: who gets what. This is where most wills differ, so we have included a number of clauses to help you. The main thing to remember is to make your gifts as clear as possible, so there is no question as to which items or how much money or what percent of your estate goes to whom. If you're giving someone a particular object, such as a painting, identify it completely, including the artist's name, if known. If you're giving your house to someone, identify it by its correct street address. It also makes things easier if you give the full name and address of every person to whom you are making a gift or appointing as executor.

You will see that some of the clauses require the beneficiary to survive you by thirty days in order to receive his or her gift. This is to cover the situation in which you and the beneficiary are injured in an accident together, and the beneficiary lives a few days longer than you. Without this provision, in this situation your gift would end up going to the named beneficiary's heirs instead of to your alternate selection.

1. Gift of All Property to Your Spouse
I give all of my property, real, personal, or mixed, to my [husband/wife] if [he/she] survives me for thirty (30) days and if [he/she] does not so survive me, then I give all of my property, real, personal, or mixed to ___[my children in equal shares or other persons]___ .

2. Gift of Everything to Children in Equal Shares
I give all of my property, real, personal, or mixed, to my children who survive me for thirty (30) days, in equal shares. If a child of mine does not survive me for thirty (30) days, and that child leaves issue surviving, I give such issue the share my child would have received had he or she survived me by thirty (30) days, by right of representation. If a child of mine fails to survive me for thirty (30) days and does not leave surviving issue, then that share shall be distributed equally among my surviving children. If none of my children survive me, and they leave no surviving issue, then I give all of my property, real, personal, or mixed, to _____.

3. Gift of All Property in Percentages
I give all of my property, real, personal, or mixed, as follows:
Forty percent (40%) to _____;
Forty percent (40%) to _____;
Twenty percent (20%) to _____.

If one or more of them shall have died before me, then such share or shares shall be divided equally between the survivors or all to the lone survivor, as the case may be.

4. Gift of Your House

I give my house, located at 1234 Main Street, Springfield, Illinois, to _____, if [he/she] survives me for thirty (30) days, and if [he/she] does not so survive me, I give said house to _____.

5. Gift of Furniture, Furnishings, and Household Goods

I give all of my furniture, furnishings, and household goods to _____.

6. Gift of Cash

I give the sum of _____ dollars ($_____.00) cash to _____.

7. Gift of Stocks and Bonds

(a) Gift of All Stocks and Bonds. I give all stocks and bonds that I own at the time of my death to _____.

(b) Gift of Particular Stock. I give all shares of XYZ Corporation stock that I own at the time of my death to _____.

8. Gift of Automobile

I give any automobile that I own at the time of my death to _____.

If you wish to give a particular car to someone, identify it by year, color, make, model, and license plate number. But if you sell or give that car to someone else before you die, the gift in your will is void.

9. Gifts of Clothing, Jewelry, and Personal Effects

(a) Gift of All Personal Effects. I give all of my jewelry, clothing, furs, and other personal effects to _____.

(b) Gift of Particular Item. I give my four-carat diamond solitaire ring to _____.

10. Naming a Guardian for Your Minor Children

If you have minor children and want to name a guardian for them, use this clause:

If my [husband/wife] does not survive me and at my death any of my children are minors, I nominate __*[name and address]*__ as guardian of my minor children. If _____ fails or refuses to qualify or ceases to act as guardian, then I nominate __*[name and address]*__ as guardian of my minor children.

Remember to talk it over with the person before naming him or her as the guardian of your minor children. Also, if you're married, who will serve as your minor children's guardian in the event both of you die should be a mutual decision.

The Residuary Clause

The residuary clause of a will is a catchall clause that essentially provides for the distribution of all property not otherwise specifically covered in the will. It also governs the disposition of any gifts if the intended beneficiary is dead or refuses to accept the gift. If your will gives all of your property to one person, a residuary clause is not necessary. But if you're making several gifts, a residuary clause is a good idea, as it dictates who gets the property if a beneficiary of a specific gift dies before you. A typical residuary clause reads:

> I give the rest, remainder, and residue of my estate, real, personal, or mixed, to _____, if [he/she] survives me for thirty (30) days, and if [he/she] does not so survive me, then I give the rest, remainder, and residue of my estate, real, personal, or mixed, to _____.

Naming Your Executor or Executrix

The first paragraph below is used to name the executor or executrix of your will. Be sure to get the person's consent before appointing him or her as executor or executrix. In addition to appointing the executor, the paragraph also waives the bond the executor would otherwise be required to post (at the expense of your estate). If you want the bond posted, simply omit the relevant sentence. The second paragraph gives the executor the right to deal with the property pretty much in the same manner as you could. Without this authority, the executor may constantly have to go back to court to get permission before doing many routine things. The extent of the powers you give your executor depends on how much you trust your executor. Since you usually trust the person you name as executor very much, we have assumed you want to give him or her broad powers. Omit the second paragraph if you don't want to give your executor this much power.

> I hereby nominate _____ to serve as the [Executor/Executrix] of this will. If _____ refuses to or cannot qualify, or ceases to act as the [Executor/Executrix], then I nominate _____ as the [Executor/Executrix]. It is my wish that no bond shall be required of any person named as Executor or Executrix in this will.
>
> I give my Executor or Executrix the power to act as I could act if living, including, but not limited to, the powers to invest and reinvest any surplus money in my Execu-

tor's or Executrix's hands in every kind of property and every kind of investment that persons of prudence, discretion, and intelligence acquire for their own account; to sell, with or without notice, at either public or private sale, and to lease any property, real, personal, or mixed, for cash, partly for cash and partly for credit, or entirely for credit; to partition, allot, and distribute my estate in kind, or partly in cash and partly in kind, or entirely in cash. I further authorize my Executor or Executrix to either continue the operation of any business belonging to my estate for such time and in such manner as my Executor or Executrix may deem advisable and for the best interests of my estate, or to sell or liquidate the business at such time and on such terms as my Executor or Executrix deems advisable and for the best interests of my estate. Any such operation, sale, or liquidation by my Executor or Executrix in good faith, shall be at the risk of my estate and without liability on the part of my Executor or Executrix.

The Signature Clause

There is no particular wording that must precede your signature. In fact, you can simply date and sign the will. We do, however, suggest that you use the following clause:

I subscribe my name to this will this _____ day of _____,
20_____, at ___[city]_____, County of _____, State
of _____.
___[sign your name here]___.
Type your name

Keep in mind that your signature should be at the end of the will. Nothing—except the attestation clause and witnesses' signatures—should follow your signature. If you make any additions or notations after your signature, a court usually will ignore them. If you discover you forgot to put something in your will, either draw up a new will or prepare a codicil (see below) after the will has been signed and witnessed.

The Attestation (Witnesses' Clause)

As with the signature clause, there is no requirement that any particular wording precede the signatures of the witnesses. Still, it is a good idea to have a witnesses' clause, if only because it reinforces that the signature and the witnessing of the will were done correctly. Use the following clause—called the "attestation clause"—in your will:

On the date last above written, ___[your name]___ declared to us, the undersigned, that the foregoing document was [his/her] Last Will and Testament, and requested us to act as witnesses to it. [He/She] thereupon signed this will in our presence, all of us being present at the same time. We now, at [his/her] request, in [his/her] presence, and in the presence of each other, subscribe our names as witnesses.

We believe that the [Testator/Testatrix] is over age 18, is of sound mind, and is under no constraint or undue influence.

_____   _____   _____
[signature of witness]   [signature of witness]   [signature of witness]

We declare under penalty of perjury that the foregoing is true and correct and that this declaration was executed on ___[date]___, 20 _____, at ___[city]___, County of _____, State of _____.

_____   _____   _____
[signature of witness]   [signature of witness]   [signature of witness]
Name and Address: Name and Address: Name and Address:
_____   _____   _____
_____   _____   _____
_____   _____   _____

Make sure you know how many witnesses are required by your state. As mentioned earlier, all states require two witnesses, except Maine, New Hampshire, South Carolina, and Vermont, which require three witnesses. Louisiana requires that the two witnesses sign in front of a notary public, who then attaches his or her seal verifying that the witnesses are who they claim to be. (You can check the current requirements by calling the clerk of the probate or surrogate court.) Lawyers frequently have one more witness sign than is necessary. For example, if the law requires two witnesses, a lawyer may have three witness sign. This is to protect you in case the court rules that one of the witnesses was ineligible to witness your will. (Who should witness your will is discussed below.)

Examples of Complete Wills

Here are examples of complete wills for guidance in writing your own. The first two are the mutual wills of a husband and wife, in which each gives the estate to the other, and to the children when both die. If none of the children survives, the will provides accordingly. The third example is one that a single person with no children or grandchildren might make. Remember that these wills are only examples. You can adapt them to your own situation by using the information and clauses provided above, keeping in mind the cautions about doing it yourself found at the end of the previous chapter.

LAST WILL AND TESTAMENT

OF

JOE SMITH

I, JOE SMITH, a resident of Hometown, Lincoln County, State of _____, hereby make, declare, and publish this, my Last Will and Testament.

1. I am married to JANE SMITH, and all references to "my wife" are to her. I have two (2) children now living. Their names and dates of birth are:

   JACK SMITH   Born: January 2, 1990
   SHERRY SMITH   Born: April 4, 1995

   I have no deceased children.

2. I hereby expressly revoke all wills and codicils that I have previously made.

3. It is my intention to dispose of all property, whether real, personal, or mixed, and wherever located, that I own or have an interest in or which I have the right to dispose of by will.

4. I give all of my property, real, personal, or mixed, to my wife if she survives me for thirty (30) days, and if she does not so survive me, then I give all of my property to my children who survive me for thirty (30) days, in equal shares. If a child of mine fails to survive me by thirty (30) days, then I give that child's share to his or her living issue, by right of representation, and if he or she leaves no surviving issue, then my surviving child shall receive all of my property. If neither my wife nor any of my children or their issue survive me, then I give all of my property, in equal shares, to my brother WILLIAM SMITH, who lives at 1234 Main Street, Hometown, and to my wife's sister, MARGIE JONES, who lives at 987 Elm Street, Mayfield, or to the survivor of them.

5. If my wife does not survive me and at my death any of my children are minors, I nominate my brother, WILLIAM SMITH, as guardian of my minor children. If for any reason WILLIAM fails or refuses to qualify as guardian, or ceases to act as guardian, then I nominate my wife's sister, MARGIE JONES, as guardian of my minor children.

6. I nominate my wife to serve as the Executrix of this will. If she refuses to or cannot qualify, or ceases to act as the Executrix, then I nominate my brother, WILLIAM SMITH, as the Executor. It is my wish that no bond shall be required of any person named as Executor or Executrix in this will.

I give my Executor or Executrix the power to act as I could act if living, including, but not limited to, the powers to invest and reinvest any surplus money in my

Executor's or Executrix's hands in every kind of property and every kind of investment that persons of prudence, discretion, and intelligence acquire for their own account; to sell, with or without notice, at either public or private sale, and to lease any property, real, personal, or mixed, for cash, partly for cash and partly for credit, or entirely for credit; to partition, allot, and distribute my estate in kind, or partly in cash and partly in kind, or entirely in cash. I further authorize my Executor or Executrix to either continue the operation of any business belonging to my estate for such time and in such manner as my Executor or Executrix may deem advisable and for the best interests of my estate, or to sell or liquidate the business at such time and on such terms as my Executor or Executrix deems advisable and for the best interests of my estate. Any such operation, sale, or liquidation by my Executor or Executrix in good faith, shall be at the risk of my estate and without liability on the part of my Executor or Executrix.

I subscribe my name to this will this _____ day of _____, 20_____, at ___[city]_____, County of _____, State of _____.

_____
JOE SMITH

On the date last above written, JOE SMITH declared to us, the undersigned, that the foregoing document was his Last Will and Testament, and requested us to act as witnesses to it. He thereupon signed this will in our presence, all of us being present at the same time. We now, at his request, in his presence, and in the presence of each other, subscribe our names as witnesses.

We believe that the Testator is over age 18, is of sound mind, and is under no constraint or undue influence.

_____   _____   _____
[signature of witness]   [signature of witness]   [signature of witness]

We declare under penalty of perjury that the foregoing is true and correct and that this declaration was executed on _____[date]_____, 20_____, at ___[city]_____, County of _____, State of _____.

_____   _____   _____
[signature of witness]   [signature of witness]   [signature of witness]

Name and Address: Name and Address: Name and Address:

_____   _____   _____

_____   _____   _____

_____   _____   _____

LAST WILL AND TESTAMENT
OF
JANE SMITH

I, JANE SMITH, a resident of Hometown, Lincoln County, State of _____, hereby make, declare, and publish this, my Last Will and Testament.

1. I am married to JOE SMITH, and all references to "my husband" are to him. I have two (2) children now living. Their names and dates of birth are:

JACK SMITH   Born: January 2, 1990
SHERRY SMITH   Born: April 4, 1995

I have no deceased children.

2. I hereby expressly revoke all wills and codicils that I have previously made.

3. It is my intention to dispose of all property, whether real, personal, or mixed, and wherever located, that I own or have an interest in or which I have the right to dispose of by will.

4. I give all of my property, real, personal, or mixed, to my husband if he survives me for thirty (30) days, and if he does not so survive me, then I give all of my property to my children who survive me for thirty (30) days, in equal shares. If a child of mine fails to survive me by thirty (30) days, then I give that child's share to his or her living issue, by right of representation, and if he or she leaves no surviving issue, then my surviving child shall receive all of my property. If neither my husband nor any of my children or their issue survive me, then I give all of my property, in equal shares, to my husband's brother, WILLIAM SMITH, who lives at 1234 Main Street, Hometown, and to my sister, MARGIE JONES, who lives at 987 Elm Street, Mayfield, or to the survivor of them.

5. If my husband does not survive me and at my death any of my children are minors, I nominate my husband's brother, WILLIAM SMITH, as guardian of my minor children. If for any reason WILLIAM fails or refuses to qualify as guardian, or ceases to act as guardian, then I nominate my sister, MARGIE JONES, as guardian of my minor children.

6. I nominate my husband to serve as the Executor of this will. If he refuses to or cannot qualify, or ceases to act as the Executor, then I nominate my husband's brother, WILLIAM SMITH, as the Executor. It is my wish that no bond shall be required of any person named as Executor in this will.

I give my Executor the power to act as I could act if living, including, but not limited to, the powers to invest and reinvest any surplus money in my Executor's or Executrix's hands in every kind of property and every kind of investment that persons of prudence, discretion, and intelligence acquire for their own account; to sell, with or without notice, at either public or private sale, and to lease any property, real, personal, or mixed, for cash, partly for cash and partly for credit, or entirely for credit; to partition, allot, and distribute my estate in kind, or partly in cash and partly in kind, or entirely in cash. I further authorize my Executor or Executrix to either continue the operation of any business belonging to my estate for such time and in such manner as my Executor or Executrix may deem advisable and for the best interests of my estate, or to sell or liquidate the business at such time and on such terms as my Executor or Executrix deems advisable and for the best interests of my estate. Any such operation, sale, or liquidation by my Executor or Executrix, in good faith, shall be at the risk of my estate and without liability on the part of my Executor or Executrix.

I subscribe my name to this will this _____ day of _____, 20_____, at ___[city]_____, County of _____, State of _____.

_____
JANE SMITH

On the date last above written, JANE SMITH declared to us, the undersigned, that the foregoing document was her Last Will and Testament, and requested us to act as witnesses to it. She thereupon signed this will in our presence, all of us being present at the same time. We now, at her request, in her presence, and in the presence of each other, subscribe our names as witnesses.

We believe that the Testator is over age 18, is of sound mind, and is under no constraint or undue influence.

_____ _____ _____
[signature of witness]   [signature of witness]   [signature of witness]

We declare under penalty of perjury that the foregoing is true and correct and that this declaration was executed on ___[date]___, 20_____, at ___[city]_____, County of _____, State of _____.

_____ _____ _____
[signature of witness]   [signature of witness]   [signature of witness]

Name and Address: Name and Address: Name and Address:

_____ _____ _____

_____ _____ _____

_____ _____ _____

Example of a Single Person's Will

LAST WILL AND TESTAMENT
OF
RHONDA BARNES

I, RHONDA BARNES, a resident of the city of Hometown, Lincoln County, State of _____, hereby make, declare, and publish this, my Last Will and Testament.

1. I am not married, and I have no children or other issue, living or deceased.
2. I hereby expressly revoke all wills and codicils that I have previously made.
3. It is my intention to dispose of all property, real, personal, or mixed, I own or have an interest in or which I have the right to dispose of by will.
4. I give the sum of ten thousand dollars ($10,000.00) to GEORGE JOHNSON, whose address is 456 Washington Blvd., Canton, Ohio.
5. I give the sum of five thousand dollars ($5,000.00) to the AMERICAN HEART ASSOCIATION.
6. I give the sum of five thousand dollars ($5,000.00) to the RED CROSS, Hometown chapter.
7. I give all of my clothing, jewelry, and other personal effects to SUSAN STANTON, whose address is 34262 Birch Street, Hometown.
8. I give any automobile that I may own at the time of my death to GUS ADAMS, whose address is 5432 Feynman Way, Springfield.
9. I give the rest, remainder, and residue of my estate, real, personal, or mixed, to BEVERLY HANSON, whose address is 5647 Bright Street, Hometown, if she survives me for thirty (30) days, and if she does not so survive me, then I give the rest, remainder, and residue of my estate, real, personal, or mixed, to MARGARET BATES, whose address is 7890 Comstock Avenue, Hometown.
10. I nominate BEVERLY HANSON to serve as the Executrix of this will. If for any reason she refuses or cannot qualify, or ceases to act as the Executrix, then I nominate MARGARET BATES as the Executrix. It is my wish that no bond shall be required of any person named as Executrix in this will.

I give my Executrix the power to act as I could act if living, including, but not limited to, the powers to invest and reinvest any surplus money in my Executrix's hands in every kind of property and every kind of investment that persons of prudence, discretion, and intelligence acquire for their own account; to sell, with or without notice, at either public or private sale, and to lease any property, real, personal, or mixed, for cash, partly for cash and partly for credit, or entirely for credit; to partition, allot, and distribute my estate in kind, or partly in cash and partly in kind, or entirely in cash. I further authorize my Executrix to either continue the operation of any business belonging to my estate for such time and in such manner as my Executrix may deem advisable and for the best interests of my estate, or to sell or liquidate the business at such time and on such terms as my Executrix deems advisable and for the best interests of my estate. Any such operation, sale, or liquidation by my Executrix, in good faith, shall be at the risk of my estate and without liability on the part of my Executrix.

I subscribe my name to this will this _____ day of _____, 20_____, at ___[city]_____, County of _____, State of _____.

_____
RHONDA BARNES

On the date last above written, RHONDA BARNES declared to us, the undersigned, that the foregoing document was her Last Will and Testament, and requested us to act as witnesses to it. She thereupon signed this will in our presence, all of us being present at the same time. We now, at her request, in her presence, and in the presence of each other, subscribe our names as witnesses.

We believe that the Testatrix is over age 18, is of sound mind, and is under no constraint or undue influence.

_____   _____   _____
[signature of witness]   [signature of witness]   [signature of witness]

We declare under penalty of perjury that the foregoing is true and correct and that this declaration was executed on ___[date]___, 20_____, at ___[city]_____, County of _____, State of _____.

_____   _____   _____
[signature of witness]   [signature of witness]   [signature of witness]

Name and Address: Name and Address: Name and Address:

_____   _____   _____

_____   _____   _____

_____   _____   _____

THE SIGNING AND WITNESSING OF YOUR WILL

Now that you've printed your will off your computer or typed it up, you're ready to sign it and have it witnessed—the "execution." We already have mentioned that two witnesses are required in all states except Maine, New Hampshire, South Carolina, and Vermont, which require three witnesses. And don't forget that in Louisiana, the two witnesses must sign in front of a notary public, who then affixes his or her seal and signature attesting to the identity of the witnesses.

Who to Get as Witnesses

You can have just about any person who is 18 or older in most states, 19 or older in a few, serve as a witness to the signing of your will, as long as he or she is mentally competent. You don't even have to know the person, although it's better to have good friends witness the will. There are two reasons for this. First, a friend will be more willing to help you out and witness your will than a complete stranger or someone you barely know. The second reason is that if it is necessary to track down a witness to the will to verify his or her signature on your will, it is usually easier for the executor's lawyer to track down a good friend with whom you have kept in touch than it is to find someone you only met once or twice. Two things that may affect your choice of a witness are his or her age, and their health. As morbid as it may sound, you want to get someone to witness the will who is probably going to outlive you, so that that person will be around to verify ("attest") that he or she witnessed your signature on the will.

If a lawyer prepares your will, he or she will usually be a witness, a standard and proper procedure, assuming he or she is not receiving a gift under the terms of the will. (If you want to give something to your lawyer, another lawyer should prepare the will.) The lawyer's receptionist or secretary may also witness the will.

Who Should Not Witness Your Will

Anybody who receives a gift under the will should *not* be a witness to your will. Likewise, anyone who is entitled to a share of your estate if you die without a will should not be a witness. A husband and wife should not act as witnesses to one another's wills, nor should their children be witnesses.

In many states, a witness named as a beneficiary in the will is disqualified from acting as a witness, and his or her signature is ignored. If this happens, and you didn't have an extra witness sign the will, the will becomes invalid, and your estate passes as though there were no will at all. Some courts may find that the will is good, but the witness will have to forfeit his or her gift to the extent that it exceeds the portion of the estate he or she would have received if the deceased had died without a will. This is why lawyers often have a will witnessed by one witness more than is required by law; if one of the witnesses is disqualified, the will still stands, as there remain two (or three, as the case may be) valid witnesses.

The Procedure for Signing and Witnessing Your Will

Here is the procedure that we recommend that you follow in signing your will and having it witnessed:

Gather all of your witnesses around you and tell them that the document you are about to sign is your last will and testament. (In Louisiana, you will also need to have a notary public present to watch the signing and witnessing of the will.) Then ask the people that you would like them to serve as witnesses to your signing of the document. Read aloud the attestation clause (the clause appearing above the place for the witnesses' signatures). While the witnesses watch you, initial each page of the will in the bottom right-hand corner. (This protects you from somebody trying to slip in a phony page.) Sign the will as the witnesses watch, then have each witness sign his or her name while the other witnesses (and in Louisiana, the notary public) look on. It is not necessary for the witnesses to read the will. You have every right to keep the contents of your will confidential.

SAFEKEEPING, REVIEWING, AND CHANGING YOUR WILL

Where to Keep Your Will

You shouldn't handle your original will unless you want to revoke it or change it. Rather, you should keep a copy of it handy so you can review it periodically—something that, as discussed below, we highly recommend. If a lawyer has prepared your will, he or she will ordinarily keep a copy of it in your client file. Tell your spouse if you are married and the person you named as your executor where the will is kept, so that it can be obtained promptly when needed. It is also a good idea to give your executor a copy of your will and, if applicable, the name, address, and telephone number of the lawyer who prepared it. This way the executor can immediately notify the lawyer upon your death, obtain the original will, and get the probate proceedings started as soon as possible.

After your will is signed and witnessed, put it in a place safe from fire, flood, loss, and theft. The best place for your original will is usually your safe-deposit box or in your home in a fire-proof safe. We advise against leaving the original with your lawyer, as the lawyer may die, move away, stop practicing law, etc., and the original of your will may get lost in the shuffle. In some states, you can, but aren't required to, deposit your will with the court. We recommend against this in most cases, however, since if you want to change your will or revoke it, you will have to go to the court to get it.

Is a court order needed to get a will out of a bank's safe-deposit box after you die? Generally not. If the box is in someone else's name as well as yours, then they have every right to open it. And even if it is in your name alone, your heirs are generally free to open the safe-deposit box without a court order to get the original will and burial instructions. But not just anyone can get the safe-deposit box opened. They must have a logical reason to be looking for the will. This means that they must be the spouse, child, or other close relative of yours, your attorney, or the person named as executor in the will. They should be prepared to show a certified copy of the death certificate or other evidence that you have died. The safe-deposit box then will be opened in the presence of a bank employee, and only the will, burial instructions, and related documents can be removed from the box at this time.

When to Review Your Will

Once a will is made, it is good until you die, change it, or revoke it. If you make a will today and die fifty years from now without making any changes to it, your property will be disposed of according to the will you made a half-century earlier. As you can imagine, a few changes might have occurred over that time that would warrant making changes to your will. You should periodically review your will to make sure that it carries out your current wishes and is not adversely affected by ever-changing estate tax laws. As a general rule of thumb, you should review your will at least every four years. Many lawyers recommend that wills be reviewed every two or three years, particularly in the case of older individuals. One thing is certain, though: You can't expect to make a will today, put it in your safe-deposit box, and forget about it. It must be reviewed periodically to reflect the changes in your life.

Certain events in life especially demand that you review your will for probable revision. In the material that follows, we will consider each factor separately. Later we will tell you how to make any needed changes.

The Birth of a Child

You need to update your will if a child is born (or adopted) after you make your will. You may want to appoint a guardian for your child, set up a trust, or otherwise make provisions for your child in the event of your death.

If you don't change your will after a child is born, the law will change it for you. In almost every state, a child born after you make a will is entitled to the same share he or she would have received if you died without a will. (This amount is discussed in the preceding chapter.) If you don't update your will after a child is born, the law ordinarily presumes that you simply hadn't yet gotten around to changing your will, not that you intended to disinherit the child.

If you want to disinherit the child, you will have to make a new will or amendment ("codicil") doing just that. Adopted children usually are treated the same as biological children when it comes to omission. But if you fail to name an unadopted stepchild, that stepchild usually gets nothing.

The Death of a Close Relative or a Beneficiary

You should review your will when a close family member such as a spouse, child, or parent has died, or when a beneficiary under the will has died. If your will contains a gift to a deceased beneficiary, that gift will go to the alternate you have named, if any, and if you have named none, it will pass according to the terms of the residuary clause. If there is no residuary clause, that portion will be treated as if there were no will at all.

If You Get Married

When you get married, you will most likely want to change your will to provide for your new spouse. What happens if you don't change your will? In many states, when you get married, any will you have at the time of the marriage is automatically revoked. If you die without making a new will, the property will be distributed as though there were no will at all, even if you didn't want to make any changes to the earlier will. If you get married but don't want to change your earlier will, you should at least execute a codicil stating that the original will signed before your marriage is to remain in effect.

If You Get Divorced

If you have obtained a divorce ("dissolution of marriage") or are in the process of doing so, you should review your will for possible changes. In some states, the act of divorce automatically cuts the ex-spouse out of the will. However, in other states, the fact that a person has obtained a divorce does not automatically revoke a will. Your divorce lawyer can advise you as to what the law is in your state on this issue. In any event, we heartily advise changing your will to omit your spouse during the divorce proceedings as soon as it is clear there is no chance for a reconciliation.

If You Move Out of State

You should review your will with a lawyer for possible changes when you move from one state to another. Usually a will that was valid in the state where it was made will be accepted as valid in the state you move to. But even if it is valid in your new state, you may still want to have a new will prepared if the gift and inheritance taxes of the new state affect you. You should also consider changing your executor and the guardian for your minor children to someone who lives closer to your new home.

Changes in Your Financial Position or the Law

For a young couple starting out without a family or much property, a simple will may be sufficient. But as the size of their family and estate grows, they will need to change their wills to nominate guardians for their minor children and to set up trusts for them, and perhaps to do some tax planning to minimize the amount of federal estate and state inheritance taxes payable upon their deaths. When the children are grown and have children of their own, changes in the will again may be called for.

When there are major changes in the law, it is important to review your will. For example, if your will was prepared before the Economic Growth and Tax Reconciliation Act of 2001 was passed into law, you will want to review it with a qualified estate planning lawyer because of significant changes in the estate tax laws that may have a tremendous impact upon your will (see chapter 3).

How to Change Your Will

Reviewing your will one day, you change your mind about giving someone a particular gift. Can you just draw a line through that person's name and write the name of a new beneficiary in the margin? No. In some states, this attempted change will be ignored completely because it doesn't meet the legal requirements, and the gift will therefore go to the person whose name was crossed out. In many states, the gift to the original beneficiary is revoked, but rather than going to the new beneficiary, the gift will pass through the residuary clause.

If you wish to make a change to your will, no matter how minor it may appear to you, you have two options: make a completely new will or make a "codicil" to your existing will. A codicil is an amendment to a will and must be prepared and executed (signed and witnessed) the same as a will. A codicil is usually appropriate only when the change is relatively short, say, changing the name of a beneficiary or the executor. If the changes are long or numerous, or if you have already made a codicil or two to your will, it is usually better to prepare a new will to prevent confusion.

In states that recognize a holographic will, you can make a holographic codicil (one entirely handwritten by you, and dated and signed by you). But as we suggested in the material on making your own will, whether or not your state recognizes holographic wills and codicils, we recommend that the codicil—like the will—be a formal witnessed one. That means it should be printed out from a computer word processor or typed up, dated and signed by you, and signed by the appropriate number of witnesses (three in Maine, New Hampshire, South Carolina, and Vermont, two elsewhere, although having three sign is advisable in every state in case a witness is disqualified. And don't forget that if you're in Louisiana, you'll need your witnesses to sign the codicil in front of a notary public, who must then affix his or her notarial seal.)

Here is a sample codicil:

CODICIL

I, MARY BAKER, hereby make this Codicil to my Last Will and Testament dated November 15, 2003.

FIRST: I hereby revoke my gift to Melissa Sands of all my clothing, jewelry, and other personal effects, and instead give all of my clothing, jewelry, and other personal effects to Irma Sanchez, whose address is 6578 College Avenue, Hometown.

SECOND: I hereby withdraw my nomination of Roger Reed as the Executor of my Last Will and Testament, and instead nominate Bruce Tully to serve as Executor. Bruce Tully's address is 36975 Oates Road., Hometown. It is my desire that no bond be required of Bruce Tully if he serves as Executor of my estate.

I subscribe my name to this Codicil this _____ day of _____, 20 ____, at _____ *[city]* , County of _____, State of _____.

_____
MARY BAKER

On the date last above written, MARY BAKER declared to us, the undersigned, that the foregoing document was a Codicil to her Last Will and Testament of November 15, 2003 and requested us to act as witnesses to it. She thereupon signed this Codicil in our presence, all of us being present at the same time. We now, at her request, in her presence, and in the presence of each other, subscribe our names as witnesses.

_____ _____ _____
[signature of witness] *[signature of witness]* *[signature of witness]*

We declare under penalty of perjury that the foregoing is true and correct and that this declaration was executed on __*[date]*__, 20 ___, at _____ *[city]* , County of _____, State of _____.

_____ _____ _____
[signature of witness] *[signature of witness]* *[signature of witness]*

Name and Address: Name and Address: Name and Address:

_____ _____ _____

_____ _____ _____

The signing and witnessing of the codicil should follow the same procedures as those set forth earlier for the signing and witnessing of a will. (The witnesses to your codicil need not be the same people who acted as witnesses to the signing of your will.) Make a photocopy of the codicil so you can keep it on hand to periodically review it. Give a copy of the codicil to the person(s) you gave a copy of your will to. Put the codicil with your will in your safe-deposit box or home fireproof safe.

How to Revoke Your Will

If for some reason you decide to revoke your will completely (perhaps it is twenty years old, and it would be disastrous if your property were to be distributed according to your outdated will), there are several ways to do this. The simplest way is to rip up the original will completely. A more dramatic but equally effective way to revoke a will is to burn it. The destruction of the will must be done with the intent to revoke it, and you must be of sufficient mental capacity ("sound mind") to revoke it. A will destroyed by accident or by a person who lacks sufficient mental competency to revoke it remains in effect. When this happens, a copy of the original will can be used to verify its contents, or the lawyer who drafted the will or anyone who had read it could testify to its contents.

Another way to revoke your old will is to execute a new document stating that you revoke your will. When a new will is prepared, a clause usually is inserted stating that all wills and codicils previously made by that person are revoked. If you are making your own will, you should include a similar provision.

WHY AND HOW WILLS ARE CHALLENGED

THE MOST COMMON GROUNDS for contesting a will are that the person wasn't of sound mind; someone was exercising undue influence over the testator or testatrix or committed fraud; the will offered for probate was revoked and replaced by a later will; the will wasn't signed and witnessed according to the statutory requirements; or the will offered for probate is an outright phony, a forgery.

Undue Influence and Mental Distress

There are those who will do everything they can to coerce another person to will them property. A son, daughter, grandchild, nephew, or niece may be guilty of such behavior; there are even instances of nurses who have threatened a patient or withheld nourishment until the patient promised to prepare a will giving the nurse all or most of the estate.

Undue influence and mental coercion are found most frequently when one child or grandchild wants all to himself or herself. Over a period of years, the child or grandchild may make subtle threats to an aging parent or grandparent in order to gain an unfair advantage over others. A court will set aside a gift on the ground of undue influence only if a four-part test is satisfied. Under this test, a person claiming that another received a gift because of improper conduct must show that (1) because of advancing years or physical or mental infirmity, the person making the will could be influenced or controlled by those close to him or her; (2) the person who received the gift in question had the chance to use undue influence; (3) the person had a motive for using undue influence (usually to get a large part of the estate or to see that someone else was denied a fair share); and (4) the person making the will probably wouldn't have made this gift if somebody weren't putting pressure on him or her.

Fraud

Fraud in the preparation of a will can be of two types. The first is fraud in the execution: The person signing the will is misled as to the nature of the paper being signed or the contents of the will. For instance, an older person whose mind and vision are both slipping away may be given a piece of paper to sign that unbeknownst to him or her is a will prepared by a conniving child or nurse. The "testator" signs the document believing it to be something as innocuous as a letter. Another example: An invalid dictates a will, but the lawyer and a child conspire to change the contents and assure the testator that everything is as he or she wished, so the testator or testatrix signs the altered will. In cases of persons whose health or memory is failing, it is a good idea, in order to reduce the chances of fraud, to have a video camera record the will being read for the testator's or testatrix's approval.

The second type of fraud is fraud in the inducement, where the testator is misled about some fact that affects the provisions of his or her will. For example, one child may tell an ailing father that another child has died to induce the father to give everything to his "sole surviving heir." A court probably would invalidate the will in this case, since it was the result of the child's deliberate misrepresentation.

The Forgotten Heir

Sometimes a person will forget to provide for a close relative—say, a child or a spouse—in his or her will. Failure to include someone so close to the testator may be a factor in determining the testator's soundness of mind at the time the will was made. But assuming that the testator was of sound mind, the question becomes, What does the omitted person get, if anything?

Earlier we discussed the rights of a disinherited spouse. When there is an omission, his or her rights are usually the same: The spouse has the right to elect between the share he or she would have received if the testator or testatrix had died without a will and what the will gives him or her.

A child not mentioned in the will is a "pretermitted" heir. (This generally includes adopted and illegitimate children as well as legitimate children, but not unadopted stepchildren.) In such a case, the law presumes that the testator merely "forgot" about the child when making the will and didn't intend to disinherit the child. But if the will makes any mention of the child, this is usually enough for a court to hold that the testator was thinking of the child when the will was made and intentionally failed to give the child any property. In most states, an omitted child usually is entitled to the same share he or she would have received if the parent had died without a will. This could be as much as one-third, one-half, or even all of the estate, depending upon the state, the circumstances, and whether a surviving spouse or any other children are entitled to share in the estate.

Mistakes

What happens if someone mistakenly believes that the person to whom he or she was going to give all of his or her estate is dead and therefore gives all of the property to others? As long as no one intentionally convinced or tricked the testator into believing that the intended beneficiary was dead, the will generally is carried out as written. A judge can change the will, however, if the will clearly shows both the testator's mistaken belief as to the death of the intended beneficiary and what property the testator would have given the beneficiary had the testator known the intended beneficiary was alive. For example, suppose Becky's will reads, "I would have given my house to my friend Dorothy Dandridge, but unfortunately she is dead. I therefore give the house to my cousin Sam Goldberg." In such a case, the judge probably would award the house to Dorothy Dandridge if she is actually alive and Becky was mistaken as to her death.

Now suppose that Becky's will merely stated, "I give my house to my cousin Sam Goldberg." There is no mention of Dorothy Dandridge anywhere in the will. If Dorothy could prove that Sam (or someone acting on his behalf) deliberately led Becky to believe that Dorothy was dead so she would give the house to Sam instead of to Dorothy as Becky had planned, the judge would void the gift to Sam and give the house to Dorothy. But if Becky was merely mistaken as to Dorothy's death and no one had deliberately misled her, the house will go to Sam, as her mistaken belief of Dorothy's death does not appear on the face of the will, nor does it appear that Becky would have given her house to Dorothy had she known Dorothy was in fact living.

Here is a different type of mistake: A lawyer draws up mutual wills for a husband and wife. The husband inadvertently signs his wife's will, and the wife signs her husband's will. No one catches the mistake, and the witnesses sign the wills. When the husband dies, the mistake is discovered. Which will gets probated, the one the husband actually signed (his wife's), or the will he thought he was signing (his own, the one signed by his wife)? Neither. The husband's innocent mistake in signing his wife's will (and her mistake in signing his) invalidates the will, as the husband intended to sign his will, not his wife's. And the intent cannot be transferred from one document to another. The husband's property is then distributed as if there were no will.

Procedure for Contesting a Will

It is during the probate process that the validity of a will can and must be challenged. The procedure for a will contest varies greatly from state to state. All states' procedures have one thing in common, though: They generally must be initiated promptly, or you will lose your right to challenge the will, regardless of how meritorious your challenge may be. If you are considering contesting a will, you should consult a lawyer immediately.

Preventing a Possible Will Contest

To prevent a possible will contest, many people insert in their wills a clause to the effect that if a beneficiary challenges the will, that beneficiary automatically forfeits his or her gift. This clause is a good idea if there is a strong likelihood that a greedy beneficiary will instigate a will contest in bad faith, with no valid reason. But a no-contest clause also can dissuade a beneficiary with a legitimate challenge from pursuing it, for fear that he or she will lose what he or she already has if the challenge is not successful. Because of this, some courts do not enforce a no-contest clause if the challenge was undertaken in good faith. If a person successfully challenges the will or a provision of the will, the no-contest clause is not enforced. A no-contest provision should be prepared by a lawyer to increase the chances that a judge will enforce it.

FIVE

The Elderly

*i*N THE LAST TEN YEARS, one of the fastest growing areas of law has been that of elder law, which covers topics of special concern for those ages 55 and over. Elder law runs the gamut of the legal spectrum. Examples of elder law are found throughout this book. For instance, detailed discussions about estate planning, durable powers of attorney for property management, advance health care directives, and revocable living trusts are found in chapter 3. Wills are discussed in chapter 4. Age discrimination in employment is dealt with in chapter 13. Social Security, Medicare, Supplemental Security Income (SSI), and Medicaid are addressed in chapter 15. Go to the specific chapter for more in-depth information on each of those topics.

In this chapter, we will focus on the issues of money, housing alternatives, long-term medical care for the elderly, hospice care, selling life insurance policies ("viatical settlements"), and elder abuse.

MAKING YOUR PROPERTY WORK FOR YOU

SUPPOSE JACK AND ELIZABETH bought their house thirty-five years ago for $25,000. Today it is worth $175,000 and the mortgage has been paid off for five years. Jack, who is 70, is a retired insurance agent, and Elizabeth, who is also 70, is a homemaker. Jack receives a monthly Social Security check of $850, and Elizabeth's is $365. Between them they are able just to squeak by each month, but money is tight and little, if any, is left over at the end of the month. The cost of their prescription drugs is not covered by Medicare and takes a big chunk of their income. The house is falling into disrepair, and needs a new roof. They dread having to pay property taxes. Plus, they would like to take one last trip to their hometown of Canton, Ohio, while they are still healthy enough to be able to do so. But with their low income, they can't afford it. Is there any relief out there for them? Yes. There are a number of programs available in many areas to make life easier for Jack and Elizabeth.

Property Tax Deferrals

Many states, counties, and cities have a program that lets elderly homeowners defer paying their property taxes until they sell their house, move out permanently, or die. The programs may differ greatly in their particulars, but the basic plan lets you defer paying your property taxes at an interest rate of usually 6 to 8 percent, which is due and payable when you sell the house, move out, or die. Usually property tax deferrals are available only to homeowners whose income and assets are at or below certain levels. There may be a minimum age requirement that the homeowner must meet as well.

In some states, you must make an application to defer your property taxes with the state. The state then pays the local tax assessor for you. In other states, you must pay the property taxes first yourself and then make an application for deferral, in which case if your application is approved, the money is refunded to you. The best and easiest way is for the tax assessor simply to credit your account as being paid, without the necessity of issuing any checks. There may be a limit as to how much of the property taxes can be deferred each year, as well as a limit to how much of the property taxes can be deferred altogether.

To find out if there is a property tax deferral program in your area and if you qualify for it, contact your county tax assessor's office, state tax board, or area agency on aging.

Deferred Payment Loans

Deferred payment loans (DPLs), sometimes called "home repair loans," are made by the government and private nonprofit organizations so you can make needed repairs or certain improvements to your home. Deferred payment loans are made at no or very low interest. The loan generally does not have to be paid off until you sell your house, move out permanently, or die. Like property tax deferrals, the homeowner seeking a deferred payment loan must generally meet age requirements and have income and assets below a specified amount.

The proceeds of the loan must be used to make an improvement—such as making changes to door widths to accommodate a wheelchair or installing ramps or grab bars by the toilet and in the shower—or to make necessary repairs, such as replacing an old leaky roof or fixing plumbing or electrical problems. Generally the funds cannot be used for mere cosmetic purposes to make the house look nicer, such as painting your house. To find out whether deferred payment loans are available in your area, call your area agency on aging or the city or county housing authority.

Reverse Mortgages

Most seniors do not realize that they are sitting on (or more accurately, in) their most valuable asset: their home. Many seniors are cash poor but house rich. But how can they get money out of their house without selling it and moving? There are several things they can do with the equity in their house, the most important of which is to use it to obtain a reverse mortgage.

A reverse mortgage—technically, a "home equity conversion mortgage" (HECM)—may be the ideal thing for them. The most common HECMs offered by financial institutions are backed by the Federal Housing Administration (FHA). Some lenders offer privately backed reverse mortgages. However, only the HECMs backed by the FHA guarantee that you will receive all of your money, even if the lender goes bankrupt or otherwise shuts down.

With a reverse mortgage, instead of you paying the bank a monthly sum for the house, the bank pays *you* a sum for as long as you live in the house as your principal residence. If you are married, the sum is paid until the surviving spouse sells the house, moves out permanently, or dies.

You are not restricted to using the reverse mortgage payments for home improvements or repairs. You can use the money for anything you want: to repair the roof; to pay a domestic helper to come in several times a week to help with the shopping, cleaning, or cooking; to pay medical bills; to refurnish the house; or to take a trip while you're still healthy enough to do so—it doesn't matter to the bank how you use the money. Most seniors who obtain reverse mortgage loans do so, however, to meet monthly expenses, make necessary home repairs, pay medical expenses, buy food, and pay for other necessities of life. The money from the reverse mortgage allows them to remain in their home and meet their financial obligations.

Options as to How the Money Is Paid Out to You

You have several options as to how and when the proceeds of the reverse mortgage are paid out to you. One way is to have the loan paid out in a single lump sum (an "immediate cash advance"). Or it can be paid out in monthly installments either for life or for a set time. (If you have it paid out for a set time—a "fixed term" reverse mortgage—at the end of the set period, you have to pay back the lender, which would probably mean having to sell the home to pay off the loan.) A third option is to use the equity in your house as a credit line account that you can draw from anytime you need to.

Finally, the reverse mortgage can be a combination of all of the above: a lump-sum payment with monthly payments; a lump-sum payment with a credit line; or a credit line with monthly payments. It even can be a combination of all three: an immediate cash advance, a credit line, and monthly payments. It all depends upon what your needs are.

Can't you just get a regular home equity loan from the bank rather than a reverse mortgage credit line? You may be able to get a home equity loan from a bank, assuming you meet their income requirements. However, this would require you paying back the bank in monthly installments, an expense you just can't afford. With a reverse mortgage credit line account, you are able to use the money just like a regular home equity loan, but the primary advantage is that you don't have to pay a cent back as long as you (or your spouse, if you are married) are living in the house.

To get an idea of how much money you may be able to get in a reverse mortgage, visit the website http://www.reverse.org and use the "calculator" function. This site also has links to the American Association of Retired Persons' (AARP) website, http://www.aarp.org/revmort, which contains thorough information on the types of reverse mortgages, what they are and how they work, which is best for you, etc.

If you use all or a portion of your reverse mortgage to set up a credit line, you should set up a growing credit line rather than a flat credit line. The difference is that, with a flat credit line, the balance available to you remains the same year after year (assuming you don't draw upon it), while with a growing credit line, it earns interest each year. Suppose you have a flat credit line of $50,000 and use $10,000 of that, leaving a balance of $40,000. Five years later, your balance will still be $40,000.

But now suppose that you have a growing credit line of 3 percent a year. When you take out the first $10,000, you are still left with $40,000. However, because it grows, and assuming you don't dip into any more of the money, in five years you will have about $46,370!

How Much Can You Get?

The amount of your cash payment, credit line, or monthly payments depends upon the following factors: your age; the value of your house and its location; and the interest rate charged by the lender. Your monthly payments from the lender will be considerably less if you get a reverse mortgage when you are 65 than they would be if you apply when you are 80. This is because your life expectancy is much shorter at 80 than it is at 65. Note that your income is *not* considered in determining the amount of your loan, as you will not be making any payments on the loan.

Part of the process in applying for an FHA-approved Home Equity Conversion Mortgage is that you must undergo counseling with an agency certified by the United States Department of Housing and Urban Development (HUD). This counseling includes the pros and cons of a reverse mortgage, and other options and their advantages and disadvantages. Some states require reverse mortgage counseling in all cases, whether or not the loan is backed by the FHA.

Qualifying for a Reverse Mortgage

To qualify for an FHA-backed Home Equity Conversion Mortgage (HECM), you must meet the following requirements:

* All borrowers (and everyone whose name appears on the deed) must be at least 62 years old. If you thought you were clever when you put your son's or daughter's name on the deed as a joint tenant to avoid probate (see chapter 3), you will need that child to execute and record a quitclaim deed taking his or her name off the title.
* You must own the property outright, free and clear. If you have a mortgage balance remaining, or any liens against the house, you must pay them off either before the reverse mortgage is granted, or use a portion of the reverse mortgage to pay off the mortgage and liens immediately upon receipt of the loan proceeds.
* The house must be your principal place of residence.
* For FHA loans, your house must be a single-family dwelling, a two- to four-unit building, or a federally-approved condominium or planned unit development (PUD). Mobile homes and apartment cooperatives do not qualify. However, "manufactured" houses may be eligible if they are built on a permanent foundation, taxed and classified as real estate, and meet other requirements.

Effect on Other Benefits

If you are receiving Supplemental Security Interest (SSI) and Medicaid benefits (chapter 15), the monthly payments from a reverse mortgage will not disqualify you from eligibility for those benefits, so long as you spend all of the money in the month you receive it. If you do not spend the money in the month you receive it and let it accumulate, it will be deemed a liquid asset that may put you over the asset limit, making you ineligible to receive SSI or Medicaid, or both.

If you use the money from a lump-sum cash advance to purchase an annuity or you obtain a reverse annuity mortgage, the annuity payments reduce your SSI benefits dollar for dollar, and may also make you ineligible for Medicaid. Likewise, if you elect to accept all of the money in a single, up-front cash payment, the payment will be counted as a resource and will probably disqualify you from receiving SSI and Medicaid benefits. If you want to have a source of money for emergencies or anything else, but do not want to lose your public benefits, it is better to take out a credit line reverse mortgage to avoid its being counted against you. Before obtaining a reverse annuity mortgage or purchasing an annuity, talk with a financial counselor or elder law attorney to determine how it will affect your SSI and Medicaid benefits.

Are the Loan Proceeds Taxable?

A common question is, Do I have to pay taxes on the money I receive from the reverse mortgage? The answer is no. The money you receive from a reverse mortgage is not income, but rather a loan that you must pay back at a later date. However, if you obtain a "reverse annuity mortgage," or put some of the money from your reverse mortgage into an annuity, part of the annuity advances may be counted as income, and therefore taxed. Also, the interest earned from a growing credit line is generally taxable.

What about deducting from your taxes the interest on the reverse mortgage the bank charges? The same rules that apply to the taxability of income from a reverse mortgage apply here as well. If you are not required to include the payment on your taxes, then you are not entitled to deduct it either. The interest the lender is charging on your reverse mortgage payments is not deductible until the loan is paid back. A good certified public accountant can advise you further on this.

When Must the Reverse Mortgage Be Paid Back?

A reverse mortgage must be paid back when you die, sell the house, or "permanently" move out. You are considered to have permanently moved out of your home if you fail to live there for twelve consecutive months. (For instance, you live in a nursing home for that period of time.) Other factors that can terminate a reverse mortgage and make the loan due and payable include failing to maintain the house in good repair, failing to pay your property taxes, or not keeping the house insured against property damage. Should one spouse die or permanently move into a nursing home, the loan does not become due and payable so long as the other spouse is still living in the home.

Suppose that you choose to be paid in monthly installments, and then live a long, healthy life, so long that the payments you receive from your reverse mortgage exceed the value of your home. When you die (or sell or move out of the house), can the bank make a claim against the rest of your estate? No. Reverse mortgages are "nonrecourse" loans. This means that the most the bank can get is whatever your house sells for, and nothing more. Its only recourse is against the sales proceeds from the house. If there is anything left over after the bank is paid its accumulated interest and other costs and expenses, the money is yours (or your heirs). But if you "outlive" the amount your house is worth and get monthly payments that exceed the house's value, the bank bears the loss. The lender cannot try to collect the difference from your other assets.

How Much Will You Owe?

How much will you owe when it comes time to pay the piper, that is, when you sell the house, permanently move out, or you (or your surviving spouse) die? The bank is entitled to recover all cash payments made to you, plus the interest charged thereon and any other associated costs and expenses. Before you sign the loan you will be given a truth-in-lending statement that tells you how much the loan will cost. And remember, while you're still living in the house, the bank can't collect a dime unless you purchased a fixed-term reverse mortgage and the fixed term has elapsed.

Selling Your Home

Another way to get cash out of your house is to sell it and move to a smaller house or condominium, or move into an assisted-living apartment or other senior care facility. Selling the house you've lived in for years is especially attractive to seniors whose house is too big for them now that all the children have moved out, or for those who find they need assistance with their day-to-day needs.

Suppose that you've lived in your house a long time, say twenty-five or thirty years or more, and it has appreciated greatly from what you paid for it and what you sell it for. Won't you have to pay a lot of capital gains taxes on the difference between what it cost you and the sales price? Recent legislation has made it much easier for seniors to sell their highly appreciated home without worrying as much about capital gains taxes as before. Let's look at one example.

Suppose that Terry and Sue bought their large, five-bedroom house thirty-five years ago when their four children were growing up. Now in their late sixties, they find they don't need that much room anymore. Some years ago they took out a second mortgage on which they have five more years to pay, which, along with medical costs that Medicare doesn't cover, is draining their savings and monthly income from Social Security and pension benefits. So they decide to sell their house and move into a smaller, two-bedroom condominium to live out their golden years.

They bought their house for $50,000, but it is now worth $400,000. If they sell their house for $400,000, they will have a capital gain of $350,000 (the selling price of $400,000 minus their cost [basis] of $50,000). Will they have to pay taxes on the $350,000? No. Under current federal law, a single person is exempt from paying capital gains tax on the first $250,000 profit on the house if he or she lived in the house as his or her principal residence for an aggregate of two of the five years immediately preceding the sale. For a married couple, the exemption is $500,000, with the same requirements as to living in the house for an aggregate of two of the previous five years.

Unlike the old $125,000 one-time exemption available to homeowners 55 and over, there is no limit to the number of times you can use the new exemption rates, nor does it matter how old (or young) you are to use it. The only restriction is that it cannot be used more than once within a two-year period.

Since both Terry and Sue are living, they qualify for the $500,000 exemption. They will not have to pay any capital gains, since their $350,000 profit on the house is less than their $500,000 exemption.

Now suppose that they don't sell the house, but that Terry dies. When the first spouse (here, Terry) dies, the house is reappraised, and the surviving spouse's (Sue's) basis is "stepped up," or increased. For instance, in a community property state, the entire basis would be increased, so that the surviving spouse's (Sue's) new basis would be $400,000, the house's fair market value on the date of Terry's death.

In a non–community property state, only the deceased spouse's basis would be stepped up. Hence, Terry's basis would be increased from his original cost basis of $25,000 to $200,000, one-half of the house's fair market value of $400,000 on the date he died. Sue's new basis for the home would be $225,000—her original cost basis of $25,000 plus Terry's stepped-up basis of $200,000. Thus, if Sue sold the house for $400,000, there would still be no capital gains to worry about, as Sue's new basis of $225,000 combined with her $250,000 exemption would equal $475,000, $75,000 more than the house's selling price of $400,000.

Sale-Leasebacks and Life Estates

Another way of making your house work for you is to sell it, and then lease it back from the new owners. You can structure the sale two ways. You can have the buyers obtain a home loan and simply pay you the full amount in one fell swoop. Or you can finance the sale yourself, taking a down payment and accepting monthly mortgage payments that are several hundreds of dollars more than what you pay the new owners in rent. Since you sold the house, you no longer have to pay property taxes, homeowner's insurance (although you should have renter's insurance), and major repairs.

Yet another way of making your house work for you is to sell your house and retain a "life estate" for yourself. A life estate gives you the right to live in the house until you die. Unlike in a sale-leaseback, you will have to pay the property taxes, insurance, and do general upkeep and keep the property in good repair.

While both sales-leasebacks and retentions of a life estate have certain advantages, it is difficult to find a buyer willing to pay fair value for property he or she may not get for a number of years. You would have to sell the house at a lower price than if the buyer were allowed to take possession immediately upon the sale. Additionally, a sale-leaseback or a sale with a retained life estate may have implications on Social Security, SSI, Medicaid, and tax consequences and should be entered into only with the advice of an attorney skilled in this field.

One option that is attractive to seniors—particularly those with no children or other close heirs—is to give their home to their favorite charity. In return, the charity gives them a life estate and pays them a monthly sum for as long as they live. When the last homeowner (that is, the surviving spouse in the case of a married couple) dies, the charity becomes owner of the house. This is known as a charitable remainder trust.

HOUSING ALTERNATIVES FOR THE ELDERLY

HOUSING FOR THE ELDERLY covers a wide range of choices, depending upon the elder's monetary situation and health condition. The options range from ritzy retirement communities that offer golf courses, swimming pools, clubhouses, dancing, and a wide variety of other activities geared toward the affluent, healthier elderly with minimal health care needs, to nursing homes where the elderly residents receive around-the-clock supervision and assistance with their activities of daily living (ADLs), such as bathing, dressing, and eating, and their instrumental activities of daily living (IADLs), such as taking medications, shopping, preparing meals, managing money, using the telephone, housekeeping, and the like.

Staying in the Elder's Own House

Many elderly persons prefer to stay in their own home as long as they are able. It is a safe, comfortable environment, and also gives the elder a feeling of independence. As time goes by, however, the elder's condition may decline, requiring more help around the house or with shopping and preparing meals or making arrangements with "Meals on Wheels" to come by the house.

When the ravages of time make their first appearance, it may be possible for family members to take care of the elder in the elder's own house. Four out of five people who take on the role of primary caretaker are relatives. Some modifications may have to be made to the elder's houses. The elderly parent may no longer be able to climb up and down the stairs of a two-story house, requiring that his or her bed be moved downstairs into the living or other room. Grab rails will have to be put in next to the toilet so the elder can get off and on the toilet more easily. Similarly, a rough surface and grab rails should be installed in the shower to prevent the danger of the elder slipping and being hurt. A new, lower bathtub may be necessary for the elder to get in and out of it without harming himself or herself.

If the elder's condition deteriorates, it may be unrealistic to have a caretaker child drop in for a few hours a day. Around-the-clock supervision may be needed, thereby necessitating the hiring of a full-time companion, which can be costly.

Moving the Elder into a Child's Home

Sometimes a child will bring the elderly parent to his or her own home. This is a weighty decision, as it not only upsets the elderly parent by taking her out of her own familiar surroundings, but also interferes with the child's routine with his or her own spouse and children.

If, for instance, you bring your aging mother to live with you and she requires constant supervision, but you cannot afford not to work nor can you afford a companion to be with your mother during the day, you might get some relief from an adult day care center. There are two types of adult day care: adult day care centers, which provide the elderly with recreation and social stimulation, and adult day health care centers, which offer some medical care, including physical, occupational, and speech therapy.

Caring for an elder with Alzheimer's disease or senile dementia takes a great toll on the family that brings in the elderly parent. Similarly, an elderly patient that is frail demands a lot of time and attention. The child who moved the elderly parent in with his family may find it too burdensome after a while, and look for options in housing for the elder.

Subsidized Housing

For elders who are still able to care for themselves properly, and do their own shopping, cooking, housekeeping, and the like, federally- or state-subsidized housing may be available for elders who do not have much in assets and have low incomes. Subsidized housing usually comes in the form of an apartment building exclusively for seniors, where every senior gets his or her own apartment for a low monthly rent.

Congregate Care

Congregate care facilities are retirement apartments with housekeeping, meals, laundry, and other amenities available. They are designed for seniors with minimal medical and supervisory needs.

Board and Care

Board-and-care facilities are group homes that provide room, board, and twenty-four-hour supervision. They also help with some activities of daily living (ADLs, discussed below) and instrumental activities of daily living (IADLs). Board and care facilities generally do not provide any medical care, and may range in size from "mom-and-pop" homes of several residents to large complexes having up to two hundred residents.

Assisted Living

Assisted-living facilities are a step up from board-and-care facilities and a step below nursing homes. Besides providing room and board, assisted living facilities provide assistance with personal care and any necessary supervision, and must be licensed by the appropriate state agency. They provide small apartments—many with kitchenettes—or private rooms and baths, and there are more social and recreational opportunities than in many board-and-care facilities. More emphasis is placed on encouraging independence, autonomy, and privacy.

Continuing Care Retirement Communities

Continuing care retirement communities (CCRCs) generally require the elder to buy his or her own housing unit. They offer a wide range of care and services, from independent living apartments to assisted living to skilled nursing services, whether in the senior's own apartment or in an assisted-living wing of the complex. The elder usually is required to pay a significant one-time entry fee as well as a substantial monthly fee. These facilities are licensed by the state, and require you to sign a legally binding agreement. Because this contract has serious financial implications, you should have it reviewed by both your financial adviser and your attorney.

Skilled Nursing Facilities

Skilled nursing facilities are generally reserved for those elders who are convalescing from a serious illness or surgery and require constant observation and rehabilitation. Medicare generally kicks in only where you were hospitalized for three full days within thirty days of your admission to the skilled nursing facility. You must also require skilled nursing care seven days a week, or rehabilitation services at least five days a week.

If you meet the criteria, Medicare picks up the entire tab for the first twenty days, and a portion of the next eighty days. If you have a Medigap policy, an insurance policy that supplements Medicare coverage, it will pick up your share of the cost. Otherwise, you are obligated to pay up to $97 a day for the remaining eighty-day period. After the one hundredth day in a skilled nursing facility, Medicare benefits stop and you have to pay the hefty fee out of your own pocket.

Home Health Care

If you are housebound and require intermittent skilled nursing care or speech therapy or physical rehabilitation, you may still qualify for Medicare benefits. However, even if you qualify, the benefits are payable only for the skilled nursing or rehabilitative services. General household services such as laundry, grocery shopping, cooking, and housekeeping are not covered.

Medicare provides home health care under limited circumstances. You must meet *all* of the following four criteria:

1. Your doctor must decide that you need medical care in your home and must make a plan for your care at home.
2. You must need intermittent skilled nursing care or physical therapy or speech language pathology services.
3. You must be homebound (this means that you are normally unable to leave home; that leaving home is a major effort; that when you leave home, it must be infrequent, for a short time, or to get medical care).
4. Medicare must approve the home health care agency caring for you.

While you are getting skilled nursing care or other covered services, Medicare covers the cost of home health aide services on a part-time or intermittent basis. These services may include help with personal care, such as bathing, using the toilet, or dressing. However, Medicare does *not* cover twenty-four-hour-a-day care at home, prescription drugs, meals delivered to your house, homemaker services such as shopping, cleaning, and laundry, or personal care by home health aides when this is the only care you need.

Nursing Homes

Nursing homes provide custodial care and supervision, and skilled nursing care when called for, for elders who are no longer able to care for themselves because of senility, Alzheimer's disease, or simply old age. Some two million persons are currently in nursing homes. Nursing homes are expensive, and run from $100 to $200 or more a day, depending upon the quality and location of the home, the services offered, the number of staff, etc. Nursing homes are *not* covered by Medicare, as they are for elders who generally require only custodial care and not skilled nursing care or rehabilitation.

What to Look for in a Nursing Home

Before you place your parent, grandparent, or other elder into one of the facilities discussed above, you—and preferably the elder who will be living there, if practical—should visit the facility on several occasions at different hours. Check out the number of staff on duty at various times—such as nights and weekends—and the sanitary conditions of the facility. Talk with staff and patients who are already living there to see if they are pleased with it and the services provided.

What does the facility smell like? Does it smell clean and refreshing, or does it smell of urine or other offensive odor that shows that cleanliness is not high on their list? Contact your state department of aging to see if the home is licensed and whether any complaints have been lodged against it. Request a copy of the facility's contract that the elder (or her legal representative) will be required to sign, and have the contract thoroughly reviewed by an attorney.

Check the nursing home's most recent state inspection report. This will show whether the nursing facility is deficient in any areas. Find out how long the current staff has been working at the nursing home. If the elder has special needs because of Alzheimer's disease or other dementia, kidney disease, dependency upon a ventilator, or other condition, make sure the nursing home has experience in caring for patients who have had such a condition.

Also check to see whether the facility is financially sound. If you are required to pay a large fee up front and the facility goes out of business shortly thereafter, you may be out of a substantial sum of money. Additionally, find out whether Medicare or Medicaid will pick up any part of the cost. Medicare generally does not provide any benefits for nursing home care that is primarily custodial. Medicaid, as we shall see below, does provide nursing home coverage, but you must be virtually a pauper before you qualify for Medicaid.

A 2000 report by the United States Department of Health and Human Services stated that on the average, nursing home patients need at least two hours a day of care from a nurse's aide. However, the report found that 54 percent of nursing homes fell below this standard. The lack of adequate staff, the report showed, contributed to a rise in the number of severe bedsores, malnutrition, and abnormal weight loss among nursing home residents. Further, many nursing home residents required hospitalization for life-threatening infections, congestive heart failure, dehydration, and other problems that could have been avoided had there been more employees on staff.

Long-term-care Insurance

Long-term-care insurance (LTCI) can be an excellent way for many elders to pay for the cost of noninstitutional services or institutional care, or both. Institutional care means skilled or custodial care provided in nursing facilities or residential facilities. Noninstitutional services are provided in the community and include home health care, personal care, homemaker services, adult day care, hospice, and respite care. Exactly what is covered and to what extent depends upon your particular policy.

Generally, there are three types of long-term-care insurance policies on the market:

1. Those that provide only nursing facility care. This covers custodial care in a nursing home or other qualified residential care facility.
2. Those that provide only home health care services. This type of policy covers such things as home health care providers, adult day care, personal care, homemaker services, and hospice and respite care.
3. Policies that provide comprehensive coverage. These policies cover both long-term care in a nursing home and home health care or community care. This is more expensive than the other policies, but provides more coverage.

One downside to long-term life insurance policies is their cost. Although they are usually available for a fairly reasonable premium from the time a person turns 40 or 45, the fact is that most people do not consider LTCI policies until much later, such as when they are 65 or 70. However, a growing number of large companies are starting to offer long-term-care insurance as part of their benefits package, although the employee generally is required to pay all or the lion's share of the premium for such coverage.

The cost difference between premiums at age 45 and those at, say, age 65 or 70 is substantial. And most policies have an upper limit of age 84; beyond that you cannot obtain long-term-care insurance. And there may be severe limitations placed on those 80 and over, such as a nursing home stay only for one year. The cost of your long-term-care insurance policy will depend upon your age, health history, and amount of benefits you want.

Federally Tax-qualified and Non–tax-qualified Policies

Two types of long-term-care insurance policies exist: those that are intended to qualify for federal tax benefits (a "qualified" policy), and those that are not (a "nonqualified" policy). The qualified policies tend to cost a little bit less, but it is harder to get benefits from them than from a nonqualified policy. Qualified policies allow you to deduct the cost of your premium as a medical expense if you itemize your tax deductions on your federal tax return on IRS Schedule A. (Currently, under federal law, health costs are deductible only to the extent they exceed 7.5 percent of your adjusted gross income.) You cannot deduct the cost of premiums for nonqualified policies.

Additionally, benefits paid from a qualified policy are not intended to be taxed as income. The law is unclear as to whether or not benefits paid by a nonqualified policy are taxable as income. You should consult a tax attorney or certified public accountant to help you to determine whether or not the payments from your nonqualified policy are classified as income or not.

While it might be more attractive to get a policy that qualifies for tax benefits, it is generally easier for benefits to start being paid with a nonqualified policy. With qualified long-term-care insurance policies, for benefits to begin a physician or registered nurse must certify that you will need assistance with at least two of *six* of the designated "activities of daily living" (ADLs) discussed below. Under a nonqualified policy, you are required to be unable to do at least two of *seven* ADLs.

A qualified policy generally prohibits the payment of benefits for services covered by Medicare, and benefits cannot be applied to pay for Medicare deductibles or copayments. For nonqualified policies, there are usually no limitations regarding the use of policy benefits for Medicare-related services.

The Activities of Daily Living (ADLs)

A long-term-care insurance policy begins paying benefits upon the occurrence of a "triggering event." This is either the inability to do two of six (for federally-qualified policies) or seven (for non–federally qualified policies) activities of daily living (ADLs) or cognitive impairment (discussed below). Benefits begin with a federally tax-qualified policy if you are unable to perform two of the six following ADLs:

* bathing
* dressing
* continence (incontinence problems)
* toileting (using the toilet unassisted)
* transferring (such as moving from the bed to a chair)
* eating

While qualified policies require a person to be unable to do two of six ADLs, non-qualified policies require a person to be unable to perform two of seven ADLs. In addition to the six ADLs listed above, the seventh is "ambulating" (walking), which, studies show, is the number-one difficulty that the elderly have. Accordingly, it is easier to start receiving benefits from a non-qualified policy than it is to begin getting benefits from a qualified policy.

Cognitive Impairment

As an alternative to being unable to do the requisite number of ADLs, LTCI benefits begin for federally tax-qualified policies when a person requires *substantial* supervision due to a *severe* cognitive loss. "Cognitive impairment" means the deterioration or loss of intellectual capacity due to organic mental disease, including Alzheimer's disease and other forms of senile dementia that require substantial supervision to protect the afflicted person or others.

For a nonqualified LTCI policy, the triggering event occurs when the elder suffers from a cognitive impairment that requires supervision to protect the elder from himself or others. Note that it is easier for benefits to begin with a nonqualified LTCI policy for cognitive impairment than it is for a qualified LTCI policy.

What to Look for in Your Policy

Nursing homes and home health care services get more expensive every year due to higher operating costs brought about by inflation and the increased needs of patients. Therefore, your LTCI policy should include "inflation protection." Three alternatives generally are offered: no inflation; 5 percent simple interest; and 5 percent compound interest. To be sure you are adequately covered in the future, you should opt for the 5 percent compound interest choice.

Your LTCI policy should not require a period of hospitalization before it will begin paying you benefits. You also will want a policy that waives the premium while you are receiving benefits. In other words, while you are in the nursing home, the long-term-care insurance policy should be paying the expenses, and you should not be required to pay the premiums. You also should scrutinize the LTCI policy to see whether it has a preexisting clause exclusion and how that impacts your situation.

If you are under 80, you will have a choice of how long the benefits last. Depending on the policy, it can be from two years until lifetime. Many policies provide benefits for up to two or three years in a nursing home and four to six years of home health care. When deciding how much coverage you need, keep in mind that over one-half of those persons requiring nursing home care will stay at least one year, and 21 percent (one in five) will stay five years or more.

For persons 80 to 84 applying for an LTCI policy, generally only one year of nursing home care is covered. Long-term-care insurance is not available to persons over 84.

Affording Long-term-care Insurance

Long-term-care insurance generally is recommended for persons having at least $50,000 in liquid assets such as bank accounts, stocks and bonds, certificates of deposit (CDs), mutual funds, and the like. The reason for this is that the cost of an LTCI policy is high, and if you have less than $50,000, it might be too burdensome to pay the insurance premiums. It generally is recommended that your long-term-care insurance premiums not exceed 7 percent of your monthly income.

The Elimination Period

LTCI policies usually have an "elimination" period. This is a fancy way of saying a deductible period during which you do not receive any benefits. Depending on the policy and state, this may run anywhere from zero days to one year. The length of your elimination period will be determined by your LTCI policy. The longer the elimination period, the lower the premium will be. However, when the time comes that you need nursing home care or home health care, you are going to have to pay the cost of the elimination period out of your own pocket (unless you are in a skilled nursing facility and are receiving Medicare benefits for the first one hundred days).

Nonforfeiture Provisions

Let's assume that you bought a long-term-care insurance policy, but three years later your income declines and you are no longer able to afford to pay the premiums. Does this mean you lose all of your benefits under the policy? Not necessarily. If it is a nonforfeiture policy, and you have paid your premiums for at least three years, you still will receive benefits based on the three years that you paid your premiums before you let the policy lapse. The payments may be less or the time they are paid out shorter, but still it is better than nothing.

Comparing Policies

Don't buy the first LTCI policy you see. Rather, you should compare at least two and preferably three LTCI policies from different insurance companies, as the premiums may vary greatly. Make sure that you are comparing apples and apples; that is, that the policies you are comparing provide substantially the same coverage. It does not give you an accurate picture if you are comparing a policy from one company that provides only nursing home care with a policy from a second company that provides nursing home *and* home health care.

One thing you don't want to happen is to pay premiums for ten or fifteen years, only to find out the company is going bankrupt and you will not be receiving any nursing care benefits. All your money will have been paid in vain. Therefore, be sure that the insurance company you decide to go with has a good rating with A.M. Best Company or Standard & Poor's to ensure the company will be solvent to pay you your benefits when they are needed. You usually can find this information at your local library, or ask your insurance agent to provide proof of the insurance company's rating.

Thirty-day Cancellation Period

Suppose you purchased an LTCI policy, but two weeks later decide that you can't afford the premiums and change your mind about the policy. Can you cancel the policy and get any money you paid back? Yes. You have a thirty-day period to return the policy either directly to the insurer or to the insurance agent who wrote out the policy. They must promptly refund any and all monies you paid on the policy.

Medicaid Payment of Long-Term Nursing Home Care

Medicaid in general is discussed in chapter 15. Here we are concerned with Medicaid's unique role in paying for long-term nursing home care. Over half of the patients in nursing homes have their health care bills paid by Medicaid. As noted in chapter 15, Medicaid is a poverty-based government health care program available to low-income seniors, the blind, persons of any age with a physical or mental disability, and families receiving Temporary Assistance to Needy Families (TANF). Unlike Medicare, which is managed by the federal government and has uniform rules and regulations throughout the United States, Medicaid (Medi-Cal in California) is administered by the individual states. Therefore, eligibility for the plan and payments can vary greatly from state to state.

The following discussion deals with the issues of having your long-term nursing home care paid for by Medicaid. Medicaid is a poverty program (like SSI), and is very strict about the amount of assets and income a person may have to qualify for Medicaid benefits.

Note that *Medicare does not pay for long-term care.* As discussed earlier, the most Medicare pays is up to one hundred days in a skilled nursing facility (and the last eighty of those days require a daily copayment from you up to $97). Most elders, however, do not require skilled nursing or rehabilitation care. Rather, they need only custodial care and assistance with their activities of daily living or mere supervision due to cognitive impairments such as Alzheimer's disease, which Medicaid covers for qualified persons.

Nursing homes are not required to accept Medicaid patients. They may limit their clientele to those who are paying out-of-pocket or have insurance coverage. Or they may allow Medicaid patients, but have only a certain number of beds for them. If you have found a nursing home you like, see whether any of its Medicaid beds are available if you will be relying on Medicaid to pay the nursing home.

Who Is Covered

Medicaid pays for those persons who are "categorically needy" or "medically needy." In most states, a person is categorically needy if he or she meets the financial eligibility tests and is either blind, disabled, or at least 65 years old. A person who is receiving Supplemental Security Income (SSI) benefits is usually automatically eligible to receive Medicaid benefits.

A person is "medically needy" if his or her resources and income are more than that allowed, but their medical bills are so great that they reduce the person's income to the level required to be eligible for Medicaid. Some states impose even more onerous limitations, while a few provide less stringent requirements.

A dozen or so states do not have a "medically needy" program, but instead focus eligibility requirements on the monthly income a person has. These are known as "income cap" states. If a person makes one penny over the limit, he or she is not qualified for Medicaid assistance. Generally, the amount of income permissible is three times the SSI benefit. In the year 2000, the maximum amount a single person could receive in SSI benefits was $512 a month, so three times that would be $1,536. If the person's monthly income does not exceed that figure, he or she qualifies for Medicaid under the income cap provisions, providing he or she met the other requirements of age, blindness, or disability.

The At-Home Spouse's Allowance

To protect at-home spouses of nursing home residents from becoming poverty-bound themselves, in cases where Medicaid is used to pay for a nursing home, Medicaid permits the non-institutionalized spouse to keep a certain amount of monthly income and assets in excess of that usually required by Medicaid. This is called the minimum monthly maintenance needs allowance (MMMNA). There is also a monthly allowance for minors and disabled children.

Because Medicaid is a combined federal and state program, the exact figures for benefits vary from state to state. The amount of assets and monthly resources the at-home spouse is able to keep can vary widely from one state to the next.

Not counted toward the assets and resources are your house, household goods up to $2,000, wedding rings (regardless of value), an automobile worth up to $4,500 (or an unlimited amount if it is used in business or for medical transportation), an irrevocable burial insurance policy of not more than $1,500 (two such policies for a married couple), and machinery and equipment used in business. The house is only exempt if, on the Medicaid application form, you answer "yes" to the question whether you intend to return to your home after you leave the nursing home. And as long as the noninstitutionalized spouse is living in the house, Medicaid cannot touch it, even after the institutionalized spouse's death.

Name on the Check Standard

In determining an individual's income, Medicaid follows a "name on the check" policy. For instance, Terry's paycheck to him is considered his resource, since it is made out to him only. Income checks made payable to Sue, Terry's wife and the institutionalized spouse, count against her for eligibility and spending-down purposes. What about checks made payable to both Terry and Sue? When a check for income is made to both spouses, each spouse gets one-half. Terry can keep his one-half, while Sue's one-half will go to the nursing home or other medical expenses.

Suppose Terry's monthly income is below the minimum monthly maintenance needs allowance. Can he dip into Sue's income to make up the difference? Yes, assuming that Sue is getting any income, that amount of her income that would raise Terry's income to the minimum monthly allowance automatically is assigned to Terry. Additionally, if Terry's monthly income allowance is not enough to provide for his needs, he may seek an amount greater than the state allowance in cases of hardship or special need. This hearing will be before a Medicaid board or through a court proceeding.

The "Look Back" Period

When applying for Medicaid to pay the costs of a nursing home, Medicaid will look back thirty-six months (sixty months for transfers made from a trust) to see whether you made any gifts or sales for less than fair market value so you could qualify for Medicaid earlier. This is referred to as the "penalty period." For instance, to qualify for Medicaid, suppose you have some stock worth $40,000 that you gave to your daughter just before applying for Medicaid to pay for the $4,000 monthly cost of the nursing home you are going into. Medicaid will "look back" thirty-six months and include this gift of stock into the computation of your period of eligibility for Medicaid. You will not be eligible to receive any Medicaid benefits for ten months, as the gift totaled ten months' worth of Medicaid benefits.

Nancy Jones, a widow, has an income of $1,000 per month, savings of $30,000, and incidental monthly expenses of $150. The nursing home she is staying at has a private pay rate of $4,000 monthly. Nancy will have to "spend down" her savings at a rate of $3,150 ($1,000 in income plus $3,150 in savings are needed to meet the monthly total expense of $4,150). At this rate, Nancy's savings will be depleted to the Medicaid level of $2,000 in approximately one year. At that point, Medicaid will take over Nancy's payments to the nursing home.

If you make a transfer of money or other item of value during the thirty-six months before you apply for Medicaid, there is no limit as to how far back Medicaid can penalize you. For instance, John gives his son Thomas $150,000 within the thirty-six-month Medicaid look-back period. The nursing home charges $3,000 a month. Medicaid will not pay for John's nursing home costs for fifty months. However, had John made the gift more than thirty-six months before applying for Medicaid, he would not be penalized at all.

The home is exempt while the noninstitutionalized spouse lives in it, or when the institutionalized person is expected to be able to return home. The house is also exempt if there is a child under age twenty-one, or blind or disabled living in it. The house is also exempt if a brother or sister owns part of the home and has lived there for at least one year immediately before the person went into a nursing facility. The house is also exempt if an adult child lived in the house for at least two years before the elder was admitted to a nursing facility, and during that time was the elder's primary caretaker whose assistance allowed the elder to remain in the house.

You also can convert a countable asset to an exempt one. For example, you could sell some stock for say, $25,000, and use the proceeds in home improvements such as a new roof or redoing the kitchen or adding a room. Or you could sell the old car and buy a new one if it is used for business or medical transportation. Talk with a qualified elder lawyer before taking any steps.

Hospital Stays

Let's say that, because of your frailty, you fall in the nursing home and break your arm and must be hospitalized for a while. Will your bed at the nursing home still be there for you when you get out of the hospital? Yes, if your stay in the hospital does not exceed fourteen days.

Medicaid pays up to fourteen days to "hold" your bed for you should you need hospitalization. But if you break, say, your hip, and need longer care in the hospital, your bed will be given up and you will need to find a new one when you finally are released from the hospital.

Reimbursement of Medicaid

Medicaid laws require the states to seek reimbursement from the estates of persons for whom they have paid nursing home costs. One may ask why they go to this trouble, when a person must be essentially a pauper to qualify for Medicaid benefits. However, the house, which initially was exempt from assets counted in determining whether the person qualifies for Medicaid, can be sold to pay the debts.

When you apply for Medicaid benefits, one of the questions the government asks is whether you intend to move back to your home after you are released from the nursing home. If you answer yes, Medicaid will not count the house as part of your assets. However, if the house is part of your estate when you die, Medicaid will try to recover its costs by placing a lien against the house and enforcing it by a sale. The lien cannot be enforced under a few exceptions, the most common being that the surviving spouse is living in it.

Some institutionalized seniors deed their share of the house to the community spouse, which reduces the institutionalized spouse's estate. (Remember that transfers between spouses do not count in determining Medicaid benefits.) However, there may be problems of taxes, trust law, and probate law by doing this. Transferring of an interest in a house by an institutionalized spouse to the at-home spouse should only be done after thorough consultation with a lawyer experienced in this area.

Need for a Lawyer's Assistance

Planning for Medicaid benefits to cover your nursing home stay (or other benefits, such as home health care services, adult day care, and the like) is an extremely complex area that demands the experience of a good lawyer knowledgeable in the field of elder law. How to find a lawyer is discussed in chapter 24.

Hospice Care

Hospice care is designed for elders (and others, such as late-stage AIDS and cancer patients) who suffer from a terminal illness, disease, or condition and are likely to die in the next six months. The patients often are bedridden and demand constant attention and supervision.

Hospice care is designed not to treat the illness or condition the patient suffers from but to make the dying person more comfortable during the last months, weeks, and days of his or her life. The care may be provided in the patient's home, or, depending on the patient's condition, in a hospice facility, hospital, or nursing home. When you elect to receive hospice care,

Medicare does not cover treatment to cure your terminal illness. You receive only palliative care, care to ease your pain and make you more comfortable while in the hospice or at home.

Hospice care is covered by Medicare Part A (hospital insurance). You are eligible for Medicare hospice benefits when your doctor and the hospice medical director certify that you are terminally ill and probably have less than six months to live. Additionally, you must sign a statement choosing hospice care instead of routine Medicare-covered benefits for your terminal illness, and you must receive care from a Medicare-approved hospice program.

Pursuant to its hospice coverage, Medicare pays for a wide variety of services, including doctor services, nursing care, medical equipment (such as a wheelchair or a walker), medical supplies (such as bandages and catheters), and drugs for symptom control and pain relief. It also covers short-term care in the hospital, including respite care so the primary caretaker can have some time off. Medicare hospice coverage also pays home health aide and homemaker services, physical and occupational therapy, speech therapy, social worker services, dietary counseling, and counseling to help you and your family deal with grief and loss.

Generally, one family member—a spouse or a child, for example—is the primary caretaker. To give the spouse or child a rest, "respite care" is given by another caretaker while your main caretaker takes a break. During a period of respite care, you will be cared for in a Medicare-approved facility, hospital, or nursing home. You will be required to pay 5 percent of the cost of inpatient hospice care. Thus, if the hospice care is $150 a day, you will be required to pay $7.50 a day. Additionally, you can be charged up to five dollars for each prescription for outpatient drugs or other products for pain relief and symptom control. You can stay in a Medicare-approved hospital or nursing home up to five days each time you get respite care. There is no limit as to the number of times you can get respite care.

Suppose you have received hospice care benefits for six months but are still alive. Does this mean you lose your right to any further hospice benefits? Not at all, as long as your doctor recertifies that you are terminally ill. Hospice care is given in periods of care. As a hospice patient, you can get hospice care for two ninety-day periods followed by an unlimited number of sixty-day periods. At the start of each period of care, your doctor must certify that you are terminally ill for you to continue receiving hospice care.

If, say, you are a cancer patient and your cancer goes into remission so that your condition is no longer terminal, you are no longer eligible for hospice care. However, should your cancer return, you are again eligible for hospice care, provided your doctor certifies you are terminally ill and not expected to survive six months.

To get more information about hospice care, you can contact:

The National Hospice Organization
1901 N. Moore St., Suite 901
Arlington, VA 22209

telephone: (800) 658-8898
website: http://www.nho.org

or

The Hospice Association of America
228 7th St., SE
Washington, DC 20003
telephone: (202) 546-4759
website: http://hospice-america.org

Life Insurance Policies and Viatical Settlements

Another method for help in paying long-term health care is to sell your life insurance policy at a reduced benefit for ready cash. Your policy may have a "living benefits" rider that provides accelerated death benefits that pay out during the insured's lifetime, generally anywhere from 40 percent to 60 percent, depending upon how long you have paid the policy's premiums.

Suppose, however, that your life insurance policy does not have a living benefits rider. Is there any way you could sell the insurance policy for a reduced amount of its payout? Yes. You may be able to sell your policy to a company or an individual investor that will give you a "viatical settlement." In a viatical settlement you sell your life insurance policy for immediate cash at a discounted price. The person wishing to sell his or her life insurance policy must generally be diagnosed as terminally ill, with a prognosis that he or she will not live beyond two years. Some states permit viatical settlements but regulate them closely, while other states forbid them altogether. In some states, viatical settlements must be registered as securities with the department of corporations unless they are being sold to investors who have $250,000 in investments or who make $100,000 or more a year and have an investment portfolio of at least $150,000. The viatical settlements can only constitute 10 percent of the person's investment portfolio. To find out whether they are legal in your state, you should talk to your life insurance agent, investment advisor, and a good elder law lawyer.

Living benefits' riders and viatical settlements have proven to be a godsend and big business for AIDS and cancer patients and other terminally ill persons facing the prospect of expensive hospice or other health care. Without the substantial, albeit partial, payment of their life insurance, they would live in utter squalor and pain. At the same time, however, they are easy prey for coldhearted investors who put profit first by trying to purchase the policy for as little as possible. Keep in mind that if you are receiving SSI or Medicaid benefits, a lump-sum payment may put you over the individual or married asset thresholds, terminating your eligibility for SSI and Medicaid.

ELDER ABUSE

IT IS A SAD COMMENTARY on our society that over two million elders are abused or neglected in the United States each year. However, only about one in fifteen cases of abuse is ever reported. Why are so few cases reported? It could be because up to 75 percent or more of all elder abuse is committed by a relative of the elder, either in the elder's own home or in the abuser's home, where he or she is taking care of the elder. The caretaker may have threatened the elder that if the elder tells anyone about the abuse, the caretaker will kick the elder out into the street or use physical or chemical restraints to keep the elder in line.

Approximately 25 percent of elder abuse occurs in nursing homes and other retirement facilities. Federal law covers abuse in nursing homes under the Nursing Home Reform Act. If you suspect that nursing home personnel are abusing or neglecting your elder, notify the nursing home's ombudsman or the local police department.

Elder abuse can take many forms. It may be done by an affirmative act, such as hitting the elder, or by fondling or otherwise sexually abusing the elder. Or it can be a negative act, such as deliberately failing to feed or provide adequate hydration (water and other fluids) to the elder. It may also consist of psychological abuse, such as yelling at the elder or threatening him or her with physical abuse or the withholding of food, or putting the elder in isolation.

Depriving the elder of medical care for physical and mental health needs is another form of elder abuse. Other examples of elder abuse include: failing to assist the elder in personal hygiene; failing to provide adequate clothing; providing inadequately heated and underventilated shelter; and failing to protect the elder from health and safety hazards. Also considered elder abuse are failing to provide or arrange transportation to medical appointments or adult day care centers; neglecting or abandoning the elder; physically or chemically restraining the elder as punishment or for longer than is necessary; and otherwise failing to provide assistance necessary to keep the elder safe, well-fed, well-groomed, and comfortable.

Elder abuse can even be financial, such as using the elder's Social Security and other funds for one's own use and not for the elder's benefit. Or the caretaker can take the elder's money for his or her own self rather than use it for the elder's benefit. For instance, suppose Victor has his elderly mother move in with him because she cannot live on her own anymore. Victor is the "designated payee" on his mother's Social Security payments, and is also on her bank accounts. Victor uses the money to support his cocaine habit, and little goes to the benefit of his mother. This is a clear case of financial elder abuse.

The law requires that health care workers, including doctors and nurses, and social workers promptly report any suspicions of elder abuse to the proper authorities. A doctor or psychologist treating an elderly patient who appears to have been physically, sexually, psychologically, or otherwise abused or neglected must report these suspicions to the appropriate authorities. A person who is taking full- or part-time care of an elder is generally legally bound to notify the proper authorities of elder abuse. The problem is that the full-time caretaker is most likely the one to be inflicting the abuse. If you believe that an elderly person is being abused, promptly report it to the department of social services or to the police.

SIX

Real Estate

*t*HE LAW OF REAL ESTATE ("real property" in legalese) covers a wide range of subjects, of which buying and selling a house are the most important for us. Other topics included in this chapter are trespassing, nuisance, and property condemnation. This chapter also discusses your liability as a homeowner for injuries others sustain on your land, although technically this is a part of tort law (chapter 10). Real estate law also covers leases and landlord-tenant relations, which because of their special complexities are treated in the next chapter.

Ownership of land has long been considered one of the fundamental rights we enjoy in America. In the early days of the United States, particularly in the West, you acquired title to land simply by living on the property and perhaps building a fence around it. If anyone dared challenge your title and claimed the land as his or her own, a shotgun decided the question, not a judge. Today, title to real estate is almost always obtained by acquiring a deed from the land's owner. And if a dispute does arise as to who owns the land, we now settle it in court, using legal precedents and title searches instead of bullets.

BUYING AND SELLING A HOUSE

FOR MOST OF US, a house is the largest and most important purchase in our lifetime. Unfortunately, all too often the purchase of that dream home turns into a legal and financial nightmare for buyer and seller alike. The buyer may be surprised, to say the least, to find out several months after buying the house that it is slowly sinking into the ground or that the plumbing is falling apart. For the seller, problems may arise because the real estate broker doesn't try very hard to find a buyer or misrepresents the condition of the house. Or the broker may claim that a commission is owed even if the sale falls through or the seller finds the buyer without the broker's help.

A brief overview of the events that take place between your first offer to buy a house and the time you take possession of it will make it easier to understand this chapter. First, a seller usually lists the house for sale with a real estate broker, who will advertise it and help negotiate a deal between the buyer and seller. When the buyer and seller agree on the price and terms, in many states they will sign a binder, and the buyer will make an "earnest money deposit." A binder is a short form that basically states nothing more than that the seller agrees to sell the house—and the buyer agrees to buy the house—for a specified price, contingent upon the parties signing a purchase and sale contract within a designated period, say three to five days. Several days later, the buyer and seller will sign a complete purchase and sale contract covering all of the terms of the agreement. The buyer may be required to make a larger deposit at this time. An escrow is then opened. This means that the contract and other documents and the buyer's deposit are entrusted to an independent third party, usually an escrow company or one party's lawyer.

Over the next few months, a number of things happen. The buyer obtains financing, arranges for homeowner's insurance, and has termite and building inspections done. A title insurance company or a lawyer will research the title to the property to make sure the seller in fact owns it, that no one else has an interest in it (such as an easement, which is discussed later in this chapter) that may affect its use, and that there are no judgments or liens outstanding against the property. This protects you from buying a house for, say, $250,000 and then learning that, for example, the government has a $50,000 lien against the house for back taxes the seller owes, giving the government the right to foreclose on the property.

If everything is in order—there aren't any termites, the house is sound, the title is good, and the buyer's loan application is approved—escrow will close. The close of escrow is referred to commonly as the "closing." At the closing, all of the parties—the buyer and seller, perhaps their attorneys, the bank's representative, and someone from the escrow company—assemble. The buyer shows the bank proof that the house is insured, the bank lends the buyer the money, the buyer gives the money to the seller, and the seller signs the deed and hands it to the buyer. The buyer now owns the house and is ready to move in.

Real Estate Brokers and Agents

Most houses in the United States are sold with the assistance of real estate brokers. It's all right to sell your own house without being a licensed broker. But if you're going to arrange the sale of someone else's house and charge a fee for your services, then you have to be either a licensed broker or a real estate agent working through a licensed broker. In several states, attorneys can act as brokers, but they can't hire real estate agents to work for them. A person who sells real estate without a license to do so not only risks being prosecuted for breaking the law, but also will not be able to sue for the commission if the seller refuses to pay it.

The real estate broker is required to use reasonable efforts to find a person who is interested in buying your property, help you negotiate a deal, assist in finding financing, and otherwise aid in the consummation of the sale. The seller normally hires the broker, and the broker is considered the seller's agent. If you're interested in buying a house, be advised that while the broker must deal fairly and honestly with you, the broker's ultimate loyalty is to the seller.

The Listing Agreement

If you decide to sell your house through a broker, the broker will have you sign a written "listing agreement." This gives the broker the authority to find a buyer for your house and also obligates you to pay the broker a commission if the broker locates a willing and qualified buyer. There are several different types of listing agreements: the open listing, the exclusive agency listing, and the exclusive right-to-sell listing.

Open Listings

When you give a broker an open listing, you reserve the right to list the house with other brokers or sell it yourself. You only have to pay a commission to the broker who supplies the buyer. If you find your own buyer, you don't pay a commission to anyone. In an open-listing agreement, you usually can revoke the agreement at any time by giving written notice to the broker.

Exclusive Agency Listings

Under an exclusive agency listing, you agree to let only one broker sell your house. If you list the house with a second broker, and he or she sells the house, you'll have to pay two full commissions: one to the broker who found the buyer and one to the broker to whom you originally gave the exclusive agency listing.

Although an exclusive agency listing prohibits you from listing your house with another broker, it does allow you to sell the house yourself, and you won't have to pay the broker a commission if you do.

Exclusive Right-to-Sell Listings

An exclusive right-to-sell listing entitles the broker to a commission if the house sells during the term of the agreement, regardless of who sells it. Even if you find the buyer and handle all the details yourself, you'll still have to pay the broker's fee.

An exclusive right-to-sell listing must clearly state that you are liable for the broker's commission even if you sell the house yourself; otherwise it usually is considered to be only an exclusive agency listing.

Which listing agreement is best? The open listing gives the seller the greatest rights, but real estate brokers rarely accept property on an open-listing basis. And if they do, they're not going to put in much effort trying to sell the house if the seller can cancel the listing at any time. The exclusive right-to-sell listing is least advantageous to the seller because the broker gets a commission even if he or she doesn't do a single thing to sell the house. The most popular listing is the exclusive agency listing because it strikes a nice balance between the rights of the seller and the broker.

Most listings—even exclusive listings—give the broker the right to place the house on a "multiple-listing service." This is particularly true in metropolitan areas.

The multiple-listing service is a directory of all houses for sale in the area, regardless of who the broker is. When a house is placed on the multiple-listing service, other brokers can try to find a buyer for the house but must go through the original broker to sell the house. The two brokers then split the commission any way they agree, although it is usually fifty–fifty.

How long does a listing agreement last? Ordinarily the length of the listing is stated in the agreement, often sixty or ninety days. In open listings, as already noted, the seller usually can cancel it at any time. Suppose, however, you give a broker an exclusive right-to-sell listing for six months, but the broker doesn't do a single thing to find a buyer. Can you cancel the listing agreement? Usually you can, because the broker must make a reasonable effort to sell the property. But before canceling the listing, write a letter to your broker, informing him or her of your concerns. In the letter, state that unless you get some assurances in the next week or two that the broker is doing something to promote your property, you will consider the broker in breach of the agreement, leaving you free to list it with another broker.

Before signing the standard preprinted listing agreement form, read it over carefully. Take the agreement home to read if you feel pressured in the broker's office. These forms are prepared by the real estate industry and favor the broker over the seller. If you object to any provisions, discuss them with the broker and see if they can be deleted or changed before you sign it. And don't hesitate to call your lawyer if you don't understand anything in the agreement.

Brokers' Commissions

Brokers earn their living by charging a fee for selling your property. Usually the broker takes a percentage of the property's final selling price. Less frequently a flat fee is charged, regardless of how much the property sells for. Ordinarily the seller pays the broker's commission at the close of escrow (discussed later) from the money the buyer paid for the house.

Typical commission fees charged by brokers run from 4 percent to 8 percent of the selling price, with 5 and 6 percent being the most common. In more expensive properties, the commission percentage usually decreases as the price increases. For example, the broker's fee schedule may start out at 6 percent of the first $500,000 of the purchase price, 5 percent of the next $300,000, 4 percent of the next $200,000 and 3 percent of the rest.

Before signing a listing agreement, shop around and see what other brokers are charging. The percentage of the broker's commission is always negotiable; don't let anyone tell you otherwise. Any agreement between real estate brokers in an area to set a standard rate violates federal antitrust laws. If one broker refuses to bargain, find one who will. But don't opt for a low commission if the broker's not going to do much to find a buyer. Find out exactly what services the broker will be rendering and how hard he or she will work to find a buyer for you.

The following provisions of the broker's commission agreement should be included in the written listing agreement: what the amount of the broker's fee is (percentage or flat fee); how the fee is determined (normally from the actual selling price); who pays it (usually the seller); and, most important, when it is due. Keep in mind that unless a clause in the listing agreement states otherwise, the broker's fee usually is earned when he or she presents a person who wants to buy the property and who has the money or can qualify for a loan—someone who is "ready, willing, and able" to purchase your house. The commission is payable even if the sale is never actually consummated. Suppose you change your mind at the last minute and decide not to sell. Or suppose there is a problem with the title that causes the sale to fall through. Unless the listing agreement states otherwise, the broker is still entitled to the commission, because the broker has done what he or she agreed to do: bring you someone who wants to and is qualified to buy your house at an acceptable price.

Obviously, you should negotiate for a listing agreement more to your advantage. You can, for example, provide in the listing agreement that the broker's commission is payable only if and when escrow closes. This protects you from having to pay the broker's commission if the purchase doesn't go through. At the very least, you, as seller, should insist upon including a clause in the listing agreement stating that if the sale is not consummated because of anyone's acts other than your own, the broker does not get a commission.

Let's say that one day your broker comes by with a couple—the Robinsons—who look the place over, but they don't show any apparent interest in buying. Two weeks later, the Robinsons drop in alone and offer to buy your house for 3 percent less than your asking price, saying, "Let's just forget about the broker and split the difference you'll save in the commission." You agree and sell them your house. A month later, your broker finds out about the sale and demands the full 6 percent commission.

Or suppose your broker is showing the Hansens a number of houses. She drives them by your house, but they feign indifference. You know nothing of the whole matter. The next day, the Hansens knock on your door, say they heard about your house from a friend, and ask to look around. The Hansens decide to buy, and you close the deal yourself. No mention is made of your broker. Your broker gets wind of the sale and threatens to sue if you don't pay her fee.

In both of the examples above, your broker is entitled to the commission, even if you've reserved the right to sell the house yourself if you find the buyer. It was your broker's efforts that brought the buyer to your house, and that's what the listing agreement is really all about. Were it not for your broker, the buyers would not have seen your house. But if the buyers pretended they didn't go through your broker, and you lowered the price because you thought you were saving the broker's commission, ask the buyers to reimburse you for some or all of the broker's commission. If they refuse, consider seeing a lawyer or suing them in small claims court.

Duty of Seller or Broker to Disclose Defects

For centuries, the rule of caveat emptor—"buyer beware"—applied in the sale of real estate. If the seller or broker (or broker's agent) did not tell you, the buyer, of a defective condition in the house, such as a leaky roof, you had no recourse against the seller when you discovered the defect. The law traditionally required you to inspect the house carefully and thoroughly before buying it, and to ask specific questions relating to any defects.

Under the common law rules, there really were only two situations in which the seller or broker was liable for failing to disclose a defective condition. The first instance occurred when the seller or broker falsely answered a buyer's question—for example, if you asked whether there was any problem with termites, and the seller answered "no," even though he or she knew full well that a termite problem existed, having spent $10,000 in the last two years to eradicate—unsuccessfully—the menace. You could then sue the seller for intentionally misrepresenting the condition of the house.

The second situation occurred when the seller or broker deliberately concealed a defect to make it appear on the surface that there was no problem. For example, to hide the fact that the roof leaks, the seller painted over the watermarks running down the walls. You looked at the ceiling and walls for evidence of leaks, and seeing none, assumed the house was watertight. When the first rains came, you learned just how porous the roof was and sued the seller. In this case, you would not have to ask any questions regarding the defective condition—the leaky roof—as the problem was not apparent and the seller intended to mislead you by concealing the problem.

Today, you also have legal recourse if the seller or broker negligently misrepresents the condition of the house. For instance, the seller might state that the electrical wiring is in good condition, without knowing one way or the other what condition the wiring is in. If it turns out that the wiring is bad, you can sue the seller for the cost of replacing it. The difference between a negligent misrepresentation and an intentional one is that in the intentional misrepresentation, the seller knows that he or she is lying. But to you, the buyer, it really doesn't matter if the misrepresentation was deliberate or not; the bottom line is that the house isn't as the seller said it was, and you got less than what you had bargained for.

Until recently, brokers could list a house and rely on what the seller told them about the condition of the house. They could take it for granted that what the seller was saying was true, and if they said the same thing to the buyer, the buyer couldn't sue the broker if it later turned out the information was false. A number of states now require a broker or agent to inspect the property before making any representations. If there is a significant defect that a careful inspection would have revealed, the broker must tell you about it. If the broker doesn't do this, and if you buy the house, you can sue him or her when the truth comes out.

The Binder

Say you're shopping for a house, and you find one that you want to buy. You make an offer to the seller, the seller makes you a counteroffer, and the two of you negotiate from there. Once you strike a deal, in many states you will probably be asked to sign a "binder," or "earnest money deposit receipt." This is usually a preprinted, one-page form that the seller (or his or her broker) supplies. (Binders can be picked up at a stationery store that carries legal forms.) The binder essentially signifies that the buyer and seller have reached an agreement and that each is committed to going through with the deal.

The binder usually contains the barest of information: the names and addresses of the buyer and seller, the street address of the property for sale, and the purchase price. If a broker is involved, the binder frequently will specify this fact and the amount of his or her commission. The buyer usually is required to make a deposit when the binder is signed, usually around $1,000 to $5,000. As the buyer, you should negotiate to pay as little as possible as the deposit. The amount of your deposit should, of course, be included in the binder.

A binder is usually not intended to set forth the complete terms and conditions of the agreement. In fact, it should contain a clause calling for a complete contract to be prepared and signed within a specific length of time (usually three to five days) and stating that if the contract isn't drawn up by that time, your entire deposit will be immediately refunded upon your request.

Before signing the binder, both the seller and the buyer should read it thoroughly. Generally, you don't need to have a lawyer review it, but if you don't understand something or if any questions do spring up, don't hesitate to get legal advice.

The one chance you take by not signing a binder is that someone else will come along and sign it. The seller then is obligated to sell the house to that person. Since you had no written agreement with the seller, you can't sue the seller for selling the house to someone else. If you do sign a binder, remember: Put as little information in it as possible; pay as little as possible; and make the sale contingent upon signing a complete purchase and sale contract within three to five days or you get all of your money back.

Option Contracts

Patty has just finished reading a book on making money by investing in real estate. Scanning the real estate section in Sunday's paper, she finds an older house offered at a low price. She looks the property over and decides she can quickly find someone to buy it for $25,000 more. Patty doesn't really want to buy the house herself, so she shouldn't sign a binder. But she wants to keep the property off the market for a month or two while she tries to find a buyer. She offers the sellers $1,000 if they will give her the exclusive option of buying the house for their asking price during the next sixty days. If the seller agrees to this, then Patty has sixty days to buy the property. This is an example of an "option contract." During this time, the sellers cannot sell the property to anyone else. If Patty exercises her option—agrees to buy the property—before sixty days go by, the sellers must sell it to her at the agreed-upon price. If Patty doesn't find a buyer, then at the end of sixty days, the sellers are free to sell the house to anyone else. Of course, Patty loses the $1,000 she paid for the option.

Option contracts are used primarily in transactions involving commercial and industrial real estate. In recent years, however, many more people are using option contracts to do what Patty did: to buy time to find someone else who will purchase the property at a higher price, so they can make a tidy profit with little effort or risk.

If no buyer is found, all that is lost is the money paid for the option.

What happens if the seller sells the property to someone else before the option has expired? If you can prove that you would have been able to sell the property to someone else at a higher price before the option was up, you can recover your "lost profit" and other damages. For example, if Patty had an option to buy the property for $175,000, and she found a person willing to pay $200,000 for it, she could recover her lost profit of $25,000 and other damages from the sellers. Even if Patty would not have found a buyer, she should still ask the sellers to return the money she paid for the option since they breached the contract by selling the property to someone else before Patty's sixty days had passed. She also can recover any out-of-pocket expenses, such as her advertising costs.

An option contract for the purchase of real estate should be put in writing and signed by both parties. It should include the names of the parties, the street address of the property, the selling price, when the option expires, and the amount of money paid for the option.

The Contract

Once you are ready to buy a house, all of the terms of the sale must be put in a written contract, usually called the "purchase and sale agreement." The provisions listed below should be in the contract to deal with the legal situations most likely to arise in the purchase of real estate. Don't sign the contract until you have thoroughly reviewed it. Get a copy of it and take it home to look it over before you sign. Compare the provisions in the contract with the information in this chapter to see what your rights are. And if you still have any questions, talk to a lawyer. An hour or two in legal fees now could save you thousands of dollars later.

Description of Parties and the Property

The contract should contain the full names and current addresses of the seller and the buyer and an adequate description of the property. The street address is usually sufficient to identify the property at this stage.

The Purchase Price and Deposit

The sales contract must include the purchase price of the property. Unless otherwise stated, the full amount is due when escrow closes. The contract should provide that the sale is contingent upon the buyer's ability to obtain financing (unless, of course, the buyer will be paying from cash on hand). If the seller will be financing any part of the price (see below), the contract also should state the amount financed and all terms of the loan. If you, as buyer, plan to assume the existing mortgage, this fact, too, should be noted in the sales contract. Because many mortgages are not assumable, you should insert a clause stating that the deal is canceled if the bank, savings and loan association, or other lender refuses to let you assume the outstanding mortgage.

The amount of money you give as a deposit—usually 10 to 20 percent—should be noted in the contract. Don't trust this money to the seller. The money should be entrusted to your attorney, the seller's attorney, or a reputable escrow company. Suppose you hand the money over to the seller, who then uses it as a down payment on his or her next house. If your deal falls through, you'll probably find yourself waiting until the seller sells the house to someone else before you get your money back. (If this happens to you, consider seeing a lawyer immediately; otherwise, you might find yourself waiting months to get your deposit back.) Usually the deposit is given to the seller's broker, who holds it or puts it in his or her trust account until escrow is opened.

What Comes with the House?

Are the stove and refrigerator included in the sale? The washer and dryer or other appliances? Any furniture, tools, or equipment? How about the lighting fixtures, drapes, and the like? Generally, except for built-in appliances such as the oven and dishwasher, these things are not included in the sale of a house unless they are specifically included in the sales contract. These items are not permanently attached to the house and can be removed with little or no damage to the house. In legalese, those objects are considered "personalty" and do not lose their status as such just because they are attached to the house by a few bolts, nails, or hoses. Before you sign on the dotted line, identify in the contract each item that goes with the house.

Inspection and Repairs

If you haven't had the chance to inspect the house thoroughly before signing the contract, insist upon a provision stating that you can back out if a termite or building inspector's report shows any problem whatsoever. Do this even if the seller agrees to guarantee that the house is free from termite infestation, structural damage or weakness, and so forth. What happens if the seller refuses to make his warranty good after you buy your house? You'll have to hire a lawyer to sue him or her. Better to find out now, before you buy the house, if there are any problems.

Suppose that your inspection reveals a problem—say, a leaky roof. You like the house but you don't want to buy it unless the seller fixes it before you move in. The seller agrees to do this but balks when you start to write it in the contract. In this case, either tell the seller that you won't sign the contract unless the provision is in there, or be prepared to pay for the repairs out of your own pocket. If such a clause is not in the written contract, the seller generally is not legally obligated to make any repairs to the property. Another alternative is to get a couple of estimates of what it will cost to fix the problem, then negotiate a corresponding reduction in the price and take care of the repairs yourself.

The contract should state that all repairs must be completed before escrow closes. If a repair cannot be made by that time, your best bet is to find out how much the repair will cost, then get the price of the house reduced by that amount. Don't rely on the seller to take care of these things once the money changes hands.

The Defect Disclosure Form

Many states now require the seller of real estate to fill out, under penalty of perjury, a form in which he or she must disclose any and all defects the property has that he or she knows about or should know about through a reasonable investigation. If the seller fails to disclose such a defect, he or she may be required to reimburse the buyer the cost of repairing it. If it is a major defect, the buyer may be able to cancel ("rescind") the sale and get all of his or her money back.

Damage to the House

One week after you sign the sales contract, the house burns down. You, the buyer, did not think about buying property insurance until escrow was due to close, another seven weeks away. Can the seller force you to go through with the deal? In some states, unless the contract provides otherwise, you become the owner of the house when the contract is signed, even though escrow doesn't close until two or three months later. As owner, you assume the risk of any damage to the property. In many states, however, you do not assume these risks until escrow closes and title passes. In any event, the sales contract should always include a provision stating that if the house is damaged before escrow closes, the seller must repair it or the buyer can cancel the deal. Likewise, the contract should give the buyer the right to cancel if the house is destroyed or substantially damaged. One thing you, as the buyer, should do to protect yourself is to arrange for homeowner's insurance to take effect immediately when escrow closes (or as soon as the contract is signed, if you are assuming the risk that the house will be damaged or destroyed before escrow closes).

The Title, Deed, and Encumbrances

The sales contract should always state that the sale is contingent upon the seller's ability to give the buyer a "marketable title." The type of deed (such as a warranty deed or grant deed, discussed below) that the seller must give the buyer should be noted. If the contract doesn't specify the type of deed to be used, the law presumes that you intended to use the type of deed customarily used in your area. All existing encumbrances, liens, easements, covenants, restrictions, and so forth (which are discussed later) affecting the property should be included.

The Broker's Fee, Adjustments, and Escrow

If a broker is involved, the contract should state what the broker's commission is, when it is due, and who is responsible for paying it. Any adjustments that will be made concerning taxes, insurance, and other expenses already paid by the seller (see discussion below) should be noted in the purchase and sale contract. The contract also should set forth information concerning escrow, such as when and where it will be opened, who will pay the closing costs, and when and where escrow will close.

Making Sure the Seller Is Out When You're Ready to Move In

Escrow closes; your furniture is loaded onto the moving van and taken to your new house. But when you get there, the sellers and all their furniture are still there. They tell you that their new house won't be ready to move into for another two weeks or so. And when the sellers finally are out, you open the door and find it looks as though a tornado hit the place.

The sales contract should explicitly require the seller to move out and leave the house in a clean condition before escrow closes. Ideally you don't want escrow to close until the seller is out (unless you have agreed to lease the property to the seller for a while) and you have looked the place over. This gives the seller an extra incentive to be out of the property on time and to leave it clean. You will want to include a provision stating that if the seller is not out of the house on time, the seller has to pay your lodging and storage costs until the seller is out. If there is a tenant who has some time remaining on a lease, or there is some other reason why you won't be able to move in when escrow closes, this should be noted in the contract.

Signing the Contract

The seller and buyer must both sign the contract. If the buyer is married, his or her spouse usually should sign the contract as well. If the seller is married, both the husband and wife should sign the contract even if the title is in the name of only one of them. (The fact that title is in one spouse's name does not necessarily mean that the other spouse has no rights in and to the property.) The contract should require the spouse whose name does not appear on the deed to sign a "quitclaim deed" releasing all interest in the property before escrow closes.

If the property is being sold by a corporation or a general or limited partnership, the contract should state that the seller has the authority to bind the corporation or partnership. The buyer should request and review copies of all documents giving the seller this authority, and these documents should be incorporated into the contract. If two or more people own the property but do not have a partnership agreement (say, two friends who hold title to the land as tenants in common), have each of them sign the contract if you're buying more than one person's share of the property.

Changing the Contract after It Is Signed

The building inspector you hired to check out the house tells you that everything is fine, except that a new heating system is needed. You get some estimates and learn that it will cost about $5,000 to install a new one. You call up the seller, who agrees to reduce the price by this amount. You figure you can trust the seller, so you don't ask to have this put in writing. The next week escrow closes, but at the original contract price. Why? Because you didn't change the contract properly.

Like any other type of contract, a contract for the sale of real estate can be changed at any time by mutual agreement of the parties. But ordinarily in real estate transactions these changes must be put in writing and signed by both buyer and seller to be enforceable. An oral modification usually is not sufficient, since the original contract—one for the sale of real estate—is required by the statute of frauds to be in writing and can be changed only by an instrument of "equal dignity."

Financing the Purchase Price

Most people who buy a home today don't have the money to buy it for cash and have to finance a large portion of the price. Most of the time, the loan comes from a conventional source, such as a bank or savings and loan association. Or, the financing of the house may be made possible through the FHA (Federal Housing Administration), which often loans money for homes at a lower rate than conventional sources. Qualified veterans may obtain a loan from the Veterans Administration (VA), which requires a minimal down payment and offers a lower interest rate than even the FHA loan. Sometimes the seller will finance all or a portion of the price.

You may want to take over ("assume") the existing mortgage on the property because it has a lower interest rate than today's loans. Loans are not as freely assumable as they once were, however. Most loans cannot be assumed without the bank's permission unless the loan agreement expressly states that it is assumable. (Loans with variable interest rates are more likely to contain this kind of provision than other loans are.) If you plan on assuming a loan, get the details worked out with the bank before escrow closes. You don't want to get caught in the situation of closing escrow and then finding the bank calling in the loan when it learns of the sale.

Suppose you let the buyer assume the outstanding mortgage on your home. Two years later, the house burns down. The buyer didn't have insurance on it and can't afford to rebuild. The buyer walks away and defaults on the loan, the bank forecloses, and the property is sold at auction, but the money isn't enough to pay the balance of the loan. The buyer can't be found or doesn't have the money to pay the balance. Can the bank sue you? Generally, yes. You are still liable for the loan, although the bank must first try to get the money from the buyer. But if the buyer doesn't have the money, the bank can come looking for you. Some states, however, have "antideficiency judgment" laws, which limit the bank to selling the property. If that isn't enough to cover the loan, the bank is stuck. Before agreeing to let the buyer assume your mortgage, see if the bank will release you entirely from your obligations under the loan. Otherwise, make sure the buyer is responsible and can be counted on to make the payments, keep the property in good shape, and maintain adequate insurance on it at all times.

When money is lent to buy a house, a mortgage or deed of trust is used to secure the lender's interest in the property. Although there are some differences between the two, the effects are the same: They give the lender the right to foreclose on the property if the buyer defaults on the loan.

If you are seeking financing from a bank or savings and loan, shop around to make sure that you are getting the best deal possible. Calling three different financial institutions on the same day may get you two or three different interest rates quoted. Carefully consider all costs of the loan and the period of time in which it must be paid back. Find out what the total cost of the loan will be, including "points," which is a fee based on a percentage of the loan amount. For example, if you are borrowing $200,000, and the bank charges 2 points, you have to pay a $2,000 "loan fee," which is usually due when escrow closes. Also find out whether there is a "prepayment penalty" if you refinance the loan when interest rates come down and pay it off earlier than it is due.

The term "creative financing" has become part of the real estate industry's vocabulary. Creative financing cannot be defined with any exactness, except to say that it is anything different from the traditional twenty- or thirty-year mortgage. For example, the loan may require the buyer to pay only interest for five years and then pay the entire loan back in one "balloon payment." Or, a bank may be willing to lend only a certain amount of money on the property, so the seller agrees to finance the rest ("carry paper").

Creative financing has allowed many people to purchase a home when they otherwise would not have been able to. But at the same time, creative financing has caused great suffering to some. For example, if the buyer can't make that balloon payment, the lender forecloses, and the buyer loses the house. Many sellers who finance the price face the expense and trouble of having to foreclose when the buyer defaults. If you will be using creative financing, make sure you know just what you're getting into. In some cases, for instance, the buyer's payments for the first few years are not enough even to pay the interest on the loan. When this happens ("negative amortization"), the interest that isn't paid off is added to the purchase price. In a few years, the amount of your monthly payment will increase—perhaps by as much as several hundred dollars—to cover both the principal and the interest. By that time, however, the price of your $225,000 house may have risen to $240,000 or more with the accumulated back interest.

The Closing

After the purchase and sale contract is signed by both the buyer and the seller, you, as the buyer, will need to do a number of things, including arranging financing, getting a title search done (see discussion below), having termite and building inspectors check the property out, obtaining insurance for the property, and perhaps having a survey done. As the seller, you may have to make some repairs to the house or clear up some problems with your title (such as paying the landscaper $250 to release the lien filed against your property).

Most contracts for the sale of real estate state that "time is of the essence." This means that escrow must close on the day and time specified, and not a minute later. If you won't be ready to close escrow on that date, call the seller or broker, let him or her know why you can't close escrow then, and state when you will be ready to close escrow. As long as you're making a solid effort to do what you have to do to close the deal, there shouldn't be any problem getting a reasonable extension of time to close escrow. Be sure to get the other party to sign a written document agreeing to the time extension and file it with the escrow company. Keep a copy for yourself in case a problem arises later.

When everything is finally in order, escrow will close. Several people may be present at the closing, including the buyer, the seller, perhaps their attorneys, the real estate broker, the bank's representative, and someone from the escrow company. A number of things happen in sequence. The buyer shows the bank the title insurance company's report (discussed below) and also proof of property insurance if this hasn't been given to the bank already. The bank lends the buyer the money to purchase the property. The buyer gives the money to the seller, who in turn signs a new deed transferring title to the buyer, which is notarized by a notary public (usually the person from the escrow company). The seller also pays off the balance of his or her mortgage on the property. If a broker is involved, the commission is paid at this time. Adjustments are made to reimburse the seller for various expenses that he or she has paid already but that will benefit the buyer. For example, if the seller has prepaid the full year's property taxes of, say, $4,500, and there are six months left in the year, the buyer will give the seller an additional $2,250 to adjust the taxes. A closing statement listing all monies, costs, expenses, and deductions is prepared (usually by the escrow company or by one of the party's attorneys) and given to each party. The deed is then recorded in the county recorder's office.

If the Sale Falls Through

When a sale falls through for some reason—if, for example you can't get financing or your building inspector finds a big crack in the foundation—you usually can cancel the sale and get your deposit back. But what happens if either the buyer or seller backs out without justification and refuses to go through with the deal?

If the seller backs out, the buyer is entitled to recover any money he or she has actually paid, including the deposit, escrow expenses, and costs of a building inspector and title search. The buyer also can sue for the difference between the contract price and the cost of buying a comparable house from someone else. For example, if you agreed to buy the house for $225,000, and it costs you $240,000 to find a comparable house, you are entitled to recover the $15,000 difference. But what if you really want the property in question rather than another house? Frequently you can go to court to compel the seller to sell the house to you. This is known as "specific performance." Courts routinely will force a seller to sell the property to the buyer if the buyer has done everything the contract required but the seller reneges without justification.

Now suppose that you are the seller, and the buyer backs out for no reason. If you end up selling the house for a lower price, you can make the buyer pay the difference. You also can recover any additional out-of-pocket expenses, such as advertising expenses that would not have been necessary if the buyer had gone through with the deal. If you had to pay a commission to a broker when the buyer backed out, the buyer can be held liable for this, too.

Here is the most commonly encountered scenario when the sale of a house is aborted: Sidney agrees to sell his house to Frank for $235,000 and they sign a written contract. The next week, Nancy offers Sidney $250,000, which Sidney likewise accepts, and a contract between Sidney and Nancy is signed. Sidney calls Frank up and tells him that he has changed his mind and is not going to sell the house after all. Frank tells Sidney they have a signed contract, and he will take the case all the way to the Supreme Court if Sidney backs out. When Frank learns of the deal between Sidney and Nancy, he calls Nancy and tells her that Sidney sold him the house first. Nancy says she doesn't know a thing about that, and as far as she is concerned, she owns the house. Both Frank and Nancy want the house, and each refuses to back down. Who wins? If Nancy knew of the signed contract between Frank and Sidney before she signed her contract, Frank will win. But if Nancy did not know of the earlier agreement, the issue may be resolved on the basis of who recorded a signed contract or a deed first. Many states hold that in this situation, who gets the house depends on who was the first to record a deed with the recorder's office. If Nancy recorded her deed first, she would win, even though she was the second buyer. One way to avoid this problem is to record the binder and purchase and sale contract as soon as they are signed. A final note: If separate brokers brought Frank and Nancy to Sidney, Sidney probably will wind up paying them each a full commission. (If the same broker that closed the deal between Frank and Sidney also closed the deal between Nancy and Sidney, Frank would be able to sue the broker for inducing Sidney to break the contract with him.)

Selling Your House and the Capital Gains Tax

Suppose you bought your four-bedroom home with a swimming pool in 1965 for $20,000 to accommodate your growing family. Now it is 2004 and you decide the house is just too big to take care of now that the children are grown and have moved out. Nobody uses the pool anymore and keeping it clean is more trouble than it's worth. So you decide to sell it and move into a nice two-bedroom apartment in a seniors-only complex. You contact a real estate agent and learn much to your delight that your home is now worth $345,000. Let's say that after the real estate agent and other fees and expenses have been paid, you net $320,000 from the sale. Will you have to pay taxes on this $300,000 capital gain (the net sales price of $320,000 minus your cost, or "basis," of $20,000, assuming you made no improvements to the property).

The old rule used to be that, for people 55 and older there was a one-time exemption of $125,000 from capital gains tax upon the sale of a house. Using the example above, that would leave you with a capital gain of $175,000 (the net sales price of $300,000 minus the $125,000 exemption) on which you would have to pay taxes.

Today, however, the exemption rates are $250,000 for a single person and $500,000 for a married couple. And there is no age limit—you don't have to be over 55. If you are 35 and single and were fortunate enough to have bought a home that appreciated in value $250,000 in say, ten years, you won't owe a dime in capital gains taxes if you sell it.

To qualify for the exemption, you must have lived in the house as your principal place of residence for an aggregate of two years in the five years before you sell it. Hence, you need not live in the home for a continuous two years. You could live there in increments of six months for four years in the five years immediately preceding its sale. However, it must be your principal place of residence.

How is your principal place of residence determined? By such factors as whether you are a registered voter in the county where the house is, whether your car is registered in the state where the house is located, whether you refer to the property as your home rather than your vacation hideaway, whether you obtained or renewed your driver's license in that county, and the like.

The one principal limitation on the $250,000 (single) or $500,000 (married) exemption is that it can be used only once every two years. Thus, if you claim the exemption in March 2004, you cannot claim it again until March 2006. Other than that, there is no limitation on the number of times you can use the exemption.

New House Warranties

What happens if you buy a new home and later discover that the built-in dishwasher doesn't work, or the electrical wiring is all bad, or, worse yet, the house is slowly slipping into the ground, and huge cracks are developing in the walls, ceilings, and floor?

When the defect is in an appliance, such as the oven, dishwasher, water heater, air conditioner, microwave oven, or trash compactor, the first thing you do is check the manufacturer's warranty card, which should have come with the house. Is the appliance still covered by the warranty? If so, contact an authorized service company to repair or replace it according to the terms of the warranty. If the defect is due to an error in its installation, however, you'll have to look to the general contractor or developer to fix it. Call or write the contractor and identify the problem. If the manufacturer told you the problem was one of installation rather than manufacturing, be sure to tell this to the contractor.

If the defect is with the house itself, such as faulty electrical wiring or leaky plumbing, contact the general contractor or developer. If the wiring or plumbing needs replacing, this should be done as soon as possible, at no cost to you. You are entitled to be compensated for any inconvenience to you, including the cost of lodging if it becomes unbearable for you to stay in the house because of, for instance, a prolonged lack of water or heating. If the defect is structurally related and serious—say, the house is slipping down a hill, or the roof is slowly collapsing—you should hire a lawyer as soon as possible to represent your interests.

CONDOS, TOWNHOMES, AND COOPS

Most of what has been covered already in this chapter also relates to buying a condominium, townhouse, or cooperative. But these involve a few different considerations—particularly as to just what you own.

When you own a condominium, you generally own only the living space of a particular unit. Exactly what you own is determined by the deed, the declaration of covenants, conditions and restrictions (CC&Rs), and other documents. Sometimes you own the inside walls. Other times, you own only the airspace inside the walls. The condominium homeowners' association owns all or most of the building and all of the land and communal structures, such as a clubhouse or swimming pool.

The main difference between a townhouse and a condominium is that with a condominium, the homeowners' association owns all of the land, while with a townhouse you usually own the land beneath your townhouse. You also own the walls, inside and outside, except for "party walls"—walls you share with your neighbor—which you only own the inside of.

Cooperatives ("coops") chiefly are found on the East Coast, particularly in the major metropolitan areas. A coop is unique in that the only thing you own is stock in a corporation. The corporation owns all of the land and the apartment building and gives you a "proprietary lease" to live in a particular unit. This lease lasts for as long as you own your stock in the corporation. If you want to live in a coop, you will have to submit the necessary application to the board of directors for review. You can be turned down for a variety of reasons, but not because of your race, national origin, or religion.

A coop is managed by the corporation's board of directors, who usually hire a management company to take care of the building. Condos and townhomes are governed by a board elected by members of the homeowners' association. Regardless of whether you live in a coop, townhome, or condo, you'll probably have to live by a number of rules and regulations concerning the use of your unit and the common area, some of which may be contained in the corporation's or partnership's bylaws or CC&Rs you received with your deed or stock.

In addition to the regular mortgage payment, you probably will pay monthly or annual dues to the homeowners' association or maintenance fees to the coop corporation. Before you buy, find out what the dues currently are and how much they have increased in the past two or three years, then figure this amount into your monthly payments to see if your budget can handle it. This money is used by the homeowners' association or coop to maintain and repair communal structures, to pay for gardening and the like, and to buy insurance for the building and land. Depending on exactly what you own, you may need to obtain property insurance to cover your particular unit in case of fire or other damage. (And in any case, you'll still need to buy insurance if you want your personal belongings—furniture, jewelry, appliances, and so forth—covered.)

ESTATES, MARKETABLE TITLES, AND DEEDS

Estates—What You Get for Your Money

When purchasing land, you need to know exactly what you are buying. Not all "estates," or interests, in land are equal. You can have anything from the absolute right to do whatever you want with a piece of property to a mere license to come onto the land for a specific purpose.

Fees

The most common interest in land is the "fee simple absolute," or just "fee simple." When you buy a piece of land, you usually become the owner of a fee simple absolute. This is the largest interest you can have in real estate. You own the property lock, stock, and barrel, no strings attached (except maybe a mortgage or trust deed). You are free to sell the land as you see fit. When you die, the property is passed according to the provisions of your will or living trust; if you die without a will or living trust, the land goes to your next of kin (see chapter 3). Sometimes the developer, seller, or a previous owner will retain certain rights, such as the rights to any gas or minerals under the property.

The other type of fee is the so-called defeasible fee. Unlike a fee simple absolute, which you own forever, you can lose a defeasible fee when a specified event or condition occurs. For example, the deed may give you the property "so long as liquor is never sold on the premises." If you open a market and sell liquor, you lose the land. The title to the land reverts to the original owner (or his or her survivors). Defeasible fees are not too common, but if you ever run across any type of restriction or condition on the title that could result in your losing it, you should talk to a lawyer before buying the land.

Life Estates

A life estate gives you the right to live on a piece of land for as long as you live. (A life estate also can let you live on a piece of land for as long as someone else lives.) The owner of the life estate is called a "life tenant." If you own a life estate, you can do what you want with it: You can live on the land; you can sell your interest; or you can give it away. But when you die, your life estate is terminated automatically. Life estates usually are found in the context of wills and estates, as when one spouse by will or living trust gives the other the right to live on any property for as long as he or she lives, and someone else (such as the children) gets it afterward.

When you own a life estate, you must leave the property in substantially the same condition as it was in when you received it. You can use reasonable amounts of the natural resources on the property—timber, water, minerals, and the like—but usually you can't exhaust them unless the deed granting you a life estate specifies differently. The person who is to receive the property after you can get a court injunction to stop you from unreasonably depleting the resources. You also are obligated to make ordinary repairs to the land and structures but don't have to spend more money in repairs than you receive in profits (from timber, gas, and mining, for example) and rent from the land.

Future Interests

A future interest gives you a right in the property at some later date. In the case of a life estate, for example, the person who gets the property after the life tenant dies has a future interest. Someone who owns a future interest must wait until a specified event happens—say, the life tenant dies—before taking possession of the property.

Easements, Profits, and Covenants

An "easement" involves the right to go onto another's property for some purpose. A common example of an easement is the right to use a road on your neighbor's property to get onto and off your own land. Easements typically are granted to public utility companies to run power, water, sewer, gas, and telephone lines over or through property. Easements also can prohibit you from using your property in some way. For example, if Marilyn divides her property in half and sells you one lot, she may place a restriction in the deed preventing you from building a house or other structure in a way that will interfere with the view from her structure.

A "profit" gives you the right to take some resource, such as timber, minerals, dirt, gravel, or oil, from another's land. A profit necessarily includes an easement to go onto that person's land to get the resource. The profit may be an exclusive or a nonexclusive one. If you get an exclusive profit, you and you alone can take the resource from the land. But the profit can restrict how much of the particular resource you can take. In a nonexclusive profit, the owner of the land can give others the right to take the same resource from the land.

A "covenant" is a promise found in a deed concerning the use of the land. An affirmative covenant requires that you perform a specified act—mow your lawn every week, for example. Far more common, though, are negative covenants, which prohibit certain acts or uses of property. For example, a covenant may prevent you from painting your house purple or operating a business out of your home. Covenants are particularly important in communal living arrangements, such as condominium complexes.

Easements, profits, and covenants ordinarily must be put in writing to be enforceable. The document giving you the right to use the land should be recorded in the county recorder's office, especially if you want to enforce it against future buyers of the property. If you don't record your easement or other interest, you may lose it when the land is sold. But if your use of the land is obvious from looking at the land itself, this is usually enough to notify a purchaser of your interest. To avoid disputes and costly legal proceedings, you should always record an easement, profit, or covenant.

If you misuse an easement or profit, you risk losing it altogether. Suppose Mary gives Jane an easement to drive her car over Mary's property so Jane can get to her own property. Jane opens a twenty-four-hour convenience market on her land, and her customers use Mary's road to get to it. Can Mary sue to stop this? Yes. At the time she gave Jane the easement, Mary did not contemplate a steady stream of cars going over her property at all hours of the day and night.

Licenses

A license gives you permission to go onto another person's land for some reason without being a trespasser. When you go to the stadium to watch a football or baseball game, the ticket gives you a license to be on the premises. Without the ticket or other consent of the owner or lessee of the property, you would be a trespasser. When you let an advertising company put a billboard on your land, the advertising company has a license to keep its sign there. If the sign is put there without your consent or the advertising company fails to remove it when the license expires, the advertising company is trespassing on your land. When you check into a hotel, you acquire a license to use a room.

Marketable Title

When buying land, you want to make sure that the seller has a good, or "marketable," title. A marketable title is one free from problems: No one else claims to own the land; there are no outstanding liens, judgments, mortgages, or other encumbrances against it; and there are no easements other than the typical easements for power, water, sewer, gas, and telephone lines.

A title is rendered bad ("unmarketable") by such things as a defective deed (perhaps it was not notarized or the description of the property is incomplete or wrong), an easement, or an encumbrance—a mortgage, judgment, or lien—that the seller cannot or will not remove. Title also can be bad because of a "break," or gap, in the "chain of title"—somewhere along the line, somebody failed to record a deed.

There are two main ways to find out if a title is good. One is to obtain a title insurance policy from a reputable title insurance company. Prior to insuring the title, the title insurance company will have its employees thoroughly research the title to see if it is marketable. You need to be aware, though, that the typical title insurance policy only protects you against recorded documents. If someone claims ownership or an easement through adverse possession (see discussion below), the ordinary policy doesn't cover this. You should always personally visit the land before buying it to see if anyone else claims to own any part of it. A more expensive policy protecting you against things that are not in the official records also usually can be purchased.

The second method of ascertaining whether a title is marketable is by having a lawyer do a "title abstract." This was the uniform method of ensuring a marketable title before title insurance companies sprang up and is still the standard practice in some states. An attorney skilled in title searches will go through the official records and then issue an opinion as to whether or not the title is marketable.

The protection you get from an insurance company usually is greater than what you get from a lawyer who does an abstract. If a lawyer makes an error, you can recover damages only by proving that the lawyer was negligent in some way, that the lawyer overlooked something that a careful lawyer would not have missed. And if the lawyer does not carry adequate "errors and omissions" insurance (legal malpractice insurance), you might not be able to collect the full amount of your damages. On the other hand, if a title insurance company makes an error, it usually has to pay your damages, regardless of whether or not it was negligent.

If the title search reveals a defect—a "cloud" on the title—the seller must clear this up before escrow closes. If the seller is unable to deliver a marketable title, however, you can either call the deal off or go through with the purchase and assume the risk of the defective title. Whether or not you should accept an unmarketable title depends on how serious the problem is. It's a good idea to talk to a lawyer before buying the property, even if the defect appears minor. In exchange for accepting a less than marketable title, you may wish to negotiate a lower price to reflect the risk you are taking.

The Deed

The seller's interest in the property does not pass to you until the seller signs a deed containing an adequate "legal description" of the land. Originally, the legal description, which governs what you own, was based on "townships," six-mile squares consisting of thirty-six sections. Reading such a legal description could give you the same feeling Alice had when walking through the looking glass: "The northeast quarter of the southwest quarter of the southeast quarter of the northwest quarter . . ." Today, especially in tract housing, the legal description is based on a tract map filed by the developer and is much easier to read.

You may want to have the property surveyed to make sure the visible boundaries (fences, for example) correspond with the legal description. A survey may reveal some problem—that the garage is encroaching two feet onto the neighbor's property, for instance. If this is the case, you will want to get an easement or other agreement with the neighbor before buying the land.

Following are the various types of deeds that are used to transfer ownership of real estate:

General Warranty Deed

In a general warranty deed, the seller promises that he or she owns the land, has the right to sell it, and that there are no encumbrances (mortgages, liens, judgments, and the like) against the property. The seller also promises to defend the title against third parties who claim to own all or part of the land, and to compensate the buyer if a third party manages to remove the buyer from the property. A "full warranty deed" includes the additional promise that the seller will do anything necessary to clear up any questions about the title. A warranty deed gives the buyer the greatest protection of all the deeds, but even so, this protection is no match for a title insurance policy.

Grant Deed

In a grant deed, the seller warrants that he or she has not conveyed the same property to anyone else and that the property is free from encumbrances other than those disclosed to the buyer. The seller does not, however, promise to defend the buyer if someone else claims ownership of the property.

Bargain and Sale Deed

In a bargain and sale deed, commonly used in the Northeast, the seller makes no express warranties. The law, however, imposes the warranties that the seller has a marketable title and is transferring all of his or her interest unless the deed states otherwise. A bargain and sale deed with a covenant against the seller's acts warrants that the property is not encumbered except as specified in the deed.

Quitclaim Deed

A quitclaim deed merely releases the seller's interest in the property, if he or she has any interest at all. If the seller is the sole owner of the property, and no one else claims an interest therein, the quitclaim is sufficient to transfer the title. Quitclaim deeds are usually the least preferred type of deed when land is being sold. The worst way of buying property would be to use a quitclaim deed and not get a title search done by a title insurance company.

When you are buying land with someone else, you need to consider how you will hold title: as joint tenants, tenants in common, community property, or tenants by the entirety. The differences among these are discussed in chapter 3. Suffice it to say here that tenancy by the entirety and community property (which exists in only nine states) can exist only between married couples, and joint tenancies and tenancies by the entirety have an automatic right of survivorship. This means that when one owner dies, the surviving owner automatically owns the other's share of the property.

Homeowner's Insurance

When you buy a home, you need two types of insurance: title insurance and homeowner's insurance. Title insurance is to ensure that there are no problems with the chain of title, that it is in fact the seller's property and there are no liens or other "clouds" on the title that could make it unmarketable (discussed above).

The second type of insurance you need is homeowner's insurance to cover damage to your house and contents from, for example, fire. The most common type of homeowner's insurance in the United States is a policy known as homeowners-3 (HO-3). It covers a wide range of damage to your house, such as losses due to fire, lightning, tornadoes, windstorms, hail, explosion, smoke, vandalism, and theft. Damage from wind may be limited on the Atlantic and Gulf coasts, so you will want to go over it with your insurance agent to make sure you have adequate coverage.

The most important thing you want is to have your house insured for replacement value, not for your actual cash basis, that is, the price you paid for it. For instance, if you bought your house for $75,000 and it is now worth $225,000, you want to make sure it is covered for the full $225,000 replacement value. If you only insure it for your purchase price ($75,000), you will have to come up with the extra $150,000 to pay to replace the house.

In the typical HO-3 policy, you are not covered for either flood or earthquake damage. Whether you should get such damage depends mainly on where you live. Persons in Southern California, where earthquakes are fairly common, may consider it prudent, albeit expensive, to have earthquake coverage. Likewise, people who live along a delta or river that is known to flood every so many years should get flood insurance. Flood insurance is provided by the federal government, under a program run by the Federal Insurance Administration. Damage to homes caused by mudslides also is covered by flood policies. Your insurance agent can give you further information on what flood policies do and don't cover and how much it costs.

Suppose a pipe breaks and water inundates the floor. Are you covered? Under an HO-3 policy, yes. You are covered for damage caused by the accidental discharge of water from a plumbing system. Assume, however, that your basement floods from water seepage from the ground. Is this damage covered? No. Water seepage is excluded from an HO-3 policy, and flood insurance does not cover it either. The best thing to do is to make sure the basement is properly waterproofed.

Are you covered if, during a heavy storm, a large tree is blown over and damages your roof? Yes and no. You are covered for the damage to your roof, but not for the removal of the tree. Your trees and shrubbery are covered for losses due to acts like vandalism, theft, or fire, but not wind damage. Insurance is available that would cover not only the removal of the tree and damaged shrubbery, but also their replacement value. Your insurance agent can advise you further on this.

Unscheduled jewelry usually is limited to $1,000; hence, if you have expensive jewelry, you should itemize them on a schedule and purchase higher limits. You may want to add a "floater" to your policy to cover specific items, such as expensive artwork, and silverware. Suppose you left some items of jewelry, artwork or other valuable personal property in your car and someone breaks into the car and steals it. Does your homeowner's insurance cover this? Yes. Your homeowner's insurance, and not your automobile insurance, covers damage to or the loss of personal property kept in a motor vehicle.

Let's suppose that you've invited a friend over for lunch one day. You have just finished waxing your kitchen floor and it is slippery, but you do not tell your friend about it. Your friend goes into the kitchen to get a glass of water and slips on the slick floor, falls, and breaks her hip. Will your homeowner's insurance policy protect you in this situation? Yes. Generally, the standard homeowner's policy will have personal liability limits of $100,000/$300,000. This means that the most insurance covers for any single individual is $100,000, to a maximum of $300,000 total to all claimants arising from a single (nonautomobile) accident. You should consider buying an "umbrella" policy of $1,000,000 that would supplement both your automobile and homeowner's insurance. An umbrella policy is surprisingly inexpensive for all of the additional coverage it provides, and may save you from financial ruin in the event you severely injure someone.

Adverse Possession

Usually you become the owner of a piece of land by buying it from the person who owns it. You also can become the owner simply by taking possession of the land and living there or using it long enough. This is the doctrine of "adverse possession."

To acquire property by adverse possession, you must actually live on or use the property, and this fact must be clear if the owner inspects the land; it doesn't count if you're hiding your presence. You must be in "continuous and peaceable possession" of the property for the statutory period of time, which varies from five to twenty years, depending on the state. Some states also require that you pay taxes on the property for a certain number of years. Your possession of the land must be "hostile." This means that you must claim to be the owner of the property, even though there may be no justification for the claim. Once you have done all of this for the requisite length of time, you become owner in fee simple absolute of the property. But if you build a house on a far corner of a thousand-acre spread, you can't claim title to the entire property. You only get the property immediately surrounding the house, including the land you farm or have otherwise been using throughout the required time period.

If you own land somewhere remote from where you live, land that you don't get to very often, you should make it a point to check it out—either in person or through a local real estate agent—every few years to make sure people have not settled in. If they have, give them a written notice that you own the property, that they are trespassing, and that you demand that they move at once. If they don't, it would be best to hire a lawyer to start proceedings to remove them, rather than risk losing the property by doing nothing.

Trespass

A person who walks across your land without your permission is trespassing, even if the property isn't in the slightest way damaged. And a person doesn't actually have to walk on your land to commit a trespass. Throwing a rock or other object onto the land constitutes a trespass, as does firing a shot across the land, even though the bullet doesn't touch the ground or any structure on the property.

Consent of the property owner or other person in lawful possession of the land (such as a tenant) is a defense against a trespass action. The person must not exceed the scope of that consent, however, and if the consent is revoked, the person must promptly leave the grounds. An example: Charles gives permission to a local Boy Scout troop to spend one night camping out on a remote corner of his farm. The boys like it so much, they decide to spend a second night but don't bother asking Charles if it's okay with him. By staying a second night, the boys have exceeded Charles's consent to use the property and are now trespassing.

Necessity can be a valid defense against a trespass action. For example, if a weekend sailor is out on the lake when a storm suddenly threatens the safety of the boat and persons aboard, the sailor can tie up at a nearby pier. But if the boat does any damage to the pier during the storm, the sailor must pay for the repairs. On the other hand, if the pier's owner untied the boat before the storm ended, and the sailor or anyone else aboard was injured or if the boat was damaged, the pier's owner is liable.

In certain cases, you can go onto another's land to recover possession of something that was stolen from you. This usually is allowed only if you are in "hot pursuit" of the person who took it, and you generally can go only onto the land; you can't, for example, break down a door and enter the house.

The most pressing questions many people have about trespassing concern how much force they can use to remove a trespasser from their land. You are entitled to use only "reasonable force" to remove the trespasser. What amount of force is "reasonable" depends on a number of things, including the danger the trespasser poses to your safety. If the trespasser is a harmless tramp, you can ask that he or she leave and gently escort him or her off your property. But you can't use excessive physical force to get someone off the land, unless he or she is threatening immediate serious harm—for example, trying to burn your house down. Ordinarily, you cannot shoot a trespasser unless it is a matter of justified self-defense. If someone refuses to leave your property after being asked to do so, it is usually best to call the police and have them remove the trespasser.

A trespasser is generally liable for all damage done to your property while trespassing upon it, even though the damage is accidental. If, for example, Tony decides—without Victor's consent—to camp out on Victor's property and lights a campfire that through no fault of his spreads and burns down Victor's house, Tony is liable for the damage done, even though he did not intend to damage the house.

OWNERSHIP OF AIRSPACE AND SUBSPACE

Years ago, when you bought a piece of real estate, you became owner of more than just the house and the surface of the land. You also owned the air above ("airspace") as far as you could see and the ground below ("subspace") to the center of the Earth. Anyone crossing above or below your land, no matter how far, was trespassing upon your land unless you permitted it. If your neighbor was mining under your house without your consent, for instance, you could sue to stop it and also get paid for the minerals already taken from your land.

Subspace rights have remained essentially the same over the centuries. Ownership of airspace, on the other hand, has changed considerably. Today, you own only so much of the airspace above your property as you can occupy or use in connection with the land—the "immediate reaches." If an aircraft flies over your land, the pilot is not committing a trespass unless the plane is flying below the altitude prescribed by federal laws or in a way that is dangerous to persons or things on the land.

Nuisance

Penny, your entrepreneurial neighbor, has come up with another scheme to make money: starting a chicken ranch in her backyard. She builds some cages and buys one hundred chickens. Within days, your peaceful solitude is transformed into a dusty, smelly, noisy hell. You ask Penny to get the chickens off her land, but she refuses. What can you do about it? You can sue her for maintaining a nuisance.

There are two distinct types of damages you can ask for in nuisance actions: money damages to compensate you for any injuries or inconveniences you suffered from the nuisance, and an injunction ordering Penny to "abate the nuisance"—to stop the dust, smell, and noise, or completely and permanently shut down the chicken farm. If Penny fails to remove the chickens after being ordered to do so, she can be found in contempt of court and jailed until she gets them out of there.

Not every unpleasant smell or noise is a nuisance, however. The thing must be offensive to the point where it greatly interferes with your use and enjoyment of your property. Minor annoyances are just a fact of modern life that we all have to put up with.

Let's say that a new airport is built near you. The noise, smoke, and vibrations are more than you can stand, so you sue the airport for creating a nuisance. The airport contends that the government authorized the location, and therefore it cannot be held liable. Will that defense succeed? No. The fact that a business of any kind is operating under a government permit and in an area zoned for that kind of activity usually does not prevent you from suing it for being a nuisance.

Suppose that for twenty years, Filbert has been operating a dairy farm about ten miles outside of Metropolis. Although the farm has produced a lot of noise and strong odors throughout its history, no one has ever complained, since the nearest neighbors were two miles away. Metropolis grows, a developer buys the land beside the farm, and a subdivision springs up. The owners of the new homes sue Filbert to abate the nuisance. Filbert argues that he should not be enjoined (stopped) from operating the farm because the developer and homeowners were fully aware of his farm when they bought the land. Will Filbert win with his argument that the people "moved to" the nuisance? No. Simply because he has used his farm in an offensive manner for many years does not give Filbert the right to continue the nuisance. His new neighbors are entitled to enjoy their property free from excessive noise and foul odors and can bring a lawsuit to stop the nuisance.

Overhanging Branches

One frequently encountered problem is that of a neighbor's tree that has grown so large that its branches overhang your property and drops leaves on your otherwise pristine lawn. For example, suppose Les and Sandy own a house. Their next-door neighbors, Tom and Pam, have a large olive tree that overhangs Les and Sandy's yard and pool, and drops olives and leaves onto Les and Sandy's property, creating quite a mess that must be cleaned up every week. Can Les and Sandy force Tom and Pam to cut their olive tree down, or at least trim it back so that it no longer encroaches over Les and Sandy's property?

The rule used in this type of situation is one of "reasonableness." According to this rule, Les and Sandy have the right to trim back the olive tree to their property line, *so long as it does not result in the tree's death*. If the tree is in fact killed by cutting it back, Les and Sandy will have to pay to have the dead tree removed and a new one planted.

If Les and Sandy are otherwise on good terms with Tom and Pam, they might suggest to

Tom and Pam that they split the cost of trimming or removing the tree. Although Tom and Pam are not legally obligated to do so, they may be willing to split the costs with Les and Sandy.

WATER RIGHTS

THE TWO TYPES OF water disputes that arise most frequently are those involving surface water and those involving rivers, lakes, and streams.

Surface Waters

Every spring since he bought his house eight years ago, Dean's property has been flooded with the runoff from rains. He decides to take action and erects some barriers and digs some ditches to divert the water. When the rains come this year, Dean's property is protected. But the water now flows onto Sylvia's land, where it does considerable damage. Sylvia sues Dean to pay for the damage and to remove the barriers and ditches. Who wins?

In some states, Dean wins because surface waters—runoff from rain, melting snow, and springs—are considered a "common enemy." You can divert the water any way you want without worrying about the effects on others. In other states, Sylvia wins because the law prevents you from doing anything that interferes with the "natural flow" of water—you generally must sit back and let the water run its course, even if damage to your property will surely result. Some states permit you to make reasonable changes in the natural flow of the surface water, so long as you avoid unnecessary harm to your neighbors' property.

Watercourses

Suppose that your land borders on a small river. For years, you have been using the water to irrigate your garden, water your cows—whatever. One day you go to dip your bucket in the river, only to find it's all dried or polluted because of a new factory upstream. What can you do about it?

In many states, primarily those east of the Mississippi River, if you own property alongside a watercourse—a river, stream, or lake—you can take a reasonable amount of water from the river, so long as you don't interfere too much with the water supply to others along the river. In many western states, where water is scarcer, the rule is "prior appropriation"—essentially, "first come, first served." The person who uses the water first has priority. If you've been using the water and someone new comes along and interrupts its flow to you, you can sue to stop that person from interfering with your rights. Regardless of which law is applied, you would most likely win a lawsuit to keep the upstream owner from interfering with your water supply.

CONDEMNATION

THROUGH ITS POWER OF "eminent domain," the government can condemn your land—force you to sell it. But the government can't go around condemning land any time it wants for just any purpose. There must be a sufficient public interest, such as making way for a freeway, redeveloping a blighted area, or providing water or electricity to the community.

Usually the government deliberately condemns a house, as when it plans the route of a new road and condemns all the houses in its path. Sometimes, though, the condemnation is the unintended result of another act that effectively makes it impossible for you to live in your house any longer. For example, if the government builds a new airport, and your house is now right beside the runway, the noise and exhaust from the planes make it unhealthy for anyone to live there. This is called "inverse condemnation."

All or only part of the property can be condemned. In either case, you are entitled to be paid the fair market value—"just compensation"—for the land (or portion of land) the government takes from you. Fair market value is the amount a willing buyer would pay a willing seller for the property if the government was not going to condemn the property to build a freeway or a new airport. If you don't think the government is offering enough, you can challenge the amount in court. At the trial, the evidence mainly consists of real estate appraisers testifying as to the value of the land based on sales of comparable parcels in the area. If your land is being condemned, and you want to challenge either the government's right to do so or the amount of money it wants to pay, you're usually better off hiring a lawyer to help you, preferably one experienced in this area of the law.

LATERAL AND SUBJACENT SUPPORT

SUPPOSE THAT YOUR NEIGHBOR decides to put a swimming pool in his or her backyard. One day you come home and find a big crack in your kitchen floor. Looking out the window, you see the cause: the hole for the pool has caved in, taking a good chunk of your property with it and undermining your house's foundation. Is your neighbor liable for damage? Yes. Your neighbor cannot do anything that adversely affects the stability of your land, either from the side ("lateral support") or beneath it ("subjacent support").

The right to lateral and subjacent support generally applies only to land in its natural condition—that is, a vacant, undeveloped lot. Your neighbor might not have to pay for the damage to your house if it can be proved that your land would not have collapsed were it not for the house.

Suppose that one night your daughter leaves a roller skate on the walk leading up to your front door. A person walking to your door slips and falls on the skate and is injured. Are you liable for those injuries?

Historically, your liability to someone injured on your land depended in large part upon who the person was—a trespasser, a visiting friend, a solicitor, the letter carrier, a business client, and so on. You generally weren't liable to trespassers, especially if you didn't know they were there. If the person was on a social visit or was a door-to-door solicitor, you weren't liable unless you knew the skate was there—in which case, you either had to make the walkway safe by moving the skate or warning the visitor of the danger. If the person was the letter carrier, a meter reader, a trash collector, a repairperson, a delivery person, or a business customer, you were liable even though you didn't know the skate was there. To these "business visitors," you owed a duty to inspect your property for dangerous conditions and remove them or to have warned your business visitors of the danger. But you usually didn't have to warn your visitor if the danger was obvious.

Most states have abolished these classifications as arbitrary and hold that a landowner owes only one standard of care toward all people—the duty to exercise reasonable care depending on the situation. (Some states have, however, retained the distinction of trespasser and continue to hold that no duty is owed to the trespasser.) Under the new rule, you must keep your land in a reasonably safe condition and warn anyone who comes onto your property of dangers that are not obvious.

Injuries to Passersby

If someone is injured on a public street or sidewalk while passing by your property—say, on foot, on a bicycle, or in a car—you're generally not liable for their injuries. There are several important exceptions to this rule, however. The first is that you must not do anything on your property that poses a danger to persons off your property. For example, when burning brush on your property, you must do it in a careful manner. If the fire goes out of control and injures others, you are legally responsible for the damage. Another exception is that if you dig a hole on the land next to a public street or sidewalk, you must take adequate precautions to protect passersby from falling into it.

Suppose, for example, that Melinda is walking on a public sidewalk in front of Eric's house, slips on a sheet of ice, and falls and breaks her arm. Can she make Eric pay? The general rule is that a landowner doesn't have to keep public sidewalks clean and free from danger. That is the city's job. So if the sheet of ice resulted from the natural runoff of water or melting snow from Eric's property, he is not liable. But if the ice sheet was formed by a structure on Eric's land—such as the discharge from the eaves—Eric is liable because he created the danger. Eric then has an obligation to keep the sidewalk free of the ice that forms beneath his eaves, and if he doesn't do so, he is liable for the resulting damage.

Fred is walking beside Joanne's property when a branch from a tree in Joanne's yard falls on him. Fred inspects the tree and finds that it is old and rotted and should have been removed years ago. Is Joanne liable to Fred? If Joanne lives in a rural area, probably not, because a rural landowner generally does not have to inspect the trees growing naturally for disease, age, and weakness. On the other hand, if Joanne lives in the city, she must periodically inspect the trees to make sure they are not a danger to anyone. If she doesn't, she is liable for injuries to passersby. These same rules apply if the branch falls onto your neighbor's land and damages your neighbor's car.

Injuries on Recreational Land

Steve owns several acres of land that are used by off-road enthusiasts for motorcycle riding and such. Bert jumps his motorcycle over a small hill, lands in a deep hole hidden on the other side, and is seriously hurt. Bert sues Steve for failing to post a warning that the hole was there. Who wins the case? In many states, Steve will win because a person who lets others use his or her land without charge for recreation is not liable for their injuries. This rule encourages landowners to keep their property open for recreational use of every kind. Without it, landowners, fearing lawsuits, would fence off their property, and the public would suffer. But the landowner is liable for someone's injuries if he or she expressly invited the person onto the property, charged the person a fee for using the land, or deliberately injured the person.

Injuries to Firefighters and Police Officers

A policeman chasing a burglary suspect on the second floor of a building falls through a hole and is injured. Can he sue the building's owner? Usually not. Most states follow the "fireman's rule," which bars a firefighter or police officer injured in the line of duty from suing a landowner for negligence. The reason behind this rule is that firefighters and police officers have chosen professions voluntarily with all sorts of inherent dangers. In other words, they generally assume the risk that they will be injured on the job.

Some states realize that, while they may assume the risk of being shot or burned, police officers and firefighters do not usually assume the risk of being hurt because a building is unsafe. These states allow firefighters and police officers to sue the building's owner for damages and injuries that result from a dangerous condition in the building.

Suppose you hire Bill's Construction Company to add a new bedroom and bathroom to your house. You pay Bill the entire cost up front. You receive "preliminary notices" from the electrician, plumber, and other subcontractors stating they will be improving your house. Not thinking them terribly important, you put them aside. Halfway through the job, Bill walks away from the project. A few weeks later, you start getting notices from the electrician, plumber, and other subcontractors or their attorneys informing you that they will foreclose on the "mechanic's lien" they recorded against your house with the county recorder's office unless immediate payment is forthcoming. What can you do in this situation?

If you can find Bill, you can sue him to recover the money you paid him and pay the subcontractors off. However, by the time you go through this process—assuming you could find Bill in the first place and he has the money to satisfy the judgment against him—the subcontractors will have enforced their mechanic's lien by foreclosing on your property. The main way you can prevent this is to pay the subcontractors out of your pocket. You may be able to negotiate with them to lower their fees. You probably will need to consult with a lawyer in this situation to see just what your rights are and to make sure the subcontractors are in strict compliance with the mechanic's lien laws.

How do you protect yourself in such a situation? Your first mistake was paying Bill's Construction the entire cost up front. You should only pay as much as is needed for each stage of the construction. For instance, if Bill says he needs $7,500 for the electrician, you should get a copy of the electrician's invoice from Bill and then pay Bill the $7,500. When the electrician is paid, you should check with Bill to make sure the electrician was in fact paid in full. The electrician should also sign a full release of lien (and have it notarized so it can be recorded) so he cannot come back and sue you. Only by paying the general contractor in increments and getting the notarized releases from the subcontractors as they do their work can you protect yourself from Bill's skipping town. When you hire a contractor, you should provide in the contract that you will be withholding a certain amount of the price, say 20 percent, until the project is finished and you have received notarized releases from all of the subcontractors.

Suppose a subcontractor files a mechanic's lien against your property, is paid off in full, but then fails to record the full release of the mechanic's lien with the county recorder's office and disappears. The contractor has no idea where he moved. What can you do to get the mechanic's lien removed from your house? About your only recourse when a subcontractor skips out without filing a release of a mechanic's lien is to file a petition to release your property from the mechanic's lien in court. You will need to hire an attorney to do this for you, as mechanic's lien law can be very complicated and technical.

SEVEN

Landlord-Tenant Issues

WITH THE RISING COSTS of homes in the last twenty years, it is a sure bet that owning a house—long the American dream—will be beyond the reach of many. This means that the number of people who rent apartments, houses, condominiums, and townhomes is certain to keep increasing steadily.

In the landlord-tenant relationship there are reciprocal rights and duties that each side should respect. Much too often, landlord and tenant view each other as adversaries, to be hated and feared. As the tension mounts, problems seem to grow until finally one side explodes: The landlord orders the tenant to leave or changes the lock, or the tenant refuses to pay the rent or abandons the apartment without warning and disappears.

Both landlord and tenant alike should realize that each is dependent upon the other and should strive toward a businesslike—or at least tolerable—working relationship. A landlord wants the peace of mind that comes from knowing that the rent will be paid on time, that the tenant will keep the apartment clean and not damage it, and that the tenant will not interfere with the landlord's or other tenants' enjoyment of their units by, for example, excessive noise. The other side of the coin? A good landlord will lease the apartment in a clean condition and will ensure that all repairs to appliances, fixtures, and the building are made promptly. A good landlord will respect the tenant's right to privacy and not enter the unit without giving the tenant a day or two's notice, unless there is an emergency.

A landlord is generally free to accept or reject prospective tenants as he or she sees fit. The landlord's main interest, of course, is to find tenants who will be able to pay rent on time and won't damage the apartment. But there are some restrictions on the landlord's ability to refuse a prospective tenant. A landlord cannot refuse to rent the apartment to you because of your race, national origin, religion, or sex. In some states, except in senior-only complexes, a landlord usually cannot turn you down (or end your lease) just because you have children, even if the apartments are advertised as adults-only.

Animals are quite a different matter. Landlords have the right to limit or prohibit animals on their property. You'll usually need the landlord's written consent to have a pet live with you. You'll also probably have to pay a higher security deposit to cover any damage the animal may do to the premises.

TYPES OF LEASES

THE TWO MOST COMMON TYPES of leases are the "month-to-month" lease and a lease for a specific period of time—often six months or a year. A month-to-month lease, or "periodic tenancy," is one that continues until the tenant or the landlord notifies the other that he or she is terminating the lease. A periodic tenancy is renewed automatically for another term if neither party gives the other "timely" notice to end it. How much notice do you have to give your landlord—or does your landlord have to give you—to end the lease? If it's a month-to-month lease or greater (for instance, year to year), only thirty days' notice before the lease ends usually is required, unless the written lease agreement provides for a longer time. Some states require the landlord to give the tenant sixty days' notice. But if it's a week-to-week tenancy, only seven days' notice by either party is needed.

A tenancy for a definite time—a "tenancy for years"—is a lease for a certain period of time: one year, five years, two months, even fifteen days—any definite time period. (But when you go to a hotel, motel, or inn and request a room for, say, three days, this does not create a tenancy for years; you merely receive a "license" to use the room.) When the last day of this type of lease arrives, the lease ends automatically. Neither landlord nor tenant has to notify the other that the lease is over; the tenant is expected to be out of the apartment unless a new arrangement has been made.

Two other types of tenancies less frequently encountered are "tenancies at will" and "tenancies at sufferance." In a tenancy at will you can live in the apartment for as long as the landlord says. (Some tenancies at will are at the will of the tenant; you can live there as long as you want.) A tenancy at will ends when either you or the landlord dies, when the landlord sells the property, when the landlord tells you to leave, or when you move out. Many states require that the landlord give you notification of a certain amount of time—such as thirty or sixty days—that the lease is over. Other states still apply the old common law rule that a tenancy at will ends immediately when the lease expires. In other words, you have to pack up and get off the property without delay when the landlord tells you to leave.

A tenancy at sufferance arises when you stay in the apartment without paying rent after the lease is over. You can stay as long as the landlord lets you, or until the landlord begins legal proceedings to evict you. When you stay on after the lease ends, you are a "holdover tenant." If the landlord accepts a rent check from you, however, you now have a periodic tenancy (usually a month-to-month tenancy), and your landlord will have to give you proper notice to end the lease. Say that you have leased an apartment for two years at $800 a month. Two years later, the lease automatically ends. The next day, you give your landlord a check for $800, which is cheerfully accepted. You now have a month-to-month tenancy. You must give your landlord thirty days notice if you plan to leave, and your landlord must likewise notify you thirty to sixty days in advance if he or she wants to terminate your lease.

The Written Lease

Leases for one year or more generally are required to be in writing. Although month-to-month rentals don't have to be in writing, it is always best to have a written lease. The reason is that most of your rights and obligations as either a landlord or tenant are determined by the provisions of the lease agreement. A few rights—such as the right to a livable apartment ("the implied warranty of habitability")—are imposed by law regardless of what the lease says or doesn't say. Having the terms of the lease in writing and signed by both landlord and tenant reduces the chances for disputes over how much the rent is, how long the lease is, and who has to do what.

Most landlords use a standardized lease form bought from the stationery store, one prepared by the real estate industry to favor landlords. Before signing a lease and moving in, read it over carefully and thoroughly. Make sure that the lease you get is legible, not a copy of a copy of a copy that was bad to begin with. If you can't read the copy you're handed, ask for one that is clear.

As a tenant, it is to your benefit to negotiate the most favorable provisions before you sign the lease and move in. If you find something objectionable, mention it before you sign. But let's look at this realistically. If you live in a big city, where rents are high and vacancies low, when you find an apartment you like and can afford, the landlord is going to shove a lease under your nose with the admonishment "Take it or leave it." Face it—the average person doesn't have much bargaining strength when it comes to leases. You either agree to everything the landlord says and sign the lease, or you keep looking. The only time you have a real shot at changing some provisions of an apartment lease is if you're in an area where the vacancy rate is high or if you're dealing with someone who is new to the business of landlording.

The lease should contain the basics: who the landlord is; who the tenant is; the address and unit number of the apartment; how long the lease lasts; and the amount of rent and when it is due (for instance, the first day of the month). If the tenant has the option to renew the lease at a set price, this too should be included.

The lease should specify everything that is included in the rental price. For example, is a garage or outdoor parking space included? If so, clearly spell this out in the lease. Who pays the apartment utilities—electricity, gas, water, and trash collection—the landlord or the tenant? If the landlord tells you that the rent includes, say, water and gas, make sure you get this in the lease. Other things, such as who has to make repairs, whether the tenant can paint or make other improvements to the unit, and what the landlord's rights are if the tenant abandons the apartment without paying rent should also be included in the lease.

Many leases have a grace period of two to three days after the due date for the rent. After that, a penalty of, say, $25 is charged. Can the landlord charge this fee? Technically, no. The courts generally do not look favorably upon penalties and therefore do not enforce them. However, if you don't pay the late fee, you probably can expect to receive a notice of termination of the lease. You could fight it in court and probably win, but it would cost more time and be more of a hassle than it's worth. The moral here: Pay your rent on time.

If you have been a good tenant for a while and always paid your rent on time, suppose your rent check is going to be two weeks late because of a foul-up at the home office in processing your paycheck. Should you mention that to your landlord and ask for an extension of time? By all means, yes. Without telling your landlord of the delay, your landlord may slap a "pay rent or quit" notice on your front door and have one hand-delivered to you telling you that if you don't pay your rent in three days, you'll be evicted. But if you've been a good tenant and inform your landlord of the anticipated delay in paying your rent, your landlord should be understanding. Who knows, your landlord may even waive the late fee!

If You Have a Roommate

If you're renting an apartment with someone else, the landlord usually will have each of you sign the lease. Both of you then become "jointly and severally" liable for the rent. This means that each of you is individually liable for the full amount of each month's rent. If your cotenant doesn't pay his or her share, you will have to pay it as well as your own share or face eviction. You can ask the landlord to include a clause in the lease that makes you liable for only your share of the rent, but few landlords will agree to this.

If you are planning on sharing an apartment with someone else, you should lay down certain ground rules—preferably in writing—to prevent disputes. First, reach an agreement about the amount of rent each will pay. Will it be split in half, or will some other arrangement be made? If there is a one-car garage, who gets it? Will utility bills be split in half? Take note that if you signed the utility service agreements, such as the telephone company, the phone company can seek full payment from you—even if it was your roommate who made all those long-distance calls. If you have a roommate, the best thing to do is to get a separate telephone line for each of you in your own separate names. If your roommate tells you he or she can't get a phone number in his or her own name, let this serve as a warning that your roommate may have a problem racking up long-distance bills and then being unable to pay for them.

SECURITY DEPOSITS

THE LANDLORD WILL REQUIRE every new tenant to pay a certain amount of money as a "security deposit" before leasing the apartment. The purpose of the security deposit is to protect the landlord from tenants who abandon the apartment without paying the rent or to pay for damages tenants have done to the unit.

Most states now have laws regulating how much of a deposit the landlord can ask the tenant to pay for security. In many states, a landlord of a residential unit can ask a new tenant to deposit an amount of up to two months' rent as security. This includes security however it may be disguised: as a security deposit; the last month's rent; or a cleaning deposit. For instance, if the monthly rent for the apartment is $800, the landlord can require the tenant to post up to $1,600 as a deposit. (This $1,600 is in addition to the first month's rent, so it will cost the tenant $2,400 to move in.)

The lease should state clearly how much money the landlord receives from the tenant and include an itemized account of what each sum represents. For example, if $800 was for the first month's rent, $800 for the last month's rent, $500 for a security deposit, and $300 for cleaning costs, this should be specified in the lease before you sign it. Any other sums paid by the tenant—as a deposit for the keys, for example—also should be listed separately. Some states require the landlord to place the security in a separate bank account, and some make the landlord pay the tenant interest on the money so deposited.

RIGHTS AND OBLIGATIONS OF THE LANDLORD AND THE TENANT

Moving into Your New Apartment

The landlord must have the apartment ready for you to move into on the agreed date. If it isn't ready when promised, you are entitled to damages resulting from the landlord's breach of this duty. For instance, if it costs you $500 to live in a hotel and store your furniture while you wait for the apartment, the landlord has to pay this. The landlord can, however, deduct from this the amount of rent you would have paid for the apartment during this same period; so if you would have paid $200 in rent to the landlord for the time you spent in the hotel, the landlord owes you $300.

If the previous tenant refuses to move out, the landlord may start legal proceedings to evict him or her. If, for any reason, the landlord doesn't have the apartment ready for you within a reasonable length of time after it was promised, you usually can treat this as a breach of the lease. You are now free of your obligations under the lease and even can sue the landlord for any damages you suffer. If you had a six-month lease, for example, and it costs you an extra $150 a month to rent a comparable apartment, you can sue the landlord for the additional $150 per month for the length of the lease.

Before signing the lease and moving in, inspect the apartment to see if it is clean and undamaged. If you run across any defects, such as a hole in the wall or a leaking toilet, write them all down on a piece of paper and ask the landlord to sign it. This protects you from a landlord who tries to charge you for "your" damage later on. Also get written assurance from the landlord that all of the problems will be corrected promptly. If the landlord refuses to sign your inventory of defects, seriously think about finding another apartment. If you still want to move into the apartment despite the landlord's refusal to sign an inventory of defects, take pictures of the defects to prove they existed when you moved in should there be any dispute when you move out.

Making Changes to the Apartment

Most residential leases prohibit you from making any changes or additions to the apartment—painting, wallpapering, or paneling, to name a few. All you're usually allowed to do is move your furniture in and hang a few pictures on the wall. Before making any changes or improvements, carefully read your lease. Does it forbid alterations or "fixtures" without the landlord's prior written consent? A fixture is something that is attached to the building, such as a shelf that is nailed to the wall. (Fixtures are much more frequent in business leases, which are discussed below.)

When you move out, can you take your improvements with you? Again, what does your lease say? If it states that all fixtures become the property of the landlord, you must leave them there, even if you put them in with the landlord's permission. You usually can remove your own fixtures only if you can do so without much damage to the apartment. And if there is any damage to the apartment from the installation or removal of an improvement, you must pay to have the damage fixed.

Who Is Responsible for Making Repairs?

You've been living in your apartment for five months, when all at once everything seems to start falling apart: the air conditioner or heater stops working; there's no hot water; and the kitchen faucet is leaking. Whose responsibility is it to fix these things, yours or the landlord's? First look at your lease. What does it say? Whatever the lease provides is what a judge ordinarily will follow.

But if the lease doesn't mention a thing about repairs, then the first thing to consider is what is customary in the area. If tenants usually take care of leaky faucets and burned-out lightbulbs, then you probably will have to do these things yourself. More major repairs are usually the responsibility of the landlord, although the extent of the landlord's duty to make repairs sometimes depends in part upon what is being rented. If the tenant is renting one apartment in a large apartment building, generally the landlord has to take care of all the repairs. But if the tenant is renting a house, the tenant may have to make minor repairs, such as fixing leaky faucets and small holes in the roof.

With apartment leases, most states have shifted the burden of making all but the most minor repairs onto the landlord. Without an agreement to the contrary in the lease (perhaps the tenant has agreed to make certain repairs in exchange for lower rent), for the typical apartment rental, the landlord usually must fix all damage and defects, except for those caused by the tenant. If you caused the damage, you must either repair it yourself or pay the landlord the cost of repairing it.

As a tenant, you have the responsibility to inform the landlord promptly when a repair is needed. If you wait awhile before telling the landlord and the condition gets worse, you may have to pay for some of the repairs. The landlord must make the repairs a reasonable time after being notified by the tenant. What is a reasonable time depends on the circumstances—for example, a heater failing in the dead of winter requires faster action than one that breaks down in the summer. If the landlord fails to make the needed repairs within a reasonable time after being notified of the problem, some states permit you to make the repairs yourself (or hire someone to do it for you) and deduct the cost of repairs from your rent.

Your right to make repairs and deduct the cost from the rent is limited; it may be as little as $100 a year, and the most any state allows you to deduct is not more than the equivalent of one month's rent each year. Before you resort to doing the repair yourself, notify your landlord in writing that if the repairs are not done within a certain period of time (for example, one week), you will go ahead and make the repairs yourself and deduct their cost from your rent. This is often enough to spur the landlord to action.

Some states do not let the tenant make the repairs and deduct the cost from the rent. In this situation, the only way you can get an unwilling landlord to make a repair is to bring a lawsuit against the landlord. Before suing your landlord, write him or her a letter specifying what the defect is and requesting that it be fixed promptly. Keep a copy of the letter for your files. If you can, take several pictures of the defect, so you can show the judge what you're talking about if it gets that far. Have a repair company inspect the damage and give you a written estimate. If the defect threatens your health or safety, a call or visit to the health department may help you get some results. A complaint to the housing or building department may be in order if the problem is related to the structure. Note that if you decide to do the repairs yourself, you are entitled to be reimbursed by the landlord for your costs of the materials used; you are not, however, entitled to charge for your time and labor in making the repair.

Injuries to Tenants and Their Guests

As you climb the stairs leading to your friend's apartment, your foot hits a loose step. You fall and break your arm. Who is liable, the landlord or the tenant? Usually the landlord. Why? Because the injury occurred in the "common area." The common area is everything outside of the tenants' apartments: hallways, stairs, the grounds, the parking lot, the swimming pool—any place that other tenants or members of the public are permitted to go.

Unlike the individual apartment units, which the tenant has exclusive possession of, the landlord retains control of the common area. It is the landlord's duty to keep the common area in a safe condition so that tenants and their guests do not injure themselves. The landlord must, for instance, provide adequate lighting to illuminate walkways, maintain stairways in good repair, and keep the elevator operating safely. If there is a swimming pool, recreation facilities, and the like, the landlord must keep them clean, sanitary, and safe. The landlord must also keep the building safe and in good shape. If a tenant or guest falls from an unguarded second-story balcony or slips on a steep stairway that doesn't have a handrail, the landlord may be liable.

A tenant is not liable to a guest injured in the apartment's common area unless the tenant created the danger. If you put your bicycle on the landing in front of your apartment, for example, and it falls on a guest who is walking up the stairs, you are liable. Although the guest was injured in a common area—the stairs—you created the danger by putting your bike there.

Your friend Theresa is cooking dinner for you in your apartment. She pulls on the oven door, but it doesn't open. She tugs a little harder, and the door falls off its hinges and lands on her foot, breaking several toes. You forgot to tell her to be careful because the oven door is broken. Are you liable for her injuries, even though the stove belongs to your landlord? Yes. You must warn your guests of dangers in your apartment, even if the thing doesn't belong to you. Can Theresa sue your landlord as well? If you haven't yet told your landlord of the loose oven door, your landlord probably isn't liable to Theresa. But if you notified your landlord of the problem a while ago, and it still hasn't been fixed, your landlord may also be liable. Once informed that something needs repair, the landlord must repair it within a reasonable time or risk being sued by someone who is injured by it. In any event, you are personally liable to Theresa for failing to warn her of the broken door, which is one reason you should have renter's insurance (discussed below).

Suppose that Tony has a vicious German shepherd, which he keeps at his apartment. One day Ted, a repairman, comes to fix the refrigerator. While Ted is working, the dog attacks and severely injures him. Tony is liable to Ted, since Tony owns the dog. But is Tony's landlord liable as well? In a number of states, a landlord is liable for injuries caused by a tenant's pet if the landlord knows the animal is dangerous before renting the apartment or renewing the lease yet still rents the apartment to the tenant. Some states hold that if the landlord has the power to end the lease, he or she must order the tenant to get rid of the animal or terminate the lease.

Les hires George as night janitor for his apartment building without checking into his past. A few weeks later, George uses his passkey to enter an apartment and rapes the tenant inside. It turns out that George had just been released from prison after serving several years for rape. Is Les liable to the rape victim for failing to investigate George's background before hiring him? Yes. A landlord must take care in hiring employees, particularly employees who will have access to the tenants' apartments. A landlord must make a reasonably thorough search of the prospective employee's background. In this case, a search no doubt would have revealed George's recent criminal history. A prudent landlord would not have hired George, or at least would have supervised him closely and not have given him free use of the passkey.

Suppose that a tenant is raped or robbed on the apartment grounds by an unknown assailant, someone who was not an employee. Is the landlord liable to the tenant in this situation? Some states hold that a landlord is not liable for criminal assaults by unknown persons. A number of other states, however, hold the landlord responsible if previous assaults or robberies have occurred on the grounds, yet the landlord hasn't done anything to discourage the criminals. For instance, the landlord must see that the hallways and grounds are well lit at night. In some cases, the landlord must hire a security guard to protect the front door or to patrol the grounds and buildings.

If you are a landlord and are interested in protecting both your tenants' safety and yourself from a lawsuit, you can take several simple steps to reduce the risk of criminal attacks and your liability for them. First of all, every apartment door should be equipped with a dead-bolt lock. Windows should also be equipped with some type of locking device. The stairwells and common area should be kept well lit at night. If the apartment building is in a high-crime area, you may wish to install a fence or other enclosure around the building and keep it locked. Give the tenants their own keys to it, and install a telephone or intercom system so guests can let tenants know they're there. You should also conduct a thorough check of the background of any person before hiring him or her and keep track of all master passkeys.

"Quiet Enjoyment": Your Right to Peace and Quiet

When you rent an apartment you expect to have some peace and quiet. Whether it is stated or not, every lease comes with a promise of "quiet enjoyment"—that the tenant will be free from unwarranted intrusions by the landlord or other tenants. Certainly complete silence is impossible in today's society, particularly in crowded cities. But you don't have to put up with a landlord who barges in unannounced or neighbors who are exploring new decibel levels with their stereos.

Does this mean the landlord can't ever enter your apartment? Not at all. Your landlord can enter the unit to inspect it for damage, make repairs, or show it to a prospective tenant after you have given notice that you are moving out. Before entering the unit, however, the landlord must give you reasonable notice of the entry. Unless it's an emergency, the landlord should notify you at least twenty-four hours before the planned entry. A landlord who enters without giving the tenant adequate notice may be committing a trespass and invasion of privacy. And if your landlord continually enters your apartment without reason or notice, you may have the right to end the lease, move out, and sue your landlord for damages.

If another tenant in the building is driving you crazy with noise, and your landlord has done nothing about it despite your repeated requests, again you may have the right to move out and sue your landlord. Likewise, if threats from other tenants make you fear for your safety, and the landlord ignores your complaints, you are being denied your right to "quiet enjoyment" of your apartment.

Renter's Insurance

So, you're renting an apartment; no need to get renter's insurance since the landlord's insurance covers not only damage to the structure, but also damage to or loss of your belongings, right? Wrong. When you rent an apartment, the apartment owner's insurance policy covers only damage to or destruction of the physical structure, that is, the building, as well as persons injured on common ground. It does not cover loss of or damage to your property, or persons injured by your negligence.

Basic renter's insurance policies cover losses to your personal property from perils such as fire, smoke, water, electricity, theft, automobiles, lightning, wind, explosion, riot, damage by glass, and more. Flood and earthquake coverage is also available, but they have to be purchased by a separate policy or rider on your renter's policy.

When buying a renter's policy, you will have a choice between buying a policy that gives you the actual cash value of the property at the time it was destroyed or stolen, or the replacement cost, which is the price of going out and buying a new item of the same kind to replace the destroyed or stolen property. Suppose you bought a television five years ago for $600. If your policy is one for actual cash value, your insurance company will pay only what the television was worth when it was destroyed or stolen. As a rule of thumb, in such cases insurance companies deduct 10 percent depreciation a year, so your actual cash value would be only $300, since you had had it for five years, which would result in a 50 percent depreciation. You also would have to pay the deductible of, say, $100, so you would net only $200.

Replacement value coverage costs more than actual cash value but will pay more if you ever need to make a claim. Using the example above, the replacement value would be at least $600 (minus any deductible). Because it provides a higher payout, replacement value insurance costs more than insurance that provides only actual cash value.

If you have any particularly valuable items, such as jewelry or an expensive coin or stamp collection, make sure you let your insurance carrier know about them so a special rider can be used to cover them. Computers are generally insurable only for the hardware and software equipment and not for the information you have stored on them.

Renter's insurance is also important because it provides liability protection. If you injure someone in an accident other than one that is automobile-related (in which case your automobile insurance applies), your renter's insurance will provide you protection up to the stated amount, which we recommend should be at least $100,000 per person to a maximum of $300,000 per incident. For instance, if someone is visiting your apartment and slips on a puddle of water in the bathroom that you forgot to wipe up and breaks his or her leg, your renter's insurance liability coverage will take care of it. The liability coverage is not limited to injuries occurring in your apartment. It covers injuries you inflict no matter where you are. The two main exceptions to coverage are automobile accidents (as we have already seen) and injuries based on your intentional conduct, such as punching another person in the nose and breaking it.

If you are thinking about getting a dog, you may want to think twice about the breed you are getting. Most insurance companies are reluctant about writing policies for owners of certain breeds: Doberman pinschers, rottweilers, and pit bulls, for example. You may be able to obtain coverage, but it can be quite expensive.

Discounts typically are offered for smoke and fire detectors, burglar alarms, and fire extinguishers. Some insurance companies may offer discounts to persons who buy both automobile insurance and a renter's policy from them.

Rent Increases and Rent Control

You have been living in your apartment for six months, when your landlord slips a note under your door stating that beginning next month, your rent is being increased. Do you have to pay the increase? If your lease provides that you are renting the apartment for, say, one year at $800 per month, your landlord cannot raise the rent during that time. The landlord has made a contract to rent you an apartment for a specified price for a definite term and is bound by the terms of the contract. If, however, you have a month-to-month lease, and it is silent as to any rent increases, then in the absence of rent control laws, when your lease expires, the landlord can raise your rent as much as he or she wants.

Because of escalating rents, a number of cities and counties have passed laws limiting rent increases to no more than a specified maximum amount, such as 8 or 10 percent per year. The amount of increase is supposed to give the landlord a fair return on his or her investment, taking into account the cost of repairs, improvements, and depreciation of the buildings, among other things. If the landlord wants to raise the rent more than the maximum allowed, he or she will have to get permission from the proper governmental agency. A public hearing may be required, at which the tenants can appear and voice their objections to the proposed hike. Many rent control laws apply only to apartment buildings of a certain size—more than four units, for example. If a building is exempt from rent control, the landlord can raise the rent as much as he or she wants.

Ceilings on rent increases usually apply only to tenants who remain in their apartments. Once a tenant moves out, under many ordinances the landlord can raise the rent to what the market will bear. If you are a landlord or tenant in a district covered by rent control, you should scrutinize carefully all applicable rent control laws before increasing rent or challenging a rent increase. You will find the rent control laws in your city and county ordinances at the public library. There may be a rent control office at city hall that also can answer your questions.

Whether or not rent control is in effect, a landlord must give the tenants proper notice of the rent increase. Generally, the landlord must give each tenant thirty days' written notice before the increase takes effect. Suppose the landlord wishes to increase the rent on July 1. All tenants must receive written notice of the increase on or before June 1. If notice is given after June 1, normally the landlord is not able to enforce the rent increase until August 1.

Subleases and Assignments

Most residential leases prohibit a tenant from subleasing the apartment or assigning the lease without the landlord's prior written consent. A "sublease" involves a transfer of less than all the lease. For instance, if you're living by yourself in a two-bedroom apartment and decide to rent the spare bedroom out to someone else, that is a sublease. Or, if you rent the whole apartment to someone for a couple of months while you're traveling across the United States that, too, is a sublease. In an "assignment," you transfer the entire lease to another person. For example, if a new job requires you to move out of state, and there are six months remaining on the lease, it is called an assignment if someone agrees to take over the lease for you.

Suzanne's lease prohibits her from assigning it without the landlord's written permission but doesn't say a word about subletting. Can she sublet the apartment to her friend? Yes; if the lease states only that an assignment is forbidden, the tenant still can sublet the apartment. Conversely, if the lease bars only subletting, the tenant can assign the lease without the landlord's approval. Both actions are prohibited only if the lease says that the tenant cannot sublease the apartment or assign the lease without the landlord's consent. Note, however, that some cities, such as New York, have ordinances regulating subleases that take precedence over private agreements.

Unless it states otherwise, when the lease prohibits you from subletting or assigning without your landlord's consent, ordinarily the landlord can arbitrarily refuse to permit a sublease or assignment. Some states and many leases now provide that the landlord must not unreasonably withhold consent to a sublease or assignment, however. So if you find someone who will be at least as good a tenant as you—who will pay the rent on time, not play the stereo too loud, and so on—the landlord must accept your subtenant.

When you sublease your apartment, you remain liable for the rent. Your subtenant ordinarily doesn't have to answer to the landlord, only to you. Your landlord generally can sue only you for the rent. If your subtenant doesn't pay the rent on time, your landlord can start eviction proceedings against you. If several months' back rent is due, you are responsible for it, just as you ultimately remain responsible for keeping the apartment in good shape. What can you do if you end up paying the delinquent rent or for repairs on damage your subtenant did to the apartment? You can ask your subtenant to reimburse you for this money and take him or her to small claims court if he or she refuses to pay (or hire a lawyer if the amount is substantial).

Unlike in a sublease, in an assignment if the subtenant (technically, the "assignee" of your lease) fails to pay the rent, the landlord can sue your assignee. The landlord also can sue your assignee for any damage to the apartment that he or she is responsible for. Be aware, however, that your landlord normally still can sue you as well, even if the landlord consented to the assignment.

Before you sublease your apartment or assign the lease, make sure your subtenant or assignee is a responsible person who will pay the rent on time and will not damage the apartment. In a sublease or assignment, you become a landlord to your subtenant or assignee. You should protect yourself just as any landlord would: demand a security deposit equal to at least one month's rent and put the terms of the sublease in writing, including the length of the sublease or assignment, the amount of rent, when and to whom it is payable, late charges, payment of damages, and so on. Many stationers have standard sublease and assignment forms that will cover you adequately. Make sure you read a form over carefully before using it, as the forms published by one company can be much different from those of another. If you are assigning your lease, be sure to include a provision that you have the right to reenter the apartment and retake possession of it if the assignee fails to pay the rent. This gives you some additional protection if the assignee defaults on the lease.

What if you have to move out of the apartment for some reason, say, six months before your lease expires, but you don't want to worry about a subtenant or assignee? Your lease may give you the right to cancel it by giving two or three months' notice. (In a month-to-month lease, you usually can end it by giving your landlord thirty days notice; see below.) If it doesn't, one thing to consider is offering to find a new tenant (subject to your landlord's approval, of course) at your trouble and expense. When you do find someone suitable, ask the landlord to sign a document releasing you from the lease. Arrange for the new tenant to pay the required security deposit, and ask that yours be returned. The landlord will want to have the new tenant sign a lease. If your landlord will do this, you are no longer liable for the rent or for the acts of the new tenant. This solution should be acceptable to a reasonable landlord.

If the Tenant Moves Out or Abandons the Apartment

When Your Lease Is Up and You Move Out

In a month-to-month lease, when you decide to move out you will have to notify your landlord in writing thirty days ahead of time. If you have a tenancy for a certain period of time—

say, one year—at the end of the year, you have to be out unless your landlord renews the lease. You should talk to your landlord about renewing the lease at least one to three months before it expires.

Suppose you took possession of the apartment on September 1, on a month-to-month lease. On December 15, you notify your landlord that you will be moving out in thirty days. Your landlord tells you that you have to pay rent through February 1 because you have to give thirty days' notice from the first of the month, since you moved in on the first. Is that true? No. Generally, you only have to give thirty days' notice whenever you want—the beginning, the middle, or the end of the month, or anytime in between. Your lease then expires thirty days from the date you notified your landlord that you are leaving.

You must be out of the apartment on or before the date the lease expires. When you leave, the apartment must be in the same condition as it was when you moved in, except for normal wear and tear—some wear on the carpet, a few small holes in the wall where you hung your pictures, and the like. If you aren't out of the apartment on time, the landlord can charge you rent for every day you or your furniture remains in the apartment. The landlord also can collect any other damages suffered because of your delay in moving out. For instance, if the landlord has to pay the next tenant for storing his or her furniture while waiting for you to leave, the landlord can seek reimbursement of these costs from you.

Suppose you have notified your landlord that you will be moving out at the end of next month. When the first of the month comes, your landlord knocks on your door, asking for this month's rent. You tell the landlord to use the security deposit. Your landlord refuses, threatening that if you don't pay the rent tomorrow, eviction proceedings will be started against you, and you'll be thrown out of there in a week. Who's right? It boils down to what the lease agreement provides. If a certain sum was designated in the lease as the last month's rent, then you have every right to tell the landlord to use that money to pay the last month's rent. On the other hand, if the lease refers only to a "security deposit" or "cleaning deposit," then you do have to pay the last month's rent.

Before vacating the premises and giving the landlord the key back, you should arrange to meet the landlord (or apartment manager) in the empty, cleaned apartment to discuss any deductions the landlord intends to make from the cleaning deposit. If you feel that the apartment is in the same or better condition than it was when you moved in, tell the landlord so. The landlord should be specific about complaints of damage or uncleanliness if all or part of the security deposit will be withheld. If you have the landlord inspect the apartment a day or two before the lease officially ends, and the landlord points out some problems, consider doing the extra work yourself. This way you can get back more or all of your deposit. If you don't agree with your landlord's assessment of the apartment's condition, a lawsuit in small claims court may be the best way of getting your money back. It is a good idea to take pictures of the apartment after you cleaned it to support your position to the judge. Some states now require the landlord, upon receipt of the tenant's notice that he or she will be vacating the apartment in thirty days, to give the tenant written notice of the right to request an initial inspection with the landlord prior to the move-out inspection.

State laws often require the landlord to return what's left of the security deposit within a certain time—say, two weeks after you move out. Some states require the landlord to include an itemized statement of damages or cleaning costs to account for the amount deducted from the deposit. If the landlord doesn't return your full security deposit, and there is no statement of charges, you should write the landlord and ask for a full explanation of how the money was used. If you don't agree with the itemized statement, your letter should be clear and specific as to why you disagree. A second letter demanding the return of your full security deposit may be in order if you're not satisfied with the landlord's response or if the landlord doesn't respond at all. If this doesn't solve anything, then filing a suit in small claims court may be your next step (see chapter 19).

If Your Apartment Becomes Unlivable

The landlord must deliver the apartment to you in a clean, sanitary, and otherwise livable condition. And after you move in, the landlord must do his or her part to keep the apartment and building fit for human living: The trash must be removed from the hallway and other common areas; heaters and plumbing must be repaired when they break down; rats, mice, and other vermin must be controlled; and so forth. This is known as the "warranty of habitability." You must do your share to keep the apartment habitable by cleaning it regularly. You generally cannot claim that the place is unfit to live in if you are responsible for the unsanitary condition.

If the apartment becomes unfit for you to live in, you have several options. You can keep paying rent and sue your landlord for damages (ordinarily the difference between the amount of rent you are paying and what a fair rent is in light of the apartment's condition); you can terminate the lease and move out; or, in some states, you can stay in the apartment without paying rent for as long as the apartment remains uninhabitable. The apartment must actually be unlivable to take advantage of these options. If living in the apartment is merely unpleasant or inconvenient, then your sole option generally is to sue the landlord for a reduction in the rent.

Before taking any action, document your complaints as thoroughly as possible. Send the landlord a letter or two clearly identifying the problems and asking that they be corrected immediately. (Remember to keep copies of everything you send the landlord so you can show them to a judge, if you need to.) If possible, take pictures of the problem; for example, show the hallway with the mounds of garbage and the rats crawling over it. Keep a journal of the problems and your efforts to get some action. Get written and signed statements from friends, visitors, and neighbors to support your complaints. Another thing you can do is contact the local health department and complain to them. This may be enough to motivate the landlord into resolving the problem.

If you live in an apartment building and the unsanitary conditions are widespread, consider joining forces with the other tenants in the building. There is strength in numbers, particularly in landlord-tenant disputes. The landlord may not pay any attention to a single tenant, but you can bet your voices will be heard if, say, fifty percent or more of the tenants get together to demand action. If you still don't get any satisfaction, the tenants may be able to go on a "rent strike." In a rent strike, all rent money is placed in a special bank account, frequently under the supervision of the court, rather than being paid directly to the landlord. The landlord gets the money only when the repairs are made, or the money can be used to make the repairs. Rent strikes should be undertaken only upon the advice of a lawyer, particularly since not all states allow them.

Suppose your landlord is letting the building deteriorate: the heating breaks down; the trash hasn't been taken out; and rats are running all over the building. You have complained repeatedly to your landlord, but nothing has been done, so you go to the health department. Your landlord finds this out, tells you to leave today, and changes the locks. Can your landlord get away with this? No. A landlord cannot evict a tenant in retaliation for the tenant's attempt to enforce a legal right. This is called a "retaliatory eviction." If this happens to you, you should see a lawyer immediately. The lawyer may be able to keep you in the apartment. And even if you are forced out of the apartment, you can still sue your landlord for damages.

If the Tenant Abandons the Apartment

Six months remain on your lease, but you've decided to move. You talk to your landlord about it, but he or she refuses to let you out of the lease. So one night, without any warning to your landlord, you move all of your furniture out of the apartment and disappear. By abandoning the apartment, you "surrender" it to the landlord. The first question is whether the landlord accepts your surrender. If he or she does, you are completely out of the lease, although you are still obligated to pay any rent that is past due and for any damage to the apartment in excess of your security deposit. But if the landlord doesn't accept your surrender, you remain responsible for the full rent to the end of the lease. How do you know if the landlord has accepted your surrender? Sometimes, if the landlord can find you, the landlord will tell you directly—in person or by letter—whether or not he or she accepts the surrender and releases you from the lease. More often, the landlord's actions indicate whether or not your surrender of the apartment is accepted. If the landlord doesn't make any attempt to relet the unit, your surrender isn't accepted. But if the landlord does rent the apartment to someone else, this indicates that he or she has accepted your surrender.

A number of states require the landlord to make a good faith effort to relet the apartment after a tenant abandons it. But if it takes two months to find a new tenant, and the landlord did not expressly accept your surrender when you left, you are responsible for the rent during those two months that the apartment remained empty. Suppose the landlord manages to rent the apartment to another tenant but for, say, $150 less a month than you were paying. Can the landlord require you to pay that $150 for each month remaining on your original lease? Again the question is whether or not the landlord accepted your surrender. If he or she did, then you don't have to make up the difference in rent. But if your surrender was not accepted, you do remain liable for the $150 a month. In this situation, many states require the landlord to send you a letter informing you that he or she is not releasing you from your obligations under the lease and is reletting the apartment on your behalf. If the landlord doesn't send such a letter, you are released from the lease when it is relet.

Let's say you abandon the apartment with ten months remaining on the lease, at $800 monthly, and the landlord refuses to accept your surrender of the unit. Can the landlord file a lawsuit the next day for the balance of the rent—that is, the full $8,000? No. The landlord can sue only for rent that is past due at the time the lawsuit is filed. So when you don't pay your rent on the first of the month as required by the lease, the landlord can sue you, but only for that month's rent. To sue for the entire $8,000 the landlord could file ten separate lawsuits—one for each month—or wait and file one lawsuit for the full $8,000 ten months later. (Remember, in the meantime the landlord may have a legal obligation to attempt to find a tenant to take your place.)

Here is a practical note for landlords: If a tenant abandons the apartment without notice and without leaving a forwarding address, it can be more trouble than it's worth to find the tenant and get the rent. You may be better off simply applying the tenant's security deposit to the remaining rent and trying to lease the apartment to someone else. In some states, you may also be able to sell any furniture the tenant leaves behind and use the money toward the rent. Any costs you incur in storing the tenant's furniture usually can be deducted as well, as can your attorney's fees in many cases (see discussion below). If any money is left over after the balance of the rent is paid, you must try to return it to the tenant. In some states, if the proceeds of the sale of the tenant's property is under $300, the landlord may keep it. But if it exceeds $300, the landlord must pay it to the state, which will put it in a special fund waiting to be claimed by the tenant. Before selling a tenant's furniture, you should consult an attorney to make sure that you follow your state's procedure to the letter. If the sale of the property is unlawful, you may be liable to the tenant for conversion (theft) of the property. Always make sure that the tenant has in fact abandoned the apartment, never to return, before taking this kind of action.

If the Landlord Evicts the Tenant

An eviction occurs when, for any reason, the landlord removes the tenant from the apartment. The eviction may be lawful, through the courts, or unlawful, as when the landlord changes the locks and throws the tenant's furniture into the street. In the event of an eviction, whether lawful or not, the tenant's obligation to pay rent ceases, except for any rent owed up to the date of the eviction.

The most common reason for eviction is the tenant's failure to pay the rent. But the landlord can also lawfully evict a tenant for major breaches of the lease. For example, if a tenant is using the apartment as an illegal drug factory or to run a prostitution ring, the landlord can evict the tenant.

Suppose that you've gotten a little behind in the rent. One day you return to your apartment to find your furniture on the front lawn and all the locks changed. Your landlord has taken the law into his or her own hands and has evicted you without bothering to go through the court system. Can your landlord get away with this? Not anymore. Almost every state has a statute expressly forbidding this type of "forcible entry." The only way a landlord can evict a tenant is to go through the legal system.

Most states now have a quick way—a "summary procedure"—for a landlord to get a court order to evict a tenant who is behind on the rent. Usually the landlord must notify the tenant to either pay the rent within, say, three days or leave ("quit"). If, at the end of the three days, the tenant has done neither, the landlord can file an eviction proceeding in court. This type of action goes by several different names, the most common of which is an "unlawful detainer proceeding." Many states let the landlord sue the tenant for back rent as well as to evict him or her.

Shortly after the unlawful detainer action is filed and served on the tenant (within, for instance, fourteen days), a court hearing is held to determine who has the right to the apartment—the landlord or the tenant. The judge may let the tenant remain in the apartment if the tenant brings the rent up to date at the court hearing. If you are the tenant and are claiming to have paid your rent on time, you will have to show the judge some cold, hard proof: your canceled check, for instance, or a receipt from the landlord if you paid by money order, traveler's checks, or cash.

But let's say your landlord sues to evict you because you didn't pay the rent. Is there any way to get out of it? Yes—if you can convince the judge that you had a legal reason for not paying the rent. One such reason (discussed earlier) is that the apartment is uninhabitable. You'll have to show the judge adequate evidence of the apartment's unlivable condition. This is where pictures, testimony of friends and neighbors, and copies of your letters to the landlord come in handy. If the judge agrees with you, you may not owe anything. And even if the judge rejects your argument that the apartment was unfit for you to live in, you may still get a reduction in the rent of, say, 25 percent if the landlord refused to make repairs.

Another legal way to defend the eviction proceeding is by proving that you put the rent money toward necessary repairs that the landlord refused to make, up to the amount permitted by your state's law. Remember, though, that you can only count the money you actually spent to purchase the parts or to hire someone to do the job for you. You can't claim money for the hours of labor you put in fixing something yourself. A final way of stopping the eviction is possible in some states, which let you stay in the apartment if you pay all of the back rent (plus interest and other expenses of the landlord, including the landlord's attorney's fees) before the court orders the eviction.

Should the judge rule in favor of the landlord and order the tenant evicted, the tenant usually is given a day or two to move out. If the tenant still isn't out after two days, can the landlord physically remove the tenant? No. The landlord ordinarily must have the sheriff or marshal do the actual evicting if that becomes necessary.

Constructive Evictions

Not all evictions result from the landlord getting a court order to remove you or throwing you out and changing the locks. Sometimes the eviction happens because something makes it impossible for you to remain in the apartment. When, through no fault of your own, the apartment becomes dangerous to your health or safety, you are forced to move out the same as if the landlord had picked you up and thrown you into the street. This type of eviction is called a "constructive eviction."

As an example, suppose the ceiling in your apartment is old and weak. When it rains, the ceiling sags and the water pours through. You have complained a number of times, but your landlord refuses to do anything about it. A particularly heavy rainstorm comes, the weight is too much for the ceiling, and the ceiling collapses. Your living room is now under two feet of rubble and water. There are another six months to go on the lease, but you want to end the lease and move out today. Can you? Yes. You can terminate the lease and move out without worrying about the remaining rent. You also can sue your landlord for any damages you suffer from the constructive eviction, including damage to your property. Some things that can constitute a constructive eviction include the landlord's prolonged failure to provide water or heat, failure to stop continuous loud noise or threats of other tenants, and an apartment that is often flooded.

Making the Other Party Pay for Attorney's Fees

Suppose you have to hire a lawyer to sue your landlord to get repairs made. Or suppose your landlord has to sue you to evict you or to collect money to pay for damage to the unit. Can you collect your attorney's fees from your landlord, or vice versa? That depends on what your lease states. If the lease doesn't say a thing about attorney's fees, most courts will not award attorney's fees to either side. Many leases specify only that if the landlord has to sue you in court to collect the rent, evict you, or make you pay for damages to the apartment, you must pay the landlord's attorney's fees. The courts will enforce this provision against the tenant only if the landlord wins. And even though the lease mentions only the landlord's right to recover attorney's fees from the tenant, many courts will apply it both ways: if you win, the landlord will have to pay your attorney's fees. Many leases now state that if either party brings a lawsuit against the other, the loser must pay the winner's attorney's fees.

Landlords are usually in a position to afford a good lawyer to advise them. But what about tenants who can barely afford to pay the rent and buy food, let alone pay a lawyer a retainer?

For many tenants, good and inexpensive legal advice can be found at the local Legal Aid office. Try to contact the Legal Aid office while a problem is still developing—before it gets out of hand and you find yourself being evicted.

BUSINESS LEASES

THERE IS A WORLD OF DIFFERENCE between leasing a building or suite for a business and leasing an apartment or house to live in. Generally, the residential tenant has greater rights in most respects. The business tenant is treated as in the days of old: Once the landlord gives the business tenant the keys to the front door, and the tenant takes possession of the building, floor, or suite of rooms, the landlord ordinarily is relieved of any further duties. Why? Because a commercial tenant frequently makes extensive changes to the interior of the building, floor, or suite, to accommodate particular needs. In fact, the whole nature of the building or floor may change drastically after the business tenant moves in.

The large business tenant, such as a manufacturing or processing plant or a warehouse, usually has the burden of making substantially more modifications to the property than the residential tenant does. The extent of the modifications the business tenant must make depends on such factors as the terms and length of the lease and the nature of the business the commercial tenant is engaged in. Because the business tenant usually has a greater duty to maintain the premises and make repairs, there generally is no warranty of habitability in the lease of business property. The tenant must keep the leased premises safe, clean, and free of, among others, safety and health code violations.

Some states have expanded the rights of commercial tenants, particularly if the tenant makes few or no changes to the building, floor, or room of suites after taking possession. A self-employed person who rents a small suite in an office building and makes little or no modifications, for example, should be entitled to expect that the landlord will keep the premises relatively safe and clean, keep the heating and air conditioning working properly, and so on. In this situation, the landlord should be required to make most repairs to the building. It is not fair to require the tenant to make extensive repairs—to fix a leaky roof, for instance—if the tenant didn't cause the damage.

Provisions regarding installation, removal, and ownership of fixtures are found much more often in business leases than in residential leases. For example, a retail business may install display racks on the wall, attach lighting fixtures to the ceiling, and so on. It is important that the lease lay out the rights of the tenant to remove the fixtures when the lease ends. Generally, a business lease provides that the tenant can remove all fixtures the tenant installed but must repair any damage to the building caused by the fixtures. In most cases, it is well worth having a lawyer review a business lease before you sign it.

EIGHT

Gays, Lesbians, Bisexuals, and Transgenders

GAYS, LESBIANS, BISEXUALS, and transgenders (GLBTs) make up a significant portion of the United States population. Just how many there are is hard to ascertain, as many still have not "come out" publicly out of fear of reprisal. Yet estimates reveal that 5 to 8 percent of adults living in the United States comes within one of these categories. Despite these figures, however, GLBTs continue to be among the most discriminated against groups in the United States.

SODOMY AS CRIMINAL CONDUCT

BEFORE THE 1970s, all fifty states had laws making it a crime to engage in sodomy (anal or oral sex), even if the participants were consenting adults doing it in the privacy of their own home. Today, thirteen states still have antisodomy laws on the books, even though they are rarely enforced. Of those thirteen states, four—Kansas, Missouri, Oklahoma, and Texas—criminalize consensual sodomy only between members of the same sex, while the remaining nine make it a crime even between willing members of the opposite sex as well, married or not. These states are Alabama, Florida, Idaho, Louisiana, Mississippi, North Carolina, South Carolina, Utah, and Virginia.

Like a number of states, in the 1980s Georgia still had a law on the books prohibiting sodomy, even between consenting adults. Accordingly, a gay man was arrested for the crime of committing sodomy on another man, even though it was consensual and in the privacy of his own bedroom. The district attorney declined to file charges unless further evidence could be gathered. The gay man who was arrested then went to federal district court to get an order preventing the state of Georgia from prosecuting him for sodomy. The man claimed that as a homosexual he was in imminent danger of arrest and that the law making it a crime to engage in even consensual acts of sodomy was unconstitutional. The case made its way through the judicial process, finally settling at the United States Supreme Court's door in 1986. The nation's highest court held in the landmark case of *Bowers v. Hardwick* that the law banning sodomy—even between consenting adults—was constitutional, and that the man could be prosecuted and punished for violating the law. The court noted that laws against sodomy had ancient roots, and concluded that the Constitution did not protect this type of behavior, even when conducted in the privacy of one's own home.

In 1998, however, the Supreme Court of Georgia held that its state constitution protected "private, non-commercial acts of sexual intimacy between persons legally able to consent." The court thereupon ruled that the law prohibiting consensual sodomy violated the state's constitutional guarantee of the right to privacy.

On June 26, 2003, the United States Supreme Court revisited the issue of sodomy in *Lawrence v. Texas*, in which two gay men had been convicted of engaging in anal sex. The Texas law in question forbade certain "deviate sexual conduct" between members of the same sex but not members of the opposite sex. The high court overruled *Bowers v. Hardwick* and held that the law violated the men's due process rights. In upholding the right of the homosexual men to engage in intimate sexual acts in the privacy of their own home, the Supreme Court stated: "[This case involves] two adults who, with full and mutual consent from each other, engaged in sexual practices common to a homosexual lifestyle. The [gay men] are entitled to respect for their private lives. The State cannot demean their existence or control their destiny by making their private sexual conduct a crime. Their right to liberty under the Due Process Clause gives them the full right to engage in their conduct without intervention of the government." This should put an end to the validity of all sodomy laws, so far as they relate to acts done between consenting adults in private places.

HOMOSEXUAL AND BISEXUAL RELATIONSHIPS AND MARRIAGES

WE NOTED EARLIER (see chapter 1) that a marriage can exist only between members of the opposite sex. If members of the same sex get "married" (other than those who follow the statutory procedure for "civil unions" set forth in Vermont), their marriage is void from the outset and need not be terminated by a divorce or an annulment, since a marriage never existed. If a partner to a same-sex "marriage" later decides to marry a member of the opposite sex, it is not necessary to obtain a divorce or annulment from his or her same-sex "spouse," and he or she can marry without fear of being guilty of bigamy. (In Vermont, the opposite is true: The partner to a same-sex civil union must get that union legally terminated before he or she may legally marry a member of the opposite sex; otherwise, he or she is guilty of bigamy.) Polls of attitudes toward gay marriages clearly demonstrate that the vast majority of Americans are against same-sex marriages, on the basis that marriage is a sacred union entered into only between a man and a woman.

With proper planning, same-sex couples can have some of the rights that married couples enjoy. For instance, by preparing and signing a durable power of attorney for property management (see chapter 3), a GLBT can select his or her life partner as the primary attorney-in-fact in a power of attorney to take care of his or her financial affairs in the event he or she is incapacitated by injury, disease, or illness and unable to do so himself or herself. With an advance health care directive (chapter 3), a GLBT person can name his or her life partner as the agent to make health care decisions on his or her behalf in the event the GLBT is incapable of doing so. Also, with a revocable living trust (chapter 3) or a will (chapter 4), a GLBT can make provisions for his or her life partner after death. If one member of a same-sex relationship were to die without a will or living trust, the estate would go to his or her "next of kin," which is determined by blood lines and marriage and would not include a life partner (except in Vermont and California, but only if the couple have registered as domestic partners, as discussed below), regardless of how long the two had been together.

Since same-sex couples do not acquire any rights under traditional family law concepts of marriage, the rights and obligations when a same-sex relationship ends must be based on a contract theory of the type found in *Marvin v. Marvin* (see chapter 1). But a court might refuse to enforce the agreement because of some abstract "public policy" argument that the law should not intervene in same-sex relationships.

There is no legal reason why a court should permit a *Marvin*-type action between unmarried persons of opposite sexes but not allow such an action between partners of the same sex. In neither relationship can the contract be based upon the performance of sexual services. Rather, it is the giving up of certain rights, such as the right to pursue one's own career to its fullest and performing household work and other chores that often serve as the legitimate legal "consideration" to make the contract binding and enforceable. Still, same-sex couples must realize that not all states agree with the *Marvin* decision, and even some courts that allow a *Marvin*-type action for unmarried cohabitants of the opposite sex may not allow such an action between members of a same-sex couple.

Members of the same sex who already are living together or buying a house or other property together should have a written agreement (preferably drawn up by a lawyer) fully setting forth the rights and responsibilities of each partner. If one partner in the relationship had substantial assets before the relationship began, the agreement should identify those assets in detail to prevent the other partner from claiming at a later date that the property was acquired with the earnings of both partners after they began living together, should they later split up.

As with unmarried heterosexual partners, an unmarried homosexual person usually is not liable for injuries his or her partner inflicts on a third person. If, however, a same-sex person causes an accident while driving a car owned by his or her lover, the lover may be held liable under the "permissive user" statute (see chapter 2) relating to the operation of a motor vehicle. Liability also could be imposed if the wrongdoer was acting at the request of or working as an employee of the same-sex lover. If one partner in a same-sex relationship is injured or killed by another person's wrongful act, except in Vermont and California, the surviving same-sex partner does not have any right to bring a lawsuit against the third person for wrongful death or loss of consortium (comfort, care, and society). However, the married partner of a bisexual or transgender person can bring such a lawsuit.

In a precedent-setting move, California's state tax board ruled that a lesbian supporting her life partner and her life partner's child qualified for status as head of the household for income tax filing purposes. The child was born of the life partner through artificial insemination. The two women had agreed that the child's biological mother (the life partner) would stay at home for the first few years taking care of the child, and the other woman would be the primary breadwinner. This decision gives some recognition to a family headed by a same-sex couple as a valid, legal entity.

Suppose a bisexual man marries a heterosexual woman but does not tell her of his sexual orientation. When she discovers his bisexuality, what are her rights? She may be able to file for an annulment of the marriage based on his failure to tell her of his sexual orientation. (For the bases for obtaining an annulment in general, see chapter 1.) What if the bisexual man cheats on his heterosexual mate with another man; is this adultery, or is it adultery only if you have sexual relations with a member of the opposite sex? This is the type of questions that can drive a judge mad. The judge has to go by the letter of the law. If the statute states that adultery is sexual relations with a person of the opposite sex, then having sex with a member of one's own sex is not adultery. However, if the statute simply states that adultery is having sexual relations with a person other than one's spouse, then it would be considered adultery.

Same-Sex Civil Unions in Vermont

On December 20, 1999, the Supreme Court of Vermont ruled that it was unconstitutional to deny marriage licenses to same-sex couples living in that state. The high court of Vermont ordered that state's legislature to enact a law recognizing same-sex marriages. Consequently, on April 26, 2000, Vermont governor Howard Dean signed the comprehensive "civil union" bill permitting same-sex couples to enter into a formal legal relationship with all the rights and responsibilities of traditional marriage. The members of a same-sex civil union in Vermont now enjoy all of the more than three hundred rights historically reserved for heterosexual marriages, such as the right to inherit property, make medical decisions when the other is incapacitated, transfer property, and tax breaks. Town clerks are authorized to issue same-sex couples licenses to enter into a civil union, and clergy, justices of the peace, and judges may formalize the union, just as in a marriage. And as in a marriage, should the union suffer a breakdown, the civil union can be dissolved by a family divorce court applying the same rules it applies to heterosexual marriages.

Before and after the Vermont Supreme Court's decision, other states, through legislation and initiatives, passed laws declaring that marriages can exist only between members of the opposite sex. Some of these laws also state that if a gay couple legally "married" in Vermont (or any other state that in the future permits same-sex unions) moves to its state, the state will not recognize the civil union. This poses an interesting constitutional question, as the United States Constitution requires one state to give "full faith and credit" to another state's law. What this means is that if the civil union was entered into validly in Vermont (the only state to date that permits same-sex civil unions), and the couple later moves to a state that forbids same-sex unions, the new state must nonetheless recognize the gay couple's union as legal and binding by giving full faith and credit to Vermont's law.

A good corollary to the giving of full faith and credit to Vermont's civil union laws is the status of common law marriage. In a common law marriage (see chapter 1) a couple decides to marry and thereafter hold themselves out to the public as being married. They do not go through the formalities of getting blood tests, being married by a clergymember or judge, etc. If the state they do this in recognizes common law marriages, their marriage is legal and binding even if they move to a state that does not permit common law marriages to be made in that state. Under the "full faith and credit" clause, the new state must recognize their marriage as lawful, even though it would not be had they done the same thing in the new state.

Because of the perceived threat of states passing laws permitting same-sex unions, in 1996 Congress passed and then President Clinton signed into law the Defense of Marriage Act (DOMA). Many states subsequently passed similar laws. DOMA defines marriage as "a legal union between one man and one woman as husband and wife," and defines a spouse as "a person of the opposite sex who is a husband or a wife." What DOMA also purports to do is to declare the full faith and credit clause invalid by giving states the right to refuse to recognize same-sex marriages or civil unions lawfully entered into in another state. The full faith and credit clause requires the states to recognize the "acts, records and proceedings" of all other states.

However, an act by the United States Congress or a state legislature cannot be in derogation of the United States Constitution, or it is invalid. Only an amendment to the Constitution can change its provisions, not a piece of legislation. It will be interesting to see what a court does when the question of whether these laws take precedence over the full faith and credit clause of the federal Constitution is presented to it, as it surely will be in the future. Because these laws fly in the face of the Constitution's explicit guarantee of full faith and credit, one would think that the appropriate ruling would be that these laws are unconstitutional.

Trying to predict what a court will hold in the future is usually an exercise in futility; trying to predict what a court will hold in the future in a case involving GLBTs is a voyage into the surreal. An example: A woman underwent a successful sex change operation; however, the surgeon left the ovaries in, stating that they would present no problem to the "new man." When the transsexual applied for health insurance, he checked off the "male" box on his application form. Unfortunately, he developed ovarian cancer. His health insurance carrier refused to pay for any expenses related to ovarian cancer on the basis that he was a man, men do not have ovaries, and therefore he could not possibly have ovarian cancer. The man took his case to court, which denied him relief on the same reasons the insurance company had turned him down!

CALIFORNIA'S DOMESTIC PARTNER REGISTRATION LAW

IN 1999, CALIFORNIA ENACTED the Domestic Partner Registration Law, which defines domestic partners as two adults who have chosen to share one another's lives in an intimate and committed relationship of mutual caring. Besides applying to members of the same sex, it also applies to a heterosexual domestic partnership where one or both of the persons are over the age of 62. This latter provision is to help out senior citizens who live together but choose not to marry because, among other things, it would lower the amount of Social Security benefits one person—usually the woman—would receive if they were to marry. We will focus here on domestic partnerships involving members of the same sex.

A domestic partnership exists when:

* two members of the same sex share a common residence;
* they agree to be jointly responsible for each other's basic living expenses incurred during the domestic partnership;
* neither partner is married or a member of another domestic partnership;
* the two persons are not related by blood in a way that would prevent them from being married to each other in California;
* both partners are at least 18 years old;
* both persons are capable of consenting to the domestic partnership;
* neither partner has previously filed a Declaration of Domestic Partnership that has not been terminated for at least six months, unless it was terminated by death or marriage of the other partner; and
* they file a Declaration of Domestic Partnership with the secretary of state (the appropriate form is available from the secretary of state or the county clerk).

In September 2002, the California legislature passed a law that made the surviving domestic partner a beneficiary of a deceased partner's separate property if that partner died without a will ("intestate"; see chapter 3). The surviving partner is entitled to one-third, one-half, or all of the deceased partner's separate property, depending upon whether the deceased partner left any surviving children or other descendants, parents, or brothers or sisters or their surviving issue. This law was the direct result of the dog-mauling death of the lesbian San Francisco woman discussed in chapter 9; because under the law as it existed then, it did not recognize any inheritance rights of unmarried persons who were not related to the deceased person by blood or marriage, thereby prohibiting her life partner from suing the dog's owners for wrongful death.

The domestic partnership is terminated when one of the partners dies or marries, when the couple no longer share the same residence (temporary absences don't count), or when one of the domestic partners gives or sends the other partner a written notice by certified mail that he or she is terminating the partnership. When a domestic partnership has been terminated, at least one of the former partners must file a notice of termination of domestic partnership form with the secretary of state by sending it via certified mail.

SAME-SEX COUPLES AS PARENTS

THERE ARE ANYWHERE from six to ten million gay, lesbian, and bisexual parents in the United States, having an estimated six to fourteen million children. The vast majority of these children were born while the homosexual or bisexual parent was in a heterosexual relationship. However, more and more gay men and lesbian women are adopting children and lesbian women are having children, through artificial insemination.

Whether GLBTs may adopt a child is not a question that can be answered in a few short paragraphs. Some states expressly forbid adoption by homosexuals and bisexuals; other states expressly permit it; while others are silent on the issue, leaving the decision up to the social services agency and the presiding judge on a case-by-case basis. A lesbian or bisexual woman has the option of getting pregnant, either the traditional way or by being artificially inseminated with a donor's sperm. The woman may prefer to be impregnated with the sperm of a male friend, or go through the process of being inseminated with an anonymous donor's sperm through a sperm bank or physician. The woman (and man) should be aware of the rights and obligations that come with being artificially inseminated, be it by a friend or an anonymous donor (see chapter 1). However, problems arise when the nonbiological, same-sex life partner wishes to adopt the child. The courts are split on whether such a partner can adopt the child. If you are planning on adopting your same-sex life partner's child, you should do so only with the guidance of an attorney well versed in this area.

Psychological studies show that there is no valid reason why gay, lesbian, and bisexual couples who otherwise meet the same criteria as heterosexual couples cannot provide a child with a warm, loving, nurturing environment and would raise healthy, well-adjusted children. In an Illinois case, the children were removed from the custody of their bisexual mother after it came out that she was in a relationship with another woman. The children were taken from the mother's custody following a lengthy hearing at which everyone agreed that the children were doing very well in their mother's custody. On appeal, the Illinois Appellate Court held that the fact that a parent is homosexual or bisexual, is living with her same-sex partner, or may face community disapproval or charges of immorality were not valid reasons to change custody. The court utilized a "sexual-orientation neutral" standard in determining the bisexual woman's right to custody.

Suppose a lesbian couple decides to have a baby. One of the women is artificially inseminated with an anonymous donor's sperm and all is well for five years. The child is brought up with both women acting as parents. However, after five years the two women have relationship problems and decide that it would be best for them to split up. Can the nonbiological "parent" assert any rights to custody of or visitation with the child? This is a very complex issue. Many judges rule that there is only one parent—the biological one—and therefore the nonbiological same-sex parent has no right to request custody or visitation. Other judges recognize the bond that has formed between the child and the nonbiological parent and *will* award visitation rights, finding it to be in the best interests of the child.

If you are a GLBT and are considering adopting a child, or already have a child but are contemplating leaving your life partner, you should consult a good family law attorney experienced in these issues. This is not an area you should try to navigate by yourself.

HOUSING DISCRIMINATION

Jack and rick are a gay couple who have made the decision to live together as life partners. They find a nice one-bedroom apartment in a trendy area that fits within their budget. However, when they apply for the apartment, the apartment owner refuses to rent it to them because their homosexuality violates the owner's religious or personal beliefs regarding members of the same sex living together. Can the apartment owner get away with this? In most states, yes.

Only about a dozen states have laws prohibiting discrimination on the basis of sexual orientation when it comes to housing issues. A growing number of cities and counties have ordinances prohibiting discrimination on the basis of sexual orientation when it comes to renting apartments and houses.

Suppose that Jane and Wanda, two lesbians, have been living together in their rented condo for thirteen years. Jane originally rented the apartment by herself, and Wanda moved in three years later when they decided to become life partners. Jane is killed in a tragic automobile accident, and now the owner wants Wanda to move out, even though there are two years remaining on the lease, which only Jane signed. Can the owner force Wanda out? Generally, yes. In most instances, the law protects only heterosexual spouses from displacement after the other spouse dies or leaves. Since only Jane signed the lease, Wanda would have no claim to remain in the rented condo.

DISCRIMINATION IN THE WORKPLACE

Title VII of the Civil Rights Act of 1964 (Title VII) makes it unlawful for an employer to, among other things, discriminate against any individual with respect to his or her compensation, terms, conditions, or privileges of employment because of the individual's race, color, religion, *sex*, or national origin. Can a gay, lesbian, or bisexual person who is being harassed or discriminated at work because of his or her sexual orientation bring a suit for such harassment or discrimination under Title VII? The answer, surprisingly, is no. The courts have stated that, in passing Title VII, "Congress manifested an intention to exclude homosexuals from Title VII coverage." That discrimination based upon sexual orientation is not actionable was embraced emphatically by the First Circuit Court of Appeals when it stated: "[W]e regard it as settled law that, as drafted and authoritatively construed, Title VII does not proscribe harassment simply because of sexual orientation."

In one case, a gay male nurse brought a suit for sexual discrimination in the workplace based on the conduct of a homophobic doctor. The nurse contended that the doctor harassed him by screaming at him over the telephone, lisping while talking to him, flipping his wrists in an effeminate manner, and making jokes about homosexuals, thereby creating a hostile environment in which the nurse could not work. The court rejected the nurse's lawsuit on the basis that he was claiming harassment because of his homosexuality and not because of his sex. The court made a thorough examination of the difference between one's "sex" (gender) and one's sexuality or sexual orientation, and concluded that only discrimination based on the former was unlawful. The court noted that same-sex sexual harassment is actionable under Title VII to the extent that it occurs because of the worker's sex. According to the court, the phrase in Title VII prohibiting discrimination based on sex means that it is unlawful to discriminate against a woman because she is a woman and against a man because he is a man. In other words, the court stated, Congress intended the term "sex" to mean biological male or biological female, and not one's sexuality or sexual orientation. Therefore, harassment based solely upon a person's sexual preference or orientation (and not one's sex) is not an unlawful employment practice under Title VII.

A woman sued Price Waterhouse for sexual discrimination for being denied partnership in part because she was too "macho." The female employee was advised that she could improve her chances for partnership if she walked more "femininely," talked and dressed more femininely, wore makeup, had her hair styled, and wore jewelry. The United States Supreme Court held that this was impermissible sex discrimination, and that "[i]n the specific context of sex stereotyping, an employer who acts on the basis of a belief that a woman cannot be aggressive, or that she must not be, has acted on the basis of gender."

In another case, the attorney general of Georgia revoked a job offer to a woman to become a staff attorney after learning that the woman had gone through a purported marriage to another woman. The aggrieved woman brought suit, claiming she had unconstitutionally been discriminated against. The Eleventh Circuit Court of Appeals rejected the woman's claim, stating that it could not say that the attorney general "was unreasonable to think that [the woman's] acts were likely to cause the public to be confused and to question the Law Department's credibility; to interfere with the Law Department's ability to handle certain controversial matters, including enforcing the law against homosexual sodomy; and to endanger working relationships inside the Department." The court also stated that it could not say "that the Attorney General was unreasonable to lose confidence in [the woman's] ability to make good judgments as a lawyer for the Law Department." The court stressed in this case the sensitive nature of the professional employment, holding that the state of Georgia's interest as an employer in promoting the efficiency of the law department's important public service outweighed the woman's personal associational interests.

A few courts have suggested that discrimination based on a failure to conform to gender norms might be allowed under Title VII. One court remarked that Title VII encompasses instances in which "the perpetrator's actions stem from the fact that he believed that the victim was a man who 'failed to act like' one." Another court stated that "just as a woman can ground an action on a claim that men discriminated against her because she did not meet stereotyped expectations of femininity, a man can ground a claim on evidence that other men discriminated against him because he did not meet stereotypical expectations of masculinity."

The reality is that the courts continue to hold that there is a distinction between one's sex and one's sexuality under Title VII, and that the statute only prohibits employers from harassing employees because of their sex. Thus, unless there is a state law that prohibits discrimination and harassment based on sexual orientation, employers and employees can subject gays, lesbians, and bisexuals to taunts, name-calling, homosexual jokes, stereotypical conduct, and other antihomosexual harassment with impunity. The harassment can be pervasive and create a hostile or abusive work environment for the homosexual or bisexual worker, but the homosexual or bisexual person cannot pursue a claim of sexual discrimination.

At the time of this writing, only eleven states have laws prohibiting discrimination based on sexual orientation in both the private workplace and the public sector. Those states are California, Connecticut, Hawaii, Massachusetts, Minnesota, Nevada, New Hampshire, New Jersey, New York, Rhode Island, Vermont, and Wisconsin. Ten other states—Colorado, Iowa, Illinois, Maryland, North Carolina, New Mexico, New York, Pennsylvania, Washington, and West Virginia—have laws or executive orders signed by the governor prohibiting discrimination based on sexual orientation that apply to public employees. Additionally, a number of cities and counties throughout the nation have statutes or ordinances making it unlawful to discriminate against a worker or prospective worker on the grounds of sexual orientation. The states of Iowa and Minnesota and approximately thirty-one cities and counties have laws prohibiting discrimination in private or public employment, or both, against gender identity.

While in office, President Clinton signed an executive order prohibiting discrimination on the basis of sexual orientation of federal employees.

A few states and a number of municipalities offer "domestic partner" benefits such as insurance coverage to unmarried couples, be they heterosexual or homosexual. A growing number of companies also provide domestic partner benefits. In fact, many cities now will not hire outside contractors that do not provide domestic partner benefits for their employees and their partners, regardless of whether the partner is of the opposite sex or not. However, these benefits are considered taxable by the Internal Revenue Service unless the noncovered spouse qualifies as a dependent. Traditionally, a dependent has been defined as having lived in the taxpayer's household for the entire year and the employee must provide for more than half of his or her support.

GLBTS AT SCHOOL: AS STUDENTS AND TEACHERS

GAY, LESBIAN, AND BISEXUAL high school students have attempted to form clubs to meet on school grounds before or after school, like any other club. High schools are faced with the choice of permitting such clubs to meet, or abolishing all nonacademic clubs from meeting. In one high school where students sought to start a gay/straight alliance club, the school initially threatened to ban all nonacademic clubs from meeting on school grounds. A federal lawsuit was filed, with the end result being a settlement that provided that the Gay/Straight Alliance could meet on school grounds like any other group, but the members of the club (and all other school clubs for that matter) could not talk explicitly about sex acts or sexual organs. However, they remain free to talk about sexual orientation and problems and issues related to it.

Gay, lesbian, and bisexual students are often the recipients of taunts and harassment at school and school-related functions. Can teachers and administrators sit silently by and not intervene to stop the harassment? Not any longer. In 1999, the United States Supreme Court held that a school board can be held liable for student-to-student sexual harassment when it is deliberately indifferent to sexual harassment of which it has actual knowledge, and the harassment is so severe, pervasive, and objectively offensive that it can be said to deprive the victim of access to the educational opportunities provided by the school.

Suppose a parent wants to remove his or her child from a classroom because the teacher is GLBT. Can that be done? This issue arose in California, where a labor commissioner reprimanded a school district for granting a parent's request to remove her child from the teacher's class solely because the teacher was a lesbian. The labor commissioner's decision was upheld by California's department of industrial relations. The teacher had taught in the school district for eighteen years and had been awarded prizes for her work. It must be noted, however, that California is generally in the forefront of GLBT rights, and has laws prohibiting employment discrimination based on actual or perceived sexual orientation. Other states may not reach the same conclusion.

Can a teacher not be hired or be fired simply and solely because he or she is GLBT? In states that do not have a law prohibiting discrimination in employment on the basis of sexual orientation, which is most states, the answer is yes. In those states that make it unlawful to discriminate against an employee or prospective employee because of his or her sexual orientation, the answer is no.

California high school biology teacher Dawn Murray, a nationally recognized and award-winning teacher, was subject to years of harassment and discrimination by other teachers and administrators based on her sexual orientation as a lesbian. She was denied a promotion even though she was the most qualified person for the position, was called derogatory names, was the target of homophobic graffiti, and was victimized by false rumors spread by the school staff of her engaging in public sexual activity. The school district claimed that Murray had not been discriminated against, as she had not been terminated from her job. However, the California appellate court held that under California's Fair Employment and Housing Act (FEHA), it clearly provided protection against harassment in the workplace based on a person's sexual orientation. The court held that in addition to pursuing her sexual harassment claim, Murray could pursue a claim for intentional infliction of emotional distress (see chapter 10) and was not barred by the exclusivity provisions of worker's compensation laws that generally bar an injured party from bringing a lawsuit against his or her employer (see chapter 13). Again, it is worth noting that California is generally a leader in the rights of GLBTs, having enacted laws to prevent discrimination and harassment based on sexual orientation in a variety of situations.

SAME-SEX PARTNERS AND IMMIGRATION

UNDER CURRENT IMMIGRATION LAW (see chapter 21), a United States citizen or permanent resident (one who holds a "green card") cannot petition the Immigration and Naturalization Service (the INS) to bring into America their same-sex life partner. As a result of this, thousands of same-sex couples are forced to separate, or the noncitizen, nonresident member enters or remains in the United States unlawfully, living in constant fear that they will be found and deported and separated from their loved one. Two California cities—San Francisco and West Hollywood—have declared themselves to be cities of refuge to gays, lesbians, and bisexuals who find themselves in this situation.

In February 2000, New York Democrat Jerrold Nadler introduced into the House of Representatives the Permanent Partners Immigration Act, which would have modified the existing law to give same-sex partners of U.S. citizens and lawful permanent residents the same immigration rights that married spouses of U.S. citizens and permanent residents have. However, that bill did not make it into law. Only thirteen countries currently recognize gay and lesbian couples for purposes of immigration. These are: Australia, Belgium, Canada, Denmark, Finland, France, Iceland, the Netherlands, New Zealand, Norway, South Africa, Sweden, and the United Kingdom.

In August 2000, the Ninth Federal Circuit Court of Appeals unanimously held that a gay man from Mexico who presented himself as a female was being persecuted in his home country as a result of his sexual orientation and granted him asylum in the United States. In so ruling, the court stated that sexual identity and orientation is "so fundamental to one's identity that a person should not be required to abandon them." The primary issue before the court was whether gay men with female sexual identities in Mexico constituted a protected "particular social group" under the asylum statute. The court defined a "particular social group" as one that is "united by a voluntary association, including a formal association, or by an innate characteristic that is so fundamental to the identities or consciences of its members that members either cannot or should not be required to change it." The court went on to say that sexual identity is inherent to one's very identity as a person, and therefore concluded that the man was entitled to asylum and the withholding of the deportation proceedings that were pending against him. (It is worth noting here that the Ninth Circuit Court of Appeals is considered the most liberal of all of the federal circuit courts of appeals, and that the decision may have been otherwise had the case been brought in a more conservative jurisdiction.)

The United States has given protection to gays seeking asylum from persecution in their native lands since 1994. In 1990, the Board of Immigration Appeals (BIA) held that sexual orientation can be the basis for establishing a "particular social group" for asylum purposes. That case involved Cubans who had been harassed and persecuted over a number of years. In 1994, Attorney General Janet Reno issued an order designating the BIA's decision as "precedent in all proceedings involving the same issue."

In 1993, then–attorney general Janet Reno issued an order making gay men, lesbians, and persons afflicted with HIV eligible for political asylum in the United States if they could show a reasonable fear of persecution in their home country based on their sexual orientation. However, proving that they have a "reasonable fear of persecution" has not been easy for gays seeking political asylum in the United States. In one case, a lesbian introduced evidence as to how she was arrested, imprisoned in a mental institution, and physically abused because of her sexual orientation. Despite this evidence, the judge ruled that her experiences did not constitute a reasonable definition of persecution and denied the woman's application for political asylum.

ANTI-GLBT LEGISLATION

IN THE LATE 1980s and early 1990s, a number of Colorado cities passed ordinances banning discrimination based on sexual orientation in housing, employment, education, public accommodations, health and welfare services, and other transactions and activities. In response to this, Colorado voters approved Amendment 2 to the state constitution, which barred all legislative, executive, and judicial action at any level of state or local government designed to protect the status of persons based on their "homosexual, lesbian or bisexual orientation, conduct, practice, or relationships." In 1996, the United States Supreme Court held that Amendment 2 to the Colorado constitution violated the equal protection clause of the fourteenth amendment to the United States Constitution.

The Supreme Court stated that Amendment 2 "is a status-based enactment divorced from any factual context from which we could discern a relationship legitimate to state interests; it is a classification of persons undertaken for its own sake, something the Equal Protection Clause does not permit. [C]lass legislation . . . [is] obnoxious to the prohibitions of the Fourteenth Amendment." The Supreme Court concluded that "Amendment 2 classifies homosexuals not to further a proper legislative end but to make them unequal to everyone else. This Colorado cannot do. A State cannot so deem a class of persons a stranger to its laws. Amendment 2 violates the Equal Protection Clause."

HOMOSEXUALS AND THE MILITARY

BEFORE BILL CLINTON WAS elected president, gays, lesbians, and bisexuals were not allowed to serve in the military. In 1993, Congress passed and then President Clinton signed into law the National Defense Authorization Act. This act created the "don't ask, don't tell" policy regarding persons in or who want to be in the armed forces. The act declares that "military life is fundamentally different from civilian life" and that "success in combat requires military units that are characterized by high morale, good order and discipline, and unit cohesion." Congress further determined that "the prohibition against homosexual conduct is a long-standing element of military law that continues to be necessary in the unique circumstances of military service." Congress also found that service members who demonstrate a propensity or intent to engage in homosexual acts create "an unacceptable risk to the high standards of morale, good order and discipline, and unit cohesion that are the essence of military capability."

To avoid those risks, the act provides that service personnel shall be discharged or otherwise separated from the armed services if: (1) the service member engaged or attempted to engage in a homosexual act; (2) the service member married or attempted to marry a member of the same sex; or (3) the service member publicly stated that he or she was a homosexual, unless the service member demonstrates that he or she is not a person who engages in, attempts to engage in, or intends to engage in homosexual acts. If a service member merely states that he or she is a homosexual, then a presumption arises that he or she engages in or attempts or intends to engage in homosexual acts. The service member must then rebut (disprove) the presumption or face discharge.

In 1996, the federal Fourth Circuit Court of Appeals upheld the constitutionality of the National Defense Authorization Act. The court affirmed the action of the Navy in giving a Navy lieutenant—who had a stellar and unblemished record—an honorable discharge after he wrote letters to four admirals in which he stated that he was gay and voiced his opposition to laws banning or limiting gays in the military. The court held that, while the lieutenant had presented evidence of his good performance, he failed to offer any evidence to rebut the presumption that he engaged in or attempted to or intended to engage in homosexual activity, and therefore the decision to honorably discharge him was constitutional.

Other courts likewise have upheld the "don't ask, don't tell" policy of the National Defense Authorization Act. The courts reason that military life is uniquely different than civilian life, and that having an open homosexual in a small unit would threaten the cohesion and trust of that unit. One court remarked that "[t]he prohibition against homosexual conduct is a long-standing element of military law that continues to be necessary in the unique circumstances of military service."

The "don't ask, don't tell" policy has been roundly criticized as abysmal by both sides of the issue, and in practice has proved unfair to many young men and women who would otherwise make good servicemen and -women if given the chance.

GLBTS AND PRIVATE ASSOCIATIONS

CAN A PRIVATE ASSOCIATION ban homosexuals from joining, or revoke the membership of a person once it is found that he or she is homosexual? Yes, said the United States Supreme Court in the case of *Boy Scouts of America v. Dale*, decided in a 5-to-4 decision on June 28, 2000. In that case, an assistant scoutmaster had his position revoked when the Boy Scouts learned that he was an avowed homosexual and gay rights activist. The Supreme Court found that the Boy Scouts is a private, not-for-profit organization engaged in instilling its system of values in young people, and that homosexual conduct was inconsistent with those values. The assistant scoutmaster filed suit in New Jersey, claiming discrimination on the basis of sexual orientation in places of accommodation.

The Supreme Court found that homosexual conduct is inconsistent with the values embodied in the Scout oath and law, especially those represented by the terms "morally straight" and "clean." The high court also found that the Boy Scouts of America does not want to promote homosexual conduct as a legitimate form of behavior. The gay assistant scoutmaster's presence, the Court stated, would interfere with the Scouts' choice not to propound a point of view contrary to its beliefs. The Supreme Court ruled that forcing the Boy Scouts to retain a homosexual assistant scoutmaster would significantly burden the organization's right to oppose or disfavor homosexual conduct.

As a result of the fallout from that decision, a number of schools, churches, and other meeting places refused to permit the Boy Scouts to meet on their premises. And some major charitable groups stopped giving donations to the Boy Scouts. On the other hand, however, some charitable groups gave money to the Boy Scouts to show their support of its antigay policy.

GLBTS AND PARADES

As ANOTHER EXAMPLE OF permissible discrimination against gays, lesbians, and bisexuals, the United States Supreme Court held that gays, lesbians, and bisexuals could be barred from marching in a St. Patrick's Day parade because it would send the wrong message from that which the promoters were trying to send. The case involved the South Boston Allied War Veterans Council, an unincorporated association of individuals elected from various veterans' groups. The council was authorized by the city of Boston to hold an annual St. Patrick's Day–Evacuation Day Parade. The Gay, Lesbian, and Bisexual (GLIB) group was organized solely to march in the parade behind a banner simply stating "Irish American Gay, Lesbian and Bisexual Group of Boston." The veterans council denied GLIB permission to march in the parade because it would be conveying a message that the council did not wish to convey. GLIB contended that the ban on their presence in the parade violated, among other things, a state law prohibiting discrimination on the basis of sexual orientation in places of public accommodation. The case made its way to the United States Supreme Court, which ruled that Massachusetts law could not force the veterans council to accept a group to march in the parade where the group's message was one that the veterans council did not wish to convey. The Supreme Court observed that GLIB wanted to make its message part of the parade, rather than an independent, separate message. The Supreme Court stated that, as a part of the first amendment right to speech, the speaker has the right to determine what is *not* said as well as what is said.

HATE CRIMES AGAINST GLBTS

Although crime in general has decreased in the past few years, hate crimes against gays, lesbians, bisexuals, and transgenders have increased dramatically. In 1999, the last year for which statistics are available, hate crimes based on sexual orientation reported to the FBI's Uniform Crime Reporting Program ranked third of all hate crimes, behind race and religion. Since the FBI first began gathering statistics on hate crimes based on sexual orientation, the number of such crimes tripled from 1991 to 1999 and continue to rise annually. Hate crimes based on sexual orientation accounted for 16.7 percent of all hate crimes in 1999, and it is believed that such crimes go widely unreported because of stigmatism and possible reprisal.

Worth mentioning here is the federal Hate Crimes Sentencing Enhancement Act, which is part of the Violent Crime Control and Law Enforcement Act of 1994, which calls for a longer sentence if it is proved beyond a reasonable doubt that the crime was committed out of hate. On the average, these tougher sentences result in an enhanced sentence of one-third the time actually served. However, the Hate Crimes Sentencing Enhancement Act applies only to crimes committed on federal property.

About half the states currently have laws making a crime based upon sexual orientation a hate crime, resulting in enhanced punishment of the offender. Most of the remaining states have hate crime laws, but do not explicitly include crimes based on sexual orientation among them.

FOR FURTHER INFORMATION

IF YOU FEEL THAT your civil rights have been violated because you are or gay, lesbian, bisexual, or transgender, or are HIV-positive or have AIDS, you should contact the Lambda Legal Defense and Education Fund. Their national headquarters is at 120 Wall Street, Suite 1500, New York, NY 10005-3904; telephone: (212) 809-8585. They also have branch offices in Los Angeles, Chicago, and Atlanta. They maintain an excellent website on the Internet, http://www.lambdalegal.org. They represent or file *amicus curiae* briefs on behalf of victims of sexual orientation or HIV or AIDS discrimination.

Another place to look is the Human Rights Campaign, which works for equal rights for gay men and lesbians. Their office is at 919 18th Street, NW, Suite 800, Washington, DC, 20006; telephone: (202) 628-4160. They also maintain an informative website at http://www.hrc.org.

NINE

Animals

WITH PET OWNERSHIP come a number of legal responsibilities. In chapter 4, we discussed two legal considerations regarding animals: whether a pet can inherit your estate, and your right to order that your pet be put to sleep when you die. This chapter discusses legal problems most commonly faced by pet owners.

IF YOU DISCOVER THE PET YOU BOUGHT IS DISEASED OR SICK

SUPPOSE YOU BUY A PET—let's say a dog—from a pet shop for $250. Three days later, the dog seems ill. You call the pet shop, but they brusquely inform you that "All sales are final; the dog is now your problem, not ours." You take the dog to a veterinarian, who informs you that it is diseased. In fact, it was diseased long before you bought it and is now so sick that it should be put to sleep. You tell the vet to go ahead and euthanize the dog and pay the bill of, say, $150. You return to the pet store with copies of the store's receipt for the dog and the vet's bill and demand $400. The pet shop refuses, so you sue it in small claims court. Will you win? Yes. When a store sells a pet, the law assumes that the pet is healthy at that time, unless the store clearly tells you otherwise before you buy it. Since the dog was diseased when you bought it, the pet shop should have refunded your money or given you a new dog when you first told it of the problem. If the illness is not life-threatening, the pet shop should pay the vet's bills. In legal terms, by selling a diseased dog, the pet shop breached the "implied warranty of merchantability," that is, that the dog was healthy and fit for sale.

Now suppose that instead of buying the dog from a pet store, you buy it from a private party we'll call Jane. Is Jane liable under the same circumstances? If she regularly sells this type of animal—for instance, if she routinely breeds her own dog and sells the litter—she is considered a "dealer" and generally has the same obligations as a pet store. On the other hand, if Jane doesn't make a business of it—this is just a one-time sale, perhaps because she is moving—Jane is liable for your damages only if she knew the animal was sick or diseased when she sold it to you and didn't tell you. But if she had no idea the animal was ill, you are stuck with the bill.

Note that the above rules apply only when the animal was diseased or otherwise defective at the time of purchase. If the animal was healthy when you bought it and contracted a disease later, you usually cannot sue the person who sold it to you, whether a dealer or a private party.

RESTRICTIONS ON KEEPING A PET

As AN ANIMAL OWNER, you need to be aware of applicable zoning laws so you do not violate the law by keeping a particular animal in a prohibited area. Zoning laws are especially important if you live in an urban area and want to keep, for example, a horse or cow on your property. While certain domesticated animals, such as dogs, cats, and birds, are permitted (in reasonable numbers, of course) in any neighborhood, horses, cows, chickens, pigs, sheep, goats, and so forth are not ordinarily allowed in urban neighborhoods. (Dangerous wild animals such as lions, tigers, alligators, and piranha fish generally are barred from being kept on private property anywhere without a special permit.) Before buying a horse, cow, pot-bellied pig, or other such animal that you intend to keep on your land, check with city or county authorities to see if any local zoning ordinance would prohibit you from keeping the animal on your land. These ordinances can also usually be found in the public library.

Many rentals, condominiums, and cooperatives restrict your right to keep a pet in your unit. Some limit you to keeping, for instance, one cat or a dog weighing not more than, say, twenty-five pounds. Most leases prohibit pets in the apartment without the landlord's written consent. Restrictions on pets are generally legal and enforced by the courts. If you have several pets or a large dog and are planning on buying a condo or a coop, carefully read all the conditions, covenants, and restrictions (the CC&Rs—see chapter 6), and rules, regulations, and other legal documents pertaining to the unit before signing anything. If you are moving into an apartment, get the landlord's written permission to let you keep the animal before you sign the lease. You may face a tough choice: finding another home for your pet or finding another home for yourself.

Even if you can keep certain animals on your property, you must still respect the rights of your neighbor to be free from a nuisance. If your animals make too much noise or cause a constant offensive odor, your neighbors can sue you for damages and force you to remove the animals (see chapter 6).

DOG LICENSES

Most areas require dogs to be licensed annually. (Other domesticated pets ordinarily don't have to be licensed.) Two things are usually necessary to get the license: You must present a veterinarian's certificate showing the dog was given a rabies shot, and you must pay the license fee. Do you really need to license your dog? Unequivocally, yes. Failing to renew your dog's license each year surely will subject you to a fine if you're caught. (It's surprising how well the animal control authorities can track down owners of unlicensed dogs.) As a practical matter, you should get a license so your dog can be identified in case the animal control authorities ever pick it up.

What happens if your dog is found roaming the streets without a dog license tag or other identification? It will be impounded at the animal shelter nearest to where the dog was found. If you don't contact the shelter within a specified number of days—say, three—the dog can be destroyed or offered for adoption. Suppose you learn a few weeks later that someone else has adopted your dog. Can you get it back? Usually not. You can tell the person your story and hope he or she is sympathetic and returns the dog, but you can't force the new owner to give it up. By failing to license the dog and claim it within the prescribed time, you forfeit your ownership rights.

Another thing to consider if you don't bother to license your dog or get it immunized against rabies: You might be held liable for the damages if your dog bites someone and infects him or her with rabies. In some states, you are guilty of a crime if you know your dog is rabid but do nothing about it, and your dog bites somebody.

INJURIES BY OR TO ANIMALS

If a Dog or Cat Hurts Someone

Under the traditional rule, the owner of a dog or cat is not liable for the injuries the pet causes unless the owner knew or should have known of the animal's dangerous propensity to do the type of act in question. Take, for example, a dog that chases after a boy riding his bicycle down the street and knocks him over. If the dog had never done anything like this before, its owner is probably not liable for the boy's injuries. But if the dog previously had chased other bicyclists, and the dog's owner saw the incident or learned about it from others, the owner is probably liable if he or she didn't take precautions to restrain the dog. As the following examples demonstrate, many states now have laws that make the owner liable in many situations for injuries inflicted by a dog or cat even though the owner had no idea the pet would do this sort of thing.

Let's say that you're walking by your neighbor Hank's house when his dog Rex runs over and bites you in the leg for no reason. Sixteen stitches are required to close the wound, and your doctor orders you to take the next week off from work. You ask Hank to reimburse you for the medical costs and your lost wages, but Hank refuses, saying that Rex has never bitten anyone. If you sue Hank, who will win? In a few states, Hank will win, because they apply the old law: The first bite is free. This rule comes to us from old England, when you had to prove that the dog's owner knew or had reason to know that the dog had bitten someone else before ("scienter") and therefore should have taken steps to prevent it from biting you. Most states today, however, have laws that make the owner liable for all bites—the first as well as the last—regardless of whether the owner knew if the dog had ever bitten anyone before.

Now suppose Rex comes bounding at you, but instead of biting you, leaps at your chest and knocks you down. Is Hank liable for your injuries if Rex had never done anything like this? In many states, no. If Hank was unaware that Rex had a tendency to jump on people, he doesn't need to take precautions to prevent it. Some states, however, now have laws that make the dog's owner liable for all injuries and damage the dog inflicts, regardless of whether the dog had done anything similar before.

Let's say that you are attacked and clawed by your neighbor's cat. Does your neighbor have to pay for your injuries? Again, the question is whether your neighbor should have realized the cat's propensity to attack and claw people. If the owner knew that the cat had a history of clawing people, he or she is obligated to take reasonable precautions against it—for example, declawing the cat, keeping it in the house, or putting it in another room and closing the door while people are visiting. Some states also have a statute that makes the cat's owner liable for all injuries it inflicts, regardless of whether the animal had ever done anything like it before.

One day you're walking toward Carla's front door, when her dog leaps at you, its teeth bared in a threatening manner. Afraid that the dog is about to attack, you jump out of the way, fall, and break your arm. Carla contends that she isn't liable for your injuries, because the dog didn't actually touch you. Besides, the dog was chained and couldn't get to you if it wanted to. Can you make Carla pay for your injuries, even though the dog didn't—and couldn't—touch you? Yes. Since you honestly thought the dog was going to attack you, and you didn't know it was chained, Carla is responsible for your injuries.

Does it make any difference if a dog or cat attacks you while you are in a public place or on its owner's private property? Generally not—at least not if you are on the land with the owner's permission. In many states, even trespassers can recover their damages from the pet's owner, unless the person trespassed in a way that would normally excite and provoke the pet—a burglar climbing through a window, for instance.

Your six-year-old daughter is clawed by a cat, and you sue after the owner refuses to pay for the damages. The owner claims the cat injured the child because she was pulling its tail. Who wins in this situation? Generally the cat's owner does, if he or she can prove that the girl was in fact pulling the cat's tail. By pulling its tail, the girl provoked the cat to take some defensive action. In other words, she asked for it. If the girl was very young, though—so young that she couldn't understand what the cat might do if she pulled its tail—the owner may be liable for her injuries. And if the girl was just petting the cat when it clawed her, and was not teasing or taunting it, this ordinarily is not considered "provocation." These same rules of provocation apply equally to injuries caused by dogs.

In some states a dog's owners may escape liability for injuries the dog inflicts to persons on the owner's land if a large BEWARE OF DOG or GUARD DOG ON DUTY sign is posted in a conspicuous place on his or her property. A person who sees the sign and disregards it is held to have assumed the risk of being bitten or attacked by the dog. But the sign may not apply to children who can't read, or who can read but really don't understand the full import of the warning.

Criminal Liability for Your Animal's Behavior

Suppose you have a ferocious dog and are out walking it. You lose control of the dog and the dog attacks a person, killing him or her. Can criminal charges for murder be brought against you? This happened in a 2001 San Francisco case wherein two large vicious dogs, a Canary Island dog and a Canary-mastiff cross, attacked and mauled to death a woman who was trying desperately to get into her locked apartment. A husband and wife owned the dogs, and the wife was present at the time but could not control the dogs. Criminal charges were brought against the wife for second-degree murder, involuntary manslaughter, and failing to control a mischievous animal that harmed a human. The husband was charged with the two lesser counts of involuntary manslaughter and failing to control a mischievous animal. The case was tried before a jury and the jury returned a verdict against the wife convicting her of second-degree murder. The husband was found guilty of the charges against him.

This was the first time in memory that criminal charges were brought against the animal's owners for injuries or death inflicted by the animal. It should serve as notice to those who harbor ferocious pets, especially those who train their dogs to fight, that they must control their animals and keep them from attacking other people, lest they themselves face criminal charges should their pets injure innocent people.

Damage to Another's Property—Leash Laws

You look out your window one day and see your neighbor's dog digging up your prize begonias. By the time the dog leaves, your flowers are ruined. Does your neighbor have to pay you for the damage? This usually depends on whether your neighbor knew that the dog had a habit of digging up yards. If this is the first time the dog has ever done something like this, your neighbor normally isn't liable. But if the dog had dug up someone's yard before, your neighbor is liable to you for the damage.

Many cities now have leash laws that require dogs to be on a lead no longer than, say, five or six feet when they are on public property. (Some places require cats to be on leashes, too.) Not only can you be fined for violating the leash law, but also, under many of these laws, you are liable for all injuries and damages your dog causes while wandering about the community unleashed. You can't get out of the fine by arguing that your dog is trained to obey your voice, hand, or whistle commands. A number of cities also now require pet owners to pick up their animals' waste from public streets, sidewalks, and parks and to dispose of it properly.

Let's say that you're taking your daily constitutional with your dog on its leash, when another dog attacks your dog, injuring it. Must the dog's owner reimburse you for your vet's bills? Yes. But if both dogs were roaming the neighborhood unleashed, the other dog's owner is usually not liable for your damages, unless your dog was acting purely in self-defense.

Suppose that your dog is in heat. You have been very careful about keeping it away from other dogs, but one day your neighbor's dog jumps your fence and gets to your dog. Is your neighbor liable for the veterinarian costs, food for the litter, and so forth? Yes. But if your dog was roaming the streets, then the answer is no. (As a practical matter, you should have your pets—male and female—neutered or spayed if you don't intend to breed them.)

Damage Done by Horses, Cattle, and Livestock

The owner of a domestic animal—a horse, cow, sheep, pig, turkey, chicken, and so forth—is not liable for injuries to people inflicted by the animal, unless the owner knew or should have known that the animal was likely to do this kind of harm. The injured person normally must prove that the animal had done this type of thing before and that the owner knew of it. For instance, if a horse bit you, you would have to prove that the horse had bitten others before and the owner knew or should have known of the previous bite. Proving that the horse had injured others by, say, kicking them ordinarily would not be sufficient. What if a neighbor's cow, horse, or chicken strays onto your land and damages your property? In that case, the animal's owner is usually liable for the damage, regardless of whether the owner had any idea that the animal was likely to do such a thing. For example, if your neighbor's cow comes onto your land and eats your crops or infects your animals with a disease, your neighbor must pay you for the damage. The reason that horses, cows, chickens, and the like are treated differently from cats and dogs when it comes to trespassing upon another person's land is that cats and dogs are unlikely to inflict serious damage to property. Also, dogs and cats by custom have enjoyed considerable freedom to roam about the community.

Suppose that one day while driving down a country road, you turn a corner, see a cow standing in the middle of the road, swerve to avoid it, and hit a tree. Can you sue the cow's owner for your injuries and the damages to your car? In most states, the cow's owner is liable only if he or she knew the animal was likely to get out yet failed to take adequate precautions to prevent it. For example, if the cow escaped through a hole in the fence that the owner had been meaning to fix for some time, the owner is probably liable. But if the hole is new and the animal's owner didn't know about it, the owner is probably not liable.

Injuries Inflicted by Wild Animals

The owner of a wild animal—a bear, lion, tiger, elephant, wolf, monkey, zebra, elk, moose, leopard, and so forth—generally is liable for all injuries inflicted by that animal, regardless of how hard the owner tries to protect others from the animal. The reason for this rule is that wild animals are instinctively dangerous and cannot truly be tamed. If you're going to take a dangerous animal out of the wild and put it where it can hurt people, you will have to pay the price. Zoos and circuses are liable when a caged animal escapes or reaches through the bars and injures a visitor standing in the public area. But suppose a young child crawls under a bar to get near a tiger's cage, and the tiger claws the child's face. Is the zoo or circus liable, even though the child would not have been injured if he or she had not crawled under the barrier? Yes—at least if the child didn't understand the danger of being so close to the animal. But if an adult does the same thing and is injured by the tiger, the zoo or circus probably is not liable. The adult assumed the risk of being injured and therefore cannot recover damages.

A not infrequent occurrence, unfortunately, is for an elephant in a traveling circus to go berserk and run amok, causing death and injuries to its handlers and spectators alike. In such a case, the circus owner and operator are liable for the injuries and damage caused by the stampeding elephant. Animal rights groups are adamantly against the use of elephants, tigers, and other wild animals in traveling circuses, claiming that the animals are treated brutally, and their destructive conduct is precipitated by inhumane care.

If Your Pet Is Injured or Killed

When someone is at fault and kills your pet—shoots it without reason, perhaps, or runs over it because of careless driving—how much money does he or she have to pay? Usually all you can recover is the value of the animal at the time it was killed. So, if your cat is a run-of-the-mill tabby, or your dog a regular mutt, its value—as measured by the law—is low indeed. For instance, if you can prove your cat was worth $100 when it was killed, that is all you can get. If the person deliberately killed your pet, you can ask for "punitive damages" to punish that person (chapter 10).

Suppose that your dog is run over and injured by a driver who wasn't paying attention. The driver of the car admits responsibility and agrees to pay you for the damages. What are the types of damages you can recover in this situation? Veterinarian bills ordinarily constitute the bulk of damages when an animal is injured. But let's say the dog loses a leg in the accident. In that case, in addition to the vet's bills, you are entitled to recover the difference in value between what the dog was worth with four legs and what it is worth with three. If you're talking about a champion show dog or a trained dog used in the movies, then the damages may be substantial. But for the average dog, the damages (exclusive of veterinarian bills) are usually not going to be very much. If the dog was worth, say, $400 with four legs, it will be worth about $300 with three.

As callous as it is, the law still views animals as inanimate objects—just like cars, furniture, or bowling balls—for purposes of valuing their injuries. If you used the dog for a special reason—to guard your factory, for example, or for hunting trips—and the dog can no longer adequately do its job, you can recover the full value of the dog at the time it was injured, the same as if it had been killed.

If your dog was a champion that you rented out for, say, $250 in stud fees, and the dog is killed or so seriously injured that it can no longer be used for stud purposes, you are entitled to recover from the party at fault the amount of stud fees the dog would have generated had it not been killed or injured.

Many people who have pets treat them as one of the family. And when the pet is injured or killed, they suffer almost as much as if it had been a child that was hurt. But you cannot make the other person pay for your mental anguish when your pet is injured or killed. Even if you see the accident happen, courts refuse to let you recover damages for your own mental anguish when your pet is injured or killed. A few courts, however, let you recover damages for your emotional distress when someone unlawfully and deliberately kills the pet without justification—if a person shoots it for no reason, for instance.

Removing a Trespassing Animal from Your Yard

You are entitled to use a reasonable amount of force to get your neighbor's dog or cat off your property. What is reasonable depends on the circumstances, however. Hitting the animal on the haunches with a broom or spraying it with water from a hose is usually reasonable, since the animal won't be seriously hurt. On the other hand, shooting the animal or hitting it over the head with a heavy piece of wood is usually excessive force, unless the animal was threatening to attack you or someone else. If you use too much force to remove the animal or kill it in the process, you may have to pay the owner for the damages you inflicted upon the animal, but only if the animal was not posing a threat of harm to anyone.

If a dog bites you or a cat claws you while you're trying to shoo it away, does the animal's owner have to pay for the damages? Most courts hold that you are well within your rights to try to remove the animal, and the animal's owner must pay your damages. Some courts, however, will not let you recover your damages from the animal's owner because you assumed the risk that it would turn on you. Before trying to physically remove a potentially dangerous animal from your yard, you should first contact the owner if possible and ask that he or she come get the animal off your land. If you don't know the owner or if a call to the owner would be futile, a call to the animal control department is in order, especially if the animal is large, vicious, or possibly rabid.

VETERINARIANS

SUPPOSE THAT YOU TAKE your dog in for its annual vaccination shots and it bites off the vet's ear. Can the vet sue you? Usually not. Veterinarians and their assistants generally assume the risk that they may be bitten, clawed, or otherwise injured by the animals they treat. But if your pet is unusually vicious for its breed, you must warn the vet about it or you could be liable to the vet for any injuries your pet inflicts upon the vet.

In many states, a veterinarian who treats your pet has a lien on the animal to the extent of the services rendered. If you refuse to pay your bill, the vet can keep the pet as collateral until you do pay. And all the while the vet is keeping your pet, you may be incurring additional fees for boarding. The vet can sell your pet to pay the bill but first must usually notify you in writing of that intention so you can pay the balance and get the pet back. If you get into a dispute with your vet over a bill, it is usually best to pay the bill in full, get your pet back, and then file suit in small claims court or complain to the consumer affairs agency.

DESTRUCTION OF DANGEROUS PETS

A DOG ESCAPES FROM its owner's yard and for no reason attacks and mauls a child walking down the street. Can the dog be destroyed against the owner's will? Yes—but only after the dog has been found to be a danger to society. The animal control board will first investigate the facts to determine whether the animal is indeed a public danger. If it finds the animal dangerous, it will then refer the case to the office of the district attorney, who will file a complaint to have the dog declared a menace and destroyed.

A court hearing will be held to decide the dog's fate. The pet's owner must be given notice of the hearing so he or she can present evidence to refute the charges. If the judge declares the pet to be vicious and dangerous to society, the pet usually will be destroyed. In lieu of ordering the animal destroyed, the judge may order the owner to take sufficient safety precautions to prevent the same thing from happening again—such as putting the animal in a large enclosed cage to keep it from getting out. Rabid and other seriously diseased animals can also be destroyed in the interests of public safety.

WE USUALLY THINK OF cruelty in terms of mercilessly beating or torturing an animal. But cruelty is not limited to these "affirmative" acts; it also includes failing to give your pet proper care and attention. For example, if you underfeed your pet, if you don't supply adequate water, if you keep the animal in a closed hot shelter (such as in a car with the windows rolled up in summer), if you don't give it prompt medical attention when needed—these, too, constitute cruelty. At the very least, you must give your pet sufficient food, water, exercise, and fresh air. And you can't simply abandon your pet when it becomes sick, injured, or old. In most states, it also is considered cruelty to train your pet for prizefighting, such as dog fighting or cockfighting.

Where is the line drawn between cruelty and allowable discipline or punishment of a pet? The question generally is one of excessiveness. Striking a dog a time or two with a newspaper because it soiled the carpet is reasonable punishment. Brutally kicking it a number of times or hitting it with a heavy branch is too much.

If you are suspected of being cruel to your pet, you can be charged with a crime (usually a misdemeanor), and your pet can be taken from you. Usually the pet cannot be taken away until after a court hearing at which it has been determined that you are guilty of animal cruelty. But when the animal's life is threatened, it can be taken away immediately and the hearing held afterward. If you are found innocent of cruelty, the animal must be returned to you. If you are found guilty, not only can the animal be taken away, but you also can be fined and even sentenced to jail. If the judge is satisfied that you will change your ways and care for the animal properly, you may be allowed to keep it, subject to periodic visits by the animal control authorities to make sure you are taking good care of the animal—a "probation" of sorts.

Animals and Scientific Research

Medicine and other disciplines long have used animals for various purposes. For example, at one time rabbits (and other animals) routinely were sacrificed to diagnose whether women were pregnant or not. Urine was taken from a woman suspected to be pregnant and was injected into a female rabbit. Several days later, the rabbit was killed and its ovaries examined for telltale signs that the woman was pregnant. Tests since have been developed that can diagnose pregnancy without using animals. In fact, home pregnancy test kits can be found on the shelves of drugstores throughout the United States.

The use of animals undeniably has led to important medical advances. Without it, important discoveries in the treatment of diabetes, polio, and heart disease, to name a few, would never have been made. What happens when the rights of animals to be free from cruelty clash with the use of animals in scientific research? This is a difficult question.

Certainly animals should not be subjected to needless experimentation and its attendant tortures and injury. On the other hand, animal research can expand man's knowledge and lead to medical breakthroughs. Recognizing that some experimentation on animals is unnecessary or unduly harsh, in December 1985, Congress passed a law that strengthened the Animal Welfare Act of 1966. Among other things, it requires researchers to exhaust other avenues before turning to animal experimentation. As a result of growing community awareness of what the animals are sometimes subjected to, the use of animals in many fields is being reduced. Also, the use of alternative methods, including tissue and cell cultures, computer simulations and analyses, models and genetic engineering, makes it possible to do much research without animals.

One controversial area between animal rights activists and cosmetic companies involves the practice of many of the cosmetic manufacturers to test their products on animals. For instance, some cosmetic companies would take their product—say, mascara or eyeliner—and rub it directly onto the eyes of rabbits to see if there was a toxic or allergic reaction. Fortunately, through public awareness and animal rights advocacy, these practices have diminished greatly. Many cosmetic manufacturers now proudly boast that their products were not tested on animals.

TEN

Civil Wrongs: Torts

WHEN YOU ARE INJURED or your property is damaged, your rights are determined by the law of torts. The English word tort is taken from a French word that means "wrong." The most common example of a tort is the automobile accident caused by one driver's carelessness. A driver who is speeding and causes an accident commits the tort of "negligence" and must pay for the personal injuries and property damage resulting from this conduct.

WHAT IS TORT LAW?

THE LAW OF TORTS can be boiled down to this: When someone is in the wrong and injures you or damages your property, that person must pay you for the damage done. This is only fair; we expect others to pay for any damages they cause us, just as they expect us to pay if we harm them or their property.

But the mere fact that someone injures you or damages your property does not automatically mean that that person has committed a tort and must pay for your damages. A person must pay for your damages only if he or she was somehow at fault. Some accidents are truly unavoidable; they happen even though everyone involved was paying attention and no one was at fault. When that happens, each party involved bears the cost of his or her own injuries and damage. A person is responsible for your injuries and damage only if his or her conduct is "tortious"—of such a nature that it is fair to make him or her pay for your damages. The three types of tortious conduct, discussed below, are (1) negligence; (2) intentional misconduct; and (3) strict liability.

Most of the time, the victim of a tort is compensated by a sum of money for the injuries and damages he or she suffers. Usually the sum includes damages for any medical expenses, lost wages for any time the person is out of work, "pain and suffering," and the cost of repairing or replacing any damaged property. Money is admittedly a poor substitute for some things—a lost arm, for instance—but what else is there? In some cases, such as a nuisance or trespass, you can go to court to get an injunction ordering the person to stop committing the tort.

Some specific tort situations are dealt with in other chapters of this book. For instance, the right to sue members of your family is discussed in chapter 1; automobile accidents are covered in chapter 2; trespassing and nuisance are explored in chapter 6; suing a landlord for injuries is discussed in chapter 7; chapter 9 covers injuries caused by animals; chapter 11 deals with medical malpractice; chapter 12 concerns defective products; and employee-related torts are contained in chapter 13. If the particular topic you are looking for is not in this chapter, a review of the table of contents or index will guide you to the proper page. Even though the specific tort you are interested in is dealt with in another chapter, however, you should still review this chapter in full in order to get a complete picture of your rights when you are the victim of another's tort.

How Torts and Crimes Differ

What is the difference between a tort and a crime? In tort law, it is you, the individual, who have been wronged; you seek damages for your own injuries by filing a lawsuit in your own name in civil court. In criminal law, by contrast, the community as a whole seeks justice. Crimes like murder, arson, rape, and burglary, to name a few, cannot be tolerated by society, and one who commits such acts must be dealt with appropriately. A criminal complaint is filed in the name of the people (or the state), not the victim's name. While tort law compensates the victim by awarding a sum of money designed to make him or her "whole," criminal law punishes the criminal, usually by imprisonment or fine, or both.

The fact that some crimes are also torts is one reason for much of the confusion between a tort and a crime. Battery, for instance, is both a crime and a tort. If someone hits you, you can sue the person in a civil court for the tort of battery to recover your damages. The state also can prosecute that person for the crime of battery. Many crimes do not have a specific tort counterpart, but you can still sue the person in civil court for your injuries. For example, there is no tort called "rape." But a rape victim can sue her assailant in civil court for the torts of assault, battery, false imprisonment, and intentional infliction of emotional distress.

SHOULD YOU SEE A LAWYER?

Wʜᴇɴ sᴏᴍᴇᴏɴᴇ ᴇʟsᴇ ɪɴᴊᴜʀᴇs ʏᴏᴜ, should you see a lawyer? Generally, yes—even if your injuries seem relatively minor to you. Most lawyers don't charge for the initial consultation fee in personal injury cases, so you can usually get at least a half-hour's worth of free legal advice for your problem. That half-hour combined with the advice in this book may be all you need to see just where you stand. And if you do hire a lawyer for a personal injury case, it normally is on a contingency fee basis; you pay the lawyer a fee only if you win the case. The lawyer's fee comes out of the money that you receive, often paid by an insurance company. The contingency fee basis relates only to the lawyer's fees. It does not apply to the "costs and expenses" of litigation, such as the cost of filing the complaint. You are liable for the full amount of all costs and expenses (to the extent they are reasonable) incurred by your lawyer, regardless of whether you win or lose the case. (Finding the right lawyer and fee arrangements are discussed in chapter 24.)

One definite advantage to hiring a lawyer is that even after paying the lawyer a fee, the chances are that you will get more with a lawyer than you will if you try to represent yourself in injury cases. Studies by independent think tanks as well as those by the insurance industry itself consistently reveal that at least in the realm of automobile accidents, victims represented by attorneys win more often and end up with more money even after paying the lawyer his or her fee than those who try to do it themselves.

NEGLIGENCE

Tʜᴇ ᴍᴏsᴛ ᴄᴏᴍᴍᴏɴ ᴛᴏʀᴛ is the tort of negligence. Negligence can be defined simply as carelessness: failing to pay sufficient attention under the circumstances. Some everyday examples of negligence include automobile accidents caused by speeding, disobeying traffic signs and signals, tailgating, making an unsafe left turn, driving while drunk, and not keeping the brakes in good shape; falling in a store, theater, or even your neighbor's house because of a loose stair or carpet or a slippery floor ("slip and fall" cases); being injured by the carelessness of a doctor or dentist; or being hurt when the bus you're riding in makes a jolting start or an unexpected sudden stop.

How can you tell whether the person who hurt you was negligent or not? The standard used is whether that person was exercising a reasonable amount of "due care" under the circumstances. What due care is depends upon a number of factors—the circumstances, the ages of the parties involved, whether anyone has a physical or mental disability, and the like. Conduct is measured against what a "reasonable person" would have done in the same situation. For example, a reasonable person would not make a left turn until it was safe to do so; negligence occurs when someone tries to make a left turn when it is not safe.

This "reasonable person" against whom your conduct is measured generally is considered to be an adult of unspecified age who has no physical or mental disabilities and who is careful without being overly cautious. (The exceptions to this are discussed below.) Is reasonable conduct always the same? No, it changes from situation to situation. For instance, you are not expected to act the same in an emergency as you would in a nonemergency, when you had time to assess the situation and weigh the alternatives.

Children and the Elderly

The standard of conduct expected of a child is measured by what a reasonably careful child of like age, intelligence, and experience would have done under the same circumstances, not by what an adult would have done. A 2-year-old child may not realize the danger in pulling a dog's tail, but a 7-year-old should. Very young children—usually under 7 years old—are legally incapable of being negligent in many states. In other words, you can't sue a child under 7 for injuring you. (Some states do not have a set age limit, but the courts often tend to settle on 4 years as the age at which a child becomes liable for negligence.) You can, however, sue a child under the set age limit for an intentional tort, such as battery, if the child understood the wrongfulness of the act yet still went ahead and did it.

When a child engages in an activity traditionally reserved for adults—driving a car, for example—his or her conduct is measured by the higher adult standard. So if a 13-year-old boy takes his parents' car for a spin and gets into an accident, his conduct is measured by what an adult would have done while driving. The boy is not liable just because he was driving without a license. You still must prove that an adult driver would not have done what the boy did under the circumstances.

What difference does it make how old a child must be before you can sue him or her or what the applicable standard of conduct is, since a child ordinarily doesn't have the money to pay any judgment even if you win? The difference is that if you can sue the child you may be able to collect under the parents' insurance policy. (In actuality, the issue of whether a child was negligent is more often raised when the child is injured and sues someone. The person being sued may claim that the child's own negligence caused or contributed to the injuries and therefore any monetary recovery by the child should be denied or reduced.)

At the other end of the spectrum, advanced age alone does not have any effect on the general standard of care applicable to all adults. An 85-year-old driver, for instance, must use the same degree of care that a 25-year-old driver must use while driving a car.

Physical and Mental Disabilities

A person who has a physical disability is not held to the same standard of care as a person without any disabilities. A physically disabled person is required to use only that degree of care and caution that a reasonable person with the same disability would use. A blind man, for instance, must exercise the same degree of care for his own safety that a reasonably prudent blind man would use in crossing a street, and a paraplegic must use the same care in his or her activities as a careful paraplegic would. It would be unfair to require people with physical disabilities to act the same way as people with no disabilities where it is physically impossible for them to do so.

Although the law makes a concession for physical limitations, no allowances are made for people who suffer from mental disabilities or retardation. A person who is psychotic or mentally retarded generally is held to the same standard of care as the person of average intelligence. An insane, psychotic person who injures another person or damages another's property is civilly liable for the damages, even though the person doesn't know what he or she is doing at the time. (But the law relieves a person of criminal responsibility if he or she was insane at the time of the act; see chapter 23.)

Proving Negligence

How much care a reasonable person would use in a given situation usually is decided by a jury, based on all of the facts presented during the trial. Frequently, the process involves an inexact analysis: One could argue that a reasonable person would have done this, or a reasonable person would not have done that. And in fact, the standard of care often is supplied by custom and common sense. Many times, however, it is imposed by a statute. All states, for example, have laws for driving a car: You must stop for a red light; you can't exceed the posted speed limit; and so on. These laws set the minimum standard of care that you must follow. If you break any of these laws and cause an accident, you are usually liable for the injuries and damage. You are presumed negligent because you violated the law.

Sometimes an accident is so unusual that the mere fact that it happened is enough to infer that someone was negligent and must pay you for your injuries. This is the doctrine of *res ipsa loquitur,* which literally means, "the thing speaks for itself." It applies only when the defendant had the exclusive control of the thing that hurt you, you did not contribute to the accident, and the accident normally wouldn't have happened unless somebody was negligent.

The classic case of *res ipsa loquitur* involved a man who was walking down the street when a barrel of flour rolled out of a window above a shop, seriously injuring him. The man could not prove exactly how or why the barrel fell from the window, and the owner of the shop wouldn't admit to any fault. Because this type of accident normally would not have occurred unless someone was negligent, and since the store owner had the means to discover why the accident happened, it was up to the store owner to prove that he was not negligent. Without this rule, the store owner—who could get at the truth much more easily than the injured person could—would be able to avoid responsibility simply by remaining silent and pretending to be ignorant of what caused the accident.

Another example: Sara goes into the hospital to have some surgery done on her knee. When she wakes up after the operation, she discovers a serious burn on her chest. None of the doctors, nurses, or other staff will admit knowing anything about how the burn got there. The hospital and its employees are presumed at fault: A patient normally wouldn't be burned like this unless someone was negligent; the hospital employees had exclusive control of the operating room; and Sara, who was unconscious when the accident happened, in no way contributed to her own injury.

Res ipsa loquitur also is applied to cases involving airplanes that suddenly drop out of the sky on a sunny day and crash. The law presumes negligence of some kind—any kind—on the part of the airline: Maybe there was pilot error, or the mechanics were careless. It is up to the airline to refute any possibility that it was negligent—by presenting the testimony of its mechanics that everything was done properly and by offering flight recorder data showing that the pilots didn't do anything wrong, for example. In practice, however, it is virtually impossible for the airliner to overcome this presumption of negligence on its part.

Proving Notice of a Dangerous Condition If You "Slip and Fall"

If you injure yourself on someone else's land, is that person liable for your injuries? The answer depends on whether the person had notice that a dangerous condition existed on the land, and if so, whether he or she had a reasonable amount of time to either remove the danger or warn persons on the land that the danger was there. (Other issues relating to a landowner's liability to persons injured on his or her land are discussed in chapter 6.) Say that Peggy is doing her weekly grocery shopping at the supermarket, when she slips on a piece of fruit that had fallen out of its bin and breaks her arm. If she sues the store for payment of her doctor bills and other damages, will she win? It depends on how long the fruit had been on the floor before Peggy stepped on it. If the fruit had fallen out of the bin only moments before Peggy walked down the aisle, the supermarket probably is not liable; it did not know the fruit was there. But if she could prove that the fruit had been lying on the floor for an hour or two, Peggy most likely would win her case on the basis that the store should have known of the fruit on the floor after a sufficient time and cleaned it up.

How do you prove how long the fruit has been on the ground? Asking other shoppers who had been in that area before Peggy fell, or if a supermarket employee had cleaned the area only minutes before, it is likely that the fruit had fallen out of the bin only moments before the accident. But if several shoppers noticed the fruit on the ground and told the manager about it half an hour earlier, this shows that there was enough time for the store to clean it up.

Another example: Samuel leaves the balcony at the movie theater to go to the lobby for refreshments. On the way down the stairs, he trips over a loose piece of carpet and is hurt seriously. Again the question of whether the theater is liable depends on whether the theater knew or should have known that the carpet was loose and had a reasonable amount of time to correct the dangerous condition, put a barrier around it, or post a warning until the carpet was fixed. One way to prove that the theater knew of the dangerous condition is by previous reports of people tripping over the carpet at an earlier show. Another way is to prove that someone had informed a theater employee that the carpet was loose or that a theater employee saw the loose carpet but did nothing about it. Yet another way to prove the theater should have known the carpet was loose is by analyzing the loose carpet and surrounding area for signs that the carpet had been loose for a while. But if Samuel is the first one to report the danger, and all the evidence shows the carpet had not been loose for very long, the theater is probably not liable for Samuel's injuries.

Defenses to Negligence

Even though someone has been negligent and hurt you, there are several defenses that can relieve him or her of having to pay for part or all of your damages. These are the defenses of contributory negligence, comparative negligence, assumption of risk, and releases.

Contributory Negligence

At one time, all states held that if you were at all responsible for your own injury, you usually could not collect a dime from the other party. If you were in an automobile accident, for instance, and were 25 percent at fault and the other driver was 75 percent at fault, you could not recover anything from the other driver. This is the rule of "contributory negligence."

Comparative Negligence

Most, if not all, states have abandoned the strict rule of contributory negligence in favor of the doctrine of "comparative negligence." Under comparative negligence, your negligence is compared to the other party's negligence, and the damages you are entitled to recover are reduced by your own percentage of fault. Say you suffered $50,000 worth of damages in an accident in which you were 25 percent responsible and the other party was 75 percent at fault. You can sue the other party for your damages, but your damages will be reduced by $12,500 (25 percent of $50,000). Who determines the amount of your fault, and how? The jury decides, based on all of the evidence presented during the trial.

Suppose you were injured in an automobile accident, and the jury rules that you and the other driver were each 50 percent at fault. Does the other driver have to pay you anything? The answer depends on what state you're in. Some states have a "pure" system of comparative negligence, which lets you sue the other party no matter how much you were at fault. If you were 99 percent negligent and the other party was only was 1 percent negligent, you could sue the other party; of course, you'd only collect 1 percent of your damages. So when you're 50 percent at fault, the other driver has to pay for half of your damages. (You, in turn, are liable for 50 percent of the other driver's damages.)

Other states let you collect from the other party as long as you weren't more negligent than he or she. In this case, since you were 50 percent at fault, the other driver must pay for half of your damages. But if you had been 50.01 percent or more responsible for the accident, you couldn't recover any damages. Finally, some states make the other party pay only if you were less at fault than he or she. Since you were equally at fault, the other driver owes you nothing. In those states, you only can recover if you were no more than 49.99 percent responsible for the accident.

Assumption of Risk

You generally cannot sue a person for injuring you if you knowingly and voluntarily assumed the risk that you might be injured. This is the legal doctrine of "assumption of risk." Suppose you're leaving your friend's house one winter day. She walks you to the door, looks at the walkway, and says, "You'd better not go out that way because there's ice all over the walk. Use the back door." You reply that you'll be okay and use the front walk—and then slip, fall, and hurt yourself. You have assumed the risk of being hurt because you knew the danger (ice) was there and voluntarily approached it, even though there was a way of avoiding the danger.

If you participate in a sport, you assume the risk that you may be injured. This is true whether you are a professional, high school, or college athlete, or a novice playing a sandlot game on Sunday. Suppose you are playing in a basketball game at the local park when a player on the other team comes up from behind and deliberately pushes you into the pole holding the backboard, breaking your nose and causing other facial injuries. Does assumption of risk bar you from suing that player? No. You only assume risks that are inherent in the sport—a "part of the game." Assumption of risk does not prevent you from suing a player who intentionally injures you.

In a professional ice hockey game between the Boston Bruins and the Vancouver Canucks on February 21, 2000, in the waning seconds of the game, notorious Bruins's "enforcer" Marty McSorley skated up from behind Canucks's forward Donald Brashear and struck Brashear on the side of the head with his hockey stick, causing Brashear serious injury. The National Hockey League suspended McSorley indefinitely, causing him to miss the final twenty-three games of the season.

Criminal charges were filed against McSorley in Vancouver. The court found McSorley guilty of assault with a weapon. The court did not give McSorley any jail time, rather putting him on probation for eighteen months and ordering him not to play in any game against Brashear during that time, in Canada or the United States. If Brashear chose to, he could file a civil action for battery against McSorley, as McSorley's action fell outside of the risks assumed in a normal hockey game. Hockey is a rough game, and hard bodychecking is part of it. But deliberately hitting another player on the head or in the face with a stick goes beyond the boundaries of permissible conduct.

McSorley was not the first hockey player ever to be tried in a criminal court for on-the-ice conduct during the course of a game. In 1988, Dino Ciccarelli, then with the Minnesota North Stars, was sentenced to one day in jail and fined $1,000 for deliberately hitting Toronto Leaf player Luke Richardson with his stick.

What if you're a spectator? Do you assume the risk of being struck by an errant baseball or hockey puck? By sitting near a tight corner at an automobile race, do you assume the risk that a car may crash into the barrier, sending up debris that can injure or kill you? Ordinarily, you do assume these risks at a sporting event, but only if the arena has provided a sufficient number of screened or otherwise protected seats for fans who could be expected to ask for them. About the only way you could recover damages is by proving that you asked for a protected seat, but they were all sold out. You can sue the stadium if you think you have found safe refuge behind the screen, but, for instance, a ball is hit through a hole in the screen and injures you.

Releases

Suppose you are hit by a baseball while attending a professional game. The stadium claims that you not only are barred from suing them because you assumed the risk, but you also are barred by the "release" on the back of the ticket, which states that you agree that the stadium cannot be held liable for any injuries you suffer on the premises. Does this release prevent you from suing the stadium? The answer can depend upon a number of things. First of all, it depends on whether the release was conspicuous and clear. If you didn't see it because, for example, it was in fine print, it doesn't count. Neither does a release that is so poorly written that you can't understand it. Another important factor is how you were injured. If you were struck by a foul ball, the release may be valid. But if you were injured by a defective seat or loose railing, for instance, you can sue because a facility that is open to the public ordinarily cannot disclaim liability for its own negligence. And a release also will not be enforced to block your suit against someone who deliberately hurt you.

INTENTIONAL TORTS

An "INTENTIONAL TORT" is one in which the person deliberately means to hurt you or damage your property. If someone punches you, purposely rams his or her car into yours, threatens to shoot you, throws a bottle or a rock at you—all of these are intentional torts. In intentional torts, the person's state of mind when he or she was performing the act is the critical element. If the person meant to hit you, it is considered battery. But if the person was merely careless and didn't intend to hit you, then the tort is negligence.

The most important legal difference between an intentional tort and negligence is that if you are the victim of an intentional tort, you are entitled to recover an award of punitive (or "exemplary") damages in addition to all of your other damages. Punitive damages are designed to punish the person for doing the wrongful act and to deter him or her from doing it again in the future. How much in punitive damages can you get? That's really up to the jury; it could be as little as $1 or as much as $100,000 or more, depending upon the facts of the case. In cases involving deliberate misconduct by a large corporation, punitive damages can run into the millions.

Suppose you are standing near Bob. Hal throws a rock at Bob, Bob ducks, and the rock hits you. Can you sue Hal for an intentional tort (battery) even though he meant to hit Bob, not you? Yes. Since Hal intended to hit Bob with the rock, that intent is "transferred" to you. The legal effect is that Hal is liable just as if he had meant to hit you with the rock in the first place.

Let's say that one night Ernie sees his girlfriend on the other side of the street. He crosses the street, sneaks up behind her, abruptly grabs her, turns her around, and kisses her. He then realizes that the woman isn't his girlfriend but another woman who resembles her. If the woman sues Ernie for battery, can Ernie get off the hook by proving that he was mistaken— that he didn't intend to kiss this woman but his girlfriend? No. The fact is he did intend to kiss this woman. His mistake as to the woman's identity is of no legal consequence.

Assault

In tort law, an "assault" consists of a deliberate act that causes you to fear that you are in imminent danger of being struck—by a fist, bullet, or whatever. If, for example, a person starts to take a swing at you or pulls a gun out and threatens to shoot you, the person is guilty of an assault because you reasonably feared that you were going to be hit or shot right away. Actual physical contact is not required for an assault to be committed. If you manage to step out of the way of the fist, for instance, or if the person doesn't fire the gun, it is still an assault.

You also do not have to fear that you will be injured from the contact. Suppose that Tiny Tom, standing three-feet-eight-inches and weighing all of eighty-five pounds, gets mad and takes a swing at George Foreman, former heavyweight boxing champion. Is this an assault, even though Foreman was in no danger of being hurt by the blow? Yes. Foreman needs only to realize that Tiny Tom is about to hit him.

In fact, for an act to be an assault, you need only have a reasonable belief that the other person intends to hit you. The person's outward actions, rather than his or her subjective intent, are what determine an assault. If John takes a swing at Alan, even though he intends only to scare Alan and not actually hit him, John commits an assault. To Alan it looked as though John was going to hit him. Likewise, if John points an unloaded gun at Alan and threatens to shoot him, in most states, John commits an assault. Although John knew the gun was unloaded and couldn't possibly hurt anyone, Alan had no way of knowing whether the gun was loaded or not. He believed—as would most anyone else in his place—that the gun was loaded. In a few states, John is not liable for an assault unless there were bullets in the gun.

John must have had the "actual ability" to commit battery. But Alan still could sue John for the tort of intentional infliction of emotional distress (see discussion below).

Suppose Howard shakes his fist at Martha, saying, "If you weren't a woman, I'd hit you." Is this an assault? Probably not, since his words contradict his actions. But this is not always true. If Howard was shaking his fist so vigorously and his face was so flushed that Martha justifiably feared an immediate strike—despite what Howard was saying—Howard is liable for an assault.

Battery

A person who deliberately hits or touches you without your permission commits the tort of "battery." As with other intentional torts, the person's mental state is all-important. Accidentally jostling someone in a crowded hallway while you're in a hurry is not battery, but purposely shoving a person out of your way is. Whether something constitutes battery often is determined by socially acceptable standards of conduct. Certain deliberate physical contact, even with a stranger, is not battery if it is commonplace. For instance, tapping a person's shoulder to ask for directions or the time is not battery. But if the contact is harmful or offensive, it is battery.

Suppose Beth walks up to you and deliberately knocks your hat off your head. Is she guilty of battery, even though she didn't touch your body? Yes. Anything you are wearing or holding is so closely identified with your body that it is considered battery to touch it. So if a person intentionally grabs your coat while you're wearing it or yanks your briefcase from your hand, that person has committed battery. What if you're sitting in your car and someone deliberately runs into you? This too is battery; the car is considered an extension of your body while you are in it. But if your coat and briefcase were lying on a bench when they were grabbed, or you were across the street from your car when it was hit, there is no battery. (The person may still be liable for a "trespass to chattels" or even "conversion," discussed below.)

You do not have to suffer any injury in order to sue for battery. Any unlawful touching, regardless of how slight, is all that is required, if it is offensive. For instance, if a man lightly, yet intentionally brushes his hand over a woman's breasts without her consent, he is liable for battery, even though the woman isn't physically injured. But the absence of physical injury is germane to the question of how much money you can ask for—indeed, to whether it is worth it to sue the person in the first place. You probably would get a lot more money if someone breaks your leg than if someone knocks your hat off your head. In some cases, however, such as where the conduct is very offensive, you may get a large award of punitive damages even though your physical injuries were next to nothing. In our example using the man who slightly brushes his hands against the woman's breasts, the jury could be expected to make a significant award of punitive damages for his reprehensible conduct.

Assault and battery seem to go together like ham and eggs; you usually don't think of one without the other. But just as an assault can occur without battery, battery can happen without an assault. Suppose you're asleep when someone you don't know kisses you. There is no assault because you weren't aware that the person was going to kiss you. But there is battery because the person touched you without your permission—you don't have to be aware of the contact when it happens. Another, perhaps more readily imaginable, example of battery without an assault would be if someone sneaked up from behind and hits you. Since you did not suspect anything until you were struck, there was no assault, but there was battery.

It is not battery if you permit someone to touch you. A man who kisses a woman with her consent, for example, does not commit battery. But the consent must be voluntary. If a man holds a knife to a woman's throat and says, "Kiss me or I'll kill you," and she complies, it is still battery; the woman did not freely consent to the contact. The person must be legally and mentally capable of consenting to the act. The consent of a child, a drunkard, or an insane or mentally retarded person may not be good.

Let's say Ron is drinking in a bar and gets into a shouting match with Mike, another customer. Mike asks Ron to step outside so they can settle their dispute in the alley. Ron says, "That's fine with me; let's go." Mike breaks Ron's nose in the ensuing fight; Ron sues Mike for battery. Mike contends that Ron consented to the fight and therefore can't sue him. Who wins? In some states, Ron wins because you can sue your opponent even if you were a willing participant in the fight. This is because you can't consent to an illegal act—here, a fight. Other states recognize consent to a fight as a valid defense; by voluntarily engaging in fisticuffs, you know you are going to be hit and likely injured and therefore can't sue the other person.

Someone is about to hit you, but you strike first, breaking his or her nose. Do you have to pay the other person for the damages? Not if you were acting in self-defense or to protect someone else. The one restriction on this is that you are only permitted to use "reasonable force" to defend yourself. How much force is reasonable force depends on the situation. You can use deadly force—force capable of inflicting death or serious bodily harm, such as wielding a gun or a lead pipe—only if it is necessary under the circumstances. If you use too much force—if you shoot someone to prevent him or her from merely touching you, for instance—you can be held liable for battery. (You may be guilty of a crime if you use excessive force and hurt or kill someone.)

One day Ken starts insulting Rodney. Rodney tells him to stop, but Ken keeps egging Rodney on. Rodney finally says, "Listen, if you don't shut up, I'm going to belt you one." Ken doesn't stop, and Rodney hits him, breaking his jaw. Ken sues Rodney for battery; Rodney contends that Ken provoked him. Who wins? Ken. Verbal provocation is normally not considered to be a good reason to commit battery.

False Imprisonment

"False imprisonment" occurs when someone intentionally confines you against your will. We ordinarily associate false imprisonment with being locked in a room or a cell. But it also can occur, for example, when someone grabs you outside and prevents you from getting away. The confinement can also be psychological—if someone tells you that he or she will shoot you or a loved one if you try to leave an unlocked room, for instance.

You are not imprisoned if there is a reasonable way to escape from the confined area. If you can safely escape from a locked room through an open window, for example, there is no false imprisonment.

False imprisonment frequently is alleged by a person who feels that he or she was unlawfully arrested. If the police did not have "probable cause" to arrest you (see chapter 23), you can sue them for false imprisonment. ("False arrest" is really just a type of false imprisonment.) If someone files a false police report that ends in your arrest, you can sue that person for false imprisonment. For example, Dennis calls the police and informs them that he saw Ted committing a burglary. Dennis knows that this is untrue and is filing the false report to get back at Ted. The police arrest Ted and put him in jail. Ted can sue Dennis for false imprisonment because it was Dennis's act—filing a false police report—that got Ted arrested. The police are liable for false imprisonment if they knew Dennis was lying when he made the report but still went ahead and arrested Ted.

Suppose you're walking out of a store when the manager asks you to follow her to a back room. Once there, she informs you that the store has had a problem with shoplifters and that she would like to take a look inside your shopping bag. You tell her that you have nothing to hide and dump the bag's contents onto a table. The manager goes through everything, finds nothing, thanks you, and tells you that you're free to go. The whole thing takes about five minutes. Can you sue for false imprisonment? Probably not. A store owner or employee who suspects a person of shoplifting generally can detain that person for a reasonable time to investigate a possible crime. But what if you refuse to let the manager look inside the bag; can she do it anyway? Generally not. About the only times the manager can look inside the bag over your objections is if she or another employee actually saw you steal something and put it in the bag, or if a stolen item is in plain view (a stolen sweater is sticking out of the bag, for example). Otherwise the manager would have to let you go or call the police to conduct any further investigation.

The investigation must be done in a reasonable manner; the owner or employee cannot loudly accuse you in front of other customers and must not be rude or offensive while questioning you. And the investigation must not take an unnecessarily long time—ten to fifteen minutes is often the most that is needed. This is known as the "shopkeeper's privilege" or "merchant's privilege."

Damage to Personal Property

The act of deliberately damaging or interfering with the use of another's personal property is called a "trespass to chattels." Personal property (chattel) is anything other than real estate—your car, books, clothing, and furniture, to name a few examples.

Suppose you see someone sitting on the hood of your car. Can you sue that person for a trespass to chattels? No. The interference with your car is minimal. It's not enough to worry about, so the law doesn't. But if the car is damaged in any way—for instance, if the hood gets scratched—you can sue for a trespass to chattels.

When a person damages your property ordinarily he or she must pay you the cost of having it repaired. If someone dents your fender, and it costs you $500 to get it fixed, that person has to pay you $500. Suppose that Ellen runs into your car and does $3,500 damage to it, but your car is old and worth only $2,500. How much does Ellen have to pay you, the full $3,500 to get it fixed or only $2,500, the value of your car. The answer is $2,500. If it costs more to repair the property than the thing is worth, you get the smaller value—in our example, the value of your car before it was damaged. Another way of calculating damages is the difference between the value of the property before it was damaged and what it is worth afterward. For example, if you could still sell the car for $1,000 after the accident, then Ellen only has to pay you $1,500—the difference between what the car was worth before the accident ($2,500) and what it was worth after ($1,000).

Theft or Destruction of Personal Property

Someone who steals or deliberately destroys your personal property is liable for the tort of "conversion," and you are entitled to be compensated for the value of the property at the time and place of the conversion. For example, if someone smashes your watch with a hammer, he or she has to pay you the value of the watch at that time. If the watch cost you $250 two years ago, and a new one costs $300 today, but yours was only worth $100 when it was destroyed, that's all you can get for it. (You can, however, also sue for punitive damages.)

Suppose your television set is stolen from your house. Two months later, you find it for sale at a swap meet. You tell the man selling it that it is your stolen set and that you want it back. He tells you that he bought the set at a garage sale and that it's now his to do with as he pleases. Who is in the right? You are. A thief does not acquire title to stolen property and so has no title to give to someone who buys the property from him or her. In other words, a person who buys something that was stolen owns nothing. You are entitled to get your property back without paying the seller a dime. This is true even if the seller is totally innocent, had no idea that the property was stolen, and paid good money for it. His only recourse is to try to get the money back from the person who sold it to him. What if he refuses to return the property to you? Can you just pick it up and take it away? No. Ordinarily you must go through the courts to get the property back. The best thing to do in this situation is to call the police and tell them that you've located your stolen property and ask for their assistance. They'll impound the set, and if you can prove that it's yours, they'll return it to you when they no longer need it for the criminal case.

Let's say that in the middle of the night you're awakened by a noise in your driveway. You look out the window and see somebody stealing the CD player from your car. Can you shoot that person to prevent the theft? No. You can use reasonable force to defend your property from theft or damage. But the right to use force to your property does not include the right to use deadly force. Why? Because when it comes down to choosing between human life and property, human life always wins. It's another matter, however, if a burglar breaks into your house and confronts you, threatening your safety and the safety of your family. You may be justified in using deadly force in that situation, because you're protecting more than just your property; you're protecting yourself and your loved ones as well.

Misuse of the Judicial System

Suppose you are a tenant and your landlord files eviction proceedings against you, knowing there is no reason to do so. Or suppose someone signs a false criminal complaint against you, knowing that you haven't committed a crime. In either case, you can sue the person for the tort of "malicious prosecution." Malicious prosecution is the filing of a civil lawsuit or the making of a criminal complaint against someone without "probable grounds" for doing so. (In the second example, if you are arrested and taken into custody, you can sue the person for false imprisonment as well.)

You cannot sue for malicious prosecution until the original bogus case is terminated, and then only if the case ends in your favor. If the other person wins, the law presumes that he or she had sufficient reason to bring the complaint in the first place. This is true even if the case is reversed on appeal and you ultimately prevail.

Let's say that you file a lawsuit on the advice of your attorney, but you lose the case, and the other person sues you for malicious prosecution. You contend that you brought the suit because your attorney told you that you had a good chance of winning. Who should win the lawsuit? You should. As long as you told your attorney all the facts of the case before he or she advised you to file it, you are deemed to have probable cause to file the suit. But if you withheld some important facts from the attorney, you cannot hide behind the attorney's advice to sue the other person.

Another tort involving the misuse of the judicial process is "abuse of process," which is the misuse of the court system to achieve an improper goal. Unlike in malicious prosecution, where there is no justification to file the lawsuit, in abuse of process the lawsuit is justified, but one party uses the court's power to achieve an impermissible result. For example, after a lawsuit is filed against you, the other party starts harassing you with court motions and procedures to coerce you into settling the case, rather than using them for the purposes they were intended to achieve.

Fraud

Let's say that you're interested in buying a horse and find one that you like. The owner tells you that the horse is only four years old and is in excellent health. In reality—as the owner well knows—the horse is eight years old and sickly. You buy the horse, but a month later you take it to the vet because it seems ill. Your vet looks the horse over and tells you the truth about it. Is there anything you can do? Yes. You can sue the person who sold you the horse for fraud. Fraud is committed when a person tells you something that he or she knows to be untrue, knowing that you will rely on this falsehood in making your decision.

The falsity usually must be one of fact, not opinion. For instance, if a used-car salesman tells you a car is a 2001 model when in fact it is a 1999 model, that is a misstatement of fact. But if the salesman tells you the car is good and will last a long time, this is only an opinion or permissible exaggeration—"sales talk" or "puffing."

INVASION OF PRIVACY

THE FIRST AMENDMENT of the Constitution guarantees the right to free speech. But what if you don't want to listen? Do you have the right to be left alone? Yes. You have the right to privacy, and if someone invades your privacy, you can sue to recover damages for any harm you suffer. And if the person threatens to continue invading your privacy in the future, you can get a court order to prevent it.

The tort of invasion of privacy really comprises four separate and distinct torts: (1) the unreasonable intrusion into your private life; (2) the public disclosure of private facts; (3) portraying you in a false light in the public eye; and (4) using your name or likeness for a commercial purpose without your consent.

Intrusion into Your Private Life

You have the right to be free from unwanted invasions into your privacy. Someone who breaks into your home is clearly guilty of invading your privacy (and of trespassing as well). But the intrusion doesn't have to be physical. The unauthorized use of wiretaps or other electronic listening devices to listen in on your private conversations is also an invasion of privacy, even if all the equipment is across the street on public property. Other examples of invasion of privacy include bill collectors and others who harass you with persistent telephone calls or knock at your door at all hours of the day and night, or someone who goes onto your lawn and looks through the window—a "peeping Tom."

Suppose a stranger takes a picture of you while you are in a public square or on a public beach. Is this an invasion of your privacy? Not by itself. You don't have as much right to privacy in a public place as you do at home. A person can follow you around in public, even take your picture without your consent and over your objections, since everyone has a right to be on a public street or sidewalk. (It becomes an invasion of privacy, however, if the picture is used in a way that portrays you in a false light or if the person uses the picture for commercial purposes without your consent, as discussed below.) There is one important limitation to the rule that you can be followed or photographed in public: If the trailing or shadowing turns into harassment, it becomes an invasion of privacy, and you can sue to stop the person from following you and to collect damages. Jacqueline Kennedy Onassis, for example, obtained a court order requiring a particular photographer who continuously overstepped the bounds of reasonableness to keep his distance. Private detective agencies have been successfully sued when their tailing operations of subjects proved less than clandestine.

Public Disclosure of Private Facts

What rights do you have if someone learns of a private fact about you and tells it to others? This is a form of invasion of privacy called a "public disclosure of private facts." You have a right to sue the person for your embarrassment and other damages that you suffer from it.

The most common example of a public disclosure of private facts involves debts. The fact that you owe somebody money is generally a matter between only you and the creditor. A creditor cannot tell others that you owe money in order to humiliate you or to coerce you into paying it back. For example, if a store tapes your bad check to the cash register—in plain view of the customers—with your name and address and the words "Returned for Insufficient Funds" marked in bold red letters, that is an invasion of privacy. Likewise, posting a list of names on a piece of paper headed "No Checks Accepted" where other customers can see it is also an invasion of privacy.

Public disclosure of private facts constitutes an invasion of privacy only if the information is offensive and objectionable to a person of ordinary sensibilities. You can't sue for an invasion of privacy if the information is innocuous or flattering. If you did a good deed—returned lost money or saved a child from drowning—and someone told others about it, that isn't an invasion of your privacy. Telling others information that is contained in public records—a court file or the county clerk's office, for instance—also does not constitute an invasion of privacy.

The press can report "newsworthy" events, even though the facts are private. For example, murder cases, divorces, deaths from drug overdoses, or children with rare and unusual diseases—these are all considered newsworthy, and can be written about even if the person does not consent to the story.

Portraying a Person in a False Light

Suppose that near election time, you are reading the paper when you see a political advertisement containing your name among the list of supporters for a particular candidate—a candidate that you can't stand. Is this an invasion of your privacy? Yes. The ad places you in a "false light in the public eye" by making it appear that you endorse someone you abhor. This form of invasion of privacy originated in England in the early 1800s, when Lord Byron sued to stop the circulation of a bad poem that was falsely attributed to his pen. It is still an invasion of privacy to credit a person with writing a book he or she did not write or to state that a critic recommends a certain book, film, or play when it is not true.

Someone's use of your photograph to illustrate certain types of stories also can place you in a false light in the public eye. For example, suppose you are a used-car salesman—an honest used-car salesman. A magazine uses your picture without asking you to illustrate an article on used-car salesmen who lie and use every dirty trick in the book. Can you sue the magazine for an invasion of privacy? Yes. A reader who sees your picture naturally will think that you are a dishonest salesman.

Appropriation of a Name or Likeness for Commercial Use

Suppose a soft drink company uses in its advertising campaign, without your permission, a picture of you drinking its product. Is this an invasion of privacy? Yes. No one can use your picture, name, or likeness for commercial purposes unless you agree. But a newspaper or television news story might be able to use the same picture in a report on the soft drink industry—the picture isn't being used to promote a particular brand but is merely used in connection with a newsworthy story.

Celebrities, who work hard to have their faces and names known to millions of people, have a "right to publicity." Hence, you can't use a celebrity's name or likeness without his or her consent. If you do, the celebrity can sue to stop it and also can recover damages—including any money you made from the unauthorized use. Movie stars and rock stars, for example, have sued successfully to stop companies from selling without their consent novelty items featuring their names or likenesses.

SLANDER AND LIBEL

"DEFAMATION" IS A FALSE STATEMENT that tends to diminish your reputation so that other people think less of you and don't want to associate with you. The key word is "false"; you can't sue for defamation if the statement a person makes is true. (You may, however, still be able to sue for an invasion of privacy or infliction of emotional distress, depending on the nature and content of the statement.)

There are two types of defamation: slander and libel. Slander refers to spoken words, while libel encompasses written communications. A hundred or so years ago it wasn't too difficult to tell whether a false statement was slander or libel. But the invention of television, radio, the phonograph, CDs, motion pictures, DVDs, computers, the Internet, and other kinds of modern technology have brought new problems in determining whether something is libel or slander. If a person ad-libs a defamatory statement on radio or television, for example, it is slander. But if the defamatory statement is read from a script or other prepared text, it is libel.

Say you're all alone in your office when someone comes in and starts calling you a crook, a liar, and a cheat. Can you sue that person for defamation? No—even if you aren't a crook, a liar, and a cheat. Why can't you sue? Because the defamatory remarks must be heard (or read, in the case of libel) by someone besides yourself.

Now suppose that your secretary heard the person call you a crook and such but didn't believe a word of it. Does this prevent you from suing the person for defamation? No. It doesn't matter whether the person who heard the false remarks believed them or not. All that matters is that he or she heard the untrue statements and knew that they referred to you. The fact that nobody believed the false statements does, however, have a bearing on how much you will recover in damages. If no one believed the remarks, your business didn't suffer, and you lost none of your friends, your damages are minimal. On the other hand, if a major client of yours took his or her business elsewhere after hearing the statement, you'll collect much more in damages.

Can you sue if somebody makes a defamatory remark concerning a dead relative? No. Under the current law, you can say anything you want about someone who has died, no matter how vicious and untrue it may be, and not have to worry about defamation.

Sometimes a statement is defamatory only if you are able to put two and two together. If, for example, the local society columnist reports that Mrs. Janice Jones is pregnant with her second child, this may seem innocuous enough on its face. But if the statement is untrue, and Mrs. Jones has been widowed for two years, the statement takes on new meaning. A person who knows Mrs. Jones can put the missing facts together to get the underlying—and defamatory—meaning of the statement.

Public figures—politicians, celebrities, star athletes, and so forth—have a tougher time suing a newspaper, magazine, or radio or television station than the average person does. In addition to proving that the statement was false and defamatory, the public figure must prove that it was made with "malice." Malice here means saying something that you know is false or making the statement with reckless disregard for the truth; you say it even though you have no idea whether it is true or not.

The difficulties a public figure faces in trying to win a defamation suit against the media received international attention when former Israeli defense minister Ariel Sharon sued *Time* magazine. In its February 21, 1983, issue, *Time* published an article that included a paragraph describing Sharon's alleged role in the 1982 massacre of seven hundred Palestinians in two

Beirut refugee camps. The jury found that the paragraph in question was false and that it did defame Sharon. But the jury also concluded that *Time* did not act with malice, so Sharon lost the case. (In an unusual move that highlights the problems in this area of the law, the jury wrote a note stating that *Time* had acted carelessly and negligently in reporting and not verifying the story. But carelessness and negligence are not enough to make the media liable to a public figure for false statements.)

INFLICTION OF EMOTIONAL DISTRESS

ONE AREA OF PERSONAL injury law that has undergone significant expansion in the last thirty years is your right to recover damages when you suffer emotional or psychological injuries because of another's wrongful act. This development in the law has paralleled the developments in psychology and related disciplines. An early fear of the law was that psychological injuries could be faked easily. Because there were no sure means of verifying these injuries, the danger was that many sham claims would be successful. Today psychological and emotional injuries and other mental disorders can be diagnosed with a good deal of certainty, so the chances that a fraudulent claim for emotional distress will succeed are no greater than for any other type of injury.

Emotional Distress Resulting from Another Person's Negligence

Say that Denise is stopped for a red light when Stan runs into her car from the rear. Stan clearly is at fault. Denise is not physically injured, and the damage to her car is only a few hundred dollars' worth. But Denise soon develops a fear of driving, of even being a passenger in a car. Treatment for her psychological injury runs into thousands of dollars and Denise endures several months of severe anxiety. Must Stan pay for these injuries as well as for the damage to the car? Yes. When you are injured by the negligence of another, you are entitled to be compensated for your emotional distress as well as the physical injuries or property damage you may suffer.

Suppose you are looking out the window, watching your five-year-old daughter, Louise, playing on the lawn. Suddenly, a car screeches around the corner, jumps the curb, and runs over Louise, seriously injuring her. The shock of seeing your daughter run over is more than you can bear, and you suffer deep psychological problems. There is no question that the driver was at fault and must pay for Louise's injuries. But does the driver have to pay for your emotional injuries, as well?

Under the old rule, you could not recover damages for your emotional injuries because you were not struck by the car. You could recover damages for your emotional injuries if the car actually touched you—even if the contact was very slight and didn't physically injure you. If you were in actual physical danger of being hit—in the "zone of danger"—you could sue even though you weren't actually hit. But in the example above, you couldn't sue because you were inside the house and well away from the street.

Today, however, most states allow you to recover damages for your emotional injuries if you witnessed the accident involving your daughter—even if you weren't in the zone of danger. But you must witness the actual accident; learning about it afterward is normally not enough. You cannot recover for your emotional damages if you heard about your daughter's accident while you were at work and first saw her in the hospital emergency room. But "witnessing" an accident does not necessarily mean you have to see it. Say that you park your car on the street outside your house. You and your son walk to the back of the car to get the groceries out of the trunk. You pick up a sack, turn your back, and start walking away. Seconds later—while your son is still standing behind the trunk—you hear the sounds of brakes squealing, bones crunching, and a car hitting another car. Instantly you know what has happened: Your son has been struck by another car. You turn around, but by that time the accident is over. Can you sue? Yes. Although you did not see the other car hit your son, you knew as it was happening just what was going on.

Can you sue anytime for emotional injuries you suffer from seeing someone injured or killed by another's negligence? No. You must be a close relative of the victim—usually limited to a spouse, parent, child, or brother or sister. And it must in fact be your relative who is injured. You can't sue if you mistakenly believe the victim is your son or daughter, when in fact it is someone else's child.

When Someone Deliberately Causes You Emotional Distress

Suppose a coworker tells you that he will break your arm or kill you if you don't agree to go on strike with the rest of your colleagues. Afterward, you dread going to work; you lose weight, can't sleep at night, and can't keep your mind on your job. You even become physically ill and can't go to work. Can you sue your coworker for your injuries, for missing work, and other damages? Yes. A person who deliberately causes you to experience severe mental anguish ("emotional distress" or "mental suffering") is liable for your injuries.

This doesn't mean, however, that you can sue anyone who insults you or calls you a name. You are allowed to recover only for "outrageous" conduct—conduct that nobody should have to tolerate. Modern life requires all of us to have a certain amount of hardness; we must brush off mere insults, profanities, and minor annoyances.

Suppose you are an extrasensitive person. Someone says things to you that an ordinary person would shrug off, but the remarks cause you serious mental anguish. Must that person pay for your damages? Only if he or she knew that you were unusually sensitive and would probably suffer emotional injuries upon hearing the remarks.

STRICT LIABILITY

"STRICT LIABILITY" usually is applied only to situations that are extraordinarily dangerous and that pose a great likelihood of harm, particularly when something goes wrong. Unlike negligence and intentional misconduct, which look at the conduct and mental state of the person doing the act, strict liability is concerned only with the nature of the activity. Extraordinarily dangerous activities include: chemical spraying and crop dusting; conducting blasting operations; operating nuclear power plants; running an oil well; and the like. The broadest application of strict liability is in cases of persons who are injured by defective products, which is discussed in chapter 12.

If you are injured as a result of another person's extraordinarily dangerous activity, you usually are allowed to recover your damages without proving that he or she did anything wrong. The nature of the activity is so inherently dangerous that it alone is sufficient to impose liability. For instance, if your neighbors are doing some blasting on their property and some debris injures you or damages your property (or you are injured or your property is damaged from the shock waves), your neighbors must pay for the damage. They cannot get out of it by saying that they did everything correctly and were as careful as anyone could be. In strict liability cases, how careful a person was is generally irrelevant to the question of whether or not he or she is legally responsible for your damages.

TORT REFORM

BECAUSE OF HIGH JURY VERDICTS in some tort cases, many states have passed laws limiting various aspects of such cases. California passed one of the first such laws in 1974 when it made drastic changes to its medical malpractice laws, including limiting the innocent victim's recovery of "noneconomic" damages (pain and suffering) to a maximum of $250,000 (see chapter 11). Since 1986, forty-five states and the District of Columbia have enacted various tort reforms into law.

In December 2002, Mississippi enacted a comprehensive tort reform package; in October of that year, the governor of Mississippi signed into law a separate measure setting limits on damages in medical malpractice cases. Under the new Mississippi laws, some of the changes are a system of graduated limits on punitive damages (see chapter 10) that cap judgments against the biggest companies at $20 million. The smallest firms—those whose net worth is $50 million or less—could be ordered to pay no more than 4 percent of their value, up to $2 million in punitive damages.

The legislation also changes products liability law (chapter 12) by relieving retailers from liability for selling defective products they did not design or produce. Where there is more than one defendant being sued, each defendant must pay its proportionate share of the victim's noneconomic loss (pain and suffering). However, the victims won a partial victory in that there is no cap on the amount of noneconomic damages, such as pain and suffering. Mississippi became fertile ground for tort reform efforts after a series of large money jury verdicts. In the seven years preceding the enactment of the legislation, there were seven jury verdicts of $100 million or more in as many years. They included a $150 million judgment for five plaintiffs who sued the manufacturer of one of the diet drugs in the fen-phen combination after they reported health problems caused by the drugs. In 1995, a jury awarded $500 million against a Canadian funeral home company, which later settled for about $175 million. And in 2001, a jury awarded $150 million to six men who sued asbestos manufacturers for asbestos-related diseases. However, these awards are usually drastically reduced before they are paid out.

The Deep South has long been a favorite place for plaintiffs' lawyers to file suit, as the typical southern juror—especially in rural counties—is poor and sympathetic toward victims in claims against big corporations. Ironically, though, the largest punitive damage award ever given to a single plaintiff was $28 *billion* awarded by a Los Angeles jury on October 4, 2002, to a 64-year-old woman with lung cancer in her case against tobacco giant Phillip Morris. The trial judge, however, reduced the amount to $28 million, and Phillip Morris has appealed the case.

ELEVEN

Medicine, Malpractice, and You

*t*HE LAW now recognizes that modern medicine is more than just the science of healing; it is also big business. Some of the most important developments in law in the last fifty years have been in the area of your rights as a patient, particularly your rights to quality medical care and to sue when you are injured by a doctor's carelessness.

A discussion of your rights as a patient necessarily revolves around "medical malpractice." Medical malpractice is simply the negligence (carelessness) of a doctor in diagnosing or treating your condition, which results in injury to you. A few examples of malpractice include reading an X-ray backward so that your healthy left kidney is removed rather than the diseased right one; your good right knee is operated on instead of your bad left one; using an unsterilized needle or thermometer, resulting in an infection to you; leaving a sponge or surgical instrument in a patient after an operation; injuring an infant during delivery because of too much pressure on the forceps; misreading an X-ray so a broken bone goes undetected; performing unnecessary surgery; failing to advise you of the possible consequences of an operation or the side effects of a drug; carelessly performing surgery so that an artery is severed or an organ is damaged; allowing a semiconscious or elderly patient to fall out of a hospital bed because the guardrails were down; and subjecting a patient to too much radiation.

Not every untoward result means the doctor has committed malpractice. Unexpected things sometimes happen despite the best of care. The doctor is liable for injuring you only if he or she used less skill and care than other doctors use in doing the same thing. In legal terms, the question is whether the doctor failed to "possess and use that degree of learning, skill, and care in diagnosing and treating the patient's condition that a reasonably competent doctor would employ in the same circumstances." In plain English, the question is whether the doctor made a mistake that another doctor would not or should not have made under the same or similar circumstances.

Medical malpractice isn't limited to just doctors. It applies to "health care providers" of every kind—hospitals, nurses, medical technicians, dentists, psychiatrists, psychologists, optometrists, chiropractors, osteopaths, acupuncturists, and others. For ease in reading, throughout this chapter, "doctor" will be used to include all other types of health care providers.

THE PHYSICIAN-PATIENT RELATIONSHIP

Must a Doctor Accept You as a Patient?

Suppose you consult a doctor for the first time, but after several minutes the doctor tells you that he or she cannot or will not accept you as a patient and advises you to find another doctor. Can the doctor do this? Yes. A doctor generally need not accept every new patient that comes to him or her. A doctor might refuse to accept a new patient for a number of reasons: The doctor is too busy to take on new patients; your ailment is beyond the doctor's competency; or there is a personality clash between the two of you. A doctor's right to reject potential patients is endorsed by the American Medical Association, whose principles of medical ethics state: "A physician is free to choose whom he will serve."

On the other hand, a hospital emergency room cannot turn you away if your problem is serious or life-threatening and you need immediate care. While doctors are essentially free to decide whom they wish to treat, hospitals with emergency rooms open to the general public must treat anyone needing emergency care for a serious injury or illness. An emergency room that refuses to examine or treat you in a true emergency is liable for your damages if you suffer further injury because of the delay in treatment that results from having to go to another hospital. For example, suppose that Collette takes her daughter to an emergency room after the girl falls off her bike and strikes her head. The girl complains of dizziness and vomits several times—signs of potentially serious head injuries. Collette tells the emergency room admissions nurse what has happened and describes her daughter's symptoms. The nurse refuses to have the girl examined, forcing Collette to take her to another hospital thirty minutes away. By the time they get there, the girl's condition is much worse, and she dies shortly after arrival. An examination shows that the girl would have lived if the first emergency room had treated her. The hospital that refused to treat the girl is liable for her death because it rejected her in an obviously serious emergency.

Now suppose that Collette receives welfare and is eligible for Medicaid, but in her haste to get to the emergency room, she forgets to bring her Medicaid card. The admissions nurse is interested only in how Collette plans to pay the hospital's bill and refuses to let a doctor examine the child until Collette proves that she is covered by Medicaid. Collette returns home to get her Medicaid card, taking her daughter with her; the girl dies in the car on the way back to the hospital. Was the nurse wrong? Yes. In a true emergency, an emergency room cannot refuse to examine or treat you for any reason, including your inability to show proof that you will be able to pay the bill. The hospital must treat you first; later it can worry about how you're going to pay the bill. The nurse clearly should have realized that the girl's injuries could have been very serious and should have called for a doctor to examine the girl as soon as she was brought in. The doctor's examination would have revealed that the child had suffered severe head injuries that required immediate treatment. Collette would have a good case against the hospital for malpractice.

Your Right to Confidentiality—The Physician-Patient Privilege

Your doctor cannot properly treat your condition unless he or she knows all of the symptoms and possible causes—regardless of how embarrassing or "shameful" they may be. But you're not going to tell your doctor something delicate unless you are absolutely certain it will remain confidential. What legal assurance do you have that the doctor won't tell others what you say? The law requires the doctor to keep in strictest confidence anything you say for the purposes of treatment. Ordinarily, the doctor cannot reveal anything you say unless you permit him or her to do so. This is known as the "physician-patient privilege."

What can you do if a doctor tells others your confidences without your consent? You can sue for the damages and humiliation you suffer. In one case, a psychiatrist who had treated a husband and wife wrote a book containing verbatim reports of their thoughts, emotions, sexual fantasies, and the disintegration of their marriage. Although the book did not identify the patients by name, the court held that the psychiatrist breached his promise to hold in confidence all disclosures made by his patients by writing the book.

Is a physician ever required by law to disclose to others a patient's confidences? Yes. Occasionally society at large has a special interest that is greater than the patient's right to confidentiality—such as protecting the public from injury or from serious communicable diseases. Many states, for instance, require a doctor to report cases of suspected child or elder abuse to the police. If the police question the doctor, the doctor must tell anything the patient said relating to being a child or elder abuser. Another example: If a patient has infectious hepatitis—particularly if he or she works at a job involving food—the doctor may be required to report it to the health department. In addition, when you file a lawsuit claiming that you were physically or emotionally injured by the defendant, your medical history may be opened to the person you are suing so he or she and his or her attorney can determine whether your injuries are the result of the person's acts or some other source.

Diagnosing Your Condition

A doctor must use due care in diagnosing your illness, so that appropriate treatment can be prescribed without undue delay. To diagnose your condition properly, the doctor generally must take an adequate history of your previous health and medical conditions, as well as significant medical conditions of your immediate relatives—cancer, diabetes, heart disease, and the like. The doctor must also get a detailed description of your current symptoms and must examine you and order any diagnostic tests that are reasonably required to diagnose your condition.

The failure to perform certain tests can sometimes be malpractice in and of itself. Suppose, for instance, a middle-aged, overweight man complains to his doctor of heaviness and severe pain in his chest. The doctor doesn't order an electrocardiogram—which would reveal that the man had suffered a heart attack—and sends him home with a diagnosis of heartburn. That evening the man dies from the heart attack. Or suppose a woman who was injured in a car accident complains of a serious leg injury, but the doctor doesn't take an X-ray, telling her the leg is just bruised. An X-ray would have shown that the leg was broken. Because the bone isn't set properly, the leg becomes deformed. In both of these examples, the doctor is guilty of malpractice for failing to order diagnostic tests that were called for under the circumstances.

When a doctor commits malpractice and misdiagnoses your condition, you can sue for any and all injuries that result from being given unnecessary or harmful treatment and for any injuries you suffer because proper treatment was delayed. For example, a doctor carelessly diagnoses your rather harmless condition as a serious form of cancer. Chemotherapy and radiation treatment are started immediately, and you suffer serious side effects: nausea, pain, vomiting, hair loss, and so forth. Three months later, the doctor realizes the mistake, and the cancer therapy is stopped. In your malpractice case against the doctor, you can recover damages for all of your hospital, doctor, and other medical expenses; for lost wages from time off work; and for any injuries you suffered. You also are entitled to compensation for the pain and suffering you experienced, not only for the suffering as a result of the radiation and chemotherapy, but for the mental anguish of being wrongly told you had cancer as well.

Now consider the reverse situation: a doctor negligently diagnoses a mole as benign, when it really is cancerous. Because of the erroneous diagnosis, no treatment is prescribed, and the cancer worsens. By the time the doctor realizes the mistake, the cancer has spread to the point where radical and dangerous treatment is necessary. Had the doctor recognized the mole as cancerous earlier, it could have been excised with little risk to you. You could sue the doctor for the injuries you suffer because the doctor didn't diagnose the condition correctly earlier.

Referring You to a Specialist

When your condition is beyond the competency or expertise of a particular doctor, that doctor must refer you to another doctor or a specialist for diagnosis or treatment. If the first doctor continues to treat you anyway, he or she is liable for any injuries you suffer from inappropriate treatment and the delay in getting proper treatment. Suppose, for example, you visit an optometrist who finds evidence of possible disease in your eye. The optometrist concludes that it isn't serious, however, and doesn't refer you to an ophthalmologist. But the disease turns out to be more serious than the optometrist thought and you eventually lose your eye because proper treatment was delayed. If the optometrist had referred you to an ophthalmologist, your disease would have been treated, and your eye would have been saved. Is the optometrist liable to you? Yes. Although optometrists are trained to recognize symptoms of many eye diseases, they are not allowed to make definite diagnoses of those diseases. That is the responsibility of a qualified medical doctor—an ophthalmologist in this case.

Providing You with Effective Treatment

Once your condition has been diagnosed, the doctor must—to the extent possible by modern medicine—prescribe an effective method of treatment to cure or alleviate the ailment. Does the doctor guarantee to cure you? Usually not. The doctor promises only to use his or her medical training, skill, and best efforts to treat your condition.

Once in a while, a doctor will promise to cure a patient. If that is the case, the patient can sue the doctor for breaking that promise, even though the doctor did not technically commit malpractice. Some states require such guarantees to be in writing in order to be valid. But telling you that you will be pleased with the results of surgery or will feel like a new person afterward is not a guarantee of any kind but, rather, merely a general therapeutic assurance. If you aren't happy with the results, or if you feel like your old self afterward, you can't sue your doctor if he or she has done nothing wrong.

Suppose there is more than one approved way of treating your condition. Is the doctor guilty of malpractice for choosing one method over the other, even though the chosen method later proves less desirable? Usually not. The doctor has the right to use his or her "best judgment" to determine which course of treatment appears best for you, based on your condition and medical history. The doctor doesn't even have to use the method preferred by a majority of other doctors; only a "respectable minority" of physicians need endorse the type of treatment used. So long as the doctor follows the treatment procedure correctly, there is no malpractice, even if you do not respond as the doctor had hoped. When it becomes evident that you aren't responding to the treatment, however, then the doctor may be required to change course. Indeed, it may be malpractice if the doctor doesn't try something else if your condition doesn't show any improvement within a reasonable time.

Suppose your doctor has been treating you for six months, but you aren't getting any better. As a matter of fact, you feel worse now than you did the first time you saw the doctor. You decide to consult another doctor, who tells you that the other doctor has been using an unaccepted and experimental method of treating you. The second doctor prescribes an established treatment program for you and within days your condition begins to show great improvement. Is your first doctor guilty of medical malpractice? Yes. Medicine must experiment to progress—that cannot be denied. But this does not give a doctor a license to use you as a human guinea pig to try out experimental techniques, only to discover afterward that the techniques are ineffective—even downright harmful. Your rights as a patient dictate that accepted, effective, and safe treatments be used first. Only after established treatments fail should experimental treatment be considered—and then only if there is some reasonable medical basis for believing that it may work without unnecessarily endangering the life or health of the patient. And before the doctor can administer an unproven treatment, he or she must tell you that it is new and experimental and that neither its effectiveness nor its side effects are fully known.

Your Right to a Second Opinion

Before undergoing any type of surgery or medical treatment, or if the treatment of your disease, illness, or physical or mental condition is not progressing the way you think it should be, you should usually seek a second opinion from another doctor. (But never postpone an operation to get a second opinion without first asking your doctor if the delay may worsen your condition, such as an appendix about to burst.) Each year unnecessary operations needlessly subject many patients to the risks and complications inherent in every surgery. You have a right to a second opinion, and if the first doctor is put off by this, so be it. Most patients, however, will be pleasantly surprised to find how receptive their doctors are to their getting a second opinion. In fact, many doctors suggest that their patients get a second opinion, particularly if the patient has any doubt whether the operation is necessary or if the method of treatment he or she is proposing or using is appropriate. Sometimes the doctor on his or her own initiative will ask another doctor to evaluate a patient's condition to confirm the need for surgery or to confirm that he or she is choosing or following an appropriate treatment plan.

Many insurance companies now encourage you to get second opinions and even pay some or all of the costs of having another doctor review the case to see if surgery is necessary or the method of treatment the primary care physician is proposing or has been using is appropriate. This benefits the insurance company because it saves money by reducing the number of unnecessary and expensive surgeries or results in changing treatment plans to one that is more effective. Review your policy to determine whether it covers second opinions, and contact your health insurance representative if you're not sure. Medicare pays for second opinions for surgery at the same rate that it pays for other services, and most state Medicaid programs also cover much of the cost of second opinions.

Your Right to Know the Risks

Before performing any diagnostic procedures or offering treatment of any kind, the doctor normally must have your consent. You can give your permission to the doctor in writing or orally. Frequently your permission is implied by your conduct: You call the doctor's office, make an appointment, show up, and let the doctor examine and treat you, even though you never once expressly tell the doctor that he or she can examine you. In the case of a minor or mentally incompetent person, the consent of a parent or legal guardian usually is required. If the doctor touches or treats you without your consent, he or she may be liable for committing the intentional tort of battery (see chapter 10).

One instance when a doctor can treat you without first getting your consent, however, is when you are unconscious and in need of emergency treatment to save your life. The law assumes that you would have consented to the treatment had you been conscious, and therefore your consent is implied. For example, Sally is injured severely and knocked unconscious in a car accident. She is rushed to the hospital, and emergency treatment is administered to save her life. When Sally regains consciousness, she is distraught to learn that she received a blood transfusion, since this is contrary to her religious beliefs. If she sues the doctor, however, the doctor will win. Even though Sally would not have permitted the blood transfusion if she had been asked, the doctor was unaware of her religious beliefs, and the blood transfusion was needed to save her life.

Consent is much more than just saying yes or no to a proposed treatment. If you don't understand the risks involved, your consent isn't worth much. You must give the doctor an "informed" consent, one based on all the facts. To enable you to do this, the doctor must explain not only the benefits of a proposed procedure to you, but also the risks of the procedure, as well as the alternatives: What other procedures are available and what their risks are. The doctor must also inform you of the dangers of not treating the condition.

Suppose a doctor prescribes medication to a pregnant woman but fails to warn her of one important side effect: The drug can cause birth defects. The woman later gives birth to a deformed baby, and a thorough investigation establishes that the drug caused the deformities. The woman did not give an informed consent to the drug treatment because she wasn't aware of all important facts and risks. If she had known of the hazards to the child, she could have chosen a less dangerous drug or some other type of treatment. Or, if her condition was not life-threatening, she could have postponed treatment until after the baby was born.

If you were facing surgery, and there was a less drastic alternative—drug therapy or radiation, for example—you'd want to know. And if that is a reasonable alternative, the doctor must tell you so, even if the doctor prefers surgery. The doctor can recommend one procedure over the other but must at least explain both alternatives, what their dangers are, their rates of success, and the like. The final decision, however, is yours alone to make.

A doctor must even inform you of the risks of refusing to submit to a risk-free diagnostic examination. In one case, a woman decided not to undergo a Pap smear, a simple and painless procedure designed to detect cervical and other vaginal cancers. Although the doctor recommended the procedure, he did not tell the woman why it was important and what could happen if she turned it down. The woman later died of cervical cancer. The court held that the doctor should have advised the woman of the risks of declining the Pap smear. Since she had no idea why the test was important, the woman did not give an "informed rejection."

Who determines how much information you need to be told, you or the doctor? In some states, your doctor must disclose only the amount of information that other doctors disclose to their patients. Other states apply the rule that the amount of information the doctor must disclose is set by the patient's needs and desires. Under this standard, the doctor must inform you of all "material" risks—risks that a reasonable person would consider important in deciding whether or not to proceed with the proposed treatment. What are considered material risks? Death, loss of limb, paralysis, stroke, brain damage, or any other serious injuries certainly are material and must always be disclosed to the patient if they are a possibility. Less serious but more common side effects, such as drowsiness, diarrhea, heartburn, and dry mouth, to name a few, also should be disclosed in appropriate situations.

Say that before surgery you sign a written informed consent form handed to you by the doctor, a nurse, or a hospital administrator. Does this prevent you from later suing the doctor or hospital for operating without your informed consent? No. The issue isn't whether or not you signed a piece of paper. Rather, it is whether the risks of and alternatives to the treatment were explained to you fully. Blanket consent forms often do not apprise you of just what risks apply to your treatment. A written consent is no substitute for a doctor's complete explanation of the risks of the proposed treatment and the alternatives. In fact, the doctor or nurse may even tell you that signing the form is "just a formality." If the doctor assures you that nothing will go wrong, and something does go wrong, you can sue and win despite what the form you signed states.

As another example, suppose your doctor tells you that there is a 90 percent chance that a proposed operation will be successful and a 10 percent chance that it will not improve your condition. You sign an informed consent form, and the doctor operates, but your condition is worse after the operation than it was before. Your doctor never said the operation could make your condition worse, and had you known there was that danger, you never would have agreed to the operation. You can sue your doctor for operating without your informed consent, despite the fact that you signed the consent form.

A doctor isn't always required to inform you of the risks before treating you, however. If it's an emergency, the doctor can go ahead and treat you without advising you of the risks. As one court noted, a doctor need not discuss possible consequences and methods of treatment with a snakebite victim while the venom is being pumped through the victim's body.

If you are likely to become so upset by news of the risks that you won't be able to make a rational decision or it would hinder the treatment, the doctor does not have to tell you of those risks. For example, a patient who was paralyzed from an operation for a suspected aneurysm (a bulge in an artery caused by a weakening of its wall) sued his doctor for failing to inform him that the operation could paralyze him. The information had been withheld because the patient was extremely nervous and suffered from coronary and kidney disease, and the doctor feared that the patient's health would be jeopardized seriously if he were told of the risks. The court dismissed the patient's lawsuit because under the circumstances, the doctor clearly was justified in withholding the information from the patient.

Your consent to an operation can be conditional, and the doctor must honor those conditions. Suppose a pregnant woman tells her doctor to perform a sterilization procedure (tubal ligation) after her child is born—but only if the baby is healthy and free of any abnormalities. The doctor delivers an obviously deformed child but does the tubal ligation anyway. Will the woman win if she sues the doctor? Yes. The doctor has committed malpractice because the woman's consent was based upon the birth of a healthy, normal baby. Some states hold the doctor liable for the intentional tort of battery (see chapter 10) in this situation.

Let's say that you've agreed to an operation to remove a gallstone. While you're under the knife, the surgeon decides to remove your appendix. Is the surgeon liable to you for removing your appendix without your consent? That depends on whether the appendix posed an immediate threat to your life or health. If your appendix was healthy, the surgeon was legally wrong in taking it out. But if your appendix was diseased and ready to burst, jeopardizing your life, the surgeon would be justified in removing it.

Suppose that the day after surgery, you learn that a medical student or a doctor you never heard of actually performed the operation, rather than the surgeon you thought was going to do it. Can you sue the person who did the surgery for operating without your consent? Yes. Ordinarily you must be informed of exactly who will be doing the surgery. If someone else steps in without your knowledge and consent—so-called ghost surgery—he or she can be held liable for committing battery on you.

Most surgeons now have patients sign a document that states that other doctors, associates, or residents may assist in or actually perform the surgical procedure. Such a form generally will protect a doctor in a "ghost surgery" case. However, the surgeon must generally be present supervising the operation, and take over if the operating resident or other surgeon is not doing a good job.

ENDING THE PHYSICIAN-PATIENT RELATIONSHIP

IF YOU ARE NOT SATISFIED with your doctor and decide to find another, your current doctor can't stop you from leaving. You can terminate the doctor's services unilaterally, with or without a reason—even without notifying the doctor. Your doctor must forward your medical records to your new doctor at your request. All your old doctor is entitled to is to be paid for all medical services rendered up to the time you leave.

But just as you have the right to end the doctor's services unilaterally, the doctor has a right to unilaterally stop treating you. There is, however, one important restriction on the doctor's right to cut you off: he or she cannot simply abandon you if you still need treatment. The doctor must give you a fair amount of time to find a new doctor and must continue treating you until that time passes.

GETTING COPIES OF YOUR MEDICAL RECORDS

SUPPOSE YOU WANT TO LOOK at your medical records. Or you want your lawyer to review them to see if you have grounds to sue your doctor or a hospital for malpractice. Must the doctor or hospital honor your request and give you your records or copies of them? Until the 1980s, you ordinarily couldn't just go in and ask to see your records, let alone copy them. About the only time you could get access to your medical records was if you sued your doctor for malpractice. Why couldn't you see your records? Doctors felt that medical records were beyond the understanding of the average patient, and reading them could frighten the patient unnecessarily. Doctors also contended that the records and charts were prepared only as work sheets for medical personnel and never were intended for review by the patient. Some doctors feared that the patient—or the patient's lawyer—would find some mistakes or omissions and would respond with a malpractice suit.

Today you generally can obtain copies of your medical records simply by making a written request to the hospital or your doctor and paying a reasonable charge to have them photocopied. Patients in Veterans Administration hospitals have had this right since 1974, when the Federal Privacy Act was passed.

HOW MALPRACTICE AFFECTS YOU AND YOUR DOCTOR

The Medical "Conspiracy of Silence"

Since the average juror usually can't tell whether a doctor was careless or if the injury was just "one of those things" that occasionally happens, in most malpractice lawsuits you must have a doctor testify on your behalf that the doctor who treated you committed malpractice. Not all that long ago, this requirement stopped many potential malpractice suits dead in their tracks. It wasn't that the cases were unfounded; rather, it was nearly impossible to find a doctor who would criticize a colleague, in or out of court, even if the claim of malpractice was fully justified. The hesitancy of doctors to criticize colleagues has come to be known as the "conspiracy of silence." This conspiracy is not imaginary. Back in 1956, the supreme court of Kentucky acknowledged its existence when it observed: "The notorious unwillingness of members of the medical profession to testify against one another may impose an insuperable handicap upon a plaintiff who cannot obtain professional proof."

Why are doctors unwilling to speak badly of a fellow doctor's performance? The main reasons are fear of ostracism by colleagues or medical societies; "professional courtesy" or loyalty to fellow practitioners; a belief that if they protect their colleagues, their colleagues will protect them if necessary; and fear that even if they never commit malpractice, their medical malpractice insurance rates nevertheless will get out of hand as a result of large verdicts against doctors who have erred.

How strong is this conspiracy of silence today? Fairly strong, but generally not as strong as it used to be. In large metropolitan areas, it is still somewhat difficult but usually possible to find a doctor to testify against a colleague who has committed malpractice, at least in cases where the mistake is obvious. But in rural areas, it is still difficult to get a local doctor to testify against a fellow practitioner in the same area, making it necessary in most cases to get a doctor from another town to testify.

The Medical Malpractice "Crisis"

The mid-1970s saw the beginning of the widely publicized medical malpractice "crisis," with insurance companies, hospitals, and doctors claiming financial hardship from the growing number of malpractice lawsuits. The crisis subsided for a bit but reared its head anew in 1983 and then again in 2002. What exactly is this alleged crisis?

Insurance companies, hospitals, and doctors contend that because of a startling increase in both the number of medical malpractice lawsuits and the amounts of money sympathetic juries are awarding, medical costs and malpractice insurance premiums are rising out of sight. At one point, threats abounded that unless something was done, insurance premiums would soar to the point where many hospitals would be forced to close their doors and thousands of doctors would quit practicing medicine. Some doctors even went "bare" and practiced medicine without malpractice insurance. (These doctors were taking a big chance: If they were sued by a patient and lost, their life savings could be wiped out.)

On the other side of the fence, lawyers for malpractice victims claim that the only "crisis" is that so much medical malpractice is happening in the first place. They claim that the problem of increasing costs stems not so much from sue-happy patients as from shoddy medical treatment. The focus, they contend, should be on getting rid of bad doctors and on improving medical care—not on adding to the malpractice victim's burden by making it harder for him or her to sue a careless doctor. Additionally, the rise in malpractice insurance premiums is due to low returns on poor investments by the insurance companies.

How the Malpractice "Crisis" Affects You

Due to this medical malpractice "crisis," insurance companies, hospitals, and doctors began an intensive lobbying effort at national and state levels to make it more difficult for victims of a doctor's carelessness to sue a doctor for malpractice. These efforts have proven quite successful, resulting in the passage in most states of many laws favorable to doctors, hospitals, and insurance companies. These laws vary from state to state and cover a wide range of subjects. Here are a few examples: requiring you to submit your case to arbitration before filing suit in court; limiting the amount of money you can recover for some types of damages, particularly "pain and suffering"; requiring that your lawyer send the doctor a letter informing him or her a certain amount of time—say ninety days—beforehand that you will be filing suit; requiring your lawyer to get a certificate from another doctor stating that he or she has reviewed the facts of the case and feels that the malpractice suit is warranted; and limiting how much the attorney who represents the victim can charge (though there are no limits on how much the lawyer representing the doctor or insurance company can charge). In September 2002, the House of Representatives passed a bill that would: limit so-called "noneconomic damages" (which mainly consists of pain and suffering) to $250,000; restrict an award of punitive damages to twice the amount of economic damages or $250,000, whichever is greater; and limit the fees that victims' lawyers could charge, among other things. Again, no limit is put on the fees that the insurance company's lawyer can charge to defend the action.

Many of the laws were passed ostensibly to weed out nonmeritorious cases against doctors. But two reasons not connected with insurance costs have already greatly reduced the threat of spurious lawsuits against physicians: (1) Lawyers representing victims on a contingency fee basis will not accept a case if it doesn't appear that the doctor was negligent and that there's a reasonable chance of success; and (2) doctors are fighting back by suing litigious patients and their lawyers for malicious prosecution (see chapter 10) if the malpractice suit was unjustified.

How has the medical malpractice crisis changed the practice of medicine? Some doctors now view every patient as a threat, a potential adversary in a malpractice suit. New patients may be evaluated for "litigiousness"—will they be likely to sue the doctor? For a while, there was even a company that doctors could call to find out whether a new patient had ever sued a doctor before. (Lawyers who represent victims of doctors' negligence responded with lists of doctors who had been sued successfully for medical malpractice.) Even today, some doctors are more detached from their patients, dealing in a colder, more businesslike manner than before. Some doctors are practicing "defensive medicine," with an eye as much toward defending a lawsuit as toward whether the treatment is appropriate or necessary in a particular case.

HEALTH MAINTENANCE ORGANIZATIONS (HMOS)

THAT MEDICINE HAS turned into a big business is demonstrated by the proliferation of health maintenance organizations (HMOs) in the last fifteen years or so. Employers like HMOs because they let them provide health care benefits to their employees at a reduced rate. Seniors in some parts of the country like Medicare HMOs because they offer some important services and benefits that Medicare does not provide—particularly a prescription drug benefit (although there may be an annual dollar limit as to how much the HMO will pay out for prescription drugs). However, HMOs do require sacrifices of care you receive from the fee-for-service methods of traditional doctors.

HMOs make up for their lower fees by dealing in volume business. The typical doctor is given about five to seven minutes with a patient. In this short time, the doctor must take an oral history of the patient's illness or disease, conduct a physical examination as needed, make a diagnosis, and prescribe an appropriate remedy, whether that be prescription drugs or something as simple as, say, bed rest for a week.

Although HMOs offer prescription drug benefits (you will generally have a copay, though), the doctor usually is limited to prescribing drugs on the approved "formulary" drug list. Instead of prescribing the latest, most effective drugs, the doctor must generally stick to drugs on the approved "formulary" drug list. The formulary drug list usually contains drugs that are lower in cost, usually have been around for some years, are available in generic form, and may not be as effective as the newer drugs. If a patient wants a drug that is not on the formulary list, he or she will have to pay a higher copay to make up the difference.

But all is not well with HMOs. In the late 1990s and early 2000s, a number of HMOs either went out of business completely or pulled out of certain unprofitable states. Some HMOs are increasing the premiums paid by the HMO member to keep a sufficiently profitable margin. For example, Medicare HMOs for seniors have premiums as high as $179 a month and have a limit of just $500 a year for medications.

If you are covered by an HMO, you usually must deal with a doctor who is part of the HMO plan. If you are a new HMO subscriber, your selection of doctors is limited greatly. Chances are that the family doctor whom you've been seeing for years is not a member of your new HMO, so you'll have to start from zero.

Doctors who are part of an HMO plan are strongly encouraged to keep costs low, and typically receive bonuses from the HMO at the end of the year for keeping costs down. Unfortunately, this is often at the patient's expense of getting high quality medical care. To control costs, the HMO doctor may not order tests that a reasonable doctor would order to obtain or confirm a diagnosis. Additionally, HMO doctors may be encouraged not to send the patients to specialists because of the added cost. This results in the patient receiving less than adequate health care and the possibility of a worsening of his or her medical condition.

If an HMO doctor wants to send the patient to a specialist or have surgery performed, the doctor generally must get permission from higher-ups to do so. For a while the person making the ultimate decision of whether you needed to see a specialist or needed surgery, or another medical decision, was an administrator, not a doctor. The administrator who made the final decision might have been at most a registered nurse. One lawsuit was brought against an HMO on the basis that since nondoctor administrators were making ultimate medical decisions that affected a patient, they were practicing medicine without a license. Amid all of the complaints and threats of lawsuits, HMOs now have a doctor review the file to determine whether a specialist or surgery is necessary. Still, the final decision of whether you need to see a specialist or need surgery is being made by a person or panel that has not examined you personally.

HMOs are able to keep their costs down by having a patient sign a document that waives his or her right to sue the HMO for medical malpractice in court and requires them to arbitrate the matter instead. Arbitration tends to favor health care organizations, and the arbitrator's award to the patient or patient's family is almost always less than it would be had a jury of one's peers rendered a verdict after a trial in open court.

TWELVE

Products Liability

*a*FAULTY HEATER CAUSES A FIRE; a house burns down; and the family inside is killed. A man walking behind a car that is idling in park is run over when the transmission slips into reverse. A five-year-old girl is paralyzed when the heavy lid on her toy trunk falls onto her neck while she is reaching inside. A tire on a sports utility vehicle (SUV) separates, causing the SUV to go out of control and roll over, killing two people and injuring three others. A young woman taking an over-the-counter diet aid or cough remedy suffers a stroke due to one of the ingredients. A young woman's nightgown brushes against a stove burner and bursts into fire, severely burning her; she is permanently disfigured. A man falls off the back of a moving boat and is injured severely by an unguarded propeller.

Millions of products of every type and description are made each year. Mass production and mass consumption of products has also meant mass injuries. Statistics released by the Consumer Product Safety Commission (CPSC) show that tens of thousands of Americans die and millions of others are injured annually in accidents involving consumer products. Many others are harmed or killed by accidents that do not come within the jurisdiction of the CPSC—industrial and farming machines, for example. Sometimes the injuries are purely accidental, the fault of neither man nor machine. Many injuries, however, are caused by products that are defective in one way or another—products that, if they had been made or designed safely, would not have caused the injury or death.

A hundred and twenty-five years ago, if you were injured by a defective product, you were pretty much left out in the cold when it came to trying to collect damages for your injuries from the manufacturer or seller. Caveat emptor—buyer beware—was the order of the day. The law assumed that you had ample opportunity to inspect the product for defects before buying it; if you decided the product was safe enough when you bought it, you could not later claim otherwise.

Caveat emptor developed in a time when products were much simpler than they are today. There were fewer products, with fewer moving parts. You usually could tell if something was built well by looking it over carefully, even trying it out a time or two. You didn't have to be a mechanical engineer to inspect a buggy for sound construction.

The average modern consumer is generally incapable of determining whether many products are safe and sound—even if given the chance to inspect and test them prior to purchase. Often, many components are hidden from view and can't be inspected without taking the whole product apart. And even if you could take the cover off, say, a television set or other product before buying it, you would need degrees in electrical engineering and many other disciplines to determine whether the product was designed and built safely. (You'd also probably void any warranty that came with the product if you took it apart before buying it to see if it was made properly.)

LIABILITY OF A PRODUCT MANUFACTURER OR SELLER

The Law of Strict Products Liability

One of the most important developments in the law regarding consumer protection was the birth of the doctrine of "strict products liability," which makes it much easier for you to recover damages from a manufacturer or seller when you are injured by a defective product. Strict products liability also has served as a strong incentive for manufacturers to design and make safer products.

Under the law of strict products liability, a product manufacturer, distributor, or seller is liable for marketing a defective product that is "unreasonably dangerous" and causes injury to the unwary consumer or user. All you need to show is that the product was defective and was allowed to get into the stream of commerce and that your injuries were caused by the product's defect. You normally do not have to prove that anyone was negligent. As discussed in chapter 10, a number of states have passed laws exempting retailers from strict products liability, where they did not alter the product.

The rationale behind strict liability is that as a part of its cost of doing business a manufacturer must compensate consumers for injuries sustained from its defective product. The manufacturer can pass along the expense to the consumer by increasing the price of each unit sold. The consumer bears the ultimate cost, but when that cost is spread among hundreds of thousands or even millions of consumers, it is minimal as far as each consumer is concerned.

Say that you buy a new air conditioner at American Hardware Store and have it installed in your house by Tom's Air-Conditioning Installation and Service Company. The first time you turn the air conditioner on, it blows up and injures you. It turns out that when the air conditioner was made, someone at the factory reversed two wires. American Hardware Store is strictly liable to you, since it sold you the unit. The company that made it is strictly liable as well. But how about Tom's? Is it also strictly liable for your injuries? No. The law of strict products liability does not apply to persons who are engaged primarily in the business of providing a service—installers, repair people, cleaners, doctors, lawyers, accountants, and so on. Tom's did not sell you the air conditioner; it merely provided the service of installing it. Tom's would be liable for your injuries only if it installed the air conditioner incorrectly and that mistake caused your injuries.

Suppose you buy a used toaster from Andy's Thrift Store, take it home, plug it in, and it blows up. Your house burns down, and everything in it is destroyed. Does strict liability apply to Andy's? In most states, no; strict liability applies only to those who deal in new products. Andy's is liable to you only if it was negligent in some way—if, for instance, Andy's had repaired the toaster, and its faulty repair work caused the fire. Some states do apply strict liability to persons who regularly sell used merchandise, and would make Andy's pay you. This rule does not apply to a person who only occasionally sells his or her unwanted items at a garage sale or swap meet, for example.

What Makes a Product Defective

There are three broad types of product defects: (1) defects in making the product—manufacturing defects; (2) defects in the product's design; and (3) failure to give the consumer adequate instructions concerning use or assembly of the product or sufficient warnings concerning its dangers.

Manufacturing Defects

A "manufacturing defect" is one that happens when the product is being produced. Something happens so that the product that hurts you is made differently from the others: a nut isn't tightened; a weld is missed; the wrong type of metal is used; a smaller screw or nut and bolt are substituted for the proper size; the product is subjected to too much (or not enough) heat or cold; a piece is missing; or the product is assembled improperly. The result is that the product is not made according to specifications and leaves the factory in a faulty and dangerous condition.

Design Defects

A design defect exists when something is wrong in the specifications for the product; the product is inherently dangerous even when made according to the plans. An example will help explain the difference between a manufacturing defect and a design defect. Suppose that you are injured when your car axle breaks. Metallurgists examine the axle and find that the metal was too weak to support the weight of the car. If the design for the car called for a stronger metal to be used—one that would have supported the weight of the car—the defect is one of manufacturing, because an inferior grade of metal was in fact used. But if the design called for the grade of metal that was actually used—the inferior grade—then the defect is one in design. All cars made according to the design would share the same defect: a weak axle that is likely to fail.

A product's design also can be defective because it omits adequate safety devices to protect against injuries. A power saw, for instance, must be equipped with a guard over the top part of the blade to prevent injuries. Lack of safety devices is especially important in commercial, industrial, and farming machinery. One slip by the worker or other user could mean the loss of an arm, a leg—even his or her life. Machines must therefore be designed with an eye to protecting the user from accidents that are likely to happen.

Since hundreds of thousands of automobile accidents occur every year, an automobile manufacturer can expect its products to be involved in an accident. A motor vehicle must therefore be designed to withstand a certain amount of contact with other vehicles and stationary objects, such as telephone poles. Because of the foreseeability of accidents, an automobile manufacturer must design its products to be reasonably "crashworthy." For example, cars flip over in some accidents. Accordingly, the manufacturer must make the roof of the car strong enough to support the weight of the car to prevent it from collapsing, resulting in the occupants being crushed should the car roll over. The car only has to be crashworthy, not crashproof. A manufacturer is not required to design a car that will provide protection in all situations. For instance, no car is expected to withstand crashes and flips at, say, one hundred miles per hour.

Lack of Adequate Instructions or Warnings

A product can be defective because it does not come with complete instructions on how to use it correctly or because consumers aren't sufficiently warned of its dangers. Products that the consumer assembles must include clear and complete instructions to ensure that the product is put together properly.

Certain dangers are inherent in some products, and removing the dangers would remove the effectiveness—indeed, the purpose—of the products. Drain cleaners, for instance, contain caustic chemicals without which they couldn't do their job. When a product has a danger that cannot be removed, the manufacturer must warn purchasers and users of the product of its dangers. The warning must be specific. A generalized statement such as "Warning: Dangerous If Used Incorrectly" isn't enough; it doesn't tell you why or how the product is dangerous. A warning that doesn't expressly designate each and all of the product's dangers that can cause serious injury is not legally adequate.

Does a manufacturer have to place a warning on a knife stating that the blade is sharp and could cut somebody, or that a bow and arrow can hurt others? No. A manufacturer need not warn of dangers that are obvious and understood, even expected, by everyone. In one case involving the sale of a slingshot to a young boy, the manufacturer was not liable for failing to include a warning of the dangers of a slingshot. The court stated: "Ever since David slew Goliath, young and old alike have known that slingshots can be dangerous and deadly. There is no need to include a warning." Similarly, it has been held that there is no need for a manufacturer to warn of the dangers of shooting a BB gun at another person.

The warning on a product must be conspicuous; it must catch the attention of the average person and must be written in language that is readily comprehensible to the average consumer. When non-English-speaking people can be expected to use the product, the manufacturer may be required to communicate the warning by signs or even in other languages.

Inadequate Packaging

An important development in the law of products liability involves defects in packaging. (Technically, this is a subcategory of design defects.) For example, dangerous household chemicals should be sold in childproof containers; if they are not, the manufacturer may be liable if a child gets into the product and swallows it. If the product cannot be made child-safe, it must be accompanied by clear warnings of its specific dangers and cautions that it should be kept out of the reach of children.

In 1982, seven people in the Chicago area died after taking the pain reliever Tylenol in capsule form that had been laced with cyanide. The bottles had been deliberately contaminated by an unknown person sometime after they left the factory. As a result of this tragedy, manufacturers have become increasingly aware of the need to make a tamper-resistant product. Most packages of headache relievers and many other products are now sealed in various ways to reduce the possibility of undetected tampering.

How far must a manufacturer go to protect its product from intentional outside interference? This decision is made on a case-by-case basis. But one thing is certain: The manufacturer must take some precautions to prevent tampering with its product after it leaves the factory. The question is really one of cost versus benefit. The manufacturer's cost to make each package tamper-resistant is minimal and can be passed on to the consumer by an insignificant increase in the price of each product. On the other hand, there is a great benefit to the consumer—protection against serious injury or death.

When a Manufacturer Knowingly Markets a Dangerous Product

Sometimes a manufacturer or seller knows that its product is likely to cause great harm but still lets it reach the public without removing or warning of the danger. This was the charge against Ford Motor Company in a suit involving the Ford Pinto. Richard Grimshaw was a passenger in a Pinto when it stalled on the freeway. Another car rammed into it from behind. The Pinto's gas tank exploded, and Grimshaw was burned severely. Grimshaw and his lawyers contended that Ford had known of the dangers associated with the gas tank, yet had not taken prompt steps to correct the problem or at least to warn the public. Grimshaw's attorneys discovered that Ford had conducted a cost-analysis survey that compared the costs of lawsuits against Ford for deaths and injuries resulting from gas tank explosions with the cost of eliminating the problem. The analysis concluded that by leaving the problem uncorrected, Ford would save $100 million, and this even after paying for expected deaths and injuries. To correct the problem—at the expense of $11 per car—would have cost Ford $137.5 million. Other documents showed that Ford decided to delay changing the fuel tank to save over $20 million. The jury awarded $2.8 million in compensatory damages and $125 million in punitive damages. The judge reduced the award to $3.5 million, and the case was later settled out of court while on appeal.

Express Warranties and Defectiveness

Express warranties are the bases for some lawsuits when a person is injured, even though the product is not defective in the usual sense. An express warranty is created when the manufacturer or seller makes a specific promise or representation concerning the quality or ability of its product. Manufacturers often make certain statements in their advertisements to entice you to buy their product, and you naturally rely on the truth of these statements when buying the product. Suppose you weigh 225 pounds, for example, and need a ladder. You want to make sure that the ladder you buy will support your weight, so you buy the one whose label states that it can hold 250 pounds. But back at home, the ladder buckles under your weight when you climb it. You fall to the floor and are injured. The manufacturer must pay for your injuries even if the ladder was designed and made properly, because the label constitutes an express warranty. The ladder could not do what the manufacturer distinctly said it could, and that is why it is "defective."

SUING FOR YOUR INJURIES IF YOU'VE BEEN HURT BY A DEFECTIVE PRODUCT

Can You Sue?

At one time, you could sue a product manufacturer or seller only if you were in contractual "privity" with it. This meant that you had to have bought the defective product directly from the manufacturer or the seller to be allowed to sue for your injuries. This requirement came from the historic 1842 English case of *Winterbottom v. Wright*. Mr. Winterbottom was injured seriously when the mail coach he was driving broke down because it had not been kept in good repair by Mr. Wright, who had a contract with the postmaster general to keep the coaches in safe condition. Mr. Winterbottom sued Mr. Wright, but the judges threw the case out of court because Mr. Winterbottom did not have a contract (was not "in privity") with Mr. Wright. The postmaster general, the court declared, was the only party who could sue, because it was to him that Mr. Wright had promised his services. One judge commented that if Mr. Winterbottom were allowed to sue, then "every passenger, or even any person passing along the road, who was injured by the upsetting of the coach, might bring a similar action. Unless we confine the operation of such contracts as this to the parties who entered into them, the most absurd and outrageous consequences, to which I can see no limit would ensue."

American courts generally required privity until 1916, when Judge Benjamin Cardozo of the New York Court of Appeals (New York's highest court) handed down the decision in the famous case of *McPherson v. Buick Motor Co.* Mr. McPherson was injured when the wooden wheel on the car in which he was riding crumbled and he was thrown from the car. Judge Cardozo decreed that if the manufacturer knows that its product will be used by persons other than the purchaser, the manufacturer owes a duty to such persons to make the product carefully, lack of contractual privity notwithstanding.

Today the purchaser of a defective product can sue the manufacturer even though he or she didn't buy it directly from the manufacturer. You also can sue if you weren't the actual purchaser of the product but were an "ultimate user" of it. An ultimate user is someone who is likely to use the product: a member of the purchaser's household; a friend; an employee; or a person who buys the product from the original purchaser; among others. But what if you neither bought the product nor were using it, but you were merely a bystander injured by the product? The steering linkage of a car breaks, sending the car out of control. The car jumps the curb and hits you, or you are injured when you fall jumping out of the car's way. Is the manufacturer strictly liable for your injuries? In most states, yes. A few states, however, have refused to extend strict liability beyond consumers and users of the product. Thus, bystanders, unless they are in the "zone of danger"—the area where they risk being struck themselves—cannot sue on a theory of strict products liability. (They might, nevertheless, be able to collect from the manufacturer if they can prove that it was negligent in making or designing the product.)

Who Is Liable for Your Injuries?

If you are injured or your property is damaged by a defective product, in most states you can sue the manufacturer, distributor, wholesaler, retailer, and anyone else involved in the chain of distribution—the "stream of commerce"—for your damages. Let's say you are injured by a defective lawnmower. The lawnmower was made by X Corporation and is distributed nationally by Y Company. Z Wholesalers markets it in your state, and you bought it at Joe's Lawn and Garden Shop. In most states, you can sue all of them for your injuries.

Suppose Acme Department Store markets its own brand of clothes. The clothes are made by Fashion, Inc., which also sells clothes nationwide under its own name. You buy a sweater with the Acme label (made by Fashion, Inc.) and are hurt when an errant cigarette touches the sweater and it goes up instantly in flames. Is Acme strictly liable to you because the sweater was not sufficiently fire-retardant, even though Fashion, Inc., not Acme, actually made the sweater? Yes. A company that puts its label on a product made by another and markets it as its own is deemed a manufacturer. Some department stores, for example, put their own names on tools, appliances, and clothes made by other companies. When they do, they are liable as if they had made the products themselves. Would Fashion, Inc., the actual makers of the defective sweater, also be liable for your injuries? That depends on the type of defect and Fashion, Inc.'s involvement. If it is a manufacturing defect—the wrong material was used, or the fabric was doused with some highly flammable liquid—then Fashion, Inc. is jointly liable with Acme Department Store. But if Acme furnished the specifications for the product, and Fashion, Inc., made it according to the designs, Fashion, Inc., may not necessarily be strictly liable. Fashion, Inc., would be liable if the design was clearly dangerous and it did not eliminate the danger or put an adequate warning to consumers on the product.

Limitations on the Manufacturer's Liability

If you are injured by a defective product, there are several factors that can relieve the manufacturer or seller of liability in whole or in part. One restriction is that the product must reach the consumer in substantially the same condition as it left the factory. If the product was altered significantly by a supplier, seller, or the consumer himself, the manufacturer ordinarily is not strictly liable if the injury is attributable to the change. This rule does not apply to products that require some alteration after they leave the factory so they can be used, however—in particular, products that you must put together before you can use them. Also, the manufacturer remains liable if the alteration had nothing to do with the cause of the injury.

Suppose the head on your new hammer is loose and flies off while you're using it, hitting you in the face and knocking out an eye. Whether the manufacturer is liable for your injuries depends on whether you knew the head was loose before you used it. If you didn't know it was loose, you can collect damages from the manufacturer, even if an inspection of the hammer before you used it would have revealed the defect. But if you realized the head was loose and still went ahead and used the hammer, you may be barred from suing the manufacturer because you assumed the risk that the head could come off.

Now suppose that you are an employee and you realize that the machine you work with is defective. You inform your boss that the machine is dangerous and that you don't want to use it. Your boss tells you that if you don't get back to work on it immediately, you'll be fired on the spot. You go back to the machine and twenty minutes later are hurt. Is the machine's manufacturer off the hook because you assumed the risk that the defective machine could hurt you? At one time you would have been barred from recovering your damages from the manufacturer. Today, though, many courts recognize that employees who use machines may be doing so not because they assume the risk of being injured, but rather out of fear that they will be fired if they don't. When it comes right down to it, the employee really doesn't have much of a choice. Therefore, an employee who continues to use a defective machine rather than face unemployment often can sue the manufacturer if the machine injures him or her. (Workers' compensation laws usually prevent the employee from suing the employer; see the discussion in chapter 13.)

The fact that you assume some risks of being hurt by a product does not prevent you from suing if your injury was caused by a risk you didn't expect. When you use an ax, for instance, you assume the risk that if you are careless, you can injure yourself or others. But you don't assume the risk that the ax is defective in any way. Suppose you are chopping wood with a new ax, and the wooden handle breaks, and the blade cuts your leg. The manufacturer is liable for your injuries. Similarly, if the blade is made from an inferior material and breaks or splinters while you're using it correctly, the manufacturer must pay for your injuries. Clearly, these dangers are beyond what you normally expect when using an ax.

To avoid or reduce their liability, manufacturers frequently assert that the person was misusing the product at the time he or she was hurt. But just because you were using a product for something other than its primary function when you were injured doesn't mean that you can't sue the manufacturer. Suppose you want to hang a picture high on the wall—too high for you to reach—so you stand on a chair. The chair breaks under your weight, and you are injured. Are you barred from suing the manufacturer or seller because you were using the chair in other than its intended manner? No. The issue is whether your misuse of the product was "reasonably foreseeable" or not. A manufacturer of a chair can expect someone to stand on its product, so a chair must be designed and made strong enough to withstand a person's full weight. On the other hand, the maker of, say, a glass beer bottle would not expect people to use it as a hammer. If someone does and the bottle shatters and hurts persons nearby, the manufacturer of the bottle is not liable. Even if the manufacturer could expect that someone might use the bottle as a hammer, it would be impossible to make a glass bottle that could survive such a use intact.

What to Do If You Are Hurt by a Product

The most important thing to do when you are hurt by a product—after getting proper medical attention, of course—is to keep the product or its remnants. For example, if a bottle explodes, keep all of the pieces; if a child gets into a dangerous chemical, keep the container; if you are hurt by a machine that you rented, take pictures of it, write down the name of the manufacturer, the model, and the identification number and keep your receipts from the rental company. When you return the machine, inform the rental company that you were injured by it. The product that hurt you is obviously a critical piece of evidence that may have to be analyzed by experts to determine exactly how the injury happened. But don't despair if you've already disposed of the product or if the product was consumed in the accident. In many cases, it is possible to reconstruct the cause of the injury by analyzing other similar products.

When a defective product injures someone, a lawyer usually should be consulted as soon as possible. (Chapter 24 tells how to find a lawyer even if you think the injury was partly your fault.) Frequently it turns out that many injuries that appear on the surface to be the user's fault are really due solely to a defective product. And even if the injury was partly your fault, under the rules of comparative negligence (see chapter 10)—called "comparative fault" in strict liability cases—you may still be able to collect part of your damages from the manufacturer, wholesaler, or seller.

THIRTEEN

Employees

EMPLOYEES ARE COVERED by a wide range of laws dealing with many subjects: minimum wages; safe working conditions; the right to form a union; and so on. This chapter discusses the areas that today's workingmen and -women most frequently consult an attorney about: compensation for on-the-job injuries; race, sex, and age discrimination; sexual harassment; rights when a worker is fired without reason; owner of patents, inventions, and copyrights made on and off the job; misuse of confidential information; and agreements not to compete. Discrimination on the basis of a physical or mental disability is discussed in the next chapter.

JOB DISCRIMINATION AND HARASSMENT

PEOPLE SHOULD BE HIRED, fired, and promoted on the basis of their ability to do the job—not because of their sex, their race, the color of their skin, their religious beliefs, or their national origin. Nor should they be subjected to intolerable working conditions and harassment because they are different from other workers. Many laws at both the federal and state level guarantee just this.

The following discussion is limited to federal laws, which generally apply to employers who have more than fifteen or twenty workers. Some laws apply only to employers who have fifty or more employees. Many states have their own laws (usually modeled on the federal laws) extending the same rights to employees of smaller businesses or to those that are not engaged in interstate commerce.

If You Are Discriminated Against Because of Your Race, Religion, or Sex

The federal Civil Rights Act of 1964 and the Equal Employment Opportunity Act of 1972 guarantee to all workers the right to be free from discrimination because of race, color, national origin, sex, and religious beliefs. In addition to protecting you from being fired or not being hired or promoted because of any of these things, these laws also ensure that you will be given the same training and opportunity for advancement and equal pay for equal work.

Not all discrimination is unlawful. An employer can refuse to hire or promote you if a different race, color, national origin, sex, or religious belief is a "bona fide qualification" of the job. For instance, a woman cannot sue for sexual discrimination if she is turned down for the job of men's locker room attendant, since being male would be a legitimate qualification for the job. True instances of permissible discrimination are rare, however.

Often discrimination takes a subtler form. Women have been discriminated against by job disqualifications regarding minimum height, weight, and physical abilities that are not reasonably related to the job. The qualifications usually favor the average American male over the average American female. Many police forces, for instance, used to have rather strict minimum requirements concerning height, weight, and physical abilities that tended—intentionally or unintentionally—to discriminate against women who wanted to become police officers. But since many women could still do a police officer's job without meeting the minimum requirements, the requirements had to be revised so women were not discriminated against.

Suppose that you are African-American and your Caucasian boss wants to fire you because of your race. Your boss knows that it's against the law to fire you because of your race, so he or she waits for you to do the slightest thing wrong. And when you do, your boss immediately calls you into his or her office, tells you that the company can't tolerate employees who foul up, and fires you on the spot. You later discover that other workers—all of them white—had made the same mistake but weren't fired for it. If you sue your employer for unlawful discrimination, will you win? Probably. The fact that other workers of a different race—the same race as your supervisor—were not terminated for the same mistake shows that your race and not your job performance was the motivating factor behind the decision to fire you.

If you claim that you were not hired or promoted because of your sex, you need to prove that you were qualified for the job or promotion in question, that you applied for it, that you were not hired or promoted although a vacancy existed, and that similarly situated members of the opposite sex with comparable or lesser qualifications were hired or promoted at the time your request for hiring or promotion was denied. Likewise, if you claim that you were not hired or promoted because of your race or religion, you must prove that you were qualified for the job in question, that you applied for the position, and that other workers with comparable or lesser qualifications—but of a different race or religion—were given the job. The first time you are passed over for a job or promotion, it may be difficult to prove that the employer was motivated by an unlawful purpose. But the second or third time the same employer passes you over, the intent to discriminate against you because of your sex, race, or religion usually will become clear.

Sexual Harassment

As an employee, you have the right to be free from unwarranted sexual advances and offensive or obscene remarks that make your working conditions intolerable. We generally think of sexual harassment in terms of a female employee who is the target of the sexual advances of her male boss and male coworkers. This is certainly the most common type of sexual harassment. But sexual harassment also exists when a male employee is sexually harassed by a female supervisor or female coworkers, or even when the sexual discrimination is by members of the same sex. Discrimination based on one's sexual orientation is discussed in chapter 8.

What type of conduct constitutes sexual harassment? The federal Equal Employment Opportunity Commission defines sexual harassment as any verbal or physical conduct of a sexual nature that unreasonably interferes with the performance of your job and that creates an intimidating, hostile, or offensive working environment. The conduct must be both undesirable and offensive. And it must be so significant and pervasive that it creates an abusive working environment, one that seriously affects your emotional or psychological well-being.

The clearest example of sexual harassment takes place when your superior requires you to submit to his or her sexual advances in order to keep your job or get a raise or promotion. Touching a female employee's breasts or the genitals of an employee of either sex is also sexual harassment (and battery as well). If your boss or coworkers continuously make lewd comments and sexually offensive suggestions or jokes to you or frequently touch you in a sexual manner, that too is sexual harassment. In the case of coworkers who are sexually harassing you, your employer usually is not liable for sexual harassment unless he or she directly participates in the harassment or knows that your fellow employees are sexually harassing you but doesn't do anything to correct the situation.

Casual or trivial events usually are not enough to constitute harassment; neither are most isolated events, such as a single obscene joke. But if your boss or coworkers persist in telling such jokes, it can be harassment—particularly if you make it clear that you are offended by the lewd jokes and ask that they not be told in your presence, and you complain to your supervisor or human resources department about it. The more offensive the conduct is, the less frequency is required to constitute sexual harassment. For instance, if your supervisor gropes you and asks you to have sex one time with him or her, telling you that your job or promotion depends upon it, that is sexual harassment even if it only happened once.

An essential element of sexual harassment is that it must be unwelcome. You can't complain of sexual harassment if you invited, participated in, or otherwise encouraged the sexual advances or lewd remarks of your boss or coworkers. But this doesn't mean that you must put up with the offensive conduct indefinitely. Even though you originally encouraged or put up with the lewd remarks or conduct, you can change your mind and request that it now be stopped.

If the sexual harassment is less serious—say, crude jokes rather than pressure to have sex with your boss—you should talk to the offender directly, or if that would do no good or you wish not to confront him or her, complain to your supervisor and the coworker's supervisor and the human resources department. Your employer must take prompt action to stop the harassment after you complain. If this doesn't make a significant difference or if the harassment is of a more serious nature, then other action (discussed below) is appropriate. You don't have to get used to the offensive conduct or lewd language, nor can your employer simply tell you to laugh it off, that your coworkers don't really mean anything by it.

What to Do If You Are a Victim of Discrimination Or Harassment

If you feel that you have been the victim of unlawful discrimination or harassment, you should promptly file a complaint with the local office of the Equal Employment Opportunity Commission (EEOC). Even if the EEOC doesn't have jurisdiction over your employer, it usually can advise you which federal or state agency to contact. If you belong to a union, talk to your shop steward about filing a complaint with it as well. It is usually a good idea to contact an attorney who is experienced in unlawful discrimination or harassment cases as soon as you decide to take action to learn of your full rights and to assist you with filing complaints with the various state and local agencies, as well as filing a lawsuit against the offender and your employer if it comes to that.

If you have been unlawfully fired, demoted, or not promoted because of your race, color, national origin, religion, or sex, you are entitled to be reinstated and to receive back pay starting with the day of your termination or demotion or the date on which you should have been promoted. You may also be entitled to recover lost benefits, damages for your emotional suffering, and punitive damages. (You may also be eligible for workers' compensation benefits if you are able to prove you are unable to work because of the stress you suffered from the unlawful conduct.) If for some reason you are fired and can't get your old job back, you can recover damages in place of reinstatement. Your employer may also have to reimburse you for your attorney's fees.

WORKERS' COMPENSATION LAWS

A WAITRESS CARRYING A TRAY of food slips on a loose tile, falls, and breaks her wrist; she is out of work for three months. A maintenance worker changing a lightbulb falls off a ladder and is paralyzed, never to work again. A loading-dock worker is run over by a forklift and killed. All of these workers have one thing in common: They or their families are probably entitled to receive workers' compensation benefits.

Workers' compensation laws are designed to provide an expeditious system of compensating an employee who was injured—or the family of an employee who was killed—in a work-related incident. Employers are required to purchase workers' compensation insurance to protect their employees. (Some states require employers to contribute to a state fund, out of which the benefits are paid to injured employees.) In return, employers receive the guarantee that they generally can't be sued by their employees and exposed to the higher amounts a jury might award. Employees are guaranteed that they will receive benefits if they are injured on the job, regardless of who causes the injuries (unless the employee deliberately hurts himself or herself). Workers' compensation acts also are intended to reduce the role of attorneys, so that all or most of the benefits go to the injured employee or to the family of an employee killed on the job.

Workers' compensation laws are based on the theory that "the cost of the product should bear the blood of the workman." In other words, as a cost of doing business, an employer is required to pay for injuries its employees suffer on the job. The employer offsets this increased cost of doing business by raising its prices to the general public. Spread out over hundreds of thousands or millions of customers, the increase is generally rather small.

Before there were workers' compensation acts, employees had a tough time collecting any money for the injuries or for the wages they lost when they were injured on the job and were off work temporarily or permanently. It was true that they could sue their employers, but winning was another story. First, the worker had to prove that the employer or one of his or her employees caused the accident, which was not easy to do. And even if the worker succeeded at this, the employer still won many cases by claiming that the employee had assumed the risk of injury or had partially caused his or her own injuries. The "fellow servant" rule usually barred the employee from suing coworkers who had injured him or her unless the fellow employee acted intentionally.

Recognizing how unfair this situation was to injured workers, New York enacted the first workers' compensation act in 1910. Within the next ten years, most of the other states had passed similar laws. Today, all fifty states and the federal government have workers' compensation laws, protecting about 90 percent of the nation's workforce.

Have workers' compensation laws lived up to their goals? Not really. The biggest complaint is that the benefits paid to the injured worker are woefully inadequate, especially when the injuries are extensive. One court acknowledged this fact when it stated: "It is common knowledge that workmen injured or killed in construction work do not receive full compensation under the Workmen's Compensation Act for damages that they sustain, notwithstanding the commendable purpose of such legislation." In many cases there are no time savings in processing an injured worker's claim because of administrative delays and lengthy appeals. And many employees—particularly those who are injured seriously—find that being represented by an experienced lawyer is essential to getting maximum benefits. So rather than alleviating the problem, in many cases workers' compensation laws have made it worse.

Who Is Entitled to Receive Benefits

To be eligible to receive workers' compensation benefits, you must be an employee of a covered company at the time of the accident. All employees are presumed covered unless the law specifically excludes their class of workers from coverage. Farmworkers, domestic help, voluntary workers, and people who work for nonprofit organizations are excluded from coverage in many states. Occasional temporary employees are usually not entitled to benefits, but regular part-time employees are. In some states, employers of a small number of workers (usually less than three, four, or five) do not have to provide workers' compensation protection for their employees.

Suppose that you have your own air-conditioning business and are hired by Sunset Construction Company to install air conditioners in a new building. While doing so, part of the ceiling falls and injures you. Can you collect workers' compensation benefits from Sunset Construction Company? No. You are considered to be an "independent contractor" rather than an employee of the prime contractor, here Sunset Construction Company. However, if you can prove an employee of Sunset Construction Company was negligent in installing that part of the ceiling, you would be entitled to sue and recover from Sunset.

Limitations on Your Right to Benefits

Workers' compensation benefits are payable only if your injury is related to your job. The clearest example of a work-related injury occurs when you are hurt on your employer's premises during working hours, while you are doing your job and getting paid for it. You usually are entitled to benefits if you are injured in the company lunchroom during a rest break.

Can you get benefits if you are injured in a traffic accident on the way to work? Usually not. Under the so-called "going and coming" rule, you are generally not entitled to workers' compensation benefits if you are injured while commuting to and from work. If, however, you are an outside salesman and call on clients between your home and the office, you are probably eligible for benefits.

You can't get benefits if you deliberately injure yourself. (But you can get benefits if you were injured by your own carelessness.) Many states deny you benefits if the injuries happened because you were drunk or high on drugs. But the intoxication must have been a cause of the accident. If you are walking down an aisle of a warehouse when a lightbulb explodes and injures you, for instance, you can recover workers' compensation benefits even if you were drunk, since your drunkenness had nothing to do with the accident.

Most workers' compensation acts also limit benefits to cases where physical injuries are suffered. Disease and illness often aren't covered by workers' compensation laws (but other laws may cover industrial diseases). Things like emotional distress and mental suffering, violation of your civil rights, defamation, and invasion of privacy are all beyond the scope of many workers' compensation acts, although, as discussed below, you may have the right to sue in court your employer or fellow employee who infringed upon your rights.

How Benefits Are Determined

The amount of benefits you receive depends on the seriousness and permanence of your injuries and the amount of your weekly salary. You'll get less for a temporary partial disability than you will for a complete and permanent disability. If you break your arm, for instance, you will be given a certain percentage of your weekly wage for a specified number of weeks. If you lose a foot, you will receive a larger amount for a longer period of time.

You are considered totally disabled if you can't work at your old job or at another job for which you are suited without experiencing substantial pain. But if you're able to work at another job without too much discomfort, you are only partially disabled. A temporary disability is one that is likely to last a certain period of time, whether several days, weeks, or months. You are permanently disabled when your physical condition, combined with your age, training, and experience, prevents you from obtaining anything more than sporadic employment for an indefinite period of time.

If you are killed in a work-related accident, your dependents are entitled to death benefits under the workers' compensation act. A "dependent" typically is defined as anyone living under the same roof as you and who receives most of his or her support from you. Does this mean that your spouse doesn't get anything if he or she earned more than you? No. Your spouse is entitled to full death benefits (up to the maximum amount) regardless of whether he or she made more than you.

How to Claim Your Benefits

When you suffer a work-related injury, you should notify your employer or superior as soon as possible and ask for a claim form to fill out. You will have to report the basic information—where, when, and how you were injured—and submit proof of your injury, including doctor's bills. If your claim is accepted, your benefits should commence promptly, usually on a weekly basis. If your claim is denied partly or completely, you can have it reviewed by the workers' compensation appeals board (WCAB). You can sue the WCAB if you don't agree with its decision and have the extent of your disability, its permanence, and the amount of your benefits decided in court.

You usually don't need an attorney to help you with your workers' compensation claim, at least not if your injury is relatively minor and you are out of work for only a short time. But if the injury is fairly serious, or the worker was killed, it is best to be represented by an attorney. You should certainly hire an attorney if problems arise in the processing of your claim or if you plan on appealing the initial decision.

When Even Maximum Benefits Are Too Small

Anytime workers' compensation benefits don't adequately compensate you, you should consider whether your employer, a fellow employee, or a third party was responsible for the accident and is liable for the rest of your damages. This is an especially important concern in cases involving serious injuries or death. The following situations are among the more common ones when you can sue others for job-related injuries and deaths.

Suing Your Employer

Workers' compensation benefits usually are referred to as the employee's "exclusive remedy" against the employer. This means that you can receive only the workers' compensation benefits and are barred from suing your employer, even if the injury was your employer's fault. In several situations, however, you can sue your employer in addition to or in place of collecting benefits under the workers' compensation act.

No Workers' Compensation Insurance. If your employer fails to carry workers' compensation insurance as required by law, you usually have the choice of collecting workers' compensation or suing your employer in court. In some states, you can do both: You can collect workers' compensation benefits *and* sue your employer in court. Whether you should just take the workers' compensation benefits or sue your employer depends on a number of factors, including whether your employer was at fault, whether your employer has any defenses that may bar or substantially reduce the amount you can recover in damages (for instance, perhaps you were partially or largely at fault for your own injuries), whether your injuries are serious, whether workers' compensation benefits are sufficient, and whether the employer will be able to pay the judgment if you win a lawsuit in court. You should discuss all of these matters with your attorney before making your decision to accept workers' compensation benefits or sue your lawyer in court.

Excluded Employment or Injuries. Earlier we noted that certain types of workers (such as farm workers, domestic help, temporary workers, and others) and injuries (emotional suffering and invasion of privacy, for example) often are excluded from coverage under workers' compensation acts. If workers' compensation laws don't cover you or the particular injury you suffer, you may be able to sue your employer.

If your injury occurs outside the course of employment, you can sue your employer (or co-employee, if a co-employee injures you). For example, let's say that your employer invites you to a baseball game on a Sunday afternoon. On the way to the ballpark, you are hurt in an automobile accident caused by your employer. Since the baseball game had nothing to do with your job, you can sue your employer and have his or her automobile insurance company pay the damages.

Intentional Misconduct of the Employer. Suppose your employer punches you in the face and breaks your nose while you are at work. Can you sue your employer, or are you limited to workers' compensation benefits? Some states let you sue your employer for deliberately breaking your nose. Other states, however, prohibit you from suing your employer even in this situation. Some states will allow you to recover benefits under the workers' compensation system, and then receive additional benefits up to a stated limit, such as 50 percent of your workers' compensation benefits.

The "Dual Capacity" Doctrine. Let's say that you work for American Ladder Company, which makes ladders that are sold to the public. While using one of American's ladders at work to change a lightbulb, the ladder breaks because of a defect; you fall and are injured seriously. Can you sue American Ladder, or are you limited to workers' compensation benefits? Some states let you do both under the "dual capacity" doctrine. The ladder company wears two hats with respect to its employees—that of employer to employee and that of product manufacturer to consumer. The ladder company has a duty to the general public—for whom its product is intended—to make a safe product. You have the same right to a safe product that any other member of the general public has.

The dual capacity doctrine is not restricted to employees who make products for public sale. It applies anytime your employer treats you as he or she treats a member of the public. Suppose, for example, that you are a nurse and strain your back on the job. Your employer-doctor treats you but is negligent (medical malpractice), and your condition gets worse. You can sue your employer-doctor for the worsened condition because he or she assumed a dual role toward you—that of employer and that of doctor. As a patient, you have the same rights as any other patient, even if you happen to work for the doctor.

Suing Fellow Employees

Fellow employees generally have the same immunity from a lawsuit as your employer. In other words, you usually cannot sue a coworker who accidentally or carelessly injures you at work, and you are limited to the recovery of workers' compensation benefits. Most states, however, let you sue fellow employees who deliberately hurt you.

Let's say that you are riding to work with a coworker and are injured in an accident caused by your coworker. Do workers' compensation laws bar you from suing your coworker? Generally not. Your coworker's automobile insurance normally would cover the incident. Now suppose that you are injured by a coworker in an automobile accident in the company parking lot. You probably are entitled to workers' compensation benefits in this situation. But can you sue your coworker as well? The states are split on this question: Some let you sue your coworker, while others don't.

Suing Third Parties

Although you generally are barred from suing your employer and coworkers for on-the-job injuries, you usually can sue anyone else (a "third party") who injures you while you are working. You may also be able to sue that person's employer if the person was acting within the course of his or her job when you were hurt. For instance, if another company's delivery van backs into you because the driver wasn't looking, you can sue the driver and the company he or she works for for negligence. Likewise, if you are a traveling salesman and are injured on a business trip in an automobile accident caused by another person, you can sue that person for your injuries in addition to collecting workers' compensation benefits. Or suppose that you work for Les's Tool and Die and are injured by a defective machine made by ABZ Corporation. You can collect workers' compensation benefits from Les's, since you were an employee injured on the job. You also can bring a lawsuit against ABZ Corporation for manufacturing and distributing a defective machine.

You Can't Get Paid Twice

Suppose in the example last used above that you collect workers' compensation benefits for the on-the-job injuries while working for Les's Tool and Die, and you take ABZ Corporation to court, where the jury awards you a nice sum. Do you get to keep both the money you received from workers' compensation and the money you got from ABZ Corporation? No. You can't recover twice for the same injuries. If you received workers' compensation injuries and a settlement from the other driver's insurance company, usually workers' compensation would have the right to be reimbursed from the settlement proceeds for any money it paid you.

IF YOU ARE FIRED OR LAID OFF

IF YOU ARE TERMINATED by your employer, that doesn't mean the end of your rights. In fact, getting laid off may activate a whole new set of rights. We already have seen, for example, that you can't be fired because of your race, color, national origin, sex, or religious beliefs, and you can take action against your employer if you are. And even if you are terminated for a lawful reason you may still have some rights, such as the right to collect unemployment insurance benefits. If you discover that you are being terminated and you belong to a union, you should immediately contact the union; a collective bargaining agreement may give you some rights to job security, reinstatement, or benefits—rights that a nonunion employee ordinarily doesn't have.

Unemployment Insurance

Suppose that you are terminated through no fault of your own—you are laid off during a slow period, for instance, or fired without cause (that is, you didn't do anything wrong, like stealing or being habitually late). Do you have any rights? If you have worked at your job long enough and have earned enough, you ordinarily are entitled to receive unemployment benefits. The amount of your benefits depends on how long you were working and how much you earned.

One thing is certain, though: Unemployment benefits do not replace your earnings in full. And if you are self-employed, you cannot collect unemployment benefits. You only get unemployment benefits if you worked for someone else.

You usually cannot collect unemployment benefits if you voluntarily quit your job, regardless of how long you were employed. But if your employer coerced you into quitting—by making working conditions so intolerable for you that you were forced to quit, for example—you may still be able to collect unemployment benefits. Unemployment benefits may also be available if you have to quit your job for health reasons.

Ordinarily, you have to be out of work for at least one week before you can receive unemployment benefits. (Apply for the benefits at your local unemployment office as soon as you can.) Benefits usually last for up to twenty-six weeks. But if unemployment levels are exceptionally high, you sometimes can get benefits for up to thirteen weeks more. If you go back to work—even if to just a low-paying part-time job—unemployment benefits usually stop. In most states, you must be totally unemployed to be eligible to receive unemployment benefits. A few states, however, give you reduced benefits if you take a part-time job that doesn't pay much.

What are your rights if the unemployment office turns down your claim because it feels your employer had cause to fire you, but you disagree? The procedure varies from state to state, but generally you are entitled to an administrative hearing in front of someone who was not involved in the denial of your application for benefits. If your claim is still denied, you may be able to sue in court.

You have to make an effort to find a job while you receive unemployment benefits; in fact, if you don't actively look for a new job, your benefits can stop. Usually you've at least got to go to the unemployment office once a week to check the job list. Suppose you're offered a job but you turn it down because it's not quite what you're looking for. What then? Your benefits can be cut off if the job was reasonably suited for you, taking into account your education and skills and the type of work you've been doing.

Retaliatory and Wrongful Discharge of an Employee

Suppose you have been working for your employer for twenty years. All of your job performance evaluations have been satisfactory, you get to work on time, work hard, and no one has complained about your work product or behavior. You expect to work for the company until you retire when, Bam!, out of nowhere your boss tells you that you are being laid off. Doesn't the company owe you something for your years of loyal service? In a word, no. Unless you have an employment contract guaranteeing that you will be employed for a set period of time or for life as long as you perform satisfactorily, you are an "at-will" employee.

Being an at-will employee means that you can be fired at any time at the will of your employer without recourse. As an at-will employee, your employer can fire you for any reason or no reason at all. Long duration of service, regular promotions, favorable performance reviews, praise from supervisors, and salary increases do not imply an employer's contractual intent to relinquish its at-will rights. The only limitation is that your employer cannot fire you for the wrong reasons, such as race, color, ethnic origin, religion, sex, pregnancy, age (if you're forty or over), physical or mental disability (see chapter 14), or if you have an employment contract for a set period of years (discussed below).

You cannot be fired in retaliation for exercising your legal rights or informing the authorities of your employer's unlawful business practices ("whistle-blowing"). For example, you can't be fired (or demoted) in retaliation for filing a workers' compensation claim, a complaint of unlawful discrimination or harassment, or a complaint of unsafe working conditions. You can't be terminated for refusing to participate in illegal activities or to commit perjury, or for reporting the criminal acts of your fellow workers or employer. If you work around food, you can't be fired for reporting to the health department that your employer is selling tainted or spoiled food. If you work in a state that prohibits employers from requiring employees to submit to a lie detector (polygraph) test, you cannot lawfully be discharged for refusing to take the test. Your employer also can't fire you close to your retirement just to avoid having to pay your pension or other retirement benefits. In each of the above examples, you would have the right to sue your employer for lost wages you would have earned and benefits that would have accrued had you not been fired.

If you have an employment contract with a company that calls for you to be employed for a set period of time, the company can fire you before the time in the contract has expired only if it has "good cause" to do so. Good cause would be such things as embezzling company funds, chronic tardiness, failing to do competent work, and the like. However, if you perform your job in a workmanlike manner, are a conscientious worker, always on time, etc., the company cannot fire you prior to the expiration of the time period provided in the employment contract.

Let's say that you have an employment contract with ABC Company for five years. Two and a half years into it, you get wind that the company would like to fire you, but since it has no cause to do so—you have performed your job competently—it knows that if it fires you now, it will be deemed in breach of contract. Therefore, the company goes on a vendetta to make working conditions as hellish as possible for you. They make your working conditions so intolerable and unsafe that you have no choice but to quit. Because you quit rather than were fired, does this preclude a breach of contract lawsuit against ABC Company? Not at all. If a reasonable employee could not work under the same or similar conditions as you were forced to work, your leaving is considered involuntary, the same as if you had been fired—in legalese, a "constructive discharge."

If you feel that you have been wrongfully fired from your job in violation of the law or a contract, you should contact an attorney immediately. The attorney can assist you in filing a complaint with the EEOC if that is in order, as well as notifying your union, if you belong to one.

Should you feel that you have been terminated wrongfully, you have an affirmative duty to "mitigate," or lessen, your damages by seeking alternative employment as soon as possible. You don't have to accept just any job, though; it must be similar in skill requirements and pay to your old job. But if you make no attempt to get new work (to "mitigate your damages"), you may be prohibited from recovering damages from your former employer, or your damages may be drastically reduced by the amount you probably would have made had you actively sought and obtained another job.

COBRA BENEFITS

WHEN AN EMPLOYEE IS voluntarily or involuntarily terminated, the employee generally loses all work-related benefits, one of the most important of which is group health insurance coverage. To provide a terminated employee with health care insurance protection until he or she can find another job, the Consolidated Omnibus Budget Reconciliation Act (commonly known as COBRA) gives the former employee (and the employee's spouse and dependent children) the right to continue in the health plan for a certain period of time. The cost to the former employee will be higher than when he or she was working, as the employer will no longer be paying its share of the cost. COBRA benefits apply only to employers who have a group health plan and had at least twenty employees, either full- or part-time, for more than 50 percent of the previous year.

If the employee is voluntarily or involuntarily terminated, or had his or her hours reduced so that the employee is no longer covered by the health plan, the employee, his or her spouse, and any dependent children can continue their health coverage for up to eighteen months by paying the premium themselves. If the employee becomes entitled to Medicare, dies, or becomes divorced or legally separated from his or her spouse, the spouse and any dependent children can continue coverage for thirty-six months. Special rules apply to a beneficiary who qualifies for Social Security Disability Insurance (SSDI).

For instance, suppose a worker is laid off in a downsizing of the company. The worker then has the right to elect and pay for a maximum of eighteen months of coverage by the employer's group health care plan at the group rate. Now suppose that Hal, the covered ex-employee, divorces his wife, Thelma. Thelma has the right to purchase coverage with Hal's health care plan for a maximum of thirty-six months.

COBRA coverage is especially valuable where there is a preexisting condition that a worker's new employer does not cover for a specified period of time, such as six months. For example, Martha leaves her job when she is four months pregnant and gets a new job. However, the new employer's health care plan has a six-month exclusion period for preexisting conditions. Martha would most likely choose to continue her insurance with her previous employer at least through the birth and the first six months of employment at her new job.

WHO OWNS INVENTIONS OR COPYRIGHTS DEVELOPED AT WORK

Suppose that you develop a patent, an invention, or copyrighted material during the course of your job. Who owns the rights to it, you or your employer? To determine the answer to this question, first look at your employment contract, if you have one, to see what it provides. For example, the employment contract may state that all inventions, patents, and copyrighted material that you develop on your employer's premises belong to your employer. If you are hired to assist in the development of something specific, say, a particular product, computer program, or book, the employment contract normally will provide that all rights in and to the end product, and any new discoveries made along the way, are the exclusive property of the employer.

Let's say that a computer software company hires you to develop a new data management program. At night, in your own home, on your own time, using your own computer, you create a game program that turns out to be quite successful. Your employment contract, however, states that all inventions, patents, or copyrights you develop belong to the employer. Does your employer have any rights to the game program? Probably not, since the game program does not relate to the terms of your employment, and you developed it at home, on your own time, and with your own equipment. But if it were a data management program that you developed at home rather than a game program, your employer probably would own it, since this was exactly what your employer hired you to do.

A "work-for-hire" is copyrighted material that you specifically are commissioned to create: For example, a magazine hires you to write an article on a specific subject, or a computer company employs you to write a technical manual for one of its programs. Copyright law (see chapter 20) provides that in a work-for-hire situation, the employer is considered the author of the copyrighted work. Accordingly, the employer owns all rights to the work, including the right to publish it whenever, wherever, and as often as he or she wants. The employer also has the right to receive all of the profits from the work. Your only compensation, unless your agreement states differently, is the money you were paid to create the work. Work-for-hire agreements must be in writing; otherwise the copyright generally belongs to the person who created the work rather than to the employer.

If you have developed or are interested in developing an invention, patent, or copyrighted material, consider talking to an attorney who specializes in "intellectual property" to see just what your rights are. As an example, if you don't have any type of agreement with your employer and you invent something on company time, you generally own the invention; your employer, however, usually has the right to use it without having to pay you any royalties or other expenses ("shop rights").

MISUSE OF AN EMPLOYER'S CONFIDENTIAL INFORMATION

YOUR JOB MAY GIVE YOU access to confidential information—information that is vital to your employer's continued success in its field. Inside information is the most valuable asset of many businesses, which take numerous precautions to ensure that it does not fall into the hands of the competition. When you leave a company, inevitably you take with you some knowledge and skills you acquired from your job. The longer you work in your field, the more you learn about the ins and outs of the business. The law will not deprive you of the right to use the skills and experience you gain by working in the profession over the years.

The law draws a distinction, however, between using your new skills and experience and exploiting your former employer's confidential information. Suppose you leave a company and take some confidential information with you; you start your own firm or take a position with a competitor and use your former employer's confidential information to compete with it. Your former employer can sue to prevent you from using any "trade secrets" and to force you to pay it any money you made from using the secret information.

A trade secret is something that gives one company an edge over its competitors. It can be a number of things: a formula (such as the recipe for Coca-Cola); a manufacturing process; a product design; a list of customers (discussed below); or a private computer program, to name a few examples. Whether something is in fact a trade secret depends on the novelty of the idea. Is it really the trade secret of one company, or is it a general secret of the whole industry? If the latter, there is no protection for the "secret."

The most important trade secrets of many businesses are the customer and client lists they have developed through the years. If an employee leaves and starts soliciting the customers on the ex-employer's secret list, the company will do whatever it can to stop the former employee's actions. A company can stop an ex-employee from using a list of customers only if that list meets the requirements of a "confidential customer list." "Confidential" here means that the names are not available to a reasonably diligent competitor or salesman. The list is not considered confidential if the names are readily accessible from sources outside the former employer's business—the telephone book or a business directory, for instance. But even if the names of potential customers are accessible to others in the business, a company's confidential customer list can sometimes still be protected. A list of customers who actually have purchased the product or service in question is infinitely more valuable than a list of people who might only be interested in buying it.

Patient and client lists are of the utmost importance to doctors, dentists, law firms, accountants, and other service professionals. If you use your former employer's confidential list to solicit patients or clients, your former employer may be able to get an injunction to stop you. But merely sending an announcement that you have left your previous employment and are now with another employer or are on your own usually is not considered an unlawful solicitation. Another important factor: The courts recognize that the customer has the right to hire whatever company he or she wants. So long as your conduct is not unfair, the court will not stop you from competing with others in the same business, including your ex-employer.

AGREEMENTS NOT TO COMPETE

When you buy an established business, you don't want the seller to open a new shop across the street from you and put you out of business before you get a chance to establish yourself. Usually, when a business is sold, the contract requires the seller not to engage in the same or a similar business within a certain geographical area for a specified length of time. This is called a "covenant not to compete."

Occasionally, in offering you a new job, an employer will require you to agree not to accept similar employment or start your own business in the same geographical area for a specified number of years after leaving. A court will more readily enforce an agreement not to compete when it involves the sale of a business than when it involves one that an employee is required to sign. Why? Because when you apply for a job, the employer generally has the upper hand. You usually are offered the job and the agreement not to compete on a "take it or leave it" basis. But when you buy a business, the law assumes that the buyer and seller stand on relatively equal footing. Each of you knows what you are getting into and can protect your interests accordingly.

Agreements not to compete are enforced only if the restrictions are reasonable in terms of time, activity, and geographical area. An agreement that bars you from engaging in any type of business in any given part of the United States for the rest of your life is invalid; you have the right to make a living.

Let's say that you want to buy a restaurant, but only if the seller promises not to open another restaurant in the area for several years. The contract provides that the seller agrees not to operate another restaurant within a five-mile radius for a period of three years. But six months later the seller opens a new restaurant half a mile from your restaurant, and your business drops to nothing; many of your customers have gone to the seller's new place. You most likely would be successful in a lawsuit against the seller because the restrictions as to time (three years) and place (a radius of five miles) are reasonable to protect your legitimate business interests. What type of damages could you recover in your lawsuit? You could get an injunction to stop the seller from operating the new restaurant in violation of your agreement. You also could ask the court for damages for business the seller took away from you and other damages you suffered as a result of the seller's violation of the agreement.

FOURTEEN

The Physically and Mentally Disabled

*A*PPROXIMATELY FORTY-FIVE MILLION Americans suffer from some type of physical or mental disability that affects their daily living. They may suffer from severe physical disorders such as paraplegia or quadriplegia, multiple sclerosis, AIDS, Alzheimer's disease or mental disorders, such as schizophrenia, bipolar disorder (manic depression), major depression, or panic disorder. Chances are that if you do not have such a disability, someone in your family or someone that you know does indeed suffer from a physical or mental disability. Unfortunately, the disabled are often shunned by society and live lives of isolation and segregation. However, if given the chance and reasonable accommodations, many disabled persons can and do achieve amazing heights. One need not look far for examples. The blind and deaf Helen Keller and the brilliant physicist Stephen Hawking, who suffers from amyotrophic lateral sclerosis (commonly known as ALS or Lou Gehrig's disease), come immediately to mind. Ludwig van Beethoven was deaf when he wrote some of his most acclaimed compositions. Many writers, artists, and composers over the years have suffered from mental disorders such as major depression and bipolar disorder, yet they still managed to put forth a vast array of outstanding work.

But for the average person suffering from a physical or mental disorder, life has not been easy. Besides suffering the pain and ignominy of their disorders, they face discrimination by others in all phases of life and work. Fortunately, the federal government has passed important laws protecting the rights of the disabled and helping to integrate them into the workplace and society in general. We shall discuss several of the most important acts.

THE AMERICANS WITH DISABILITIES ACT

THE AMERICANS WITH DISABILITIES ACT (ADA) was passed by Congress and signed into law by President George H. W. Bush in 1990 and took effect in 1992. The ADA was Congress's response to its finding that in 1990, some forty-three million Americans suffered from one or more physical or mental disabilities, and that this number was growing annually as the population as a whole is growing older. The ADA also was passed in recognition of the fact that historically society has tended to isolate and segregate individuals with disabilities, and despite some improvements, discrimination against persons with physical or mental disabilities continues to be a serious and pervasive social problem.

Persons with disabilities were being discriminated against in such areas as employment, housing, public accommodations (stores, cinemas, theaters, libraries, sporting arenas, etc.), education, transportation, communication, recreation, institutionalization, health services, voting, and access to public services. Unlike those who experience discrimination based on race, color, sex, national origin, religion, or age, there were few if any laws protecting the disabled person from discrimination.

The ADA is divided into several titles; we will discuss only the first three titles here. Title I deals with discrimination in employment by state and local governments, and employers with fifteen or more employees. Title II covers discrimination in services and activities of state and local governments. Title III concerns public accommodations and commercial facilities (private businesses and nonprofit business providers).

Title I: Discrimination in Employment

Title I of the ADA prohibits discrimination against disabled persons by private employers, state and local governments, employment agencies, and labor unions. The Rehabilitation Act of 1973 (discussed below) is the model upon which the ADA is based. At first the ADA applied only to employers who had twenty-five or more employees. Since July 26, 1994, the ADA applies to employers who have fifteen or more employees. The ADA prohibits discrimination in all employment practices, including job application procedures, hiring, firing, promotions (advancement), compensation, training, and other terms, conditions, and privileges of employment. It applies to recruitment, advertising, tenure, layoff, leave, fringe benefits, and all other employment-related activities.

Employment discrimination is banned against "qualified individuals with disabilities." This includes applicants for employment as well as employees. The ADA defines a disability as (a) a physical or mental impairment that substantially limits one or more of the major life activities of a person; (b) a record of such an impairment; or (c) being regarded as having such an impairment. The ADA also protects persons who are discriminated against because they have a known association or relationship with a disabled individual. An example of this group would be a worker who has a spouse at home with Alzheimer's disease or other physical or mental illness who, the employer fears, will take extra leave and days off to stay at home to care for the ailing spouse.

The Social Security Administration's definition of "disability" (see chapter 16), as well as those of most disability insurance plans, differs materially from the ADA's definition of a "qualified individual with a disability." Accordingly, the "disabled" person is free to come forward with additional evidence to show that he or she could perform the essential duties of the desired position with or without reasonable accommodation, despite the fact that he or she might have been deemed disabled under some other law or insurance contract.

The first part of the ADA's definition of a disability makes it clear that the ADA applies to persons who have impairments that substantially limit major life activities (discussed below). Expressly excluded from the definition of disabled is a person who is a transvestite, homosexual, bisexual, pedophile, exhibitionist, or voyeur. Others explicitly excluded from the term "disabled" under the ADA are persons having gender identity disorders not resulting from physical impairments, or other sexual behavior disorders. Compulsive gamblers and persons suffering from kleptomania or pyromania also are considered not disabled solely because of their status. Additionally, persons having psychoactive substance use disorders resulting from current illegal drug use are expressly beyond the scope of the definition of disabled or persons with a disability. Individuals who currently engage in the illegal use of drugs are excluded specifically from the definition of a "qualified individual with a disability" protected by the ADA when the employer takes action on the basis of their drug use.

A person who uses alcohol is not automatically denied protection under the ADA. An alcoholic is a person with a disability and is protected by the ADA if he or she is qualified to perform the essential functions of the job. An employer may be required to provide an accommodation to an alcoholic. However, an employer can discipline, discharge, or deny employment to an alcoholic whose use of alcohol adversely affects his or her job performance or conduct. Additionally, an employer may prohibit the use of alcohol in the workplace, and can require that employees not be under the influence of alcohol during working hours.

The second part of the definition of a disability, protecting individuals with a record of a disability, would cover, for instance, an individual who has recovered from cancer or a mental illness. The third part of the definition protects individuals who are regarded as having a substantially limiting impairment, even though they may not have such an impairment. For example, this provision would protect a qualified individual with severe facial disfigurement from burns from being denied employment because an employer fears the negative reaction of customers or coworkers.

The ADA protects only "qualified individuals with a disability." A qualified individual with a disability is a person who meets legitimate skill, experience, education, or other requirements of an employment position that he or she holds or seeks, and who can perform the essential functions of the position with or without reasonable accommodation. Requiring the ability to perform the *essential functions* of the job assures that an individual with a disability will not be considered unqualified simply because he or she is unable to perform marginal or incidental job functions. If the employee or prospective employee is able to perform essential job functions except for limitations caused by a disability, the employer must consider whether the person could perform these functions with reasonable accommodation.

The ADA does not require employers to develop or maintain written job descriptions. However, if a written job description was prepared in advance of advertising or interviewing applicants for a position, this will be considered as evidence—although not conclusive evidence—of the essential functions of the job.

An employer is not required to give preference to a qualified applicant with a disability over nondisabled applicants. The employer is free to choose the most qualified applicant available and to make decisions based on reasons unrelated to a disability. For instance, suppose two persons apply for a job as a word processor, an essential function of which is to type seventy-five words per minute accurately. One applicant who has a disability is given reasonable accommodation for a typing test, and types fifty words per minute. The other, nondisabled applicant is able to type seventy-five words per minute accurately. The employer can hire the nondisabled applicant if typing speed is needed for successful performance of the job.

"Substantially Limited"

When referring to the major life activity of working (see below), the Equal Employment Opportunity Commission (EEOC) defines "substantially limited" as "significantly restricted in the ability to perform either a class of jobs or a broad range of jobs in various classes as compared to the average person having comparable training, skills and abilities." Accordingly, a person must be regarded as precluded from working at more than a particular job or narrow range of jobs. "Substantially limited" is viewed against what the average person in the general population can do.

Factors looked at in determining whether a person is substantially limited in the major life activity of working include the number and types of jobs utilizing similar training, knowledge, skills, or abilities, within the geographical area reasonably accessible to the individual, from which the individual also is disqualified. Thus, to be regarded as substantially limited in the major life activity of working, one must be regarded as precluded from more than a particular job. Their condition must significantly restrict their ability to perform either a class of jobs or a broad range of jobs in various classes as compared to the average person having comparable training, skills, and abilities. A physical or mental impairment that disqualifies a person from only a narrow range of jobs is not considered a substantially limiting one for the purposes of determining whether a person is disabled within the meaning of the ADA. Intermittent, episodic impairment is not considered a disability under the ADA.

In one case, a man with high blood pressure who was taking medication to control his condition was hired by United Parcel Service (UPS) as a mechanic. The job required driving commercial vehicles on the highway. The Department of Transportation (DOT) erroneously granted him certification to do so. However, when the DOT discovered its mistake, it revoked its certification based on the fact that the man's blood pressure exceeded DOT requirements. Unmedicated, the man's blood pressure was approximately 250 over 160. With medication, however, the man's blood pressure did not significantly restrict his activities and in general he could function normally and could engage in activities that other persons normally do. The undisputed evidence showed that the man was otherwise generally employable as a mechanic, and there was uncontroverted evidence that he could perform a number of mechanic jobs. Consequently, the man failed to show that he was regarded as unable to perform a class of jobs. Rather, the evidence demonstrated that he was at most regarded as unable to perform only a particular job—driving a commercial vehicle on the highway— which was insufficient to prove that the man was regarded as substantially limited in the major life activity of working.

An airline pilot who was unable to fly due to mental and emotional problems was not considered disabled under the ADA, as nonpiloting jobs existed in the pilot's area that utilized similar training, knowledge, skill, or abilities, including pilot ground trainer, flight simulator trainer, flight instructor, aeronautical school instructor, and consultant to aircraft manufacturers.

However, in a case decided by the United States Supreme Court in 2002, the nation's highest court ruled that the word "substantially" should be defined narrowly, and defined "substantially" in the phrase "substantially limited" as considerable or to a large degree.

"Major Life Activities"

"Major life activities" include such things as seeing, hearing, speaking, walking, breathing, performing manual tasks, reading, writing, learning, taking care of oneself, and working. A person with epilepsy, paralysis, HIV, AIDS, a substantial hearing or visual impairment, mental retardation, or a specific learning disability such as dyslexia also is included under this definition. Individuals suffering from a minor, nonchronic condition of short duration, such as a broken limb, sprain, or the flu, generally are not covered by the ADA.

The United States Supreme Court defined "major" in the phrase "major life activities" as "important." The court stated that "major life activities" as used in the Americans with Disabilities Act refers to "those activities that are of central importance to daily life. In order for performing manual tasks to fit into this category—a category that includes such basic abilities as walking, seeing, and hearing—the manual tasks in question must be central to daily life. If each of the tasks in the major life activity of performing manual tasks does not independently qualify as a major life activity, then together they must do so."

The case the U.S. Supreme Court ruled in, *Toyota Motor Manufacturing, Kentucky, Inc. v. Williams,* involved an automobile assembly line worker who claimed her carpal tunnel syndrome and related injuries rendered her disabled as they substantially limited her ability to perform the range of manual tasks associated with her assembly line job. The employee claimed that her impairments prevented her from gripping tools and doing repetitive work with her hands and arms extended at or above shoulder level for extended periods of time.

The high court held that, "to be substantially limited in performing manual tasks, an individual must have an impairment that prevents or severely restricts the individual from doing activities that are of central importance to most people's daily lives. The impairment's impact must also be permanent or long-term."

The Court went on to hold that, when addressing the major life activity of performing manual tasks, the central inquiry must be whether the employee is unable to perform the variety of tasks central to most people's lives, not whether the employee is unable to perform the tasks associated with her specific job. The Court found that repetitive work with hands and arms extended at or above shoulder level for extended periods of time is not an important part of most people's lives. Rather, the Court noted, evidence such as household chores, bathing, and brushing one's teeth are relevant to the types of manual tasks of central importance to people's daily lives that should be part of the assessment of whether an employee is substantially limited in performing manual tasks.

The Court noted that the employee still was able to do the manual tasks required by her original two jobs, and that even after her condition worsened, she still could brush her teeth, wash her face, bathe, tend her flower garden, fix breakfast, do laundry, and pick up around the house. However, the evidence also showed that the employee's medical condition caused her to avoid sweeping, to quit dancing, to occasionally seek help dressing, and to reduce how often she played with her children, gardened, and drove long distances. The Court concluded that such changes in her life did not amount to such severe restrictions in the activities that are of central importance to most people's daily lives that they established a manual-task disability as a matter of law. Rather, it was for a jury to make such decision.

Pre- and Post-Employment Medical Examinations

Can a prospective employer require a job applicant to take a medical examination before offering the applicant a job? No. Neither can the employer ask any questions of the job applicant about a disability or the nature or severity of a disability. The employer may ask questions about the individual's ability to perform specific job functions and may—with certain limitations—ask a disabled person to describe how he or she would perform these functions.

While an employer cannot require a job applicant to take a medical examination before offering the applicant a job, the employer may condition a job offer on the satisfactory result of a medical examination or medical inquiry after a job offer is made. However, this required medical examination or inquiry must be required of *all* entering employees in the same job category. The employer may not single out the disabled person for a medical examination. Note that the postoffer medical examination or inquiry need not be job-related or consistent with business necessity. But if a person is not hired because the postoffer medical examination or inquiry reveals a disability, the reason for not hiring the person must be job-related and consistent with business necessity. The employer must also show that no reasonable accommodation was available that would enable the individual to perform the essential job functions, or that accommodation would impose an "undue hardship" on the employer.

A postoffer medical examination may disqualify an individual if the employer can demonstrate that the individual would pose a "direct threat" in the workplace that cannot be eliminated or sufficiently reduced through reasonable accommodation. An employee poses a direct threat in the workplace if he or she poses a significant risk of substantial harm to the health or safety of the individual or others. A postoffer medical examination may not disqualify an individual with a disability who currently is able to perform essential job functions because of mere speculation that the disability may cause a risk of injury sometime in the future.

Once a person starts work, a medical examination or inquiry must be job-related and consistent with business necessity. Employers may conduct employee medical examinations where evidence exists of a job performance or safety problem, examinations required by other federal laws, examinations to determine current fitness to perform a particular job, and voluntary examinations that are part of employee health programs. Information from all medical examinations and inquiries must be kept separate from general personnel files as a confidential medical record, available only under limited conditions. You should be aware that tests for the illegal use of drugs are not medical examinations under the ADA and are not subject to the ADA's restrictions of such examinations.

Establishing a Prima Facie Case of Employment Discrimination

A disabled plaintiff establishes a prima facie case of employment discrimination in violation of the ADA by proving that: he or she was disabled within the meaning of the ADA; he or she was qualified for the position, with or without accommodation; the employer knew or had reason to know of the employee's (or potential employee's) disability; the employee or prospective employee suffered an adverse employment decision with regard to the position in question (that is, was rejected for the position, passed over for promotion, was demoted, or was discharged); and after his or her rejection or discharge, the job remained open or a nondisabled person replaced him or her. If the employee can prove all of these facts, then he or she is entitled to the mandatory inferences that the adverse employment decision was made solely because of his or her handicap.

If the employee proves a prima facie case of disability discrimination under the ADA, the burden shifts to the employer to prove a legitimate nondiscriminatory reason for discharging the employee. Accordingly, where a truck driver was terminated in violation of the employer's policy and Department of Transportation regulations in falsifying his logs and thereby obtained unearned pay, this constituted a legitimate, nondiscriminatory reason in ADA action for discharging the truck driver. However, where the employee can prove that the employer's asserted nondiscriminatory reason for terminating the disabled employee was merely a pretext for illegal discrimination, a jury reasonably can reject the employer's reason for firing the disabled employee.

An employee established a prima facie case that his employer discriminated against him because of his epileptic condition, where the evidence included the employer's own admission that the employee was discharged due to his epileptic seizures.

Mitigating Measures

Whether a person is disabled is determined by looking at the person with mitigating or corrective measures he or she employs, such as eyeglasses or medications. For instance, if a person suffers from high blood pressure, that pressure is determined by what it is while he or she is on antihypertensive medications. For persons suffering from, for instance, bipolar disorder (manic depression), whether they are disabled under the ADA likewise is determined while they are in a medicated state. If the person suffers from impaired vision, the extent of his or her impairment is determined by what the person's vision is while wearing corrective eyeglasses or contact lenses. A hearing-impaired individual's disability is measured by taking into consideration any hearing-aid devices the person may be using.

Sutton v. United Air Lines Inc. involved severely myopic twin sisters whose uncorrected vision was 20/200 or worse, but with corrective measures (eyeglasses or contact lenses), both functioned identically to individuals without similar impairments. They applied to defendant United Air Lines Inc. for employment as commercial pilots, but were turned down because they did not meet United's minimum requirement of uncorrected visual acuity of 20/100 or better. The twins thereupon brought suit under the Americans with Disabilities Act, and the United States Supreme Court ultimately heard their case. The nation's highest court ruled that the twin sisters did not have a claim under the ADA for an actual physical impairment that substantially limited them in one or more major life activities. The Supreme Court held that because the sisters alleged that with corrective measures their vision was 20/20 or better, they did not suffer a disability as that term is defined in the ADA.

Reasonable Accommodations

A reasonable accommodation is any modification or adjustment to a job or the work environment that will allow a qualified applicant or employee with a disability to participate in the application process or to perform essential job functions. A reasonable accommodation also includes adjustments to assure that a qualified individual with a disability has rights and privileges in employment equal to those of employees who do not have a disability. Examples of a reasonable accommodation include making existing facilities used by employees readily accessible to and usable by an individual with a disability; restructuring a job; modifying work schedules; acquiring or modifying equipment; providing qualified readers or interpreters; or modifying examinations, training, or other programs. A reasonable accommodation may also include reassigning a current employee to a vacant position for which the employee is qualified if the employee is unable to do the original job—even with a reasonable accommodation—because of a disability. There is, however, no obligation to find a position for an applicant who is not qualified for the position sought. While "reasonable accommodation" may require an employer to transfer a disabled employee to a vacant position, it does not impose a duty upon the employer to create a new position for the disabled employee.

An employer is not required to reallocate essential functions of the job which a qualified individual must perform to make a reasonable accommodation under the ADA. Employers are not required to lower quality or quantity standards as an accommodation, nor are they obligated to provide personal use items such as eyeglasses or hearing aids.

The decision as to the appropriate accommodation must be based on the particular facts of each case. In choosing the particular type of accommodation to provide, the principal test is that of effectiveness, that is, whether the accommodation will provide an opportunity for a disabled person to achieve the same level of performance and to enjoy benefits equal to those of an average, similarly situated person without a disability. The accommodation need not ensure equal results or provide exactly the same benefits.

An employer is only required to accommodate a *known* disability of a qualified applicant or employee. No accommodation need be made for disabilities of which the employer is unaware. A disability usually will become known to the employer by a request for accommodation from an individual with a disability, who frequently will be able to suggest an appropriate accommodation. Accommodation must be made on an individual basis because the nature and extent of a disabling condition and the requirements of a job will vary in each case. If the disabled individual does not request an accommodation the employer is not obligated to provide one, except where an individual's known disability impairs his or her ability to know of—or effectively communicate a need for—an accommodation that is obvious to the employer. If a person with a disability requests, but cannot suggest, an appropriate accommodation, the employer and the individual should work together to find one.

Undue Hardship

An employer is not required to make a reasonable accommodation for a disabled individual where making a reasonable accommodation would impose an "undue hardship" on the operation of the employer's business. Undue hardship is defined as an "action requiring significant difficulty or expense" when considered in light of a number of factors. These factors include the nature and cost of the accommodation in relation to the size, resources, nature, and structure of the employer's operation. Undue hardship is considered on a case-by-case basis. Where the facility making the accommodation is part of a larger entity, the structure and overall resources of the larger organization are considered, as well as the financial and administrative relationship of the facility to the larger organization. Generally, a larger employer with greater resources will be expected to make an accommodation requiring greater effort or expense than will be required of a smaller employer with fewer resources.

If one accommodation would be an undue hardship, the employer must attempt to find another accommodation that would not pose such a hardship. Additionally, if the cost of an accommodation would impose an undue hardship on the employer, the disabled individual should be given the chance to pay that portion of the cost that would constitute the undue hardship.

Altered or reduced production standards or designation of lighter workload was not a reasonable accommodation for former employees who were unable due to alleged disabilities to meet their employer's new production standards for grocery selectors, which required them to accomplish their jobs filling orders in the warehouse in a shorter amount of time. The employer was not required to reallocate job duties, which would alter essential functions of the grocery selector job. The proposed accommodation would result in other workers having to work harder or longer hours, slow the production schedule, or assign lighter loads to employees in violation of a collective bargaining agreement.

Where and When to File Complaints of Discrimination

Complaints of employment discrimination (Title I) by the state or local government or by private employers should be filed with the Equal Employment Opportunity Commission. Call (800) 669-4000 (voice) or (800) 669-6820 (TDD) to find the field office in your area. The headquarters for the EEOC is as follows: U.S. Equal Employment Opportunity Commission, 1801 L Street NW, Washington, DC 20507.

If you feel you have been discriminated against on the basis of a disability under Title I of the ADA, you must file a complaint with the EEOC within 180 days of the date of the alleged discrimination, or 300 days if the charge is filed with a designated state or local fair employment practice agency. You may file a lawsuit in federal court for violation of Title I of the ADA only after you receive a "right-to-sue" letter from the EEOC.

If you are successful in an employment discrimination lawsuit under Title I of the ADA, the damages you are entitled to include: hiring, reinstatement, promotion, back pay, front pay, restored benefits, reasonable accommodation, attorneys' fees, expert witness fees, and court costs. You may also be entitled to compensatory and punitive damages in cases of intentional discrimination or where an employer fails to make a good faith effort to provide a reasonable accommodation.

ADA Title II Discrimination

Title II of the ADA prevents state and local governments from discriminating against a disabled individual from all of their programs, services, and activities (such as public education, employment, transportation, recreation, health care, social services, courts, voting, and town meetings). A state or local government must eliminate any eligibility criteria for participation in programs, activities, and services that screen out or tend to screen out persons with disabilities, unless it can establish that the requirements are necessary for the provision of the service, program, or activity. The state or local government may, however, adopt legitimate safety requirements necessary for safe operation if they are based on real risks, not on stereotypes or generalizations about individuals with disabilities. Finally, a public entity must reasonably modify its policies, practices, or procedures to avoid discrimination. If the public entity can demonstrate that a particular modification would alter fundamentally the nature of its service, program, or activity, it is not required to make that modification.

Title II of the ADA prohibits all public entities, regardless of the size of their workforce, from discriminating in employment against qualified individuals with disabilities. In addition to Title II's employment coverage, Title I of the ADA and section 504 of the Rehabilitation Act of 1973 prohibit employment discrimination against qualified individuals with disabilities by certain public entities.

A public entity must ensure that individuals with disabilities are not excluded from services, programs, and activities because existing buildings are inaccessible. A state or local government's programs, when viewed in their entirety, must be readily accessible to and usable by disabled persons. This standard—known as "program accessibility"—applies to facilities of a public entity that existed on January 26, 1992. Public entities do not necessarily have to make each of their existing facilities accessible to the disabled. They may provide program accessibility by a number of methods, including alteration of existing facilities, acquisition or construction of additional facilities, relocation of a service or program to an accessible facility, or provision of services at alternate, accessible sites.

All new buildings constructed by a state or local government must be accessible to the disabled. Additionally, when a state or local government makes alterations to a preexisting building, it must make the altered portions accessible to the disabled. State and local governments are required to follow specific architectural standards in the new construction and alteration of their buildings to accommodate the disabled.

Public entities are not required, however, to take actions that would result in undue financial and administrative burdens. They are required to make reasonable modifications to policies, practices, and procedures where necessary to avoid discrimination, unless they can demonstrate that doing so would alter fundamentally the nature of the service, program, or activity being provided.

Where and When to File Complaints

Complaints about violations of Title II by units of state and local governments may be filed with the Department of Justice within 180 days of the date of discrimination. Complaints should be sent to: Disability Rights Section, Civil Rights Division, U.S. Department of Justice, P.O. Box 66738, Washington, DC 20035-6738.

You may also call them at (800) 510-0301 (voice) or (800) 524-0383 (TDD). Title II discrimination may be enforced through private lawsuits in federal court. Unlike Title I discrimination cases, it is not necessary to file a complaint with the Department of Justice, EEOC, or any other federal agency, or to receive a "right-to-sue" letter before going to court.

Public Transportation

Title II of the ADA prohibits discrimination against disabled persons by public transportation services, such as city buses and public rail transits (for example, subways, commuter rails, and Amtrak). Public transportation authorities must comply with requirements of accessibility in newly purchased vehicles; make good faith efforts to purchase or lease accessible used buses; remanufacture buses in an accessible manner; and, unless it would result in an undue burden, provide paratransit where they operate fixed-route bus or rail systems. Paratransit is a service where individuals who are unable to use the regular transit system independently (because of a physical or mental impairment) are picked up and dropped off at their destinations.

Where to Ask Questions and File Complaints

Questions and complaints about public transportation should be directed to: Federal Transit Administration, U.S. Department of Transportation, 400 Seventh Street, SW, Washington, DC 20590.

Information, questions, and complaints can be made at (888) 446-4511 (voice/relay), (202) 366-2285 (voice); or (202) 366-0153 (TDD). Documents can be obtained and questions answered at (202) 366-1656 (voice/relay) and legal questions addressed at (202) 366-4011 (voice/relay).

ADA Title III: Public Accommodations

Title III of the ADA prohibits discrimination against physically or mentally disabled persons by businesses and nonprofit service providers that are public accommodations, privately operated entities offering certain types of courses and examinations, privately operated transportation, and commercial facilities. Public accommodations are private entities that own, lease, lease to, or operate facilities open to the public, such as restaurants and bars, retail stores, inns, hotels and motels, cinemas, live theaters, bakeries, grocery stores, clothing and hardware stores, shopping centers and other sales or rental establishments, private schools, private museums, doctors' and dentists' offices, homeless shelters, transportation depots, zoos, funeral homes, convention centers, day care centers, and recreation facilities (including sports stadiums and fitness clubs). Title III of the ADA also covers transportation services provided by private entities. However, private clubs and religious organizations are exempt from Title III's requirements for public accommodations.

Public accommodations must comply with basic nondiscrimination requirements that prohibit exclusion, segregation, and unequal treatment. They must also comply with specific requirements related to architectural standards for new and altered buildings; reasonable modifications to policies, practices, and procedures; effective communication with people with hearing, vision, or speech disabilities; and other access requirements.

Additionally, public accommodations must remove physical barriers in and around existing buildings where it is easy to do so without much difficulty or expense, given the public accommodation's resources. The removal of a physical barrier that is "readily achievable" means that it is easily accomplishable without much difficulty or expense. The readily achievable requirement is based on the size and resources of the business. Larger businesses with more resources are expected to take a more active role in removing barriers than are small businesses. The ADA recognizes that economic conditions vary. When a business is doing well and has the resources to remove barriers to disabled persons, it is expected to do so. However, when profits are down, the barrier removal may be reduced or delayed. Note that barrier removal is an ongoing obligation—the business is expected to remove barriers in the future as resources become available.

Architectural barriers are physical features that limit or prevent people with disabilities from obtaining the goods or services that are offered. They can include parking spaces that are too narrow to accommodate people who use wheelchairs; a step or steps at the entrance or part of the selling space of a store; round doorknobs or other door hardware that is difficult for a disabled person to grasp; aisles that are too narrow for a person using a wheelchair, electric scooter, or a walker; a high counter or narrow checkout aisles at cash registers; and fixed tables in eating areas that are too low to accommodate persons using wheelchairs or that have fixed seats that prevent persons using wheelchairs from pulling their wheelchairs under the table.

For many recreational golfers, riding a golf cart is part of the game. However, in events that are sanctioned by the Professional Golf Association (PGA), golf carts are strictly prohibited. Professional golfer Casey Martin suffers from a rare circulatory disorder that makes his right leg extremely weak. Throughout his college years at Stanford, where he played on the same team as Tiger Woods, Martin's condition steadily worsened as the disorder eroded the bones in his right leg. The only way he could make it through a round of golf was to use a golf cart, which the NCAA allowed him to do.

After graduating from Stanford, Martin turned professional and wanted to enter golf tournaments put on by the PGA. However, the PGA refused to let Martin use a golf cart and required him to walk the full course like other players who were not similarly disabled. Martin filed suit, claiming that the golf courses were public accommodations as defined by the ADA and that he suffered from a disability that affected one or more of his major life activities (walking) and was therefore entitled to the reasonable modification of using a golf cart. The United States Supreme Court agreed with Martin's argument, holding that the essence of the game of golf was shot making, and allowing a disabled person to use a cart rather than walk the course would not fundamentally alter the nature of the game.

Courses and Examinations

Title III of the ADA provides that any person who offers courses and examinations related to applications, licensing, certification, or credentialing for professional or trade purposes shall offer such courses and examinations in a place and manner accessible to persons with known physical or mental disabilities or offer alternative accessible arrangements for such individuals. The examination must be selected and administered to reflect accurately the individual's aptitude or achievement level, rather than his or her impairment. "Physical or mental impairment" includes specific learning disabilities. Appropriate accommodations may include changes in the length of time permitted for completion of the examination.

Where to File Your Claim

Complaints of Title III violations may be filed with the Department of Justice. In certain instances, cases may be referred to a mediation program sponsored by the DOJ. The DOJ is authorized to bring a lawsuit where there is a pattern or practice of discrimination in violation of Title III, or where an act of discrimination raises an issue of general public importance. Title III may also be enforced by a private lawsuit. It is not necessary to file a complaint with the DOJ or any other federal agency as a prerequisite to filing a private lawsuit, nor is it required that the victim of the discrimination receive a "right-to-sue" letter before going to court. For further information or to file a complaint, contact: Disability Rights Section, Civil Rights Division, U.S. Department of Justice, P.O. Box 66738, Washington, DC 20035-6738.

You may also call them at (800) 514-0301 (voice) or (800) 514-0383 (TDD).

If your complaint involves access in and to buildings or barriers in transportation, contact: Architectural and Transportation Barriers, Compliance Board, 1331 F Street, NW, Suite 1000, Washington, DC 20004-1111; telephone: (800) 872-2253 (voice and TDD).

THE REHABILITATION ACT OF 1973

THE REHABILITATION ACT OF 1973 was the first federal law protecting the rights of the disabled to be free from discrimination in employment by certain agencies of the federal government and contractors doing business with the federal government, and in programs or activities receiving federal financial assistance. For the purposes of the Rehabilitation Act of 1973, the definition of a "qualified individual with a disability" is the same as that used by the Americans with Disabilities Act.

Section 501 of the Rehabilitation Act requires federal agencies of the executive branch to create affirmative action programs to hire the disabled and not to discriminate against them when hiring, promoting, firing, etc. If you work for or have been turned down for a job with a federal agency with the executive branch of the federal government, and believe it is due to your disability rather than your qualifications, you should contact the Equal Employment Opportunity Office in your area to get more information and to file a complaint. The office for your area can be found in the front of your telephone book in the United States government listings.

Section 503 of the Rehabilitation Act of 1973 requires that any contract in excess of $10,000 entered into by any federal department or agency for the procurement of personal property and nonpersonal services—including construction—for the United States must contain a provision requiring the contractor to take affirmative action to employ and promote qualified individuals with disabilities. Similarly, if a subcontractor enters into a contract with the prime contractor for the sale of personal property or nonpersonal services for more than $10,000, the subcontractor must have in place or create an affirmative action and advancement programs for qualified individuals with disabilities. If you are disabled and feel that you have been discriminated against by a contractor or subcontractor doing work or selling personal property to the United States or any of its departments or agencies, you should contact: Office of Federal Contract Compliance Programs, U.S. Department of Labor, 200 Constitution Ave., NW, Washington, DC 20210; telephone: (202) 219-9423 (voice/relay).

Section 504 of the Rehabilitation Act of 1973 states that no individual with a disability shall be excluded from the participation in, be denied the benefits of, or be subjected to discrimination under any program or activity that either receives federal financial assistance or is conducted by any executive agency or by the United States Postal Service. Each federal agency has its own set of regulations that apply to its own programs. Agencies that provide federal financial assistance also have regulations covering entities that receive federal aid. Common requirements of these regulations include reasonable accommodation for employees with disabilities; program accessibility; effective communication with people who have hearing or vision disabilities; and accessible new construction and alterations. Each agency is responsible for enforcing its own regulations. Section 504 violations may also be enforced through private lawsuits. It is not necessary to file a complaint with a federal agency or to receive a "right-to-sue" letter before going to court. For information on how to file a Section 504 complaint with the proper agency, contact: Disability Rights Section, Civil Rights Division, U.S. Department of Justice, P.O. Box 66738, Washington, DC 20035-6738, telephone: (800) 514-0301 (voice), (800) 514-0383 (TDD).

DISCRIMINATION IN HOUSING

EXCEPT FOR FEDERAL PUBLIC HOUSING, the Americans with Disabilities Act does not cover discrimination against the disabled in housing issues. These are covered by the Fair Housing Act as amended in 1988, which prohibits housing discrimination on the basis of race, color, religion, sex, *disability*, familial status, and national origin. Its coverage includes private housing, housing that receives federal financial assistance, and state and local government housing.

It is unlawful to discriminate in any aspect of selling or renting housing or to deny a dwelling to a buyer or renter because of the physical or mental disability of that individual, of an individual associated with the buyer or renter, or of an individual who intends to live in the residence. Other covered activities include, for example, financing, zoning practices, new construction design, and advertising.

The Fair Housing Act requires owners of housing facilities to make reasonable exceptions in their policies to give people with disabilities equal housing opportunities. For instance, a landlord with a "no pets" policy may be required to grant an exception to this rule and allow a person who is blind to keep a guide dog in his residence. The Fair Housing Act also requires landlords to allow tenants with disabilities to make reasonable access-related modifications to their private living space, as well as to common use spaces. Note that it is the tenant, and not the landlord, who is required to pay for the changes. The Fair Housing Act further requires that new multifamily housing with four or more units be designed and built to allow access for persons with disabilities. This includes accessible common use areas, doors that are wide enough to accommodate wheelchairs, kitchens and bathrooms that allow a person using a wheelchair to maneuver, and other adaptable features within the unit.

Complaints of Fair Housing Act violations may be filed with the U.S. Department of Housing and Urban Development. For more information or to file a complaint, contact: Office of Program Compliance and Disability Rights, Office of Fair Housing and Equal Opportunity, U.S. Department of Housing and Urban Development, 451 Seventh Street, SW (Room 5242), Washington, DC 20140.

You may also call the Fair Housing Information Clearinghouse at (800) 343-3442 (voice) or (800) 290-1617 (TDD).

The DOJ can file cases involving a pattern or practice of discrimination. The Fair Housing Act may also be enforced through private lawsuits.

THE DISABLED AND FLYING

THE ADA DOES NOT COVER discrimination against disabled persons flying. However, the Air Carrier Access Act and the Department of Transportation rule that implements it set out procedures to ensure that disabled individuals have the same opportunity as anyone else to enjoy a pleasant flight. A person may not be refused air transportation based on a disability or be required to have an attendant or produce a medical certificate, except in certain limited circumstances.

Airlines must provide personnel and equipment to assist the disabled individual for getting on and off a plane and to a connecting flight. Some small commuter aircraft may not be accessible to passengers with severe mobility impairments. If you suffer from a severe mobility impairment and will be flying to a small city, you should check in advance on the type of commuter aircraft you will be flying in and find out whether it can accommodate you and your wheelchair or other assistive equipment.

Aircraft terminals and airline reservation centers must be equipped with TDD telephone devices for persons having hearing or speech impairments. Passengers having vision or hearing impairments must have timely access to the same information given to other passengers at the airport or on the plane concerning gate assignments, delayed flights, safety, and the like. New wide-body aircraft must have a wheelchair-accessible lavatory and an onboard wheelchair. Airlines must put an onboard wheelchair on most flights upon a passenger's request. Be aware that forty-eight hours' notice is required for this. Air carriers must accept wheelchairs as checked baggage, and cannot require passengers to sign a liability waiver for them, except for preexisting damage. Most new airplanes must have movable armrests on half of the aisle seats, and onboard stowage for one folding passenger wheelchair.

Air carriers must allow service animals such as guide dogs for the blind to accompany passengers in the cabin, as long as they don't block the aisle or other emergency evacuation routes. The Federal Aviation Administration (the FAA) safety rules set standards for passengers permitted to sit in emergency exit rows. Such persons must be able to perform certain evacuation-related functions. The FAA rules also prohibit passengers from bringing their own oxygen aboard a plane. Most airlines will provide aircraft-approved oxygen for a fee, but are not required to.

Where to File a Complaint

To file a complaint of discrimination based on a disability against an air carrier or for more information, contact: Departmental Office for Civil Rights, Office of the Secretary, U.S. Department of Transportation, 400 Seventh Street, SW, Washington, DC 20590.
They may be reached by telephone at (202) 366-4648 (voice) or (202) 366-8538 (TDD).

You may also contact: Aviation Consumer Protection Division, C-75, U.S. Department of Transportation, 400 Seventh Street, SW, Washington, DC 20590, telephone: (202) 366-2220 (voice), (202) 755-7687 (TDD).

FIFTEEN

Computers and the Internet

COMPUTERS ARE EVERYWHERE TODAY: in homes, in businesses, in schools, in libraries, in hotels, even in cyber coffee shops. And if the place you're going to doesn't have its own computer, no problem—you can bring your own laptop computer with you. Computers are used for all things serious to all things entertaining. They may be used in a business to keep track of inventory, do the bookkeeping, send notices to employees, do word processing, keep calendars, and more. At home, computers are used by kids to do homework and play games, by mothers to keep address books and to store recipes, among other things. And of course, there is "surfing the Internet," which consumes computer time use both at home and at work (much to the chagrin of the boss). With all the time and money we invest in computers and the Internet, one wonders how we ever managed to do without them.

THE COMPLEXITY OF COMPUTER LAW

COMPUTER LAW CAN BE one of the more complex areas of the law. It involves that branch of the law known as "intellectual property," which involves such things as copyrights, trademarks and service marks, patents, and trade secret laws, as well as contract law and the laws of defamation. Contrary to what many people think, the information on the Internet generally cannot be downloaded and used for any purpose the person wants. Almost all of the material on the Internet is copyrighted. As we will see in chapter 20, material is copyrighted as soon as it is put in a "fixed" form. It is not necessary to put a copyright notice on the work to get the protection of copyright laws. (However, putting a copyright notice on the work does go to the question of damages available and whether or not you can collect attorney's fees in an action for violation of copyright. See chapter 20.)

Downloading material from a website for your own personal (noncommercial) use probably does not violate copyright laws. This is akin to videotaping a television show to watch at a later date. However, if you use some or all of the downloaded material in a school project, business presentation, book, your own website, etc., this goes beyond "fair use" and runs afoul of the copyright laws.

Who owns a copyright for a work made on the job is discussed in chapter 13. Briefly, when an employee creates copyrightable material on the job, or has signed an agreement with the employer that all copyrightable material made on the job belongs to the employer, the copyright belongs to the employer. This is the "work made for hire" rule. This rule applies to works made by the employee within the scope of his or her employment. If the employee creates the copyrightable material outside the scope of his or her employment (such as at home on his or her own time after work), the copyright generally belongs to the employee.

Unlike copyright law, patent law does not have a "work for hire" rule. However, if an employee creates a patentable invention within the scope of his or her employment, the employee may have a legal obligation to transfer ownership of the patent to the employer under the patent law's "hired to invent" rule. As a condition of employment, the employer usually has the employee sign an agreement stating that any patents developed by the employee within the scope of his or her employment belong to the employer.

Trademarks and service marks are names, words, symbols, jingles, and the like used by manufacturers and service providers to distinguish their goods and services from goods and services manufactured and sold by others. A domain name (discussed below) can be used as a trademark. You cannot use another company's trademark or service mark, nor can you use one which is "confusingly similar" without express permission from the trademark or service mark holder. Does registering your trademark or service mark with the United States Patent and Trademark Office give you an irrefutable right to use the trademark or service mark and protect you from all others who would use the same mark? No. There is a "common law" trademark that gives protection to persons or companies who simply adopt a trademark or service mark and use it in connection with goods or services. This protection generally is limited to the geographic area in which the trademark or service mark actually is being used. A trademark or service mark may be registered with the appropriate state agency for state protection.

WHAT IS THE INTERNET?

JUST WHAT IS THE INTERNET? In a 1999 case, the federal Court of Appeals for the Tenth Circuit made the following observations about the Internet:

The Internet is a decentralized, global medium of communication that links people, institutions, corporations and governments around the world. It is a giant computer network that interconnects innumerable smaller groups of linked computer networks and individual computers.

As you can see, it is difficult to explain just what the Internet is and how it works. There is no central location for the Internet; it is everywhere, and yet it is seemingly nowhere. You cannot write a letter to the keeper of the Internet, as no such person or entity exists. As another judge wrote of the geographically borderless nature of the Internet,

> [It] negates geometry . . . it is fundamentally and profoundly anti-spatial. You cannot say where it is or describe its memorable shape and proportions or tell a stranger how to get there. But you can find things in it without knowing where they are. The [Internet] is ambient—nowhere in particular and everywhere at once.

The Internet and the World Wide Web offer a tremendous and seemingly endless supply of information about every subject one could possibly think of. It is estimated that there are well over one billion pages of information on the World Wide Web just waiting to be accessed. The websites range the gamut from sports and games to dating tips to physics and astronomy to rocket science. You can do your banking online, do your clothes and grocery shopping, and look for a job or an apartment to rent or a house to buy. The possibilities on the Internet really do seem endless.

Internet Service Providers (ISPs)

Notwithstanding the conceptual difficulties we may have with just where and what the Internet is, one thing is certain: You need an Internet Service Provider (ISP) to get access to it. Some of the better known ISPs are America Online (AOL), CompuServe, Prodigy, the Microsoft Network (MSN), and Earthlink, although many smaller companies exist as well. America Online is the largest ISP provider, with well over twenty million subscribers. Several companies sprang up that offered free Internet access; in return, the user would have to put up with advertisers' banners taking up one-third of the screen. At first the notion of free Internet access appealed to many, but users quickly tired of the advertisements and went back to traditional ISPs.

When choosing an ISP, you should make sure that they have a local number for you to connect to the ISP. Once you are on the Internet you can access sites all over the world for free. But if it is a long-distance charge to connect your computer to your ISP, you will find your telephone bill running into the hundreds of dollars, depending upon how much you use the Internet.

Domain Names

Suppose you are an entrepreneur who wants to register "Madonna.com" as a website, in the hope that the singer/actress Madonna will pay you hundreds of thousands, even millions, of dollars for the "domain name" Madonna.com. Can you do this? Many people register a domain name that they know someone else probably would want for various reasons. These people are known as cybersquatters.

Cybersquatters, also called cyberpirates, register a domain name with the intent of selling it for a handsome profit either to the trademark holder or to a third party. The trademark holder has a choice to make: either pay the cybersquatter or engage in costly, possibly protracted litigation with no guarantee of winning.

For instance, one person registered the domain names "jethrotull.com" and "jethro-tull.com" after the popular musical group Jethro Tull. The musical group took action to win back its name and won on the basis the domain names were registered in bad faith. Actresses Julia Roberts and Nicole Kidman and singer Madonna have taken their cases to a three-member panel in Geneva, Switzerland (at the World Intellectual Property Organization, or WIPO for short), that decides such issues and won.

Popular singer Sting was not so lucky, however. He attempted to claim all rights to the domain name "sting.com," which was owned by an online gambler. The arbitrator found that the gambler was *not* acting in bad faith and permitted him to keep the domain name. Similarly, rock star Bruce Springsteen lost his request that a Canadian man and his fan club relinquish their Web address, www.brucespringsteen.com. The World Intellectual Property Organization ruled that the Canadian man had a legitimate interest in the Web address name. The tribunal also found that Springsteen failed to show that the name was registered and used in bad faith, or that the Canadian man had ever attempted to sell it. At least one state has passed new laws that bar the registration of website names that are "identical or confusingly similar" to the names of people, living or dead.

That has not put an end to cybersquatting, however. People will register catchy names in the hope of selling them later at a handsome price. One such name, "business.com," sold for the hefty sum of $7.5 million. The search engine altavista paid over $3 million to purchase the rights to the domain name "altavista.com."

What is the criteria used in determining whether a person's domain name is legitimate or simply that of a cybersquatter hoping to sell the name for big bucks? Under the Uniform Domain Name Dispute Resolution Policy, which took effect on January 3, 2000, a three-part test is used in making this determination. These are:

1. The domain name is identical or confusingly similar to a trademark or service mark in which the person complaining has rights; and

2. The domain name holder has no rights or legitimate interests with regard to the domain name; and
3. The domain name has been registered and is being used in bad faith.

If all three parts of the test have been satisfied, the person who registered the domain name will be deemed to be a cybersquatter and will lose the right to keep the name.

Libel on the Internet

If you write anything defamatory about someone on the Internet, you can be sued for libel (chapter 10). But can you sue the Internet Service Provider (ISP), such as America Online or the Microsoft Network, on which the website resides? No. ISPs are granted immunity against lawsuits for defamation on the basis that they are like a bulletin board of information, where anyone can post any message. An ISP does not act as a newspaper editor responsible for the electronic bulletin board's content.

Suppose a student writes some anonymous comments defamatory of a teacher on a website designed for students to post remarks about their teachers. Can the teacher sue the webmaster (the person in charge of running the website) for the anonymous—and defamatory—critiques? Probably not. Although no case law exists on the question, legal experts on the first amendment and the Internet believe that a webmaster is similarly immune from liability for defamatory or obscene messages.

What about offensive, indecent, or libelous e-mails? The same rule applies. An ISP and its webmaster cannot be expected to read every one of the millions of e-mails sent every day to ensure that their content is not libelous or offensive. The ISP is considered a mere conduit of the message and therefore cannot be held liable for defamatory or indecent e-mails.

Fraudulent Manipulation of Stock Prices

Rumors of projected corporate gains or losses, mergers and acquisitions, and other corporate activities abound on the Internet. Some Internet users engage in fraudulent and deceptive practices by sending out phony press releases or rumors so they can manipulate a stock's price and make money in the process.

In one case, a fourteen-year-old boy made a large killing by buying large blocks of penny stocks, then hyping them on financial message boards. After purchasing the stocks the boy sent false e-mails to Internet message boards, each under a fictitious name, touting the stock he had purchased. For example, one message stated that a stock currently trading at $2 a share would be trading for more than $20 per share "very soon." Another message stated that a stock would be the next stock to gain 1,000 percent. Investors seeing the positive remarks bought the penny stock, causing the stock's price to increase. The youth then sold off his stock at a handy profit, totaling over $270,000. Of course, many investors who relied on the stock tips ended up losing money when the stocks went down.

In another case, a twenty-three-year-old man was indicted on eleven counts of securities and wire fraud in an online scheme to defraud investors in a high-tech company. The man was accused of issuing a false press release that sent the price of the stock plummeting as much as 62 percent in one day, most of that in a fifteen-minute period. The man needed the stock price to fall so he could buy back shares and cover a margin call issued by his online brokerage firm. The man was facing a loss of $97,000 after selling short several thousand shares of a company. (Selling a stock short means selling shares borrowed from a stock brokerage and then replacing those stocks later.) The indictment charged that the man made more than $241,000 trading in the stock in question. He faced a cumulative prison term of one hundred years and fines of $9.5 million if convicted of all charges.

Anyone can place a rumor or authentic-looking press release on the Internet. You must be extremely careful when acting on such information or you can get burned badly. Remember, the Internet is not like a newspaper. There are no editors or fact-checkers looking over an article for accuracy and objectivity before it is published. You can write anything you want on the Internet. (Of course, you will have to pay the consequences if it is illegal or causes damage to others.) Before relying on an Internet rumor, particularly of a stock's impending rise or fall, it is best to check it out with a reputable stockbroker.

Electronic Mail

Electronic mail (e-mail) is a popular method for people to stay in touch without having to go through the day or two delay of the post office. E-mail is instantaneous—once you compose your message and press the send button, your e-mail is sent immediately to its recipient. One of the major differences between "snail mail" (that is, letters sent via the regular United States Postal Service) and e-mail is privacy. When you send a letter via the postal service, once you lick the envelope and seal it shut, you expect it to remain that way—unopened and unread—until it reaches the addressee.

E-mail is not as private (secure) as a letter. It can be intercepted at several stages. This is one of the reasons you should never send confidential information—such as your Social Security number, credit card number, or a personal identification number (PIN)—over unsecured e-mail. When you are buying something online, you should make sure that your credit card number is encrypted (scrambled) before you send it.

Spam—Junk E-mail

E-mail "spam" (not to be confused with the luncheon meat trademarked by Hormel) is the Internet's version of junk mail or telephone solicitations. It is unwanted, unsolicited advertisements offering products, services, extensions of credit, etc., for lease, sale, rental, gift, or other disposition. Spam can range from a mere annoyance to a time-consuming problem that clogs up your e-mail. Spamming is attractive to advertisers because it can reach hundreds of thousands, even millions of Internet users for much less than it would cost to do a direct mailing to them.

A typical spam message comes from a business with which you have had no previous relationship. The message does not clearly identify the person or group that has sent it. The message itself often is illegitimate or misleading. When you try to remove your e-mail address from the e-mail address given, it is simply ignored and you continue to get spam from the unknown site. Spammers usually disguise their true e-mail addresses by using fictitious addresses or e-mail accounts set up for the sole purpose of spamming that one message.

Because of the unscrupulous practices of most spammers, many states have passed laws requiring that the spammer include in its message a toll-free telephone number or a valid sender-operated return e-mail address that you, the recipient of the unwanted e-mail (spam), may call or e-mail to notify the sender not to e-mail any further unsolicited documents. Bills currently are pending in the House of Representatives and the Senate that would put limitations on spam, such as prohibiting a person from sending a message unless the message contained a valid e-mail address, conspicuously displayed, to which a recipient could send notice of a desire not to receive further messages. (A similar law was passed to outlaw spam faxes.) To keep up on the latest of this legislation, log on to http://www.cauce.org, the website of the Coalition Against Unsolicited Commercial Email.

Employees

Many business employees spend time they should be working writing personal e-mail or surfing the Internet. A 2000 survey found that 38 percent of major United States companies check their employees' e-mail, and 54 percent monitor their Internet use. Seventeen percent of the companies responding to the survey stated that they had terminated employees for misusing the Internet; 26 percent had given workers formal reprimands; and 20 percent had issued informal warnings.

Employers who fear they are losing employee working hours by employees surfing the net or chatting online can buy software that allows them to take a snapshot of an employee's computer screen from every minute to every three hours. This allows the employer to see just how much time the employee spends surfing the Internet and not working at his or her job. If an employee knows that the employer is conducting surveillance of the employees' Internet use, the employee is more likely to reduce his or her surfing time on the Internet and use it instead to conduct his or her employer's business.

Hackers and Crackers

Computer hacking consists of the unlawful and unauthorized entry into another person's or business's computer or computer system. In 1999, there were more than 35,000 reports of computer security breaches affecting more than 4.3 million computers. "Hackers" may attempt to gain entry to secure government computers containing classified information or break into their school's computer to change their grades. Website hackers range from teenage pranksters to foreign powers seeking classified intelligence, to everyone in between. Many hackers tend to be bright, loner teenagers or men in their early twenties. Software now exists that makes hacking much harder and more sophisticated than it was ten years ago, but getting around these programs just increases the thrill of the challenge for the serious hacker. In response, software manufacturers have come out with "firewall" programs designed to thwart hackers.

The motivation of one hacker and the next may differ. One hacker may just seek the thrill of the challenge of getting into the government's (or other entity, such as a business's or a bank's) secure system. Others engage in hacking to acquire secret governmental information or business trade secrets (industrial espionage) to sell to a third party. These hackers are known as "crackers." A cracker is a hacker with a criminal intent. Crackers sabotage computers, steal information on secure computers, and cause disruption to computer networks for personal or political reasons.

In the mid-1990s it was estimated that there were about one hundred thousand hackers, up to one thousand of whom were in the hacker "elite," skilled enough to penetrate corporate network systems and to get past corporate security. One estimate is that employees commit 80 percent of the attacks on a company's computer systems. Disgruntled employees who steal confidential information and trade secrets are thought to comprise 35 percent of the theft of a company's proprietary information.

With the spread of high-speed Internet access over digital telephone lines and cable television lines, computer users are facing a greater chance that a hacker will break into their computer. Internet users with cable modems or digital subscriber lines (DSL) can surf the net much faster than those with traditional dial-up connections. And unlike those with dial-up connections, computers using cable modems or DSL are online twenty-four hours a day.

Computer Viruses

There are a few sick individuals who get their kicks out of disabling computers or wiping out all of the information stored on computer hard drives by "infecting" them with a computer "virus." A computer virus is a rogue computer program, usually a short program designed to disperse copies of itself to other computers and disrupt those computers' normal operations. A computer virus usually attaches to or inserts itself into an executable file or the boot sector (the area that contains the first instructions executed by a computer when it is started or restarted) of a disk. While some viruses are merely disruptive, others can destroy data or cause an operating system or applications program to malfunction. Computer viruses are spread via floppy disks, networks, or online services.

Often a virus comes in over the Internet in the form of an innocuous e-mail, such as the infamous "I Love You" virus. You are directed to open an attachment, and when you do, the virus takes over, infecting your computer. Once the virus has done its damage, it is difficult to retrieve the disrupted material or otherwise bring things back to normal. You may have to hire a company specializing in restoring data recovery at considerable cost. This goes to show how important it is to back up your work on floppy disks, zip drives, or other data-saving equipment.

If you have a stand-alone computer that is not connected to the Internet, you do not have to worry much about viruses. About the only time your computer could be infected by a virus is by using shareware (free software containing software programs and sometimes viruses). But if you are connected to the Internet, you must be ever vigilant of viruses hidden in e-mails with attachments or pictures. If you are not sure who is sending you the e-mail, it is best to delete it rather than risk opening the attachment or picture only to find a virus lurking inside.

To prevent viruses from infecting your computer, you should have antivirus software installed in your computer. There are several excellent programs commercially available for just this purpose. However, you will need to update your antivirus software regularly to protect it against newly created viruses. Some of the best-selling antivirus programs have a system whereby each month you can download antivirus programs for new viruses.

Besides a virus, there are other disruptive programs, such as a "bomb," a "worm," and a "Trojan horse." A bomb is a program that sits silently in a computer's memory until it is triggered by a specific condition, such as a date. A worm is a destructive program that replicates itself over a network, reproducing itself as it goes. A Trojan horse is a malicious program that reproduces itself over a network, and like a virus must be distributed by diskette or e-mail.

Protecting Minors from Indecent Material

There are at least thirty-thousand adult sites promoting pornography on the World Wide Web. Parents, educators, librarians, lawmakers, and others are justifiably concerned about the harmful effect such sites may have on children who innocently or intentionally visit such sites. Because of this, several laws have been passed in recent years in an attempt to regulate the content of pornographic websites and protect minors from viewing harmful material. As we shall see below, however, such attempts to regulate website content basically have failed, the courts holding that the laws unconstitutionally infringe on the website publisher's first amendment guarantee of freedom of speech.

The Communications Decency Act (CDA), passed in 1996, prohibited Internet users from using the Internet to communicate material that under "contemporary community standards" (see chapter 20) would be deemed patently offensive to minors under the age of 18. The United States Supreme Court ruled that the CDA was unconstitutionally vague, as it failed to define key terms. Additionally, the high court noted that the breadth of the CDA was "wholly unprecedented" as, for instance, it was not limited to commercial speech or commercial entities, but rather its open-ended prohibitions embraced all nonprofit entities and individuals posting indecent material or displaying them on their own computers.

Most troubling to the Supreme Court was the "contemporary community standards" criterion as applied to the Internet. The Supreme Court found that applying such a test would effectively mean that because all Internet communication is made available to a worldwide audience the content of the conveyed message would be judged by the standards of the community most likely to be offended by the content. What this means is that the content of the website could not be any more liberal than that permitted by the most conservative community, such as Utah. Hence, material that would not be offensive in a more liberal community, such as California, would be banned, an infringement upon the latter's citizens' first amendment right to free speech.

Other types of speech, such as direct-mail letters, can be targeted to a specific geographical area. Even with "dial-a-porn" telephone services, the operator of the telephone service can screen its calls and accept a call only if its point of origin is from a community with standards of decency that are not offended by the content of their pornographic telephone message. This permits the publisher of pornographic material and the pornographic telephone operator to convey its material to communities whose mores would not be offended by its content and to avoid sending the material to more conservative communities whose sensitivities would be offended.

The Web, however, is without boundaries. Once something is published on the World Wide Web, it is immediately available throughout the world. There is currently no way of blocking out specific countries, let alone specific states. Accordingly, the United States Supreme Court concluded that "the 'community standards' criterion as applied to the Internet means that any communication available to a nationwide audience will be judged by the standards of the community most likely to be offended by the message." Hence the Supreme Court ruled that the CDA violated the first amendment, because people living in more liberal communities who would not be offended by the material would not have access to it.

The CDA was followed by the Child Online Protection Act of 1998 (COPA), which attempted to cure the constitutional flaws of the CDA. COPA prohibited an individual or entity from knowingly and with knowledge of the character of the material making any communication on the World Wide Web for commercial purposes that is available to any minor and that is harmful to minors. COPA attempted to restrict its scope to material on the World Wide Web only rather than on the Internet as a whole, to target only those Web communications made for "commercial purposes," and to limit its scope only to that material deemed harmful to minors. Whether material was harmful to minors was determined by a three-part test:

1. The average person, applying contemporary community standards, would find, taking the material as a whole and with respect to minors, that it was designed to appeal or pander to the prurient interest.
2. The material depicted, described, or represented, in a manner patently offensive with respect to minors, an actual or simulated sexual act or sexual contact, an actual or simulated normal or perverted sexual act, or a lewd exhibition of the genitals or postpubescent female breast.
3. Taken as a whole, the material lacks serious, literary, artistic, political, or scientific value for minors.

Like the CDA, COPA also provided affirmative defenses to those subjected to prosecution under that law. An individual could qualify for a defense if he or she, in good faith, restricted access by minors to material that is harmful to minors: (a) by requiring the use of a credit card, debit account, adult access code, or adult personal identification number; (b) by accepting a digital certificate that verified age; or (c) by any other reasonable measures that were feasible under available technology.

In June 2000, the United States Court of Appeals for the Third Circuit ruled that COPA was invalid because, like the CDA, it was unconstitutionally overbroad based on its definition of "harmful to minors" applying "contemporary community standards." According to the third circuit, the main problem with COPA was applying contemporary community standards in the face of the fact that the World Wide Web is without boundaries. The court observed that information published on the Web cannot be tailored to specific geographical areas, that once published on the Web the material is available worldwide. The Third Circuit Court of Appeals agreed with the United States Supreme Court's analysis of the CDA, finding that to comply with the requirement of applying "contemporary community standards" to determine the offensiveness of the material, material published on the Web would have to be judged by the most restrictive definition in order not to be considered patently offensive. This would result in an infringement of first amendment rights to free speech of members of more liberal communities. Additionally, minors still could access potentially harmful offensive matter on websites that originate in cities in other countries, such as Amsterdam, which is far more liberal in what it considers harmful to minors than even the most liberal American states.

However, in May 2002 the U.S. Supreme Court held that COPA's reliance on "community standards" to identify what material is "harmful to minors" does not by itself render COPA substantially overbroad for first amendment purposes, and vacated the Third Circuit Court of Appeals's decision. The U.S. Supreme Court sent ("remanded") the case back to the third circuit to determine whether COPA is substantially overbroad for other reasons, whether COPA is unconstitutionally vague, or whether COPA likely will not survive strict scrutiny analysis (see chapter 20) once the case is tried at the district court level.

The courts' decisions on CDA and COPA demonstrate just how difficult it is crafting a law that protects minors but does not run afoul of the first amendment rights of others. Rather than relying on the law to protect their children, parents should take proactive steps on their own to ensure their young children are not exposed to harmful material.

Buying blocking or filtering software is one possibility. However, such software programs may be overinclusive or underinclusive. Numerous products are on the market that purport to block or filter objectionable websites so a parent assumedly can allow a minor child to use the Internet unsupervised, without fear that he or she accidentally or intentionally will stumble across adult-oriented sexually explicit sites. However, you need to be aware that none of these filtering programs are perfect, and nothing substitutes for good old-fashioned parental supervision. A study published by *Consumer Reports* in its March 2001 issue found that, on the average, one in five objectionable sites made it through the filtering software. (The study did not reveal how many perfectly harmless sites filtering software blocked.)

How does blocking and filtering software work? Some block key words while others filter objectionable websites, of which there are currently more than thirty thousand. The latter takes much more time and upkeep, as new websites spring up daily. The problem with blocking and filtering software that is word-oriented is that it does not look at the context the word is in. For instance, the word "sex" is a red flag that would result in the web page being blocked or the whole website being filtered. The problem is that the filter does not distinguish between the contexts in which the word is used. For instance, if the word "sex" is used in a romantic, innocuous poem about "the fairer sex," with no objectionable carnal connotations whatsoever, the page or entire website would nonetheless be blocked because of the objectionable word "sex."

Similarly, the word "breast" likely would result in the blockage of the web page or entire website. That means that not only would recipes calling for chicken breasts be blocked, but also valuable medical information on breast cancer would be filtered as well. Information on sexually transmitted diseases (STDs) would be blocked, despite the need for sexually active teens to be made aware of unsafe sexual practices.

Hence, a better monitoring system is to have parental supervision of the child's use of the Internet and not let him or her have free rein over the Internet for hours at a time. You should instruct your child on what to do if he or she accidentally stumbles onto a pornographic website, such as immediately clicking on the "back" icon.

Effective April 2001, a federal law requires libraries and schools that receive certain federal funds to install blocking and filtering programs on computers used by children to access the Internet. The law, known as the Children's Internet Protection Act (CIPA), requires libraries and schools to install computer filtering software that screens out "visual depictions" that are obscene, harmful to minors, or child pornography. While the aim of the legislation is laudatory, as discussed above, one in five objectionable websites get through the filtering software. Further, the filtering software blocks important material on health, sexuality, and social issues of great import to teenagers. During the trial of this case, it came out that the filters screened out a site for aspiring dentists, a site to promote federalism in Uganda, and a third site that sold wooden wall hangings of scenes from the Bible.

The law was struck down as unconstitutional in the district court, and that decision was affirmed by the Third Circuit Court of Appeals, which concluded that thousands of nonpornographic websites wrongly were excluded by filtering software now on the market. In ruling that CIPA violates the first amendment because it would screen out too much material that is both harmless and useful, the third circuit noted that no presently conceivable technology can make the judgment necessary to determine whether a visual depiction is obscene or pornographic. On June 3, 2003, the United States Supreme Court held that CIPA was constitutional and does not violate the First Amendment.

Libraries should be the bastions of the first amendment right of free speech and should not be strong-armed by the federal or any other government or agency into prohibiting materials that some patrons may find objectionable. As more than one librarian has said, if the government were to use an equivalent filter to that used on computers to the books in the library, the library shelves would be almost bare. This we must not allow to happen. Free speech is one of our most valuable and treasured rights and should be protected at all costs, even though it offends some people.

Downloading Copyrighted Music for Free

Suppose you are a musician whose main source of income is the royalties paid each time one of your CDs or audiocassettes is sold. Imagine how much it would hurt you financially if people were able to download your songs from the Internet for free. This issue arose in relation to the program Napster, which allowed Internet users to download songs from the Internet without having to pay a cent to the record company or the artist who recorded or wrote the song. More than twenty million Internet users downloaded Napster to give them the capability of copying their favorite songs off the Internet for free. Many musical groups objected to this practice as a violation of the copyright laws. The groups reasoned that, why should a person buy a copyrighted CD or cassette of their songs when they could download their favorite songs from the Internet for free?

There is no doubt that the downloading of copyrighted songs from another person's computer is a violation of copyright laws. After months of contentious legal negotiations, Napster agreed to block access to at least one million copyrighted songs, preventing an estimated sixty-four million users from accessing certain tracks. Napster tried to survive as a "pay-for-play" website in which each computer user who downloaded a song would be required to pay a fee, part of which would go to the artists who wrote and performed the song. However, few users were willing to do this, especially due to the fact that there are other websites on the Internet that allow users to do the same thing as Napster. For instance, in the week before Napster's announcement that it would be blocking one million songs, computer users downloaded more than two hundred thousand copies of a software program by an Israeli-based company that offers a service almost identical to that of Napster. Napster ultimately went out of business and declared bankruptcy.

Shopping on the Internet

Shopping on the Internet can be a very convenient way to purchase new items from name-brand stores, often at a discount from what the item sells for in their "bricks-and-mortar" stores. But if you're not careful, you can wind up paying for merchandise that never arrives or is substantially different than it was represented to be. You should shop only with companies you know. If you want to buy something from a store you've never heard of, ask them to send you their latest paper catalog or brochure so you can get a better idea of what they sell and their services. Also, be sure to find out the company's return and refund policies;

these should be posted clearly on the website. One advantage to buying online is that unless the company has a bricks-and-mortar store in your state, you don't have to pay sales taxes on your purchase. However, you will have to pay shipping and handling fees, so it all works out in the wash.

When you buy something online, use your credit card whenever possible. This will give you rights under the Fair Credit Billing Act (chapter 18). Additionally, the Mail/Telephone Order Merchandise Rule applies to online purchases. Pursuant to this rule, the seller must deliver your merchandise within the time period stated, or if one is not stated, within thirty days. If there are going to be any delays, the company must notify you, giving you the right to cancel the transaction. Before paying for merchandise online by charge or credit card, make sure that the website has proper security measures to scramble or "encrypt" your card number to prevent others from getting it. Some websites use a picture (icon) of a closed lock to indicate it is a secure site. You always should print out a copy of your purchase order and confirmation number in case a problem with the order arises.

OnLine Auctions

Online auctions, or e-auctions (for electronic auctions), are one of the hottest activities on the Internet. One need only log on to www.eBay.com and browse for a few minutes to get a feeling of just how big e-auctions are. At the time of this writing there are over four million items in thousands of categories for sale on eBay alone! There are a number of other auction sites, but eBay is by far the largest and most active. There are auction sites that deal in anything and everything—like eBay—and there are auction sites that limit themselves to one type of item, such as sports memorabilia or rare coins and stamps.

Not only do individuals use e-auctions to sell their wares; many businesses do too. The advantage to buying from a business is that usually you can pay with your credit card and get certain rights and warranties. Most of the time, though, you are buying directly from an individual and not from a business or the website itself. The auction website usually acts as a mere broker in bringing the seller and buyer together. When you are buying from a business or a website, you usually are buying new items unless otherwise specified. If you are not sure whether the item being offered is new or not, you can e-mail the seller to get this question answered before you place your bid. Most sellers include a picture of their item on eBay.

You must be at least 18 years old to participate in auctions. This is because a completed auction is a binding legal contract (chapter 16), and minors do not have the legal capacity to enter into a binding contract. When a seller places an item for auction, he or she is legally placing an invitation to accept offers for his or her wares. When the buyer makes a bid, this is a legally binding offer, which the seller can accept, resulting in a binding contract. The seller accepts the highest offer, unless he or she has placed a "reserve" on the item that has not been met. A "reserve" is the minimum amount the seller will sell the item for.

To avoid getting ripped off (such as sending in the money but never getting the item from a fraudulent seller), you should check the "feedback forum" on the seller. The feedback forum contains comments from other buyers on how they rate the seller. The feedback forum lets you rate whether your transaction was positive, neutral, or negative, and lets you write a brief comment on your experience with the seller.

Suppose that you have five of the same items. You could hold five separate auctions. Or you could hold a "Dutch auction." In a Dutch auction, all five items are up for bid at the same time. All items are sold for the lowest successful bid. For example, suppose Jeri has five of the same porcelain doll that she decides to sell at auction. At the end of the auction, the top five bids are as follows: one for $50, two for $42.50, one for $40.00, and one for $35.00. Since it was a Dutch auction, all of the dolls are sold for $35.00, the lowest successful bid.

Rather than bidding and then returning to the website day after day to see if someone's outbid you, you can bid by "proxy bidding." For instance, suppose there is a baseball card you want. You're willing to pay $100 for it. The current bid is $35, and bid increments must be at least $5. When you bid, your bid will be listed as $40. If someone comes in and bids $45, your proxy automatically will increase your bid to $50. If someone bids over $100, you will not get the item. (You could, however, raise your bid if you wanted the card. You'll know that someone outbid your proxy bid, as the auction site will notify you of such fact by e-mail.) But if the last high bid is $70, your proxy automatically will bid $75, and if no one bids higher, you have the card you wanted.

After the bidding has ended, the auction website will notify the seller and the highest bidder via e-mail, giving them the other's e-mail address. The seller and winning bidder must then deal directly with each other in closing the deal. Generally, the winning bidder and the seller must contact each other within three days after being notified that the auction has closed and that the particular buyer was the highest bidder. The winning bidder and the seller then will mutually agree on the way to ship the product to the winning bidder. Normally the winning bidder pays all shipping costs. Depending upon the item bought and its cost, the buyer may want to consider having the seller insure the product when shipping it, again at the buyer's cost.

Some websites provide auction insurance to protect you from getting ripped off by a scam artist. For instance, eBay will reimburse you up to $200 with a $25 deductible. Amazon auctions will indemnify you for up to $250 with no deductible. In mid-October 2000, www.Yahoo.com entered into an insurance agreement with Lloyd's of London whereby Yahoo! will insure the winning bidder for purchases for as much as $250 with a $25 deductible. Yahoo! does, however, place a lifetime limit of two claims for fraudulent transactions. If you purchase anything directly from Yahoo!'s own shopping site, the buyers are protected free of charge for the full value of the item up to a maximum of $750.

If you are purchasing a large ticket item that exceeds the insurance limits, you should consider having an escrow service handle the sale. If you are buying something from an eBay auction, you probably will want www.iescrow.com (i-escrow) to handle the escrow. With an escrow service, you send your money to it and the seller sends it the item you purchased. Upon receipt of your funds, the escrow company will send you the item. You will then have the opportunity to inspect the item to ensure that it is as it was represented to be. If it is unsatisfactory, the deal is off. You return the item to the escrow company and get a full refund of your money (less any escrow fee).

But beware: There is the possibility for being scammed on e-auctions. The Federal Trade Commission reports that the number of complaints of e-auction fraud rose from about 100 in 1997 to 10,700 in 1999. You may send the seller your money and never receive the product, or the product may not be what it was represented to be or a much cheaper version than the seller described. Another fraudulent practice committed by some sellers is known as "shilling." They will bid on their own product under a different name to drive the price up. One warning sign of this possibility is if the Internet Service Provider (ISP) domain name is the same as that used by the seller. In one case, eBay canceled a $135,805 sale of an abstract painting because the seller had violated its rules by bidding on the painting himself.

If you feel that you are the victim of e-auction fraud, you should contact the National Consumers League at www.nclnet.org or call them at (800) 876-7060. They can help you file a complaint with the Federal Trade Commission. You also can file a complaint with the Federal Bureau of Investigation (FBI), which has set up the Internet Fraud Complaint Center, which is a joint operation of the FBI and the National White Collar Crime Center. Their website is www.ifccfbi.gov.

A French court ordered that Yahoo! stop computer users in France from accessing auctions of Nazi paraphernalia. France has very strict hate laws that make it illegal to display or sell racist material. One item on the Yahoo! auction site being offered by a user in the state of Washington was an "Ultra Rare Nazi Banner MUST SEE!!" for $600. As we mentioned at the beginning of this chapter, the Internet knows no boundaries; once something is posted on the Internet, it is available worldwide, and there is currently no technology to block it from reaching specific communities or countries. A French judge gave Yahoo! three months to find a way to prevent French users from accessing auction pages with Nazi-related objects. If Yahoo! did not comply within that period, it would be fined $13,000 for each day after the deadline that it did not comply. Other auction sites also sell Nazi and other hate and racist material but warn residents of France, Germany, and several other countries not to bid on the items.

SIXTEEN

Social Security, Medicare, SSI, and Medicaid

*t*HE GREAT DEPRESSION completely wiped out the savings accounts and stocks that many Americans were counting on to provide security for their retirement. The young were relatively fortunate; they could start over and build anew. But the elderly did not enjoy this luxury; many lived out their last days in poorhouses. To prevent the elderly from ever facing this prospect again, on August 14, 1935, President Franklin D. Roosevelt signed into law what has come to be widely regarded as the most important program spawned by this tragic period in American history: the Social Security Act.

Social Security consists of several different plans. The main one is Old-Age, Survivors, and Disability Insurance (OASDI), which provides benefits when a worker retires, becomes disabled, or is killed. Unlike workers' compensation benefits, the worker's disability or death does not have to be job-related in order for the worker or his or her family to be entitled to Social Security benefits. Social Security also provides health insurance through Medicare, discussed later in this chapter.

This chapter discusses your legal rights to Social Security benefits, Social Security Disability Insurance (SSDI), Medicare, Supplemental Security Income (SSI), and Medicaid (Medi-Cal in California). As with many government programs, your rights are determined by a maze of regulations. The material that follows will help you discover just what your rights are in many areas involving Social Security, SSDI, Medicare, SSI, and Medicaid.

HOW SOCIAL SECURITY IS FINANCED

Who pays for Social Security? If you are employed (or self-employed), the chances are that you do. Nine out of every ten workers contribute regularly to Social Security through a tax on their earnings. Your employer deducts 7.65 percent of your wages from your paycheck and then matches this from his or her own pocket. If you're self-employed, you pay the entire amount—15.3 percent—yourself, although you do get to deduct one-half of your self-employment tax from your tax return (IRS Form 1040). Self-employed individuals must file Schedule SE, Computation of Social Security Self-Employment tax, with their annual federal income tax returns.

As of 2001, the maximum earnings taxed for Social Security is $80,400, for a total of $4,984.80. Anything you make over that is free from Social Security taxes (but you still have to pay income taxes on it). This amount automatically increases each year as earning levels throughout the nation rise. If you work for two or more employers in one year and earn more than the maximum amount, be sure that you don't wind up paying too much to Social Security. For instance, suppose you worked for Company A for the first six months of the year and made $40,000. You then worked for Company B for the last six months and earned $45,000—a total of $85,000 for the entire year. If both companies deducted full Social Security taxes from your wages, you can claim a refund of the overpayment when you file your tax return. (If you worked for only one employer and too much was deducted, ask your employer to refund the excess.)

The maximum monthly Social Security retirement benefit for a person retiring at age 65 in 2001 is $1,536. For a person retiring at age 62 in 2001, the maximum monthly retirement benefit is $1,314. You can get an estimate of how much your Social Security retirement, survivor, or disability benefits will be by accessing the Social Security Administration's website at http://www.ssa.gov/top10.html and clicking on the "Retirement, Disability or Survivors planners and calculators" link.

Most jobs in the United States are covered by Social Security and are subject to the same rules. If your type of employment is covered, you don't get to choose whether or not you want to participate in Social Security; your participation is mandatory. There are a few employees who are subject to special rules. These include persons who do housecleaning, gardening, or baby-sitting in private homes; students who are employed by their school or college; farmworkers; members of religious orders; persons who get cash tips on the job (waiters and waitresses, for instance); employees of international organizations; and persons who work outside the United States. If you fall into any of these categories, contact your local Social Security office for information regarding your situation. Railroad workers and federal employees are covered by their own plans but may have some rights to Social Security and also should contact Social Security to see what their rights are.

QUALIFYING FOR BENEFITS

You are entitled to Social Security benefits only if you have earned sufficient "work credits" (sometimes referred to as "quarters of coverage"). How many credits you need depends upon how old you are and what the benefits are for—retirement, disability, or survivor's benefits. The number of credits you need to be eligible for retirement benefits after 1991 is forty. The number of credits necessary for disability and survivor's benefits is shown in Table 16.1. (Depending upon your financial condition, if you aren't eligible for Social Security benefits, you may be able to get Supplemental Security Income (SSI, discussed below) or other public assistance.

In 2001, you received one credit for each $830 you made, up to a maximum of four credits for the whole year. (The amount you need to earn for a credit goes up each year. For example, in 1999, it was $740, in 2000, it was $780, and in 2001, it was $830.) You can earn four credits in one month, or you can work all year and still not earn a single credit. For instance, if you made $3,320 or more in January of 2001, you earned four credits for that year, even if you didn't work another day. If you made only $69 a month, you wouldn't get a single credit, since your total earnings for all of 2001 would be only $828. If you earned $140 a month—$1,680 for the year—you would receive two credits for the whole year.

Would you have received additional credits if you earned more than $3,320 in 2001? No. The most credits you can earn in a single year are four. That doesn't mean your earnings above $3,320 aren't taken into consideration. They are used to determine the size of your Social Security check when you retire. The greater your earnings, the larger your Social Security check will be—up to a point.

Suppose Heather has been working for several years and has earned ten credits. She decides to have a baby and quits working for a time. Does she lose those ten credits? No. Once you've earned a credit, it's yours for good; nobody can take it away from you. You don't lose any credits, even if you stop working before you qualify for Social Security benefits. When you go back to work, the new credits will be added to the credits you already have.

It's a good idea to check your Social Security earnings record every three years or so to make sure your earnings are being reported correctly. You can get a free postcard form for this at any Social Security office. Be sure to notify Social Security if you change your name (for example, when you get married and change to your husband's name, or get divorced and return to using your maiden name) to insure that you receive credit for all of your earnings under your new name. You will have to show sufficient proof to establish your identity, such as a driver's license, marriage certificate, decree of divorce, or court order granting a name change.

RETIREMENT BENEFITS

THE BULK OF SOCIAL SECURITY benefits is paid out in retirement to workers who earned enough work credits, as previously discussed. If you retire in 2003 or thereafter, you must have accumulated at least forty credits to be eligible for Social Security retirement benefits.

If you have earned enough credits, you can retire and receive Social Security benefits as early as your sixty-second birthday, although your benefits will be reduced permanently if you retire before 65 (or your full retirement age if you retire after 2002, discussed below). But you won't get any benefits unless you apply for them. You can work hard all your life and retire at age 65, but the Social Security office is not going to start sending you checks automatically. Ideally, you should notify your local Social Security office three months before you retire. Even if you won't be retiring, you should still contact Social Security three months before your sixty-fifth birthday in order to get Medicare coverage.

To apply for Social Security retirement benefits, call Social Security toll-free at (800) 772-1213. If you are deaf or hard of hearing, call them at (800) 325-0778 (TTY). You also can call or visit your local Social Security field office. Their number is found in the government pages in the front of your telephone book. Or you can find the nearest Social Security field office by going on the Internet to http://www.ssa.gov/top10.html and clicking on the "How to Contact a Local Office" link. You also can apply for Social Security retirement benefits on the Internet by going to http://www.ssa.gov/top10.html and clicking on the "Apply for Social Security Retirement Benefits Online" link.

Suppose you retire at your full retirement age but forget to apply for Social Security benefits for three months. Do you lose your benefits for those months? No. You can receive back payments for up to six months after you retire. But if you retire *before* your full retirement age, generally you can only get benefits starting with the month in which you apply for them. So if you retire at, say, age 63 in March but wait until August to apply for retirement benefits, your benefits will begin with August.

When applying for retirement benefits, you'll need your:

* Social Security card (or a record thereof);
* birth certificate;
* children's birth certificates (if they are applying);
* proof of U.S. citizenship or lawful alien status if you were not born in the United States;
* spouse's birth certificate and Social Security number if he or she is applying for benefits on your record;
* marriage certificate (if applying on a spouse's record);

* military discharge papers if you had military service;
* W-2 form from the previous year, or your last year's tax return if you are self-employed.

Amount of Your Retirement Benefits

When you retire at your full retirement age (see Table 16.1), you are entitled to full retirement benefits (assuming you have earned enough credits to qualify). In calculating your benefits, Social Security will take an average of your thirty-five highest earnings years. If you have less than thirty-five years of earnings, Social Security will average in years of zero earnings to bring the total number of years to thirty-five. Thus, the amount of your monthly Social Security check will depend on how much, on the average, you made each year for your thirty-five years of highest earnings; the more you made, the higher your benefits will be (up to the maximum). You can retire as early as your sixty-second birthday, but if you do, your monthly checks will be reduced permanently to 80 percent of the full benefit. For example, the maximum monthly retirement benefit check for a worker who retired in 2001 was $1,536, but only $1,314 if he or she retired at 62—a monthly difference of $222. For the worker who retired in 2001 at the full retirement age of 65, it will take twelve years to make up the difference. If you retire at age 62, for instance, and receive $1,314 a month, by the time you reach 65, you already will have collected $47,304 in retirement benefits. If you retired at age 65 (or later full retirement age), it would take 17.75 years for your checks ($222 larger per month) to make up this difference.

If you retire before your sixty-fifth birthday (or later full retirement age, if applicable), the amount by which your monthly check is reduced depends upon how many months short of your full retirement age you retire. If you retire at age 62, you will receive a smaller check than if you retired at 64. By the same token, if you decide not to retire when you reach 65 (or later full retirement age, if applicable), your benefits will increase for each month that you continue working. Your monthly checks will increase automatically each year as the national cost of living goes up. Under the current regulations, if the cost of living increases by, say, 3 percent, your benefits will rise by the same amount.

Table 16.1 shows the increasing full retirement ages for people born in 1937 compared to those born in 1960 or later. Note that the full retirement age for purposes of collecting full Social Security benefits starts at age 65 for persons born before 1938 and rises to 67 years for persons born after 1959.

FULL RETIREMENT AGE

Year of Birth	Full Retirement Age
1937 or Earlier	65
1938	65 and 2 months
1939	65 and 4 months
1940	65 and 6 months
1941	65 and 8 months
1942	65 and 10 months
1943 to 1954	66
1955	66 and 2 months
1956	66 and 4 months
1957	66 and 6 months
1958	66 and 8 months
1959	66 and 10 months
1960 and later	67

Table 16.1: Table showing increasing ages for full retirement age.

Retirement Benefits to Spouses and Children

If you have been married for at least one year when your spouse retires and begins receiving Social Security retirement benefits, you may also be entitled to spouse's benefits (also called "auxiliary benefits"), even if you don't qualify for benefits on the basis of your own work record. You can apply for benefits as early as age 62, but, as with a worker who retires before his or her full retirement age (65 years and two months in 2003), your benefits will be reduced permanently. If you wait until your full retirement age to apply for your benefits, you will get one-half of the amount your spouse receives. You also can receive retirement benefits based on your spouse's record if you are under 62 and are caring for a child who is under 16 or disabled and who is receiving Social Security benefits based on the retired worker's earnings. If you also worked and earned enough credits on your own record, but your benefits as a spouse are larger, you will receive the larger amount.

Even though you are divorced, you may still be eligible for retirement benefits based on your ex-spouse's record. If you are 62 or older, single, and were married to your ex-spouse for at least ten years, you can receive retirement benefits when your ex-spouse starts to collect them. If you were married for at least ten years and have been divorced for at least two years, you can receive retirement benefits as early as age 62 even if your ex-spouse isn't receiving them (but your ex-spouse must be eligible to receive retirement benefits). Although your retirement benefits based on your ex-spouse's record end when you remarry, they can start again if your new marriage ends in divorce, annulment, or death.

When a worker who is receiving retirement benefits has unmarried children—including stepchildren, adopted children, and dependent grandchildren—under age 18 (or under 19 if they are full-time high school students), those children can receive supplemental benefits, as can single children 18 or over who were disabled severely before age 22 and who continue to be disabled. Illegitimate children may also be eligible for benefits. Social Security benefits to a worker's child generally end when the child marries and commence again only if the marriage is annulled.

If You Go Back to Work While Receiving Retirement Benefits

What happens to your Social Security retirement checks if you go back to work? That depends on how old you are. Nothing happens to them if you're at least your full retirement age when you go back to work; your benefits remain the same regardless of how much you earn after reaching your full retirement age; see Table 16.2. This is due to the Senior Citizens' Freedom to Work Act of 2000. But if you're under your full retirement age, your checks may be reduced, depending upon how much you make. In 2001, if you were between 62 and 65, you could have earned up to $10,680 in 2001 and still have received your full retirement benefits. If you are under your full retirement age when you start getting your Social Security payments, $1 in benefits will be deducted for each $2 you earn above the annual limit.

In the year you reach your full retirement age, $1 in benefits will be deducted for each $3 you earn above a different limit, but only for earnings before the month you reach the full retirement age. For 2001, this amount is $25,000. For instance, suppose that you were 64 at the beginning of the year but turned 65 in August 2001. You earned $40,000 during the year, $28,000 of which was earned in the first seven months from January through July. You would give up $1,000 in benefits: $1 for every $3 of the $3,000 you earned above the $25,000 limit through July.

With benefits of $800 a month, you would still receive $4,600 out of your $5,600 benefits for the first seven months. You would get all $4,000 for the months of August through December after you turned 65. Hence, even though you earned $40,000 in 2001, you would still get $8,600 of your Social Security benefits. After you reach your full retirement age, you can earn an unlimited amount without it affecting the amount of your Social Security benefits. Note that if you go back to work after getting some Social Security retirement checks, your new earnings may result in higher benefits being paid to you, as they will be credited to your record, and Social Security will refigure your benefits automatically.

What kind of income is taken into account in determining whether it reduces your benefits? Money paid to you as an employee—including cash tips, bonuses, vacation pay, and severance pay—and your net profit from self-employment are all counted. If you do work in exchange for room and board—if you manage an apartment building, for instance, or do maintenance work in return for a free apartment or reduced rent—you must include the value of that in your total earnings. The monthly income from your "nest egg"—things like savings accounts, IRAs, stock dividends, 401(k)s, annuities and other insurance, gifts and inheritances, rents from real estate, and other investments—ordinarily does *not* count against you.

Suppose that in 2001 you turn 63 and decide to retire in July of that year, but you've already made more than $10,680, the maximum amount a person receiving retirement benefits who has not yet reached his or her full retirement age could earn in 2001 without a reduction in benefits. Does this mean that your retirement benefits will be reduced for the rest of the year? No. You can still retire and collect your full benefits for each month your income falls below a certain amount. If you retired in 2001 after making more than the base amount for the year, you can get full benefits (to the maximum allowed) for any month your earnings do not exceed $890 if you were between 62 and your full retirement age (65 through 2002). This way you can retire in the middle or near the end of a year and still receive full retirement benefits for the remaining months. This special monthly test is applied only in the first year you retire.

If you have reached full retirement age, but elect to continue working and not receive Social Security retirement benefits, you receive a special credit (a "delayed retirement credit") for each full month before you turn 70 in which you were eligible for but did not receive Social Security benefits. This will result in an increase in your retirement benefits.

Low-income Medicare Beneficiaries

Stephen is receiving Medicare benefits and his earnings are just below the poverty level. However, he has more than $2,000 in countable assets and therefore is ineligible for Medicaid (see below). Because he earns so little, Stephen cannot pay all of his medical bills, and oftentimes faces the choice between using his money to buy food or pay for health care services. Is Stephen up the proverbial creek without a paddle? Not necessarily.

Stephen may be eligible for Medicaid assistance as a qualified Medicare beneficiary (QMB). To qualify as a QMB, a single person's countable assets must not exceed $4,000; a married couple's countable assets can be no more than $6,000. In determining the amount of assets a person or couple has, the home and household goods, personal effects, a car under $4,500—or unlimited if used for business—burial plot, and business property are not included in the count. Additionally, the person's income must be at or below the poverty level as annually adjusted.

If Stephen meets the requirements for becoming a qualified Medicare beneficiary, then he is able to get some Medicaid assistance. Medicaid will pay his Medicare Part B monthly premium and all Medicare deductibles and coinsurance.

If Stephen makes more than the poverty level line, but his income is not more than 150 percent above the poverty level (the exact percentage is determined by each state; many limit it to 120 percent above the poverty line), assistance is available under the specified low-income Medicare beneficiary (SLMB) program. This program pays the monthly Medicare premium.

DISABILITY BENEFITS

You AND YOUR DEPENDENTS are entitled to receive Social Security disability benefits if you are disabled before your full retirement age and have earned enough credits. If you are disabled after your full retirement age, you will receive retirement benefits rather than disability benefits. The amount of your disability benefits is based on your age, how long you have worked, and how much you have earned before becoming disabled.

You are considered disabled when you suffer from a physical or mental condition that is terminal or expected to last at least twelve months and that prevents you from doing any "substantial gainful activity" (see below). You are considered blind and disabled if, even with glasses or corrective lenses, your vision is no better than 20/200 or your field of vision is 20 degrees or less.

Qualifying for Disability Benefits

As with other Social Security benefits, you must earn sufficient credits to qualify for disability benefits. The number of credits you need to be eligible for disability benefits is determined by how old you are when you become disabled. If you are between 24 and 31 when you become disabled, you must have earned credits for half the time between your twenty-first birthday and the time you become disabled. For example, if you become disabled on your twenty-eighth birthday, you need fourteen credits—one-half of seven years—to qualify for disability benefits. If you are disabled at age 31 or later, you generally need at least twenty credits in the ten years preceding your disability.

Disability benefits may also be available to a disabled widow or widower (and in some cases, to a disabled surviving divorced spouse) who is 50 or older, if the worker was insured at death.

Applying for Disability Benefits

If you are born after 1929 and become disabled at age	Credits needed to qualify for benefits
44	22
46	24
48	26
50	28
52	30
54	32
56	34
58	36
60	38
62 or older	40

Table 16.2: Credits needed in order to qualify for benefits if you become disabled at age 44 or older.

If you can't work because of a physical or mental disability that is expected to last at least twelve months or to result in your death, you should apply for disability benefits without delay. Although you usually won't receive any benefits until you've been disabled for five full months, it is better to apply immediately so Social Security can verify your disability and send you your checks as soon as you are eligible for them. You will need to give Social Security the names, addresses, and telephone numbers of the doctors, hospitals, and clinics that have treated you for the disability, and the approximate dates of treatment. You will have to tell Social Security what your illness or injury is, when the illness started or the injury was sustained, how it keeps you from working, and the date you stopped working. Be prepared to tell the Social Security caseworker the restrictions your doctor has placed on you and the names and dosages of all medications you are taking currently.

Your Social Security caseworker will request all medical evidence from you regarding the doctors, hospitals, and clinics that treated you. Your claim then will be sent to the disability determination services in your state, where a disability evaluation specialist and a physician will review the evidence. They may ask your doctors about your condition, the diagnosis, the extent to which your working ability is impaired, the treatment that has been provided already, and what treatment may be required in the future. You may have to submit to a special examination or test—at no cost to you—to verify your claim.

Disability claims ordinarily are processed in three to six months, after which you receive written notice informing you of whether your claim has been approved or denied. If it is approved, the notice will show the amount of your monthly payments and the date when they will start. For most people, there is a five-month waiting period after the date they become disabled and the date the payments begin. No wait, however, applies if you are disabled before your twenty-second birthday and qualify for Social Security benefits on the record of a parent. If your disability claim is rejected, the written notice must explain why benefits were turned down. You have the right to appeal the decision if you don't agree with it (see discussion below).

Why and When Disability Checks Stop

Disability checks continue for as long as you can't perform any "substantial gainful activity." Each case is reviewed periodically—usually every one, three, or seven years—to determine whether the worker is still disabled. Should Social Security determine that your condition has improved to the point where you are ready to go back to work, you will be notified of that decision. You will then receive three more monthly disability checks. You have the right to appeal this determination, and you can ask that your benefits continue in the meantime. Ordinarily, this request must be made within ten days after you are notified that your disability checks are going to stop. If you lose your appeal, you will be asked to repay the benefits you received while you were appealing the termination of your benefits.

You usually can go back to work for as long as nine months (sometimes longer) on a trial basis without losing any disability benefits. A "trial work month" is one in which you earn $530 or more or work at least eighty hours in a month at your own business. The trial work months do not have to be consecutive; they can be separated by months, even years, during which you don't work. When the trial period is over, the Social Security office will decide whether you can go back to work. If it determines that you can, your disability benefits will stop after another three months.

You generally are considered to be doing "substantial gainful work" if you make over $740 or more a month in 2001 in gross wages ($1,240 a month in 2001 if you are blind). In figuring your gross wages, you are allowed to deduct certain expenses related to your disability that you need in order to work, such as medical equipment, drugs, services, and nurses or attendants. For instance, if for March 2001 you were paid $900, but you spent $350 on medical equipment and drugs so you could work, your gross income would be $550. If you are self-employed, the amount you make is not the sole consideration. Other factors, including the general state of the economy, the type of work you did, and your ability to manage your business, also are taken into account.

If you are still disabled and go back to work, then stop working less than one year after your disability checks have stopped, you don't need to make a new application for disability benefits. But before your disability checks will be resumed, you do have to inform your local Social

Security office that you have stopped working. And you may be required to undergo a new medical evaluation.

Suppose you are disabled, recover, and go back to work, but become disabled again two years later. Do you have to make a new application for disability benefits? Yes. But if you are disabled within five years after your disability benefits stop, you won't have to wait five months for the disability benefits to start the second time.

Note that after you have been receiving Social Security Disability Insurance benefits for two years, you automatically are enrolled in Medicare (discussed below).

Survivors' Benefits

When a worker dies, his or her spouse, children, and other dependents may be eligible for monthly survivors' benefits if the worker had earned enough credits of coverage needed for disability benefits. In addition to the monthly benefits, a one-time lump-sum death benefit of $255 is available to an eligible surviving widow or widower or child. Under a special rule, the minor children and their mother or father can receive survivors' benefits if the worker had earned at least six quarters of coverage (one and a half years) in the three years before his or her death. The wife and children of a deceased worker usually can get benefits if the marriage lasted at least nine months.

A surviving widow or widower under age 60 generally can receive survivors' benefits only if he or she is caring for the worker's child(ren) under 16 (or if the child is disabled), and the child is receiving benefits based on the record of the deceased worker. But when the child's benefits stop (discussed below), so do the benefits of the surviving widow or widower. The widow's or widower's benefits also stop if the child moves out. Survivors' benefits are also available to a surviving widow or widower who is 60 or older (50 or older if the surviving spouse is disabled within seven years of the worker's death), regardless of whether he or she is caring for any children.

If you are divorced, you can still receive survivor's benefits when your ex-spouse dies if you are not married, are 60 or older (50 or older if you are disabled within seven years of the worker's death), and were married to your ex-spouse for at least ten years. A divorced spouse under 60 who meets the other qualifications may be eligible for survivors' benefits if he or she is caring for the deceased worker's child (who is receiving Social Security benefits based on the deceased worker's earnings). But, as with benefits received by a widow or widower who is caring for a child of the deceased worker, the benefits stop when the child turns 16 or moves out. The child's own benefits, however, continue until the child turns 18 (19 if he or she is a full-time high school student), or longer if the child is disabled. Survivors' benefits to widows, widowers, and divorced spouses usually stop if they remarry before they are 60, but start again if the remarriage ends.

Unmarried children—including stepchildren, adopted children, even illegitimate children—under 18 (19 if they are full-time high school students), usually are entitled to survivors' benefits when the worker dies. Benefits are also payable to unmarried children 18 or older who were severely disabled before age 22 and continue to be disabled. For most children, survivors' benefits stop when they marry and start again only if the marriage is annulled.

The parents of a deceased adult worker can receive survivors' benefits if the parent is 62 or older and received at least half of his or her support from the deceased adult child. A grandchild who is living with and being supported by a grandparent who is covered by Social Security may be eligible for survivors' benefits when the grandparent dies. This applies only if the grandchild is under 18 and his or her biological parents are dead or disabled.

If your spouse or parent (or child or grandparent upon whom you were dependent) dies, you should contact your local Social Security office as soon as possible. Widows and widowers can apply for survivors' benefits in the month after the worker's death and still receive benefits for the month of death. (The one-time death benefit of $255 usually can be applied for up to two years after the worker's death.) You will need the deceased worker's Social Security card or a record of that number, your marriage certificate, the birth certificates for your children, if any, and a certified copy of the deceased worker's death certificate. If you are applying for benefits as a dependent parent of a deceased child or as a dependent grandchild of a deceased grandparent, you will have to prove that the worker was in fact supporting you. Your local Social Security office can tell you what type of documentation you need to prove your dependency.

SOME THINGS YOU NEED TO KNOW ABOUT SOCIAL SECURITY

How Payments Are Handled

Social Security benefits are paid only for a full month. If you have been receiving Social Security checks since before May 1997, your check is due to arrive on the third day of the month. For persons who began receiving Social Security benefits after May 1997, the benefits are staggered throughout the month. If your date of birth is on the first to the tenth day of the month, your Social Security benefits check is due the second Wednesday of the month. If your birthday is on the eleventh to the twentieth of the month, the check is due the third Wednesday of the month, and if your birth date is on the twenty-first through the thirty-first of the month, the check should arrive on the fourth Wednesday of the month. To avoid delays in the mail, as well as the possibility of a thief intercepting your check before it reaches you, you should consider having the check deposited directly into your bank account. If your check does not come on the date due, Social Security advises waiting three days and, if it still hasn't come, calling the Social Security Administrator at (800) 772-1213, or if you are deaf or hard of hearing, at (800) 325-0778 (TTY).

You can arrange to have your monthly Social Security checks deposited directly into your checking or savings account by going to your bank and filling out the proper form—Form SF-1199. How can you be sure that the bank has received your check? The bank can do one of the following things: Within two business days of receipt, it can notify you that your check was received; it can notify you that your check was not received within two business days after it should have been received; or it can set up a telephone number for you to call to find out whether your check was received and deposited (this number must appear on your bank account's periodic statement).

When to Notify Social Security

If you are receiving benefits, here are some of the times when you need to contact your local Social Security office:

* If you move, change your mailing address, or change your name. (Be sure to report your address change even if the checks are deposited directly into your bank account, because the checks can be stopped if Social Security cannot get in touch with you.)
* If your checks are deposited automatically into your bank account and you change banks or accounts.
* When the beneficiary of Social Security benefits dies, you should call the Social Security Administration at (800) 772-1213 or (800) 325-0778 (TTY) immediately to notify Social Security of the beneficiary's death. Do not cash any checks received for the month the beneficiary died or thereafter. You can, however, retain and cash checks for the months prior to the month in which the beneficiary died. For instance, if the beneficiary dies in August, the Social Security check he or she receives in August is payment for July's benefits and does not have to be returned. However, future checks must be returned to your local Social Security office. If the benefits were being deposited directly into the beneficiary's bank account, promptly notify both Social Security and the bank of the beneficiary's death.
* If the person receiving the benefits becomes physically or mentally incapable of managing his or her funds. Social Security can arrange to send the checks to a "representative payee," such as a close relative or a trusted friend.
* If you get a divorce or an annulment and receive benefits as a spouse, a surviving or divorced spouse, a parent, or a child of the worker.
* If a child receiving benefits becomes disabled or is a full-time high school student (otherwise, benefits automatically terminate when the child turns 18). Also notify Social Security if a child over 18 who receives benefits as a full-time student leaves school.
* If you are receiving retirement benefits, are under your full retirement age, and go back to work and expect to make more than the annual exempt amount for the year. If you are under the full retirement age and work or are self-employed outside the United States,

you must notify the nearest U.S. embassy, consulate, or Social Security office promptly and inform them of this fact.

* If your condition improves or when something happens that could affect your status as a disabled person (if you receive disability benefits). Also notify Social Security if you go back to work, regardless of how much or how little you expect to earn.

* If you will be traveling abroad for more than thirty days. Also notify your local Social Security office if you will be visiting Albania, Cuba, Democratic Kampuchea (formerly Cambodia), North Korea, or Vietnam, even if the trip will be shorter than thirty days. Your local Social Security office can provide you with the informative pamphlet "Your Social Security Checks—While You Are Outside the United States," which discusses how traveling abroad affects your Social Security check.

* If a person receiving benefits is convicted of a felony and sent to prison. Although benefits are not ordinarily payable while a person is in prison, benefits to family members do continue.

Your Right to Have Someone Act for You

You have the right to appoint an attorney, a relative, or even a trusted friend to act on your behalf with Social Security if, for example, you are bedridden, suffer from Alzheimer's disease or other dementia, or just don't want to do it yourself. Your representative can do just about anything you can. To arrange for a representative, you must fill out and sign Form SSA 1696-U3, "Appointment of Representative" (available from your local Social Security office).

Some people are able to deal with Social Security at the initial application stage without the assistance of an attorney, close relative, or trusted friend. Others are confused by the amount of paperwork they need to fill out, and the assistance of an attorney well versed in this area is helpful. If you're having trouble getting a claim accepted—particularly if the claim is a major one—you should seriously consider hiring an attorney experienced in Social Security claims to represent you.

Before you give anyone the authority to represent you, find out what fee, if any, he or she intends to charge you, and make sure to get this in writing and signed by the attorney or other person you are hiring to represent you. Will you have to pay a fee only if the attorney or other person is successful with your claim? If so, make sure that, too, is written down. Before you have to pay anything, the person who represented you must file a petition with Social Security showing the fee requested, the nature and extent of the services performed, and the dates the services started and ended. Social Security usually decides the amount of the fee, but if you go to court, attorney's fees cannot exceed 25 percent of what you recover. If you disagree with the fee approved by Social Security, you can ask your local Social Security office to review it. You must make this request in writing within thirty days of the time you received notice of the approved fee. Your representative likewise has a right to have the fee reviewed if he or she feels that it is too small.

If an attorney represents you, Social Security usually withholds 25 percent of your back payments for the attorney. If this is not enough to pay all of the attorney's fee as approved by Social Security, you must make up the difference from your own pocket. If the amount withheld is too much, you will be sent the excess. If your representative is not an attorney or if your claim is unsuccessful, you usually must pay your representative his or her fee directly.

Appealing Social Security Decisions

What can you do if your Social Security claim is denied or if you feel the amount of benefits you are awarded is too little? Within sixty days after you receive notice of the decision on your claim, you can send a written request for reconsideration to your local Social Security office. You can do this on a form available from Social Security (which we recommend using), or you can simply write a letter appealing the decision. Your local Social Security office can tell you what information your letter should contain and to whom the letter must be addressed. The main objective should be to present enough solid evidence to support your position. You are well advised to consult a lawyer who handles Social Security cases at this point.

If you disagree with the decision after reconsideration, your next step is to make a written request for a hearing before an administrative law judge of the Office of Hearings and Appeals of the Social Security Administration. (If your claim involves a Medicare hospital insurance claim of less than $100, you do not have the right to a hearing; your only recourse is to ask for reconsideration of the claim's original denial.) You can represent yourself at this hearing or appoint someone to represent you. Or you can waive the hearing and have the case decided on the basis of the written evidence submitted to the judge. If you still aren't satisfied after the administrative law judge makes a decision, you can request a review by the Appeals Council. The Appeals Council chooses the cases it hears; you do not have a right to have it hear yours. If the Appeals Council refuses to hear your case, or hears your case but rules against you, you can then file suit in federal court. Generally, you have only sixty days to appeal each action to the next stage, and appeals to Social Security usually must be made on a special form available at your local Social Security office. Appealing denials of a Social Security claim often requires the assistance of an attorney experienced in this area of law.

MEDICARE BENEFITS

MEDICARE PROVIDES HEALTH SERVICES for people who are 65 and older, persons who have been receiving Social Security disability insurance payments (SSDI) for at least two years, and those who suffer permanent kidney failure. Medicare consists of two parts: Part A—hospital insurance—and Part B—medical insurance. Part A is paid for from your Social Security taxes.

Part B is supported in part (one-third) by the small monthly premiums required of each person who enrolls. The remaining two-thirds comes from general federal revenues.

You are eligible for Medicare Part A hospital insurance if you are 65 or older and are entitled to monthly Social Security benefits (you don't have to be receiving any Social Security benefits, however). Your spouse, divorced spouse, widow or widower, or dependent parents are also eligible for Medicare at age 65. If you are under 65, you are automatically eligible for Medicare if you have been receiving Social Security disability benefits for at least twenty-four months.

Widows and widowers between 50 and 65 who have been disabled for at least two years may be eligible for Medicare, even if they have not applied for disability benefits because they were receiving other Social Security benefits. Disabled surviving divorced spouses under 65 and disabled children 18 or older are eligible for Medicare in some cases.

Even if your work record does not qualify you for Medicare, you still can enroll in the program by paying a monthly premium if you are 65 or over.

Applying for Medicare Benefits

Some people are enrolled in Medicare automatically; others are not covered unless and until they apply. You are enrolled in Medicare automatically when you turn 65 (or full retirement age after 2002) if you took an early retirement and have been receiving Social Security checks or if you are under 65 and have been receiving Social Security disability benefits for twenty-four months.

If you plan to retire (or even to keep working) after you reach your full retirement age, you need to apply to be covered by Medicare. In either event, it is a good idea to apply three months before your sixty-fifth birthday so your Medicare benefits will start as soon as you are eligible. Disabled widows and widowers between 50 and 65 must also apply to be covered. If you have any questions about whether you need to enroll in Medicare to be covered, contact your local Social Security office. (You can postpone filing for Part B medical insurance, with no penalty, if you or your spouse is still working and have medical insurance through work.)

Medicare Hospital Insurance

Medicare hospital insurance (Part A) helps pay for treatment in participating hospitals and skilled nursing homes. It also covers services for in-home care and, under certain conditions, hospice care. Medicare will pick up only a portion of the "approved costs" of services. Approved costs are based on what charge is considered reasonable in your area for the same procedure. For instance, if your doctor charges $1,500 to perform a certain procedure, but the average cost in your area is only $1,200, the "approved cost" of $1,200 will be used to determine the amount of your Medicare benefits.

Should you need inpatient care in a hospital, Medicare helps pay the cost during the first ninety days in a participating hospital. In 2001, Medicare paid for all but $776 of the covered medical services during the first sixty days you were hospitalized. "Covered services" include a semiprivate room, your meals, regular nursing services, operating and recovery room costs, intensive care and coronary care, drugs, lab tests, medical supplies and appliances, and rehabilitation services. For days 61 through 90, as of 2001, you pay $194 each day, and Medicare pays the rest of all covered services.

Medicare pays the above benefits for each "benefit period." A benefit period begins the day you enter the hospital and stops sixty days after the medical services end. For example, if you're in the hospital for sixty days, you're discharged, and then six months later you're back in the hospital for another sixty days, the second hospitalization constitutes a new benefit period. Instead of combining your two hospital stays into a single benefit period of 120 days, your two separate stays are counted as separate benefit periods of sixty days each.

Let's say that during one benefit period you're in the hospital longer than ninety days—120 days, for instance. Since Medicare covers only the first ninety days of hospitalization in a single benefit period, do you have to pay for the other thirty days out of your own pocket? No— at least not if you haven't used up your sixty "reserve days." These reserve days were designed to help you during longer periods of hospitalization. But there's a catch: Reserve days are not renewable. That means, once you use a reserve day, it's gone forever. By using thirty of your reserve days to cover your 120-day hospital stay, you're left with only thirty reserve days. Also, for reserve days, in 2000, you must pay $388 a day; Medicare pays the rest.

If you need inpatient skilled nursing care or rehabilitation services after you leave the hospital following a three-day hospital stay, Medicare will pay benefits for up to one hundred days in a participating skilled nursing facility. In 2002, Medicare paid for all covered services a person received in the nursing home for the first twenty days, and paid all but up to $97 a day for the next eighty days. Covered services in a skilled nursing facility include a semiprivate room, all meals, regular nursing services, rehabilitation services, drugs, and medical supplies and appliances.

When people are confined to their homes and meet other criteria, Medicare pays the fully approved cost of home visits from a participating home health agency. Medicare also pays benefits for hospice care provided by a Medicare-certified hospice to eligible terminally ill beneficiaries, to a maximum of two ninety-day periods and one thirty-day period.

Medicare Medical Insurance

Medicare medical insurance (Part B) helps pay for doctor's services, outpatient hospital services, and other medical items and services not covered by Medical hospital insurance. If you are 65 or older or are eligible for Medicare hospital insurance (Part A), you are usually eligible for Medicare medical insurance. When you apply for Medicare Part A hospital insurance, you are automatically enrolled in Part B medical insurance unless you tell the people at Social Security that you don't want it. The basic premium for Medicare medical insurance in 2003 is $58.70 a month. There is also a small annual amount (a "deductible") you must meet each year before Medicare medical insurance takes over. In 2003, the annual deductible is $100.

Medicare Part B medical insurance pays 80 percent of covered services. Among them are treatment by a doctor anywhere in the United States, including surgery, diagnostic tests, and X-rays; medical supplies (if furnished in a doctor's office); services of the office nurse; emergency room and outpatient clinic services; and home health visits (if you meet certain conditions). Other services covered under certain conditions include ambulance transportation; artificial eyes and limbs; home dialysis equipment, supplies, and periodic support services; laboratory tests; outpatient maintenance dialysis; outpatient physical therapy and speech pathology; and X-rays and radiation treatment. Some prescription drugs are now covered.

Permanent Kidney Failure

If you are insured under Social Security (or are receiving monthly Social Security benefits), and you, your spouse, or your children suffer from permanent kidney failure, Medicare Part B medical insurance covers the costs of maintenance dialysis or a kidney transplant. If anyone in your family suffers from permanent kidney failure, contact your local Social Security office to see if you are covered by Medicare.

Supplementing Your Medicare Coverage

Because Medicare does not pay 100 percent of your hospital and medical bills, you should seriously think about supplementing your Medicare protection. Most people on Medicare need to consider additional protection, but some don't. For example, low-income people who qualify for Medicaid (discussed below) usually can do without protection from a private insurance company. Many private insurance companies offer insurance plans to supplement Medicare. Before you buy from any of these companies, compare the prices of the policies and the benefits each policy offers, since the benefits and cost of a policy can vary widely from one company to the next. Social Security has a pamphlet—"Guide to Health Insurance for People with Medicare"—that you should read before buying a supplemental policy.

Medicare HMOs

Because of the restrictions on what Medicare covers—or more precisely, what it doesn't cover, specifically prescription drugs—some people choose to have their health services dispensed by a Medicare health maintenance organization (HMO). HMOs do their utmost to contain costs so they can make a reasonable profit while still providing competent medical services to their patients. (HMOs are discussed in more detail in chapter 11.) While some HMOs do provide a prescription drug benefit, there is usually a limit, and the drug ordinarily must be on the approved "formulary" list. What this means is that instead of getting the newest, most effective drug for your ailment, you most likely will be prescribed an older drug that is a generic version and costs considerably less than the newer, more effective drug. Plus, to see a specialist you must get a referral from your general practitioner, who generally has a financial incentive not to refer patients to specialists except in the most serious of cases. Additionally, your doctor usually will see more patients in a day than a non-HMO doctor, cutting down the time he or she has to listen to your symptoms, examine you thoroughly, and make a proper diagnosis.

SUPPLEMENTAL SECURITY INCOME (SSI)

SUPPLEMENTAL SECURITY INCOME—SSI for short—is a special program to help out aged, disabled, or blind persons with low incomes and limited assets. Although SSI is administered through Social Security, in many respects it is considerably different from retirement, disability, and survivors' benefits. For one, your eligibility for SSI doesn't hinge on whether you've earned a certain number of quarters of coverage ("credits"); you can be eligible for SSI benefits even if you've never worked a day in your life. And unlike Social Security, the money for SSI comes from the general funds of the U.S. Treasury, rather than from a special tax on earnings.

Who Is Eligible for SSI?

You are eligible for SSI benefits if you meet the financial limitations discussed below and are at least 65 years old; are any age and can't work for twelve months or more because of a physical or mental impairment (or you are expected to die from the condition); or you are visually handicapped—you cannot see better than 20/200 with corrective lenses or have a visual field of twenty degrees or less. (Even if your sight is not that bad, you may still qualify for benefits as a disabled person.) In some states, if you qualify under more than one category—if you are over 65, for example, and blind—you get the higher benefits—in this case the benefits for being blind. Your local Social Security office will help you to determine which category will give you the higher benefits.

To be eligible for SSI benefits, you must be a citizen of the United States, and you must be a resident of the United States or the northern Mariana Islands. SSI benefits have been severely restricted to lawfully admitted immigrants. You are generally *not* eligible for SSI benefits if you live in a public institution, such as a jail or certain hospitals. You may, however, be eligible for SSI if you live in a publicly operated community residence of no more than sixteen people. Temporary residents of a public emergency shelter may also be eligible for SSI payments for up to three months during any twelve-month period.

The Amount of Your Assets and Income

Since SSI is designed for people who have low incomes and limited assets, how much property you own and the money you make are of the utmost importance. Currently, you are eligible for SSI only if your assets do not exceed $2,000 if single, and $3,000 for a married couple. Things that are counted include any wages you earn, bank accounts, Social Security checks, alimony, cash on hand, workers' compensation benefits, retirement benefits, stocks and bonds, the cash value of any life insurance policies, insurance annuities, and real estate (other than your home).

Items that are *not* used to determine the extent of your assets include your home, burial plots for your immediate family, and, depending upon their value, your personal and household items, a car, and burial funds. Food stamps are not counted either. Although you can receive SSI benefits even if you also are getting Social Security benefits, you can't receive benefits from both SSI and Temporary Assistance to Needy Families (TANF) at the same time.

The standard federal SSI payment in 2001 for an eligible single adult or child was $530 a month, and for an eligible couple $796 a month. Your income (or the parents' income in the case of a child) for the month may prompt a reduction in the amount of your check. The first $20 of income you have each month usually is not counted, regardless of where it comes from. All "unearned income" (such as stock dividends or interest from your savings account) over the first $20 of income ordinarily will reduce the amount of your SSI check. But the first $65 of "earned income" (wages) you have each month is not counted against you in determining your SSI benefits. If you earn more than that in a single month, your SSI payment is then reduced by $1 for every $2 you make above $65.

If you think that you may qualify for SSI benefits, you should apply for them immediately at your local Social Security office. SSI benefits can only begin with the day on which you apply for them (or on the date you become eligible for SSI benefits, if that is later than the date you apply).

MEDICAID AND MEDI-CAL

MEDICARE IS A GOVERNMENT health program based on age (65 or older) or two years of disability. Medicaid (called Medi-Cal in California) is a government program that is based on financial need. Unlike Medicare, which is available to everyone over 65 or on Social Security disability for at least two years, Medicaid is a poverty-based, financial-need program which is based on the amount of your assets and resources and wages you earn.

Medicaid is a jointly funded, federal-state health insurance program for low-income and needy persons. It covers approximately thirty-six million persons, including children, the elderly, the blind, and the disabled, and people who are eligible to receive federally assisted income-maintenance payments. The federal government sets broad national guidelines within which each state establishes its own eligibility standards; determines the type, amount, duration, and scope of services; sets the rate of payment for services; and administers its own program. Accordingly, the Medicaid program varies considerably from state to state, as well as within each state over time.

Who Qualifies for Medicaid?

Generally speaking, the requirements for obtaining Medicaid are the same as those required for obtaining Supplemental Security Income, discussed above. Hence, if you are receiving SSI benefits, in most states you automatically qualify for Medicaid. In some states, however, the qualifications for eligibility for Medicaid may be more restrictive. Younger, impoverished persons are also eligible for Medicaid benefits if they are receiving Temporary Assistance to Needy Families (TANF), the successor to Aid to Families with Dependent Children (AFDC). These classes of persons (and a few others) are referred to as "categorically needy" persons.

Other categorically needy persons include:

* low-income families with children who meet certain eligibility requirements;
* infants born to Medicaid-eligible pregnant women (Medicaid eligibility must continue throughout the first year of life so long as the infant remains in the mother's household and she remains eligible for Medicaid, or would be eligible if she were still pregnant);
* children under six years old and pregnant women whose family income is at or below 133 percent of the federal poverty level. (The minimum mandatory income level for pregnant women and infants in certain states may be higher than 133 percent of the federal poverty level, if as of certain dates the state had established a higher percentage for covering those groups.) States are required to extend Medicaid eligibility under age 19 to all children born after September 30, 1983 (or such earlier date as the state may choose), in families with incomes at or below the federal poverty level. This coverage was phased in, so that by the year 2002, all poor children under 19 were covered. Once eligibility is established, pregnant women remain eligible for Medicaid through the end of the calendar month in which the sixtieth day after the end of the pregnancy falls, regardless of any change in family income. States are not required to have a resource test for these poverty-level-related groups. However, any resource test imposed can be no more restrictive than that of the TANF program for infants and children and the SSI program for pregnant women;
* special protected groups who may keep Medicaid for a period of time. One example of such a group is persons who lose SSI payments due to earnings from work or increased Social Security benefits.

States also have the option to provide Medicaid coverage to other categorically needy groups, such as:

* infants up to age 1 and pregnant women not covered under the mandatory rules whose family income is below 185 percent of the federal poverty level (the percentage to be set by each state);
* optional targeted low-income children;
* certain aged, blind, or disabled adults who have incomes above that requiring mandatory coverage, but below the federal poverty level;
* children under 21 who meet income and resource requirements for TANF but who are otherwise ineligible for TANF;
* institutionalized persons with income and resources below specified limits;
* persons who would be eligible if institutionalized but are receiving care under home and community-based services waivers; and
* tuberculosis-infected persons who would be financially eligible for Medicaid at the SSI level (only for TB-related ambulatory services and TB drugs).

The state has the option to have a "medically needy" program to extend Medicaid eligibility to additional qualified persons who may have too much income to qualify under the mandatory or optional categorically needy groups. This option allows the qualified person to "spend down" to Medicaid eligibility by incurring medical and remedial care expenses to offset his or her excess income, thereby reducing it to a level below the maximum allowed by that state's Medicaid plan. States may also allow families to establish eligibility as medically needy by paying monthly premiums to the state in an amount equal to the difference between family income (reduced by unpaid expenses, if any, incurred for medical care in previous months) and the income eligibility standard.

Eligibility for the medically needy program does not have to be as extensive as the categorically needy program. However, states that elect to include the medically needy under their plans are required to include certain children under age 18 and pregnant women who, except for income and resources, would be eligible as categorically needy. They may choose to provide coverage to other medically needy persons: aged, blind, and disabled persons; certain relatives of children deprived of parental support and care; and certain other financially eligible children up to age 21. In 1995, there were forty medically needy programs that provided at least some services to recipients.

The Amount of Your Assets and Income

As with SSI, generally a single person must have no more than $2,000 in assets and a couple must have no more than $3,000. (Remember from the discussion on Medicare above: You can still apply for certain Medicaid assistance as a qualified Medicare beneficiary [QMB] if your assets do not exceed $4,000 if you are single or $6,000 for a married couple.) Not all resources are counted, however. Your house usually is exempt, as are most of your household goods and personal effects, as well as your wedding rings, regardless of their value. One car is exempt, so long as its value does not exceed $4,500 (unless it is used in your business, in which case its value is irrelevant). Burial plots are exempt, as are irrevocable burial plans. Burial bank accounts of up to $1,500 are exempt as well. Assets used in your business, such as tools and machinery, also are excluded, regardless of their value.

What Medicaid Covers

Medicaid covers doctors' bills and time in the hospital, and—to the great delight and relief of many elderly—home health care services and long-term nursing home care (discussed in chapter 5), neither of which is paid for by Medicare. Other medical expenses that Medicaid pays for include part-time skilled nursing care; at-home services for persons who would otherwise be put in a hospital or long-term nursing facility; home-health and homemaker services provided by certified home health agencies; and prescription drugs.

Depending on the state, Medicaid also covers such things as clinic services, medical equipment, dental care, optometry care and eyeglasses, foot care, various diagnostic, screening and rehabilitative services, and the cost of transportation to and from your doctor, hospital, or other facility where you obtain medical care.

Receiving Both Medicare and Medicaid

Suppose you qualify for both Medicare and Medicaid. Must you make a choice as to which one to obtain? No. You can obtain both Medicare and Medicaid so long as you qualify for both of them.

When a person is covered by both Medicare and Medicaid, Medicare is the primary insurer and Medicaid the secondary insurer. That means that bills are first submitted to Medicare for payment, and what Medicare doesn't pay is then submitted to Medicaid.

Many doctors do not accept Medicaid coverage because they feel what it pays for medical fees is too low. Some states require that Medicaid beneficiaries join a designated health maintenance organization (HMO) or other managed plan.

SEVENTEEN

Contracts

*M*ENTION OF THE WORD "contract" often conjures up terrifying visions of endless pages of yellow parchment written in obscure legalese. Nothing could be further from the truth. Of all the areas of law, perhaps none is encountered more frequently in day-to-day living than the law of contracts. Contracts are everywhere. You've probably made at least ten contracts this week without even thinking about it. You made a contract when you bought your groceries at the supermarket. If you ate at a restaurant last night you had a contract: You paid money in exchange for food. Your savings account is the subject of a contract between you and the bank. Your credit cards are another example of a contract. Your electricity and gas are provided by the public utilities under a contract: You have agreed to pay them the going rate for the services they furnish. The same is true of the telephone company. In fact, when you bought this book, you entered into a contract. You gave the salesperson a certain amount of money and in return received this book.

What is it about the word "contract" that so intimidates the average person? Perhaps it is because we usually reserve its use for more significant things—buying real estate or cars, for instance, or employment contracts. But the general rules of contract law that govern your relationships are the same as those that protect your rights when you, say, hire a company to do extensive and costly home improvement work to your house. The law of contracts, as you'll soon discover, is one of the most methodical areas of the law. It flows logically and chronologically from the time an offer is made until the contract is breached or successfully and unproblematically concluded. This chapter gives you the information you need to understand your basic rights when making an agreement. After reading the following material, you'll never again cringe upon hearing the word "contract."

First, several introductory remarks about contracts are in order. Except for a few types of contracts (discussed below), an oral contract is just as good as a written one. But it is always preferable to have the contract in writing and signed by each party. The terms of the contract should always be spelled out with specificity so that the other party can't claim that there wasn't a contract or that the terms were different than those agreed upon. If it comes down to a lawsuit—even if it's only in small claims court—it's much easier to prove the terms of a written contract than those of an oral one. Plus, it is easier for the other party to claim there was no agreement where the alleged agreement was oral rather than in writing and signed by him or her.

We've all been warned never to sign a contract without first reading it. Just how important is this? It can be very important. Suppose you sign a contract without reading it and later discover that some of the provisions are different from those you thought you had agreed to. Can you get out of it? Generally not. You normally are bound by the terms of the contract you signed. So before you sign your next contract, take whatever time you need to read it carefully, and ask for explanations if you don't understand something. And if you don't get a satisfactory explanation, talk to a lawyer, especially if the contract involves a significant amount of money. Above all, don't feel pressured into signing a contract without being given the chance to read it.

MAKING A CONTRACT

FOUR THINGS ARE ESSENTIAL for a contract to be legally binding: (1) both parties must have the legal capacity and authority to make a contract; (2) there must be an offer; (3) there must be an acceptance of that offer; and (4) there must be "consideration"—something you give (money, for instance) or do (provide a service) in return for something else.

Legal Capacity and Authority to Make a Contract

Having "legal capacity" to contract means in part that you are old enough to make a contract. A minor (in most states, a person under 18; in a few, under 19) is legally incapable of making a binding contract. A minor who enters into a contract with an adult really has the best of both worlds. The adult cannot enforce the contract against the minor, but the minor can enforce it against the adult. The minor can reap the benefits of the contract while avoiding any obligations. If an adult sues a minor for breach of contract, the minor simply can assert his or her minority as a complete defense. One exception is that a minor is usually liable for the reasonable value of any "necessities of life"—food, clothing, shelter, and medical care—given directly to him or her. What happens after the minor comes of age? The contract can be enforced against the minor if he or she does not "disaffirm" (cancel) it within a reasonable time after reaching the age of majority. In a few states, however, the only way a minor can ratify (affirm) a contract after coming of age is in writing. When a minor cancels a contract, he or she ordinarily must return what was received (or what is left of what was received) from the other party.

Legal capacity to contract also means that you have sufficient mental capacity to understand what the contract is all about. A person who is insane (psychotic), mentally retarded, or suffering the ravages of Alzheimer's disease or other dementia, for instance, normally lacks the mental competency to enter into a contract. If a guardian has been appointed for a person, only the guardian can make contracts on his or her ward's behalf. Contracts made by persons who are lacking mentally are usually void and unenforceable. A number of courts, however, hold that if you don't know that a person is mentally incompetent, and the person doesn't exhibit bizarre conduct or do anything else to indicate a problem, and you fulfill your part of the agreement, you can enforce the contract against him or her. And, like a minor, a mentally deficient person still can be liable for the necessities of life that he or she receives.

A person who is so drunk or high on drugs that he or she doesn't understand the nature and effect of the contract is not bound by it. When the person sobers up, he or she has the option of canceling or ratifying the contract. If the person chooses to cancel a contract in this situation, he or she promptly must return any money or property received from the other party. (Of course, the person would be entitled to the return of anything he or she gave to the other party as well.)

"Legal authority" to make a contract is important when you or the person you are dealing with represents someone else. Suppose, for example, a friend asks you to sell her car while she is in Europe and gives you the necessary papers to transfer title. You now have the legal authority to make a contract on her behalf to sell her car. When you give someone the authority to make contracts on your behalf, you are the "principal"; the other person is your "attorney-in-fact." You have the "power of attorney" to act on that person's behalf. Powers of attorney may be oral or written. If the statute of frauds (discussed below) requires the contract to be in writing, as when real estate or personal property valued at over $500 is the subject of a purchase contract, the power of attorney permitting the agent to act on your behalf must also be in writing. In any event, it usually is recommended that if you are giving a person a power of attorney to act in your behalf in buying, selling, or doing something, that it be in writing.

Whenever you are dealing with an attorney-in-fact, ask to see written authority (preferably notarized, especially when real estate is involved) from his or her principal. And when giving someone the right to contract for you, put in writing exactly what authority your attorney-in-fact has. For example, if you're giving someone the power of attorney to sell your car for you, describe the car and state the lowest price that your attorney-in-fact can sell it for and the terms of the sale (cash, cashier's check, or money order only, for instance). That way, should your attorney-in-fact sell your car for less than you authorized or on different terms (such as monthly installments), the other party may not be able to enforce the contract against you if you object to it, as your attorney-in-fact acted beyond the powers you had given him or her.

The Offer

The first step in making any contract is the "offer"—a proposal to buy, sell, or do something in exchange for something of value. The person who makes the offer is the "offeror"; the person to whom it is made the "offeree." The offer may be preceded by "preliminary negotiations" in which one party feels the other party out about the price range he would be willing to accept for his goods or services.

The most important thing to know about an offer is that the proposal must be sufficiently clear and definite as to its terms. At least four things should be spelled out in the offer: the names of the parties, the subject matter of the contract, the price, and how soon the contract must be performed. In order to avoid problems of fraud and misrepresentation, which can give the other person a way out of the contract (see discussion below), the offer should accurately and honestly describe what you are selling or promising to do. If you forget to agree on when the contract is completed—the money given, the work performed—the law implies a reasonable time, usually no more than thirty days (see below).

Suppose Joanne tells Elizabeth that she will sell Elizabeth her $25,000 car for $1,000. Elizabeth goes to her bank and withdraws the money, but when she tries to give it to Joanne, Joanne refuses to take it, saying she was only kidding. Can Elizabeth hold Joanne to her "offer"? No. An offer made in jest is not binding if a reasonable person in the offeree's position would have realized it was in fact made in jest. The price Joanne was asking was clearly out of line with the car's value, and anyone in Elizabeth's position would have known that Joanne was not serious. But if someone makes you an "offer" that he or she secretly intends as a jest, but the offer outwardly appears reasonable and serious and you accept that "offer," a valid contract is formed. And even though, to a reasonable person, the offer would seem adequately fair, you cannot enforce it against the person making the offer if you subjectively knew it was made in jest.

When Does an Offer End?

To determine how long an offer is good for, first look at the offer itself to see if it states how long it is open. For instance, if Jane offers to sell you her car for $10,000 and gives you a week to think it over, the offer is good for one week. But what if Jane doesn't say anything about the time that the offer is open? When no time is stated, the offer expires within a reasonable time. What constitutes a reasonable time depends on the circumstances. Offers made face-to-face generally can be accepted only on the spot if no time limit is specified.

Suppose Jane told you that she'd keep the offer open for a week but the next day informs you that she's changed her mind about selling her car. Can you force her to sell you the car since the full week hasn't passed? No. Jane was within her rights to revoke the offer before you accepted it. But if you had given her, say, $100 to keep the offer open for the week, she could not revoke it until the week was up. You would have an "option contract" that allowed you to buy the car at the set price for the entire week.

What happens to Jane's offer if she dies or if the car is totaled in an accident while the offer is still open? The offer automatically ends. Similarly, if someone offers to sell you an animal, but it dies before you accept the offer, the offer dies with it.

Let's say that when Jane first offers to sell you her car for $10,000, you decline. A few hours later, though, you change your mind, call her up, and tell her that you'll buy it. She informs you that the price has gone up from $10,000 to $11,000. Can she do this? Yes; when you said no to the original offer, you rejected that offer and it legally died at that instant. There was no longer any offer for you to accept. When you called Jane later that day, you were making your own offer—an offer to buy the car for $10,000—that she was free to accept or reject. What Jane actually did was make you a "counteroffer." The legal effect of that counteroffer was to reject your offer of $10,000 and make you a new offer to sell the car for $11,000.

The Acceptance

Once there is an offer, a contract is made only if the person to whom the offer was made accepts it while it is still open. Normally, only the person to whom the offer is made has the power to accept the offer. If Doris offers to sell you her stereo system for $500, you and you alone can accept that offer. Suppose that Peter is also present when Doris makes you the offer. Can he accept it? No. If Peter hands Doris the money, Doris is not obligated to accept it. But when an offer is made to the public in general, anyone has the right to accept it.

An acceptance must be unconditional and unequivocal—that is, with no strings attached. Suppose Bert says to Andy, "I'll sell you my sailboat for $15,000," and Andy replies, "You have a deal, but only if you outfit it with a new mainsail first." Has Andy accepted Bert's offer? No. Andy has changed the terms of Bert's offer by adding a new and material condition. Andy's "conditional acceptance" has the same legal effect as a counteroffer; it terminates Bert's original offer and acts as a new offer, which Bert can accept or reject as he pleases.

A "grumbling acceptance" is one in which the offeree accepts the offer but makes a statement of dissatisfaction. For example, suppose Bill is interested in buying a 1955 Ford Thunderbird, a collector's item. In his part of the country, 1955 Ford Thunderbirds are a rare commodity indeed. After six months of searching the classified ads and classic car publications, Bill finally finds one advertised for $50,000, well above the going rate given the condition of the car. Bill says, "I think the price is outrageous and this is highway robbery. But I want one so badly I guess I'll have to pay through the nose for it." Bill then takes out his checkbook, writes out a check for $50,000, and hands it to the seller. Is the seller obligated to accept it? Yes. This is a classic example of a grumbling acceptance. Bert has purchased the car for $50,000 and his grumbling neither adds to nor takes away from the validity of the contract.

Unilateral and Bilateral Contracts

A "unilateral contract" is one in which someone promises to give you something or do something for you in exchange for your doing a specified thing. For example, if someone offers to sell you a table for $500, this is a unilateral contract: You accept the offer only by giving the $500. A "bilateral contract," on the other hand, is one in which both sides *promise* to do or give a certain thing. If the person selling you the table had said, "I'll sell you the table if you promise to pay me $500 next Tuesday," it is a bilateral contract: The contract is made as soon as you promise to pay the money next Tuesday. The distinction between a unilateral contract and a bilateral contract is not always an easy one to make, but it can be critical in determining the rights of the parties if a disagreement arises before both parties have performed their obligations completely.

Unless the offer states otherwise, you can accept a bilateral contract in person, over the telephone, by mail, or by telegraph, by promising to do what the offer requires, and your acceptance is good at the time it is dispatched via any reasonable means of communication. If you mail your acceptance, most courts hold that the acceptance is effective once you drop a properly addressed and stamped envelope into the mailbox. If you put too little postage on the envelope or make a mistake on the address, the acceptance is good only if and when it actually reaches the other person.

A unilateral contract is accepted only when you do what the offer calls for. For example, if Pam tells you that she will give you $350 for your bookcase if you deliver it to her house on Saturday, you can accept the offer only by delivering the bookcase to her house on Saturday. It is not necessary, nor does it have any legal effect, for you to say something like, "You have a deal; I'll be there Saturday morning." You don't have to say anything; all you have to do is show up at Pam's house on Saturday with the bookcase.

Suppose that Brad offers Gene $1,500 if he digs a hole for a spa in Brad's backyard—a unilateral contract. Gene can accept Brad's offer only by digging the hole. Does that mean that Brad can revoke his offer before the work is completed, even if Gene has started digging already and is, say, half done? No. Once Gene begins work, Brad must give him a reasonable time to finish the work and accept the offer.

Consideration: The Heart of the Contract

The final thing a contract needs in order to be legally binding and enforceable is "consideration." Consideration is something you give or do in return for something; it is the heart of the contract, the very reason for its existence. You give up something to get something. Suppose you buy a new sofa for $2,500. Your consideration is paying $2,500; the other person's consideration is giving you the sofa. Or suppose you get your car washed. Your consideration is paying money and the other person's consideration is washing your car. Money is frequently one party's consideration in a contract, but bartering goods or services is just as valid.

The amount of the consideration given is generally not important, except to the extent it bears on whether the offer was made in jest or whether it wasn't a contract at all but really a gift. If, for example, you pay $1,000 for a painting that is worth $15,000, the contract is binding unless the other party claims to have been "only joking" when he or she made the offer. In some states, contracts in writing are presumed to be supported by consideration and are therefore enforceable.

You can enforce a contract, but you ordinarily cannot enforce a gift against a person who promised it. For instance, if a solicitor from Community Chest, a charitable group, calls you on the phone, and you agree to pledge $500, are you legally obligated to pay that amount? Generally not. This is not a legally binding contract because, although you're giving something up, you aren't receiving anything in return. As it is only a gift, it cannot be enforced against you in court. Once you make the gift, you normally don't have any right to force the recipient to return it to you.

Sometimes a contract can be enforced against you even though you didn't receive any consideration in return for what you gave. Suppose, for example, that your niece wants to open her own business but doesn't have enough money. She needs $50,000 to get it off the ground but has only $35,000. You tell her that you'll give her the other $15,000. She signs a lease, buys the necessary equipment, and otherwise gets things moving. Can you back out of your offer now on the basis that you're not getting anything in return? No. You could have gotten out of it if you had told your niece you'd changed your mind before she signed the lease and bought the equipment. Since your niece relied to her detriment on your promise, it is only fair and just that you be held to your word. This is the doctrine of "promissory estoppel."

WHEN A CONTRACT MUST BE IN WRITING

IN ENGLAND IN 1677, a statute of frauds and perjuries was enacted that required certain contracts to be in writing in order to be enforceable. Because some agreements were more susceptible to fraud than others, they had to be in writing to protect the parties involved. If the contracts were not in writing, the courts would not intervene.

All fifty states and the District of Columbia have adopted versions of this law, which has come to be known as the "statute of frauds." The main types of contracts that must be in writing in order to be enforceable in court are:

* contracts dealing with interests in real estate, except for leases of less than a year;
* contracts for the sale of goods priced at more than $500;

* contracts that cannot be performed within one year from the date when the contract is made or that require services for the lifetime of either party;
* contracts in consideration of marriage, such as premarital agreements; and
* promises to pay another's debts.

To be enforceable, the written contract need contain only the bare requirements: the names of the parties; the subject matter; the price; and when the contract is to be performed. Most states require that the other party sign the contract before it can be enforced against him or her. (On the other hand, if you don't sign it, the other party can't enforce it against you.) A few states require that both parties sign the written agreement. The written agreement can be made and signed after an oral agreement is reached. But until the essential terms of the contract are put in writing and signed by the other party, you generally can't enforce it in court against him or her.

Under certain circumstances, a court will enforce an oral contract for the sale of goods for more than $500. If you've already paid for the goods, you can enforce the contract against the seller or at least get your money back. Conversely, if you accept the goods, the seller can enforce the contract against you; you can't take the goods and then get out of paying for them because the contract isn't in writing.

If your contract requires you to perform services for more than one year, after you do all that the contract requires of you, you can enforce it against the other party even though it's not in writing. If you've only partially performed, you can still recover the reasonable value of any benefits that the other party received from your work.

THREE-DAY RIGHT TO CANCEL

MANY PEOPLE MISTAKENLY BELIEVE that once they have signed a contract, they have three days to back out. This is true, but only in a very limited number of circumstances. The general rule is that a contract is valid and enforceable as soon as you sign it (or shake hands on it). If you then try to back out of it, the other party can sue you for breach of contract and recover damages for such things as lost profits. The three-day right to cancel (legally, "rescind") a contract mainly applies only to contracts that were made by door-to-door salesmen and certain home improvement contracts. Before you sign a contract, read if carefully—the back as well as the front—to see whether it contains a three-day right to cancel clause. If you can't find the relevant clause or don't understand it, ask the salesperson to show it to you or explain it to you. Don't rely too heavily upon the salesperson's explanation, however, since his or her main interest is closing the sale and he or she may say anything to consummate the deal.

If the contract is sizable, it might be worth spending $150 or $200 to have a lawyer look it over to see what protections you have. Remember, the company that wrote the contract is only interested in protecting its own rights, not yours. Plus having a lawyer review the contract before you sign it shows the company that you will not hesitate to get legal assistance to enforce your rights if the company tries to substitute an inferior product, takes longer than promised in finishing the work, does a sloppy job, doesn't complete the work, or otherwise breaches the contract.

Remember to review the contract with the lawyer *before* you sign it. If the salesperson says you have a three-day right to cancel the agreement but that right is not mentioned anywhere in the contract, you might not have that right. The salesman easily can deny ever saying you had a three-day right to cancel and expensive litigation might ensue. If no mention is made in the body of the contract of a three-day right to cancel but the salesperson says there is, have the salesperson write it in the contract and initial it before the two of you sign the contract.

MODIFYING A CONTRACT AFTER IT IS MADE

ONCE A CONTRACT IS MADE, it usually can be changed only if both parties agree; ordinarily, neither party can change the contract unilaterally. For example, if Jane has agreed to sell her car to Virginia for $10,000, then calls her several days later and says she's changed her mind and now wants $11,000 for the car, Jane is not entitled to the extra $1,000. Most of the time, even if both parties agree to change the terms of the contract, the change is not effective unless it is supported by new consideration—until the parties give or get something more than the original contract called for. So even if Virginia initially agrees to pay the higher amount, if she later changes her mind, she doesn't have to pay the additional money. Jane is already contractually obligated to sell her the car for $10,000. (Of course, because this contract is for the sale of goods having a value of over $500, it must be in writing and signed by Jane in order for Virginia to enforce it. If there were no written agreement signed by Jane promising to sell her car to Virginia for $10,000, Virginia would be out of luck. For purposes of our example, we will assume that there is a written contract.)

Nothing, however, would prevent Jane from calling Virginia and telling her that she wants to raise the price to $11,000 and in return will add four new tires. If Virginia agrees, she is bound by the new terms because she would be getting more than she was originally entitled to. Of course, Virginia does not have to accept Jane's proposal and can demand that the contract be carried out as they originally agreed.

Once in a while, one party can make a unilateral demand that the contract be changed. This happens when something comes up that neither party could have anticipated when the contract was made. Say that you hire Reliable Pool Company to put a swimming pool in your backyard for $30,000. Soon after it starts digging, Reliable discovers that instead of the typical dirt and clay found in the area, your yard has a protrusion of solid granite. Reliable informs you that it will cost an additional $7,500 to get the granite removed and that unless you agree to this extra amount, it will walk off the job. Is Reliable bound to do the work for $30,000 as originally agreed in the contract, the granite notwithstanding? Generally, no. In this case, Reliable can demand that the contract be changed to provide for the new difficulty, since neither of you could have expected it at the start. To require Reliable to do the work at the original price would impose a substantial hardship on the company.

A written agreement usually can be modified by an oral agreement of both parties, even if the contract expressly provides that it can be changed only by a written modification. A written modification normally is required only when the statute of frauds requires the original agreement to be in writing, or if a statute (a law passed by Congress or a state legislature; see chapter 25) expressly provides that written contracts can be changed only by written modifications. But even if a statute does require a written modification, an oral modification is valid and enforceable once it is completed. The other person can't then get out of the terms of the modification by claiming that the contract required all changes to be in writing. It is usually best, however, to put the modification in writing and have both parties sign it to avoid later misunderstandings.

Here are some examples of the rules regarding contract modifications:

1. Dennis hires Phil's Construction Company to add a new room onto his house. The original contract calls for a ten-feet-by-fifteen-feet single-story addition for $15,000. After the contract is signed, Dennis decides that he wants a larger room, with a bathroom. Phil tells Dennis it will cost $25,000 to install a fifteen-feet-by-twenty-feet room with a bathroom. Dennis agrees. In this situation, the modification is effective, since each party has given new consideration: Phil must now build the larger room with a bathroom, and Dennis must now pay $25,000 instead of $15,000.

2. Let's say that the contract for the construction of the ten-feet-by-fifteen-feet room addition for $15,000 is signed, and Phil has started work. Dennis now tells Phil that he wants an extra window in the new room. Phil refuses to do this because it would require considerable time and effort to change the plans and have them approved by the city building department, and work would be delayed several weeks while they waited for the framing. Dennis tells Phil that he will pay Phil a fair amount to cover the cost of the window and related expenses, but Phil still refuses to agree to the change. Phil does not have to accept Dennis's offer to change the contract and can continue work according to the terms of the original agreement. If Dennis tells Phil to stop working, Dennis will be in breach of contract.

3. Ace Painting Company agrees to paint Patty's house for $5,000. When the job is about half done, Ace tells Patty that it will finish the job only if Patty agrees to pay $1,000 more and threatens to walk off the job if Patty refuses. Telling Ace that it is "putting a gun to my head," Patty reluctantly agrees to pay the additional amount, since she wants the work completed before her family arrives for a visit. After the job is finished, Patty

refuses to pay Ace the extra $1,000. If Ace sues in court for the $1,000, who will win? Patty. She only has to pay the $5,000 as they originally agreed, as she is getting nothing more in return for the additional $1,000. The terms of the original contract entitled Patty to have her house painted a certain color with certain paint. Under the "modification," Patty receives the same thing, only now at a higher price. If Ace required Patty to pay the extra $1,000 before it finished the job, Patty could sue them in small claims court, where she would likely win (see chapter 19).

WHEN A PARTY BREACHES THE CONTRACT

A CONTRACT IS "BREACHED" when one party unjustifiably refuses to do something that the contract requires of him or her; if, for example, the work you contract for isn't done correctly or on time; if the other person refuses to pay you for work done; or if the product you bought is defective or not what the seller represented it to be. What are your rights when the other party is in breach of the contract? If the breach is a minor one, the contract remains intact—you must still do what the contract requires you to do—but you are entitled to be compensated for any damages you suffer from the other party's breach. If the breach is a major one, you have a choice: You can treat the contract as continuing and seek reimbursement for your damages, or you can treat the contract as completely breached, in which event the contract is over, you are relieved of your obligations under the contract, and you can demand compensation from the other party for the damages you suffer as a result of his or her breach.

When the other person is in breach of the contract, you have a few alternatives: You can forgive ("waive") the breach; you can agree to modify the old contract; or you can release the other person from all or part of the contract. In some situations, you can unilaterally cancel ("rescind") the contract and get your money (or whatever you gave for consideration) back.

Money Damages

When the other party to the contract breaches it, you are entitled to monetary damages to compensate you for your losses. The idea is to give you the "loss of your bargain" and put you in the position you would have been in if the contract had been carried out to the letter. For example, suppose Standard Paint Company agrees to paint your house for $4,000, then backs out on the deal, and it costs you $4,500 to get someone else to do the job. You are entitled to recover $500 in damages from Standard Paint—what it cost you extra to get the job done.

Now consider the opposite side of the coin: You are the painter and have a signed contract to paint the house for $4,000. The day before you start, however, the homeowner calls you and tells you that he or she has changed his or her mind and doesn't want the house repainted after all. The homeowner is in clear breach of the contract. How much can you, the painter, recover in damages? You generally are entitled to your lost profit. Say the paint and other materials for the job would have cost $1,500, leaving you with a net profit of $2,500. You would be entitled to recover the $2,500 damages in lost profit. What if you already had purchased the paint and materials for the job; could you recover the extra $1,500 for that as well? That depends on whether you can use the paint for another job. If you can, you can't recover its cost. But if you placed a special order with your paint distributor for it and no one else wants that color, then you can recover your cost of the paint as well.

When the other party breaches the contract, you must make a reasonable effort to "minimize your damages." Suppose you have an employment contract for two years and are fired without cause after six months. You must minimize your damages by attempting to find a comparable job—one doing similar work for similar pay. If you make no effort to reduce your losses, you may not get anything.

Suppose you buy a new mountain bike made by American Bike Company. The first time you ride it, the front wheel collapses and you are thrown to the ground and injured. The registration card that came with the bike states that if the bike is defective, American Bike's sole liability is to repair or replace it and that this warranty is in place of any and all other warranties. In accordance with the warranty, American Bike Company offers to give you a new wheel but refuses to pay for your medical bills and other expenses. Can American Bike do that? No. A manufacturer cannot disclaim liability for personal injuries resulting from the use of its defective products.

Say, though, that the bike broke down on your way to work. You weren't injured, but you missed work and were docked the full day's pay. Whether American Bike has to reimburse you for those lost wages depends initially on whether you saw the warranty disclaimer on the registration card before you bought the bike. A disclaimer is usually effective only when it is "conspicuous"—in larger or bolder type than the rest of the information—so that your attention is naturally drawn to it. A disclaimer in fine print usually doesn't count, so American Bike may have to pay for your lost wages. But if the disclaimer is in large bold type, American Bike may not have to reimburse you for your lost pay, since this is a purely economic loss.

Some contracts provide for a certain amount to be paid as "liquidated damages" in lieu of any other damages if either party breaches the contract. Many contracts for the purchase of real estate, for example, provide that if the buyer backs out of the deal, the earnest money deposit is forfeited to the seller as liquidated damages. A court will enforce a liquidated damages clause only when the actual damages are difficult or impossible to ascertain, and the amount of the liquidated damages is reasonable under the circumstances; otherwise the judge will ignore the liquidated damages clause as a prohibited penalty and invalidate the liquidated damages clause. Say you signed a contract to buy a house for $250,000, put down 10 percent ($25,000) and then change your mind a week later. The seller refuses to return your deposit on the basis of the contract's liquidated damages clause. If you sue the seller, who will win? You should. The $25,000 is clearly out of line with the seller's actual damages. The judge will most likely rule that the liquidated damages clause isn't really a provision for damages but a penalty against you, the buyer. Courts will enforce legitimate liquidated damages clauses, but never one that is really just a disguised penalty.

Specific Performance: Ordering You to Uphold Your Part of the Bargain

Sometimes the judge will order the party in breach to do what the contract requires of him or her, to "specifically perform." Specific performance is granted only when money is not adequate under the circumstances. Suppose, for example, you agree to buy an original painting from Gloria's Art Mart for $5,000. Before you pick up the painting, Gloria receives a higher offer from someone else and refuses to go through with your deal. Because original paintings are "one of a kind," no amount of money can really replace them. Unlike a mass-produced product, you can't just go to another art gallery and buy the same painting. You can therefore sue in court to force Gloria to sell you the painting for $5,000.

The courts often order specific performance when one party backs out of a contract that requires him or her to sell land to someone else. The law views each piece of land as wholly unique and different, even if the parcels stand side by side. So if someone contracts to sell you his or her house, then tries to back out and sell it to someone else at a higher price (or decides not to sell at all), you usually can sue to compel the sale of the house to you (see chapter 6).

One important limitation on specific performance is that a court cannot order a person to work under a personal services contract, because of the thirteenth amendment to the Constitution, which abolished slavery and involuntary servitude. For example, suppose Tony's Italian Restaurant hires an acclaimed chef to work for it for two years. After eight months the chef quits. The court will not order the chef to work for Tony's because that would amount to forced labor. But one thing the court can do is prohibit the chef from cooking for any other restaurant. The chef is given a choice: cook for Tony's Italian Restaurant or cook for no restaurant until the balance of the two years is up. The court could not, however, prevent the chef from working at a different type of job, such as selling insurance or repairing cars. In effect, the court can say to the chef, "You can do any type of work you want, but if you want to cook, then you can cook only for Tony's until the two-year time limit specified in the contract expires."

Rescission and Restitution

In some situations, a contract can be canceled ("rescinded"), and each party gives back anything received from the other party ("makes restitution"). This serves to nullify the contract; it is as if the contract never existed. An everyday example of rescission and restitution: Suppose you buy a pair of shoes without trying them on in the store. You get home, put them on, and discover that they're too small. You go back to the store, and since it doesn't have a pair that fits you, you return the shoes and the store gives you your money back. It is now as though the contract never existed: You have your money and the store has the shoes.

Before a court will order rescission and restitution, you must return or attempt to return anything you received from the other party unless it is worthless. One exception, however, is that if you received money from the other party, you can credit it against the value of any services you performed or any property you gave. You must offer to make restitution promptly after learning of the other party's breach, or you may forfeit your right to this remedy. Do you have to give the other party what you received if he or she refuses to return what you gave? No. You can make the other party's restitution a condition of your own.

Accord and Satisfaction

An "accord and satisfaction" takes place when you and the other party disagree on what the contract requires to be paid or done and then you compromise. The terms of the compromise, not those of the original contract, then govern your rights and duties. For instance, suppose you owe Harry money for some work he did for you. You claim the amount owed is $1,500; Harry claims it is $2,000. If you send a check for $1,500 and write "Payment in Full" or something similar on the back of the check, does that mean you don't have to pay the remaining $500 if Harry endorses the check and cashes it? In many states, yes. Because the amount owed is in dispute, Harry is accepting the "accord" by endorsing the check. It will have no effect if Harry crosses out the words "Payment in Full" and writes something like "Compromise not accepted" before signing the check; he has accepted the accord by cashing the check, regardless of what he writes on the check. Some states have changed the old rule, such that when the amount owing is disputed, writing "Payment in Full" does *not* act as a settlement and accord if the person to whom the check is made out crosses out the restrictive endorsement (that is, the "Payment in Full" or similar language) and cashes it. That person is still able to seek the amount in dispute from the other party.

Suppose that you don't dispute the amount owed is $2,000, but you send a check for only $1,500 and write "Payment in Full" on the back. If Harry endorses the check, will that release you from having to pay the other $500? No. Accord and satisfaction applies only if there is a dispute. When there is no dispute as to the amount owed, in most states, Harry can endorse and cash the check and still collect the remaining $500 from you.

When you want a check to act as an accord and satisfaction of a disputed amount, write on the back of it something like "Accepted as Payment in Full of the Disputed Debt Involving the Contract Dated _____, 20 _____." With it, include a cover letter stating why you feel you owe the smaller amount and informing the other person that by endorsing the check, he or she accepts it as an accord and satisfaction. Keep a copy of the letter, as well as the canceled check.

How a Judge Interprets a Contract in Dispute

What happens when you and the other party disagree on the meaning of a word or sentence and can't work it out yourselves? In resolving disputes of how the words and terms of a contract should be interpreted, a judge uses the following guidelines: The contract is construed as a whole. An individual provision, sentence, or word is read in relation to the entire contract and the expectations of the parties. Nothing is considered alone or out of context. Words are given their ordinary meaning unless a special business or technical usage is apparent from the contract. Previous dealings between the parties are taken into consideration, as are trade customs in appropriate situations. Doubts and ambiguities in terms are resolved against the party who prepared the contract, since that party was in a better position to avoid them.

A special rule applies to written contracts that the parties intend as the "complete and final expression" of their rights and obligations. This is the "parol evidence rule," which generally prohibits the judge from considering earlier agreements or understandings that would change the terms of the written contract. Under this rule, the judge ordinarily cannot look beyond "the four corners of the contract" to resolve the dispute. This rule does not apply to modifications made after the contract was signed, however. Judges are hesitant to rule that a contract is the final and full expression of the agreement and normally will do so only when the contract contains a provision to that effect and the contract lays out the whole agreement.

THINGS THAT MAY GO WRONG

Satisfaction Guaranteed?

Can you get out of paying on a contract if you're not satisfied with the work? That depends on the nature of the contract. Unless they explicitly provide otherwise, most contracts require only that the performance be acceptable to a reasonable person. If a reasonable person would be satisfied with the results, you cannot refuse to pay even if it wasn't up to your own standards. You can change this rule by specifying in the contract that you must be "personally satisfied" with the other party's performance. You can even provide in the contract (if the other party agrees) that it must meet with the satisfaction of a third person.

When the subject matter is personal, it must meet *your* standards, unless the contract specifically provides otherwise. If you hire a photographer to take wedding pictures, for example, you must be happy with the final product. If you aren't, you don't have to pay the photographer. (Of course, you won't get the pictures either.) It makes no difference that a reasonable person would accept the work. This is because the subject matter of the contract—the photographs—involves personal taste.

How Mistakes Affect a Contract

Suppose Molly sells you a champion male show dog for $2,500, and you have plans to breed it. After several months of failure at breeding it, your vet tells you that the dog is sterile. If Molly knew why you were buying the dog but didn't know it was sterile, you can rescind the contract based on your mutual mistake and get your money back. (If Molly knew her dog was sterile before selling it to you and knew why you wanted it, you would have a good case for fraud.)

Not every mistake is enough to justify rescission of the contract, however. It must go to the heart of the matter. For example, Susan has inherited her uncle's estate. She holds a garage sale to clear out what she doesn't want to keep for herself. One of the items is an old clothes wardrobe her uncle had for years. Because it is old and needs refinishing, Susan puts it up for sale at $50. You buy the wardrobe, take it home, and later learn that it is a rare antique worth several thousand dollars. If Susan finds out about this, can she demand that you return the wardrobe or pay more for it? No. This type of mistake is not enough to invalidate the contract because you got what you both thought you were buying: an old wardrobe. In the example with the dog, by contrast, you both thought that you were getting a dog capable of breeding, when in fact it was sterile.

Your Rights When a Contract Is Grossly Unfair

Sometimes a court will not enforce all or part of an agreement against you if it is "unconscionable"—grossly unfair and oppressive. Suppose you buy a sofa from Jack's Furniture Store for $1,500 on time payments. After paying off all but $100, you buy a china hutch from Jack's for $1,000, also on time. You pay Jack's another $500 and then miss a few payments. Jack's attempts to repossess both the sofa and the china hutch, claiming that the credit contract gives it this right. Can it do this? No. This is an example of a once prevalent practice that has been denounced as unconscionable—giving the seller an indefinite security interest in all property it ever sells you. You've more than paid off the sofa, and it would be patently unfair to let Jack's take it away from you now. The remaining security (the china hutch) is enough to protect Jack's interests.

Unconscionability can come in a number of forms: high-pressure sales tactics; a seller's unfair security interests or repossession rights; sales contracts that result in your paying much more than the product is actually worth (say three or four times its actual value); excessive penalties or charges if you default on your payments; or long, confusing contracts that can't be understood even by the average lawyer. Unconscionability is particularly important in consumer transactions, since the ordinary consumer has little or no bargaining power and is handed the contract on a "take it or leave it" basis.

Suppose you quit making payments on a time contract you believe is unconscionable and are sued. If the judge agrees with you that the contract is grossly unfair, he or she will do one of three things: (1) enforce the contract without the unconscionable provision; (2) limit the unconscionable provision to a more reasonable standard; or (3) completely refuse to enforce any part of the contract.

Fraud and Misrepresentation

Let's say that you buy a used car. The seller falsely states that it is a 2002 model, when in fact it is a 2000 model. The seller also tells you the car has only fifteen thousand miles on it, but what he doesn't tell you is that he disconnected the odometer for a couple of years, and the true mileage is close to fifty thousand. What can you do when you learn the true facts and the seller refuses to return your money? You can sue to rescind the contract and get all of your money back. You also can sue the seller for the tort of fraud (see chapter 10). If the seller honestly, though mistakenly, believed the car to be a 2002 model, you can still rescind the contract and get your money back on the grounds of misrepresentation: What you bought was not what the seller led you to believe you'd be getting. If you decide to keep the car, you can ask the seller to refund you the difference in price between the value of the car as he represented it to be and its actual value. If you paid $20,000 for the car (thinking it was a 2002 model), and 2000 models (the car's real year) in a similar condition were selling for $15,000, you'd be entitled to the difference of $5,000.

When you learn that you are the victim of fraud or misrepresentation involving a contract, you must take prompt action to cancel the contract, or you may lose your right to do so. For instance, if after you discover that the car is two years older than the seller represented, you drive it for another six months, putting ten thousand miles on it, you can't expect to cancel the contract and get all of your money back. But you still might be able to sue the seller for the difference in the car's value. If you want to cancel a contract, you should consult a lawyer as soon as you discover the truth.

Illegal Contracts

Contracts involving illegal acts or things (for example, contracts to kill someone or contracts to purchase illegal drugs or stolen property) are usually void and cannot be enforced in court. If a hired assassin fails to kill the targeted person, the person who hired the assassin cannot sue in court to enforce the agreement or to recover damages because the assassin breached the contract. Conversely, if the assassin does the job but the person who hired him refuses to pay him, the assassin will not be able to get a court judgment against him.

Knowingly selling, buying, or receiving stolen property is illegal, and contracts involving stolen property are usually unenforceable in court, unless you didn't know the property was stolen. Suppose Ted offers to sell you a Brand X car stereo system with CD player worth $750 for $500. Ted tells you that he has a brother in the wholesale business, but in fact Ted stole it from an auto stereo store. You have no reason to suspect the stereo is stolen, and you buy it. A week later the police confiscate your stereo, or it stops working. Can you sue Ted to get your money back? Yes. Because you had no reason to suspect that the stereo was stolen, you can recover your $500 from Ted. But if you knew or suspected that the stereo was stolen, the court would not let you recover your money, since you were a party to an illegal act.

Lending money at a rate above the lawful interest rate is usury. If you quit paying the excessive interest and the lender sues you, the court will not order you to pay the illegal interest charges just because the contract requires it; the lender can sue you only for interest up to the legal rate. And in some states, the lender forfeits *all* interest and can collect only the amount that was lent (the principal).

SPECIAL TYPES OF CONTRACTS

Mail-Order Contracts

Millions of products are sold each year by mail-order companies that advertise their wares on television, in just about every magazine, newspaper, and other publication imaginable, over the Internet, and through letters and catalogs sent directly to prospective buyers' homes and offices. Some mail-order companies have been in business for decades and enjoy solid reputations. Others seem to come and go every month.

Like any other big business, mail order has its share of consumer grievances. Of the millions of complaints the Better Business Bureau receives each year, about 20 percent concern products ordered through the mail, over the telephone, or on the Internet. The most common complaints are slow delivery, delivery of damaged goods, and problems with credit or billing. (Problems with credit or billing are discussed in chapter 18.)

When you order something by mail, telephone, or over the Internet, the seller must ship it to you by the date promised or you can cancel the order for a full refund. How soon must something be shipped to you? If the ad doesn't specify when to expect a product, you must receive it no more than thirty days after your order and payment have been received by the company, or thirty days after your credit account has been charged for a credit purchase.

If the company can't ship the product on time, it must notify you of the new delivery date. If that date is more than thirty days after the original date, the company must send you a prepaid postcard or envelope so you can let it know whether you wish to cancel the order. If the shipping delay will be less than thirty days, you can cancel your order only by sending the company a letter to that effect.

Anytime you wish to cancel an order, do so in writing and keep a copy for your records. If you cancel the order by telephone, follow it up with a letter confirming the cancellation. Keep a copy of the letter in case a dispute arises as to whether or not you notified the company.

When you cancel an order, the mail-order company must refund your money in full within seven working days after it receives your letter. If you paid for the merchandise with a credit card, it must credit your account within one billing cycle after it receives notice of your cancellation.

Suppose something comes in the mail that you didn't order. Do you have to pay for it or send it back? No. You can treat unordered merchandise as a gift and keep it without any obligation. (But first make sure neither you nor anyone else in your family ordered it.) The mail-order company cannot force you to pay for something you didn't order. If you want, you can offer to return the product unused—but only if the company advances the postage.

What should you do if the mailman or delivery service rings your doorbell and tries to hand you a package that is badly torn, crushed, or otherwise damaged? If a package obviously is damaged, you should simply refuse to accept it and send a letter to the mail-order company informing it of what you did and asking for another shipment. If you weren't home at the time and the damaged package was left on your doorstep or with a neighbor, return it to the mail or delivery service unopened. Tell them that you were not at home when the package was delivered and that you refuse to accept the package in such a damaged condition.

Now suppose that the package looks fine on the outside and you accept it, but when you open it, you discover the product in a thousand pieces. If that happens, immediately return the product to the mail-order company with a letter stating why you are returning it. You ordinarily will have to pay the postage, but reputable companies may let you charge the postage to its account, so call first.

Let's say that you open the package and the product is fine except for one thing—it's not what you ordered or what you expected. Perhaps a mistake was made in the order fulfillment department or in shipping; perhaps the product you ordered was out of stock so another one was substituted; or perhaps the picture of the product in the catalog or on the Internet misrepresented the product. What are your rights in this situation? You can return the merchandise to the seller, and the seller must give you a full refund and reimburse you for the postage for returning it.

If you feel that you are the victim of mail fraud, you can call the United States postal inspector's office to file a claim at (800) 372-8347. The necessary form is also available at your local post office, or can even be filled out and transmitted over the Internet at their website: http://www.usps.com/postalinspectors. Note that while the United States Postal Service Inspection Service cannot resolve routine business disputes between a company and its customers, it can act against a company or an individual if there is a pattern of activity suggesting a potential scheme to defraud. If your matter is urgent, you should contact your local authorities or the fraud division of your local district attorney's office immediately.

Advertisements

An advertisement, whether appearing in a newspaper, in a catalog, on television or the radio, on a website, or in a circular delivered to your home or office, is usually not deemed an offer, but merely an invitation for offers. By advertising, the retailer is just informing the general public that it has certain items for sale and is asking the customer to come in and make an offer. If a store advertises a twenty-five-inch stereo digital television set for $750, the legal effect of that advertisement is to notify potential customers that it has the television set for sale and that it requests an offer of $750. When the customer takes the television set to the checkout stand and hands over a check or credit card for $750, the store then accepts the customer's offer.

Does this mean that a store can advertise a television for $750, and then raise its price to $1,000 when you're in the store? Not at all. Although an advertisement legally is not an offer, many laws protect consumers from unfair, misleading, and outright fraudulent advertising practices. For instance, a store can't advertise a product at one price, then charge more for it in the store (unless the mistake was an innocent typographical error). Stores cannot advertise one item for sale and then substitute another of inferior quality at the same price or another one at a higher price ("bait and switch"). Unless the ad states that only a limited number of items are available at the sales price, the store must have a reasonable supply of the advertised item to meet expected demand. If you feel a company's advertisement is deceptive or misleading, you can complain to your local office of the Federal Trade Commission and your state attorney general's office.

Auctions

When you make a bid at an auction, you are offering to buy the item for a certain price. Someone else may bid a higher amount, which is a new offer to the auctioneer. In some cases, a minimum bid may be required. If no bid reaches this minimum, the item can be withdrawn from the auction. An auction can be held "with reserve" or "without reserve." "With reserve" means that the item will not be sold if the highest bid is not high enough. When an auction is "without reserve," the seller must sell to the highest bidder.

Suppose you make a bid but then change your mind. Can you withdraw your offer? Assuming no one has bid higher than you, you can withdraw your offer if the auctioneer hasn't yet accepted it. If, for instance, as the auctioneer shouts, "Going once, going twice . . . ," you yell something like, "I withdraw my bid," before the auctioneer's gavel comes down a third and final time and the auctioneer declares the item "Sold!" your offer is withdrawn. But if you change your mind after the auctioneer has called "Sold!" you generally are obligated to buy the item.

EIGHTEEN

Consumer Credit, Debt Collection, and Bankruptcy

*a*MERICANS LIVE on the "buy now, pay later" plan. In fact, living beyond one's means has become an accepted way of life. The federal government leads the way with deficit spending, so it is no surprise that the average citizen follows suit. But with credit come a number of potential legal problems. Laws have been passed to protect you when you are applying for or have credit. Laws protect you from creditor harassment if you fall behind on your payments. And if you find yourself so deeply in debt that you can't see a way out, you can use bankruptcy laws to get a new start in life.

Good credit is a necessity in today's society. It takes years to build up a good credit rating but only a couple of missed payments to destroy it. Reestablishing your credit can be a long, difficult process. Because of this, if you ever find yourself facing a problem with getting credit, you should take action immediately. There are a number of steps that you can take yourself, and those are discussed in this chapter. But if you find that you're not making any progress toward resolving the problem on your own, get to a good lawyer immediately. A lawyer often can help save your credit rating or at least minimize any damage.

A disturbing trend has been taking place in the last ten years: The number of young adults filing for bankruptcy has risen drastically. In 1993, only 1 percent of personal bankruptcies were filed by those 25 years of age or younger. By 1998, however, that number had jumped sharply—to almost 5 percent. One of the main reasons for this rise is the increased availability of credit cards to young adults. Previously, credit cards generally were not made available to young adults who were still in school, as the credit card issuer was concerned that since the students didn't yet have jobs, they wouldn't be able to pay the balances on their credit cards.

Today, however, applications for credit cards are found all over every university and college. The credit card companies rely on the students to make the payments with their student loans or other sources, including hitting up good old Mom and Dad. Even with the number of defaulting students factored in, at the interest rate they charge the credit card companies still are making considerable money off the majority of students who pay their bills on time. Plus, it sets the pattern for the student to use credit in the future, so that when the student finally graduates and gets a job, he or she will already be conditioned to charging things he or she otherwise could not afford.

CONSUMER CREDIT AND YOUR RIGHTS

If a Lender Discriminates Against You

Lenders mainly look at three things in deciding whether or not to grant you credit: (1) your ability to repay the loan, based on how long you have been working for your present employer, how much you make, whether you have additional sources of income, and the amount of your outstanding obligations (including alimony and child support); (2) your reputation for paying loans back—your "credit history"; and (3) your ability to pledge sufficient collateral as security for the loan so the lender can get paid if you default.

Sometimes, however, a lender makes the decision to deny or limit credit based on something that has nothing at all to do with your ability and likeliness to repay the loan. The Equal Credit Opportunity Act prohibits lenders from discriminating against you on the basis of your race, national origin, color, sex, marital status, religion, and age. It also prohibits discrimination against you if you receive public assistance such as Social Security, veteran's benefits, or welfare. If you meet the particular lender's basic standards for creditworthiness, your credit application ordinarily must be approved.

Discrimination often manifests itself as a refusal to lend you money even though you meet all of the lender's objective standards; discouraging you from applying for a loan; or lending you money on terms different from those given to persons of, say, a different race, with similar credit qualifications—lending you money at a higher interest rate or for a shorter period of time, for instance, or requiring a larger down payment when making a credit purchase.

Traditionally, much credit discrimination has been directed against women. If you are a woman, you cannot be denied credit or otherwise be discriminated against because you are single or divorced, nor can the lender ask you whether you plan on having any children. In fact, the lender cannot deny you credit on the assumption that you may have children in the future.

You are entitled to have alimony and child support that you receive from a former husband or the father of your child counted as part of your income, if you so choose.

If you are a married woman, you can apply for credit in your own name—either your married name or your maiden name—and the lender cannot turn you down because of your sex or marital status. Your husband usually cannot be required to sign the loan application if your income and assets alone meet the lender's standards for creditworthiness. You also cannot be denied credit because your husband declared bankruptcy, nor can your credit cards be canceled immediately and arbitrarily when your husband dies—even if your husband was listed as the "basic" cardholder and you are named as a "supplementary" account holder.

Another group that has been the target of credit discrimination is the elderly. Lenders had a history of cutting off or reducing a person's credit as soon as he or she reached a certain age, often 60. The Equal Credit Opportunity Act prohibits a lender from discriminating against you because of your age. A lender cannot refuse you credit or charge you more than it does others because of your age, nor can the lender close your account or require you to reapply for credit because of your age. The lender can, however, take your age into consideration in determining how much longer your income will continue at its present rate and what your sources and amount of income will be after you retire. Like anyone else, you have to demonstrate that you will have the financial wherewithal to make the payments for the term of the loan.

Your Credit History: The Fair Credit Reporting Act

When you apply for a loan (or an apartment, insurance, or some jobs), your credit history will be checked to determine whether you are "creditworthy." A credit reporting bureau compiles information from various sources—stores where you have charge accounts, the bank where you have your car loan or bank charge cards, and the like—and puts together a credit report on you. A credit report essentially is a list of your current and previous loans, credit cards, and other debts, and your record of paying them. The date each loan was made or each charge account opened is listed, as are the initial loan amounts or credit limits and the current balances of each loan or credit account. The amount of the monthly payment and other terms are shown also. Most important to the prospective lender and your credit rating are any delinquencies, including missed payments, past due accounts, whether a company has ever written off a loan, whether you have been arrested or sued, and whether you have filed for bankruptcy.

What rights do you have if your application is denied because your file at the credit bureau is incomplete or contains inaccurate information that indicates that you are a bad credit risk? The Fair Credit Reporting Act protects consumers from having inaccurate, incomplete, and obsolete information about their credit histories circulated. (Under the Fair Credit Act, a credit report is called a "consumer report," and the credit agency that furnishes the report is a "consumer reporting agency.") The Fair Credit Reporting Act mandates that bad credit marks—"negative information"—can be kept on file for no more than seven years, except bankruptcy, which can be reported for up to ten years. It also requires credit reporting agencies to adopt fair standards for gathering, maintaining, and reporting information concerning your credit. The Fair Credit Reporting Act applies only to consumer credit and insurance, and does not cover commercial credit or business insurance.

Credit reports are not available to everyone. Only people or companies with a legitimate business reason are entitled to see your credit report, such as a prospective lender, credit card company, employer, insurer, or landlord. This protects your privacy from being invaded by people who have no real need for the information. And credit reports must be obtained with your knowledge—although they need not be obtained with your consent. Someone who obtains your credit report under false pretenses or who uses it for an improper purpose may be subject to criminal penalties. You may also be able to sue that person for an invasion of your privacy.

You have a right to obtain a copy of your credit report from a credit bureau, which may charge you a reasonable fee, ranging from $1 to $10, depending on which state you live in. Most states permit credit bureaus to charge you $8 to $8.50 per report. There is no fee, however, if you have been turned down in the preceding sixty days for credit, employment, insurance, or a rental unit because of information in your credit file. The credit bureau must provide someone to help you interpret the information in your credit file.

You are entitled to one free copy of your credit report each year if you are unemployed and intend to apply for employment in the next sixty days; if you receive public welfare assistance; or if you have reason to believe that there is inaccurate information in your credit report due to fraud. In any event, you should order your credit report at least once a year to ensure that it is accurate and includes only those debts and loans that you have incurred. If you suspect that someone has stolen your identity and is opening new accounts and charging things in your name, you should get a copy of your credit report immediately. To get a copy of your credit report, call one of the credit bureaus listed below to find out how much it will cost for your state. If you have access to the Internet, you can go directly to their websites and find out what that fee is. You may also be able to order your credit report with a credit card using the credit bureau's website. Note that the information on the three major national credit bureaus listed below is not identical; one may include information that the other two do not have:

Equifax
P.O. Box 740241
Atlanta, GA 30374-0241
(800) 997-2493
http://www.equifax.com

Experian (formerly TRW)
National Consumer Assistance Center
P.O. Box 2002
Allen, TX 75013-0036
(888) 397-3742
http://www.experian.com

Trans Union
Consumer Disclosure Center
2 Baldwin Place
P.O. Box 1000
Chester, PA 19022
(800) 888-4213
http://www.tuc.com

The Fair Credit Reporting Act requires the credit bureau to give you the information without charge if you ask for it within thirty days after your application for credit is denied. If you wait more than thirty days to ask for it, the credit bureau can charge you a reasonable fee for providing the information.

If your credit report contains incomplete or inaccurate information, you should request in writing that the credit reporting bureau reinvestigate its information. (If the information is more than seven years old—ten if it's a bankruptcy—demand that the credit bureau immediately remove it from your file.) Also inform the credit bureau why you feel the information is incomplete or inaccurate. Once you have asked to have the information reinvestigated, the credit bureau must do so, unless the dispute is frivolous or not relevant to the report. If you do not hear back from the credit bureau within two weeks to a month, call it to find out what the results of its reinvestigation are.

If the information is found to be incorrect or cannot be verified, ask that the credit bureau immediately remove it from your file. Also ask the credit bureau to notify everyone who has received a credit report on you within the last six months that certain information has been deleted or corrected, which the credit bureau must do at no cost to you. After a few weeks have passed, you should contact those people or companies to determine whether they have in fact received the new information. If they have not, get in touch with the credit bureau and remind it of its obligation to furnish this updated information to those companies.

As long as your request for a reinvestigation is not frivolous, you can sue a credit bureau that refuses or fails to reinvestigate your credit history. You also can sue if the credit bureau fails to correct the information and forward it to companies that have refused you credit within the past six months.

Traditionally, credit reporting bureaus were not required to verify information before including it in their reports. They have been allowed to rely on the integrity of the company or store that reports the information. A number of courts now recognize that a credit reporting bureau cannot simply report any and all information it receives without making some effort to determine its accuracy. Credit reporting bureaus today have a duty to follow reasonable procedures to ensure the accuracy of all credit information they report.

What can you do if the credit bureau reinvestigates your complaint but refuses to change its records because it believes the information is correct? You can write a short statement (no more than one hundred words) spelling out your side of the disagreement and have it placed in your file. This statement must then be included in all future credit reports. You also can demand that the credit bureau send your statement to companies that have requested a report within the previous six months. The credit bureau must send a copy of your statement without charge to companies that turned you down if you make your request within thirty days of the adverse action. Otherwise you may have to pay the credit bureau a reasonable fee to send your statement.

The typical credit report contains only information reported to, say, department stores, banks, credit card companies, and the like. A report that includes interviews with third persons concerning your character, reputation, or manner of living is called an "investigative consumer report." You have the right to be notified any time a business makes an investigative report on your background, and the business must give you information about the nature and scope of the investigation if you request it. You also have the right to learn the substance of the information gathered for the investigative report, although the names of the sources of that information are considered confidential and need not be disclosed to you.

If a credit reporting bureau negligently or intentionally violates a provision of the Fair Credit Reporting Act, you have the right to sue the agency and collect damages, including punitive damages for a willful violation. If you win the case, you are entitled to have the credit agency pay your attorney's fees and court costs as well.

The Truth in Lending Act

The Truth in Lending Act—part of the Consumer Credit Protection Act of 1968—was designed primarily to let you know exactly how much a loan is going to cost. It requires the lender to tell you the amount being financed, the finance charge, the annual percentage rate, and the total amount of the payments. This information must be given to you before you sign the credit contract.

The finance charge includes the total amount of the interest charges you will pay, any service charges, and other costs. The annual percentage rate is the most important rate in determining what the true interest rate of the loan is. Suppose, for example, you are borrowing $5,000 at 10 percent interest for one year, and the lender requires you to pay all of the interest

($500) up front. Your net proceeds from the loan then amount to just $4,500. So you're really paying $500 interest on $4,500—an annual percentage rate of almost 11.2 percent.

The length of the loan will determine how much interest you will pay eventually, as well as the amount of your monthly payments. The shorter the term of the loan, the less you will pay in the long run in interest, but your monthly payments will be more than if you spread the loan out over a longer period of time. How long the loan should be depends in part on the size of the monthly payment you can afford.

Ordinarily, you are not required to purchase disability or accident or life insurance to pay off the loan in the event you are injured or killed and unable to meet your obligations. That insurance is usually optional and is more for the lender's protection than it is for yours. Before signing a loan application, make sure that the lender hasn't included an insurance premium if you don't want it.

Under the Truth in Lending law, if a company advertises some of the terms of a loan, it must advertise *all* important terms of the loan. For instance, if a car dealer advertises a car for $299 a month, it must also tell you how much the down payment is, what the annual percentage rate is, the length of the loan, the total payments, and the cash price for the car.

If a company violates the Truth in Lending Act, you can sue it for damages—including, in many cases, double the amount of finance charges—and for your attorney's fees as well. Criminal action also can be taken against companies in appropriate cases. Your local office of the Federal Trade Commission can direct you to the proper authorities if you suspect a criminal violation.

The Truth in Leasing Act

As an alternative to purchasing major items—especially cars, trucks, and sport utility vehicles (SUVs)—many people are deciding to lease them instead. The Truth in Leasing Act requires the lessor (the company that leases you the vehicle or other product) to tell you the basic facts about the terms and cost of the lease, in order to help you decide whether leasing is as attractive as it appears.

Before you sign the lease, the lessor must give you a written statement of the costs involved. This must include the amount of the security deposit required, your monthly payments, and the total amount of fees you must pay for license, registration, taxes, and documentation. You must also be given a written statement of the terms of the lease: who is responsible for repairing and maintaining the property; the insurance you are required to maintain on it; any warranties that come with it; and whether you have an option to purchase the property when the lease is over. Standards for determining what wear and tear on the product is considered reasonable must also be included.

The Truth in Leasing Act applies only to products leased for more than four months and that are used for personal, family, or household purposes. It does not apply to real estate (apartment leases, for example), nor does it apply to daily or weekly rentals of cars or other products.

There are two types of leases: "open-end" leases and "closed-end" leases. A closed-end lease usually costs more each month than an open-end lease, but at the end of a closed-end lease, you simply give the property back and walk away. (If there was an option to purchase the property, you have the right to do so at the agreed price.)

An open-end lease may cost less each month, but at the end of the lease, you may have to make an additional payment (a "balloon payment") when you return the property. The balloon payment usually cannot be greater than three times the amount of the average monthly payment, unless there is excessive wear and tear on the property. In the lease, the lessor will estimate how much the property will be worth when the lease is over. If, when you return it, the product is worth less than the lessor had estimated, you will have to make up the difference. If you disagree with the lessor's valuation of the property at the end of the lease, you have the right to have an independent appraiser value the property—at your cost.

Errors on Your Credit Card Statement

Sometimes an item that you never bought appears on your credit card statement. Or the price billed is more than what the price tag or sales advertisement said. There are other types of billing errors: the statement may show a wrong date of purchase (so you may wind up paying more in interest); errors in computation; purchases made by someone not authorized to use your credit card; and a failure to credit your account properly. Your rights when faced with a billing error are covered by the Fair Credit Billing Act.

If you suspect that your bill contains an error, you must give the creditor *written* notice within sixty days after the bill was mailed to you. You can telephone the creditor, but doing so will not preserve your rights under the Fair Credit Billing Act. Only a letter containing your name, address, account number, the dollar amount of the suspected error, copies of receipts and other documents supporting your position, and why you believe there is an error will preserve your rights. Keep a copy of this letter and supporting documents for future reference.

The creditor must acknowledge receipt of your letter within thirty days, unless it can resolve the problem by then. Meanwhile, you do not have to make any payments on the disputed charge. But you still have to pay any charges that you don't dispute. Interest on the disputed amount will continue to accrue until the matter is settled. If you win, you won't have to pay either the charge or any of the interest attributed to it. If you lose, you'll have to pay both.

While your complaint is being investigated, the creditor may not report you as delinquent to a credit reporting bureau, nor may it take any action to collect the disputed charge. It can, however, apply the disputed amount against your credit limit. For example, if your credit limit is $5,000 and you already have $2,500 in charges, and another $1,000 is in dispute, the creditor can apply the disputed amount against your credit limit so that you have only $1,500 credit available. The creditor also is prohibited from making any threats to damage your credit rating unless you pay the disputed amount. It can, however, report you to the credit bureau for failing to pay an undisputed charge and can even take steps to collect a delinquent undisputed amount.

Within two billing periods, but never more than ninety days, the creditor must either correct the error or give you a written explanation telling you why it believes the bill is correct. If the creditor made a mistake and admits it to you, you do not have to pay any charges, including any finance charges, on the disputed amount. If the creditor feels the bill is not in error, it must promptly send you an explanation of its reasons for thinking the charge is correct and a statement of the amount you still owe. You then are obligated to pay the disputed amount, as well as any finance charges that may have accumulated from the date when the item was first charged to your account.

Once the creditor gives you a written explanation of the charge, it has met all of its legal obligations under the Fair Credit Billing Act and can treat the charge as correct. If you still believe that the charge is wrong, you should pay the amount in question and write a short letter to the creditor, explaining your position. Ask that a copy of this letter (no more than one hundred words) be included in your file at the credit bureau and copies be sent to those persons or companies whom the creditor notified of the delinquency. If you continue refusing to pay, your credit history may be damaged. The creditor can report you to a credit bureau as being delinquent and can take action to collect the debt. The creditor must also report that the bill is being challenged, however, and must give you a list of the names and addresses of all persons or companies to whom it gave credit information on you. The creditor must notify these same people of the outcome when the dispute finally is resolved. If you wish, you can file a lawsuit in small claims court to have a judge settle the controversy, or you can seek the advice of an attorney.

Credit Repair Companies

Credit repair companies spring up from time to time that claim to be able to clear your credit report of all adverse information such as late payments, charge-offs, even bankruptcies, and leave you with a crystal clear credit report. These companies charge a hefty fee to do so—usually all up front, of course.

The plain truth of the matter is that these credit repair companies can do nothing more than you can do yourself, which is to dispute *factual* errors. They cannot get negative information taken off your credit report unless there is a legitimate reason to do so, such as the information is too old. Many of these companies stay in business only a few short months, just long enough to collect some hefty fees from desperate consumers and then they close up shop and move on to another town.

One trick of these credit repair bureaus is to obtain a federal employer's identification number (E.I.N.) for you, which does not have any credit history, good or bad, on it. You then are instructed to open a bank account using the E.I.N. as your taxpayer ID number and use this as your credit reference when applying for a credit card or a loan. This way, when the potential seller checks your credit, it comes back clean, as you have no history of bad (or good) credit information on it. Most lenders are wise to this trick and will refuse to consider extending you credit unless you give them your Social Security number as well so they can check your personal credit.

Your Rights If You Buy Defective Merchandise with a Credit Card

Let's say that Thelma Lou uses her A. B. Nickel Department Store credit card to buy a toaster for $45 from her nearby A. B. Nickel store. When she gets home and plugs the toaster in, it explodes. Thelma Lou takes the toaster back to the store, but they refuse to replace it or credit her account. Can Thelma Lou refuse to pay the bill for the toaster when it comes? Yes.

Under the Fair Credit Billing Act, if you buy defective merchandise with the store's own credit card, you do not have to pay the balance. Before you can do this, though, you must make an honest, good faith attempt to return the product or to settle the dispute with the store that sold it to you.

If Thelma Lou had bought the toaster with, say, her MasterCard or Visa, the outcome would have been different. When you use a credit card other than one issued by the store, you are not required to pay for a defective product only if the product cost more than $50 and the sale took place in the state in which you live or within one hundred miles of your home if the store is in another state.

HARASSMENT, REPOSSESSION, AND OTHER DEBT COLLECTION PRACTICES

CREDITORS EXPECT DEBTS to be paid in full and on time. If you miss a payment or two, you can bet that the creditor will take steps to collect it. First you'll get a polite letter reminding you that your payment is past due. If you don't respond with a check, other letters will follow, each firmer in tone than the last. The second or third letter may threaten to turn the matter over to a collection agency or to the creditor's lawyer. If you ignore these letters, you'll soon receive a letter or telephone call from a collection agency or a lawyer. And if that doesn't prompt you to pay up, you may find yourself being sued by the creditor. But there are limits to how far a creditor or collection agency can go to collect a debt.

Let's say that your debt has been turned over to a collection agency, and the collection agency starts calling you at all hours of the day and night, at home and at work. The debt collector calls you names and even goes so far as to threaten to call your boss and get you fired if you don't pay up immediately. Can you do anything to stop this harassment? Yes. A number of laws now protect you from creditor harassment and other strong-arm tactics. The most important of these is the federal Fair Debt Collection Practices Act, which protects you from "debt collectors"—persons who regularly collect debts for others. The creditor is not covered by this act, but states usually prohibit them from harassment and other excessive collection tactics. Attorneys who collect debts on a regular basis are subject to the provisions of the Fair Debt Collection Practices Act.

One thing that is quite common when you fall behind in your payments is a letter from your creditor asking for the full balance of the loan even though there may be, say, two more years to go. Suppose, if you will, that your loan calls for you to make twenty-four monthly payments of $100. After making six payments, you miss two. The creditor sends you a letter stating that you are in default of the loan and that it is accelerating all of the future payments, so that the entire balance of the loan—$1,800 plus interest to date—is immediately due and payable. Can the creditor do this? Yes—if the loan agreement contains an "acceleration clause" (which written loan agreements ordinarily do). Usually, though, if you bring the delinquent payments up to date, the creditor won't make you pay the rest at once. But if you don't make up the back payments, the creditor will most likely accelerate the payments and demand the entire amount, and take you to court if you don't pay it.

What a Debt Collector Can and Can't Do

A debt collector can contact you in person, by telephone, telegram, mail, or fax. If he or she contacts you in person or by telephone, it must not be at unusual or inconvenient times or places. A debt collector may not contact you before 8:00 A.M. or after 9:00 P.M. unless you agree to it. You cannot be contacted at work if your employer objects, and many state laws prohibit a debt collector from contacting you at work unless you agree to it.

A debt collector must tell you his or her name and cannot lie and say that he or she is from a credit reporting agency or is an attorney or government representative. Within five days after the debt collector contacts you, the debt collector must send you a written statement showing how much you owe and to whom. The debt collector must also tell you what to do if you don't think you owe the money. If within thirty days you send the debt collector a letter stating that you do not owe the money, the debt collector can contact you again and resume trying to collect the debt only if he or she sends you proof of the debt, such as a copy of the bill, credit card purchase receipt, or your returned check.

A debt collector is prohibited from harassing you or embarrassing you in front of others. For example, the debt collector can't keep calling you ten times a day, use profanity in talking with you, or threaten you with physical harm if you don't pay up. A debt collector can't call you a deadbeat in front of your friends or coworkers. The debt collector also cannot tell you that he or she will ruin your reputation if you don't pay up immediately. The debt collector can't threaten to call the police and accuse you of a crime if no crime has been committed. Nor can a debt collector threaten to take any other kind of legal action against you unless the legal action is permitted and the debt collector intends to take it. A debt collector also cannot telephone debtors without identifying themselves, nor can they advertise the fact that you owe a debt. The latter would be an invasion of privacy for which you could sue the debt collector and the company he or she works for.

Debt collectors may not misrepresent the amount of your debt or the involvement of an attorney in collecting a debt. Nor can a debt collector tell you that papers being sent to you are legal papers when they are not; similarly, he or she may not tell you that papers being sent to you are *not* legal documents when in fact they are.

The fact that you owe somebody money is usually a matter between only you and the person or company to whom the money is owed. A debt collector cannot tell your friends or coworkers that he or she is a debt collector and is looking for you to discuss a delinquent debt. A collection agency can't even send you a letter that notes on the envelope that the sender is a collection agency. The creditor may be liable for invading your privacy if he or she tells others of your debt.

A debt collector can, however, contact your friends and coworkers for the limited purpose of finding out where you live or work. They usually are permitted to contact each person once, but cannot tell them that they are looking for you because you owe them or the company they represent money.

Sometimes a creditor will sell a delinquent debt to another company for less than the amount of the outstanding balance. The creditor is relieved of the burden of trying to collect the debt, and the company that buys it will make a vigorous attempt to collect the full debt. Suppose that you buy a used car from Swift Jim's Used Car Company for $9,995. You pay $3,000 down, and Swift Jim's finances the rest. Soon after you get the car home, you discover the salesman grossly misrepresented the car: It's three years older than the salesman said; the odometer was turned back twenty thousand miles; and so on. After you unsuccessfully try to return the car to Swift Jim's, you quit making the payments. Swift Jim's sells the debt to Speedy Collection Services, and one of Speedy's employees—we'll call him Gus—contacts you. You tell Gus that you're not going to pay Speedy a dime because Swift Jim's committed fraud. Gus tells you that that is a matter between you and Swift Jim's, not you and Speedy, and that since Speedy is the legal owner of your debt, you'd better pay up immediately or face a lawsuit. Is this permissible? No. Although your debt can be sold to another company, you are still free to assert any legal defenses you have against the original creditor. So anything you could prove against Swift Jim's to get you off the hook can be used against Speedy. Speedy is guilty of an unfair debt collection practice by telling you otherwise.

How to Stop Debt Collectors from Harassing You

How can you stop a collection agency from bothering you? Simply by writing a letter to the collection agency telling it that you won't or can't pay the debt and to leave you alone. This bars the collection agency from contacting you again, except to say that there will be no further contact or that some specific action—a lawsuit, for instance—will be taken against you (but only if the collection agency intends to do so). This rule usually applies only to collection agencies and lawyers who regularly collect debts as part of their practice. The creditor (that is, the store where you charged the item) can continue contacting you, so long as it does not harass you.

If a debt collector continues to call or otherwise contact you even though you've sent a letter demanding that it stop contacting you, you should contact an attorney immediately to get the debt collector off your back. One nice thing about hiring a lawyer is that once your lawyer notifies your creditors and debt collection agencies that he or she represents you, your creditors and the collection agencies must deal with your attorney, not you.

Other things you can do when you feel that you are the victim of a debt collector's unlawful harassment or other misconduct is file a complaint with your state attorney general's office, as well as filing a complaint with the Federal Trade Commission (FTC) at: Consumer Response Center, Federal Trade Commission, Washington, DC 20580.

While the FTC ordinarily does not intervene in individual disputes, your complaint may indicate a pattern of possible law violations by this particular collection agency and the FTC will take action against it.

Repossession: Here Today, Gone Tonight

Can a creditor repossess the merchandise you bought with a loan if you fall behind on the payments? That depends on the nature of the loan. There are two types of loans: secured and unsecured. A secured loan is one that requires you to pledge something as collateral. For instance, when you buy a car with a loan, the creditor usually will require you to put up the car as collateral. The creditor has a "security interest" in the car. An unsecured loan, on the other hand, does not require any collateral. When you buy something with a bank charge card, it is usually an unsecured loan.

If you default on an unsecured loan, the creditor's only recourse (after letters and collection agency efforts fail) is to sue you, get a judgment, then collect from any assets or money that you have. But if you default on a secured loan, the creditor can repossess the collateral you pledged and sell it to pay off the outstanding balance. If the money from the sale isn't enough to pay the loan off in full, the creditor can sue you for the rest. Conversely, if there's any money left over after the loan is paid off—a rare situation—it must be returned to you. When, for example, you buy a television set from an appliance store on an "installment contract," the appliance store often retains ownership of the set until you make the final payment. Although this is a little different from a secured loan, the rules regarding repossession are the same.

Before your creditor can repossess the collateral, you must be in default of the loan. What constitutes a default usually is defined in the finance agreement. Failure to make payments is the obvious default. But depending on the terms of the loan, you can be in default if you don't keep adequate insurance on the collateral at all times (this usually applies only to cars); if the collateral is lost, destroyed, or substantially damaged; if you die or file for bankruptcy; or if you sell the collateral without the creditor's permission.

Once you default on a secured loan, the creditor normally has the right to repossess the collateral. In most states, the creditor does not have to go through the courts to repossess the collateral, at least not if it can do so without a "breach of the peace" (discussed below). Some states require the creditor to notify you that you are in default before repossessing the collateral and give you the chance to "cure" the default—bring the payments up to date, get insurance put on the collateral, and so forth. Other states allow the creditor to repossess it without notifying you that you are in default. (In practice, most reputable creditors will notify you of the default and give you the opportunity to correct it.)

The main restriction on a creditor's right to repossess something is that it must do so without committing a "breach of the peace." This means that the repossessor must avoid the possibility of a physical confrontation with you. If it appears that the repossessor will not be able to take the collateral without a physical confrontation, the repossessor must leave and try again some other time. It is also a breach of the peace for a repossessor to enter your home or garage without your consent. Some states also bar a repossessor from breaking into a locked car to repossess it, even if the car is parked on a public street. If a repossessor does breach the peace, you can sue for the damages you sustain, including any physical injuries to you or damage to your property.

All is not necessarily lost after the collateral is repossessed. Some states give you the right to cure the default by paying all outstanding loan charges—including interest, late charges, and penalties—and reimbursing the creditor for its reasonable attorney's fees and costs of having the collateral repossessed. You may not have much time to cure the default after the collateral is repossessed, so you should act quickly and call the creditor as soon as you can bring the payments current.

Lawsuits: The Ultimate Form of Debt Collection

If you don't respond to collection attempts or can't work out some repayment agreement with the creditor, the creditor may sue you. Unless you have a good excuse—for instance, the product you bought with the loan fell apart as soon as you got it home—there's not much you can do to defend the lawsuit. If you ignore the lawsuit—and many people do in this type of case—the creditor will ask the court to enter a default judgment against you.

After a judgment is entered against you, your creditor (who is now your "judgment creditor") will try to collect the judgment. If you pledged anything as collateral, the judgment creditor will get this if it hasn't already. The judgment creditor also can get at your bank account and other assets. Some property is exempt up to a certain amount: your house; a car (unless it's security for the loan); your business tools; personal and household goods; and life insurance and retirement proceeds, to name a few. The judgment creditor may be able to garnish up to 25 percent of your wages; rather than paying the money to you, your employer pays it directly to the judgment creditor until the amount of the judgment and costs of collection are paid off.

IDENTITY THEFT

CREDIT CARDS, ATM machines, debit cards—we are accustomed to using all of these without a second thought. But what if an identity thief gets hold of your name, card number, address, Social Security number, bank account numbers, credit card numbers, debit card numbers, etc., along with your personal identification numbers (PINs), and uses them to commit fraud or theft. For instance, the thief may use your credit card information to run up thousands of dollars in charges. Or the thief gets hold of your personal telephone card number and uses it to make hundreds, even thousands of dollars' worth of long-distance calls.

If any of these things happen to you, you may be a victim of "identity theft." How is your identity stolen? The thief may steal your wallet or purse containing your driver's license and other identification, as well as your bank and credit cards. Or the thief may steal your mail, including your bank and credit card statements, pre-approved credit offers, telephone bills, and the like. The thief may engage in "Dumpster diving," whereby he or she rummages through your personal or business trash receptacles looking for personal and financial data. (You may want to consider the purchase of an inexpensive paper-shredding machine to run through data containing financial information.) The thief may break into your house and ransack it, looking for personal information, or he or she may take personal information about you off the Internet.

With your personal information, the identity thief may call your credit card company and request a change of address, then run up charges to your account. Because the credit cards are being sent to an address other than your own, it may take a month or two before you realize that you haven't been sent a credit card statement.

The identity thief may also use your name, date of birth, and Social Security number to open new charge accounts in your name. The thief then uses the credit card to make purchases and when he or she doesn't make any payments, the delinquency is noted on your credit report. The identity thief may use the information to open a wireless telephone account in your name and run up hundreds, even thousands, of dollars in charges.

What can you do to minimize the risk that your identity will be stolen? Before revealing any personal identifying information, find out how it will be used and whether it will be shared with others. Ask if you can choose to have the information kept confidential. Be aware of your billing cycles for your various creditors. If a bill does not arrive on time, call the creditor to find out whether the address has been changed on the account and when the bill was sent out.

If the address has been changed, inform the creditor of this fact and have it changed back to your mailing address. Do not keep your PIN number with your ATM card or other cards requiring a PIN number. Protect your mail from theft. Instead of leaving outgoing mail in your mailbox for hours for your mail carrier to pick up, deposit all of your outgoing mail in a collection box or at your local post office. Promptly remove mail from your own mailbox after it has been delivered.

Do not give out personal information over the telephone, through the mail, or over the Internet unless you initiated the contact and know the business or person at the other end of the line. Do not give out such information over the Internet unless it is secure ("encrypted"). Identity thieves may pose as representatives of banks, Internet service providers (ISPs), or governmental agencies in an attempt to get you to reveal your Social Security number, mother's maiden name, your birth date, bank and credit card information, and so forth. Do not carry your Social Security card with you. Leave it in safe place at home and memorize the number. Give you Social Security number out only when necessary. When you are applying for credit for, say, a new or used car or store charge card, they will ask for your Social Security number. Ask how your Social Security number will be used, and whether it will be shared with other companies.

If you suspect that someone is using your identity to open new charge accounts in your name or to get loans in your name, you should immediately contact the three major credit bureaus and tell them to flag your file with a ninety-day "security alert," which requires the creditor to confirm your identification before opening a charge account or making a loan. If someone is in fact using your credit reports, you may wish to place a seven-year "victim statement" on your account, which requires the creditor to telephone you before issuing a charge card or loan in your name. The names and numbers of the three major credit reporting bureaus to call to report identity theft are:

Equifax
(800) 525-6285

Experian
(888) 397-3742

Trans Union
(800) 680-7289

If your identity has been stolen, there are several places you should call or write. First call the Federal Trade Commission's identity theft hotline toll-free at (877) 438-4338, or write them at: Identity Theft Clearinghouse, Federal Trade Commission, 600 Pennsylvania Avenue, NW, Washington, DC 20580.

They also can be reached at their website, http://www.consumer.gov/id/theft.

If an identity thief has stolen your mail to get bank and credit card statements, pre-approved credit offers, or tax information, or if the identity thief has filed a fraudulent change of address form with the post office, report the criminal activity to your local postal inspector as soon as you become aware of it. Your local post office can give you the telephone number of the nearest postal inspection service office, or you can get their number off the Internet at http://www.usps.gov/websites/depart/inspect.

This is a good time to request a copy of your credit report from all three of the major credit reporting bureaus. Credit reporting bureaus must give you a free copy of your report if it is inaccurate because of fraud. Review your reports carefully to ensure that no new credit accounts have been opened in your name or that no unauthorized purchases have been made to your existing accounts.

If any accounts, including credit card accounts, telephone numbers, and banks and other lenders have been tampered with, immediately notify them of the fraudulent charges. Remember that with credit cards you must make your request in writing pursuant to the pro-visions of the Fair Credit Billing Act. If an account has been tampered with, immediately cancel it and open a new one with a new PIN number. Do not make your PIN number easy for an identify thief to figure out, such as your birth date or last four digits of your Social Security number.

If you discover that credit card account addresses have been changed, close the accounts immediately. Likewise, if you believe that an identity thief has gained access to your bank accounts, close the accounts immediately. If your ATM card is lost or stolen, cancel it imme-diately and get a new card with a new PIN. If your checks have been misused or stolen, cancel the checks and notify your bank immediately. Also notify the following check verification companies: Telecheck: (800) 710-9898; International Check Services: (800) 631-9656; Equifax: (800) 437-5120.

The Identity Theft and Assumption Deterrence Act of 1998 makes it a federal crime when someone "knowingly transfers or uses, without lawful authority, a means of identification of another person with the intent to commit, or to aid or abet, any unlawful activity that consti-tutes a violation of federal law, or that constitutes a felony under any applicable state or local law." A "means of identification" includes a name, Social Security number, credit card num-ber, cellular telephone electronic serial number, or any other piece of information to identify a specific individual.

In addition to taking the steps outlined above, file a report with your local police or the police in the community where the identity theft took place. You may need this to send to a bank, credit card company, or other business if they require proof that a crime has been com-mitted.

Be aware that you must act quickly when you discover that your identity has been stolen, or you may lose your rights to sue the credit reporting bureaus for wrongly approving credit for an imposter. In one 2001 case decided by the U.S. Supreme Court, a woman named Adelaide Andrews alleged that her Social Security number had been stolen by a Santa Monica medical receptionist with the same last name, Andrea Andrews, who took her Social Security number off of a doctor's information form Adelaide was required to fill out. The receptionist moved to Nevada, where she used her real name but Adelaide's Social Security number, and was able to obtain a credit card and rent an apartment based on a credit report from TRW. Andrea then failed to pay her bills on time, damaging Adelaide's credit standing. Adelaide did not learn that Andrea was using her Social Security number to get credit reports until she tried to refinance her home. TRW issued four credit reports to Andrea based on Adelaide's credit history. Adelaide did not sue TRW for its alleged misconduct on the first two credit reports until more than two years had passed since TRW committed its wrongful conduct. The Fair Credit Reporting Act states that claims for damages against credit reporting agencies must be brought within two years from the date on which liability arises. Thus, the U.S. Supreme Court held that Adelaide was barred from suing for the first two credit histories issued by TRW, but could proceed with her lawsuit based on the wrongful release of the other two credit histories. Had Adelaide not attempted to refinance her home, it is quite likely that she would not have learned about the identity theft by Andrea for more than two years after TRW issued the last credit report and would be barred from suing TRW. This is another reason why you should get a copy of your credit history at least once a year. If you find that you are the victim of identity theft, you should hire a lawyer well-versed in this area to help you out of this quagmire.

WHEN YOU'RE IN OVER YOUR HEAD: REPAYMENT PLANS AND BANKRUPTCY

WHAT CAN YOU DO when your monthly expenses exceed your income, you fall behind on some payments, your creditors are hounding you, and a lawsuit seems inevitable? You have several options, depending on just how deep in debt you are. Running short $50 each month is one thing; being a few thousand or more behind and adding to this every month is quite another.

How do people fall into a financial abyss? For some the lure of easy credit is too much to resist, and they soon find themselves overextended. But more often than not, serious financial trouble arises because a worker is laid off or there is a serious illness that drains finances. Whatever the cause of the situation, the thing *not* to do is ignore it. Ignoring the problem will not make it go away; in fact, it *will* make things worse.

You need to take stock of the situation. First determine what your monthly after-tax income is: Add up your salary, interest from bank accounts, income from investments, alimony (if applicable), and other income that you regularly receive. How much money do you have in the bank and how much in "liquid assets"—things that can be sold quickly for cash, such as stocks and bonds? Next itemize your monthly expenses. Include everything: the mortgage or rent payment; the car loan; food; clothes; utilities and telephone; gas, parking, maintenance, and other car expenses; credit card payments; all insurance premiums—home, car, medical, and life; medical and dental expenses; and so on. Comparing the totals will give you an idea of where you stand.

Now separate your "necessary" monthly bills—mortgage or rent, food, utilities and telephone, clothes, car expenses, and insurance premiums—and deduct the total from your monthly income. The difference is how much you have left over to pay the rest of your bills. If it's just a matter of being a poor manager of money, a call to a legitimate credit counselor may be in order. One credit counseling agency that can be of assistance is the Credit Counseling Centers of America (CCCA), which can be reached at (800) 493-2222, or at its website, http://www.cccamerica.org. CCCA is a nonprofit organization that will work with you and your creditors in an attempt to make your debts more manageable. CCCA is a member of the National Foundation for Consumer Credit and the Association of Independent Consumer Credit Counseling Agencies. CCCA provides free credit counseling services to persons in financial trouble. They will work with creditors to stop or lower your interest rates, stop late charges and overlimit fees, reduce your payments, and often get the debt collectors to stop calling. They also can help you avoid your wages from being garnished.

There are other legitimate companies besides CCCA that can be found in the yellow pages under the heading of Credit and Debt Counseling. But beware: There are companies with similar names that are for profit, promise the moon, and deliver little, if anything, and charge you a small fortune in the meantime. Make sure the credit counseling agency you choose is a nonprofit organization, charges little or no fees, is a member in good standing of the National Foundation for Credit Counseling, and is accredited by the Council on Accreditation. This will help you to avoid getting ripped off by a nonlegitimate company that promises you everything but delivers nothing.

Voluntary Repayment Plans and Debt Consolidation

If things aren't too far out of hand, or your financial difficulties are only temporary—say, your layoff is expected to last only a few months—you can try to work out a solution with your creditors yourself. You can ask all of your creditors to accept a smaller amount each month for a longer period of time, or you can ask that each creditor agree to reduce the amount of the debt by a certain percentage, or both. All creditors should be asked to accept the same percentage of reduction. If you can afford to pay only 60 percent of the bills each month, then ask each creditor to accept 60 percent. Try to get each creditor to waive late fees and penalties. Sometimes you can persuade a few creditors a reprieve of a couple of months so you can pay off other creditors and make your debt more manageable.

Your chance of working out a voluntary repayment plan with your creditors is best if you contact them as soon as you start receiving past due notices. Speak to the person who has the authority to approve repayment plans, and discuss your situation frankly and sincerely. Tell why you can't keep your payments up to date and exactly what you can pay. You'll need to show each creditor the worksheet with your monthly income and list of expenses, and a schedule showing how much you propose to pay each creditor.

A voluntary repayment plan can work only if all of your creditors agree to it. If even one creditor balks at your proposal and sues you for the delinquent debt, then you may have to consider bankruptcy. You sometimes can bring a reluctant creditor into line with the others by mentioning that your other creditors have agreed to the plan and that you will have to file for bankruptcy if you can't work things out on your own.

Another thing to consider if you can't quite meet all of your monthly bills is "debt consolidation." Debt consolidation usually consists of exchanging all of your smaller debts for one large debt for a longer period of time. Rather than owing, say, five creditors a total of $20,000, you get one loan so that you owe only one creditor the full amount. The advantage to this is that your monthly payments are reduced over a longer period to pay back the loan. Where can you get a debt consolidation loan? Try your bank or credit union; you may not have much luck if you don't have anything to put up as security, however. You'll often have a better chance of getting a debt consolidation loan from a finance company, although the interest rate generally will be higher.

Bankruptcy

If your creditors don't agree to a voluntary repayment plan or if your financial condition is just so bad that there is no other way out, it is time to consider filing for bankruptcy. In 2001, a record 1.4 million bankruptcy cases were filed, compared with 298,000 in 1985, according to the American Financial Services Association. Part of the reason for this is that many workers have been laid off from their jobs, while others have seen the value of their investment portfolio drop dramatically. Plus, filing for bankruptcy doesn't carry the stigma it once did; it is now an accepted solution for persons who find themselves in a difficult financial situation.

There are two types of bankruptcy available to individuals: straight bankruptcy—called "chapter 7" because it is found in chapter 7 of the federal Bankruptcy Code—in which your assets are sold ("liquidated") and the funds distributed to your creditors, and chapter 13 repayment plans. (Businesses in financial difficulty can reorganize under chapter 11.) Bankruptcy proceedings come under the exclusive jurisdiction of the federal courts; you can't file for bankruptcy in a state court.

Filing for bankruptcy does not mean that you will lose everything you own. In fact, some people lose little or nothing of what they have and still get all or most of their debts canceled. This happens because most of their assets are completely or partially exempt from bankruptcy. Your house is exempt up to a certain amount. (In some states, such as Texas and Florida, your house is absolutely exempt, regardless of how much it is worth.) Your car is exempt for up to $4,500 (or no limit, if it is used for business) and household items such as furniture, appliances, and clothing are exempt up to a certain amount. Property you use in your business or trade is also exempt. Student loans, however, are *not* dischargeable unless you can prove it would be a substantial hardship.

Most people need to hire an attorney to represent them in a bankruptcy, since the forms and procedures are usually too difficult for the average person to handle alone. A good bankruptcy lawyer will see that all of your property that is exempt from bankruptcy is protected, so you don't part with something the law says you can keep. An attorney also will save you from having to talk to your creditors—something you have probably been avoiding anyway.

You can't protect an asset from bankruptcy merely by putting it in your parents' or a friend's name. Unless it is a bona fide sale—one for fair value, not a token sum—the court usually will void any such "sale" and treat the asset as though you still own it.

Let's say that you owe your friend Gail $5,000. You know you'll be filing for bankruptcy in a week or two, but you want to make sure Gail gets everything you owe her, so you use your last cash to pay her. Is this fair? No. If your other creditors find out about this, they can require Gail to pay the bankruptcy trustee (discussed below) the amount over what she should have received. For example, if each creditor is only going to get ten cents for every dollar you owe, Gail must return $4,500 to the trustee. That $4,500 then will be divided among the remaining creditors. Money paid to a creditor within ninety days before you file bankruptcy is called a "preference payment," which the creditor may be required to return.

Chapter 13 Repayment Plans

Chapter 13 involves a repayment plan in which you pay your creditors as much as you can. Sometimes this means paying the whole debt in smaller amounts over a longer period of time. It can also mean reducing the size of the debt as well, so instead of having to pay off the full $50,000 you owe (for example), you'll only have to pay $25,000. Can everyone take advantage of the chapter 13 repayment plan? No. You must have a regular income, unsecured debts of not more than $100,000, and secured debts of not more than $350,000.

A trustee appointed by the bankruptcy court will review your proposed plan to determine whether it is made in good faith and is feasible. Some of the things the trustee (and later the bankruptcy judge) looks at are: how much of each debt you plan to pay off; the length of time of the plan; your employment history; whether you have any hardships; how often you have filed for bankruptcy; and your sincerity and honesty. Most repayment plans must be completed in three years, but the judge can extend your plan to five years if you have a good reason.

Once the bankruptcy judge approves your repayment plan, each month you will send a check to the bankruptcy trustee, who in turn will pay each creditor his or her share. What happens if you can't make the monthly payments as required? You can ask the bankruptcy court to approve a modified repayment plan that is within your financial abilities, or you can consider filing for straight bankruptcy.

If you declare bankruptcy under chapter 13 and fulfill your obligations, at the end you are discharged from all debts provided for by the plan except: certain long-term obligations (such as your home mortgage); debts for alimony or child support; debts for student loans; debts arising from death or personal injury caused by driving while intoxicated; debts that are a result of your intentional conduct; and debts for restitution or a criminal fine included in a sentence if you have been convicted of a crime. As noted above, a discharge is granted only when you have met your obligations and repaid all of your creditors according to the repayment plan. Under some limited circumstances, however, you may request the court to grant you a "hardship discharge" even though you have failed to complete your payment plan. A hardship discharge is available only to a debtor whose failure to complete plan payments is due to circumstances beyond his or her control.

Straight Bankruptcy: Chapter 7

Chapter 7 of the bankruptcy code lays out the procedure for filing for straight bankruptcy. The purpose of letting you declare bankruptcy is to let you get a fresh economic start in life. In a chapter 7 proceeding, all of your assets (except those that are exempt) are gathered up and sold, and your creditors are paid off with the proceeds. Except for a few types of obligations (discussed below), once the bankruptcy is finished, all of your debts are discharged, even if your creditors get only pennies on the dollar. Most chapter 7 bankruptcies start when you, the debtor, file for bankruptcy. Sometimes a creditor files an "involuntary petition" to force the debtor into bankruptcy. Congress has been trying to pass laws making it more difficult to file for a straight Chapter 7 liquidation bankruptcy, especially for high-income wage earners, whom they want to put in chapter 13 and force them to make partial repayment of their debts, but their efforts to date have died in the Senate.

What Happens After You File for Bankruptcy

The moment you file for bankruptcy—whether chapter 7 or chapter 13—any lawsuits pending against you for the payment of debts are suspended automatically ("stayed"), and no new actions can be filed against you. Your creditors also are prohibited from contacting you or your employer or trying to make any attempt to collect the debts owed them. You must list all of your creditors on the forms filed with the bankruptcy court. If you don't list a creditor, the debt you owe that creditor is not discharged, and the creditor can sue you for it or take other measures to try to collect it.

Shortly after you file for bankruptcy, you must appear at a court-scheduled meeting of your creditors. At this meeting, the creditors can ask you questions regarding your assets and how you got so deeply into debt. For the average personal bankruptcy, the creditors' meeting is a mere formality, lasting only a few minutes. Most of the time, no creditors even bother to show up.

Not every debt is discharged when you declare bankruptcy under chapter 7. Debts that are not discharged include debts that the debtor does not disclose on the lists and forms filed with the bankruptcy court; student loans (unless you can prove hardship); child support and spousal support (alimony); legal fines, penalties, and restitution; court fees; debts for deliberate and wanton injuries to persons or property; punitive damages; and debts for the death of or personal injury to persons resulting from your driving while intoxicated.

A creditor or trustee may file an objection to the discharge of specific items on the basis that the debtor transferred or concealed property with the intent to hinder, delay, or defraud creditors, or destroyed or concealed books or records. Other things that may affect discharge include a debtor's perjury and other fraudulent acts, failure to account for the loss of assets, violation of a court order, or an earlier discharge in a chapter 7 or 11 proceeding commenced within six years before the instant bankruptcy petition was filed.

If you file for bankruptcy under chapter 7 and the bankruptcy court approves it, you cannot file for bankruptcy again for six years. There is no such waiting period after filing for a chapter 13 repayment plan. (And remember that, as noted earlier in this chapter, a bankruptcy stays on your credit rating for up to ten years.)

NINETEEN

Suing in Small Claims Court

SUPPOSE YOU RUN into a minor legal problem and feel that the other person should pay you, say, $1,500. You don't want to hire a lawyer, but neither do you want to forget about the $1,500. What can you do? You can file a complaint in small claims court and be your own lawyer. Small claims court provides a fast, informal, and inexpensive avenue to the judicial system when the amount of money involved is relatively small. It dispenses with many traditional legal formalities in favor of a simpler process that saves time and money. In small claims court, it may take as little as four weeks from the time you file a claim until the trial is held and the judge makes a decision. Compare this with the several years it often takes to get to trial in "regular" civil courts.

Most states prohibit lawyers from appearing in small claims court except in a few situations, such as when the lawyer files his or her own claim or is being sued, or represents a corporation that is being sued. But even in states that allow lawyers to represent clients in small claims court, most people represent themselves. The cases are usually too small to justify the expense of hiring a lawyer; it could easily cost you more for the lawyer than you'll get in your judgment.

Here are some definitions of terms we'll be using throughout this chapter: The "plaintiff" is the person who files the lawsuit; the "defendant" is the person being sued. A "complaint," or "claim," is the document that the plaintiff files with the court to start the lawsuit. It lays out the basic facts of the case and states how much money the plaintiff is asking for. The "answer," or "response," is the defendant's response to the complaint. A "counterclaim," or "cross-complaint," is a lawsuit the defendant files against the plaintiff. A "judgment" is the judge's decision in the case. (A decision by a jury is a "verdict.")

WHAT TO CONSIDER BEFORE FILING A LAWSUIT

A LAWYER CONSIDERS THREE THINGS before filing suit for a client: (1) Does the client have a valid "cause of action" against the defendant? (2) Is the case barred by the "statute of limitations"? and (3) What are the chances of proving the case and collecting from the defendant? Since you will be your own lawyer in small claims court, you'll need to consider these questions before you file suit.

Do You Have a Leg to Stand On?

Whether you have a legal leg to stand on—a "cause of action" against the defendant—is the meat of the lawsuit. If you have a cause of action, it means that the defendant has committed a legal wrong against you for which you can sue. If someone damages your car in an accident, for instance, and the accident was his or her fault because he wasn't paying attention and rear-ended you while you were stopped at a red light, your legal cause of action is for "negligence" (see chapter 10).

The other chapters in this book can tell you whether or not you have a right to sue in many situations. If, after reading the relevant chapters, you're still unsure about what your rights are, discuss the specific facts of your case with a lawyer first. Some lawyers offer a free initial consultation, and many others charge only $75 to $100 for a thirty-minute consultation, which may be all you'll need. Most areas have a Legal Aid Society, which provides low-cost legal advice for people who can't afford a lawyer.

How Long Do You Have to Sue?

You don't have forever to sue someone. Every state has a "statute of limitations" that governs how long you have to sue for various types of cases. In some states, for example, you have only one year to file a suit for personal injuries. If you let more than one year pass before you file your complaint, you'll soon find that your suit is time-barred. You can go ahead and file the suit, but the other side will see that it is too late and request the judge to dismiss your claim. If the other side doesn't spot it, the judge will see it is too late and will throw it out of court. Generally, you have more time to file a lawsuit based on a contract or damage to real estate than one for personal injuries.

You can find out how long you have to sue in your own situation by calling the small claims court clerk or going to your local law library and looking it up in the codes or books of statutes (many large public libraries also have these books). As a general rule, no matter what type of case you have, you should file your lawsuit as soon as possible after you realize that you won't be able to work things out with the other person without a lawsuit.

Special rules apply if you are suing a state or municipal government or one of its agencies or divisions. (Some states do not permit you to sue the government in small claims court.) You must file a "claim" with the proper government body before you can sue in any court, including small claims court. You may have to file the claim within as few as sixty days after the incident, or the claim will be barred unless you can show a good reason for not having filed it on time. Generally, most government agencies give you six months to file a claim with them. (Claims must also be filed if you want to sue the United States, but you can't sue the United States in small claims court. Suits against the United States can be filed only in federal courts—which do not have a small claims court division—not state courts.)

Where do you file the claim? If it is against the state, call the local office of the state attorney general. Call the county clerk or district attorney's office if your claim is against a county, and the city clerk or city attorney if your claim is against a city. They can advise you on how long you have to file your claim and where to file it. Usually they also will send you a standard claim form for you to fill out, complete, and return. Be sure to keep a copy of the completed claim form. If the government agency or division doesn't use a standardized claim form, then state your claim in a letter and send it certified mail, return receipt requested. Include your name, address, telephone number, date and place of the incident, a full description of your claim (why you believe the government agency or division is liable), and the amount of money you are requesting. You should usually hear back within sixty to ninety days as to whether your claim has been approved or rejected. If rejected, you normally have six months to file your suit.

Can You Win the Case and Collect the Money?

Will you be able to convince the judge that justice is on your side? If it's just your word against the defendant's, your chances of winning are less than if you have an unbiased witness by your side backing you up. Also important: Do you have any tangible evidence to show the judge? If you were involved in an automobile collision, pictures of your car may show how it happened. Likewise, pictures of bad construction work can be most helpful in a case against a contractor. If you bought a defective product from the defendant, bring the product to court, as well as your canceled check and the receipt for the product. Depending on the nature of your case, hospital and doctors' bills, repair estimates, and other documentation are also important.

One final thing to consider before filing your small claims court suit: How likely is it that you will ever collect a dime from the defendant? Nothing can make a victory as sour and hollow as the frustration of trying to collect from a person who has no money, someone who is essentially "judgment-proof." Consider the wisdom in the saying, "You can't squeeze blood from a turnip," before filing your suit. But even though the defendant can't pay now, you may be able to collect in the future. Judgments are good for at least several years, and you may be able to get the time extended if the defendant still hasn't paid.

Sometimes a defendant will threaten to file bankruptcy if you sue. What should you do? Go ahead and sue. Threatening bankruptcy if a lawsuit is filed is a common ploy of some defendants, from individuals to big corporations alike. It is unlikely that a lawsuit in small claims court would be enough to force a person into bankruptcy. But even if it did, you could still file a claim for your money with the bankruptcy court.

HOW MUCH CAN YOU AND SHOULD YOU SUE FOR?

GENERALLY, YOU CAN SUE only for money damages in small claims court. The damages can be for just about any type of case: someone dents your car; the dry cleaner ruins your jacket; someone refuses to pay you back a loan; you bought a defective product and the store won't give you your money back; and so on. In most states you cannot file a suit in small claims court to, say, get an injunction to prohibit a person from harassing you or maintaining a nuisance, nor in most states can you evict a tenant through small claims court. Many states do not allow cases for libel or slander in small claims court. If you are suing the defendant for taking property from you, the judge can order the defendant either to return the property to you or pay you its full fair market value (to the amount permitted in small claims court).

The maximum amount you can sue for in a single small claims court action varies widely from state to state. Here is a state-by-state rundown of the current limits:

Alabama	$3,000
Alaska	$7,500
Arizona	$2,500
Arkansas	$5,000
California	$5,000
Colorado	$7,500
Connecticut	$3,500
Delaware	No small claims court
District of Columbia	$2,000
Florida	$5,000 (county courts)
Georgia	Varies greatly across state
Hawaii	$3,500 (district court)
Idaho	$4,000 (magistrate's division of district court)
Illinois	$5,000 (circuit courts)
Indiana	$3,000 to $6,000, depending on circuit court
Iowa	$4,000
Kansas	$1,800
Kentucky	$1,500

Louisiana	$5,000
Maine	$4,500
Maryland	$2,500
Massachusetts	$2,000
Michigan	$3,000
Minnesota	$7,500 (conciliation courts)
Mississippi	$2,500 (justice courts)
Missouri	$3,000 (circuit courts)
Montana	$3,000
Nebraska	$2,400 (county and municipal courts)
Nevada	$5,000 (justice courts)
New Hampshire	$2,500
New Jersey	$2,000
New Mexico	Abolished small claims court in 1980
New York	$3,000 (justice courts)
North Carolina	$4,000 (magistrate judges in district courts)
North Dakota	$5,000 (district courts)
Ohio	$3,000
Oklahoma	$4,500
Oregon	$750 must be handled in small claims court; up to $5,000, defendant may have case tried in justice court
Pennsylvania	$10,000 in Philadelphia municipal court; otherwise $8,000 in district court
Rhode Island	$1,500
South Carolina	$7,500 (magistrate courts)
South Dakota	$4,000
Tennessee	No small claims court
Texas	$5,000 (justice of the peace courts)
Utah	$5,000 (district and justice courts)
Vermont	$3,500
Virginia	$1,000
Washington	$4,000
West Virginia	No small claims court per se, but small claims procedure for evictions and civil actions where claim does not exceed $5,000
Wisconsin	$5,000
Wyoming	$3,000 (justice of the peace)

Since these figures can go up every few years, if your claim exceeds the amount listed above, you should call the clerk of your local small claims court to learn the current limit before you file suit. If it's near the end of the year and you don't have a problem with the statute of limitations, you can ask the clerk whether the limit will be increased on January 1, and, if so, hold off suing until then. In many states, the maximum amount you can sue for is exclusive of interest and your "costs" (such as the cost of filing the complaint and having someone such as the marshal or sheriff serve it on the defendant).

Determining How Much to Sue For in Your Case

How much you should sue for depends on what types of damages are recoverable in your particular case. The following discusses the kinds of damages you can recover in cases that frequently make their way to small claims court: minor personal injury cases; property damage cases; breach of contract cases; and landlord-tenant disputes. In addition to the specific damages listed below, in every type of case you can recover certain "costs" if you win. These include the costs of filing the complaint and having it served on the defendant by the marshal, as well as subpoena costs to compel the attendance of witnesses (discussed below). Some costs are not recoverable, the main ones being the time you have to take off work to appear in court and your travel expenses to and from the courthouse. Neither are you allowed to recover any fees you may have paid a lawyer you consulted to help you to determine whether you did in fact have a case that you could probably win.

Personal Injury Cases

If the defendant injured you due to his or her carelessness, you can sue for all of your medical expenses (up to the small claims court limit), including ambulance costs, doctors' fees, hospital bills, the cost of any physical therapy, prescription drugs, the costs of a cervical collar or other medical equipment, transportation costs to and from the health care providers' places of business, and other medically related expenses. How do you prove your medical expenses? By showing the judge all of your doctors' and hospital bills, receipts for prescription drugs, dates of doctors' appointments and distances traveled to and from their offices, and the like. If a number of receipts and bills are involved, summarize them on one piece of paper, and attach the summary to the stack of receipts and bills, which should be arranged in chronological order.

In personal injury cases, you also can recover damages for your "pain and suffering." This is a rather nebulous term, and pain and suffering are difficult to put a price on. The judge will consider the type and severity of your injury in deciding how much to give you for pain and suffering. Many judges tend to use a set formula, such as two or three times the medical expenses. For example, if your medical bills were $1,000, the judge might award you another $2,000 to $3,000 for pain and suffering.

If you lost money because you couldn't work for a while, then you can recover damages for your lost wages for the time you were off work because of the accident. You can prove the amount of these damages by bringing in a letter from your boss or accounting director verifying the dates of your absence and the amount of wages you lost because you were hurt and unable to work.

In personal injury cases, you should also take into account your property damage, such as the damage to your car and its contents, to your clothing, and so on.

Property Damage

There are several rules for computing damages if you are suing for damage to or destruction of property. If something is damaged, usually you can get back the cost of repairing it; if it costs $1,000 to fix the damage, for example, that's what you will get. However, if the cost of repair exceeds the value of the property, the judge will give you only the smaller amount. For instance, if someone damages your sofa, and it will cost $750 to repair it, but your sofa is old and was worth only $250 before it was damaged, the judge will award you only $250.

If your property was destroyed, lost, or stolen due to the defendant's negligence, the judge will make the defendant pay you the reasonable value of the property at the time it was destroyed, lost, or taken. You can't get the amount it costs to replace the item today (its "replacement value"), however, unless you had just recently purchased the property new. Suppose Nancy takes her two-year-old stereo to a repair shop for a minor repair, and her stereo is destroyed due to the repair shop's negligence. Nancy paid $1,250 for the stereo system, and a comparable new one would cost $1,500 today. The question is, how much was Nancy's stereo worth when it was destroyed. Invariably, the parties will disagree on the stereo's condition. Nancy likely will claim that it was in excellent condition and still worth its original $1,250, while the repair shop will contend that it was worn out and damaged before it was brought in for repairing and was worth $250 at most.

Sometimes the judge will estimate how long the product would have lasted, then deduct a certain percentage for each year you had it. For instance, the judge could determine that the stereo would have lasted ten years from the date Nancy bought it, so its value declines by 10 percent each year. Since Nancy had the stereo for two years, the judge would deduct 20 percent ($250) of the original cost ($1,250) and award Nancy $1,000. (Nancy should have the original receipt, canceled check, or other evidence showing how much she paid for the stereo, especially if the defendant disputes what it originally cost her.)

Breach of Contract Cases

How much money you can get in a breach of contract case depends on the situation. For instance, if the defendant breached a contract to sell you his or her car for $5,000, and you wound up paying $7,500 for a similar car in like condition, you can collect $2,500. If a painter walked off the job and it cost you $500 over and above what you were going to pay the first painter to get the job finished, you can recover $500 from the first painter. If you did some work for the defendant but didn't get paid, you can recover the contract amount. Other ways of determining your damages in breach of contract cases are discussed in chapter 17.

If your case involves a written contract, take a close look at the contract to see what other damages are recoverable. For example, the contract may provide that the defendant has to pay you interest on the money from the day it should have been paid to you.

Landlord-Tenant Cases

The two kinds of suits filed most frequently in small claims court by tenants against land-lords are for failing to return the tenant's security or cleaning deposit after the tenant has moved out, and for the cost of having something repaired that the landlord either refused or neglected to fix despite repeated requests of the tenant. Chapter 7 discusses the tenant's right to the return of the full security and cleaning deposit, except for a reasonable amount to cover repairing or cleaning the apartment for damage or dirt that exceeds normal wear and tear. The tenant also is entitled to recover interest on the money from the date when the deposit should have been returned. In some states, the tenant can recover two or three times the amount of the security deposit if the landlord unjustifiably refuses to return it or if the landlord does not send the tenant an itemized expense list showing how the security deposit was applied within, say, two weeks of the tenant's moving out. In repair cases, you can recover the cost of having the problem repaired or, if you did it yourself, the cost of the materials and supplies, but not your own time and labor in fixing it.

What to Consider If Your Damages Are over the Limit

Suppose the small claims limit in your state is $2,500, but the defendant owes you $3,500 for damage done to your car. Can you file two suits—say, one for $2,500 and the other for $1,000? No. You cannot split a single claim. But if the defendant owes you $3,500 from two separate transactions—for instance, you lent her $2,000 on one occasion and $1,500 on another—then you can file two separate claims.

Let's assume that the small claims limit in your state is $5,000 and the damage the defendant did to your car was $6,000. Should you file in small claims court for $5,000 and forget about the other $1,000? Or should you hire a lawyer to file in a higher court for the full $6,000? In such a situation, you're often better off filing in small claims court and forgetting about the $1,000 that is over the limit. Why? Because by the time the lawyer gets paid his or her share, you'll probably end up with less than $4,000. For instance, suppose your agreement with the lawyer calls for the lawyer to receive one-third of everything he or she recovers for you. If the lawyer manages to collect the full $6,000 for you, one-third of that is $2,000. You would be left with $4,000, *a thousand dollars less than what you would have gotten if you had done it yourself.* And many lawyers charge 40 percent if they have to take the case to trial.

Another factor to consider is the time limits involved. With a small claims action, your case usually is heard within no more than two months of filing the complaint and serving it on the defendant. In "regular" courts, however, the wheels of justice grind much more slowly, and it might take you a year or even longer to get to trial.

Nonetheless, if your damages are over the small claims court limit, you should seriously consider talking to a lawyer about representing you and suing in regular court. If a written contract is involved, read it carefully to see whether it provides for the payment of attorney's fees to the winning party. Also, some small claims courts that permit a lawyer to represent the claimant provide for the payment of attorney's fees by the losing party. Even if you decide not to have a lawyer represent you in court, it wouldn't hurt to consult a lawyer and have him or her write a letter or two on your behalf to the other party. This may be enough to show the other side that you are serious about pursuing your rights and move him or her to pay you. And in some cases, especially those involving personal injuries, the lawyer may feel that the case is worth much more than you have estimated. By having the lawyer represent you in such a case, your eventual recovery—even after paying the lawyer's fees—might be significantly more than what you could have recovered by yourself in small claims court.

MAKING A DEMAND FOR THE MONEY

You've decided how much you're going to sue the defendant for. Is there anything else you need to do before you file your complaint in small claims court? Yes. You must make a "formal demand" on the defendant to pay you the money. Do this by sending the defendant a letter that states how much money you are asking for and why you believe you are entitled to it. Include the relevant facts and dates, and send a copy of any documents, such as the contract, a repair estimate, doctors' bills, etc., to support the amount of damages you're claiming. The demand letter should give the defendant ten days to respond. Remember to keep a copy of all letters to show the judge at the trial. Also remember to send copies of the estimates, bills, receipts, etc., and keep the originals.

Do you need to send the letter by certified mail, with a return receipt requested? Usually not. But how will you know if the defendant ever received the letter if you never get a response? The law presumes that a letter properly addressed and with sufficient postage was delivered to the addressee in due course. Small claims court judges have heard the excuse, "But Your Honor, I never received the letter," so many times they rarely believe it. One problem with sending a certified letter with a return receipt requested is that the defendant may refuse to accept it. If you want a record from the post office that you mailed the letter but don't want to risk having the defendant refuse it, ask the post office for a "Certificate of Mailing." You'll have proof that you sent the defendant the letter, and the defendant will be none the wiser. Here is an example of a demand letter:

Ms. Ashley Smith
123 Zeus Way
Hometown, USA

Mr. Bill Jackson
9876 First Avenue
Bayside, USA

March 3, 2004

Dear Mr. Jackson:

I hereby demand that you pay me the sum of $3,500 for the damages you did to my car by your negligent driving on February 15, 2004.

This demand is based on the fact that while my car was stopped at the stop sign at Broadway and Main you rear-ended me and caused damage to the back end of my car. I am enclosing a copy of the police report, which shows that you were clearly at fault for this accident.

As proof of the amount of the damage, I am enclosing copies of estimates I received, one from Acme Auto Body Shop for $4,000, and one from Ray's Body Shop for $3,500.

Please send a cashier's check or money order payable to me for $3,500 by March 13, 2004, ten days from the date of this letter.

Sincerely,
Ashley Smith

Try to Settle Out of Court

The defendant's response, if any, to your demand letter will determine your next step. If you don't receive a response or if the defendant replies that he or she will not pay you anything, then you have no choice but to file in small claims court or forget the whole thing. Alternatively, you might consider having a lawyer write a letter or two on your behalf.

What if the defendant expresses an interest in settling the matter, but doesn't want to pay the full amount? If, for instance, the damage to your car is $3,500, and the defendant offers you $2,500, should you take it? That depends on how good of a case you have. If the defendant rear-ended you, in almost every case that is due to the defendant's negligence. In such a case, you would probably not want to settle the case but proceed to trial. However, if the accident arose from the two of you trying to merge into the same lane at the same time, then liability may be closer to fifty-fifty, and it might be advisable to accept the $2,500. You'll have a much better chance of settling the case if you are flexible and willing to compromise. It's usually worth it to settle the case for a few hundred dollars less and get the money in your hands today. How low you should be willing to go in order to settle depends on the facts of your case, especially on how clear the defendant's fault is. Unless the question of who is at fault is "iffy," you normally shouldn't settle for less than 75 or 80 percent of what the fair damages are.

Sometimes the defendant doesn't dispute the fact that he or she owes the money but claims that he or she can't pay you right now. In this case, offer to let the defendant pay you, say, 25 percent or more now (as much as he or she can) and then make monthly payments for the balance. For instance, suppose the defendant owes you $1,000, but doesn't have the money to pay you right now. Have him or her pay, say, $400 down and make six monthly payments of $100. If the defendant agrees to this, put it in writing and have him or her sign the agreement. Include a clause stating that if a monthly payment is more than ten days late, the entire balance becomes due immediately. That way, if the defendant doesn't make a payment or two, you can go into court and sue the defendant for the full unpaid balance.

FILLING OUT, FILING, AND SERVING THE COMPLAINT

You can get the proper forms to file the summons and complaint ("claim" or "petition" in some states) from the small claims court clerk. You should also ask the clerk if they have a pamphlet on small claims court. This contains important procedural information, such as how much you can sue for, how soon before the court hearing you must serve the defendant with the complaint, and other important information so you won't have to call the clerk every time you have a question.

The forms are usually brief and easy to fill out. The information asked for is the bare minimum: your name, address, and telephone number; the defendant's name and address; a brief summary of the case (usually just a couple of sentences); and how much money you're asking for. If a written contract is involved, attach a copy of it to the complaint. You may also want to attach a copy of estimates (in automobile cases, many judges require you to submit two estimates), invoices, medical bills, or anything else that shows your right to recover the amount requested.

Whom Should You Sue?

One problem you may face is whom to sue. If more than one person is involved, consider suing all of them. If you were injured in an automobile accident, for instance, and the person driving the car was not the owner, consider suing both the owner and the driver (see chapter 2). If at the time of the accident you didn't ask the driver to show you the registration form, and he or she refuses to send you a copy, you can find out who the registered owner is by contacting the department of motor vehicles.

If you are suing a business, you will want to find out who the owner is. For example, "Speedy Cleaners" may be owned by Cindy Edwards. You should state the owner's name and the business's name on your complaint this way: "Cindy Edwards, doing business as (or simply "dba") Speedy Cleaners." If the business is operated by a partnership, you should name each partner as a defendant, as well as the partnership itself: "Acme Repair Shop, a partnership, and Joe Brown and Sue Green, individually and as partners." Where do you find out who the owner of a business is? You can find out the names and addresses of the owners of a business by checking the "fictitious business statement" records of the county records of the county clerk in the county where the business is located. You might also be able to get this information from the city's business licensing bureau.

If the business is a corporation, you normally must sue the corporation in its name alone because it is deemed a separate, "living" legal entity. (You can still sue the particular individual who harmed you.) Call the corporations department of the secretary of state for your particular state and ask for the name and address of the corporation's "agent for service of process" (the person who is authorized to accept legal complaints filed against the corporation).

Where to File the Complaint

Once you've filled out the complaint, you'll have to file it with the small claims court clerk. But which court should you file it in, the one closest to you or the one closest to the defendant? Where you can or must file your complaint depends on the type of case you have. If you're suing for personal injuries or property damage, you can file your complaint in the county or judicial district where the defendant lives or has his or her principal place of business, or the county or judicial district where the accident occurred. For example, suppose that a defendant who lives in Lincoln County hits your car in Orange County. You live in Washington County. You can sue in either Orange County—where the accident occurred—or Lincoln County—where the defendant lives. You cannot sue in Washington County just because you live there.

For cases based on a contract, you can file suit in the county or judicial district where the defendant lives or has his or her business; where the defendant signed the contract; or where the subject matter of the contract was to be performed. For example, if you had some construction work done on your summer cottage in Adams County, and the defendant signed the contract at his office in Jefferson County (where he also lives), you could file the complaint in the small claims court in either Adams County or Jefferson County. If the contract involves something bought on time—for instance, a car or an appliance—the suit can be brought in the county or judicial district where you currently live, where you lived when the contract was signed, or where the car, appliance, etc., is kept.

Larger counties often have two or more judicial districts within them. In that case, you must file in the appropriate district, usually the one closest to where the defendant lives or has his or her business, to where the accident happened, or to where the contract was signed. If you're not sure which county to sue in, call the clerk of the small claims court in that county and ask him or her.

To file the completed and signed forms, take them to the small claims court clerk. If the forms are filled in properly, the clerk will ask you to pay the filing fee (currently running from $15 to $30, depending on the state), and will then stamp your complaint as filed. At this time, ask the clerk to set a date of the trial. The clerk will give you a choice of dates, so pick the one most convenient to you.

Serving the Defendant with the Complaint

You are now ready to "serve" the defendant with the summons and complaint. The defendant must be served with the summons and complaint a specified number of days before the trial, usually twenty to thirty days. This amount of time varies from state to state and also can vary within a state, depending on whether the defendant lives in the same county where the court-house is. The small claims court clerk can tell you how soon before the hearing the defendant must be served with the summons and complaint. If you don't serve the defendant in time, call the court clerk and ask to have a new date assigned for the trial.

There are two convenient and common ways of serving a defendant. In most states, you can ask the small claims court clerk to serve the defendant through the mail. This usually costs only a few dollars. If you opt for this route, check back with the clerk at least two weeks before the day set for trial to see whether the defendant received the letter. If not, you will have to ask for a "continuance" of the trial to a later date and serve the defendant another way.

The second—and recommended—way of serving the defendant in a small claims court action is to have the marshal's or sheriff's office do it. Although this is more costly than having the clerk mail a letter, it is usually well worth the added expense. Plus, if you win the case, the defendant must reimburse you for your costs involved in pursuing the suit, including the cost of filing the complaint and having it served on the defendant. After the marshal or sheriff serves the defendant with the summons and complaint, he or she will file a "proof of service" with the court and mail you a copy to let you know that service was accomplished. A proof of service is a legal document signed under oath stating that the marshal or sheriff served the defendant with the summons and complaint on a certain date at a certain place and time.

In most states, the summons and complaint can be served on the defendant by anyone who is over 18 (19 in a few states) and not a party to the action—a licensed process server, even a friend. Make sure that the person who serves the defendant properly fills out and signs the proof of service (which you usually get from the small claims court clerk at the time you file your complaint and the summons is issued) and that it is filed with the small claims court clerk several days before the trial.

What to Do If You Are the Defendant

Let's assume for a while that you are the defendant and have just been served with a summons and complaint for a small claims court action. What should you do? If the plaintiff never contacted you, call or write him or her and see if you can't settle the case. If you can't reach a compromise, you may want to file a response to the complaint, stating why you believe you don't owe any money or as much money as the plaintiff is asking for. The summons shows how much time you have to file a response, often fifteen to twenty days. If you plan on filing a response and it doesn't say on the papers you were served with how long you have to file it, call the small claims court clerk to see how soon before the trial you have to file an answer. In most states, you don't have to file any response and can just show up at the hearing and present your side of the case. It is better to file a response, though, so the judge can read it before hearing the trial.

If you believe that you are entitled to damages from the same transaction or accident as the plaintiff is suing you on, you must file a "counterclaim" or "crosscomplaint" against the plaintiff. If you don't you will lose your right to sue the plaintiff for those damages later on. Suppose, for example, the plaintiff is suing you for $2,500 in a breach of contract case. You claim the plaintiff breached the contract and owes you $1,500. You must file a counterclaim for the $1,500 with your response to the complaint, or you will lose your right to assert it later.

HOW TO GET THE WINNING EDGE

Preparing Your Case: The Key to Success

Regardless of how clear-cut you feel your case is, you may not win unless you prepare your case thoroughly before the trial. You'll only have a few minutes to persuade the judge of your cause, so you must make your presentation as precise and effective as possible. Know what you're going to say before you walk into the courtroom. Most presentations should be in chronological order, since this is how the law—and the judge—generally views things. Stick to the heart of the matter, and leave side issues alone. Do you have a "smoking gun"—that one piece of evidence that especially proves that justice is on your side? If so, then concentrate on it.

Practice your testimony in front of a mirror a few times, and then do it in front of family and friends. Ask if they understood it easily, if any part left them confused, and if anything is missing. If you're shy in front of family and friends, imagine how difficult it will be to present your case without practice in front of a judge and a number of spectators.

Get all of your exhibits—canceled checks, invoices, receipts, repair estimates, written contracts, medical bills, pictures of damage or substandard work, and so on—ready so they'll be handy when you need them. Make at least three copies of every document. You will hand the original to the judge at trial. Attach one copy to your complaint, have one copy ready to hand to the defendant at the trial, and keep one copy with you throughout the trial. If you have photographs, number each one on the back in the sequence in which you plan to use it, along with the date when it was taken. If a couple of photographs particularly support your position, think of having them enlarged to eight inches by ten inches. Keep all of your exhibits in the order in which you plan to introduce them at the trial so you don't get flustered by having to shuffle through them under the judge's increasingly impatient glare.

A week or two before your trial, go to the small claims court to watch the proceedings. Small claims court trials are open to the general public, and all you have to do is walk through the door and take an empty seat. By visiting small claims court before your own hearing, you will become familiar with the surroundings and know what to expect when your time comes. The last thing you need to worry about at your own trial is where the courthouse is, which courtroom to go to, where to check in, which table to sit at, and so on. You will have an immediate advantage over someone who has never been in small claims court before.

Sit through at least three or four small claims cases, preferably in front of the same judge who will be presiding over your case. Soon you will be able to see which side is better prepared and who presents his or her case with more confidence. Notice how the judge conducts the proceedings. Are the parties permitted to ramble on, or is the judge a no-nonsense type who wants "just the facts"?

You will probably immediately notice two differences between real small claims court and its television counterparts. First, each case lasts only about five to ten minutes, not the fifteen to twenty minutes you usually see on television. Also, the judge does not go back into chambers to decide each case, as television portrays. (In television courts, this is just an excuse for a commercial break.) Participants in real small claims court do not get away interrupting the other party or arguing with the judge as their television counterparts seem to do. Judges do not tolerate this in the courtroom and quickly will admonish anyone who disrupts the proceedings. Persons who continue to be unruly may find themselves being escorted out of the courtroom or even taken into custody for contempt of court.

You'll also notice that the judge does not let the parties read from prepared statements. Often when the judge tells a person to explain the situation in his or her own words, the person is totally lost; this is another reason why you should practice your presentation beforehand. But while the judge won't let you read a prepared statement, you should have a sheet of paper with some critical notes—points you want to emphasize to the judge. A skilled trial lawyer wouldn't try a case without an outline or a few notes, and neither should you.

Support Your Testimony with Witnesses

As in any court, you have the right to subpoena witnesses, including police officers, to compel their appearance in court. If a witness (or even the opposing party) has documents or pictures that you want him or her to bring to court, you can serve that person with a *subpoena duces tecum*, available from the small claims court clerk. Subpoenas, however, are rarely used in small claims court, since the witnesses are often friends, family, or neighbors. A word of caution: Never force a witness to appear at trial against his or her will. An unwilling witness might "forget" key facts, claim not to have seen anything at all, or even testify out of spite that the situation is all your fault.

Never ask a witness to testify unless you have an idea of what he or she is going to say. Nothing is as dangerous as calling a witness without knowing what he or she saw. Never assume that the witness agrees with your version of the facts. Everyone's perception of an event can be different, so talk to the person before asking him or her to appear on your behalf at trial.

How important is it for a witness to appear? It literally can make or break your case in many instances. The judge won't simply take your word that you heard the witness say that he or she saw or heard something. This is "hearsay"—saying as true something that someone else said, a second- or thirdhand statement. If, for instance, a person heard the defendant say that she was speeding at the time of the accident and tells this to you, you can't tell the judge that that person told you the defendant admitted to speeding. Only the witness himself or herself can testify to this, because the witness heard it firsthand.

What can you do if a key witness won't be around for the trial? Perhaps he or she lives in another state, is ill, will be traveling out of the country, or otherwise can't make it. If the witness is only temporarily unavailable—out of town on a business trip, for instance—ask the clerk or judge to continue the case for a week or two until the witness gets back. But if the witness won't be able to make it to the trial at all, you should have the witness sign an affidavit telling what he or she saw. An affidavit is the witness's statement signed under oath. The witness must swear to a notary public that the statement is the truth, then sign and date the affidavit, and then the notary must sign it and affix his or her notarial seal. If you can't get an affidavit from the witness, at least have the witness give you a written, signed, and dated statement, including his or her address and telephone number.

When a witness can't appear at the trial, some judges will let him or her testify by telephone. The judge's clerk can advise you on the judge's practice. If the judge does allow testimony by telephone, it is your responsibility to make sure that the witness knows the day and time of the trial and is available at a certain telephone number if the judge decides to call.

The Trial: Time for Your Hard Work to Pay Off

Before the trial, the judge may order you and the defendant to go into the hallway for a few minutes to try to settle the case. If you manage to reach a settlement, put it in writing, and both of you sign it. Then tell the judge or his or her clerk that you have settled the case, and ask if it's okay to go home.

As the plaintiff, you present your case first. The burden is on you to prove your case to a "preponderance of the evidence." You must convince the judge that your version of the facts is more likely to be true than the defendant's version. All you have to do is tip the scales of justice ever so slightly in your favor and you've won. You can do this with witnesses, pictures, canceled checks, copies of the contract, the damaged article, or any other tangible evidence. You really have *two* things to prove: liability (that the defendant committed a legal wrong against you) and damages (how much money you should get). Proving one without the other won't do you any good. All the liability in the world means nothing if you can't demonstrate any damages. Likewise, the most severe damage will get you no award if you don't prove that the defendant is legally responsible for it.

The judge may have read your complaint before the hearing, but don't count on it. Besides, the complaint often gives room for only a sentence or two, so it doesn't say much anyway. Give the judge a one- or two-sentence introduction as to what the case involves, and then get on with your story. For example: "Good afternoon, Your Honor. My name is Beth Williams. I'm suing the defendant, Honest Car Repair Company, for not repairing the transmission on my car correctly. I took the car in to Honest Car Repair on July 15 because the transmission was slipping. They told me it would cost $1,500 to fix. . . ."

There isn't much time, so stick to the relevant facts and get to the heart of the matter right away. If you have prepared your case as suggested earlier, you'll have a concise and organized presentation. Exude confidence and show courtesy to the judge and the other side. Remember to conduct yourself properly in court, and instruct your witnesses to do the same.

Show the judge your exhibits and explain each of them. Go through the receipts and records. Never hand an exhibit or receipt to the judge without first asking his or her permission first. Usually you will show the exhibit to the other side, then hand it to the bailiff, who will take it to the judge. Then have your witnesses testify. Although both parties and their witnesses will be sworn to tell the truth under penalty of perjury, rarely will the judge ask anyone to take the witness stand. You and your witnesses will tell your story from a podium or the counsel table, usually standing up. Introduce each witness to the judge like this: "Your Honor, I would like to introduce my next witness, Gloria Jones."

When you and your witnesses are done testifying, the judge will ask the defendant to present his or her case. After the defendant is finished, you will get a chance to respond to ("rebut") the defendant's assertions. Sometimes, when the plaintiff's right to recover damages seems obvious from the complaint, the judge will simply skip the plaintiff's testimony and ask the defendant to present his or her case first. If the defendant has nothing substantial to say, the judge may find in the plaintiff's favor. If the defendant does raise a defense or a doubt in the judge's mind, the judge will then give you the opportunity to present your case.

What Happens If a Party Doesn't Appear at the Trial?

What happens if the defendant doesn't show up at the trial? The judge will probably enter a "default judgment" against him or her. Before doing so, however, the judge will look at the court file for your case to see whether the defendant was served properly with the summons and complaint and notified of the correct time, date, and place of the trial. If the file doesn't show that the defendant was properly served (for instance, you forgot to file the proof of service or it isn't signed), the judge will not enter the default. If this happens, ask the judge for a continuance to give you time to serve the defendant or file the proof of service.

But if the defendant was properly served, the judge may ask you to summarize your case and justify the amount of damages you are claiming. Once the judge enters the default judgment against the defendant, you can attempt to collect from the defendant the same as if he or she had appeared at trial and fought the case and lost.

Sometimes the defendant can later convince the judge to vacate, or "set aside," the default judgment so that he or she can defend the case. For example, if the defendant could show that he or she was in the hospital on the day of the trial or was involved in an automobile accident on the way to the hearing and was unable to call the court or the opposing party to inform them of the predicament, the judge may set aside the default. But the excuse must be sufficient in the eyes of the law to justify a failure to appear—forgetting to mark the date on the calendar is normally not enough. And the defendant must act promptly after receiving notice that a default judgment was entered against him or her. The longer the defendant waits after being notified of the default judgment, the more reluctant the judge will be to vacate the judgment.

Suppose you, the plaintiff, fail to show up at the hearing without calling the small claims court clerk. If the defendant appears, the judge normally will enter a judgment against you, and you'll have a harder time getting excused for not appearing than the defendant would. If neither side shows up, the judge may simply take the case "off calendar." You will then have to call the clerk and ask for a new trial date.

If you find that you are going to be unable to appear at the trial because of, say, illness or a business trip, call the opposing party, explain your situation, and ask for a continuance of a week or two. If the other side agrees, call the small claims court clerk to get the trial date changed. If the other party does not agree to your request for a continuance, you should still call the small claims court clerk and explain your situation. You generally can get one continuance even if the other side objects. But don't expect to get one continuance after another. The judge usually will not tolerate more than one or two continuances.

The Judgment

After both parties have presented their cases, the judge will make a decision. Judges usually don't announce small claims court rulings from the bench but mail them within the next day or two. This is mainly to prevent a disappointed party from taking up everyone's time by complaining to or arguing with the judge.

What can you do if you don't agree with the judge's decision? If you're the plaintiff and you lost, you are usually out of luck. In most states, a losing plaintiff has no right to appeal a small claims decision. But if the judge finds in favor of the plaintiff, the defendant has the right to appeal the judgment. The appeal usually is heard by one to three judges and basically consists of starting all over again from scratch. There is no court reporter in small claims court, so the appellate judges have no transcript of the earlier proceedings to review. You usually can have a lawyer represent you at the appeal even if your state doesn't permit a lawyer in small claims court. But before you hire a lawyer to handle the appeal for you, consider the cost. Also consider whether a written contract or court rule provides for the loser to pay the winner's attorney's fees if the case goes to trial.

EXAMPLES OF SMALL CLAIMS COURT TRIALS

HERE ARE THREE SAMPLE trials involving disputes that frequently wind up in small claims court.

Example #1: Parking Lot Collision

In the following example, the plaintiff's (Mr. Wilson's) car was damaged in a doctor's parking lot when the defendant (Mr. Stanton) struck it while backing out of a parking space next to it. Mr. Wilson was in the doctor's office and did not see the accident happen. But an eyewitness, Mary Davis, the office manager for Dr. Marks, saw the collision and recognized the driver as being another patient of Dr. Marks. Mr. Wilson has brought two estimates to repair the damage to his car, one for $2,500, the other for $2,350.

JUDGE: Are both parties present in the case of *Wilson versus Stanton*?
PLAINTIFF (*Mr. Wilson*): I am Albert Wilson, Your Honor.
DEFENDANT (*Mr. Stanton*): I am the defendant, Bill Stanton.
JUDGE: Fine. Would you please proceed, Mr. Wilson.
PLAINTIFF: Thank you, Your Honor. I am suing Mr. Stanton for the damage he did to my car when he sideswiped it while it was parked in Dr. Marks's parking lot on November 12, 2003, at approximately 2:30 P.M. I had parked my car and gone into the doctor's office for my appointment. I did not see the accident happen, but I have a witness who did. I would like to introduce Mary Davis, the office manager for Dr. Marks, and have her explain what she saw.
JUDGE: Have you been sworn in, Ms. Davis?

Ms. Davis: Yes, sir. [*To avoid wasting time swearing in each party and witness, in small claims court the court clerk generally will swear in everyone at one time just before the judge takes the bench.*]

Judge: Then please tell me what you saw, Ms. Davis.

Ms. Davis: I had just finished helping another patient when I heard a loud "thud" come from the parking lot. I looked over and saw Mr. Stanton's car wedged against the side of Mr. Wilson's car, which was parked. Mr. Stanton then drove away without stopping to leave a note or anything.

Judge: Are you sure it was Mr. Stanton driving?

Ms. Davis: Yes, Your Honor. Mr. Stanton is also a patient of Dr. Marks. He has been coming for years, and I am also familiar with his car. I got a good look at the driver and it was Mr. Stanton.

Judge: Thank you, Ms. Davis. Mr. Wilson, do you have anything more to say?

Mr. Wilson: Yes, Your Honor. I have two eight-by-ten-inch photographs showing the damage to my car that I would like to show you. [*Hand the pictures to the bailiff, who will give them to the judge.*] I also have two written estimates for the repair work, Your Honor. One is for $2,500 and the other is for $2,350. [*You should have attached a copy of the repair estimates to your complaint. If not, hand the two estimates to the bailiff to give them to the judge.*]

Judge: Do you have anything to add, Mr. Wilson?

Mr. Wilson: No, Your Honor, that is all.

Judge: Thank you, Mr. Wilson. Mr. Stanton, what do you have to say?

Mr. Stanton: The only thing I have to say is that I didn't hit his car, Your Honor. It was somebody else. And even if I did hit it, I certainly didn't do $2,500 worth of damage. I might have scratched it a little, but that's it.

Judge: Well, these photographs show significant damage, and the repair estimates are for more than a little scratch.

Mr. Stanton: His car may already have been damaged and he's trying to make me pay the whole thing.

Judge: Mr. Wilson, was your car damaged before the date in question?

Mr. Wilson: No, Your Honor. It was in perfect shape. In fact, I had just had it painted six months before the accident.

Judge: Do either of you have anything to add to your presentations?

Mr. Wilson: No, Your Honor.

Mr. Stanton: No, sir.

Judge: Thank you. That is all. You should receive my judgment in the mail in two or three days.

The judge most likely would find in Mr. Wilson's favor and award him at least $2,350, the lower of the two estimates. If Mr. Wilson already had had the car fixed, he would have brought the invoice and receipt for the work done into court and the judge probably would have awarded him the full cost of having the car repaired. Mr. Wilson meticulously prepared his case, including taking pictures of the damage to his car and bringing in two estimates to fix it. The independent, unbiased eyewitness testimony of Mary Davis who saw Mr. Stanton hit Mr. Wilson's car certainly would impress the judge. Mr. Wilson kept his presentation short, kept to the main points, and had his exhibits in order of presentation to the judge. Mr. Stanton had no defense, and most likely when Mr. Wilson gets his mail in a day or two, he will get a favorable verdict from the judge.

Example #2: Dry Cleaners Ruined Coat

In this example, the plaintiff took her coat to the dry cleaners to have it cleaned, but when she took it out of the plastic bag three days later, she found a hole in the back.

PLAINTIFF (*Ms. Laird*): Your Honor, on December 2, 2003, I took a white coat to the defendant's dry cleaning store to have it cleaned. It was in excellent condition when I took it in. There were no rips, tears, or holes in it. I picked the coat up four days later and paid for it. I didn't take it out of the plastic garment bag until three days later, when I was going to wear it, and I found a large hole in the back. I have the coat here, and you can plainly see the big hole here. As soon as I discovered the hole, I called the dry cleaners and told them what I had found. The woman who answered the phone said she was very sorry for putting the hole in the coat and that they would dry clean another coat for me for free. I told her that wouldn't do, because the coat cost me $225, it was only a month old, and I had only worn it twice. I told her that I wanted them to pay for a new coat. She refused to pay anything. I then wrote a letter to the dry cleaners, stating what I had found and requesting $225 to replace the coat. I never received an answer to that letter. I have a copy of the letter here, if you care to see it, Your Honor.

JUDGE: Do you have anything more to say, Ms. Laird?

Ms. LAIRD: Yes, Your Honor. Although I don't have the receipt for my coat, I do have a letter here from the manager of Cindy's Fashions, the clothing store where I bought the coat. [*The letter should be on the store's stationery.*] As you can see, the manager says she remembers selling the coat to me about a month before the defendant ruined it, and that the sales price was $225.

JUDGE: Thank you, Ms. Laird. Do you have anything to say, Mr. Harper?

DEFENDANT [*Harry Harper, owner of Harper's Dry Cleaners*]: Your Honor, I would like to say two things. First, I don't believe that we caused the hole in the coat. There is simply no way we could have done that. I think that she probably ripped the coat after she got it back from us and is just trying to figure out some way of getting a new coat without paying for it. Second, the coat she has there is not worth $225, even if there was no hole. If

I could see the coat for a minute . . . thank you. As you can see, Your Honor, there is a stain on the front of the coat that can't be taken out. You can also tell by looking at the coat that it has been worn more than twice.

JUDGE: Ms. Laird, when you called the dry cleaners to tell them you had discovered the hole, do you remember who you talked to?

MS. LAIRD: Yes. I believe it was Mrs. Harper that I spoke with.

JUDGE [*to Mr. Harper*]: I presume Mrs. Harper is your wife?

MR. HARPER: Yes.

JUDGE: Is she here today?

MR. HARPER: No, sir. One of us had to stay at the shop.

JUDGE: Does either side have anything to add? If not, thank you, and you'll receive my decision in the mail in several days.

In this case, the judge likely would find in favor of the plaintiff, but might award only $150 or so depending on the condition of the coat. The defendant should have presented the testimony of his wife to the effect that she never told the plaintiff that they had caused the hole. Without that testimony, the judge probably would accept the plaintiff's version as true.

Example #3: A Landlord's Failure to Return a Tenant's Security Deposit

The following case involves a landlord's refusal to return a tenant's security deposit of $1,000. The tenant claims he left the apartment in better condition when he moved out than it was in when he moved in.

PLAINTIFF [*Bill Butler*]: Your Honor, on August 1, 2002, I rented an apartment from Mr. Turnball on a month-to-month basis. I had to pay the first month's rent of $1,000 and a security deposit of $1,000 when I moved in. I have a copy of the lease, which shows I did in fact pay the security deposit of $1,000. On December 1, 2003, I gave Mr. Turnball written notice that I would be moving out in thirty days. I managed to get all of my furniture and belongings out of the apartment before Christmas. I had the carpets cleaned by a commercial establishment, Sonny's Carpet Cleaning, on December 27. Here is the receipt from Sonny's for the work. I used Sonny's on the recommendation of Mr. Turnball, who told me that he used Sonny's to clean all the carpets in the apartment complex and that he was always pleased with their work.

I also thoroughly cleaned out the oven, refrigerator, bathrooms, and all other rooms. When I originally moved into the unit, the place was a mess. It took me a week to clean it up. I feel that I left the apartment in a very clean condition, certainly much cleaner than it was when I moved in. Unfortunately, I don't have any pictures of the apartment, but I do have a witness who can support my testimony that the apartment was clean when I left it. I would like to introduce Ms. Valerie Lopez.

MS. LOPEZ: Your Honor, I helped Bill clean the apartment, and I can assure you that it was very clean when we were done. It took us two days. We mopped the floors, cleaned all of the windows, cleaned the oven, cleaned the bathroom, and had that place looking spotless. I couldn't believe it when Bill told me that Mr. Turnball refused to return any part of his security deposit.

MR. BUTLER: Your Honor, after a few weeks, I called Mr. Turnball because I hadn't received my deposit back, nor had he sent me an itemized statement showing how my security deposit had been applied as required by the law. He just laughed at me and said it would be a cold day in July before he'd send me any money. I wrote a letter demanding the return of my security deposit—here is a copy for you to see—but he never answered.

JUDGE: Thank you, Mr. Butler. What do you have to say, Mr. Turnball?

MR. TURNBALL: First of all, Your Honor, when Mr. Butler moved into the apartment it was clean as a whistle. I make sure that all my units are thoroughly cleaned before a new tenant moves in. As to the condition it was in when Mr. Butler left, when I walked into his unit, I was shocked to see how dirty it was. The carpet was filthy, the bathrooms hadn't been cleaned, the oven had crusted food all over it, and the walls were all banged up. I had to hire carpet cleaners and a cleaning service to get the place back into good order. It cost me more than $1,000 to clean it up. I couldn't believe Mr. Butler had the nerve to ask for his security deposit back.

JUDGE: Do you have any receipts showing your costs?

MR. TURNBALL: No, Your Honor, I didn't think it would be necessary for me to bring them.

JUDGE: Do you have any pictures showing the condition of the apartment after Mr. Butler moved out but before you cleaned it?

MR. TURNBALL: No, Your Honor, I never thought to take any.

JUDGE: Mr. Turnball, did you ever send the plaintiff an itemized statement showing how the cleaning deposit was applied?

MR. TURNBALL: Yes, Your Honor, but if he didn't get it, it must have gotten lost in the mail because of his moving.

JUDGE: Mr. Butler, did you see the carpet after Sonny's had cleaned it?

MR. BUTLER: Yes, sir, I saw it the next day when Ms. Lopez and I went to finish the other cleaning.

JUDGE: How did it look?

PLAINTIFF: It was spotless. It was much cleaner than when I had moved in.

JUDGE: I'm going to break with my usual procedure and announce my verdict right now. Mr. Butler, I am awarding you $3,000. From the evidence you presented, I find that you left the apartment in a clean condition. I have your receipt from Sonny's Carpet Cleaning

Service for $250 to have the carpets cleaned, so I certainly can't believe Mr. Turnball's testimony that the carpet was filthy. This is especially true since Mr. Turnball himself had recommended that particular company. I am inclined to believe everything that Mr. Butler said and to take everything Mr. Turnball said with a grain of salt. I do not believe that Mr. Turnball ever sent a letter explaining how the security deposit was applied, as he is required by law to do. Mr. Turnball claims to have spent more than $1,000 to have the apartment cleaned, but he has no receipts or photographs to prove it. Nor has he filed a counterclaim for the difference against Mr. Butler. I am therefore awarding Mr. Butler his full security deposit of $1,000 and am tripling that amount as permitted by law to $3,000.

TURNING YOUR JUDGMENT INTO CASH

THE FINAL STEP IS to collect the judgment from the defendant. In many cases, the defendant (now the "judgment debtor") will pay the judgment, albeit grudgingly, but maybe not right away. In many states, with the notice of the judgment against him or her, the defendant also will receive a form to fill out (a "judgment debtor's statement of assets" form) that requires the defendant to list all of his or her assets and where he or she works. By the end of thirty days after the judgment, the defendant must either pay you in full or send you the completed information form so you can attempt to collect the debt.

Suppose thirty days passes and you have received neither payment nor the information form from the defendant. What should you do? Write the defendant a polite yet firm letter asking for payment of the full award within ten days or face going back to court so you can enforce the judgment. Advise the defendant that in addition to the amount the judge awarded at the trial, the law entitles you to be reimbursed by the defendant for your costs of collecting the judgment. This may be enough to persuade many defendants to pay, at least if they have the money. If the defendant can't pay you in full, consider having him or her pay as much as he or she can now and work out some monthly terms. Put the payment agreement in writing, have the defendant sign it, give him or her a copy, and keep the original.

If you are the defendant, before paying the plaintiff the full amount, obtain a "satisfaction of judgment" form from the small claims court clerk's office and have the plaintiff sign it when you pay him or her the money. If you mail the plaintiff a check, send the form with it, along with a self-addressed, stamped envelope for him or her to return the signed and dated form to you. (If you are the plaintiff, insist upon payment in cash or by cashier's check or money order. If the defendant convinces you to accept a personal check, do not sign and return the "satisfaction of judgment" form until the check clears the bank.) Once the plaintiff signs the satisfaction of judgment, the defendant should make a copy and file the original with the small claims court clerk.

Suppose the defendant refuses your attempts to collect the debt through letters and reason. What next? You'll need to find out what assets or sources of income the defendant has that you can reach ("levy on") to pay ("satisfy") the judgment. The two best ways to collect your money are from the defendant's bank account and by garnishing his or her wages. Some property is partially or totally exempt from judgments: the equity in a house; household furniture and furnishings; a car up to a certain amount; and clothes and personal effects. The defendant's wages are partially exempt. The amount of the exemption for the different assets varies from state to state, and the small claims court clerk may have a schedule for your state.

If the defendant refuses to return you a completed "judgment debtor's statement of assets," it will be necessary for you to file for a "judgment debtor examination." At the judgment debtor examination, which takes place at the courthouse, you can ask the defendant any and all questions about his or her assets and workplace. Does he or she have any bank accounts, and if so, with which banks and what account numbers? Where does he or she work and how much does he or she earn?

Once you know where the defendant's bank account is or where he or she works, you will need to fill out a "writ of execution" form (available from the small claims court clerk) and file it with the court. Ask the clerk how many copies you will need, and make an extra one for your records.

Take the writ of execution to the marshal's or sheriff's office in the county where the bank account is located. The marshal (or sheriff) will serve the bank with the writ of execution. The bank must give the marshal all money in the account over the exemption amount, if any, up to the amount of your judgment and the marshal's fee. If you are garnishing the defendant's wages, the marshal will serve the employer with the writ of execution. The employer then withholds the prescribed amount (usually 25 percent, depending on how much the defendant earns) from the defendant's regular paycheck and pays it to the marshal, who in turn pays it to you. This continues until the judgment is paid off.

If the defendant owns a business, you can have the marshal do a "till tap," in which the marshal goes to the business and takes all of the money out of the cash register, up to the amount of the judgment and the marshal's fee. Another possibility is a "keeper"—the marshal stays for a few hours or a few days and collects all the money the business takes in.

Keep track of all the expenses you incur in collecting the judgment, including the marshal's fees and the costs of filing various forms with the court, and add these to the judgment. Don't overlook the fact that you are entitled to interest at the legal rate (which varies from state to state) from the date the judgment is entered.

TWENTY

Civil Rights and Liberties

*t*HE UNITED STATES CONSTITUTION gives us many fundamental and inalienable rights: among them, the right to practice the religion of our choosing; the freedoms of speech and peaceable assembly; the right to be free from discrimination; the right to travel freely; and the right to protect our writings, creations, and inventions. This chapter is concerned not only with what these rights are, but also with when and how far the government can restrict them. (Constitutional rights related to criminal proceedings—the right against self-incrimination, for example, or the right to be free from unwarranted searches and seizures—are discussed in chapter 23.)

One thing to keep in mind throughout this chapter is that few of our constitutional rights are absolute. As the examples in this chapter will demonstrate, it essentially boils down to balancing the competing interests of the individual's rights against the government's rights. The government can limit your constitutional rights only when the public interest is so strong and compelling that it is justified in doing so.

The last section of this chapter concerns your right to sue the government for damages when you are injured by a government employee or by a dangerous condition on government land. Although most people would not consider this a civil right or liberty in the strictest sense (and indeed nothing in the Constitution gives you the right to sue the government), on the other hand, what could be a more fundamental right than holding the government liable for the injuries it causes you? The Constitution requires the government to compensate you fairly when it takes your property (see chapter 6). Nothing less should be required of the government when it takes, say, your arm or your life.

THE FIRST AMENDMENT to the Constitution begins, "Congress shall make no law respecting an establishment of religion, or prohibiting the free exercise thereof; . . ." The first part of this is known as the "establishment clause"; the second part, the "free exercise clause."

The Establishment Clause

The establishment clause was intended to prevent Congress from establishing a national religion. But it goes much further than that. The government cannot favor one religion over others, nor can it hinder or forbid a religion. Essentially, the establishment clause requires that the government not interfere in religion, that there be a "wall of separation" between the two. Is every law that affects religion therefore unconstitutional? No. Many laws passed by Congress and state legislatures directly or indirectly affect religion but are nonetheless constitutional. The establishment clause is not a precise, detailed provision in a legal code capable of ready application; in the words of the United States Supreme Court, "the purpose of the Establishment Clause was to state an objective, not to write a statute."

As the United States Supreme Court has acknowledged, the total separation of church and state is not truly possible. Given that admission, the question then becomes how much association between church and state is permissible. The United States Supreme Court has declared that a law that affects religion does not violate the establishment clause if the law has a secular purpose and its primary effect neither advances nor inhibits religion. In determining whether its primary effect advances religion, the criteria looked at are whether the law results in religious indoctrination, defines its recipients by reference to religion, or creates an excessive government entanglement with religion.

The government attempts a "benevolent neutrality" toward religion, aiming neither to promote nor to inhibit religion, but to reasonably accommodate it. This explains the tax-exempt status afforded religious organizations. Another example of the government's "hands-off" approach to religion: Disputes in internal religious matters must be resolved within the confines of the particular religious organization. For instance, if there is a disagreement as to how a particular passage from a religious writing should be interpreted, the courts will not decide which of the interpretations is correct or more acceptable.

As one court stated: The establishment clause means

at least this: Neither a state nor the Federal Government can set up a church. Neither can pass laws that aid one religion, aid all religions, or prefer one religion over another. Neither can force nor influence a person to go to or to remain away from church against his will or force him to profess a belief or disbelief in any religion. No person can be punished for entertaining or professing religious beliefs or disbeliefs, for church attendance or nonattendance. No tax in any amount, large or small, can be levied to support any religious activities or institutions, whatever they may be called, or whatever form they may adopt to teach or practice religion.

In the course of resolving specific cases, the U.S. Supreme Court has interpreted the establishment clause to mean that government may not promote or affiliate itself with any religious doctrine or organization; may not discriminate among persons on the basis of their religious beliefs and practices; may not delegate a governmental power to a religious institution; and may not involve itself too deeply in such a religious institution's affairs.

One recurring issue of religious rights involves the posting of the Ten Commandments on the classroom wall of a public school, on a courtroom or city hall wall, or even as a monument on the lawn outside a municipal building housing county offices and courtrooms. The United States Supreme Court consistently has held that such action violates the establishment clause. The religious belief that God created everything in the universe, including man ("creationism"), cannot be taught in a public school, even under the guise that creationism is a "science" and evolution is merely an unproven theory. However, public schools are allowed to lend secular textbooks and other supplies to religious schools and give other assistance. Vouchers given to parents of schoolchildren to attend private schools are constitutional, even though the vast majority of parents use the vouchers to send their children to religious institutions.

Every winter come the challenges to city or county Christmas displays, such as the nativity scene (crèche) on the lawn in front of city hall or the cross atop it. Historically the courts held that such displays violated the establishment clause, since they amounted to government promotion of a religion (Christianity). But in 1984, the United States Supreme Court held that a nativity scene erected by the city of Pawtucket, Rhode Island, was permissible because it was included with a Santa Claus house and a live Santa Claus passing out candy, a display of reindeer pulling Santa's sleigh, a "talking" wishing well, a large banner proclaiming "Season's Greetings," and other secular objects. The U.S. Supreme Court concluded that the display, taken as a whole, symbolized a secular American holiday rather than a religious one. Christmas trees put up and decorated by a government body generally are permitted on the basis that they do not symbolize any religious holiday, even though they are associated with the Christian holiday of Christmas.

In a case subsequent to that involving Pawtucket, a nativity scene replete with angels attached to the staircase and the Latin phrase meaning "glory to God" in the "main," "most beautiful," and "most public" part of the county courthouse was held unconstitutional. The court found that the display had the effect of promoting or endorsing religious beliefs. However, in the same case, an eighteen-foot menorah next to a forty-five-foot Christmas tree, at the foot of which was the mayor's name and a declaration that it was a "salute to liberty," outside the courthouse was held not to violate the establishment clause.

Whether public school students can sing Christmas carols depends upon the religious content of the individual carol. Public school students ordinarily are prohibited from singing religious carols, such as "Joy to the World." But secular carols—"Jingle Bells," for instance—are allowed.

Your Right to Practice Your Religious Beliefs

The "free exercise clause" of the first amendment guarantees you the right to practice your beliefs without government interference. Does this mean that the government cannot place any restrictions on religious practices? No. The government need not always yield to religious beliefs when secular laws and religious tenets clash. Some acts can be prohibited when the government has a "compelling interest" that overrides an individual's right to the free exercise of religion. Human sacrifice can be banned, for example (however, animal sacrifices have been upheld), as can bigamy or polygamy, even if they are sanctioned by the person's religion. The government can't, however, restrict your right to *believe* in any aspect of a religion.

Suppose a member of a religious group whose beliefs prohibit blood transfusions is injured severely and requires a blood transfusion to save his or her life. Can the religious member refuse the blood transfusion, even though it means certain death? Yes. A mentally competent adult has the right to refuse necessary—even life-saving—medical assistance if it is contrary to his or her religion. Suppose the surgeon knows of the person's religious objections to blood transfusions but goes ahead anyway to save the person's life. Can the person turn around and sue the doctor for saving his or her life by using a blood transfusion? Yes. But suppose the doctor was not informed of the patient's religious objections to a blood transfusion. Can the patient sue then and win? No. The doctor must have known of the patient's religious objections before ordering the blood transfusion. If the doctor has no reason to know that the patient would object to a blood transfusion if he or she were conscious, the doctor is immune from liability.

A different situation arises when parents who harbor religious objections to medical treatment refuse to submit to a transfusion or treatment by a physician that would save the life of their minor child, believing instead in the power of prayer to heal their sick child. In questions involving the life and death of a minor child and the parents' religious beliefs versus the government's interests in the child's welfare, the government almost always prevails. Indeed, parents who fail to provide reasonable medical care for their minor children have been prosecuted successfully for such crimes as child abuse and endangering a child's life. In fact, involuntary manslaughter charges have been prosecuted successfully against parents where the child has died from lack of medical care due to the parents' religious beliefs in the power of prayer only.

Does the free exercise clause include the freedom to use illegal drugs in religious ceremonies? For years, members of the Native American Church were allowed to use peyote (a hallucinogen) during religious services. Two Native American workers in Oregon were denied unemployment benefits after being fired from their jobs after they tested positive for peyote use. They had used the drug for sacramental purposes at a ceremony of the Native American Church, and brought suit claiming their free exercise of religion had been violated. The Supreme Court of Oregon ruled that Oregon's prohibition against controlled substances does not contain an exception for the religious use of peyote. The United States Supreme Court stated that, "although it is constitutionally permissible to exempt sacramental peyote use from the operation of drug laws, it is not constitutionally required." While the state in question—Oregon—had a law prohibiting the possession of peyote, other states, including Arizona, Colorado, and New Mexico, have laws permitting the use of peyote for sacramental purposes.

The federal government has laws that regulate who can immigrate into the United States (see chapter 21). There are formal procedures to comply with and quotas specifying how many people from a given country can move here each year. Suppose a church proclaims itself a sanctuary for refugees from countries with rampant political strife or poverty. Some church members, acting in accordance with their religious beliefs and the church's declaration, help refugees from such countries enter the United States unlawfully. Can those members be convicted of breaking the law, even though they were only following their religious beliefs? Yes; the government's interest in regulating immigration is superior to the individual's religious practices in this situation.

Another example of permissible government intrusion upon religious practices: The U.S. Supreme Court held that the Air Force could prohibit a commissioned officer from wearing a yarmulke while on duty. The Supreme Court deferred to the judgment of the Air Force that the tradition of outfitting military personnel in standardized uniforms encouraged the subordination of personal preferences and identities in favor of the overall group mission. Wearing of the yarmulke detracted from the uniformity sought by dress regulations. The effect of the Supreme Court's decision was to uphold the Air Force's distinction of banning visible religious apparel or symbols but allowing those that are hidden from view.

Whenever a person claims to be exempt from a law because of his or her religious convictions, the judge can inquire into the sincerity of the person's beliefs. The judge cannot, however, make a determination of whether a particular religious belief is acceptable, logical, consistent, or even comprehensible. But the judge can decide whether a belief properly comes under the heading of religion. For instance, one court held that whether a person is pro- or antinuclear is a political issue, not a religious one. The religion does not have to be a traditional one, nor is belief in a supreme being required. But protection is not given to "religions" that are obviously shams and whose members have no religious sincerity. "Religions" that are set up solely to get around drug or tax laws and that lack true religious foundations are not protected by the first amendment.

Religion and Schools

Much of the controversy regarding the separation of church and state involves religion's role in public schools. And in this area, nothing engenders as much dispute as whether prayer—

voluntary or forced—should be allowed in public schools. To date, the United States Supreme Court consistently has ruled that laws requiring or permitting prayer in public schools is unconstitutional. For example, the U.S. Supreme Court held that an Alabama law prescribing a one-minute period of silence in all public schools for "meditation or voluntary prayer" was unconstitutional because the law was designed solely to return prayer to public schools. Reading passages from the Bible or other religious writings in the classroom or over a loudspeaker to start the school day also is prohibited. Having a member of the clergy deliver a prayer at a graduation ceremony is likewise unconstitutional.

In June 2000, the United States Supreme Court held that a student-led, student-initiated prayer at football games violated the establishment clause. The invocation took place on school property, at a school-sponsored event, over the school's public address system, by a speaker representing the student body, under the supervision of school faculty, and pursuant to a school policy that explicitly and implicitly encouraged public prayer.

For years the courts prohibited students from forming religious clubs that met in schoolrooms before and after school to study the Bible and pray. The U.S. Supreme Court has ruled that under the Equal Access Act students in secondary schools may form religious clubs and enjoy the same benefits as other nonacademic clubs at the same school do.

The U.S. Supreme Court is getting more liberal on the type and amount of aid and assistance that a public school district can offer to private religious schools. For example, it is constitutional for a public school to lend secular textbooks, computer hardware and secular software, library services and materials (including media materials), and other curricular materials to religious schools without violating the establishment clause. Nor does it violate the establishment clause to provide a publicly paid interpreter to sign for a deaf student at a Roman Catholic high school. As part of a long-standing aid program, the federal government distributes funds to state and local government agencies, which in turn lend educational materials and equipment to public and private schools, with the enrollment of each participating school determining the amount of aid that it receives. This practice has been ruled constitutional by the courts, since the support the religious school is receiving is secular, and it is not receiving title to the material, as they are only on loan.

For years, the U.S. Supreme Court refused to permit publicly employed teachers to go on private religious school grounds to teach such basic subjects as remedial reading and math. It was constitutional to teach the students off-campus, even in a van parked on a public street adjacent to the school. However, in 1997, the United States Supreme Court overruled that long-standing law and permitted publicly employed, secular teachers to go into the classrooms of religious schools to teach their subjects—without teaching religion, of course.

Parents of children who attend religious schools are entitled to deduct on their tax forms the cost of certain tuition, transportation, and educational expenses of their children attending elementary and secondary schools. The U.S. Supreme Court found it compelling that the deduction was available for all parents with school-age children.

The United States Supreme Court's current philosophy is to treat religion as neutrally as possible. Hence, it allows a religious club to meet on school grounds the same as any other clubs. A plurality of justices of the U.S. Supreme Court stated that if aid to schools—even "direct aid"—is neutrally available and, before reaching or benefiting any religious school, first passes through the hands (literally or figuratively) of private citizens who are free to direct the aid elsewhere, the government has not provided any "support of religion."

Until 2002, the U.S. Supreme Court had ruled that the giving of school vouchers or payment of tuition for elementary or secondary students was unconstitutional, as the money typically went to private religious schools. However, in June 2002, the U.S. Supreme Court ruled that a government aid program is not readily subject to challenge under the establishment clause if it is neutral with respect to religion and provides assistance directly to a broad class of citizens who, in turn, direct government aid to religious schools wholly as a result of their own genuine and independent choice. By giving the voucher directly to the children's parents, who must then make their own "genuine and independent choice" as to which school to send their children, the government aid reaches the religious institutes only by way of the deliberate choice of individual recipients, that is, the various parents. The Supreme Court rationalized that the incidental advancement of a religious mission, or the perceived endorsement of a religious message, reasonably is attributed to the individual aid recipients (the parents) and not the government, whose role ends with the disbursement of the benefits to the parents.

Can parents refuse on religious grounds to send their children to public school? Yes, but the state can require that the children receive an equivalent instruction in a private school or at home. Parents who refuse to see to the proper education of their children can be prosecuted and punished. One interesting case in which the parents could not be punished for violating compulsory education laws involved a Wisconsin law that required all children to attend school until they reached 16. Amish parents, however, refused to let their children attend school beyond the eighth grade for fear that secondary education would expose them to outside worldly influence that conflicted with Amish tenets. The United States Supreme Court declared the Wisconsin law unconstitutional because, if enforced, it would do more harm to the Amish religion than it would do good for the children.

Can a child in a public school be forced to salute the flag and recite the Pledge of Allegiance? Not if doing so would violate his or her religious beliefs. Also, a lower court judge ruled that the recitation of the Pledge of Allegiance is unconstitutional, as it contains the words "under God" and therefore violates the establishment clause of the first amendment. That case is currently on appeal. Although the government may not make a student say the Pledge of Allegiance over his or her religious objections, the government can require all students to be vaccinated over their religious objections (or the objections of their parents) before attending public school, because of the state's overriding and compelling interest in preventing the spread of childhood diseases.

The United States Supreme Court has ruled that the federal government can give money to religious-affiliated colleges and universities to construct buildings and facilities that can be used only for secular education purposes. The government cannot, however, give construction money to a religious primary or secondary school, even if the school promises to use the proposed building solely for secular education. Why the disparate treatment? Because the curriculum in religious elementary and secondary schools involves substantial religious indoctrination, while church-related colleges and universities do not.

Religion and Your Job

Can an employee who refuses to work on his or her Sabbath be fired, demoted, transferred, or subjected to other disciplinary action? In some situations, yes. A Connecticut law prohibited employers from firing employees who refused to work on their Sabbath. The U.S. Supreme Court ruled that this law was unconstitutional because it forced employers to conform their business practices to the particular religious practices of the employee. Sabbath religious concerns automatically prevailed over all secular interests at the workplace, and the law did not take into account the interest of the employer or of other employees who did not observe a Sabbath. This Supreme Court decision does not, however, prevent a state from requiring employers to accommodate their employees' religious practices to the extent that it can be done without excessive disruption to the business or inconvenience to the other employees.

Some states still have "Sunday closing laws" that prohibit many types of businesses from operating on Sundays. Although such laws may have some religious undercurrents, the U.S. Supreme Court consistently has held that these laws are constitutional because they give the workers a needed day of rest and promote community welfare and order.

YOUR RIGHT TO FREEDOM OF SPEECH

FREEDOM OF SPEECH, guaranteed by the first amendment, lets us speak our minds without fear of government recrimination. We can give speeches, write articles and books, or hold rallies criticizing the government, advocating other political systems, or generally saying whatever we want without risking imprisonment or other punishment. And speech isn't limited to the spoken or written word. It can be symbolic, such as dancing or wearing clothing; burning a book—indeed, even the flag—is a protected form of symbolic speech, as repugnant as such acts may be to the majority of citizens.

Like most other constitutional rights, the right to freedom of speech is not absolute. Limitations can be placed on our speech when the government has a legitimate overriding interest. The classic example of speech that is not protected by the first amendment is running into a crowded theater and falsely yelling "Fire!" Preventing the high potential for injuries caused in the ensuing panic greatly outweighs the person's right to that kind of speech.

The right to free speech also does not include the liberty to slander or libel someone else (see chapter 10). If you defame someone, you cannot escape paying the damages you caused that person by claiming that you have the right of free speech. The first amendment also doesn't give you the right to ask someone else to commit a crime for you. If you do, you are guilty of the crime of solicitation (see chapter 23). The government can prohibit you from standing on the sidewalk outside a jail and talking to the prisoners inside without permission. The courts have held that all of these are valid restrictions on your right to free speech.

The Ku Klux Klan and freedom of speech were in the spotlight in 2000 and 2001 when the KKK attempted to "adopt" a stretch of Missouri highways. Under "adopt-a-highway" plans, which are in all but two states, businesses and civic groups are encouraged to "adopt" a stretch of highway typically two miles long to pick up the litter, plant trees, and generally maintain the stretch of highway. If the group does not want to do the actual maintenance, it can pay the department of transportation its cost of keeping that part of the road clean. In return, the group gets to post a sign stating "This Highway Adopted by [Name of Group]."

The Ku Klux Klan wanted to adopt part of a highway in Missouri but was turned down by the department of transportation. The Klan went to federal court, claiming that the refusal violated their right of free speech. The court agreed, and the state of Missouri appealed the decision to a federal appellate court. The appellate court held that, under the first amendment's guarantee of free speech, the state could not exclude certain groups because of their racist views. In upholding the lower court's decision, the appellate court stated that, "The 1st Amendment protects everyone, even those with viewpoints as thoroughly obnoxious as those of the Klan, from viewpoint discrimination by the state." Missouri then filed an appeal with the United States Supreme Court, which declined to hear the appeal. Because the U.S. Supreme Court refused to hear the case, the law is good in Missouri, Mississippi, and Texas (the other states over which the Fifth Circuit has jurisdiction), that is, the Ku Klux Klan cannot be denied the right to adopt a highway. It does not, however, serve as a binding precedent on the other forty-seven states and the District of Columbia. Nine other states have turned down similar requests from the Klan to adopt a highway.

Obscenity

The first amendment does not protect obscenity. The U.S. Supreme Court has defined obscenity as material that, taken as a whole by the average person applying contemporary community standards, "appeals to the prurient interest in sex, portrays sexual conduct in a patently offensive way, and does not have serious literary, artistic or scientific value." "Community standards" refers to the entire state, not each community within the state. And the standard used is that of the reasonable adult, exclusive of children. (But a state can forbid the sale of adult-oriented material to minors.) Deciding what is obscene and what is not is admittedly a difficult task, one that is done on a case-by-case basis by the judge and jury.

Although the government can prevent the sale or distribution of obscenity, it is not a crime to keep obscene material in your own home. An individual's right to privacy outweighs the government's interest in protecting society from obscenity. This protection does not, however, extend to possessing child pornography.

Speech That Presents a "Clear and Present Danger"

The fact that speech is offensive or annoying to some—or even to many or most—generally is not sufficient cause to prohibit it. In one decision of the U.S. Supreme Court, Justice William O. Douglas stated:

> A function of free speech under our system of government is to invite dispute. It may indeed serve its high purpose when it induces a condition of unrest, creates dissatisfaction with conditions as they are, or even stirs people to anger. Speech is often provocative and challenging. It may strike at prejudices and preconceptions and have profound unsettling effects as it presses for acceptance of an idea. That is why freedom of speech [is] protected against censorship or punishment.

Suppose a communist group is holding a meeting in a park near city hall. The speaker is advocating the immediate overthrow of the government by any and all means possible, including force. The crowd becomes unruly, the speaker's harangue continues, and it appears that some type of illegal action is imminent. Can the police step in, break up the meeting, and arrest the speaker and others for breach of the peace without violating the first amendment guarantee of speech? Yes. In this case, there is a "clear and present danger" of immediate unlawful action, a "call to arms," which goes beyond merely making some people angry.

On the other hand, if the speaker merely had been explaining his or her philosophical view that the forcible overthrow of the government is proper and was not advocating any specific plan, and if the crowd was not stirred to action, the police would have to let the meeting proceed. This is because the first amendment guarantees you the right to express your beliefs in any political theory in the abstract. But when you go beyond merely explaining your convictions and start advocating that something be done right now to overthrow the government, the first amendment no longer protects your speech.

YOUR RIGHT TO PEACEABLY ASSEMBLE

CLOSELY ALLIED WITH FREEDOM of speech is the freedom of peaceable assembly, also guaranteed by the first amendment. A city or county government can require you to obtain a permit or license to hold a meeting, rally, or demonstration, and it can charge you a fee to help cover the costs of police protection and the like. The permit can even impose reasonable regulations as to the time, place, and duration of the meeting, but it cannot regulate its content; in other words, the government can't censor what you say at the meeting.

A city cannot deny a group permission to meet in a public place (such as a park) or march in the streets just because the group's views are unpopular. This was made clear in a case in the late 1970s involving a pro-Nazi group that wanted to hold a demonstration in front of the town hall in Skokie, Illinois, a predominantly Jewish community. The city denied the group's request for a permit to hold a rally during which the members would be wearing uniforms with swastikas and holding signs advocating white rights. The courts overturned the city's denial of the permit, and eventually the KKK was permitted to demonstrate as originally planned.

YOUR RIGHT TO BEAR ARMS

THE SECOND AMENDMENT to the United States Constitution reads: "A well regulated militia, being necessary to the security of a free State, the right of the people to keep and bear arms, shall not be infringed." America would not have gained her independence from Britain without the Minutemen and others who were ready to pick up their guns on a moment's notice and fight for their new country. The government, however, has the power to regulate many aspects of gun ownership and possession, and there are a number of restrictions on your right to keep and bear arms. You can't, for example, carry a concealed gun with you in public without a permit, which in most counties and states is difficult to obtain. Certain types of firearms—such as assault rifles—can be banned entirely.

The federal Gun Control Act of 1968 prohibits firearms dealers from transferring handguns to any person under 21, persons not residents in the dealer's state, or those persons prohibited by state or local law from purchasing or possessing a firearm. It also forbids possession of a firearm by, and transfer of a firearm to, convicted felons; fugitives from justice; unlawful users of controlled substances; persons adjudicated as mentally defective or committed to mental institutions; aliens unlawfully present in the United States; persons dishonorably discharged from the armed forces; persons who have renounced their citizenship; and persons who have been subjected to certain restraining orders or been convicted of a misdemeanor offense involving domestic violence.

In 1993, Congress amended the Gun Control Act of 1968 by enacting the Brady Handgun Violence Protection Act (the "Brady Act"). James Brady was then–president Ronald Reagan's press secretary when he was wounded seriously and permanently disabled by John Hinckley Jr., during the latter's attempted assassination of President Reagan. Brady's wife, Sarah, vigorously campaigned for stricter gun control laws, and eventually the Brady Act was passed into law. One of the most important features of the Brady Act was to create a "national instant criminal background check system," known as the NICS, to search the backgrounds of prospective gun purchasers for criminal and other information that would disqualify them from possessing firearms. The NICS is a computerized system operated by the FBI and it searches for disqualifying information in three separate databases: (1) the NICS index, which contains records on persons known to be disqualified from possessing firearms under federal law; (2) the National Crime Information Center, which contains records on protective orders, deported felons, and fugitives from justice; and (3) the Interstate Identification Index, which has criminal history records.

Pursuant to the Brady Act, before selling a weapon, a firearms dealer must submit the prospective purchaser's name, sex, race, date of birth, and state of residence (this is known as a "Brady form") to the NICS operation at the FBI. If the firearms dealer is in a state that has elected to serve as a "point of contact" for NICS queries, the dealer must submit the inquiry to the relevant state agency. Upon receiving an inquiry, the FBI or state agency must immediately provide the gun dealer with one of three responses: (1) "proceed," if no information in the system indicates that a firearm transfer would be unlawful; (2) "denied," if the applicant may not legally possess a firearm; or (3) "delay," if further research is necessary.

In October 2001, the United States Court of Appeals for the Fifth Circuit ruled that the second amendment guarantees to individual private citizens a fundamental right to possess and use firearms for any purpose at all, subject only to limited government regulation. However, a little more than a year later, in December 2002, the United States Court of Appeals for the Ninth Circuit held that the second amendment does not give individual private citizens a right to own or possess weapons. Rather, the court held, the second amendment guarantees the right of the people to maintain effective state militias, and the federal and state governments have the full authority to enact prohibitions and restrictions on the individual use and possession of firearms. Because of this split in decisions, it is quite likely that the United States Supreme Court will agree to hear the appeal in the ninth circuit case and rule once and for all whether the second amendment guarantees the private, individual right to own and possess firearms, or whether it only confers "collective rights" to maintain effective state militias, but does not provide any type of individual right to own or possess weapons.

YOUR RIGHT TO BE FREE FROM DISCRIMINATION

A NUMBER OF LAWS PREVENT you from being singled out and discriminated against in various situations because of your race, color, national origin, religion, sex, age, or physical or mental disability. Other chapters in this book discuss discrimination in particular situations: your right to be free from discrimination and harassment in employment (chapter 13); when applying for credit (chapter 18); when buying a house (chapter 6); or when renting an apartment (chapter 7). The rights of gays and lesbians to be free from discrimination are dealt with in chapter 8, while the rights of the physically and mentally disabled are discussed in chapter 14.

Perhaps the most important—and certainly most groundbreaking and contentious—

antidiscrimination act passed by Congress was the Civil Rights Act of 1964, which barred discrimination on the basis of race, color, national origin, sex, or religion. The circumstances surrounding the enactment of that law brought about a mini–Civil War in the Deep South, where National Guardsmen were called in to escort black students into historically all-white universities.

The government or a governmental agency is barred from discriminating against you on the grounds of race, color, national origin, sex, or religion because of the fourteenth amendment guarantee of "equal protection of the laws." Discrimination by a business that is "engaged in or affects interstate commerce" is prohibited by the Civil Rights Act of 1964 and other laws. For instance, a restaurant that serves people regardless of where they live (that is, in state or out of state) cannot refuse to serve African Americans, Jews, or other minorities. Purely private and individual discrimination, however, is not prohibited. For instance, a private men's club that is supported solely by its membership dues can prohibit women and even African Americans from membership. The club generally can't, however, discriminate if persons from out of state belong as members or even if, for example, a private tennis or golf club has a regular annual match with a private club from another state. In such a situation, the club would be deemed to be "engaging in interstate commerce" and therefore subject to the Civil Rights Act of 1964 and other laws relating to discrimination.

To compensate for years of discrimination by many educational institutions and businesses against African Americans and other minorities, the federal government required them to create "affirmative action" programs to increase the opportunities for minorities. Other employers and schools voluntarily set up affirmative action programs on their own initiatives. Some businesses and universities even set up numeric quotas of spots to be filled by minorities. These programs resulted in lawsuits by white workers and students for "reverse discrimination." The gist of these lawsuits was that it is unconstitutional to give anyone better or different treatment solely because of his or her race. They argued that discrimination in any form is wrong, even if it is designed to make up for past discrimination.

The most widely known reverse discrimination lawsuit was Allen Bakke's seminal case in the 1970s against the regents of the University of California for refusing him entrance to the University of California at Davis medical school while admitting minorities whose grade-point averages and entrance examination scores were significantly lower than his. Bakke challenged the special admissions program that reserved sixteen of the one hundred positions for blacks and other specified minorities, leaving white students to compete with all other students, including blacks and other minorities, for the remaining eighty-four positions. In 1978, the United States Supreme Court held that the medical school should have admitted Bakke because his race was the only reason for his rejection. But the U.S. Supreme Court also ruled that as part of an overall admissions program, the university could consider an applicant's race to promote ethnic diversity among its student body.

A later reverse discrimination case was filed by Brian Weber against his employer, Kaiser Aluminum and Chemical Corporation, and his union, United Steel Workers of America. For years, Kaiser's workforce consisted almost exclusively of whites, even though the labor force from which it drew employees was about 40 percent black. To make up for this past imbalance, a collective bargaining agreement between Kaiser and United Steel Workers gave a promotion edge to blacks over whites with seniority. Weber contended that he had been discriminated against because a black with less seniority was selected for a training program instead of him solely because of his race. The U.S. Supreme Court rejected Weber's argument and ruled that the program was necessary to accomplish the racial balance and integration sought by the Civil Rights Act of 1964. And in yet another case, the U.S. Supreme Court ruled that an established seniority program that tended to favor whites over minorities by protecting them from layoffs did not violate the Civil Rights Act.

As far as colleges and universities are concerned, the U.S. Supreme Court has recognized that the attainment of a diverse student body "is a constitutionally permissible goal in an institution of higher learning." In that regard, "ethnic diversity" can be "one element in a range of factors a university may consider in attaining the goal of a heterogeneous student body." Race can be a factor in determining a particular candidate's potential contribution to diversity without the factor of race being decisive when compared to the qualities exhibited by others. For example, a list of factors could include, in addition to race, such qualities as exceptional personal talents, unique work or service experience, leadership potential, maturity, demonstrated compassion, a history of overcoming disadvantage, or the ability to communicate with the poor. As one federal court stated:

> So, when all is said and done, even if race is a consideration, each applicant is, in fact, treated as an individual rather than as a mere stand-in for some favorite group. The effect, then, is that each person's qualifications will have been weighed fairly, and a losing candidate will not have a basis "to complain of unequal treatment under the Fourteenth Amendment," because, even if the last available seat has been given to a person who received "a 'plus' on the basis of ethnic background," the loser "will not have been foreclosed from all consideration for that seat simply because he was not the right color or had the wrong surname."

However, over the last fifteen years there has been a movement toward eliminating race as a factor to be considered in giving a particular student an edge in admissions. Voters in California and Washington approved measures that abolished race-based preferences in state programs, including university admissions. Federal courts in Texas and Georgia have struck down the use of affirmative action in college admissions.

Since 1989, the U.S. Supreme Court has rejected affirmative action in a series of situations. For instance, the nation's highest court has ruled that cities cannot set aside some of their public contracts for African-American and Latino entrepreneurs. Until 1995, most federal agency contracts were required to contain a subcontractor compensation clause, which gave a prime contractor a financial incentive to hire subcontractors certified as small businesses controlled by socially and economically disadvantaged workers, and required the contractor to presume that such individuals included minorities or any other individuals found to be disadvantaged by the Small Business Administration. However, in 1995, the U.S. Supreme Court held that requiring such a clause must meet "strict scrutiny," that is, it must serve a compelling governmental interest and must be tailored narrowly to further that interest.

In a case involving the reapportionment of voting districts based on race, the U.S. Supreme Court ruled that a plaintiff may state a claim for relief under the equal protection clause of the fourteenth amendment by alleging that a state "adopted a reapportionment scheme so irrational on its face that it can be understood only as an effort to segregate voters into separate voting districts because of their race, and that the separation lacks sufficient justification." The high court stated that the laws may appear neutral on their face but are unexplainable on grounds other than race.

In June 2003, the United States Supreme Court addressed the issue of affirmative action in college admissions anew in two cases, one involving the University of Michigan Law School, the other the University of Michigan. The Law School's policy sought to achieve a diverse student body by reaffirming its commitment to diversity with special reference to the inclusion of African-American, Hispanic, and Native-American students, who otherwise might not be included in the student body in meaningful numbers. The University of Michigan used a selection method under which every applicant from an underrepresented racial or ethnic group was automatically awarded 20 points of the 100 needed to guarantee admission. The Supreme Court upheld the Law School's admissions policy, but held that the University of Michigan's admissions policy was unconstitutional.

YOUR RIGHT TO TRAVEL FREELY

THE UNITED STATES CONSTITUTION protects your right to travel freely in and about the United States. The government cannot restrict a person's right to travel within the United States except under extraordinary circumstances; a criminal suspect out on bail, for example, or a convicted felon on probation may be prohibited from leaving the county or state without the permission of the court or the probation officer. If you're divorced and have custody of the children, you may need court approval to take them with you if you want to move to another state, particularly if your ex-spouse objects.

The federal government can restrict your travel to "enemy" countries—countries we are at war with, for example, or with which we have no official diplomatic relations. You can't, for example, visit Cuba, Libya, or Iraq except under rare circumstances. And if you receive Social Security benefits, they may be affected while you are in certain unfriendly nations (see chapter 16).

Air Travel

When you travel by air, you may encounter some problems that are appropriate to discuss here. What, for instance, are your rights if your luggage is lost, destroyed, or damaged by the airline company? For domestic flights—flights originating and ending in the United States—the current limitation on the airline's liability is $1,250. For international flights, the current liability limit is $20 per kilo (which is about 2.2 pounds), up to a limit of 32 kilos per bag. If your luggage and its contents are worth more than the domestic or international limits as applicable, you should consider purchasing "excess valuation" from the airline at the time you check in. This is not insurance, but it will increase the airline's potential liability.

You are entitled only to the actual value of your luggage and its contents as of the date when they were lost, destroyed, or damaged. For instance, if your suitcase cost $500 but was four years old and has been heavily used, the most you'll get for it will be around $75 to $100. You won't get the amount it cost (unless it was new) or what it will cost to replace it with a comparable new one.

Suppose you purchase excess valuation of $5,000, but your baggage and its contents are worth only $3,000. If everything is lost or destroyed, how much do you get, the full $5,000 or only the $3,000? Only the $3,000. It doesn't matter how much excess valuation you purchase; you still get only the *actual value* of the property at the time it was lost or destroyed.

What are your rights if you are "bumped" from an overbooked flight? Overbooking is not illegal, and most airlines overbook their scheduled flights to make up for no-shows. Passengers sometimes are bumped from the flight as a result. When an oversale occurs, the Department of Transportation requires the airline to ask people who aren't in a hurry to give up their seats voluntarily, in exchange for compensation. Passengers bumped against their will are, with a few exceptions, entitled to compensation.

Before you voluntarily give up your seat, ask the airline employee when the next flight is on which the airline can confirm your seat. The alternate flight may be just as acceptable to you. On the other hand, if they offer to put you on standby on another flight that's full, you could be stranded. Also ask whether the airline will provide such amenities as free meals, a hotel room, phone calls, or ground transportation. If not, you might have to spend the money they offer you on food or lodging while waiting for the next flight.

The Department of Transportation does not mandate how much an airline must pay those persons who voluntarily give up their seats. This means that the airlines may negotiate with the passengers for a mutually acceptable amount of money—or perhaps a free trip or other benefits. If the airline offers you a free ticket, ask about any restrictions that may come with it. For example, how long is the ticket good for? Is it "blacked out" during holiday periods when you may want to use it most? Can it be used for international flights? And, most important, can you make a reservation, and, if so, how far before departure are you permitted to make it?

Suppose that not enough people are eager to give up their seats on an overbooked flight voluntarily. Can the airline force you to give up your seat? Yes. When an airline involuntarily bumps a person from a flight, the airline must give the person a written statement describing his or her rights and explaining how the airline decides who gets on an oversold flight and who doesn't. Those travelers who don't get to fly frequently are entitled to an on-the-spot payment of denied boarding compensation. The amount of compensation depends upon the price of the ticket and the length of the delay:

* If you are bumped involuntarily and the airline arranges substitute transportation that is scheduled to get you to your final destination (including later connections) within one hour of your original scheduled arrival time, the airline is not required to pay any compensation.
* If the airline arranges substitute transportation that is scheduled to arrive at your destination between one and two hours after your original arrival time (between one and four hours for international flights), the airline must pay you an amount equal to your one-way fare to your final destination, with a $200 maximum.
* If the substitute transportation is scheduled to get you to your destination more than two hours later (more than four hours internationally), or if the airline does not make any substitute travel plans for you, the compensation doubles (200 percent of your fare, to a maximum of $400).
* You always get to keep your original ticket and use it on another flight. If you choose to make your own arrangements, you can request an "involuntary refund" for the ticket for the flight you were bumped from. The denied boarding compensation is essentially a payment for your inconvenience.

As with all rules, there are a few exceptions:

* To be eligible for compensation, you must have a confirmed reservation. An "OK" in the status box of your ticket qualifies you in this regard even if the airline can't find your reservation in the computer, as long as you didn't cancel your reservation or miss a reconfirmation date.
* You must meet the airline's deadline for buying your ticket. Discount tickets must usually be purchased within a certain number of days after the reservation was made. Other tickets normally have to be picked up no later than thirty minutes before the flight.
* In addition to the ticketing deadline, each airline has a check-in deadline, which is the amount of time before scheduled departure that you must present yourself to the airport. For domestic flights, most airlines have a deadline of ten minutes before scheduled departure, but some can be an hour or longer. Many airlines require passengers with advance seat assignments to check in thirty minutes before scheduled departure, even if they already have an advance-boarding pass. If you miss this deadline, you may lose the specific

seats you were promised, although not the reservation itself. Check-in deadlines on international flights can be as much as three hours before departure time, due in part to security procedures. Some airlines may simply require you to be at the ticket/baggage counter by this time; most, however, require that you get all the way to the boarding area. If you miss the ticketing or check-in deadline, you may have lost your reservation and your right to compensation if the flight is oversold.

* If the airline must substitute a smaller plane for the one it originally planned to use, the airline is not required to compensate people who are bumped as a result.

* The rules do not apply to charter flights, or to scheduled flights operated with planes that hold sixty or fewer passengers. They don't apply to international flights coming into the United States, although some airlines on those routes may follow them voluntarily. Also, if you are flying between two foreign cities—for instance, from Paris to Rome—these rules do not apply. The European Community has a rule on bumpings that occur in a European country. Ask the airline for details, or contact the Department of Transportation.

* Airlines may offer free transportation on future flights in place of a check for denied boarding compensation. However, if you are bumped involuntarily, you have the right to insist on a check if that is your preference. Once you cash the check (or accept the free flight), you probably will lose the right to demand more money from the airline later on. However, if being bumped costs you more money than the airline will pay you at the airport, you can try to negotiate a higher settlement with the airline's complaint department. If this doesn't work, you usually have thirty days from the date on the check to decide if you want to accept it or not. You are always free to refuse the check and take the airline to court to try to obtain more compensation. The government's denied boarding regulation sets out the airline's *minimum* obligation to people they bump involuntarily.

The best way to reduce your chances of being bumped is to arrive at the airport and check in early. On oversold flights, the last passengers to check in are usually the first passengers to be bumped, even if they have met the check-in deadline.

One last thing worth noting here about air travel is that if a passenger is injured or killed in an accident on an international flight originating, ending, or having a stopping point in the United States, the damages are limited by the Warsaw Convention to $75,000. Let's say that Dean Banes and Sylvia Smith board an airliner at San Francisco International Airport. The plane's ultimate destination is London, where Dean is headed, with a stop in Bangor, Maine, Sylvia's final destination. The plane crashes on the way to Bangor and both Dean and Sylvia are killed. Because Dean was killed on an international flight—San Francisco to London—his survivors (his next of kin, such as his wife and children; see chapter 3) are subject to the limitations of the Warsaw Convention and can recover no more than $75,000. Sylvia's survivors, on the other hand, are not subject to any limitations, as Sylvia was on a purely domestic flight—San Francisco to Bangor. One important restriction on the Warsaw Convention's limitation on damages:

the limitation must appear on the passenger's ticket, and the language must be printed in type large enough to catch your attention, that is, it must be conspicuous. A limitation in fine print is not effective to notify the passenger of the Warsaw Convention's limitation.

YOUR RIGHT TO COPYRIGHT PROTECTION

WHEN YOU WRITE, for instance, an article, a book, a theatrical play, a screenplay, or a software program, do you have any protection against someone else using all or part of your work in his or her own article, etc.? Yes. You are protected by the Copyright Act of 1976, which applies to "works" made after December 31, 1977. (Works created prior to 1978 are protected by different laws.) The Copyright Act of 1976 protects you from others infringing upon your work by using it for their own gain or purposes, such as plagiarizing it, quoting it, adapting it (using your article or book as the basis of a movie, for example), or reproducing it (CD, videotape, or DVD piracy or "bootlegging") without your permission.

What types of works can be copyrighted? Books, newspapers, magazine and journal articles, poems, television shows, cinematic movies, theatrical plays, song lyrics, musical compositions, computer software programs, video games, photographs, paintings, drawings, catalogs, maps, compilations of information (such as a telephone directory or mailing lists), architectural plans or works embodied in a building, instruction manuals, choreographed dances (but only if they have been notated or recorded), and more, whether or not they have been published. But only original works of authorship that are "fixed" in a tangible form of expression are protected by copyright law.

Ideas, titles, names, facts, short phrases, slogans, and methods of operations are not protected by copyright laws (although other areas of the law might protect them; for instance, names, short phrases, and slogans may be protected by trademark law); neither are general plot themes. Also unprotected are works consisting entirely of information that is public property and contains no original authorship, such as a standard calendar, height and weight charts, tape measures and rulers, and lists or tables taken from public documents or other common sources.

How to Copyright Your Work

A work is copyrighted automatically at the moment of its creation; no publication, registration, or other action in the Copyright Office is required to copyright your material. A work is "created" when it is "fixed in a copy or phonorecord" for the first time. "Copies" are material objects from which a work can be created or visually perceived either directly or with the aid of a machine or device, such as a book, manuscript, film, videotape, or microfilm. "Phonorecords" are material objects embodying fixations of sound (excluding motion picture soundtracks), such as audiocassette tapes and compact disks (CDs).

Since March 1, 1989, when the United States joined the Berne Convention, it has not been necessary to put a copyright notice on your work for copyright protection. However, use of the copyright notice is still important as, among other things, it informs the public that the work is protected by copyright, identifies the copyright owner, and shows the year of first publication. Having a copyright notice on the work rebuts a copyright infringer's argument that he or she was innocent and did not know that the work was copyrighted. Also, as an incentive to copyright your work promptly, the law generally allows you to collect statutory damages only if you register your copyright of the work with the U.S. Copyright Office within three months after the date of first publication of your work. Additionally, such registration gives the court the discretion to award you attorney's fees if you are successful in your copyright infringement lawsuit. If your work has not yet been published, or if it is registered more than three months after its first publication, you can recover statutory damages and attorney's fees only for infringements that occur after the date of registration.

Only the author or the person to whom the author has transferred the copyright can copyright a work. In a "work for hire" (see chapter 13), the employer (the person who commissions the work) is considered the author of the work. All copies of the work that are distributed to the public should contain a proper notice of copyright. This is done by writing "copyright" or simply "©," followed by the year the work was finished or first published, and then your name; for example, "copyright 2004 Rita Williams" or "© 2004 Randy Barnes." Note that only the symbol "©" should be used for copyright protection internationally, as "copyright" or any abbreviations thereof (such as "copr.") are not recognized internationally.

Sound recordings are defined legally as works that result from the fixation of a series of musical, spoken, or other sounds, but not including the sounds accompanying a motion picture or other audiovisual work. Examples of sound recordings include recordings of music, lectures, and drama. A sound recording is not the same as a phonorecord. A phonorecord is the physical object in which works of authorship are embodied. Phonorecords include audiocassette tapes, CDs, LPs, as well as other formats. The copyright notice for phonorecords embodying sound recordings should contain the symbol "℗," the year of first publication of the sound recording, and the name of the owner of the copyright in the sound recording. An example of a phonorecord copyright would be "℗ 2004 XYZ Records, Inc."

The copyright notice should be affixed to copies or phonorecords in such a way as to give reasonable notice of the claim of copyright. The three elements of the copyright (that is, the symbol, the year of first publication, and the author's name) should appear together on the copies or phonorecords or on the phonorecord label or container.

Registering Your Work with the Copyright Office

You don't need to register your work with the Copyright Office in order for it to be copyrighted, but you do need to copyright it to recover damages if someone infringes upon your copyright. As noted above, if the work is registered with the Copyright Office within three months after the date of first publication of the work or prior to an infringement of the work, the copyright owner will be able to recover statutory damages and, in the court's discretion, attorney's fees in court actions in addition to other damages. If the copyright was not so registered, the copyright owner is entitled to recover only actual damages and lost profits resulting from the infringement.

To register your work with the Copyright Office, you will need to do the following:

* Send a properly completed request-for-copyright application form; to obtain a copyright application form, call the Copyright Office between the hours of 8:30 A.M. and 5:00 P.M. Eastern time at (202) 707-3000 or (202) 707-6737 (TTY); mail a request for the form to the Library of Congress, Copyright Office, 101 Independence Avenue, SE, Washington, DC, 20559-6000; or download the form from the Copyright Office's website at http://www.loc.gov/copyright.
* Send a nonrefundable fee payable to the Registrar of Copyrights in the appropriate amount for each application; you can get the current fee by calling the Copyright Office at the number above or by accessing its website.
* If the work was first published in the United States on or after January 1, 1978, send two copies or phonorecords of the best edition to the Library of Congress Copyright Office at the address noted above.

If the work is a motion picture, the deposit requirement is one complete copy of the unpublished or published motion picture and a separate written description of its contents, such as continuity, press book, or synopsis. If the work is a literary, dramatic, or musical work published only in a phonorecord, the deposit requirement is one complete phonorecord. If the work is a published or unpublished computer program, the deposit is one "visually perceptible" copy in source code of the first twenty-five and last twenty-five pages of the program. If the program is fewer than fifty pages, then a complete copy of the program must be deposited with the Copyright Office. If the work is in a CD-ROM format, then the deposit requirement is one copy of the CD-ROM, the operating software, and any manuals that accompany it. If you also want to register the computer program on the CD-ROM, you should include a printout of the first twenty-five and last twenty-five pages of source code for the program. If the work you want to copyright is three-dimensional, photographs or drawings of the work are usually sufficient.

The Copyright Act establishes a mandatory deposit requirement for works published in the United States. Generally speaking, the owner of the copyright or the owner of the exclusive right of publication in the work has a legal obligation to deposit in the Copyright Office, within three months of publication in the United States, two copies (or two phonorecords) for the use of the Library of Congress. If you fail to make the requisite deposit, you are subject to fines and other penalties. Failure to deposit a work does not, however, affect copyright protection.

Your best copyright protection is to register your work with the Copyright Office as soon as you complete it and to put the proper copyright notice on the title page of every copy (or on the label of every phonorecord) you send out. If you will be submitting your unpublished work to others—for instance, a magazine, a book publisher, a movie or television production company, or a music publishing company—keep a record of those submissions. It may well be worth the extra money to send your work via certified mail, return receipt requested, particularly if you are sending a script to a movie or television production company or music recording company. This way, if you suspect that someone is using your work without your consent and without compensating you, you will be able to prove without a doubt that the alleged infringer at least had possession of your work at the relevant time. Many cases of copyright infringement—particularly those involving musical compositions and screenplays—are won or lost on the ability to prove if and when the alleged infringer received the work. Because of the potential for fraudulent infringement claims, many television and movie production companies and record companies either return unsolicited material unread or unheard or toss it into the trash without reading or listening to it.

How Long a Copyright Lasts and Transferring Your Rights

A work that is created on or after January 1, 1978, automatically is protected from the moment of its creation and usually is given a term of the author's life plus seventy years. If two or more persons own the copyright, the copyright lasts from the death of the last of the copyright holders to die, plus seventy years. In the case of a work made for hire, by corporations (such as motion picture companies), and for anonymous and pseudonymous works (unless the author's true identity is revealed in the Copyright Office records), copyright protection lasts for ninety-five years from the date of publication or 120 years from the date of creation, whichever is shorter.

If the author owns the copyright, he or she can direct by will or living trust who will own the copyright after he or she dies. If the author dies without a will or trust and is the owner of the copyright, his or her next of kin becomes the owner of the copyright (see chapters 3 and 4). In a work for hire, the owner of the copyright can transfer it to anyone he or she wishes to.

As the author of a work, you can transfer all or part of a copyright you own to another person unless you already have assigned the copyright to someone else, such as a book publisher. Transfers of exclusive rights—such as giving a magazine the exclusive right to be the first to publish your article ("first serial rights")—are required to be in writing. But even if you're giving someone a nonexclusive right to use your work, get the agreement in writing and read it carefully. Know exactly what rights you're giving up before signing the agreement. If there's any part of the agreement that you don't understand, seriously consider talking to an experienced copyright lawyer.

What Constitutes a Copyright Infringement

If you claim that your copyrighted work has been infringed upon, you must prove three things: (1) that you own a valid copyright to the work; (2) that the infringer—the person who used your work without permission—had access to your copyrighted work (there is no copyright violation if someone else independently creates a similar work without knowing about yours); and (3) that when considered in their entirety and final form (that is, the form in which the public sees them) the two works are "substantially similar."

In determining whether two works are substantially similar, the judge considers specific similarities between the plots, themes, dialogues, moods, settings, paces, characters, and sequences of events. The mere fact that someone used your idea or plot theme as the basis for a work is not enough for a case of copyright infringement. Each case is determined on its own merits, by comparing the total concept and feel of the allegedly infringing work with the copyrighted work. Random and insignificant similarities between two works are not enough. But determining whether the infringement is "substantial" can be a difficult question.

Let's say you write an article revolving around a wealthy person living in a large mansion, who is attended to by several servants, gets around town in a chauffeur-driven limousine, eats at the best restaurants, and so on. Your article is published in a magazine, and a few months later you see an article in another magazine involving a wealthy person with similar attributes, but the plot is considerably different. Assuming you can prove that the alleged infringer read your story, if you sue for copyright infringement based on the similarities of the lifestyles of the two characters, will you win? Probably not. That a rich person lives a certain lifestyle comes under the heading of *scènes à faire*: incidents, characters, or settings that are standard to certain ideas and themes and therefore not protected by the copyright laws. Some other examples of *scènes à faire* include a church wedding, a barroom brawl, a high-speed police chase, and a formal cocktail party.

"Fair Use" of a Copyrighted Work

Not all uses of a copyrighted work without the copyright owner's permission are prohibited. "Fair use" is permitted. Fair use is "a privilege in others than the owner of the copyright to use the copyrighted material in a reasonable manner without the consent of the copyright owner." In determining whether the use of a copyrighted work comes under the heading of fair use, a judge considers the following factors:

* The purpose and character of the use, including whether the use is a commercial one or is for nonprofit educational purposes. Uses that are generally permissible include using the copyrighted material for criticism, comment, news reporting, teaching (including photocopying the material for classroom use), and research. Book reviewers, for instance, gen-

erally can quote short passages from copyrighted material without violating the Copyright Act. Not all use for criticism, news reporting, and the like is considered fair use. An example: Former president Gerald Ford had a contract with a book publisher and *Reader's Digest* to publish his memoirs. *Time* magazine agreed to pay $25,000 for the exclusive right to excerpt 7,500 words from the memoirs, which *Time* planned to publish the week before the book was shipped to bookstores. But before it did, *The Nation*, a political commentary magazine, obtained an unauthorized copy of the manuscript and used it to scoop *Time* by publishing a 2,250-word article on Ford's pardon of former president Richard Nixon. Although *The Nation* quoted a total of only three hundred words from the book, the U.S. Supreme Court found that it was guilty of copyright infringement, because the quoted material was "essentially the heart of the book."

* The nature of the copyrighted work. Works that are factual in nature can be used a little more freely than original works of fiction and fantasy, for instance.

* The amount and substantiality of the copyrighted work used in relation to the copyrighted work as a whole. There are no hard and fast rules on just how much of a copyrighted work can be used without infringing on the copyright. Each case is decided on its own facts, with the judge taking into consideration the amount of copyrighted material that was used and the length of the entire copyrighted work. For example, quoting a one hundred-word paragraph from a six-volume historical work might not be considered a substantial infringement, but quoting twenty-five words from a fifty-word poem could be. As we saw earlier in the case of the memoirs of former president Gerald Ford, a quote of only three hundred words from a book can constitute an impermissible infringement, where the quoted words are the heart of the book.

* The effect the use has upon the potential market for or value of the copyrighted work. This generally is considered to be the single most important element of fair use. The focus here is on whether the use materially impaired the marketability of the copyrighted work. If the use resulted in a significant reduction in the value of the copyrighted work, the copyright owner has a much better chance of winning a lawsuit for copyright infringement.

Your Rights When Someone Infringes Upon Your Copyright

When someone unlawfully infringes upon your copyrighted work, you usually need to be represented by an experienced copyright lawyer to enforce your rights. Depending on when you copyrighted your work, you are entitled to recover the following types of damages in a copyright case:

1. You can ask the judge for an "injunction" to stop any further infringement of your copyright.

2. You can recover money damages based on one of the following:
   (a) The "actual damages" the infringement caused you. Actual damages compensate the copyright owner for the extent that the work's market value was injured or destroyed by the infringement. If, for instance, before the infringement you could have sold the work for $10,000, but now it is worth only $1,000, your actual damages are $9,000.
   (b) The profit made by the infringer. This is the amount of the infringer's gross sales minus any costs—such as printing, promoting, and distributing the work—and overhead. In one case, a magazine used a copyrighted photograph of Raquel Welch without permission on the cover of one its issues of *High Society's Celebrity Skin*. The judge awarded 75 percent of the magazine's profit from that issue to the photograph's copyright owner because of the cover picture's importance in attracting the customer's attention.
   (c) "Statutory damages" set by federal law. Statutory damages are used when neither your actual damages nor the infringer's profits can be ascertained with a reasonable degree of certainty. At his or her discretion, the judge also can award statutory damages instead of actual damages or the infringer's profits, even if the actual damages or the infringer's profits are ascertainable. (This usually is done when the actual damages and infringer's profits are relatively small.) Statutory damages generally range from $750 to $50,000 for each infringement. If the judge finds that the infringement was "willful," he or she can triple the award up to $150,000.
3. In many cases, you also can recover your attorney's fees from the infringer if you win the case.

Before you can recover damages in court for an infringement, you must register your work with the United States Copyright Office. If you want to recover statutory damages and attorney's fees, you must register your work with the Copyright Office *before* the infringement of an unpublished work, or within three months after the first publication of a published work. If you wait until after the infringement to register your work, you will be permitted to recover only your actual damages or the infringer's profit from the infringement.

YOUR RIGHT TO PATENT YOUR INVENTIONS

IF YOU INVENT SOMETHING, you should think about protecting yourself with the rights afforded you by the law—most important, the right to patent your invention. Many types of inventions and discoveries can be patented: a new product or machine; a novel manufacturing process; compositions of matter (combining two or more ingredients to form a new compound with different or additional properties); even original designs for an "article of manufacture";

to name a few. Improvements to existing products, machines, processes, and designs can be patented in many cases. You generally cannot patent an idea, however, if you do not have the means to carry it out. Another major limitation is that an invention can be patented only if it has some "utility." You can't get a patent if your invention is useless or trivial. (The requirement of utility does not apply to patents for designs.)

A patent generally gives you the exclusive right to your invention for twenty years from the date you file your application for a patent (fourteen years for a design patent). You retain all rights to use, make, and market your invention yourself during that time, or you can give or sell some or all of these rights to others. If someone infringes upon your patent (copies or uses your invention without your consent), you can sue to stop the infringement and recover monetary damages the infringement caused you.

Only the original inventor can obtain the patent; if someone else has invented something but has not applied for a patent, you cannot apply to patent it. Your employer may have some or all of the rights to the patent if you developed it on company time, however (see chapter 13). Falsely claiming on a patent application that you are the original inventor is a serious matter.

You may lose your right to patent your invention if you don't protect yourself properly. For example, you can't patent your invention if it already has been available to the public for a year and you haven't applied for a patent. Putting "patent pending" on the invention won't help you if in fact no patent is pending; doing so may even subject you to criminal penalties. (You usually can't put "patent pending" on your invention until you have filed an application for a patent with the United States Patent and Trademark Office.)

The best thing to do if you have a finished invention—or even just an idea that you plan to pursue—is to talk to a patent lawyer. Since patent law is a very complex area, lawyers who deal in this area tend to be specialists; many of them have engineering degrees as well as degrees in law. Before filing an application for a patent, a patent lawyer will commission a search of the patent office records to see whether someone else already has obtained a patent for a similar invention. (If you're still in the idea stage, a patent search now could save you considerable time and money by preventing you from putting a lot of effort and expense into developing your invention, only to discover later that someone else already has a patent on it.)

There are companies that advertise in popular magazines and occasionally on television that they can help you develop your idea from inception to finalized invention, and assist you in the marketing of it, even create an infomercial for you. You have to be cautious when dealing with such companies, as these companies often lead the potential inventor to believe his or her invention has considerable merit and selling potential, and charge the would-be inventor thousands—in some cases tens of thousands—of dollars putting together a marketing plan for a product they know has little if any potential. To save yourself from getting ripped off, you should consult a patent lawyer before making any commitment to one of these companies. An experienced patent lawyer can give you some advice on the marketing of your invention, including telling you which companies live up to their promises and which companies to avoid. At the very least, check the company out with the Better Business Bureau. Ask the company for references, including the names and telephone numbers of others whose inventions it marketed; contact those people and ask how much the company's services cost them, what the company did, and whether they were pleased with the company's efforts. Don't sign a contract with a development and marketing company until you've read it carefully, and pay special attention to just what the contract requires the company to do. If there's anything you don't understand, or if it appears the company really isn't obligated to do anything, talk to a patent lawyer before signing the contract.

YOUR RIGHT TO KNOW WHAT THE GOVERNMENT KNOWS

THE FREEDOM OF INFORMATION ACT (FOIA), signed into law in 1966, gives you access to information the federal government has in its files. The information need not mention or even pertain to you. The idea behind the Freedom of Information Act is this: The government is "we the people," and we the people have the right to know what the government knows about us. Some states have their own version of the FOIA, giving you access to state, county, and city files.

Generally, the government can withhold requested information only when a sufficient reason exists. Many refusals, for example, are based on the assertion that to disclose the information would compromise national security. The government also won't give out information that constitutes a company's trade secrets (see chapter 13). If you don't agree with the government's refusal to furnish the information to you, you can sue in court to have a judge decide whether the government's refusal is justified.

To obtain the information, you must request it either in person or by mail directly from the appropriate government agency. Your request must identify the information as precisely as possible. Which agency you should contact depends on the type of information you're seeking. If, for example, you want to learn what the FBI knows about you, someone else, or a certain event, you must direct your request to it. The names and addresses of the federal agencies where various information is kept are published in the *Federal Register*, which is available in many large libraries. When you request information from the government, you will have to pay a "search and copy" fee, the amount of which depends on how difficult the information is to find and how many pages there are to copy.

Another law to be aware of is the Privacy Act of 1974, which regulates the government's use of information a government agency obtains on you. The Privacy Act gives you the right to demand that information important to you be used only for the purpose for which it was gathered originally. The Privacy Act also gives you the right to obtain copies of the information, correct errors in it, and make additions to it.

YOUR RIGHT TO SUE THE GOVERNMENT FOR PERSONAL INJURIES

SUPPOSE YOU'RE INJURED BY the negligence of a government employee—federal, state, county, or city—or you are hurt on government property because of a dangerous condition. Do you have a legal right to make the government pay for your injuries and associated damages, such as your medical bills, the damage to your car, the wages you lost while you were out of work, and your pain and suffering?

Historically, if you were injured by a government employee or on government property, you could not sue the government. This rule originated in old England, when the king had the ultimate authority regarding who could sue whom. Since the courts were in fact the king's courts, he naturally ordained that no one could sue the government (which was, of course, the king).

This rule of "sovereign immunity" made its way to the United States, and as a result, neither the federal government nor a state or local government can be sued without its permission. Generally speaking, today, laws permit suits against governments, their agencies, and their employees for personal injuries in some situations. If a government employee on duty driving a government-owned vehicle causes injuries due to his or her careless driving, for instance, the government is usually liable to the injured person.

If you want to sue the United States government, your injury must fall within the provisions of the Federal Tort Claims Act. State and local governments generally have laws regulating personal injury suits against them. Some states, for example, still do not permit a suit against them for medical malpractice in a public hospital.

Examples of Injuries Caused by Government Employees or Public Property

The most common injuries caused by a government employee are traffic accidents traceable to the negligence of the driver of a government-owned vehicle, such as a city or county bus, a police car or fire truck, or a city landscaping truck. Brutality and false imprisonment by police officers are other examples of personal injuries caused by government employees. One important limitation on the government's liability is that generally the employee must be on the job when he or she hurts you. Let's say you're injured in a car accident caused by the careless driving of a city police officer. If the accident happened while the officer was on duty, the city is liable for your injuries and the damage to your car. But if it happened, say, on the officer's day off while the officer was driving his or her own car, the city is not liable. In many states, the government is not liable if a police car or fire truck that is responding to an emergency call hits a person.

Governments generally have the obligation to maintain their property in a reasonably safe condition, and if they fail to do so, you can sue for your resulting injuries. For instance, if you slip on a loose tile at city hall, if your heel catches a piece of loose carpet at the Social Security office, or if you fall on a freshly waxed floor at the county courthouse where there were no warnings, the government is liable for your injuries. Defects in the design of highways and other roads also have been the basis of many successful lawsuits against governmental bodies. If, for instance, a corner is too sharp for the speed limit and there is no cautionary sign warning drivers to slow down, a car may veer off the road while trying to negotiate the curve at the posted speed limit and crash into a tree or a ditch, even into oncoming traffic. The failure to maintain landscaping on public property is another source of lawsuits against a government for personal injuries. For example, the city may permit a hedge at a busy intersection to grow too dense, making it dangerously difficult for approaching drivers to see cross traffic.

Suppose you're driving down a city street and your car hits a pothole, which causes several hundred dollars' worth of damage to your car. Is the city liable for your damage? That depends on whether the city had "notice" of the pothole. If the pothole was new and the city didn't know about it, then the city is probably not liable. But if the pothole had been there quite some time and the city either knew or should have known it was there, the city either should have repaired it or placed a warning barrier around it. Some cities have laws that make the city liable for damages caused by potholes only if the proper department had received a written notice from someone informing it of the pothole and its location.

Filing a Claim with the Government

Before you can file a lawsuit in court against the government, you must first file a "claim" with the proper administrative body, such as the city or county clerk, or the appropriate state or federal agency. The time you have to file a claim against the government is usually considerably shorter than the time you have to sue a private individual or company (the "statute of limitations"). You may be required to file your claim with the proper governmental agency within as few as sixty days of the injury-producing incident. More commonly, you have six months to file a claim. If the governmental agency rejects your claim, you then have a specific amount of time, which varies from state to state, from that date to file your lawsuit in court.

If you file the claim late, you can be excused from the time requirement if you have a valid legal reason—if you were in a coma, for example, or in the hospital due to the accident or otherwise unable to file a claim on time. But mere ignorance of the fact that you had to file the claim within six months (or whatever time is specified) is generally no excuse for not filing it or for filing it late. A claim that is filed late usually is denied without the merits of the claim even being considered, unless you show a valid legal reason why it was not filed on time. If the government agency refuses to consider your claim because it was filed late and rules that you don't have a sufficient legal reason for being excused from the time requirement, you can file a petition in court asking for relief from the time requirement.

If you suspect that a government employee or that defective or dangerous government property is wholly or partly to blame for your injuries, you should promptly consult an experienced personal injury lawyer to determine what rights you have against the government. Suits against governments tend to be more complex and must comply with many technical, formal procedures. For these reasons, a lawyer's help is warranted for most claims against a government.

If your claim is a relatively small one—within your state's small claims court's limits—and is against the city or county, you may be able to handle the claim yourself. You can get information about filing a claim against a city or county by calling the city clerk or city attorney's office or the county clerk or district attorney's office—whichever is appropriate. Ask how much time you have for filing the claim from the date of the accident, and ask whether there is a specific claims form the city or county can send you to fill out. If the claim can simply be a letter from you, include your name, address, and telephone number; the date and place of the accident; a complete description of the accident (for instance, on March 3, 2004, you were stopped at a red light on Madison Avenue when a city maintenance truck, license number 1ABC234, driven by Anthony Smith, a city employee, rear-ended you); proof of your damages (such as your doctors' bills and repair bills or estimates to fix your car); and ask for a specific amount of money (the total amount of your medical bills; damage to your car; lost wages; pain and suffering; and any other damages you suffered from the injury, such as damage to any contents in your car). If your claim is rejected, you may be able to sue the city or county in small claims court (see chapter 19). Ask the city or county clerk if you can sue the government in small claims court, as not all states, cities, or counties permit it.

TWENTY-ONE

Visas, Immigration, and Naturalization

Give me your tired, your poor,
Your huddled masses yearning to breathe free . . .
I lift my lamp beside the golden door!
—Inscription on the Statue of Liberty

OKAY, SO THE streets aren't paved with gold, and we do have our share of impoverished people, but America is still the land of opportunity, especially to those living under authoritarian rule or who go to bed hungry each night. Unfortunately, the United States cannot handle all of the people who want to immigrate here each year, and therefore closes the "golden door" after a certain number of immigrants have been allowed in each year by stopping the number of "green cards" it issues each year.

For decades, the federal Immigration and Naturalization Service (INS) had jurisdiction over matters pertaining to visas, immigration, and naturalization. However, the INS went out of existence on March 1, 2003, when it was absorbed into the new Department of Homeland Security's Border and Transportation Security Division. It was broken down into three agencies:

1. *Bureau of Citizenship and Immigration Services (BCIS).* This bureau has jurisdiction over citizenship, immigration services, and administration of services.
2. *Bureau of Immigration and Customs Enforcement.* This agency covers investigations, detentions, deportations, and enforcement operations.

3. *Bureau of Customs and Border Protection.* This bureau encompasses the border patrol, agricultural inspections, and other inspection operations of former INS and U.S. Customs Service.

VISAS

A "VISA" GIVES AN ALIEN permission to enter the United States. There are two types of visas: nonimmigrant (temporary) and immigrant (permanent). Without a temporary or permanent visa, an alien's presence in the United States is usually unlawful, and if he or she is discovered, the alien will be "removed" (deported) from the United States.

When a Visa Is Not Required: The "Visa Waiver" Program

Thanks to the visa waiver program, a visa is *not* required for people coming from certain countries. These countries must give reciprocal privileges to United States citizens; must have a nonimmigrant visa refusal of less than 3 percent for the previous year; certify that they have a machine-readable passport; and the attorney general, in consultation with the secretary of state, must determine that the country's designation for the visa waiver program will not compromise United States law enforcement or national security interests.

Countries that currently are approved for the visa waiver program are Andorra, Australia, Austria, Belgium, Brunei, Denmark, Finland, France, Germany, Iceland, Ireland, Italy, Japan, Liechtenstein, Luxembourg, Monaco, New Zealand, Norway, Portugal, San Marino, Singapore, Slovenia, Spain, Sweden, Switzerland, The Netherlands, the United Kingdom, and Uruguay. (Note that you must be a citizen of the country to be eligible for the visa waiver program.)

Persons coming from one of the visa waiver program countries are not allowed to work in the United States, nor are they allowed to stay as long as they want. There are two primary limitations on their visit to America: (1) upon arrival in the United States, the person must show a round- or continuing-trip ticket; and (2) the return or continuing date on the ticket must be no longer than ninety days from their date of entry into the United States. In short, before coming to the United States for a period of three months or less, they are not required to get their passports stamped with a visa. However, if they wish to stay in America for up to six months, then it will be necessary for them to make the trip to the consular office in their own country to get the appropriate visa stamped in their passports.

Canadians are not required to obtain a visa to enter the United States unless they are a "treaty trader" or "treaty investor" according to the laws and regulations of the North American Free Trade Agreement (NAFTA).

Nonimmigrant Visas

Nonimmigrant visas give an alien the right to stay in the United States for a specified time, with limited rights. The most common types of nonimmigrant visas are tourist visas (B-2), business visas (B-1), and student visas (F-1). The length of time you can stay in the United States depends on the category of nonimmigrant visa you have. For example, a student visa (F-1) ordinarily allows you to remain in the United States longer than a tourist visa. (Note, though, that a student visa is good only for as long as you are a bona fide student. If you drop out of school entirely, or take only one token class, you run the risk of having the Bureau of Citizenship and Immigration Services (BCIS) arrest you and start removal proceedings against you.)

The length of your stay will be assigned when you first enter the United States on the Nonimmigrant Arrival-Departure Document (Form I-94, or Form I-94W, if you qualify for the visa waiver program discussed above), which will be provided to you by the steward or stewardess of the airliner or ship you are arriving on. The expiration date of your Form I-94 will be stamped in your passport by BCIS representatives at the airport or docks and Form I-14 will be attached to your passport. A tourist or business visa normally allows you to remain in America for six months.

Getting an Extension of Your Temporary Visa

Let's say that you are in the United States on a tourist visa but want to stay longer than your visa allows because you haven't seen everything you wanted to. Or you or a close family member has become seriously ill and you can't leave by the designated time. Or you're on a business visa but your work is taking longer than anticipated. You must file an application to extend/change nonimmigrant status, along with a statement of why you need the extension. The form and supporting documents must be filed within sixty days of the date your visa is set to expire, and no later than fifteen days before it terminates.

The extension requested must be for no longer than six months. If you find that you still need more time after the first extension is granted, you may file another request for extension no later than fifteen days before your first extension expires. Be prepared to file as much supporting documentation as you can gather to justify the legitimacy of the need for your continued, albeit temporary, visa. If the BCIS determines the extension request is not being made in good faith, it will deny your petition for extension. If you file for an extension of stay in a timely manner (before your visa expires), you may remain in the United States for 120 days past your I-94 termination date while the BCIS processes your petition. If you do not hear from the BCIS within 120 days after your I-94 termination date has expired, you may ask for an extension of the 120-day period.

Overstaying Your Permitted Time

What happens if your request for an extension is denied and you stay in the United States past the expiration date on your I-94? Or you simply don't file for an extension and remain in the country after your visa expires? You do so at your own peril. You risk being jailed and having removal proceedings brought against you, with the ultimate punishment of being deported.

But what if you overstay your time in the United States and the BCIS does not find out about it, and you voluntarily return home? If your overstay was less than twelve months, you will not be able to return to the United States for three years. If your overstay was twelve months or longer, you will be banned from returning to America for ten years. As you can see, if you wish to return to the United States in the near future, you must leave the country before your visa expires.

If you have a single entry visa, you must not leave the United States and expect to reenter before your Form I-94 time expires. You will have to return to your home country and request another visa. However, if you are traveling on a "multiple entry visa," which is good for three years, you may make unlimited entries into the United States during that time.

Changing Your Status from Tourist to Student

Suppose you entered the United States on a tourist visa, but once here decide you want to go to school. Can you get your tourist visa changed to a student visa? Usually not. If you are planning on coming to the United States to study, you must state your intention to the consular office in your country or the appropriate airport personnel that you are coming here to study. The consulate or airport personnel will stamp "prospective student" in your passport. You must also show any Forms I-20 (certificate of eligibility for nonimmigrant student) you have received from schools that have accepted you, plus demonstrate that you have sufficient money in the bank or other funds to support yourself for at least one year. Additionally, you must be more certain about your intentions than you have come to the United States to "study" and not to find a United States citizen to marry to remain in the country. You should have a particular educational goal in mind. For instance, it is better to be accepted by a four-year college to work toward a four-year bachelor of arts degree in, for example, music or psychology, than taking general classes at a two-year college. Finally, you must convince the consular office or airport personnel that you intend to return to your native land or country of origin after you complete your studies.

Immigrant Visas

Unlike the case with a nonimmigrant visa, with an immigrant visa you are free to live in the United States as long as you want (that is, the visa is permanent), and more important, to work without restrictions. The immigrant visa commonly is referred to as a "green card," because it was originally green. It was white for a while, and currently is pink and blue, but it is still referred to as the "green" card.

There are limits (quotas) on each country or group of countries as to how many persons may immigrate to the United States each year. When the country's, or group of countries, quota has been fulfilled (including any unused visas from other countries), no further visas are authorized for the rest of the year. Does this mean you must start over and file a new petition each year you don't get your visa? Not at all.

The date your quota-waiting period officially begins—your "priority date"—is the date you originally filed your petition with the Bureau of Citizenship and Immigration Services (BCIS) or the American Embassy. The priority date for quota waiting in the case of employment preference visas begins the day your employer files the application for labor certification with the department of labor (discussed later in this chapter).

Your priority date is important, as it establishes when your interview with the BCIS will be. The length of time you must wait depends on how many people have earlier priority dates than you. In some countries, such as Korea, Mexico, India, and China, there is a wait of up to nine years for brothers and sisters of United States citizens. The current priority dates being processed are published once a month in *The Visa Bulletin*, a publication of the United States State Department.

GETTING A "GREEN CARD"

THE "GREEN CARD" IS known officially as the alien registration receipt card. Except for "conditional" green cards (discussed below), a green card permits an alien to live and work permanently in the United States. A green card confers essentially all of the rights and protections that a citizen has, with the major exclusion of voting, and the right to receive some welfare benefits.

Of course, besides all of the rights and protections that come with a green card, so too come all of the obligations of a citizen, the major one being the duty to pay taxes and file annual tax returns as required by the tax laws. Two main considerations exist in determining whether you will get a green card: family reunification and financial contribution. What the United States is trying to avoid is immigrants who have no family, no money, and no skills, and who must rely on already overtaxed government programs to survive.

Preferences for Immigrant Visas

The time it takes for a person to be eligible to get a green card is based on a system of preferences. There are two broad categories of preferences: family preferences and employment preferences.

Family Preferences

The Family Unity Program is designed to allow immediate family members (spouses, unmarried minor children and their children, and parents) of United States citizens or permanent residents to remain in America and work or go to school while their green cards are being processed. Otherwise the spouses, unmarried minor children and their children, and parents would have no legal status in the United States and would be subject to deportation.

The following is a list of the different preferences afforded relatives:

* Immediate relative: Immediate relatives of an American citizen are eligible for the immediate issuance of a green card; there is no limit to the number of immediate relatives that can immigrate to the United States every year. "Immediate family relatives" are limited to the United States citizen's spouse, unmarried minor children and their children, and parents. However, for the parents to be eligible, their American citizen child must be at least 21 years of age. Special rules apply to a stepparent and adoptive parents.
* Family First Preference: the unmarried children of a United States citizen who are over age 21 and unmarried.
* Family Second Preference: the spouses and unmarried children of a permanent resident (one who has a green card). Unmarried children under 21 years of age have preference over unmarried children over 21.
* Family Third Preference: the married children and their spouses and unmarried children of a United States citizen. Note that married children, their spouses, and their children of a permanent resident do *not* receive any preferential treatment.
* Family Fourth Preference: the brothers and sisters of an American citizen who is at least 21 years old.

Getting Your Fiancé(e) a Visa and a Green Card

If you are an American citizen or permanent resident and wish to marry a foreign national, you are both headed down a burdensome trail fraught with bureaucratic paperwork and cynicism. Because of the possibility of sham marriages solely to allow an alien to enter the United States and get permanent resident status (that is, a green card), the BCIS will look at your attempt to bring your fiancé or fiancée to this country with great skepticism. The BCIS generally looks upon marriages to aliens as shams. Because of the attitude of the BCIS and the number of laws and regulations, as well as the paperwork that must be filed, you would be smart to hire a competent immigration lawyer to assist you in getting your fiancé(e) admitted to America.

A special law applies to "mail-order bride" businesses to protect the bride from an abusive marriage and to help stem the number of fraudulent marriages. Studies show that many mail-order brides are the subjects of abuse by their husbands, who threaten that they will get the bride deported if she tells anyone of the abuse. The law requires that every international matchmaking organization doing business in the United States must give its "recruits" (the potential brides) information in the woman's native language regarding conditional permanent residence status and the battered spouse waiver under such status.

The organization must also inform the prospective bride, in her native language, of permanent resident status, marriage fraud penalties, and the unregulated nature of the matchmaking organization. The matchmaking organization can be fined $20,000 for each time it fails to inform one of its "recruits" of these facts.

The Penalties for a Fraudulent Marriage

The penalties for a fraudulent marriage to obtain permanent resident status is high: According to the law, "[a]ny individual who knowingly enters into a marriage for the purpose of evading any provision of the immigration laws shall be imprisoned for not more than 5 years, or fined not more than $250,000, or both."

One example of a fraudulent marriage involved an alien who admitted she went through a marriage ceremony with a citizen for the sole purpose of obtaining an immigration visa. The alien admitted that the couple did not intend to consummate the marriage, and agreed that a divorce would be obtained within six months. The court ruled that the alien was not in fact married to a citizen and hence was not entitled to an immigration visa under the circumstances.

If You Are an American Citizen

For the purpose of the following discussion, let's assume that you are a man who wants to bring your alien fiancée into the United States. Your right to do so depends on whether you are an American citizen or a permanent resident.

If you are a United States citizen who wishes to bring your fiancée to America, you must file a petition for alien fiancé(e) (Form I-129F) and an affidavit of support (Form I-134). Along with these, you must file a great deal of other paperwork to prove that you are an American citizen and in fact intend to marry your fiancée, and the marriage is not a sham. You must submit proof of your own American citizenship (such as certified copies of your birth certificate and voter registration card, or your certificate of naturalization) and proof that you can indeed support your fiancée (an employment certification, copies of bank statements, the deed to your house and any other real estate you may own, stocks, bonds, and other investments, life insurance policies, etc.).

You must also submit proof that you and your fiancée have in fact met in person within the last two years. The attorney general, in his discretion, may waive this requirement. The personal meeting requirement is to ensure that you are not entering into a fraudulent marriage with an alien who is paying you to become her husband, only to divorce you once she gets her green card. Proof that you actually have met in person within the previous two years include pictures of the two of you together, affidavits from others who saw you together, airline ticket stubs showing travel to and from your fiancée's country of residence, and the like.

You must also provide proof that you do indeed intend to marry your fiancée within ninety days of her arrival in the United States. One type of proof is a letter from the authorized person—such as a minister, rabbi, priest, commissioner, or judge—who will be performing the ceremony. Letters, invoices, or receipts from the caterer and photographer you have hired for the wedding are also helpful, as are wedding announcements or invitations showing the date of the wedding to be within the ninety-day limit.

Additionally, you will be required to submit an affidavit as to how, when, and where you met your fiancée and how and why you decided to get married. You must also lay out the details of the marriage and what your plans are for the honeymoon. If you have been married before, you must submit evidence that the previous marriage has been ended legally, such as the final divorce decree or a certified copy of the death certificate if you are a widower.

Be prepared to be called in for a personal interview with an INS representative. If you are requested to come in for an interview, bring as much documentation as you can showing that your love for your fiancée is true and that you have the means to support her once she arrives here.

If the BCIS concludes that your marriage is the real thing and not just a sham, you will be sent a notice of action telling what you must do next. When the file is completed, it will be sent to the American embassy or consulate in your fiancée's country.

What Your Fiancée Must Do

While you, the American citizen, are busy gathering and submitting documents, photographs, affidavits, and other evidence to the BCIS, your fiancée also should be getting together the documents that she will have to present to the American embassy to get permission to come to the United States to marry you. The visa classification for the fiancée of an American citizen is K-1. Your fiancée must obtain a passport for herself and for any unmarried children under 21 years old and their children who plan to accompany or follow her to America. She must also have birth certificates for herself and her children (and their children, if any) and a medical report for herself and all of her children who will be accompanying her to the United States showing that they are free of communicable diseases.

If your fiancée was married before, she must present proof that the marriage was legally terminated by divorce decree, annulment, or death. She must also bring the originals of all documents that you (her fiancé) filed with your petition for alien fiancé(e), as well as an affidavit of support from you. Among other proof she will have to file are statements from the police in all countries (except the United States) she lived in for six months or more stating she was not charged with any crimes, particularly prostitution.

Once all of the documents and photographs are gathered, your fiancée must take them to the American embassy as soon as possible to apply for a nonimmigrant visa. If the American consul concludes that your engagement is in good faith, he or she will stamp the appropriate visa in your fiancée's passport and the passports of her unmarried children under 21 years old and their children, if any, who will be accompanying her to America.

When the Wedding Must Take Place

The wedding must in fact take place within ninety days of your fiancée's arrival in the United States; otherwise, she and her children who accompanied her will be removed (deported) to her country of origin. Suppose your fiancée is in a traffic accident the day before your wedding and suffers serious injuries. There is no way you can get married within the ninety-day period because of it. If an emergency situation such as this prevents you from getting married within ninety days, you must file an affidavit with the BCIS requesting an extension of time to marry. Be sure to state the reasons in full and attach any supporting documentation (copy of medical records, hospital and doctors' fees, a letter from her attending physician, and, in the hypothetical situation we are using, a photograph of your fiancée laid up in the hospital). The BCIS is loath to grant an extension to the ninety-day time limit to get married, so make every human effort to get married within that period.

Note that your fiancée must marry *you* and not someone else within the ninety-day period. If your fiancée does marry someone else, deportation proceedings will be started against her. Also, if your fiancée does not marry you within ninety days after she and any unmarried children under 21 are admitted, she and her children will be required to leave the United States, and if she fails to do so, removal proceedings will be initiated against her and her children.

Filing for an Adjustment of Status

After marrying you, an American citizen, within ninety days of entering the United States, your new wife must file for an adjustment of status. You should also concurrently file Form I-130, petition for alien relative. This will get your new wife—and any accompanying unmarried children under 21, assuming she filed a petition for them as well—a "conditional" green card. This is valid for only two years. Within ninety days of the expiration of the two-year period, you and your spouse must jointly file a petition to remove the conditions on residence and then she will be granted a permanent green card.

Unless you can show good cause for not complying with the law, if you do not file the requisite joint petition to remove the conditions of residence by the end of the two-year conditional permanent status period, the attorney general will terminate the conditional permanent resident status of your wife as of the second anniversary of your wife's lawful admission as a permanent resident. At your wife's removal hearing (unless there is no hearing because she has voluntarily left the country), your wife has the burden of proving that she complied with all laws and time limits or has a legally recognized excuse for failing to do so.

Are both signatures necessary on the petition to remove the conditions on residence? Normally, yes. If the American citizen's signature is missing from the petition, removal proceedings may be brought against the alien spouse. The alien spouse will be removed (deported) unless she can establish a good reason for the lack of her husband's signature. A waiver is permitted if the alien spouse was the victim of spousal abuse or battery; if the couple entered into a valid marriage but it has since been terminated by the citizen's death; or the alien spouse would suffer extreme hardship if removed.

If You Are a Permanent Resident

If you are in the United States as a permanent resident (that is, you have a green card) and wish to bring your alien fiancée to America prior to marriage, unfortunately the laws discussed above do *not* apply to you. No special treatment is given to the fiancée of a permanent resident.

Termination of Conditional Permanent Resident Status

The attorney general must terminate the permanent resident status of an alien (and his or her accompanying children) if the attorney general determines that the qualifying marriage (1) was entered into for the purpose of getting the alien admitted as an immigrant; (2) the marriage was annulled or ended in divorce or was otherwise terminated, except by death; or (3) a fee or other consideration (other than a fee or other consideration paid to an attorney to help prepare a lawful petition) was paid for the filing of a petition for immigrant or permanent resident status.

For example, suppose Markie, an American citizen, is paid $10,000 for a "marriage of convenience" to an alien, so that the alien can come to and stay in the United States by filing a petition for alien fiancé(e) and acquires conditional permanent resident status. Markie and the alien do not live together, nor do they share a joint banking account; in fact, they don't even see or communicate with each other except, perhaps, for BCIS hearings and the like. This is a clear example of an obviously fraudulent marriage.

The attorney general must notify the couple of his or her decision that the marriage does not qualify as a legitimate one, and must terminate the permanent resident status of the alien involved as of the date of the decision. The alien may request a hearing to review the attorney general's decision, and the burden at the hearing is on the attorney general to prove that the qualifying marriage was improper on one of the three grounds listed above. As discussed earlier, Markie (and her alien "husband") will face up to five years of prison and a fine of up to $250,000 for her role in the fraudulent marriage. The alien husband will also be deported after serving his time in prison.

THE ANNUAL GREEN CARD DIVERSITY LOTTERY

EACH YEAR, the department of state holds a "green card diversity lottery," with fifty-five thousand green cards available to natives of certain countries as determined by a mathematical formula. Aliens from certain countries are not eligible to apply for the lottery. They are usually from countries that have a high immigration rate to the United States already. For example, in the 2001 lottery, natives of the following countries were excluded from the lottery: Canada, China, Taiwan, Colombia, the Dominican Republic, El Salvador, Haiti, India, Jamaica, Mexico, Pakistan, the Philippines, Poland, South Korea, the United Kingdom (except Northern Ireland), and Vietnam.

To be eligible for the green card lottery, you must either have a high school education or its equivalent or, within the past five years, you have had two years of work experience in a job requiring at least two years of training or experience. You must also demonstrate that you will be able to support yourself and your family, and that you have not been convicted of committing certain crimes or suffer from certain physical or mental defects.

The application period for the green card lottery generally runs from the first week of October to the first week of November. You can submit only one application; if you are married, your spouse can file his or her own application as well. If you are selected, you should hear within eight months of that fact. If not, you can register again when the thirty-day registration period reopens in October. There is no limit on the number of times you can apply. You can apply for the green card lottery either from within the United States or from your home country.

Employment Preferences

If you do not qualify for a family preference, you may be able to qualify for an employment preference if you have an employer sponsoring you. Following are the different preferences and a discussion of each.

* Employment First Preference: people of "extraordinary ability" in science, art, education, business, entertainment, or athletics, as well as outstanding professors and researchers, and executives and managers of multinational corporations; does not need a job offer but correspondence with a potential employer is advisable; does not need a labor certification.
* Employment Second Preference: persons of "exceptional ability": professionals with advanced degrees or people of exceptional ability in science, business, or the arts; usually requires a job offer and a labor certification.
* Employment Third Preference: recently graduated professionals, those with a bachelor's degree; and skilled workers in occupations requiring at least two years of training, education, or experience; requires a job offer and labor certification.
* Employment Fourth Preference: unskilled workers in occupations requiring less than two years of training, education, or experience; job offer and labor certification required.
* Fifth Preference: millionaire immigrants or alien entrepreneurs.

Obtaining a Labor Certification

Most aliens in the employment preferences category must receive a "labor certification" from the department of labor before they are eligible to immigrate to and work in the United States. This is a burdensome and time-consuming procedure. The reason for requiring a labor certificate is to ensure that an alien is not taking a job that otherwise could be filled by an American citizen or permanent resident.

The employer wishing to hire someone other than a first-preference alien (aliens of extraordinary ability, outstanding professors and researchers, and executives and managers of multinational corporations) must obtain the proper form from the Department of Labor (DOL Form ETA 750, application for alien employment certification).

The prospective employer must first advertise for the job. Before the employer may do so, however, he or she must submit a draft of the ad to the Department of Labor's advertising specialist or case manager. To enable the government agency to monitor how many American citizens and permanent residents respond to the ad, it must include the state employment agency's address rather than the employer's address and telephone number. If the ad is placed in a daily newspaper, the ad must run for three consecutive days. If placed in a weekly newspaper, it must run for three consecutive weeks. You will need to file with the advertising specialist or case manager originals of the entire newspaper pages on which the ad ran.

The state employment agency will send you the responses to your ads, and you must then interview the applicants to determine their qualifications for the job offered. You must have a valid reason for rejecting a prospective employee. If no one responded to your ad, or no one who answered the ad is legitimately qualified for the job at the wages being offered (which should be the same as what the employer actually is paying to other workers with similar experience and qualifications for the specific employment in question, or the prevailing wage for the type of work being paid by other employers), you may then file DOL Form ETA 750 with the Department of Labor, which will then make a decision on whether to grant a labor certification.

Once the Department of Labor issues the labor certification, the employer must then file INS Form I-40, immigration for alien workers. If the Department of Labor denies the request for labor certification, the denial may be appealed, and often the employer will be permitted to file extra documentation to bolster its petition.

Priority Workers

Aliens of Extraordinary Ability Because of the decreasing numbers of top-level American scientists, outstanding professors, acclaimed researchers, artists, and other gifted persons, the immigration law has been amended to allow certain aliens to work in the United States without having to go through the rigmarole of obtaining a labor certification. These are the "priority workers," who may file an immigration petition for alien worker (Form I-140) without having to get a labor certification from the Department of Labor. Qualified priority workers are limited to aliens with "extraordinary abilities," outstanding professors and researchers, and executives and managers of multinational corporations. This group of workers is known in INS parlance as "employment first preference" immigrants.

An alien of "extraordinary ability" is someone whose abilities in the sciences, arts, education, business, or athletics has been proved by sustained national or international renown, and whose achievements have been recognized in the field through extensive documentation. Winning a Nobel Prize or other internationally recognized award certainly qualifies one as a person of extraordinary ability. An alien who has not won such an award may still qualify if he or she meets other qualifications, such as winning less acclaimed prizes or awards for excellence; had articles written about him or her in a professional journal or major scholarly works; or has made original scientific, scholarly, artistic, athletic, or business-related contributions of major significance. Other accomplishments that help qualify the alien as having extraordinary ability include having written articles that have been published in professional journals or major trade publications or other media; having played a leading role for organizations or establishments that have a distinguished reputation; or having had commercial success in the performing arts.

In short, the alien must essentially be a household name in at least one country other than their home country because of his or her accomplishments. Examples of priority workers include brilliant scientists, acclaimed performing artists, economists, stellar athletes, best-selling authors, star actors, well-known film directors, and top physicists.

Although an alien of extraordinary ability does not need to have an employment offer in the United States to be admitted, he must demonstrate by clear and convincing evidence that he is coming to America to continue work in his or her particular field of expertise.

Outstanding Professors and Researchers Outstanding alien professors and researchers may petition for a green card without having to obtain a labor certification from the Department of Labor. An "outstanding" professor or researcher is one who (1) is internationally recognized as outstanding in a specific academic area; (2) has at least three years of teaching or research experience in the field; and (3) seeks to enter the United States for a tenured position (or tenure-track position) with a university or institution of higher learning to teach or conduct research.

Alternatively, an outstanding researcher who has achieved documented accomplishments in his or her academic field will be permitted to immigrate to America for a comparable position to those listed above with a private employer, if the private employer has at least three persons engaged in full-time research activities.

Some of the criteria that are looked at include whether the alien has written scholarly books or articles in international journals or has participated as a judge, either individually or on a panel, of others in the same or a related academic field. The alien must have at least three years of experience in teaching or research and have a job offer from an American university or research institute for a tenured teaching or permanent research position. Without the requisite job offer waiting for the alien, he or she will be denied entry into the United States as an immigrant.

Executives and Managers of Multinational Corporations Executives and managers of multinational corporations are also eligible for immigrant status without having to obtain authorization to work from the Department of Labor. A "multinational corporation" includes corporations with branches, affiliates, or subsidiaries located in two or more countries, but are owned by the same individual or corporation.

An "executive" is an employee who directs management of the corporation or a major component of it, has broad discretion in decision making, and is under only general supervision by higher-level executives or a board of directors. A "manager" of a multinational corporation must manage a department, subdivision, or component of the corporation, and supervise and control the daily work of other supervisory, managerial, or professional employees. The manager must also have the authority to hire and fire or promote personnel he or she supervises.

A threshold requirement to qualify as an executive or manager for purposes of immigration is that the alien must have been employed as an executive or manager by the multinational corporation or one of its subsidiaries for at least one year. Additionally, the alien executive or manager must continue working in the same or a higher capacity for the same corporation when he or she moves to the United States.

Nonpriority Workers

Professionals with Advanced Degrees and Aliens with Exceptional Ability The BCIS classifies this category as employment second preference aliens, and their visa is designated H-1B. Their spouses and unmarried children under 21 years of age obtain H-4 visas. Examples of professionals and aliens with exceptional ability include accountants, market researchers, lawyers, economists, engineers, and members of the art and performance world who are well-known in their own country but not outside it. Unlike priority workers, nonpriority workers usually must obtain a labor certification (discussed above) before their Form I-140, immigrant petition for alien worker, can be filed. However, the BCIS may waive the labor certification for this group of alien worker immigrants if it is in the national interest to do so. One example of when it is in the national interest to waive the labor certification requirement is in the case of alien physicians working in an area where there is a shortage of doctors, or if the alien physician is to go to work for a Veterans Administration hospital or other VA medical clinic or facility.

Skilled Workers and Professionals with Bachelor's Degrees This category is composed of skilled workers and professionals who hold baccalaureate degrees and are members of their profession. Examples of professionals who have baccalaureate degrees and are members of their profession include teachers, chemists, dietitians, computer system analysts, medical technicians, and journalists. Normally the professional must have at least five years of experience in his or her area of expertise.

"Skilled workers" are those workers who have at least two years of education or on-the-job training or experience. The exact length of training or experience the worker must have is set by the Department of Labor. The job the skilled worker is entering the United States for must be a permanent one and not of a seasonal or temporary nature.

Unskilled workers Unskilled workers are all other workers who, like skilled workers, enter the United States for a permanent job, and not for one that is temporary or seasonal. Remember that for unskilled workers, as well as for skilled workers and professionals not holding an advanced degree, they must obtain a labor certification from the Department of Labor before the employer can file Form I-140, immigrant petition for alien worker.

Workers Changing Jobs

An alien worker who enters the United States under the above laws legally cannot change employers. If he or she does, removal (deportation) proceedings will be brought against the alien employee, unless the employee agrees to leave the country voluntarily. For example, suppose you are a Filipino national working in the Philippines for ABC Company. Your company wants you to go to its American branch to do some work there, and files the appropriate petition with the BCIS to have you come over. You come to America, but after working two months for ABC Company, you find a better, higher paying job with XYZ Corporation and go to work for them. When the BCIS learns of this, removal proceedings will be initiated against you and you will most likely be deported to the Philippines.

One exception to the above rule involves professionals. Professionals can change jobs and remain in the country, so long as they obtain permission to do so from the BCIS. Professional athletes may change employers, providing, however, that the new employer is a team in the same sport. For instance, if Jeff, an alien, plays hockey for the New York Rangers and is traded to the Anaheim Mighty Ducks, it does not affect his status or otherwise count against him, despite the fact he has a new employer. But Jeff could not leave the New York Rangers to become a member of a team in another sport, such as the San Diego Padres baseball team.

Live-In Nannies Suppose you are a single mother who must work to support her family. Or you're a married couple who both have successful careers and neither wants to give theirs up. You decide to hire a live-in illegal (undocumented) alien nanny to help you out. How easy is it just to hire an alien as a live-in nanny? It's very easy, but also very illegal.

If you hire a so-called "illegal" alien—in legalese, an "undocumented" alien; one who has entered the country illegally or has stayed in the United States past the time his or her non-immigrant visa has expired—you, your spouse, and your alien nanny are all breaking the law. The law treats a live-in alien domestic worker just like it does any other unskilled worker. You must obtain a labor certification from the Department of Labor by filing DOL Form ETA-750. Then you must file BCIS Form I-140, immigrant petition for alien worker. To obtain the labor certification, you must go through all the steps described above that any employer must go through when hiring a nonpriority worker such as an unskilled laborer.

Once the alien acquires the labor certification, and the immigrant petition for alien worker is approved, you may hire the alien as a live-in domestic worker. However, be aware that you must treat the live-in domestic worker as an employee. This means paying at least the minimum wage, although your state may require a higher minimum wage rate for home-care workers. It also means filing for a federal employer identification number; withholding taxes for Social Security and unemployment; getting workers' compensation insurance to cover the live-in worker in case she is injured on the job; filing quarterly tax documents; and filling out and submitting any and all other paperwork to various governmental agencies as required by law.

You may not be entitled to obtain the labor certification and get your petition for alien employment application approved to hire an alien as a live-in worker if a day worker is all you need. For instance, suppose Beth and Jim want to hire a live-in nanny because both of them have good careers and need someone to take care of the children during the day. The Department of Labor or BCIS may conclude that Beth and Jim only need a day care helper, and therefore will not grant permission to work to the prospective live-in nanny and may commence removal proceedings against her.

Going through the labor certification process and the time it takes to get your immigrant petition for alien worker (BCIS Form I-140) approved is burdensome and frustrating. Additionally, you may not be able (or want) to pay the live-in nanny at least minimum wage. These factors lead many people to submit to the temptation of simply hiring illegal (undocumented) aliens as live-in help, paying them wages that are considerably below the minimum wage requirements. If caught, they face fines from the Bureau of Citizenship and Immigration Services for employing illegal help, as well as trouble from the Internal Revenue Service (IRS) for failing to report the hiring of an employee, paying less than the minimum wage, and failing to file the requisite documents required of every employer.

The minimum wage and maximum work hour provisions do not apply to persons employed on a "casual basis" to provide, for example, mere baby-sitting services. A live-in nanny certainly is hired on more than a casual basis and is expected to do more than just baby-sit. Note that a live-in nanny (one who legally is permitted to work in the United States) is *not* exempt from the minimum wage laws, but is exempt from the maximum work hour provisions of the federal law.

Millionaire Entrepreneurs To promote growth and investors in the United States, a number of visas are designated each year for certain entrepreneurs who want to start a business in the United States. The business must be a new commercial enterprise that employs at least ten American citizens or permanent residents (exclusive of the alien entrepreneur's own spouse, sons, or daughters). The alien entrepreneur must invest, or be in the process of investing, at least $1 million dollars in the business, with a few exceptions. The alien must file Form I-526, immigrant petition by alien entrepreneur.

A limited number of visas are made available each year for qualified immigrants who wish to establish a new business in a targeted area. A "targeted area" is defined as a rural area (roughly defined as a town of less than twenty thousand residents) or an area that has had high unemployment figures—at least more than 150 percent of the national average rate. The alien entrepreneur may be allowed to start his business in such areas with considerably less than $1 million, but not less than one-half of that amount (or other amount as the attorney general may set from time to time).

If the alien entrepreneur wishes to go into a nontargeted area such as a metropolitan area with an unemployment rate significantly below the national average, the attorney general may require the alien entrepreneur to invest an amount more than $1 million, up to three times greater.

The alien (and his or her spouse and unmarried children under age 21) will be given a conditional green card that is good for two years. Within ninety days of the expiration of the two-year period, the alien (and his or her spouse and children who accompanied or followed him) must file BCIS Form I-829, application by entrepreneur to remove conditions. The alien entrepreneur must demonstrate that he started a business that employs at least ten employees—American citizens or permanent residents—has invested, or is actively in the process of investing $1 million, and that the alien entrepreneur is operating or otherwise sustaining the business.

The BCIS may require the alien entrepreneur to come to its office for a personal interview.

If the BCIS approves the application to remove the conditions of his green card, he and his family will be granted a second, unconditional green card that gives them permanent resident status.

ALIENS SEEKING ASYLUM

Suppose you are being persecuted in your home country because of, say, your political beliefs or religion. You are the subject of taunts and the contempt against you by others is escalating. Threats are made against you or your family members. Can you apply to the United States for asylum? Yes; however, you must make the petition for asylum *in* the United States. It is not necessary to make the request at an official "port of arrival." You can make the request anywhere in the United States.

To qualify for "asylee" status, you must show that your life or freedom in your home country is being threatened due to your race, religion, nationality, membership in a particular social group, or political opinion. After you have been in America for one year, you may file for permanent resident status (i.e., a green card). However, you should be aware that there currently is a large backlog for asylum visas.

Asylum is not available if you can be removed (deported) to a third country where your life or liberty will not be threatened because of your race, religion, political opinions, etc. The third country must give you a full and fair procedure for determining your claim to asylum or equivalent temporary protection. Even if there is a third-party country that would accept you, the attorney general of the United States may find that it is in the public interest for you to receive asylum in the United States.

You need not file the application for asylum immediately upon arriving in the United States, although this is recommended highly. The longer you stay in the United States before making your asylum plea, the more the asylum officer may believe that it is not being made in good faith. In any event, you must show by "clear and convincing" evidence that the application for asylum has been filed within one year after the date you entered the United States.

Reasons for Denial of Asylum

You will be denied asylum if:

* you ordered, incited, assisted, or participated in any way in the persecution of any person due to race, religion, nationality, membership in a particular social group, or political opinion;
* you were convicted of a particularly serious crime, such as an aggravated felony, and pose a danger to the community in the United States;

* you committed a serious nonpolitical crime outside the United States prior to your arrival in America;
* you are likely to be a danger to United States's security;
* you have engaged in terrorist acts;
* you were "firmly resettled" in another country before arriving in the United States.

Work Authorization and Permanent Residence for Asylees

Once you have been granted asylum, you cannot be returned to your home country. In making your petition for asylum, you may also include your spouse and unmarried children under 21. Upon approval of your petition for asylum, you are entitled to a work permit ("employment authorization") and may be allowed to travel abroad with the prior consent of the attorney general.

A granting of asylum does not guarantee you permanent residence in the United States. Asylum may be revoked, for instance, if the conditions in your home country have undergone a "fundamental change in circumstances," such that your life or freedom would no longer be in jeopardy if you were to return. Similarly, asylum may be revoked if you have persecuted another because of race, religion, nationality, membership in a social group, or political opinion; are convicted of a serious crime; become a danger to United States's security; or engage in terrorist activity.

Asylum may also be revoked if you can be removed to another country—other than your home country—where your life or freedom will not be threatened. Other reasons for terminating asylum include if you voluntarily return to your home country as a permanent resident or you have acquired a new nationality and enjoy the protection of your new home country.

When you file a petition for asylum, you are not automatically entitled to a work permit. However, a work permit will be granted to you by a regulation of the attorney general. If you are not otherwise eligible for a work permit, you may not be given a work permit before 180 days after the date you filed your application for asylum. If your asylum petition is rejected, your work permit application expires sixty days thereafter or when the document is dated to expire, whichever is later.

Before you are granted asylum, a background check will be run on you to determine if there are any grounds to deny asylum or deport you. Unless there are exceptional circumstances, the asylum hearing must be heard no more than forty-five days after the date the application for asylum is filed. A decision on the application normally must be made within 180 days after the application is filed.

If your petition for asylum is approved, you can file a petition for permanent status for yourself, your spouse, and your children one year after you are granted asylee status. To qualify for the change of status to permanent resident, you must have remained physically in the United States for one year from the time your petition for asylum has been approved to the time your petition to change status to permanent resident is filed.

If You Are Denied Asylum

Suppose, however, that the asylum officer denies your petition for asylum. What are your rights then? One choice is to leave the United States voluntarily. By leaving voluntarily, you can attempt to enter America at a later time without having to wait any length of time.

If you decide to fight the denial, you can avail yourself of formal court proceedings, including a hearing before an immigration judge. Ordinarily, you have thirty days to appeal from the time your petition for asylum is denied. Should the judge agree with the denial and order you removed from the United States, your next step would be to file suit in federal court. (Of course, all of this should be done with the assistance of a good, experienced immigration lawyer.) If you ultimately lose your challenge of the adverse decision to your petition for asylum, you will be ordered removed from the United States. In such a case, you will be banned from entering the United States for five years. (Contrast this with the no-waiting policy if you choose to leave the United States voluntarily after the asylum officer originally denies your petition.)

Generally, you may not make a second claim for asylum if the first petition was rejected either because you adequately failed to establish the threat to your life or freedom or because the petition for asylum was made more than one year after you entered the United States. However, you may be granted asylum if you can prove that the circumstances and conditions in your home country have changed significantly to the point where your life or liberty would be in jeopardy or that the claim was late due to extraordinary circumstances.

ALIENS SEEKING REFUGEE STATUS

YOU ARE A REFUGEE if you are outside the country of your nationality and are unable or unwilling to return to that country because of actual persecution or a well-founded fear of persecution because of your race, religion, nationality, membership in a social group, or political opinion. In some circumstances, you may be declared a refugee even though you are still living in your own country.

The number of aliens eligible for refugee status is set by the president of the United States at the beginning of the fiscal year after "appropriate consultation." This consultation is based upon meetings between designated Cabinet-level representatives of the president who meet with members of the committees on the judiciary of the Senate and the House of Representatives and review the status of countries throughout the world. The number of refugees who may come to America must be made by the president before the beginning of each fiscal year, and is mainly based on humanitarian and political considerations.

As with asylum, a refugee may apply for permanent resident status after one year's residence in the United States from when his or her petition for refugee status was approved. The refugee may file for permanent residence for his or her spouse and any unmarried children under the age of 21.

Forced Abortion or Sterilization

Some countries limit the number of children that a woman may bear. Suppose a woman living in China already has given birth to one child—her limit—and is pregnant again. According to the laws of her country, she must submit to a forced abortion. Does she qualify as a refugee even though she still lives in her home country of China? Yes.

Special consideration is given to a woman in such a predicament. A woman who has been forced to abort a pregnancy or undergo an involuntary sterilization, or who has been persecuted for failing to abort the child or undergo unwanted sterilization, or who otherwise resists a coercive population control program is deemed to be persecuted on the basis of political opinion and qualifies as a refugee. Likewise, a woman who has a well-founded fear that she will be forced to undergo such a procedure or be subject to persecution for such failure, refusal, or resistance is deemed to have a well-founded fear of persecution on account of political opinion.

However, if that woman moves to a new country that does not restrict the number of children she may have, there is no longer any actual fear of persecution or well-founded fear of same; therefore, she no longer qualifies as a refugee according to United States immigration law.

Denial of Petition for Refugee Status

The reasons for denying a refugee's application for immigrant status are generally the same as those of a person seeking asylum, discussed above, as are the appeal proceedings in case the petition for change of status to permanent resident is denied.

TEMPORARY PROTECTED STATUS

"Temporary protected status" essentially gives humanitarian protection to aliens whose countries are undergoing strife, whether natural or man-made. If the attorney general decides you qualify for temporary protected status, you may stay in the United States, even work, during the duration of your home country's unrest.

The types of strife that qualify include:

* war within the country; that is, a civil war;
* a natural disaster, such as an earthquake, flood, drought, epidemic, or other environ-

mental disaster resulting in a substantial—but temporary—disruption of life in the affected areas;

* your home country is temporarily unable to handle the return of its own citizens adequately;

* the attorney general finds that there are extraordinary and temporary conditions in the foreign country that prevent its own citizens from returning to their country in safety.

The attorney general decides how long the foreign country is at strife. The initial period is no shorter than six months, nor longer than eighteen months. At least sixty days before the initial period ends, the attorney general, who must consult with the appropriate governmental agencies and review the situation in the foreign country, must determine whether the conditions of unrest still exist.

If the attorney general decides such conditions do in fact remain in existence, he or she may extend the "period of designation" for six, twelve, or eighteen months, as the attorney general deems appropriate. The attorney general must file notice of the extension in the *Federal Register*. When the attorney general decides the adverse conditions no longer exist, he must publish that fact, also in the *Federal Register*.

The termination of the foreign country's designation under this law takes effect six months from the date the notice was published in the *Federal Register*, or the date the last extension was granted, whichever is later. The courts have no right to review the attorney general's decision as to whether the foreign country initially qualifies under the temporary protected status law, or whether to terminate such designation at a later time.

Aliens who are not permitted to take advantage of temporary protected status include those who:

* have been convicted of any felony or two or more misdemeanors committed in the United States;

* have attempted, conspired to commit, or committed a crime of moral turpitude ("moral turpitude" is defined as a crime that is particularly morally repugnant, more so than the average crime), except a purely political offense;

* have attempted, conspired to commit, or committed a violation of any law or regulation regarding a controlled substance, or trafficked in controlled substances, unless the alien's transgression was a single instance of simple possession of thirty grams or less of marijuana;

* ordered, incited, assisted, or participated in any way in the persecution of any person due to race, religion, nationality, membership in a particular social group, or political opinion;

* are likely to be a danger to United States's security;

* have engaged in terrorist acts.

Temporary protected status is withdrawn from an alien living in the United States as prescribed if (1) the attorney general finds that the alien was not in fact eligible for temporary protected status; (2) the alien has not remained continuously in the United States from the time he or she was first granted temporary protected status; or (3) the alien fails to register with the attorney general at the end of each twelve-month period after being granted temporary protected status.

PERSONS NOT ALLOWED TO IMMIGRATE TO THE UNITED STATES

Not everyone who wants to come to America can do so. A list exists of "inadmissible aliens" who are ineligible to receive visas and be admitted to the United States. Among those who cannot enter the United States include:

* health conditions: aliens who have a communicable disease of public health significance, including acquired immune deficiency syndrome (AIDS) and tuberculosis;
* no vaccinations: aliens who have not been vaccinated for such diseases as the mumps, measles, rubella, polio, tetanus and diphtheria toxoids, pertussis, influenza type B, hepatitis B, and any other vaccinations against vaccine-preventable diseases. However, children who are 10 years old or under who are seeking an immigrant visa as an immediate relative are exempt from this requirement. The parent, adoptive parent, or prospective adoptive parent must submit a signed affidavit stating the he or she is aware of the law and will ensure that the child will be vaccinated within thirty days of the child's admission or at the earliest time when it is medically appropriate;
* physical or mental disorder: aliens who have a physical or mental disorder that may pose a threat to the property, safety, or welfare of the alien or others, including those with a history of violent behavior that is likely to recur;
* drug addicts: aliens who are drug addicts or abusers;
* criminals: aliens who have committed, or attempted or conspired to commit, a crime of moral turpitude, other than a purely political crime. Additionally, aliens who have been convicted of two or more crimes (excluding purely political crimes), regardless of whether the crimes involved moral turpitude, for which the cumulative jail sentences were five years or more;
* controlled substances violations: aliens who have violated (or conspired or attempted to conspire) any law or regulation of a state, the United States, or any foreign country relating to a controlled substance;
* drug traffickers: aliens whom the immigration officer knows or has reason to believe is or has been an illicit trafficker in controlled substances, or is or has been a knowing assister,

abettor, conspirator, or colluder with others in the illicit trafficking of controlled substances;

* prostitutes: aliens who are coming to the United States solely, principally, or incidentally to engage in prostitution, or who have engaged in prostitution within ten years of the date of their application for a visa, admission, or change of status;

* spies and saboteurs: aliens whom a consular officer or the attorney general knows, or has reasonable grounds to believe, seek to enter the United States to spy or commit sabotage, or to violate any law prohibiting the export of goods, technology or sensitive information; aliens who intend to commit any other unlawful activity; or aliens who plan to oppose or overthrow the government of the United States by force, violence, or other unlawful means;

* terrorists: aliens who have engaged in terrorist activity, or whom the appropriate officials know, or have reasonable grounds to believe, is engaged in or is likely to engage after entry into the United States in any terrorist activity; or aliens who are representatives or members of a foreign terrorist organization;

* adverse foreign policy consequences: aliens whose entry or proposed activities would have potentially serious adverse foreign policy consequences for the United States;

* communists: aliens who are or have been a member of or affiliated with the communist party or any other totalitarian party. This does not apply if the alien can convince the consular officer when applying for a visa (or the attorney general when applying for admission) that membership is or was involuntary, the alien was under 16 years of age, or it was necessary for the purposes of obtaining work, food rations, or other essentials for living;

* Nazis: aliens who, from March 23, 1933, to May 8, 1945, were members of the Nazi party or any government that was an ally of the Nazi government, and ordered, incited, assisted, or otherwise participated in the persecution of any person because of race, religion, national origin, or political opinion, or any alien who engaged in genocide;

* the poor, unhealthy, and uneducated: aliens who, taking into account their age, health, family status, assets, resources, and financial status, and education and skills, are likely to become public charges;

* unapproved workers: aliens who attempt to enter the United States to perform skilled or unskilled labor are inadmissible, unless the secretary of labor has determined and certified to the secretary of state and the attorney general that (1) there are insufficient workers who are able, willing, qualified, and available at the time and place of the application for a visa and admission; and (2) the employment of the alien will not adversely affect the wages and working conditions of similar workers in the United States.

Residency Requirements

After you have received your green card (officially, your alien registration receipt card), you again play the waiting game until you can become a citizen. Most applicants must have lived in the United States for five years immediately preceding the date they are eligible to become United States citizens. You must also have lived in the state from which you apply for citizenship for at least three months.

Alien spouses who married a United States citizen need only wait three years to apply for citizenship. Special rules apply to spouses of United States government employees who are "regularly stationed abroad," and an attorney should be consulted about what the waiting requirements are in such a case.

Taking Trips Outside of the United States

For the purposes of this discussion, we'll assume that you are like most immigrants and must wait the whole five years before getting your citizenship. Does the five-year wait mean that you must stay in the United States and can't make trips abroad either for business or pleasure, or even to your home country to see your relatives? No.

During your five-year waiting period, there is no problem with taking trips out of the United States for less than six months, so long as the total does not equal more than two and one-half years. But if you are out of the United States continuously for one year or longer, you will be deemed to have changed your mind and don't want citizenship. Such an absence will "break the continuity" of your residence.

If your trip out of the United States is longer than six months but less than one year, it will break the continuity of your residence, unless you can establish to the attorney general's satisfaction that you did not in fact abandon your residence in the United States during such time.

Special rules regarding lengthy absences from the United States apply to permanent residents who are employed by a government contractor or an American institution of research. Your employer may be able to advise you as to the special rules of residence applicable to such residents; otherwise, you will need to consult a good immigration lawyer.

Other Requirements

Other requirements for becoming a United States citizen include: being a person of "good moral character"; having the ability to speak, read, and write English (although there are exceptions to this rule for persons who are over a certain age or who have lived in the United

States for a certain period of time); having a basic knowledge of United States history and the workings of its government; and have no voluntary communist affiliation.

Filing for Citizenship

To file for citizenship, you must obtain and complete BCIS Form N-400. This form (and all other BCIS forms) may be obtained by calling the BCIS at 1 (800) 870-FORMS or by visiting your local BCIS office. You must send a cover letter to the BCIS with: the completed Form N-400; a fingerprint fee (currently $25) in the form of a check or money order made payable to the Bureau of Citizenship and Immigration Services (your fingerprints will be taken by a BCIS employee at a later date); and two color photographs of your head (there are specific requirements as to the precise size of the photograph and pose you must take, so be sure to go to a photographer who takes immigration and passport photographs on a regular basis and is familiar with the necessary requirements of the photo).

You must also send a copy of the front and back of your green card, a filing fee (currently $225) payable to the Bureau of Citizenship and Immigration Services, and a self-addressed, stamped envelope so the BCIS can return your filing receipt. You don't need to wait until the exact moment your five-year waiting period is up to file. You may file Form N-400 and the supporting documentation up to three months in advance of your actual eligibility date.

You must send all of the documents to the BCIS service center that covers your area. You should send your letter via certified mail, to prove that you did send in the forms on a specific date.

There are four service centers, whose addresses and areas covered are:

California Service Center
(for UPS and courier deliveries)
24000 Avila Road, 2nd Floor
Laguna Niguel, CA 92677
Attn: Incoming Mail Room
Telephone: (949) 360-2995
Mailing Address:
P.O. Box 30111
Laguna Niguel, CA 92607
This office covers Arizona, California, Guam, Hawaii, and Nevada.

Nebraska Service Center
(for UPS and courier deliveries)
850 "S" Street
Lincoln, NE 68508

Mailing Address:
P.O. Box 82521
Lincoln, NE 68501-2521
Telephone: (402) 437-5218

The Nebraska Service Center covers the following states: Alaska, Colorado, Idaho, Illinois, Indiana, Iowa, Kansas, Michigan, Minnesota, Missouri, Montana, Nebraska, North Dakota, Ohio, Oregon, South Dakota, Utah, Washington, Wisconsin, and Wyoming. The Nebraska Service Center also has jurisdiction over BCIS offices in British Columbia, Calgary, and Manitoba.

Texas Service Center
Attn: N-400 Unit
Room 2300
7701 N. Stemmons Freeway
Dallas, TX 75247
Mailing Address:
P.O. Box 851204
Mesquite, TX 75185-1204
Telephone: (214) 381-1423

The Texas Service Center is for Alabama, Arkansas, Florida, Georgia, Kentucky, Louisiana, Mississippi, New Mexico, North Carolina, Oklahoma, South Carolina, Tennessee, and Texas. It also has jurisdiction over the Bahamas, Freeport, and Nassau.

Vermont Service Center
(for UPS and courier deliveries)
75 Lower Weldon Street
St. Albans, VT 05479-0001
Mailing Address:
P.O. Box 82521
St. Albans, VT 05479-0400
Telephone: (802) 660-5000

You should file with the Vermont Service Center if you live in Connecticut, Delaware, the District of Columbia, Maine, Maryland, Massachusetts, New Hampshire, New Jersey, New York, Pennsylvania, Rhode Island, Vermont, Virginia, and West Virginia. The Vermont Service Center also has jurisdiction over the BCIS offices in Bermuda, the Dominican Republic, Montreal, Puerto Rico, Toronto, and the Virgin Islands.

More information can be obtained on the BCIS's official website, http://www.bcis.gov.

The Interview

After the BCIS has processed your Form N-400 and attached documents, you will be notified of a hearing date and time to meet with a BCIS examiner. At the interview, you must prove that you can read, write, and speak English. The examiner will speak to you in English and you must reply in the same language. You will be asked to write a sentence in English, but if you struggle too much, the examiner may ask you to write an additional sentence if the examiner is not satisfied with your first attempt.

You should be aware that there are several important exceptions to this requirement. First, you need not demonstrate a proficiency in English if you are unable to do so because of a physical or developmental disability or a mental impairment, such as retardation. Second, you are exempt from the English proficiency rule if you are over 50 years old and have lived in the United States for a total of at least twenty years, or you are over 55 years old and have resided in the United States for a total of at least 15 years. However, in both of those cases, the residence must be after a lawful admission for permanent residence. What that means is, if you entered the country illegally (as an undocumented alien) and never obtained your green card, you can't become eligible for citizenship regardless of how long you have lived in America.

Note that even though you qualify on the age and residency requirements for exemption from the proficiency in English requirement, you must still have a knowledge and understanding of American history and the principles and form of government in the United States. However, if you are over 65 years old and have lived in the United States for a total of at least twenty years, you may be exempt from both the proficiency in English and the knowledge of history and how the government works requirements.

If you do not qualify for an exemption, and you have demonstrated the requisite proficiency in the English language, the examiner will then ask you a series of questions regarding your knowledge of United States history and the workings of its government. Sample questions run something like the following:

* How many stars are on the United States's flag? (50)
* What do the stars represent? (each state admitted to the Union)
* How many stripes are on the flag? (13)
* What do the stripes represent? (the number of original states that made up the United States)
* How many senators come from your state? (2)
* When was the Declaration of Independence adopted? (July 4, 1776)
* Who was the main writer of the Declaration of Independence? (Thomas Jefferson)
* How many branches are there in our government? (3)
* What are the three branches? (the executive branch, the legislative branch, and the judicial branch)

* How many times has the Constitution been amended? (27)
* How many Supreme Court Justices are there? (9)
* Who was the first president of the United States? (George Washington)
* Which president freed the slaves? (Abraham Lincoln)
* How long is a congressman elected for? (2 years)
* How long is a senator elected for? (6 years)
* How long is the president elected for? (4 years)
* For how many terms may a president be elected? (2)
* What are the two major political parties? (Democrats and Republicans)
* What are the first ten amendments to the Constitution called? (the Bill of Rights)
* What is the name of our national anthem? (The Star-Spangled Banner)

The United States government publishes free study guides on the history of America for aliens who must take the citizenship test. Libraries also contain books and pamphlets specifically designed for permanent residents facing the test. In fact, most adult education programs offer classes on becoming a citizen. We highly recommend that you take one of these classes that teach the basics of American history and government—taking the test is one thing a lawyer cannot do for you!

The Final Step: Getting Sworn In

After what seems like an eternity, you finally have fulfilled all the requirements necessary to becoming a naturalized citizen of the United States of America. The final step is getting sworn in. The usual way is with a group of other people who meet at a large auditorium as specified in the notice sent to you by the BCIS. A federal judge will be there to swear you in.

After you have been sworn in, you will be given your certificate of naturalization. Congratulations! You are now officially a new citizen of the United States. Note that it is a federal offense to make copies of your certification of naturalization, so you should keep it in a secure place, such as your bank deposit box or home fireproof safe.

The first thing you should do as a new citizen is register to vote. Not only is voting one of the most precious rights of a United States citizen, your voter registration card can be carried with you in your purse or wallet at all times as proof that you are a citizen. And when it comes time to vote, become acquainted with the candidates, propositions, and issues so that you may be an informed voter. That's what democracy is all about.

TWENTY-TWO

Anatomy of a Civil Lawsuit

SOME PEOPLE HAVE CRITICIZED America as a litigious, sue-happy society, with people ready to file a lawsuit at the slightest provocation. Is this true? In the sense that we have chosen to settle our disputes in a civilized manner in the courtroom rather than in the middle of a dusty street at high noon, perhaps it is. Those who founded this country recognized that might does not mean right, and that unless given an opportunity to be heard in a fair and impartial setting, the meek would be subject to the tyranny of the powerful. The activity in our courts is really the modern incarnation of the colonial spirit that declared "Don't tread on me." When an American feels trod upon, he or she can seek justice through our court system.

When you add to the number of lawsuits filed each year the number of witnesses and jurors who can be involved in a case, it becomes clear that sooner or later you are likely to participate in a lawsuit in some capacity—if you haven't already or aren't involved in one now. To help you understand how a case proceeds through the legal system, this chapter traces the course of a civil lawsuit, from the time the complaint is filed until the jury's verdict is announced. (A criminal trial generally follows the same format, but with emphasis on the defendant's constitutional rights and due process; see chapter 23.)

For the purposes of this chapter, let's assume that you were injured in an automobile accident; you were making a left turn when the defendant—Bob Jones—who was doing 50 in a 35 miles-per-hour zone, ran into you. Your injuries substantially exceed the dollar amount you can recover in small claims court, so we'll assume that you're being represented by an attorney since, as noted in chapter 24, it's not a good idea to act as your own lawyer in court except in small claims court or traffic court. (Plus, even insurance companies' own studies reveal that persons who are injured in automobile accidents and are represented by attorneys end up with more money even after paying their attorneys than do people who represent themselves.)

STARTING A LAWSUIT

How Long Do You Have to Sue?: The Statute of Limitations

The first thing you need to be aware of is that you don't have forever to file a lawsuit. Every case—civil and criminal (except murder cases)—is subject to a "statute of limitations," a time limit within which you must file your lawsuit in court. If you do not file it within the prescribed time, you lose the right to sue the other person. The time you have to file a lawsuit varies depending on the nature of the case and from state to state. For example, depending on the state, you have from two to ten years to file a suit for breach of an oral contract and three to fifteen years if the contract was written. The statute of limitations for personal injury cases (like the one you were involved in) ordinarily ranges from one year to six years. However, if the person who hit you was a government employee acting within the scope of his employment, you normally must file a claim with the appropriate government body within as few as sixty days and rarely more than six months.

Let's say that the statute of limitations for personal injury cases in your state is two years. Suppose your 9-year-old daughter is also hurt in the accident. Do you have to file suit for her as well by the time she is 11 (two years from the date of the accident)? Generally not. In the case of a minor, the statute of limitations usually is suspended ("tolled") until the child reaches the age of majority. If the age of majority in your state is 18, then your daughter has two years from her eighteenth birthday to file her lawsuit against the person who hit her. (Other times when the statute of limitations is suspended include while the victim is insane or hospitalized because of the accident, or while the defendant is outside of the state.) If you want to file a lawsuit for your daughter while she is still a minor, your attorney will have to get a court order naming you or someone else as your daughter's "guardian *ad litem*"—literally, guardian for the lawsuit. Note, however, that while the statute of limitations is suspended for your minor daughter, it is *not* suspended for you. You must still file your own lawsuit within the prescribed time limit—here, two years—or you will lose your right to sue forever.

Although the statute of limitations may give you up to six years to file a lawsuit, you should contact an attorney as soon as possible after the accident. The attorney can gather evidence that might otherwise be lost if you wait; interview witnesses while their memories are still fresh; begin negotiations with the insurance company on the question of liability; and do other things that need to be done promptly. Your lawyer often can help you receive the proper medical attention you need and have the doctor take a "lien" on the case. That means that the doctor's fees are paid when you settle the case or get a favorable jury's verdict; in the meantime you do not need to worry about paying the doctor while he or she treats you.

Filing the Complaint

The first step in most lawsuits is the filing of a "complaint" with the proper court. (If a government employee injured you while he or she was on the job, the first step is the filing of a claim with the proper government body. A complaint is filed only after the government agency denies your claim or fails to act on your claim within a designated period of time.) Because you are filing the complaint, you are the "plaintiff"; the person you are suing is the "defendant." The complaint tells why you feel the defendant is responsible for your injuries and damages. It lays out the legal grounds for the suit, the "cause of action"—for instance, a breach of contract, a suit for false arrest, or, in our sample case, a complaint for negligence (see chapter 10). In a breach of contract action, for example, your lawyer would allege in the complaint that you had a contract with the defendant; what the terms of the contract were; that you did everything the contract required you to do; that the defendant breached the contract by not doing something that the contract required him or her to do; and that you suffered damages as a result of the defendant's breach of contract.

Before filing the complaint, your lawyer will usually first conduct a preliminary investigation to determine if there appear to be grounds for the suit. A lawyer who doesn't investigate the facts before filing what turns out to be an unfounded lawsuit may be liable to the defendant for the tort of malicious prosecution (see chapter 10). The person who told the lawyer to file the suit may also be liable for malicious prosecution.

Where is the complaint filed? That initially depends on the nature of your case. If you're filing for bankruptcy, you can only file it in the federal bankruptcy court. Such things as divorce and probate can be filed only in a state court, and usually there are courts specifically designated for these proceedings—family, or domestic, court for divorces, and surrogate, or probate, court for probates (see chapter 25). Cases for personal injuries, such as those suffered in our hypothetical traffic collision, are ordinarily filed in a state court of general jurisdiction, such as superior, or district, court.

When your lawyer files the complaint with the court, the clerk issues a "summons," which signals the official start of the lawsuit. The summons notifies the defendant that you have filed a lawsuit and that he or she must answer it within a certain time period or a default judgment may be entered against him or her.

The summons and complaint must now be delivered formally to ("served on") the defendant. Your lawyer probably will have this done by the marshal's office, a professional process server, or a member of the lawyer's staff who is over the age of majority (18 in most states, 19 in a few) and is not a party to the lawsuit. Sometimes the complaint can be served on the defendant by mail, but this is usually done only when the defendant is already represented by a lawyer and the lawyer agrees to accept service of the summons and complaint on behalf of his or her client.

The Defendant's Response to the Complaint

The defendant (through his or her attorney if he or she has one) must file a response to the complaint with the court within a specified time, usually twenty or thirty days. The most frequent response the defendant's attorney files is an "answer" that generally denies all of the complaint's allegations. In essence, a general denial states: "I deny everything; I didn't do anything wrong." The answer may contain an "affirmative defense" that something bars or limits the plaintiff's claim. The fact that the statute of limitations expired before you filed the complaint is an example of an affirmative defense that, if true, would bar the complaint. In our hypothetical case, the defendant, Bob Jones, will raise in his answer the affirmative defense that you were comparatively negligent (see chapter 10) for making the left turn before it was safe to do so. (Occasionally the defendant admits to doing the wrongful acts complained of, but argues that the amount of damages the plaintiff is asking for is too high. The case then proceeds to trial solely on the issue of damages—how much the plaintiff should get.) In addition to filing the answer, the defendant may file a countersuit, or cross complaint, against you. For instance, in our case Bob Jones's answer may deny everything and he may file a countersuit against you for his injuries and damages to his car.

Sometimes instead of filing an answer, the defendant will file a "demurrer" (in federal court, a "motion to dismiss") to the complaint. A demurrer is designed to get all or part of the complaint thrown out of court if it doesn't contain enough facts to show that the defendant did anything legally wrong—if it doesn't state a "cause of action" against the defendant. Suppose the main facts alleged in your complaint are these: "On November 15, 2003, the defendant was driving his car down Main Street and struck the plaintiff, thereby injuring her." If the defendant files a demurrer to the complaint, will the court uphold ("sustain") the demurrer? Yes. Your lawyer has not alleged any facts in the complaint to indicate that the defendant was in any way at fault. The complaint does not allege that it is illegal to drive down Main Street, or that the defendant was speeding, or that the plaintiff was in a crosswalk and the defendant failed to stop for him or her. The complaint doesn't tell how the plaintiff was injured, other than being hit by a car. The plaintiff could have been a young child who ran out into the street from between two parked cars to retrieve a ball that was hit into the street, and the defendant had no way of avoiding the accident. It may be that the defendant driver wasn't paying attention, but it could just as well be the plaintiff whose own negligence caused the accident. Neither the defendant nor the judge should have to guess at what you're claiming the wrongful conduct to be. In our case, there is absolutely no mention that the accident was caused by Bob Jones's driving 15 miles over the 35-miles-per-hour speed limit.

The first time a demurrer to a complaint is sustained, the judge normally will give your lawyer a chance to "amend" the complaint to allege the necessary facts. For instance, your lawyer could change the complaint as follows: "On November 15, 2003, the defendant was driving his car down Main Street at 50 miles-per-hour in a 35-miles-per-hour zone and because of this unlawful and negligent act, struck the plaintiff, who was lawfully making a left turn." The complaint now alleges that the defendant was doing something wrong that resulted in your being injured.

The amended complaint must be served on the defendant, or usually his or her attorney at this stage of the proceedings. If the defendant files a demurrer to your new complaint, the judge should overrule it, and the defendant will then have twenty or thirty days to file an answer to the complaint. Let's say the judge sustains the demurrer to your first amended complaint and refuses to let your lawyer amend the complaint again. What then? The complaint is thrown out of court completely. The only way you can get another chance is to appeal the judge's ruling to a higher court and try to convince the appellate court that the lower court's ruling was wrong.

What happens if the defendant simply ignores the complaint and doesn't do anything about it? When the time that the defendant has for responding to the complaint expires and the defendant has not responded, your attorney can file for a "default judgment." The judge will grant the default judgment if the court record shows that the defendant was served properly with the summons and complaint, the time for answering the complaint has run out, and the defendant was notified of the default judgment hearing. Can a defendant get a default judgment set aside so he or she can answer the complaint? Yes, but only if the defendant acts quickly after learning that the default was entered against him or her and can show some valid reason for not responding to the complaint or appearing at the default judgment hearing: if, for example, the defendant was seriously ill when he or she was served with the complaint and default judgment hearing papers and was unable to do anything about it; or the process server lied about serving the defendant and threw the summons and complaint into the trash instead of serving them on the defendant.

WHAT HAPPENS BEFORE THE TRIAL

Pretrial Investigation

After the complaint and answer have been filed and served, the formal and intensive investigation process—called "discovery"—begins. During this stage, each side gathers evidence and prepares his or her case. Your attorney will want to find out as much about the case as possible, both yours and the defendant's.

In our hypothetical case, if he or she hasn't already done so, your lawyer or an investigator may go to the accident scene to take pictures and measurements. Witnesses will be interviewed and accident reports and medical records reviewed. If there is any indication that a defective condition in either car contributed to the accident or made your injuries worse than they would have been otherwise, and your injuries justify the expense, various experts in automobile design or manufacture may be retained to study the problem for a possible lawsuit against the car's manufacturer. If you have been injured seriously, you will be evaluated by medical specialists to determine the extent and permanence of your injuries and the cost of future medical care to treat you.

The formal discovery process also gives your lawyer the chance to find out what evidence the other side will be presenting at the trial. There are several ways of doing this. One is through "written interrogatories," a list of questions asking the defendant, under oath, for information about the case: How fast were you driving at the time you struck the plaintiff's car? Where were you coming from? Where were you going? Did you have anything to eat that day? Did you have anything to drink that day? Did you take any drugs or medications in the twenty-four hours preceding the collision? Who was in the car with you? What are the names and addresses of the witnesses you plan to call at trial?

The most important—and enlightening—part of discovery in many cases is the "deposition" (in some parts of the country, the "examination before trial," or simply "EBT"). A deposition is testimony taken outside of court, where you are sworn in and give your testimony under oath, just as you are when you testify in court. You can be held guilty of the crime of perjury if you lie at a deposition.

Your lawyer will "depose" the defendant, and the defendant's lawyer will depose you. If either side will be calling other witnesses to testify, the opposing lawyer may want to depose them as well. The deposition usually is held in the office of the lawyer taking the deposition, with lawyers for both sides present. The deposition proceedings are taken down by a court reporter and can be used at trial. Some depositions are videotaped, particularly when there is a strong chance that the witness will be unable to testify at the trial because of, say, age, illness, or a move out of state.

After the court reporter has transcribed your deposition testimony, you are given the chance to review it to see if your answers were recorded accurately. You can make changes on the record but may be asked at trial to explain those changes: It's one thing to explain correcting a mistake that the court reporter made; it's quite another to explain why you changed your answer from "yes" to "no." If you say one thing at the deposition but another at the trial, your truthfulness will be questioned at trial by the opposing lawyer and the jury during its deliberations. Unless you can explain the discrepancy to the satisfaction of the jury, the jury may find it hard to believe anything you say. Because of this, you should answer deposition questions with as much care and thought as if you were testifying before a jury at trial.

The discovery stage of a trial is crucial in preventing either side from being unduly surprised by the other at trial. It is designed to provide a fair and faster trial. Unfortunately, some lawyers have gotten into the habit of using the discovery process as a means of harassing the other side rather than as a part of a good faith effort in preparing their cases. When a lawyer abuses the discovery process, many judges will impose penalties ("sanctions") ranging from monetary fines to throwing the case out of court.

Out-of-Court Settlements

The vast majority of civil disputes—more than 95 percent—are settled out of court. Some are settled before a complaint is even filed; others are settled after the complaint is filed but before trial has commenced; some are settled during the trial; and still others are settled after the trial, while the case is on appeal to a higher court.

Why are so many cases settled out of court? The main reason is that plaintiffs and defendants alike often want to avoid the risk each side faces in going to trial. No matter how strongly justice appears to be on your side, if you are the plaintiff, there is always the chance that you might lose the case or the jury will be stingy with its award. For the defendant, there is the risk that the jury will base its decision on sympathy rather than the facts and will find liability where none exists or will be too liberal in its award. Because of the uncertainties, the plaintiff may accept a sum smaller than the one he or she originally hoped for and the defendant (or his or her insurance company) may pay an amount higher than he or she would like.

Pretrial Motions

Before a trial begins, either side may make any number of motions. Three of the more frequent and important motions are motions for summary judgment, for judgment on the pleadings, and to exclude evidence at the trial ("motions *in limine*").

A motion for summary judgment is an attempt by one side to have the case decided by the judge before the trial. Let's say that your attorney feels that there are no facts in dispute and that no one could reasonably dispute your right to win the case and therefore files a motion for summary judgment against the defendant, Bob Jones. Your attorney submits a legal brief explaining your position, reciting the facts, which must be supported by evidence such as depositions and sworn affidavits or declarations (witnesses' statements signed under oath). If the defendant can't present any evidence to contradict your facts and evidence and show that material facts are in dispute, the judge will grant your motion for summary judgment. Why? Because no dispute of a material fact exists. In other words, the evidence your lawyer presented to the judge shows that you clearly are entitled to win. But if the defendant can present any evidence that contradicts any of your key assertions, the judge will deny the motion for summary judgment. For instance, if defendant Bob Jones states he was only going 35 miles an hour or that you pulled out in front of him before it was safe to do so, he has created a factual dispute as to the cause of the accident. The judge does not make a determination as to who is more likely to be telling the truth—that is left for the jury to decide at the trial. The judge can grant a motion for summary judgment only where no dispute of a material fact exists and only questions of law remain.

A motion for summary judgment may be preceded by a motion for judgment on the pleadings. This motion is made after the complaint and answer have been filed. Let's say that in our hypothetical case in which the complaint alleges that the accident was caused by defendant Bob Jones's speeding, and that Bob Jones's answer admits this and doesn't contain any affirmative defenses that would bar your suit. It is clear from the complaint and answer (the "pleadings") that you are entitled to recover monetary damages for your personal injuries and damage to your car from Mr. Jones. Your attorney therefore would file a motion for judgment on the pleadings, which would be successful. The major difference between a motion for judgment on the pleadings and a motion for summary judgment is this: In a motion for judgment on the pleadings, the judge can look only at the pleadings themselves (the complaint, answer, etc.) and the allegations contained therein, while in a motion for summary judgment, the judge can look at depositions, affidavits, experts' reports, and any other evidence submitted to him or her in addition to the pleadings.

Before the trial, motions may be made to exclude evidence from being presented at the trial for one reason or another. These are called motions *in limine*. Suppose Bob Jones had caused another accident six months before the one in which you were hurt. Your lawyer normally is not allowed to bring this previous accident up at your trial. The question is whether Bob Jones was negligent when he hit you, not when he hit someone else six months earlier. The danger in permitting evidence of an earlier accident is that the jury will find the defendant liable because of the previous accident or because he generally may be a poor driver, and not because he necessarily did anything wrong at the time in question. To prevent your attorney from making any reference to the earlier accident at the trial, Bob Jones's attorney will ask the judge for a pretrial ruling that your attorney cannot mention the earlier accident to the jury.

THE TRIAL

Jury Selection

The selection of jurors who will hear the facts and decide the case can be the most decisive part of the trial. One juror who is hostile to your case can influence others to vote his or her way or may simply hold out so that the jury is unable to reach a decision, resulting in a hung jury. In civil cases, the lone holdout juror is not as important as in criminal trials, as in most states civil cases need not be decided by a unanimous jury. For example, if there are twelve jurors, in some states only nine jurors need to be in accord; if six jurors are permitted, only five must agree.

Prospective jurors initially are chosen from the surrounding community. At one time, names of potential jurors were taken from the voter registration records. Today, a much broader base is used, including registration information from the Department of Motor Vehicles. From this group, a "panel" will be sent for questioning to the courtroom where your case will be tried (see chapter 25).

Most of the time, the lawyers for the parties question ("voir dire") the prospective jurors for possible bias for and against their clients. Some judges (especially federal judges) prefer to do most of the questioning of prospective jurors themselves. Your lawyer will try to select jurors who are most likely to be favorable to your case, and to keep off those who may side with the opposition. The defendant's lawyer will do likewise.

Suppose your lawyer feels that a prospective juror—let's say, a woman—is prejudiced against you and doesn't want her to decide your fate. How can your lawyer keep her from being a juror? By "challenging" her. There are two types of challenges used to exclude a prospective juror from hearing your case: challenges for cause and peremptory challenges. A "challenge for cause" is allowed when a prospective juror clearly is biased for or against one side or has an interest in the outcome of the lawsuit. The juror may be a friend or relative of one of the parties or the lawyers, or may be prejudiced against you because of your race, religion, or sex. Or the juror may have a preformed opinion of the case and can't objectively weigh the facts presented in the courtroom.

If the judge doesn't feel that there is sufficient cause to excuse the juror, your lawyer still can remove her by using a "peremptory challenge." A peremptory challenge can be used to exclude a juror for any reason or for no reason. Your lawyer may feel that because the woman is a redhead or thin that she may not be sympathetic to your case. Or your lawyer may have noticed that the woman gave the defendant's lawyer a smile or a nod, but when your lawyer looked at her, she had an icy glare. These things are not enough for a judge to excuse a juror for cause, but they may be enough to give your lawyer reason to excuse the person as a potential juror. Why is it important to distinguish between challenges for cause and peremptory challenges? Because your lawyer gets an infinite number of challenges for cause, but only a limited number of peremptory challenges, such as six or ten, depending on the state. Once the peremptory challenges are used up, a juror can be challenged only for cause. If the judge doesn't think the person is prejudiced, that person sits as a juror in your case.

Opening Statements

When the last juror has been selected, the trial starts. The judge may say a few words to the jury regarding what the case is about. Then your attorney gives an "opening statement" to the jury, summarizing what he or she is going to prove. An opening statement is just that: a statement of the evidence your attorney intends to present. Your attorney is not allowed to argue against the defendant's version of the facts at this point; that is reserved for the summation at the end of trial. After your attorney is finished, the defendant's attorney can make an opening statement. Or the defendant's attorney can wait and make his or her opening statement after your attorney has rested your case. Most of the time, however, the defendant's attorney will make an opening statement right after your attorney's opening statement, if only to remind the jurors that there is another side to the story and that they should keep an open mind.

Suppose your attorney forgets to state some important facts during the opening statement—that the defendant, Bob Jones, was speeding when his car hit you, for instance. When your attorney sits down, the defendant's attorney moves for a "nonsuit." A motion for a nonsuit asks the judge to throw the case out of court because your attorney hasn't alleged the basic facts to show that the defendant committed a legal wrong. In our case, your attorney forgot to tell the jury that evidence was going to be presented to show that the defendant was speeding at the time of the accident and that his speeding was the cause of the collision. Ordinarily the judge will give your attorney the chance to amend the opening statement to allege the missing facts. But if it is clear to the judge that your attorney will not be able to add anything new to the opening statement even if given the chance, the judge will grant the defendant's motion for nonsuit.

The Cases in Chief

After the opening statements, your lawyer will present your "case in chief." As this is a civil case, your lawyer has the burden of proving your case to the jury by a "preponderance of the evidence"—a "probability" that the defendant is liable for your damages. This is a much lower standard than that of "beyond a reasonable doubt" used in criminal trials. In a civil case, you just have to tip the scales of justice ever so slightly in your favor to win the case. All your lawyer needs to do is prove there is more than a 50 percent chance that the defendant is at fault and you've won the case.

During your case in chief, your lawyer will call witnesses and present evidence demonstrating your right to recover monetary damages. Expert witnesses frequently are used by both sides to support their respective positions. In a traffic accident such as in our hypothetical case, an expert in accident reconstruction may be called upon to give an opinion on the cause of the accident. Medical doctors, physical therapists, psychologists, and other health care workers may be called to the stand to describe the nature and permanency of your physical and emotional injuries caused by the accident.

Your lawyer calls the first witness to the stand (it may well be you), the clerk swears the witness in, and your lawyer proceeds with "direct examination." When your lawyer is finished questioning the witness, the defendant's lawyer has the chance to cross-examine the witness. More leeway is given to the lawyer while cross-examining a witness. For instance, leading questions—questions that suggest an answer—aren't allowed on direct examination but are permitted on cross-examination. It would be a leading question and therefore improper for your lawyer to ask you on direct examination, "You looked far down the road in front of you before making your turn and didn't see any cars, isn't that true?" That is a leading question because it suggests an affirmative answer and prodding by your lawyer. But it would be proper for the defendant's lawyer to ask something like "Isn't it true you were in a hurry to get to work that day because you were running late?" This question also suggests an answer—again in the affirmative—but because it is on cross-examination, the question is proper. Why permit leading questions on cross-examination but not on direct examination? Because there is a much greater danger that you will be led to an answer by your own lawyer than by the other party's lawyer.

Neither lawyer can badger or intimidate a witness. Television lawyers notwithstanding, lawyers are not permitted to walk up to a witness and browbeat him or her. The lawyers usually must remain at the counsel table or stand at the lectern beside it. About the only time a lawyer is allowed to approach a witness is to hand the witness a document or photograph to look at, and then only if the lawyer first asks the judge for permission to approach the witness. Failure to follow courtroom etiquette can get the lawyer a terse admonishment from the judge, and even a contempt citation if he or she continues to ignore courtroom decorum.

When your lawyer is finished presenting all of the witnesses and evidence to prove your case, he or she officially concludes ("rests") the case in chief. If your lawyer neglected to present some crucial testimony, the defendant's lawyer can make a motion for nonsuit at this point.

Assuming the judge denies the motion for nonsuit, the defendant's attorney now proceeds with the defendant's case in chief. (Sometimes the defendant's attorney will rest the case without calling any witnesses or presenting any evidence; this is more common in criminal cases than in civil cases.) Just as the defendant's attorney has the right to cross-examine your witnesses, your attorney can cross-examine each defense witness. When the defendant's attorney rests his or her case, your attorney has the opportunity for "rebuttal"—to present additional evidence that contradicts or explains the evidence presented by the defendant's attorney.

When the defense has rested its case, your lawyer may ask the judge to grant you a "directed verdict." This is a request that the judge take the case out of the jury's hands and decide in your favor because no reasonable person could dispute your right to recover damages. The judge will grant this motion only if there is no doubt as to how the jury would decide the case.

Closing Arguments and Jury Deliberations

Now that both sides have rested their cases, each attorney is allowed to make a summation, or "closing argument," to the jury. In some states the defendant's attorney goes first, then your attorney. In other states, your attorney goes first, then the defendant's attorney, and then your attorney gets a chance to say a few final words. Regardless of the procedure, your attorney gets the last word. Why? Because the burden of proving the case to a preponderance of the evidence is on your attorney.

After the closing arguments, the judge instructs the jury on the burden of proof, the law that applies to the case, and how the jury must apply the law to the facts of the case. Jury instructions can be very lengthy, convoluted, and difficult for the average juror to understand. The danger here is that the jurors may disregard the instructions and decide the case on what they feel the law ought to be, not on what it is.

The jurors retire to the deliberations room, where the first order of business is electing a foreman. (In some states the judge selects the foreman, while others have a simpler system: The first person chosen for the jury is automatically the foreman.) Back in the deliberations room, the jurors begin their deliberations. They weigh the evidence, decide which witnesses were telling the truth, and reach a verdict in favor of one party. Or they reach the conclusion that they are hopelessly deadlocked. During the deliberations, the jury may ask to see some of the exhibits again, have trial testimony reread, or have the judge give a further explanation of a jury instruction. Jurors in civil cases are almost never isolated ("sequestered") from the public and media during the course of the trial and deliberations, although they are instructed at the beginning not to talk to anyone about the case until it is over.

When a verdict is reached, the jury files back into the courtroom. The judge asks the foreman whether the jury has come to a verdict, the foreman replies in the affirmative, and the judge instructs the foreman to hand the verdict form to the bailiff. The bailiff takes the verdict form and hands it to the judge, who looks it over to make sure it is proper in form, then usually gives it to his or her court clerk to announce the verdict in open court.

Suppose that the jury returns a verdict for the defendant. What can your lawyer do? The first thing is to ask the judge to disregard the jury's verdict and instead enter a judgment in your favor. This is called a motion for a "judgment notwithstanding the verdict." The judge will grant the motion only when it is obvious that the jury's verdict is patently wrong—a rare event. If the judge denies your lawyer's motion for a judgment notwithstanding the verdict, you can appeal your case to a higher court (see chapter 25).

ARBITRATION AS AN ALTERNATIVE TO THE COURTROOM

MANY CASES ARE BEING arbitrated today rather than going through the official judicial system. Indeed, the courts encourage parties to a dispute to arbitrate their cases. The reason for this is that arbitration takes a load off the courts' busy backlog. There is no doubt that cases move more swiftly through the courts today with "fast track" programs designed to get a case to trial within two years.

Arbitration is generally a faster, less costly procedure than going through the formal legal system. Many arbitrators are retired judges or judges who have turned in their robes for the higher pay of being a private arbitrator. Arbitration is generally a faster, less costly procedure than the legal system, and the rules of civil procedure and evidence are somewhat relaxed.

The arbitration hearing usually is not held at the courthouse but in a conference room, often in the arbitrator's office. Arbitration proceedings are similar in structure to trial proceedings—with opening statements, cases in chief, rebuttals, and closing arguments—but more informal than you'll find in a courtroom. Just as in a court trial, each witness is sworn in and testifies under oath and can be cross-examined by the opposing party's attorney. There is no right to be heard by a jury, however; the arbitrator decides the case.

When does a case go to arbitration rather than through the traditional legal system? Most of the time, a dispute goes to arbitration because you signed a contract providing that any disagreements must be arbitrated. For instance, if you are a member of a health maintenance organization (HMO), you probably signed a contract that includes a paragraph stating that, if any dispute arises between the HMO and you, including medical malpractice, the dispute will be resolved by arbitration rather than judicial proceedings.

When a contract calls for arbitration of disputes, the decision of the arbitrator is usually final. Generally there is no right to appeal the arbitrator's decision, even if the arbitrator applied the wrong law. If you don't agree with the arbitrator's decision, you normally can't file in a court of law to invalidate the arbitrator's decision, even if you feel the arbitrator was prejudiced in favor of the other party. Many arbitrators who were once judges originally started out defending cases for insurance companies whose insureds were being sued. Often these arbitrators are biased in favor of insurance companies and will find in the insurance company's favor if it is a close call. Or when they do rule against an insurance company, they tend to award less money to the injured victim than a jury would.

Should you sign a contract that requires you to arbitrate the matter if a dispute arises? If you can avoid it, by all means delete the mandatory arbitration provision. Arbitration generally tends to favor the defendant. If you have any bargaining power at all, get rid of the arbitration clause. The problem is that you generally have no bargaining power and are presented with a contract with an arbitration clause on a "take-it-or-leave-it" basis. If, for example, you don't want to sign an HMO contract that requires the arbitration of disputes, the HMO simply won't accept you into its plan.

To move cases along smoothly and quickly in the legal system, judges routinely order parties in civil disputes to arbitration. Often you have the choice between binding and nonbinding arbitration. In nonbinding arbitration, the arbitrator's decision is not final; if you don't like it, you can still proceed to trial with your case. Why, then, does the judge even bother sending the case to nonbinding arbitration? Because it gives each side an idea of how strong his or her case is, and many cases sent to nonbinding arbitration end up getting settled. Hence, the court is able to reduce its backlog and move cases along.

TWENTY-THREE

Crimes and Criminal Justice

CRIMINAL LAW prescribes the rules that we as civilized people must respect and live by in order to keep our society from collapsing into chaos. Without a set body of criminal rules, administered by a fair and impartial justice system, the law would be whatever the richest person or fastest gun in the territory said it was. American history—particularly settlement of the open West—proved that while vigilante justice is swift, it is often wrong, and the punishment is frequently far worse than the crime justifies.

The number of people in the United States behind bars or on probation or parole was a staggering 6.6 *million* in 2001. This means that the number of adults under supervision by the criminal justice system was 1 in 32. Texas had more adults in prison than any other state, with 755,100; California was second, with 704,900. Texas also had the most adults on probation, 443,684, while California again was second, with 350,768.

Criminal law in the United States really encompasses two distinct areas. The first of these includes the rules defining what is a crime. The second includes the rules that the police, prosecuting attorneys, and courts must obey before a person can be convicted of and punished for a crime. The first half or so of this chapter discusses the elements of many of the more common crimes and the defenses often raised by criminal defendants. The second half deals with a person's rights when he or she is suspected of committing a crime.

This chapter is not designed as an aid to help you defend yourself against charges that you committed a crime. When you're charged with a crime more serious than a routine traffic violation (see chapter 2) or a very minor infraction (such as drinking a beer in a public park), you'll usually want to be represented by a good criminal lawyer because of the potential consequences. What this chapter will do is give you a close look at the criminal justice system to help you understand how it works.

CRIMES

Just what is it that makes an act a crime? Some acts are crimes because they are inherently evil (*malum in se*), such as murder, rape, robbery, or arson. Other acts are crimes not because they are necessarily evil, but because they are contrary to an important social objective. Such a crime is referred to as *malum prohibitum*. For instance, fishing without a license or catching more than the limit is not evil in itself. Laws prohibit this type of thing to preserve natural resources. Other acts—speeding, for instance—are prohibited to protect the safety and welfare of the driving and pedestrian public.

Crimes generally are categorized as either felonies or misdemeanors, although some are treated as only infractions or minor offenses. Felonies are the most serious types of crime. Originally, only nine crimes were felonies: murder, manslaughter, burglary, robbery, larceny, rape, sodomy, arson, and mayhem (maiming or permanently disfiguring someone). Today, many other crimes are also felonies. The punishment for a felony is stiffer than it is for a misdemeanor. In many states, the punishment for a felony is imprisonment for *at least* one year (or death in some limited cases), while for a misdemeanor it is for *no more* than one year in jail.

Two things must be present in order for a crime to be committed: an act (the physical element) and a particular state of mind (the mental element). The act is the body of the crime—the corpus delecti. In a murder, for example, it is the killing of a human being by another human being. In arson it is the burning of a structure. Sometimes the act can consist solely of words, as in solicitation (discussed below).

The mental element is the person's intent to do the illegal act. In law it is said frequently that an act is not a crime if it is done without a guilty mind. Killing someone, for instance, is not a crime if it was purely accidental or justified self-defense, because there was no wrongful intent. And just as the act needs the intent to be a crime, the intent needs an act to be a crime. Merely thinking about doing something illegal is not a crime, regardless of how evil the thoughts are.

PRELIMINARY CRIMES

The crimes of solicitation, conspiracy, and attempt are known in law as "preliminary crimes," since they occur before the intended crime. Preliminary crimes are punishable because they go far beyond merely thinking about committing an illegal act.

Solicitation

You are guilty of solicitation when you ask someone to commit a crime for you, or to help you commit a crime, or when you advise someone on how to commit a crime. The only act required for the crime of solicitation is that of asking or advising the other person to do an illegal act. Although solicitation usually is associated with prostitution, you are guilty of solicitation any time you ask someone to commit any crime for you or advise a person on how it should be done. For example, it is solicitation to ask a person to kill someone or to commit a burglary for you, or to tell him or her how to do it.

Conspiracy

A "conspiracy" is an agreement between two or more persons to commit a crime. A married man and his mistress, for example, may plot to kill his wife and collect the insurance money. But in order for the crime to be committed, more is required than a mere agreement. One of the conspirators must do an "overt act" that furthers the conspiracy. Suppose that after making the agreement with his mistress, the man buys a gun to kill his wife with. The husband and mistress are guilty of conspiracy because buying the gun to achieve the goal of the conspiracy—killing the wife—was the necessary overt act. If the two now have a change of heart and decide to forget the whole thing, they are still guilty of conspiracy. The underlying crime—here, murder—does not actually have to be completed.

Suppose Joe asks you to help steal a car. You think he is joking and say yes, but you don't really intend to assist with a theft. Joe then goes to the hardware store and buys some tools to use to steal the car (the "overt act"). Are you guilty of conspiracy because you apparently agreed to help? No. You are guilty of conspiracy only if, when you agree to assist with the crime, you actually intend to help.

Attempt

An "attempted crime" takes place when you intend to commit a particular crime and come dangerously close to completing it. This occurs when you enter the "zone of penetration"—you are close enough to the victim that you actually could commit the crime. For example, a man jumps out of the bushes at night and grabs a passing woman, intending to rape her. At that point, he has committed the crime of attempted rape. Suppose the assailant changes his mind after grabbing the woman and does nothing more, and lets the woman go. Does that relieve him of criminal responsibility for the attempted rape? No. The crime of attempted rape was complete when, with the intent of raping the woman, he jumped out of the bushes and grabbed her.

The following example shows how solicitation can escalate to a conspiracy and then to an attempted crime. Say that Ron decides to rob a liquor store and asks Scott to help him. Ron is guilty of solicitation at this point, since he has asked someone else (Scott) to help him commit a crime. Scott agrees to help, then borrows a gun to use during the robbery. Scott and Ron are now both guilty of conspiracy: by borrowing the gun, Scott has committed the necessary overt act that furthers their agreement to rob the liquor store. On the night of the planned robbery, the two men drive to the liquor store and walk in. But once inside, they see a police officer, call the whole thing off, and leave. Both men are guilty of attempted robbery because they were close enough to commit the actual crime.

ACCOMPLICES AND ACCESSORIES

A PERSON WHO GUNS DOWN another in cold blood without a valid legal excuse is guilty of the crime of murder. But what of someone who helps the killer before, during, or after the murder, or who helps anyone with any other crime? Is he or she guilty of the same crime as well, some other crime, or no crime at all?

Anyone who participates in any way in the actual crime—an accomplice—is generally as guilty as if he or she actually commits the crime. For example, if one member of a gang goes inside the bank while another waits in the car with the motor running, and a third is up the street as a lookout, the driver of the getaway car and the lookout are just as guilty as the gang member who goes inside the bank and does the dirty work.

You are an "accessory before the fact" if you incite, aid, or abet someone in the commission of a crime. For instance, if you obtain firearms or ammunition for someone else, knowing that he or she intends to use them to commit a crime, you are an accessory before the fact. Stealing a bank's blueprints to facilitate another person's burglary of it is another example of an accessory before the fact. An accessory before the fact is generally as guilty as the person who actually commits the crime.

An "accessory after the fact" is someone who knowingly conceals a criminal, helps a criminal escape, or otherwise deliberately acts to prevent a criminal's capture. An accessory after the fact is not guilty of the main crime (unless he or she had a hand in it) but is criminally responsible for harboring or concealing the fugitive. Someone who deliberately conceals another person's felony is guilty of the crime of "misprision of felony." If you accept money or property from a person in exchange for agreeing not to report or prosecute his or her crime, you commit the crime of "compounding."

CRIMES OF THEFT

Larceny

Larceny (theft) is the "unlawful taking and carrying away of another person's personal property, with the intent to permanently deprive the owner thereof." Stealing someone else's stereo system either for your own use or to sell is larceny: You took the stereo without the owner's consent, and either way you did not intend to return it.

Taking a car for a joyride usually isn't larceny (although it is its own separate crime), since there is no intent to deprive the owner of the car permanently. But if the car is destroyed or damaged in an accident during the joyride, it then becomes larceny, even if the accident wasn't the fault of the joyrider. The "borrowed" property must be returned in the same condition it was in when it was taken; otherwise, a larceny is committed. Suppose the joyride begins in Detroit, and the car is abandoned undamaged in New Orleans. Is this larceny? Yes. The car must be returned at or near the spot where it was taken to constitute joyriding; otherwise, it is larceny.

The difference between grand larceny (a felony) and petit larceny (a misdemeanor) is determined by the value of the property taken. In some states, for example, it is grand larceny if the property stolen is worth $500 or more and petit larceny if it is worth less than $500.

Embezzlement

You commit the crime of embezzlement when you wrongfully take something that someone else has entrusted to you. The main difference between larceny and embezzlement is that in embezzlement, you start off with lawful possession of the property. For example, the corporate accountant who juggles the books and skims 10 percent off the top is guilty of embezzlement, since he or she was lawfully entrusted with the money in the first place. But if a cleaning woman sees the money in an open safe and takes it, she is guilty of larceny because the company never entrusted the money to her.

Forgery

You are guilty of forgery when you make or alter a writing that has some legal significance. It is forgery to sign another person's name to a check without his or her consent. It is also forgery to change the amount on the check without the person's permission. If you pretend to be someone else and sign his or her name to a contract without the person's consent, that, too, is forgery. A contract has legal significance because it obligates a person to do certain things.

Burglary

Burglary originally was defined as the "unlawful breaking and entering into the dwelling house of another in the nighttime, with the intent to commit a felony therein." Breaking into someone's house during the day was not a burglary, nor was it a burglary to break into a commercial building, a barn, or an unattached garage. Today burglary is usually defined as entering a structure at any time with the intent to commit any felony or misdemeanor larceny. (Breaking into a car or other motor vehicle in order to steal something inside is auto burglary.)

While we usually think of burglary as stealing money or property from a house or business, it is also burglary to enter a structure to commit a murder, rape, arson, or any other felony. The crime of burglary is complete when the felon enters the structure, regardless of whether the intended felony is accomplished. Suppose, for example, that Fred decides to break into a house to steal the jewelry and cash. He pries open a window and crawls through, but when a large barking dog confronts him, he hurriedly leaves without taking anything. Fred is still guilty of burglary, since he entered the house intending to commit a felony (grand larceny).

Suppose Betty, a homeless woman, breaks into a house seeking shelter from a storm, and once inside decides to steal some money or property. Is that a burglary? No. When Betty entered the house, she did not intend to commit a felony inside. She decided to steal only after entering the house. She would, however, still be guilty of breaking and entering (using force to enter a house or other structure without permission), as well as larceny.

Robbery

Robbery is the use of force, or the threat of immediately using force, to take money or property from a person. Shoving a gun into someone's ribs and demanding all of his or her money is an obvious example of robbery, in this case armed robbery. The force can be directed against either the victim or a member of his or her family. For example, a father and daughter are walking down a street one night and are accosted by a robber. The robber threatens to hurt the daughter if the father doesn't hand over his wallet. This is a robbery, although the force is directed at the daughter, not at the father.

Stealing a wallet from an unconscious person generally isn't considered a robbery (unless the thief knocked the person out), since the victim doesn't surrender his or her money in the face of any force or threats. This doesn't mean that it's not a crime to take things from an unconscious person; it is larceny.

Extortion

Extortion ("blackmail," in everyday language) takes place when someone forces you to pay money or to hand over something by threatening to hurt you (or a member of your family) or to destroy your reputation sometime in the future. For example, if someone threatens to break your arm next Friday unless you pay him $10,000 before then, that is extortion. Extortion differs from robbery in that it involves a threat of future harm, while robbery involves a threat of immediate force if you don't comply with the robber's demands.

The crime of extortion often involves a threat to release information that could damage a person's profession or marriage. For instance, a person may threaten to expose a married woman's extramarital affair to her husband if she doesn't pay a certain sum. Or a person may threaten to expose a politician's shady dealings with a real estate developer before an election unless the politician pays $25,000.

CRIMES INVOLVING PROPERTY

Receiving Stolen Property

The crime of receiving stolen property consists of taking possession of property you know to be stolen. You can intend to keep it yourself, sell it to someone else, or even store it temporarily for the person who stole it. Can you get yourself off the hook by proving that you paid the thief or fence fair value for the property? Not if you knew the property was stolen when you bought it.

Let's say that you buy a new automobile stereo CD system from Jim, who, as you know, has a history of arrests and convictions for dealing in stolen property. The stereo is worth $750, but Jim sells it to you for only $150. You realize that the stereo is probably "hot" but decide that the risk is worth taking. Are you guilty of receiving stolen property? Yes. In this case, the circumstantial evidence is probably enough to prove that you knew the car stereo system was stolen. You don't have to know who stole the property or from whom it was stolen, only that it was wrongfully taken from its rightful owner.

Arson

Arson initially was defined as the deliberate burning of another's house. If you burned a commercial building or your neighbor's barn, you weren't guilty of arson (although you were guilty of other crimes, such as malicious mischief). Today, arson usually is defined as the deliberate burning of *any* structure owned by another person. Is it arson to torch your own house? At one time it wasn't, unless you did it for an unlawful purpose, such as to collect the insurance money on it. Many urban areas, however, now make it illegal to burn your house for any reason because of the danger to nearby structures.

Suppose Eileen sets your house on fire, but you quickly see the flames and manage to put them out before any real damage is done. Is Eileen guilty of arson? Probably. The house need not be demolished or even substantially damaged by fire. All that is required is any burn damage, even if it is mere charring. But if the only harm is smoke damage, such as blackening of the walls, the damage is not enough for arson. Eileen would be guilty of attempted arson, however.

Possession of Drugs

To establish the crime of unlawful possession of a drug, the prosecution must prove, first of all, that the drug is in fact what it purports to be (that is, it is cocaine and not, say, flour), and second, that you knew you had this drug on your person, in your car, or in your house. You are not guilty if you did not know that you had a banned or illegal substance. Suppose, for example, your friend Teri tells you that she grows her own oregano and gives you a plastic bag containing some of the leaves; you do not realize that Teri actually has given you marijuana as a joke. In this instance, you are not guilty of unlawful drug possession because you honestly believed that the leaves were a harmless spice. By the same token, if someone borrows your car and leaves a packet of drugs inside that a police officer later discovers, you can get out of any charges filed against you by proving that you knew nothing about it. But be aware that such claims are viewed with great skepticism, and you will have to clearly prove your ignorance of the drugs' presence. This may require having your friend testify that the drugs were his or hers, something your friend may not want to do.

Growing marijuana is a crime, the severity of which often depends on how many plants the person has growing. If, for instance, there is only one plant that the person grows for his or her personal use, it is often a misdemeanor. But if there are a number of plants, the assumption is made that the person is selling to others, and therefore he or she may be charged with a felony.

In 1996, California voters approved a statewide initiative called the "Compassionate Use Act of 1996" that gave seriously ill Californians the right to obtain and use marijuana for the treatment of such medical conditions as cancer, anorexia, AIDS, chronic pain, spasticity, glaucoma, arthritis, migraine headaches, or any other illnesses for which marijuana provides relief. The law basically exempted patients and their caregivers from liability for possessing a reasonable amount of marijuana for the personal use of the patient, or for growing a reasonable number of plants. The law also immunized a doctor from punishment or discipline for having recommended marijuana to a patient for medical purposes. A handful of other states subsequently passed similar laws. The proponents of the law argued that it was based on medical necessity, that the marijuana was given only to seriously and terminally ill patients, and that medical necessity was a legally recognized defense under the circumstances. However, in a 2001 decision, the U.S. Supreme Court ruled that the state laws were superseded by the federal Controlled Substances Act, which prohibited even those who had what could be termed a medical necessity from growing, possessing, or using the drug. The nation's highest court noted that the Controlled Substances Act, under which marijuana is classified as a schedule 1 controlled substance, provides only one express exception to the prohibitions on the manufacturing and distribution of the drug: that they are part of a government-approved research project. Since the marijuana in question was not part of a government-approved research project, it was illegal to grow, distribute, possess, or use the marijuana under federal law. Medical necessity was not considered a viable defense.

CRIMES AGAINST A PERSON

Assault

There are several definitions of a criminal assault. In some states, an assault is defined as attempted battery (see below), plus the ability to actually carry out that battery. Other states define assault as a deliberate threat to commit battery, even though the person doesn't intend to carry out the battery. Suppose Jack intends to scare Rodney by jumping out of the bushes at him as though he were going to hit him. Jack does not intend to hit Rodney, nor does he touch Rodney at all. In states that define assault as attempted battery, Jack is not guilty of assault, since he never intended to touch Rodney—that is, he never intended to commit battery on Rodney, only frighten him. But in those states that apply the second definition, Jack is guilty of assault because he deliberately threatened to commit battery on Rodney.

Battery

The crime of battery is defined as a deliberate harmful or offensive touching of someone else without his or her consent. Although we tend to think of battery as a violent act, such as a punch in the nose or a kick to the stomach, a light brush of the hand can be battery in some cases. A man who deliberately rubs his hand across a woman's breast without her consent, for example, commits battery, even if the woman isn't physically injured, because the touching is highly offensive to the woman.

False Imprisonment

False imprisonment is the deliberate confinement of a person without his or her consent or legal justification (a lawful arrest, for instance). The confinement can be physical, such as putting the victim in a room or cell and locking the door. Or it can be psychological—threatening to break the victim's arm if he or she tries to leave. And the fact that this takes place outside in the open air makes no difference; the victim is still frightened that she will be harmed if she tries to leave the area.

Kidnapping

A person is kidnapped when he or she is moved from one place to another against his or her will. In some states, it is also kidnapping to secretly confine the victim, even though the victim isn't taken anywhere. A kidnapping can be accomplished through force, such as knocking the victim unconscious. Or it can consist of threatening to harm the victim or members of his or her family if the victim doesn't accompany the kidnapper. Does the kidnapper have to make a demand for ransom in order for the crime of kidnapping to be committed? No; but if such a demand is made, the punishment usually is increased.

Rape

Rape—"unlawful carnal knowledge"—is sexual intercourse with a woman without her consent. (As far as the law in most states is concerned, a man cannot be "raped," although he can be sodomized.) The rapist does not have to use physical force; threats of harm are sufficient. In most enlightened states, the victim does not have to resist the rapist physically, especially where any resistance would be futile and might subject her to more danger. For example, if a rapist wields a knife in front of his victim, telling her that he will slit her throat if she does not cooperate, the woman does not have to attempt to struggle with the rapist. To do so could well mean her death.

Is it rape even if the assailant does not reach climax? Yes. The crime of rape is committed as soon as there is any penetration of the woman's vagina by the man's penis. (Inserting a foreign object into the woman's vagina is "rape by artifice." "Sodomy" is a broad crime covering any forced sexual act that is deemed unnatural, including anal or oral copulation.)

Suppose an impotent man is accused of rape. Can he be convicted of that crime? The old rule was that if he could prove his impotency he would be physically incapable of rape and therefore innocent. But with the development of Viagra and various pumps, previously impotent men are now capable of getting an erection. To prove whether the claimed impotent man was guilty of rape can be proved or disproved by DNA testing. But if the man is truly impotent, then he cannot be convicted of rape. In some states, however, he can be convicted of attempted rape. But in those states that require the actual ability to commit the crime as an element of an attempt, he could not be guilty of an attempted rape. But he could be guilty of assault, battery, and false imprisonment.

Historically, a married man could not be found guilty of raping his wife, although he could be guilty of some other crime, such as assault or battery. Today, however, most states have laws that make it rape for a married man to force himself upon his wife when she refuses to engage in sexual relations.

"Statutory rape" is sexual intercourse with a female under a certain age, usually 14 to 18 years old, depending on the state. A girl under the statutory age is deemed legally incapable of consenting to sexual intercourse because of her immature years. It therefore won't help the man to claim that the girl consented to the act. Suppose a man sees a young woman drinking in a bar and naturally assumes that she is at least 21, the legal drinking age. If the two of them have sexual intercourse, but it turns out the girl is only 17 (and in that state, the age for statutory rape is 18), and the man is prosecuted later for statutory rape, can he claim that he was honestly mistaken about the girl's age; that he just naturally assumed she must have been at least 21 since she was drinking in a bar? At one time, the only defense permitted was that the man was married to the underage girl at the time of the otherwise unlawful intercourse. Mistakes—even honest and sincere ones—were not taken into consideration. Today, however, some states do permit the man to prove that he was honestly mistaken about the girl's age if the girl intentionally misled him about her age or if his mistake about her age was reasonable under the circumstances.

Mayhem

Mayhem is the intentional act of maiming a person or causing permanent disfigurement. Years ago, mayhem was defined as cutting off the victim's limb, leaving the victim less able to protect himself or herself against adversaries. Today the crime of mayhem includes deliberate acts that cause someone to lose a limb, finger, eye, or any other part of the body, or that result in significant scarring or other permanent disfigurement, such as throwing acid into a person's face.

Homicide, Murder, and Manslaughter

A common misconception about homicide is that it is a crime, that it is in fact synonymous with murder. But homicide itself is not a crime. "Homicide" means only the killing of one human being by another human being. Some killings are not criminal: accidental killings or killings in self-defense, for example, or the state's execution of a convicted murderer who was given the death sentence and has exhausted all of his or her appeals. The types of homicide that are crimes are murder, voluntary manslaughter, and involuntary manslaughter.

Does the body of the victim have to be found in order to get a verdict of murder or manslaughter? No. The fact of death can be proved by circumstantial evidence, such as when the victim suddenly and inexplicably disappeared and the suspect had traces of the victim's blood on his or her clothes. With the advancements made in forensic sciences and crime scene investigation, detectives frequently are able to build very strong cases of a person's death despite the lack of a body.

Murder

Murder is the unlawful killing of one human being by another human being with malice aforethought. "Malice aforethought" means in a particularly evil or heinous state of mind.

Malice aforethought does not mean that the murderer thought about killing the victim beforehand or even meant to kill him or her. Rather, malice aforethought includes all of the following situations:

1. Intentionally killing the victim. One person deliberately, and without legal justification, takes the life of another person—a murder in "cold blood."
2. Intending to harm the victim seriously. Doug beats Jerry over the head with a lead pipe, intending only to knock Jerry out, but not to kill him. If Jerry dies of the injuries inflicted by Doug, Doug is guilty of murder. This is because of the likelihood that death can result from a serious injury.
3. Killing someone during the course of a dangerous felony, such as a burglary, robbery, rape, or arson. For example, during a bank robbery (actually, a burglary), the bank guard draws his gun and is shot and killed by the felon. Even though he was acting to save his own life, the felon is guilty of murder. The felon was committing a dangerous felony and in effect invited this type of reaction from the guard. Committing a killing during the course of a dangerous felony is known as the "felony-murder rule."
4. Doing something that has a high risk of death or serious injury, in disregard of the consequences. Suppose Ben shoots into a crowd but doesn't intend to shoot anyone in particular; indeed, he may not intend to shoot anyone at all. The bullet strikes a young girl and kills her. Or suppose Ben shoots at a passing train full of commuters and kills someone he never even saw. In both examples, Ben is guilty of murder because of the strong probability that his act would kill or seriously hurt someone. This type of murder is called a "depraved heart" killing.
5. Killing a police officer while resisting arrest. A person who kills a police officer while resisting a lawful arrest is guilty of murder, even if the person didn't intend to kill the officer.

Degrees of Murder Most states break murder down into at least two degrees: first and second. The difference is based on the murderer's intent in committing the murder or the manner in which he or she carried it out. The severity of the punishment also varies, with first-degree murder being subject to more severe penalties, particularly the ultimate punishment—the death penalty (see discussion later in this chapter).

Manslaughter

Manslaughter is the unlawful killing of a human being by another human being, but without malice aforethought. There are two types of manslaughter: voluntary and involuntary. Voluntary manslaughter is more serious than involuntary manslaughter, and the punishment is accordingly stiffer.

Voluntary manslaughter Voluntary manslaughter is an *intentional* killing without malice aforethought. Usually there are some mitigating circumstances that justify reducing a murder charge to the lesser offense of manslaughter. A common example of voluntary manslaughter is a killing committed in the "heat of passion" by a husband who finds his wife in bed with another man. If the wronged husband kills before a reasonable person in the same situation would have cooled off, the killing, although still unlawful, is usually reduced from murder to voluntary manslaughter. But if the husband did not act immediately and instead plotted the killing for a few weeks, there would be a good argument that he is guilty of murder because he waited beyond a reasonable cooling-off period before acting.

Involuntary manslaughter Unlike murder and voluntary manslaughter, involuntary manslaughter ordinarily is an *unintentional* killing. The death results from the person's criminal negligence, rather than from any intent to kill the victim. For example, if a driver speeding down a residential street loses control of the car and runs over and kills a child playing on the sidewalk, that is involuntary manslaughter.

A drunk driver who causes an accident resulting in the death of a person in another car or a pedestrian traditionally has been held guilty of involuntary manslaughter. But some courts have held that when an intoxicated person takes control of an automobile—in effect, a dangerous weapon—he or she acts with a reckless disregard for the safety of others and can therefore be held liable for voluntary manslaughter or even second-degree murder (see chapter 2).

OTHER CRIMES

Prostitution, Pandering, and Pimping

Prostitution is engaging in sexual activities in exchange for money, drugs, or property. It is illegal in most states, although a few parts of Nevada allow legalized prostitution to some extent. The prostitute is often the one prosecuted, but it is a crime for the customer as well.

"Pandering" is the procurement of a person to become a prostitute. "Pimping" is the crime of soliciting on behalf of a prostitute or deriving support from a prostitute's earnings. Suppose that Lance approaches a young runaway and offers her a place to stay and half of everything she makes if she will have sex with the men he finds for her. Lance finds several men who will pay to have sex with the girl. The men pay Lance, the girl has sex with them, and Lance gives her half the money. Lance is guilty of pandering, since he procured the girl to become a prostitute. Lance is also guilty of pimping, not only because he derived support from the girl's earnings, but also because he solicited the men to have sex with her.

Bigamy, Incest, and Adultery

"Bigamy" is the crime of being married to more than one person at the same time. "Incest" is marriage to, or having sex with, a close relative: a parent, child, uncle or aunt, nephew or niece, grandchild or grandparent, and, in some states, a first cousin, a former stepparent or stepchild, a former father- or mother-in-law, or a former son- or daughter-in-law. "Adultery" occurs when a married person has sexual intercourse with a person other than his or her spouse. Although it was a fairly major crime at one time, adultery is not a crime in most states today, and even where it is still on the books, it is rarely, if ever, enforced.

Loitering and Vagrancy

"Loitering" and "vagrancy" are the "crimes" of sitting or standing around in a public place with no apparent place to go. Statutes prohibiting loitering and vagrancy are often struck down as unconstitutional for being too vague or because they prohibit lawful conduct as well as illegal conduct.

Disturbing the Peace and Malicious Mischief

You disturb the peace when you do something that unreasonably disturbs the public peace and order, such as getting into a brawl in public or setting off firecrackers in the early hours of the morning. "Malicious mischief" is the defacement of property, such as spray-painting the side of a building or throwing a rock through a store window.

Perjury

A person commits perjury when he or she knowingly gives false testimony while under oath. Lying at a trial is perjury, as is lying at a deposition or other proceeding when the witness is under oath. The lie must concern a material matter; there is no perjury if it involves a trivial matter or something unrelated to the issue at hand. "Subornation of perjury" is the procuring of someone to commit perjury for you. Paying someone $2,500 to lie and establish an alibi for you, for instance, is subornation of perjury. (And the witness who lies on the stand is guilty of perjury.)

DEFENSES TO CRIMINAL CHARGES

IF YOU HAVE DONE something that ordinarily constitutes a crime, is there any way out? Yes, if you can prove that you had a legal excuse or justification—a "defense"—for your actions. Here are the major defenses that make otherwise criminal conduct lawful.

Consent of the Victim

Is an act that would otherwise be a crime still a crime if the victim consents to it? That depends on the crime involved. It's not rape if the "victim" is of age and freely and voluntarily consents to have sex with the alleged "rapist." (But if the victim is under age, her consent is ineffective, and the man is guilty of statutory rape.) Neither is it larceny if the person voluntarily parts with or abandons his or her property. But the victim's consent is never a defense to a more serious crime, such as murder or mayhem. Consent is also not a defense to crimes against the general public, such as prostitution or selling illegal drugs. Two men who agree to fight can still be guilty of a public brawl or disturbing the peace.

You Were Defending Yourself

It frequently is asserted in cases of murder, manslaughter, and assault and battery that the defendant was acting to protect himself or herself from being hurt. This is the defense of "self-defense." You are entitled to use reasonable force to protect yourself when it reasonably appears that you are in danger of immediate harm from someone else. Suppose that one night you are walking down a dimly lit street in a neighborhood known for robberies, muggings, and rapes. As you pass a bush, a man lunges out at you. Thinking he is about to attack you, you begin kicking and beating him. If the man was in fact trying to rob or assault you, no one would question your right to defend yourself. But suppose it turns out that the man works for the water company and was making some emergency repairs. As he emerged from the bush, he tripped over a branch and fell in your direction. Will your claim of self-defense hold up in this situation, even though you weren't actually in danger? Yes. In this case, your actions probably were justified, since it reasonably appeared that the man was trying to attack you. You are therefore not guilty of an assault and battery.

Your right to defend yourself includes the right to use "deadly force" in appropriate situations. Deadly force is force that is likely to result in the death of or serious injury to a person—using guns, knives, heavy pipes or branches, even moving cars, for example. You can use deadly force to defend yourself only when you are in immediate danger of death or serious injury and deadly force is reasonably necessary to protect yourself. You can't shoot someone to protect yourself from, say, a slap in the face. If you do and the person dies, you are guilty of voluntary manslaughter, maybe even of murder. On the other hand, shooting someone who is attacking you with a knife or tire iron may well be a justifiable use of deadly force for self-defense.

In a number of states you must try to back away ("retreat") before using deadly force to stop your attacker, unless you are in your home at the time or you cannot retreat safely. If someone is threatening you with a heavy pipe, for example, in these states you ordinarily must try to walk away. But you don't have to if it's apparent that the person will still come after you.

Many people mistakenly believe that they have almost a license to kill anyone who breaks into their home, especially at night. Indeed, many even think that if you shoot a potential intruder who is outside your home, then drag him or her into your hallway, your acts will not be questioned. But before you can use deadly force legally against the intruder, he or she must reasonably appear to pose a threat of imminent danger to the lives and safety of you and your family. For example, suppose that Benny breaks into the Miller house in the middle of the night while the Millers are sleeping. Mr. Miller wakes up, hears some noise in the dining room, takes his loaded revolver from his nightstand drawer, and goes to investigate. When he turns on the dining room light, he finds Benny with a bag full of silverware. Benny drops the bag, puts his hands up, and says, "Please don't shoot." Mr. Miller shoots anyway, hitting Benny in the leg. Mr. Miller is guilty of assault with a deadly weapon, since there was no reason to fire: Benny had surrendered and did not pose any apparent danger when Mr. Miller shot him.

You Were Defending Someone Else

Not only do you have the right to protect yourself from criminal assaults, you have the right to protect others as well. Originally, you could take advantage of the "defense of others" rule only when defending a member of your own family. Today you can step in and defend anyone— even a stranger—who is being attacked. You can use deadly force to protect someone else, but under the same conditions that apply when you are using it to protect yourself: the person must be in immediate danger of serious harm and deadly force is reasonably necessary to prevent it.

Suppose you come upon a fight between Jerry and Mike. Jerry clearly is pummeling Mike, so you step in and hit Jerry. When everything settles down, you learn that Mike was trying to rob Jerry, and when you arrived on the scene, Jerry had just managed to turn the tables: You rescued the assailant, not the victim. If criminal charges are filed against you, can you raise the "defense of others" defense, even though you mistakenly believed that you were protecting the victim? In some states you are guilty of an assault and battery on Jerry because mistakes don't count in this situation. You have the right to defend the person only to the extent he or she has the right to protect himself or herself; you "step in the shoes" of the person you are protecting. In this situation Mike had no right to protect himself, since he was the one who started the fight. You therefore had no right to protect Mike. In other states, however, you are not guilty of a crime if, when you arrived on the scene, it reasonably appeared that Jerry was the aggressor and Mike was the victim.

You Were Defending Your Property

You have the right to use reasonable force to defend your property in appropriate situations. For instance, if you see someone trying to break into your car, you can use reasonable force to prevent it. Before using any type of force to defend your property, you ordinarily must first warn the other person to stop and leave, unless doing so would put you in danger.

Can you use deadly force to protect your property? Generally not. If it comes down to a choice between, say, a car stereo and a human life, human life always prevails. Even if, for instance, a twice-convicted felon is trying to steal or destroy a priceless painting, you can't shoot the felon to protect the painting. About the only time you can use deadly force to protect any property is when you are protecting your house, but only if you are home at the time and deadly force is reasonably necessary under the circumstances. In this situation, you really are protecting yourself and the safety of your family as much as you are protecting your house. You can't, however, go on vacation and rig a shotgun up to go off if the front door is opened when you're not home.

Suppose you hear a noise and see someone running down the street with your toolbox. You give chase, tackle the culprit, and retrieve your toolbox. Is this within the bounds of defending your property? Yes. You were in "fresh pursuit" of your property and can use reasonable force to get it back. But if, for instance, you find out two days later who stole your toolbox, and you go to that person's house, barge in without permission, and retrieve your toolbox, you probably would be guilty of breaking and entering. If you strike the person, you would be guilty of assault and battery. The best way to handle a situation like this is to ask the person to return your toolbox and leave if he or she refuses. Then call the police and report that you have located your stolen toolbox.

Prevention of Crime

Police officers generally are entitled to use reasonable force—including deadly force, when necessary—to prevent a crime or to apprehend or prevent the escape of a person who has committed a felony or a misdemeanor involving a breach of the peace. Can the police shoot a fleeing suspect? That depends on whether the person poses a threat of harm to the community. If the person is suspected of killing several people and is fleeing with a gun, there could be sufficient reason to believe that the community is threatened. But if the crime is less serious, and the suspect has no gun and doesn't appear to be a danger to the community, the police generally cannot use deadly force to stop the fleeing suspect.

As a private citizen, you can use reasonable force to prevent a felony that is attempted in your presence, even though you yourself are not endangered by it. But if you are mistaken and use force to stop and apprehend someone who has not committed or attempted a crime, you can be held liable for the death of or injuries to the "felon."

Insanity

Insanity is a valid, though often maligned, defense to a criminal charge. The defense of insanity is rarely successful, but widespread press coverage of a few celebrated trials involving pleas of insanity has led many people to question whether we shouldn't abolish it completely.

"Insanity" is a legal term, not a psychiatric one. Indeed, psychiatry and psychology purposely avoid using the word "insane." The closest psychiatric equivalent of insane is "psychotic," which basically refers to a loss of touch with reality. To determine legal insanity, most states use the "M'Naughten Rule," which comes to us from an old English case. Under this standard, you are insane if, because of a diseased condition of the mind, you were unable to understand the nature of your act (in other words, you didn't know what you were doing), or if you knew what you were doing, you lacked the mental capacity to distinguish right from wrong. This is an extremely strict standard of insanity. The other test of insanity used by some courts is a little more liberal: You are insane and therefore not criminally responsible for your conduct if, because of a mental disease or defect, you lacked "substantial capacity" to appreciate the criminality of your conduct or to conform your conduct to the requirements of the law.

The question of insanity as a defense involves your state of mind at the time you committed the alleged crime. You could be sane before the act and sane afterward, but if you were insane while committing the crime, insanity (in this case, temporary insanity) would be a valid defense.

You Were Intoxicated

Voluntary intoxication is generally no defense to a crime, but may reduce the charge in a few cases where a specific intent is required. For instance, a man charged with first-degree murder may be convicted of second-degree murder by proving that he was so drunk that he was incapable of premeditating the killing.

Suppose at a party somebody drops a powerful drug in your drink without your knowledge. Or you've been told that the punch you're drinking is nonalcoholic, when in truth it is spiked. The next morning you wake up in jail wondering where you are and why. You soon learn that you went on a criminal rampage the night before. Can you be held guilty for your actions the night before? Not if you were so drunk or high on drugs that you didn't know what you were doing, because in this case, your intoxication was involuntary, against your knowledge and will. But you can use involuntary intoxication as a defense only if you weren't sober enough to realize what you were doing and could not control your actions.

You Were Acting Under Threats or Coercion

You are not normally responsible for crimes you commit while acting under physical duress or coercion. If John takes your son hostage and tells you that he will kill the boy unless you steal a car for him, you can avoid criminal responsibility for auto theft if you comply with John's demand. It is John who would be guilty of auto theft, just as surely as if he had done the act himself. Duress or coercion does not, however, apply in cases of murder or manslaughter—for example, someone puts a gun to your head and orders you to kill someone else or he will kill you. If you do kill the other person, you will be held criminally responsible for that person's death.

The Police Entrapped You

Entrapment is a valid defense to certain crimes, such as solicitation for prostitution and selling drugs. But it is not a defense to crimes involving physical injury or property damage, such as murder, rape, arson, or robbery. Entrapment occurs when the police talk the defendant into committing a crime that he or she was not otherwise predisposed to commit. In other words, the police put the thought of committing the crime into the defendant's mind.

Entrapment often is asserted when a person is charged with soliciting an undercover police officer for prostitution. At issue is whether the defendant approached the undercover officer and offered money in exchange for sexual services, or whether the officer approached the defendant and offered to engage in sex for a certain price. The question becomes, whose idea was it, the defendant's or the police officer's? If the latter's, the defendant is not guilty of solicitation.

Entrapment frequently is raised as an issue when the police set up an operation to catch suspected drug dealers. Entrapment is a valid defense only if you can prove that before the undercover agent approached you, you were not inclined to deal in drugs.

Domestic Authority

Parents generally are entitled to use reasonable force to discipline their children, without being criminally liable for assault or battery. If, however, the punishment is excessive and the child is injured, the privilege is lost and the parent can be held liable for child abuse. The use of deadly force to discipline a child is never permitted, and if deadly force is used, and a child dies from it, the parent can be guilty of manslaughter or even murder.

Children

Under the common law rules that some states still apply, a child under the age of seven is legally incapable of committing a crime because they cannot form the necessary criminal intent. Children between the ages of seven and fourteen are presumed incapable of committing a crime. A child can be convicted of a crime, however, if the evidence shows the child was sufficiently mature to understand what he or she was doing and that it was wrong.

Other Defenses

A person who already has been tried and acquitted of a particular crime cannot be tried a second time for the same crime. If the state tries to prosecute the person a second time, the defendant can assert the defense of "double jeopardy" (see discussion below). Another procedural defense is that the "statute of limitations"—the time that the prosecution has for filing criminal charges—has expired, and it is now too late to prosecute the person. Most crimes have a time limitation on how long after the crime charges can be filed. For instance, there may be a ten-year limitation for filing a criminal complaint for burglary. If ten years pass without the charges being filed, they generally can no longer be filed. One major exception is murder, however; there is no limit on when murder charges can be filed. If, say, the crime is solved thirty years later, the murderer still can be prosecuted for murder.

THE CRIMINAL JUSTICE SYSTEM

THE CRIMINAL JUSTICE SYSTEM sets the rules that the police, the district attorney (or other prosecutor), and the courts must abide by before you are even arrested until the time when your sentence is carried out. At the heart of the whole system of American criminal justice are the fifth and fourteenth amendments to the Constitution, which mandate that no one shall be deprived "of life, liberty, or property, without due process of law." Due process means that before you can be fined, imprisoned, executed, or otherwise punished for a crime, the government must respect your constitutional rights—specifically, the right not to incriminate yourself; freedom from unlawful searches and seizures; the right to retain an attorney or have one appointed for you free of charge if you can't afford one; the right to confront and cross-examine your accusers; and the right to have your case heard before a fair and impartial jury. When you are denied any of these and other constitutional rights, you are deprived of due process of the law, and your conviction cannot stand.

The criminal justice system is the least stable of all the areas of law. It is in a continuous state of change. Since the early 1980s, for instance, the United States Supreme Court has shifted noticeably from protecting the rights of the individual accused of a crime to expanding the powers of the police, in the interests of public safety. Proponents of this shift contend that the judicial system has long been too lenient with criminals and feel that it is about time the courts did something to crack down on crime. On the other hand, some have criticized this trend on the basis that the Constitution is designed to protect the individual from arbitrary and abusive government intrusion. The government (and therefore society) can protect its own interests much better than the individual can protect his or her own, and because of this, the rights of the individual should be paramount.

The pendulum will continue to swing back and forth as long as the Constitution endures, since the interests of the individual and those of society as a whole will always be competing with each other. Sometimes the individual will prevail; other times the government will win.

When Can the Police Stop, Question, and Frisk You?

Suppose you're walking down the street one day, doing nothing wrong, when a police officer stops you, asks for identification, and questions you for ten minutes about your activities. Can the officer do this? Only if the officer has an "articulable and reasonable suspicion that criminal activity is afoot." In other words, the police officer must have some basis for thinking that you might be committing or about to commit a crime, or have committed one already. A police officer cannot stop and question you on a whim, hunch, or simply to harass you.

In determining whether you might be up to something illegal, the officer can base his or her assessment of the situation on experience and the surrounding circumstances. For example, suppose that early one morning you're on your way home from a camping trip near Mexico. You're driving a pickup truck with a camper shell, and the truck is weighted down with all of your gear. Although you're not speeding or breaking any other traffic laws, a border patrol car pulls you over to the side of the road. The immigration officer asks for your driver's license and vehicle registration. The officer then asks where you're coming from, where you're headed to, and what you've been up to. After you answer the officer's questions, the officer informs you that the road you're on frequently is used by smugglers of illegal aliens, who drive overloaded pickup trucks with camper shells much like yours. The officer then tells you that you're free to go. Did this brief stop violate your rights? Probably not. The immigration officer had a reasonable suspicion for stopping you based on his or her experience and on the fact that your vehicle fit the method of operation (profile) of illegal alien smugglers. The officer stopped you only for as long as necessary to confirm or deny his or her suspicions, and the officer did not harass, abuse, or threaten you.

When you are stopped legitimately for questioning, can the police officer pat you down ("frisk you") for possible weapons? Yes. The officer may conduct a protective patdown for his or her own safety to determine if you are carrying any weapons. However, the search must be limited to potential weapons only. Suppose, for example, that Paula, a police officer, suspects that Denny may be intoxicated or under the influence of illegal drugs, and she goes over to investigate. Paula asks Denny for identification and asks some routine questions. Paula tells Denny that she would like to ask him some questions, but first would like to pat him down for any weapons for her safety. Denny complies with Paula's request. During the frisk, Paula does not find anything that resembles a weapon, such as a gun or a knife. However, she finds a small metal case in Denny's shirt pocket, takes it out, opens it, and finds several amphetamine tablets in it. This would most likely be considered an unlawful search because Paula had no reason to suspect that Denny might have a weapon concealed in such a small case. If Paula arrests Denny for possession of illegal drugs, more than likely Denny's lawyer will be able to get the drugs excluded from trial (see below), as Paula had no reason to search the small metal case.

Suppose that Roger is standing in an area known for its drug trafficking when a caravan of four police cars drives through the area. Fearful that the police will stop and frisk him and find a gun in the bag he is holding, Roger flees the scene. The officers in one police vehicle see Roger running away, take off after him, eventually catch him, and stop him. In the course of a patdown search, one of the officers squeezes the bag and feels a handgun. Roger is arrested for illegal possession of a firearm. In court, Robert claims that the police officers violated his fourth amendment right to be free from unreasonable searches and seizures, as they had no reason to suspect that he was doing anything criminal. Will Roger persuade the court with his argument?

In just such a case, the U.S. Supreme Court held that the officers acted properly and did not violate the defendant's fourth amendment rights. The Supreme Court ruled that sudden flight in a high crime area upon seeing a caravan of police cars created a reasonable, articulable suspicion that criminal activity was afoot, justifying a brief investigatory stop, including a protective patdown for weapons for the officers' safety. The Supreme Court held that while a person's mere presence alone in a high crime area is not by itself sufficient to give rise to a reasonable and articulable suspicion that criminal activity is afoot, a location's characteristics are relevant in determining whether the circumstances are sufficiently suspicious to warrant further investigation. Furthermore, it was the defendant's unprovoked flight that aroused the officers' suspicions. The Supreme Court observed that nervous, evasive behavior is another pertinent factor in determining reasonable suspicion for a brief investigatory stop.

In another case, two police officers in a marked patrol car spotted a man leaving a twelve-unit apartment building known for cocaine sales. The suspect began walking in the direction of the police car, but when he spotted the squad car and made eye contact with one of the policemen, he abruptly stopped and began walking in the opposite direction and entered an alley on the other side of the apartment building. Based upon the suspect's evasive behavior and the fact that he had just left a known crack house, the police officers decided to stop the suspect and investigate further. The officers pulled their squad car into the alley and ordered the suspect to stop and submit to a patdown search. The search revealed no weapons, but the officer conducting the search took an interest in a lump in the suspect's nylon jacket. The officer testified that as he patted down the front of the suspect's body, he felt a small lump in the front pocket. He examined it with his fingers "and it slid and it felt to be a lump of crack cocaine in cellophane."

The U.S. Supreme Court ruled that this search violated the fourth amendment. The

Supreme Court ruled that if an officer lawfully pats down a suspect's outer clothing and feels an object whose contour or mass makes its identity immediately apparent, there is no invasion of privacy beyond that already authorized by the officer's search for weapons. If the object is contraband, its warrantless seizure would be justified by the realization that resort to a neutral magistrate to obtain a search warrant under such circumstances would be impracticable and would do little to promote the fourth amendment's objectives. However, the U.S. Supreme Court held further that while an officer may put his hand on the clothing and feel the object, the officer may not squeeze, slide, or otherwise manipulate the object in an attempt to identify it.

A border patrol agent boarded a bus in Texas to check the immigration status of its passengers. As he walked off the bus, he squeezed the soft luggage that the passengers had placed in the overhead storage space. He squeezed a canvas bag over one passenger's seat and noticed that it contained a "brick-like" object. After the passenger admitted owning the bag and consented to its search, the agent discovered a brick of methamphetamine. The case made its way to the U.S. Supreme Court, which held that the border patrol agent's physical manipulation of the passenger's carry-on bag violated the fourth amendment's prohibition against unreasonable searches. The Supreme Court held that physically intrusive inspection is simply more intrusive than purely visual inspection.

YOUR RIGHT TO BE FREE FROM UNREASONABLE SEARCHES

THE FOURTH AMENDMENT to the United States Constitution protects citizens against *unreasonable* searches and seizures. Except as discussed below, the police normally must obtain a search warrant before searching you, your house (or apartment), or your car. To get a search warrant, the police apply to a judge (or a magistrate). The judge will issue a warrant only if the police present sufficient testimony and affidavits to establish probable cause that contraband (illegal drugs, for example, or stolen property) or evidence of a crime (the murder weapon, for instance, or the rope used to bind a kidnap victim) will be found on the person or premises to be searched. The warrant must carefully describe the person or premises to be searched, as well as the type of contraband or evidence sought.

During the search, the police must stay within the scope of the warrant, which is determined by the object they are looking for. Something that is small and easily concealed justifies a more intensive search than a large object. For example, if the warrant is for drugs or a handgun, the police can open drawers, go through cupboards, take air vents off to look in ventilation shafts, and so forth, because drugs or a handgun can be hidden almost anywhere. But if the search warrant were for a stolen twenty-seven-inch color television set, the police would not be justified in going through drawers, ventilation shafts, and other places too small to conceal the television.

When Can the Police Search You Without a Warrant?

Here are the major situations in which the police can make a search without first obtaining a warrant.

If You Consent to the Search

A warrant is not required if you voluntarily consent to be searched. But even when you permit a search, the police must stay within the bounds of your consent and must search only those areas where the object the police are looking for could physically be concealed. For instance, if you're suspected of stealing a car, the police could only look for it in your garage; they're not going to find it in a dresser drawer or in the attic.

Suppose you change your mind after giving the police consent to the search and ask the police to leave. Do the police have to stop the search? Yes. You can revoke your consent at any time, and the police normally must leave and obtain a search warrant before they can search any further. But if by the time you revoke your consent they have already found something incriminating that gives them probable cause to arrest you, they can do so on the basis of that evidence.

Can a landlord give the police permission to search a tenant's apartment (or rented house)? Usually not. A landlord does not have the authority to permit a search of a tenant's apartment; only the tenant does. Suppose your roommate tells the police that it's okay to search the apartment or house—including your bedroom and everything in it—and the police find some drugs on your closet shelf. Is that search lawful? No. Your roommate could consent to a search of his or her private area or to areas used by both of you, such as the kitchen and living room, but not to the areas that you use exclusively, such as your bedroom.

Suppose the police want to search a child's room. If the parents consent to it, will that stop the child from claiming that the search was illegal? No. Children as well as adults have the right to be free from unreasonable searches. The parents can permit the police to search areas of the child's room where the parents themselves are permitted to go. But if, say, the child has a chest that he or she keeps locked and has the only key to, then only the child can give the police the permission to open it without a warrant.

When an Object Is in Plain View

The police do not need a search warrant if the object is in "plain view." If a gun or packet of cocaine is lying uncovered on the seat of a car parked on a public street, for instance, and a police officer walks by and sees it, no warrant is necessary, since anybody passing by could have seen it. Suppose, though, that the car is parked inside your garage, and the officer—without your consent—opens the garage door and sees the illegal object on the car seat. Is the object then in plain view? No. The plain view rule applies only when the police officer has the right to be where he or she is at the time the officer sees the object. Since the officer doesn't have the right to go inside your garage without your consent or a warrant, the objects on the car seat are not in plain view.

The plain view doctrine also applies to searches conducted pursuant to a warrant. For example, if the police have a warrant to search a house for weapons and in the process find some drugs on the living room coffee table, those drugs are in plain sight and can be used in court to convict the defendant of possession of illegal drugs.

When You Are Arrested

When you are arrested lawfully, you can be searched without your consent. If you are arrested but not taken into custody, the police can search you for weapons and to prevent you from destroying any evidence. Should you be taken into custody, the police can conduct a full search of you, as well as the immediate area around you in case you hid something when the police arrived. At the police station or the jail, you may be strip-searched if there is a possibility that you may be concealing drugs, contraband, or evidence on your body. Absent extenuating circumstances, a police officer of your own sex must do the search.

When You Are in a Car, Truck, or Motor Home

If the police have probable cause to believe that contraband or evidence of a crime is in your car, truck, SUV, motor home, or other vehicle, a search warrant usually is not required. Why not? Because you could easily flee the scene before the police could get back with a warrant. Of course, a police officer can't single your car out for no reason and search it. There must be sufficient justification to conduct the search in the first place, or it is illegal.

Texas law makes it a misdemeanor—punishable only by a fine—either for a front-seat passenger in a car equipped with safety belts not to wear one or for the driver to fail to secure any small child riding in front. A woman was driving her truck with her small children in the front seat. None of them was wearing a seat belt. A police officer pulled the woman over, verbally berated her, handcuffed her, placed her in his squad car, and drove her back to the police station, where she was made to remove her shoes, jewelry, and eyeglasses, and empty her pockets. Officers took her mug shot and placed her alone in a jail cell for about an hour, when she was taken before a magistrate and released on bond. She pleaded no contest to the seat-belt misdemeanors and paid a $50 fine. The U.S. Supreme Court held that the fourth amendment guarantees against unreasonable search and seizure, and does not forbid a warrantless arrest for a criminal offense, such as a misdemeanor seat-belt violation punishable only by a fine.

Suppose that plainclothes policemen are patrolling a high drug area in an unmarked vehicle and observe a truck waiting at a stop sign for an unusually long time. When the police car makes a U-turn in order to head back toward the truck, the truck suddenly turns to its right without signaling, and speeds off at an "unreasonable" speed. The police officers follow it, and shortly catch up to the truck when it stops behind other traffic at a red light. The policemen pull alongside; one officer gets out and approaches the truck driver's door, identifies himself as a police officer, and directs the driver to put the vehicle into park. When the officer walks up to the driver's window, he immediately sees two large plastic bags of what appear to be crack cocaine in the passenger's hands. The driver and his passenger are arrested, and quantities of several types of illegal drugs are found in the truck.

The two suspects allege that the police officer's asserted ground for approaching the truck—to give the driver a warning concerning traffic violations—was a pretext to his real reason: to search them for drugs, which he did not have probable cause to do. Before their trials, the two defendants make a motion to have the drugs excluded as evidence from their trials (see below) on the basis that the search was unreasonable and therefore a violation of their fourth amendment rights. Will they win their motion? No. The police officers had probable cause to stop the vehicle because they believed a traffic violation had occurred. The U.S. Supreme Court has ruled that a police officer's subjective intentions play no role in ordinary, probable-cause searches.

Similarly, in another case a police officer stopped a person for speeding and for having an improperly tinted windshield. The officer approached the vehicle, explained the reason for the stop, and asked for the driver's license, registration, and insurance documentation. Upon seeing the driver's license, the police officer realized that he was aware of "intelligence on [the driver] regarding narcotics." When the driver opened his car door in an unsuccessful attempt to locate his registration and insurance papers, the officer noticed a rusted roofing hatchet on the car's floorboard. The officer then arrested the man for speeding, driving without his registration and insurance documentation, carrying a weapon (the roofing hatchet), and improper window tinting. After another officer arrived and placed the man in his squad car, the officer conducted an inventory search of the vehicle and under the armrest discovered a bag containing a substance that appeared to be methamphetamine, as well as numerous items of suspected drug paraphernalia. As a result of the detention and search, the man was charged with various drug offenses, unlawful possession of a weapon, and speeding. The defendant moved to exclude the evidence seized from his vehicle on the basis that his arrest was merely a "pretext and sham to search" him and therefore violated the fourth and fourteenth amendments of the Constitution. The U.S. Supreme Court affirmed its earlier ruling that a valid traffic-violation arrest will not be rendered invalid by the fact it was a "mere pretext for a narcotics search."

After stopping a speeding car in which the defendant was a passenger, a Maryland state trooper ordered the passenger out of the vehicle because of his apparent nervousness. When the passenger got out of the car, a quantity of cocaine fell to the ground. He was arrested and charged with possession of cocaine with intent to distribute. The passenger sought to have the cocaine excluded from his trial on the basis that the state trooper's ordering him out of the car constituted an unreasonable seizure under the fourth amendment. The U.S. Supreme Court disagreed and held that an officer making a traffic stop may order the passengers to get out of the car pending completion of the stop.

In a U.S. Supreme Court case originating in Ohio, a deputy sheriff stopped the defendant for speeding, gave him a verbal warning, and returned his driver's license. The deputy then asked whether he was carrying any illegal contraband, weapons, or drugs in his car. The defendant answered "No" and consented to a search of the car, which revealed a small amount of marijuana and a pill that turned out to be methamphetamine. The defendant sought to have the drugs excluded from the trial on the basis that, when he returned his driver's license, the officer should have informed him that he was "legally free to go." The Supreme Court held that the fourth amendment does not require that a lawfully seized defendant be advised that he is "free to go" before his consent to search will be recognized as voluntary. Rather, the high court stated that the question was one of reasonableness, noting that it would be unrealistic to require police officers to always inform detainees that they are free to go before consent to search may be deemed voluntary. The Supreme Court concluded that the fourth amendment test for a valid consent to search is that the consent must be voluntary, and voluntariness is a question of fact to be determined from all the circumstances.

Suppose a city sets up random checkpoints to search vehicles for illegal aliens, drunk drivers, to verify drivers' licenses and registrations, or to search for drugs. Is that legal? All but the checkpoints to search for drugs are legal, according to the U.S. Supreme Court. The Supreme Court expressly has upheld brief, suspicionless seizures at highway checkpoints for the purposes of combating drunk driving and intercepting illegal immigrants. The Supreme Court also has suggested that a similar type of roadblock with the purpose of verifying drivers' licenses and vehicle registrations would be permissible. However, the Supreme Court has held that a checkpoint program whose primary purpose is the discovery and interdiction of illegal narcotics violates the fourth amendment. The reason the Supreme Court makes the distinction is that the search for drugs is not distinct from a general purpose of investigating crime.

When Can the Police Enter and Search a House?

The police almost always need a warrant to enter and search a house. (A mobile home that is fixed to the ground is considered a "house," since, unlike a motor home, it cannot be moved readily.) One time the police do not need a search warrant to enter a house is when they are in hot pursuit of a dangerous suspect, and there is reason to believe that the suspect is inside the house. Once inside, the police can search anyone who could be a threat to them. If, while lawfully inside the house, the police spot drugs, illegal weapons, or contraband from a burglary, it is admissible in court.

Consider the following example: Responding to a call reporting an armed burglary at a liquor store, the police arrive in time to see a man fleeing from the store with a gun in one hand and a paper sack in the other. The suspect gets into a car and takes off, with the police right behind. The suspect stops in front of a house and runs inside, followed by the police. When they enter the house, the police officers see several guns and some packets that contain a white substance on the coffee table. The suspect is found hiding in the upstairs bathroom and gives up without incident. He is searched, and the police find a gun and some cocaine on him. A further search of the house turns up the paper sack containing the cash he got from the liquor store burglary. In this case, the police officers' entry into the house was justified, because they were in hot pursuit of an armed burglar. The search of the suspect also was justified, since it took place in connection with a lawful arrest. Because the police had the right to enter the house, the guns and packets of cocaine on the coffee table were in plain view and could therefore be used as evidence at the trial. Suppose, though, that there were no guns or drugs on the coffee table, but an officer rifled through the suspect's dresser drawers and nightstand and found the incriminating items there. Could the guns and drugs found in the dresser and nightstand be used against the suspect? No. Since they were not in plain view, a warrant would have been necessary to search for them in these places.

Another time the police lawfully can enter a house without a warrant is when they have reason to believe that a crime victim inside needs immediate aid. In this situation, the police also can search the house to see if there are other victims or if a suspect is still on the premises. Evidence that is in plain view of the officers would be admissible in court, but the police would have to obtain a search warrant to conduct a more exhaustive search.

When the police do obtain a warrant to search a home, ordinarily they must first knock and announce who they are and why they are there. The police usually can't just barge in unannounced, even if they have a warrant. But if they aren't let inside within a reasonable time, they then can force their way in. And the police need not knock and announce themselves if the people inside likely would destroy the evidence. If the search warrant is for drugs, for instance, the police do not have to announce themselves and wait outside while the drugs are flushed down the toilet. The police also need not "knock and announce" when doing so would put them in danger of being shot or otherwise seriously hurt by the people or animals inside.

In order to justify a "no-knock" entry, the police must have a reasonable suspicion that knocking and announcing their presence under the particular circumstances would be dangerous or futile, or that it would inhibit the effective investigation of the crime by allowing for the destruction of evidence. However, a blanket rule giving the police the right to enter a house, apartment, mobile home, etc., without knocking and announcing the fact that they are police officers is unconstitutional. Each case must be determined by looking at the totality of its circumstances.

Can the Police Tap Your Phone or Bug Your House?

Using electronic and other devices to listen in on private conversations is considered a "search." Federal law prohibits the police from listening in or tape-recording a telephone conversation without a search warrant unless one party to the conversation consents. Many states, however, require that *all* parties to the telephone conversation be informed of and consent to the eavesdropping or recording of the conversation if no warrant has been obtained.

In fact, unless the police have the consent of at least one party, they cannot use electronic surveillance equipment to listen in on *any* private conversation without a search warrant. But a warrant is not required if the police—not using any surveillance or amplification equipment—are in, say, a public park or movie theater and overhear a loud conversation.

The Exclusionary Rule

Suppose the police illegally search you (or your house, car, etc.) and discover incriminating evidence that implicates you in a crime. Can you prohibit the district attorney from using that evidence against you at trial? Yes. Evidence found in an illegal search cannot be used against you in court. This is known as the "exclusionary rule." And not only is that evidence itself not admissible in court; neither is any other evidence discovered as a result of that evidence. This is known as the "fruit of the poisonous tree" doctrine. Since the original evidence was obtained unlawfully, the other evidence bears the "taint" of that illegality. For example, the police illegally search Fred's car and find a shotgun and a bloodstained blanket in the trunk. They show this to Fred, who immediately confesses to having shot and killed his wife. Not only are the shotgun and blanket inadmissible at Fred's trial because they were found during an illegal search, but so is his confession, because it was the product of that unlawful search.

Why do we have the exclusionary rule? Suppose for a moment that the exclusionary rule didn't exist. Let's say that the police break into your house without a warrant, tear everything apart, and find evidence of a crime—say, some burglar's tools and stolen property, or drugs or illegal weapons. The police have violated your constitutional rights. But without the exclusionary rule, what recourse do you have? You can sue the police in civil court, but a jury probably won't award you very much, if anything at all. The result is that you essentially will have been deprived of your constitutional right against unreasonable searches and seizures. What the exclusionary rule does is provide a simple and effective method of deterring the police from violating your rights: It prevents the illegally obtained evidence from being used against you in court. It also serves as an incentive to prevent the police from indiscriminately searching persons for no reason at all.

Suppose you suspect your neighbor of committing the recent rash of burglaries in your neighborhood. One day while he is out, you break into his house and find items stolen from neighborhood homes. Does the exclusionary rule prevent the district attorney from using this evidence at trial? No. The exclusionary rule applies only to evidence obtained through an unlawful search conducted by or at the direction of the authorities, not to illegal searches that are completely the idea and doing of a private citizen. This is because the fourth amendment protects only against unlawful government actions, not actions of private individuals. (If you did break into your neighbor's house, however, you would be guilty of a crime and also subject to a civil lawsuit.)

The exclusionary rule is probably the most strongly criticized of all of the so-called "legal technicalities." A common misconception is that many criminals go free because the police did not conduct a search without absolute propriety. The truth is that only a minute percentage of defendants who raise this objection are successful with it. A study by the General Accounting Office of the United States suggests that less than one-half of 1 percent of all serious federal crimes are dismissed for this reason.

There is one exception to the exclusionary rule. Traditionally, if there were any faults with the search at all, the evidence would have to be excluded from trial. For instance, if a search warrant incorrectly listed the address as 123 Main Street, rather than 125 Main Street, the warrant would have to be corrected before the police lawfully could search 125 Main Street. If the police did not get the warrant changed and searched 125 Main Street, all of the evidence obtained during the search would be inadmissible in court.

The one exception now recognized by the U.S. Supreme Court is that when the police are acting in "good faith" on a warrant that turns out to be defective, the evidence is admissible if the defect was not apparent on the face of the warrant. For instance, if the judge issued the warrant based on a faulty affidavit—one based on hearsay, perhaps, rather than the witness's own firsthand knowledge—and the police did not know that anything was wrong with the warrant, the evidence obtained in the search would be admissible.

YOUR RIGHTS WHEN YOU ARE ARRESTED

UNDER WHAT CIRCUMSTANCES can the police arrest you? Anytime there is "probable cause" to believe that you are committing or have committed a crime. The police have probable cause when there are enough facts to lead a reasonable person to conclude that you are committing or have committed a crime. This is a considerably higher standard than the mere "suspicion" an officer needs in order to stop you briefly to investigate possible criminal activity.

Can a police officer make an arrest without a warrant? Sometimes. The officer doesn't need a warrant to arrest you if you commit a crime in his or her presence, for instance. A warrant also isn't necessary if the officer has probable cause to believe that you committed a felony, even though it was not committed in his or her presence. Otherwise, the officer generally needs a warrant to make an arrest.

Your *Miranda* Rights

After you are arrested, the police must advise you of your *Miranda* rights before they can question you. But in a mere "stop and frisk" situation (discussed earlier), the police do not have to advise you of your *Miranda* rights before questioning. If the police are conducting a routine investigation and asking a number of people what they know about the crime, each person need not be advised of his or her *Miranda* rights before questioning.

What are the *Miranda* rights? In the 1966 case of *Miranda v. Arizona*, the U.S. Supreme Court ruled that an incriminating statement obtained during a "custodial interrogation"—one in which you are not free to leave anytime you want—is not admissible in court unless, before the police begin to question you, they advise you of certain fundamental rights: that you have the right to remain silent; that anything you say can be used against you in court; that you have the right to have an attorney present during questioning; and that if you want to have an attorney represent you but cannot afford one, one will be provided for you without cost.

After the police read you your *Miranda* rights, they will ask whether you understand these rights. If you reply that you do, you will be asked whether, having your rights in mind, you wish to talk to the police at that time, without the presence of a lawyer. If you agree to talk to the police, you have waived your *Miranda* rights, and any confession or incriminating statements you make can be used against you in court. To ensure that there is no dispute about whether the police have read you your *Miranda* rights, some police departments will have you sign a card that contains the *Miranda* rights and states that they were read to you and that you understand them.

Contrary to what you are accustomed to seeing on television, the police do not have to read you your *Miranda* rights the moment they arrest you. They only have to inform you of your rights before they question you. Often the arresting officers will not ask a suspect any questions and will leave that task to the detectives back at the station. Since the arresting officers aren't asking you any questions ("interrogating" you), they don't need to need to advise you of your *Miranda* rights. Suppose the arresting officers don't read you your rights and don't ask you any questions, but on the way back to the station you blurt out that you are sorry you committed the crime. In this instance, the remark can be used against you at trial; the police weren't questioning you, so they didn't have to inform you of your rights.

Are there any situations in which the police don't have to read you your *Miranda* rights before questioning you? Yes. The police can question you briefly upon their arrival, and without advising you of your rights, if there is an immediate threat to public safety. Suppose the police are called to a murder site. When they arrive, they find the victim lying on the porch, dead of a gunshot wound. A crowd is gathering on the lawn in front of the house. Witnesses point out the man who apparently killed the victim. The police approach the suspect and, before advising him of his *Miranda* rights, ask him where the gun is. The suspect replies that he threw it into the bushes in front of the house. The police search the bushes and recover the weapon, which is later proved to be the murder weapon. The suspect's statement that he threw the gun into the bushes is admissible in court, even though he was not advised of his *Miranda* rights. In this case, public safety was threatened by the fact that a loaded gun may have been lying around, so the police were justified in trying to find out where it was as soon as possible.

What to Do If You Are Arrested

What should you do if you are ever arrested? The first thing is to stay calm and obey all of the police officer's instructions—even if you feel that you have done nothing wrong and that the arrest is unlawful. You don't need to have actually committed a crime to be arrested; the officer needs to have only probable cause to arrest you. And the penalty for resisting arrest can be much more serious than that for the charge on which you were arrested originally. A more practical reason for cooperating with the police officer's instructions is that by resisting arrest, you run the risk of being seriously hurt or killed by the police officer. The place to challenge the police officer's authority to arrest you is in a court of law, not on a street corner or in a dark alley.

After you have been arrested, volunteer nothing. The only information you should give is your personal information: name, address, telephone number, and the like. You have the right to remain silent, so use it. If the police read you your *Miranda* rights and then start questioning you, insist on having a lawyer present before answering any questions. Your right to have a lawyer present during questioning is your best protection when you are arrested, so take advantage of it. If you can't afford one, tell the police, and request that one be appointed for you immediately. Until you've talked to a lawyer, refuse all attempts by the police to ask "just a few routine questions."

Don't be persuaded into making a confession in return for the police officer's promise to do everything he or she can for you. Only the district attorney's office can make deals. Also, don't talk to your cellmates or anyone else about the specifics of the incident. Nothing in the law prohibits the district attorney from calling your cellmates to the witness stand to testify that you admitted committing the crime, especially if your cellmate is promised a lighter sentence if he or she cooperates with the district attorney's office.

WHAT HAPPENS AFTER YOUR ARREST

AFTER YOU ARE ARRESTED and taken into custody, you are transported to the jail, where you are "booked." Booking consists of logging your name and the reason for your arrest in the computer and taking your picture ("mug shot") and fingerprints. Your personal belongings will be taken from you and inventoried, and you will be given a receipt for them. Read the receipt carefully before signing it to make sure everything is listed. You will have the opportunity to make at least one telephone call, which should be to your lawyer if you have one, and if not, to the person you can most count on to help you—your spouse, your parents, or your closest friend, for example.

What happens next depends on how serious your crime is. If the crime is minor, you may be given the chance to post bail (discussed below). If your crime is more serious, you will be held in jail until you are arraigned and a judge sets bail.

Arraignment

At your arraignment, which takes place in court, the judge will inform you of the charges against you and ask how you plead: guilty or not guilty. You also can enter a plea of nolo contendere, or no contest, which means that you're not going to fight the charges. A plea of no contest has the same effect as pleading guilty, except that it cannot be used against you in a civil case for injuries another person suffered as a result of your criminal conduct. Suppose you're criminally charged with battery. If you plead guilty (or the jury finds you guilty after a trial), your plea of guilty can be used against you if the victim sues you in civil court for his or her injuries. But if you plead no contest to the criminal charges, it can't be used against you in the civil case. The plaintiff in the civil action then has to prove the battery against him or her. Ordinarily, you'll want to plead not guilty at the arraignment even if you committed the crime so a possible plea bargain can be reached between your lawyer and the prosecution.

At the arraignment, the judge also will inform you of some rights, including the right to have a lawyer represent you and be appointed for you if you can't afford one. The judge also will usually set the amount of bail if it hasn't been set already. If bail was set earlier, but you feel it is too high, you can ask the judge to reduce it at this time or to release you on your own recognizance ("OR").

How soon after your arrest you are arraigned depends on where and when you were arrested. If you were arrested in a small town on a Friday night, you might not be arraigned until Monday. But if you're arrested in a major city, you could be arraigned the very night of your arrest. In any event, you must be arraigned promptly, usually no more than forty-eight or seventy-two hours after your arrest if you're not released on bail.

What happens if you plead guilty at your arraignment? If the crime is minor, the judge may impose your sentence—perhaps a $100 fine or a couple of days in jail—on the spot. Otherwise, the judge will set a date for your sentencing and send your file to the probation department. There, a probation officer will review the case, your criminal record, your work history, your standing in the community, and your current situation, and make a recommendation to the judge regarding appropriate punishment.

Bail

"Bail" is the money you post with the court to insure that you will show up at the arraignment and all other court proceedings and not disappear until your case is resolved. You will get your money back at the end of trial, unless you "jump," or "skip," bail—in other words, not show up in court as you were required to. In that case, you will forfeit the bail and a warrant for your arrest will be issued. (After your arrest on this warrant, you will be required to post a new bond—at a considerably higher amount than the original bond, since you're a proven flight risk.)

The amount of bail must be reasonable in light of the crime committed, your previous criminal record, your roots in the area—how long you've lived or worked there—and the chances that you will skip bail or commit another crime while out on bail. Bail of $500,000 for a simple assault case in which the defendant has no previous record and has lived in the area all of his or her life is clearly unreasonable. But when murder is charged, a very high amount of bail is justified; in fact, many suspected murderers are held without bail.

In lieu of bail, the judge may release you on your own recognizance. All that is required in this case is your promise to appear in court at a later date. Ordinarily, you will be released on your own recognizance only when the crime is not serious, you have no previous criminal record, and you have lived and worked in the area for a substantial period of time.

Although traditionally bail could be posted only in cash, many states now let you use a bank credit card, such as Visa or MasterCard. Bail bond services—which abound near jails, open 24 hours a day, 365 days a year—will post your bail for a certain fee, such as 10 percent of the full amount, plus adequate security (such as a house) for the remainder of the bail. If, for example, your bail is set at $10,000, the bond service may charge $1,000 to post the bond. (You don't get the $1,000 back even if you attend all of the court proceedings as required.) What happens if you don't show up for your arraignment, trial, or other proceeding? The bond service has to pay $10,000 to the court. It then goes looking for you (or the person who guaranteed the bond) for full reimbursement, or will levy on the property you put up as security for the balance of the bail.

How You Are Formally Charged with a Crime

If you're accused of a misdemeanor, you are charged formally with the crime by a criminal complaint signed by the arresting officer if he or she saw you commit the crime and, if not, by the victim (the "complaining witness"). The complaint is reviewed by the district attorney's office, and if they feel it is justified, they will file it with the court.

If you're suspected of having committed a felony, you must be charged either by a judge after a preliminary hearing or by an indictment issued by a grand jury. The purpose of each procedure is the same: to determine whether there is sufficient cause for charging you with a crime.

A preliminary hearing is held before a judge (or magistrate), who decides whether there is enough evidence to hold ("bind") you over for trial. At the preliminary hearing, you can—and should—have a lawyer represent you. Your lawyer can cross-examine the witnesses called by the district attorney to see how strong of a case they have against you. The judge will order you to stand trial only if the evidence shows that it is probable that you committed a crime. (This is a lower standard than the "beyond a reasonable doubt" test needed to convict you of the crime.)

In a grand jury proceeding, the district attorney presents a document called an "indictment," or "bill of indictment," to the grand jury, a panel of residents (usually numbering twelve to twenty-four) selected from the local community. The grand jury has the power to subpoena witnesses to appear before it and can consider just about any type of evidence it wants, including evidence that may not be admissible at trial. If, after considering all of the evidence presented to it, a majority of the grand jury finds that there is probable cause to believe that you have committed a crime, the foreman will approve and sign the indictment as a "true bill."

Grand jury proceedings are an anomaly, in that they are one of the few aspects of the American judicial system that take place in private, behind closed doors, beyond the scrutiny of the public and the press. This is justified on the ground that the grand jury is merely an investigatory body trying to determine whether there is a basis for charging a person with a particular crime. And because the grand jury is merely investigating the possibility of a crime, it does not have to advise you of your *Miranda* rights before questioning you—even if you are the person under investigation—nor do you have the rights to have your lawyer present while you are questioned, to cross-examine witnesses, or even present evidence in your own defense. The one right you do retain is your fifth amendment right not to incriminate yourself. Frequently, a person under investigation by the grand jury will invoke this right and refuse to answer the grand jury's questions.

The grand jury system has been criticized for being a tool of the district attorney rather than an independent body that gives each side an equally fair chance. The district attorney runs the whole show, deciding whom to investigate and what evidence to present to the grand jury and what evidence to withhold. Because of this, many states abolished or limited the role of the grand jury in favor of the preliminary examination. (In fact, England, which created the grand jury system, has abolished it completely for these very reasons.)

PLEA BARGAINING

SOMETIME AFTER YOUR ARREST, the district attorney may be willing to "plea bargain." Plea bargaining is an agreement between the prosecution and the defendant in which the defendant agrees to plead guilty in exchange either for the district attorney reducing a more serious crime to a lesser one or recommending to the judge that the defendant receive a reduced sentence. Absent unusual circumstances, the judge will approve the sentence recommended by the D.A. But when the crime in question is serious or the defendant has a long criminal record, the judge will review the district attorney's recommendations more carefully.

Plea bargaining, though one of the most maligned practices of our criminal justice system, is a necessary evil. Why does plea bargaining exist? The answer is really quite simple: It keeps our judicial system from being flooded with inmates. Without an incentive for pleading guilty, many more defendants would ask for trials, inundating our already pressed courts. Our court system quickly would collapse if every defendant wanted a trial. To accommodate all of these trials, we would need tens of thousands more courthouses, hundreds of thousands more judges, prosecuting attorneys, and public defenders, millions more courtroom staff members, and millions more citizens for jury duty. The costs and logistics would be enormous. Plea bargaining allows the criminal justice system and everyone involved to operate at a manageable pace.

YOUR RIGHTS AT THE TRIAL

WHEN YOU ARE CHARGED with a crime, you have the right to a speedy and public trial. A state statute may require your trial to start within a certain time (say, forty-five days) after your arraignment. If your trial doesn't begin within the specified time, you can ask the judge to dismiss the charges against you. Often a criminal defendant will agree to waive the right to have a trial within a specified time, since his or her attorney usually needs more time to prepare the case for trial. Many criminal trials don't start until four months to a year after the defendant's arraignment.

You are entitled to a trial before a fair and impartial jury, unless you are charged with only a petty offense—defined as one for which the maximum penalty is imprisonment for six months or less. In that case, the trial is held before a judge. Historically, criminal trials have been heard by twelve jurors, all of whom must agree for a conviction.

The American criminal justice system presumes that a defendant is innocent until proven guilty. The prosecutor has the burden of proving that the defendant is guilty, and must do so "beyond a reasonable doubt." This is a higher standard than that used in civil trials (see chapter 22), where the plaintiff need only prove his or her case by a preponderance of the evidence, a "probability" that the defendant did what he or she is accused of.

You have the right to be confronted by and to cross-examine your accusers, and to subpoena witnesses in order to compel their attendance at the trial. Before the trial, you have the right to discover what evidence the district attorney plans to present, so that you can prepare a defense accordingly. If you feel that any of the evidence the district attorney plans to use at the trial resulted from an illegal search or from the failure of the police to advise you of your *Miranda* rights before questioning you, you can file a "motion to suppress" that evidence. If the judge agrees with you and grants your motion, the district attorney will be barred from presenting that evidence to the jury at trial.

What can you do if there is a threat that the news coverage of your case will be so widespread that it will be difficult to find a jury who has not heard or read about the incident and formed certain opinions based on those news reports? You can ask the judge to close the pretrial proceedings to the public and to issue an order prohibiting the principals from talking to the media—a "gag order." If you still can't get a fair trial because of prejudicial pretrial publicity, then you should ask the judge to transfer the case to another county (a "change of venue") where the case has not been so widely publicized. And if there is the prospect of heavy media coverage during the trial, the jury may be sequestered for the duration of the trial and deliberations.

The structure of a criminal trial is basically the same as that of a civil one (see chapter 22). First, a jury is chosen. The prosecution (the district attorney) then makes its opening statement, followed by the opening remarks of the defendant's attorney. (Or the defense attorney may wait until after the prosecution rests its case before making his or her opening statement.) The prosecution presents its case in chief, calling witnesses (whom the defendant's lawyer can cross-examine) and offering evidence. After the prosecution rests its case, the defense puts on its case in chief. Occasionally, the defendant's attorney will not present any evidence but will rely completely upon the prosecutor's failure to convince the jury or upon his or her cross-examination of the prosecution's witnesses to exonerate the defendant. The prosecutor and the defense attorney then make closing arguments. The judge instructs the jury on the applicable law, and the jury retires to the jury room for deliberations. If the jury reaches a verdict, it is read in open court, usually by the judge's clerk. If the jury is hopelessly deadlocked and unable to agree upon a verdict, the judge will declare a mistrial. The district attorney must then evaluate the case anew to see whether the chance of winning a conviction might be better at a second trial before a different jury. One important factor the district attorney considers is which way the jury was leaning. If the jury was just a vote or two shy of convicting the defendant, the chances of retrial are high. However, if the jury was just a vote or two shy of acquitting the defendant, the district attorney may decide he or she will not be able to get a conviction in that case and ask the judge to dismiss the case "in the interests of justice."

If you are acquitted, you cannot be tried a second time for the same crime. To do so would violate your constitutional guarantee against "double jeopardy." There are, however, times when you can be tried twice for the same crime. Suppose, for example, at your first trial the jury convicts you. Your attorney appeals your case and wins a reversal; the district attorney can then prosecute you again. You also can be tried twice (or more) if the jury can't agree on a verdict (a "hung jury") or if the judge declares a mistrial because of, say, the misconduct of one of the attorneys involved in the case.

JUVENILE COURT

Minors accused of crimes usually are processed through the juvenile court rather than the traditional court system. If a youth is charged with a serious crime or has a significant history of previous offenses, however, the district attorney may ask the judge to allow the child to be prosecuted in regular court as an adult. An important distinction between juvenile court and regular court lies in the focus each has: Regular court concentrates on punishment, while juvenile court emphasizes education and rehabilitation to keep the minor from being further caught up in the criminal cycle. Punishment does, of course, still play a major role in the juvenile court system.

Juvenile court is less formal than its adult counterpart, but the accused minor is still entitled to all of the major constitutional protections, such as the right not to incriminate oneself, the right to be represented by an attorney, and the right to confront and cross-examine his or her accusers. As in regular court, the prosecution must prove beyond a reasonable doubt that the youth committed the crime that he or she is accused of doing. The only major right that a minor does not have in juvenile court is the right to have the case tried by a jury. The judge alone listens to the evidence and decides whether the minor is guilty or innocent. A minor who is found guilty of committing a crime is declared a "juvenile delinquent," and the judge then determines what action would be appropriate. The youth may be sent to reform school or other public institution, placed in a foster home, or returned to the custody of his or her parents and put on probation.

AFTER THE VERDICT

Overturning the Verdict

What can you do if you feel the jury wrongly convicted you because of some impropriety before or during the trial? Your lawyer can ask the judge who presided over the case to disregard ("set aside") the jury's verdict and declare you innocent. Failing that, your lawyer can appeal your case to a higher court and ask it to reverse the jury's verdict and give you a new trial. But you should note that the alleged impropriety must be important enough that it could have affected the jury's decision (a "prejudicial error"). If the jury's result clearly would have been the same even if the impropriety never happened, the appellate court will not reverse your conviction.

Here are the main reasons a conviction can be overturned:

* The trial judge allowed the prosecution to present evidence that was obtained in violation of the defendant's constitutional rights—if, for instance, the defendant wasn't advised of his or her *Miranda* rights before police questioning and the defendant confessed, but the trial judge still permitted the district attorney to use the confession against the defendant.
* The judge admitted evidence that should not have been admitted. For example, in criminal cases, the defendant's previous arrests and conviction record normally cannot be presented at the trial for fear that the jury will convict the defendant on the basis of that record rather than on the facts of the case it is deciding. So if, for instance, the judge allowed the prosecution to show that the defendant in a robbery trial had been convicted

of three previous assaults with a deadly weapon, this could be grounds for reversing the conviction.

* The prosecution did not adequately inform the defendant of what evidence it would be presenting at the trial, so the defendant could not properly prepare a defense against it.

* The judge made a mistake when instructing the jury on the law to apply to the case. For instance, in a burglary case the judge might have neglected to instruct the jury that the defendant must have had the intent to commit a felony inside the house *before* he or she entered it.

* The prosecution did not prove its case beyond a reasonable doubt, engaged in manifestly unfair tactics, or made repeated prejudicial remarks that affected the defendant's case.

* After the trial, the defendant (or the defendant's attorney) found new evidence that was unavailable at the time of the trial. For instance, the person who really committed the crime confessed after the defendant had been convicted, or the defendant finally located the witness who could establish his or her alibi.

Suppose that after the defendant is convicted by a jury and sentenced to jail or prison, the victim states that he or she made the whole thing up, no crime happened, and an innocent person was sent to jail for a crime that was never committed. Will the defendant be released from prison because the victim has recanted his or her testimony? Not necessarily. The judicial system views recantation with considerable suspicion. If the evidence was strong enough for a jury to convict the defendant, there is usually some basis for believing that the defendant committed the crime in question. Cases that are completely fabricated from the beginning usually are discovered by the police during the investigation of the case or by the district attorney's office during its preparation of the case for trial. And a victim may recant his or her testimony for many reasons that have nothing to do with the defendant's guilt. For instance, the victim may feel that the defendant has served enough time in jail, or friends of the defendant may threaten the victim with harm if he or she doesn't recant.

Sentencing

After a defendant pleads guilty to a crime or the jury (or judge if the trial is by court) finds the defendant guilty, the judge will impose the defendant's punishment, or "sentence." Ordinarily, it will consist of time in jail, payment of a fine, a certain number of hours of community service, or a combination of any or all three. The judge often will order a defendant to "make restitution" to the victim—return stolen property, for instance, or pay the victim for the damages done to them or for destruction or loss of any property. Note that the judge imposes the convicted defendant's sentence. The jury ordinarily has no say in what that punishment will be except in death penalty cases.

In capital murder cases, the jury has a two-phase obligation: first, it must determine the guilt or innocence of the defendant, and second, if it finds the defendant guilty of murder with "special circumstances" (discussed below), it must make a recommendation as to whether to impose the death penalty (used in only thirty-eight states, see below) or to spare his or her life and recommend life imprisonment without the possibility of parole. In some states, even if the jury comes back with a recommendation for the death penalty, the judge is not bound by this and can sentence the defendant to life imprisonment without the possibility of parole. However, the judge usually goes along with the jury's recommendation and will impose the death sentence if that is what the jury recommends.

Hate Crimes

A growing and disturbing trend in the last ten years has been the proliferation of hate crimes. Crimes are being committed against innocent victims because of their actual or perceived race, color, religion, nationality, country of origin, ancestry, disability, gender, or sexual orientation. A man of African-American descent was tied to the back of a pickup truck in Texas and dragged to death. In Wyoming, a young gay man was tied to a fence, beaten, and left to die simply because of his sexual orientation. These are just a couple of examples of crimes based on hate. While violent crimes in general have remained fairly steady in the United States in recent years, hate crimes have soared dramatically.

The main bearing hate has on a crime comes in the enhancement of the punishment meted out by the judge. A crime of hate generally gets a stiffer penalty than a crime that does not fit within hate crime criteria. For example, a crime that was motivated by hate may result in a longer sentence. In a murder case, hate may be a special circumstance that warrants imposition of the death penalty in a state that imposes the ultimate punishment (see below).

Three Strikes, You're Out

Many states have enacted a "three strikes, you're out" law to keep repeat offenders off the street. Upon the commission of his of her third felony, the defendant is sentenced to a mandatory sentence of twenty-five years to life, regardless of the seriousness—or lack thereof—of the third crime. For example, in one case the defendant stole a bottle of vitamins from a supermarket. Had this been the defendant's first offense, it would have been treated as a petty theft (a misdemeanor), with a maximum penalty of a fine and six months in jail. However, because of the defendant's previous criminal history, the trial judge was required to treat the crime as a felony. Having done so, the judge was then compelled to apply the mandatory sentencing provisions of the three-strikes law and sentenced the defendant to a minimum sentence of twenty-five years to life imprisonment. While this seems a patently excessive punishment for stealing a bottle of vitamins, the sentence was upheld on appeal. And this is not an isolated incident. One man was sentenced to twenty-five years to life for stealing a piece of pizza, and another man was given a similar sentence for stealing $150 worth of videotapes from a video store.

The philosophy behind the three-strikes law is admirable: to keep repeat violent offenders off the street. However, in practice it is being used to give lengthy prison terms for relatively minor offenses that do not involve any violence. Accordingly, many judges will do what they can when faced with a criminal whose third strike is a minor, nonviolent crime. For instance, they will reduce the second conviction from a felony to a misdemeanor or engage in other legerdemain to avoid sentencing a petty criminal to a life sentence.

CRUEL AND UNUSUAL PUNISHMENT

PERHAPS THE ENGLISH DRAMATIST Sir William Schwenck Gilbert (of Gilbert and Sullivan fame and who was schooled as a barrister) said it best when he wrote, "Let the punishment fit the crime." But how do we determine which punishment fits a particular crime? What is considered reasonable punishment by one generation or society may be considered barbaric or excessive by another. For instance, in the days of the Old West, death by hanging was the order of the day for a cattle rustler. Today, that would be considered cruel and unusual punishment. A cattle thief today would most likely spend some time in state prison and probably have to pay a fine, but would be spared the gallows. In some countries, a hungry thief who steals a loaf of bread might have his hand chopped off. In America, that would be considered barbaric and therefore cruel and unusual punishment.

The eighth amendment to the Constitution states: "Excessive bail shall not be required, nor excessive fines imposed, nor cruel and unusual punishment inflicted." The eighth amendment guarantee against cruel and unusual punishments is made applicable to the states through the due process clause of the fourteenth amendment. The eighth amendment was taken essentially word for word from the English Declaration of Rights of 1689, enacted more than a century earlier. Note that the eighth amendment prohibition against cruel and unusual punishments comes into play only after a person has been convicted of (or pled guilty to) a crime. For cruel and unusual treatment by the authorities before being convicted of a crime, the prisoner has to rely on other provisions of the Constitution and its amendments.

The eighth amendment absolutely prohibits the infliction of cruel and unusual punishments. At a minimum, the eighth amendment prohibits punishments that were considered cruel and unusual at the time the Bill of Rights was adopted in 1791. The meaning of "cruel and unusual" under the eighth amendment must be interpreted in a flexible and dynamic manner, and measured against evolving standards of decency that mark the progress of a maturing society. In discerning these evolving standards, the courts look to objective evidence of how our society views a particular punishment today. The clearest and most reliable objective evidence of contemporary values are the statutes enacted by the country's legislatures.

The unnecessary and wanton infliction of pain constitutes cruel and unusual punishment, as does conduct that is barbaric. The U.S. Supreme Court has held that the eighth amendment only protects the "unnecessary and wanton infliction of pain." Besides the unnecessary and wanton infliction of pain, there must be a "culpable" state of mind on the part of the prison guard, warden, or other official meting out the punishment. As one federal appellate court stated: "The infliction of punishment is a deliberate act intended to chastise or deter. This is what the word means today, it is what it meant in the eighteenth century. . . . If a guard accidentally stepped on a prisoner's toe and broke it, this would not be punishment in anything remotely like the accepted means of the word, whether we consult the usage in 1791, or 1868, or 1985." Another court commented that "The thread common to all [eighth amendment prison cases] is that 'punishment' has been deliberately administered for a penal or disciplinary purpose."

Deliberate indifference constitutes wantonness. Accordingly, a prisoner who alleged deliberate indifference to his "serious" medical needs made out a prima facie violation of cruel and unusual punishment. However, if the inattention to the prisoner's medical problems had only been an inadvertent failure or a mere negligent misdiagnosis, it would fail to establish the requisite state of mind to constitute wantonness.

Excessive Sentences

Can a man caught with 650 grams of cocaine on his person be sentenced to life imprisonment without the possibility of parole, the second stiffest punishment permitted (execution being the first), even though it was his first offense and the sentence is clearly excessive for a nonviolent crime? Yes. The eighth amendment prohibition against cruel and unusual punishment does not have to be in proportion to the crime committed. Thus, the courts—in the absence of a state law to the contrary—can impose as harsh a sentence as they wish, short of death.

Some states have passed laws prohibiting disproportionate sentences. In those states, the basic test is whether the punishment is so disproportionate to the crime that it shocks the conscience and offends fundamental notions of human dignity. In such a state, the person convicted of having 650 grams of cocaine on his or her person would most likely not be sentenced to life without the possibility of parole, on the basis that the sentence is excessive.

The Death Penalty: Murder with "Special Circumstances"

The death penalty is the ultimate punishment, the most severe that can be handed out. Before 1972, a number of states permitted the death penalty not only for first-degree murder cases but also for lesser crimes, such as rape, armed robbery, and kidnapping. In 1972, the U.S. Supreme Court held that permitting the use of the death penalty in such cases was unconstitutional and abolished the death penalty. In 1976, however, the U.S. Supreme Court held that the eighth amendment did not prohibit the death penalty in limited cases, exclusively in murder cases where there are aggravating circumstances. The U.S. Supreme Court noted that the death penalty was allowed in these cases because (1) it was considered permissible by the framers of the Constitution and the Bill of Rights (the first ten amendments to the Constitution), and (2) the death penalty might serve two principal social purposes: retribution and deterrence.

The death penalty is permissible only in murder cases, but not every murder qualifies as a death penalty case. It must be murder in the first degree with aggravating, or "special," circumstances. Special circumstances justifying the imposition of the death penalty include:

* multiple murders in the proceedings for which the defendant is being tried;
* the murder was committed for the purpose of avoiding or preventing a lawful arrest or while attempting to escape from lawful custody;
* killings by means of a destructive device, bomb, or explosive that the defendant mailed or delivered in person;
* the victim was a peace officer or firefighter acting within the course of his or her duties and this fact was known to the defendant;
* the victim was a witness to a crime, a prosecutor or former prosecutor, judge or former judge, jury member or former jury member, and the murder was committed in retaliation for, or to prevent the performance of, the victim's official duties;
* the murder was committed by ambush ("lying in wait");
* the victim was killed deliberately because of his or her race, color, religion, nationality, country of origin, or sexual orientation (a hate crime);
* the murder was committed while the defendant was engaged in the commission of a designated felony, such as a robbery, kidnapping, rape, sodomy, the performance of a lewd or lascivious act upon a child under a certain age (such as 14 years), oral copulation, burglary, arson, mayhem, rape, carjacking, or train wrecking;
* the murder was intentional and involved the use of torture;
* the murder was committed by poison;
* the murder was deliberate and involved the shooting of a gun or other firearm from a motor vehicle at another person outside the vehicle with the intent to inflict death; or
* murders by an active participant in a criminal street gang, and the murder was carried out to further the activities of the gang.

Cruelty and the Death Penalty

In capital murder cases, "cruel" implies "something inhuman and barbarous, something more than the mere extinguishment of life." The eighth amendment bars the infliction of unnecessary pain in the execution of the death sentence. Punishments are deemed cruel when they involve torture or a lingering death.

It has been said that "The cruelty against which the Constitution protects a convicted man is cruelty inherent in the method of punishment, not the necessary suffering involved in any method employed to extinguish life humanely."

The eighth amendment requires that as much as humanly possible, a chosen method of execution minimize the risk of unnecessary pain, violence, and mutilation. If a method of execution does not meet these standards—it causes torture or a lingering death in a significant number of cases—then the method of execution violates the cruel and unusual punishment clause.

A single unforeseeable accident in carrying out an execution does not establish that the method of execution itself is unconstitutional. Accordingly, Louisiana was permitted to proceed with a second effort to electrocute a prisoner after the first attempt was aborted because of a mechanical failure.

In June 2002, the U.S. Supreme Court held that it violated the eighth amendment ban on excessive punishment to execute a mentally retarded murderer. The Supreme Court found that unlike a murderer of average intelligence, a mentally retarded murderer does not have the mental capacity to process what is happening. The Supreme Court also noted a "growing national consensus" that the mentally retarded should not face execution, stating that a number of states had passed laws prohibiting the execution of mentally retarded prisoners. Additionally, a recent Gallup poll found that 83 percent of Americans favor exempting the mentally retarded from the death penalty. According to a United Nations report, Japan and Kyrgyzstan are the only countries that still execute mentally retarded criminals.

Delays in Executing a Prisoner

A lengthy delay of fifteen years or more may take place before a convicted murderer ultimately is executed. To date, the U.S. Supreme Court has not held that such delays are cruel or unusual punishment. However, foreign countries sometimes have refused to extradite criminals to the United States because of the lengthy delay before the prisoner is executed. (The countries may also refuse to grant extradition on the basis the alleged murderer may face the death penalty, which has been abolished in most civilized nations.) Britain, for instance, refused to extradite a murderer to the United States, claiming it would be a violation of the European Convention on Human Rights, primarily on the risk of delay before execution, which the Britons found to be cruel and unusual punishment.

In 1890, the U.S. Supreme Court recognized that "when a prisoner sentenced by a court to death is confined in the penitentiary awaiting the execution of the sentence, one of the most horrible feelings to which he can be subjected during that time is the uncertainty during the whole of it." That case involved a prisoner who was required to wait *four weeks* before he was executed. That makes a strong favor of holding as cruel and unusual punishment waits up to fifteen or more years before prisoners finally are put to death.

What accounts for these lengthy delays between the time a sentence of death is given and the date the convicted defendant finally is executed? In many cases, it is the numerous appeals filed by the convicted murderer. The convict will exhaust all of his appeals in the state judicial system, and when those are exhausted, he or she will turn to the federal courts for help.

Methods of Execution

As one judge wrote back in 1947, "The traditional humanity of modern Anglo-American law forbids the infliction of unnecessary pain in the execution of the death sentence." Five methods traditionally have been used to put a person to death over the years: hanging; the firing squad; the electric chair; the gas chamber; and lethal injection. Today most, if not all, executions are by lethal injection.

Hanging

Hanging originally was thought to be a relatively quick and painless method of causing death. The mechanisms involved in bringing about unconsciousness and death in judicial hanging were believed to occur extremely rapidly. Unconsciousness was thought to be immediate or within a matter of seconds, and death was believed to follow rapidly thereafter. The risk of death by decapitation was believed to be negligible, and hanging was thought not to involve lingering death, mutilation, or the unnecessary and wanton infliction of pain. However, in practice it was found that hanging is a crude and imprecise practice that always included a risk that the prisoner would slowly strangulate or asphyxiate if the rope was too elastic or too short, or would be decapitated if the rope was too taut or too long.

One veteran prison warden described a hanging as follows:

> When the trap springs the prisoner dangles at the end of the rope. There are times when the neck has not been broken and the prisoner strangles to death. His eyes pop almost out of his head, his tongue swells and protrudes from his mouth, his neck may be broken, and the rope many times takes large portions of skin and flesh from the side of the face that the noose is on. He urinates, he defecates, and droppings fall to the floor while witnesses look on.

Only one state—Washington—still permits execution by hanging. The state of Washington's protocol details the appropriate placement of the noose knot and the width and length of the rope to avoid decapitation, and provides that the rope be boiled, stretched, and waxed to reduce asphyxiation by taking the spring out of the rope. The protocol includes a chart for determining, based on the weight of the prisoner, the appropriate distance the body should be dropped to ensure a quick and relatively pain-free death, while avoiding the risk of decapitation. Since 1963 there have been two hangings, both in Washington, one in 1993, the other in 1994.

Firing Squad

One of the most notorious executions involved the death by firing squad in Utah of Gary Gilmore. Death by firing squad, along with death by hanging, were the earliest forms of execution; they were also among the most brutal. In a 1986 Utah case in which an inmate sentenced to death claimed that the firing squad was cruel and unusual punishment, the U.S. Court of Appeals for the Tenth Circuit held that the sentence of death by firing squad was not unconstitutional, as the prisoner could choose death either by the firing squad or by lethal injection, and mandated death by lethal injection if the prisoner made no choice.

Electrocution

Electrocution was adopted as a more humane method of execution than hanging or the firing squad. However, death by the electric chair was found to have its own cruelties. Witnesses routinely reported that when the switch was thrown, the condemned prisoner cringed, leapt, and fought the straps with amazing strength. The prisoner's hands turned red, then white, and the cords of the neck stood out like steel bands. The prisoner's limbs, fingers, toes, and face were contorted severely. The force of the electrical current was so powerful that the prisoner's eyeballs sometimes popped out and rested on his cheeks. The prisoner often defecated, urinated, and vomited blood and drool.

The body turned bright red as its temperature rose, and the prisoner's flesh swelled and his skin stretched to the point of breaking. Sometimes the prisoner caught on fire. Witnesses often heard a loud and sustained sound like bacon frying, and the sickly sweet smell of burning flesh permeated the electrocution chamber. This smell of frying human flesh in the immediate neighborhood of the chair was sometimes bad enough to nauseate even the press representatives who were present. In the meantime, the prisoner almost literally boiled; the temperature in the brain approached the boiling point of water, and when the postelectrocution autopsy was performed, the liver was so hot that the examining doctors said that it could not be touched by the human hand. The body was frequently badly burned and disfigured.

The Gas Chamber

Execution by cyanide gas is "in essence asphyxiation by suffocation or strangulation." Prisoners who are put to death in the gas chamber do not become immediately unconscious upon the first breath of the lethal cyanide gas. The prisoner can remain conscious up to eight minutes. During this time the prisoner suffers intense, visceral pain throughout his arms, shoulders, back, and chest, primarily as a result of the lack of oxygen to the cells. This experience of "air hunger" is similar to the experience of a major heart attack, or to being held under water. Other possible effects of the cyanide gas include "tetany," an extremely painful contraction of the muscles, and a painful buildup of lactic acid and adrenaline. Cyanide-induced cellular suffocation causes anxiety, panic, terror, and pain.

Whether death by the gas chamber in which cyanide gas is used is cruel and unusual has been split among the courts. The federal Circuit Court of Appeals for the Ninth Circuit, generally regarded as the most liberal of all the federal circuit courts of appeals (see chapter 25), held that California's use of the gas chamber was unconstitutional. However, the California legislature then enacted a law giving a convicted murderer the right to choose between death by lethal injection and death by the gas chamber. If the prisoner failed to choose the method of his or her death within ten days of the date set for execution, he or she would be put to death by lethal injection. The Fourth and Fifth Circuit Courts of Appeals, on the other hand, have upheld the constitutionality of the gas chamber.

Since the United States Supreme Court reinstated capital punishment in 1976, not one of the twenty or so of the states to adopt new methods of execution has chosen execution by lethal gas. One by one, states that permitted execution by the gas chamber have abandoned it as inhumane and torturous.

Lethal Injection

Death by lethal injection is the most humane of the five methods of execution commonly used since the origination of the United States. The prisoner is taken into the death chamber, strapped onto a gurney, and given a sedative, which usually renders him or her unconscious within a short period of time. Intravenous tubes are hooked up to administer the lethal poisons. Once the lethal poison is administered, witnesses report that all they usually see is a single heave of the prisoner's chest. A few minutes later, a doctor examines the prisoner and declares him or her dead.

The family of the victim—if they choose to witness the execution—often is disappointed when the killer of their loved one is put to death by lethal injection, because it is so routine and sanitary. The killer does not suffer any pain, whereas the victim may have suffered tremendously before dying.

The Arguments for and against the Death Penalty

Like abortion and gun control, the death penalty generates much emotional controversy. It seems that you are either strongly for it or just as strongly against it; there is little or no middle ground. Not every state uses it. Only thirty-eight states currently impose the maximum punishment of death, and even then it is applied sparingly, with the main exception being Texas, which leads all other states by a wide margin in the number of prisoners executed.

Proponents of the death penalty argue that it deters others from committing murder. Studies have shown, however, that the death penalty does *not* serve as a deterrent to murder. In fact, in one state that outlawed the death penalty, the number of murders actually dropped when the death penalty was abolished. Proponents also argue that by executing a murderer, it guarantees that he or she will not kill again. However, by imposing a sentence of life imprisonment without the possibility of parole, that too guarantees that the murderer will be kept off the streets and out of the community, where he or she can never again take a life. Proponents argue that if the murderer is granted life imprisonment without parole, the governor can still grant the murderer clemency. While this is technically true, it is not borne out in real life.

Proponents of the death penalty complain of the high cost of feeding and housing a murderer who is sentenced to life imprisonment. Studies show, however, that it is less expensive to keep a convicted murderer in prison for life than it is to handle all the appeals for a murderer who has been sentenced to death. Death penalty advocates argue that it brings about closure for the victim's family and friends. Unfortunately, for the most part that simply is not the case. Killing the murderer does not bring back the dead victim. The family must still eat breakfast without the victim, go to church without the victim, and do everything else without the victim. Psychologists who have studied the issue have found that the death penalty may give the survivors a sense of relief for a few days or weeks, but they will soon get back to a state of emptiness caused by the deceased victim's absence.

Proponents of the death penalty argue that the death penalty is retribution for the murderer's crime. They argue an eye for an eye, a life for a life. Opponents of the death penalty argue that it is barbarous and has been outlawed as a form of punishment in most civilized nations.

But there is still the possibility that an innocent person will be convicted of murder on circumstantial evidence and sentenced to die for a crime he or she did not commit. Because of the development of DNA evidence, a significant number of death row inmates were freed when it turned out that their DNA did not match the blood or semen on the dead victim on evidence that had been preserved ten or fifteen years or more. This led to a handful of states calling a moratorium on the death penalty until better safeguards could be put in place to prevent innocent men and women from being executed. For instance, since resuming capital punishment in 1977, Illinois courts found that thirteen condemned men were freed from death row because they had been convicted wrongly. This spurred a letter of appeal from twenty-one former Illinois state and federal judges to Illinois governor George Ryan in late 2002 to commute the death sentences of any inmate whose conviction was tainted by flaws in Illinois's capital punishment system. Among the faults the former jurists noted were coerced confessions, inadequate defense attorneys, and unreliable testimony from jailhouse informants and accomplices who testified in exchange for such incentives as lenient sentences. In light of the facts, Governor Ryan put a moratorium on executions in 2000, and in June 2002 stated that he might even propose abolishing capital punishment altogether in Illinois. In December 2002, Governor Ryan commuted the sentences of all inmates on death row to life imprisonment.

Probation

As part of the sentence, the defendant may be put on "probation" for a length of time. Probation gives the convict freedom with some restrictions. If the convict violates any terms of the probation, the judge can terminate the probation and order the criminal punished according to the terms of the original sentence. For instance, suppose the judge sentences the guilty defendant to six months in jail but suspends that sentence—which means that the convict doesn't go to jail—and places the convict on two years' probation. If the convict violates the terms of the probation, the judge then can order the convict imprisoned for six months as per the original sentence. There are two main reasons for probation: to help rehabilitate the criminal and to prevent our prisons from becoming more overcrowded than they already are.

Parole and Clemency

A criminal sentenced to prison may be granted a "parole" before serving out the whole term of his or her prison sentence. A parole is essentially the same as probation; the difference lies in when each occurs. Probation is granted at the time of sentencing, while parole is granted after the person has served time in prison. Like probation, parole serves two objectives: to help rehabilitate the convict by reintegrating him or her back into society, and to prevent prison overcrowding. Parole has another objective as well: It gives prison inmates an incentive for good behavior in prison, since the better their conduct, the earlier they can be released. A parolee who violates the terms of his or her parole can be returned to prison to finish out serving the original sentence.

A state governor (in the case of a state crime) or the president of the United States (if the offense is a federal one) can alter a convict's sentence by granting "clemency" when there is clearly an injustice. The governor (or the president, as the case may be) can give clemency in any case, but in reality clemency rarely is granted.

Clemency usually means a pardon, a commutation of sentence, or a reprieve. A pardon normally declares a person innocent, ends his or her punishment, and erases the conviction from the person's record. A commutation of sentence reduces the punishment—to time already served in prison, for example—but it doesn't change the fact that the person is guilty of the crime. A reprieve (or "respite") is a temporary suspension of punishment. For example, when a criminal on death row gets a reprieve from the governor, this means only that his or her execution is postponed to a future date. If a court or the governor does not reduce the sentence to, say, life imprisonment (a commutation if done by the governor), the prisoner still can be put to death when the reprieve ends.

TWENTY-FOUR

Finding the Right Lawyer

WHEN CAN YOU BE your own lawyer? Anytime you want. You can represent yourself in court in any type of case, from a minor traffic ticket to a divorce action to a murder case. Most times, however, it's not advisable to be your own lawyer; instead you'll want to be represented by a competent, experienced attorney. As a general rule, you should never be your own lawyer in court, except in small claims court (where most states forbid representation by a lawyer) or traffic court (and then only if you're not facing punishment more serious than a small fine).

Finding a good lawyer when you need one can be a hard and aggravating task if you don't know where to look. With a little effort in the right direction, you can find a lawyer who is an honest, hardworking professional sincerely interested in protecting your interests. This chapter will give you practical advice on finding the right lawyer for you—and at a reasonable cost. It also will help you to recognize when you need a lawyer and will discuss lawyers' fees and what to do if a problem arises between you and your lawyer. One bit of preliminary advice: When you need a lawyer's advice, get it immediately. The earlier you get legal assistance, the better. A lawyer might be able to keep a difficult situation from snowballing out of control, and save you money in the process.

Although England has separate classes of lawyers—"barristers," who try cases in court, and "solicitors," who advise clients and prepare cases for barristers—we make no such distinction in the United States. "Lawyer," "attorney," "attorney-at-law," and "counselor" all mean the same thing.

WHEN DO YOU NEED A LAWYER?

Do you need a lawyer every time one of your legal rights is threatened? No. There are everyday legal situations that people handle quite well without a lawyer. (For those times, a review of the applicable material in this book will help you understand your rights and will give you the edge in dealing with the other person.) But other times you just can't do without one. How do you tell when you need a lawyer?

First, look at what's at stake. If you're talking about a $150 jacket ruined by the dry cleaners or a small dent to your car's fender, then by all means take care of it yourself. It probably will cost you more than it's worth to talk to a lawyer about the situation. But when you're dealing with something more serious—a real estate dispute, for example; severe injuries or extensive property damage; or time in jail—you would be ill-advised to attempt to try to handle it yourself. Throughout this book, there are suggestions about when you can attempt to handle things on your own and when you need a lawyer. Here is a good rule of thumb to follow: In civil disputes, you usually can try to get by without a lawyer if the amount involved is less than or near the small claims court limit in your state (see chapter 19). With the help of this book, you may be able to settle the dispute in many situations just by coming to an agreement with the other party; if you can't, this book will assist you if you decide to take your case to small claims court. But if you encounter any unexpected problems, it may be advisable for you to talk with a lawyer. In criminal matters, you need to be represented by a lawyer if more than a small fine is involved or if a conviction will result in jail time or a permanent bad mark on your record—something that could affect, say, your chances of future employment.

If the problem is borderline—maybe a lawyer is needed but maybe you can handle it on your own—one thing you can do is read the chapters in this book that apply to your situation and then see whether you think you can work the problem out with the other person (or his or her lawyer) by sitting down and discussing it rationally. If the other person isn't receptive to your settlement efforts, then you have several options, among them, contacting a lawyer, filing in small claims court, if appropriate, or simply forgetting the whole thing. You may achieve a speedier resolution by having a willingness to compromise, even if you feel that you're totally in the right.

When a dispute arises, the other person's lawyer or insurance company's adjuster may contact you; they may try to negotiate a quick settlement and have you sign a document releasing the other person from all further liability. The lawyer or insurance adjuster may even tell you that you don't need a lawyer, that a lawyer won't get you any more money and will keep as much as half of the settlement as his or her fee. Keep in mind that these insurance company lawyers and claims adjusters are highly skilled negotiators and are trying to get the best deal for their clients, the insurance companies they work for. Their sole objective is to settle the claim as quickly and as cheaply as possible. They are not looking out for your best interests. Only your attorney will do that. Unless the money or damage involved is relatively minor, it is usually advisable to hire your own lawyer as soon as you are contacted by an insurance company's claims adjuster or by the other party's attorney.

WHAT TYPE OF LAWYER IS BEST FOR YOU?

WHEN YOU NEED A LAWYER, the trick is finding the lawyer who is right for your problem. The right lawyer for your situation may not be the most expensive, the best known, or even the best in the particular field. Why spend $10,000 to get the top lawyer in town when a lawyer just out of law school two or three years can do the same thing just as well for $3,000? Then again, if you're charged with a serious crime, are in a nasty child custody suit, or were paralyzed when your car went out of control because of a defect, why save a few hundred dollars by getting a less experienced lawyer when you need as good a lawyer as you can get?

Will a general practitioner do, or do you need a specialist in the field? A "general practitioner" is a lawyer who practices many areas of law rather than concentrating in one field—the legal profession's "family doctor." (Although many lawyers call themselves general practitioners, there are few true general practitioners these days. You'll find that most general practitioners limit their practices to four or five areas of law, such as divorces; personal injury; defense of drunk drivers; wills, trusts and probate; and routine business matters.) A specialist is a lawyer who concentrates on one area of the law, such as family law, workers' compensation, tax law, or personal injury. There are even specialists within a specialty: criminal lawyers who handle only murder trials or personal injury lawyers who limit their practice to medical malpractice cases, for example.

Whether or not you need a specialist depends on the nature and complexity of your legal situation. For routine matters, a general practitioner is usually fine. But for more complex problems, a specialist may be necessary. A good general practitioner will recognize his or her limitations and will either consult with or refer you to a specialist when appropriate.

Is it better to hire a big law firm (with say, twenty-five to a hundred lawyers) than a small one (with two to ten lawyers, for instance)? Is it better to have a small firm represent you than an attorney who practices alone (a "sole practitioner")? The answer depends on your problem and how much you can afford. You'll usually get more personal attention from a small law firm or a sole practitioner than you will from a big firm. In a big firm, you're likely to get shuffled from one lawyer to another for different problems, while with a small firm you'll generally be represented by the same lawyer. Depending on their experience and areas of practice, small firms and solo practitioners are often better for routine legal matters, while larger firms can handle more complex matters—at a price, of course. Larger firms tend to charge more than small firms, and specialists usually cost more than general practitioners. If you hire a large law firm or a specialist to do some routine legal work for you—drawing up a simple will, for instance—you may have to pay as much as two or three times over what a sole practitioner would charge for the same thing.

Should you hire a lawyer with offices downtown, or will a lawyer near your home in the suburbs do? The downtown lawyer probably will charge more, if only because rent downtown is generally more expensive than in outlying areas. On the other hand, a downtown lawyer may be closer to the courthouse. Because lawyers charge for "travel time"—the time it takes to get from the office to the court and back again—it may cost you less in the long run to pay the higher hourly rates of the downtown lawyer if your case will involve many court appearances by the lawyer. But if your legal problem will involve little or no time in court, a lawyer closer to home may be able to do the job for less money.

WHERE TO LOOK FOR A LAWYER

AFTER DETERMINING THE TYPE of lawyer you need, you have to find one that fits the bill. The usual way to start is to ask relatives, friends, and neighbors if they can suggest a lawyer for your situation. If, for instance, a friend recommends a particular lawyer, ask whether your friend has ever consulted the lawyer, and if so, for what reason. Was he or she pleased with the quality of the work, and was the final charge close to the fee initially quoted by the lawyer? Did the lawyer return your friend's phone calls promptly and keep him or her informed of the status of the case? Did the lawyer take the time to explain things in plain English? What were the lawyer's shortcomings? Would your friend go back to the lawyer?

A referral to a lawyer may not mean much if the person's legal problem was considerably less complex than yours, or if it concerned a totally different area of the law. For instance, if your friend recommends the lawyer who handled his or her divorce, but your problem involves a dispute with a home-remodeling company, the lawyer might not be qualified to handle your type of case. But if your friend vouches for the lawyer's integrity, consider calling the lawyer. If nothing else, the lawyer may be able to refer you to a lawyer competent to handle your problem.

If your problem is not related to your job, ask your employer who his or her attorney is. Large companies may have an in-house attorney who can refer you to an outside lawyer (you may even be able to wangle some free advice out of the in-house lawyer). Unions often can give members referrals to good lawyers.

Another way to get a referral to a lawyer is by looking in the yellow pages under the heading "Attorney Referral Service." Most referral services use only lawyers who subscribe to them. Often they are younger lawyers who need the business. You may have no better assurance of getting a good lawyer through a referral service than by opening the telephone directory to the "Attorneys" listing, closing your eyes, and putting your finger anywhere on the page. Although it costs you nothing to call the lawyer referral service and get the name of a lawyer, the lawyer may charge you for the initial interview. This fee, if any, should be quoted to you by the referral service. Often, when you use the local bar association's referral service, the first consultation is free.

Ever since 1976, lawyers have been permitted to advertise on television and radio, but outside of the yellow pages, few lawyers take advantage of this opportunity. Large cities tend to have a few lawyers who saturate the late-night movies and daytime sitcom reruns with commercial after commercial. Should you pick a lawyer based on a television commercial? There's no reason not to—although neither is there any special reason why you should. You get no assurance that the lawyer who advertises on television or radio is any better or worse than any other lawyer.

You should be aware, however, that television advertising is expensive. To cover its cost, the advertising lawyer must do a high-volume business. You may find yourself not getting all of the attention you feel your case deserves. And the fact is that many of these lawyers rely heavily on paralegals doing much of the work. So if you go to a lawyer who advertises on television, find out just who will be doing the bulk of the work on your case, and whether the lawyer will return your telephone calls personally, rather than handing it off to a paralegal.

What if you can't afford a lawyer but need one now? That depends on the nature of your problem. If you've been injured in an accident or on the job, the lawyer usually takes his or her fee out of your settlement or award when you get paid, so your inability to pay now shouldn't make a difference. But if your situation involves paying a flat fee or an hourly charge (for instance, to defend you for driving while intoxicated or to represent you in a divorce action), you have several options.

If you're charged with a crime where the punishment may be six months or longer in jail and you can't afford a lawyer, you are entitled to have one appointed for you at the expense of the county. You usually must accept the lawyer appointed for you; you don't get to pick and choose from the public defender's staff. If your request to have a lawyer appointed for you is turned down because your income and assets are above the limits, you will have to provide your own lawyer. Many lawyers now accept credit cards for payment of their services, and others will let you make a down payment and pay the balance in monthly installments. To ensure that you make the payments, the lawyer may ask you to pledge something as collateral, such as your car or house.

If your legal problem is civil in nature, such as the drafting of a will, a divorce, or a landlord-tenant dispute, you may qualify to be represented by the Legal Aid Society, which provides legal services to the poor at little or no cost. You can get the number for your local Legal Aid office by calling your county's bar association or by looking it up in the telephone book. Many law schools also provide legal assistance programs to low-income persons at no charge. If your legal problem involves a violation of your civil rights, try the American Civil Liberties Union (ACLU) or the Legal Defense and Education Fund for the appropriate race, ethnicty, or other group, such as the National Association for the Advancement of Colored People (NAACP) Legal Defense and Education Fund.

Before you make the first appointment with the lawyer, find out how much it's going to cost. Many lawyers do not charge for the initial consultation (usually twenty to thirty minutes long); others charge a relatively small fee, such as $50 or $75.

Bring all the documentation you have concerning your situation to the interview. If a written contract is involved, take it along. In personal injury cases, the police report, medical bills, estimates, pictures of the accident scene, and any correspondence between you and the other person (or his or her insurance company or lawyer) also should be shown to the lawyer.

At the interview, be open and honest with the lawyer. The advice given and strategy planned by your lawyer are determined by the facts of the situation. Don't lie or embellish. If you don't remember something, tell the lawyer so. If something might hurt your case, don't hide it. Be up front with it. It may not be as damaging as you think. And even if it is, your lawyer often can minimize the damage if he or she knows about it first. Everything you say to the lawyer is protected by the "lawyer-client privilege"—with rare exception, the lawyer must keep everything you tell him or her in the strictest confidence.

Ask the lawyer what experience he or she has in handling your type of problem. What areas of law make up the bulk of the lawyer's practice, and what area is the lawyer most experienced in? Does the lawyer routinely send clients copies of all correspondence and legal documents involving their cases? Will the lawyer give you regular status reports informing you of what is being done on your case? Does the lawyer send regular itemized bills showing all charges, and will you get a full accounting of all money and expenses at the end of the case? Will the lawyer listen to your suggestions on how the case should be handled? As important as anything else: Will the lawyer take the time to explain things to you, and in plain English?

At this first consultation, the question of fees needs to be addressed, openly and frankly. Don't authorize a lawyer to begin work unless you know what it's going to cost.

At the end of the interview, the lawyer will make an initial evaluation of your situation and decide whether to represent you. (Sometimes the lawyer will want to do some preliminary investigation or research before determining whether to take your case.) Some of the lawyer's considerations in deciding whether to represent you: How much time your case will take; whether it is within the lawyer's fields of competence; the likelihood of success; the size of the fees involved and your ability to pay them; and whether the lawyer has a conflict of interest (for instance, the other party is a friend or former client of the attorney). The lawyer may refer you to someone else. If the lawyer feels you don't have much of a case, you should have your case evaluated by another lawyer before deciding not to pursue it—in other words, get a legal "second opinion."

A LAWYER MAY BILL YOU for legal work in a number of ways: a flat fee for the whole job, an hourly rate, or a percentage of the money the lawyer recovers for you (a "contingency fee"). The amount a lawyer charges you depends on a number of factors, not the least of which are the nature and complexity of your problem and the lawyer's ability, experience, and reputation. The more serious and difficult your situation, or the higher the stakes, the more the lawyer is likely to charge. Likewise, the more qualified and experienced the lawyer, the higher his or her fee probably will be. If it's an emergency situation requiring fast action, the lawyer usually will charge more than if the matter could be taken care of in the normal course of events. If your situation involves a novel or unsettled question of law, then the lawyer will have to spend more time researching the issue than if the law were already well established, and he or she will charge you accordingly.

How negotiable are the lawyer's fees? In one sense, not very. If a lawyer typically charges $250 an hour, it's doubtful that he or she will agree to work for $200 an hour, unless perhaps the lawyer can make it up in volume. But in another sense, attorneys' fees are very negotiable: You can probably find another lawyer who will charge only $200 an hour. That lawyer may be a little less experienced, but if your problem isn't too complex, he or she should be able to do just as good a job as an older, more experienced lawyer.

Always get the complete terms of your fee agreement in writing, and make sure the lawyer signs the written agreement. Unless an emergency precludes it, never give the lawyer authorization to go ahead and start working on your case until you have looked over the proposed fee agreement. Make sure you understand everything; if you don't, ask the lawyer to explain it to you. Because fee disputes are one of the main reasons for a client's disappointment with a lawyer, have the lawyer spell out everything in writing before you hand over a check or the authority to represent you.

One thing to remember about lawyers' fees is that time is a lawyer's stock in trade. Expect to be charged for any of the lawyer's time you take up, whether it's in person, over the telephone, or writing a letter that the lawyer must read and respond to or take action on.

Hourly Rate

Hourly rates for lawyers generally range anywhere from a low of about $150 an hour to $500 or more, depending on the ability, experience, reputation of the lawyer or the law firm he or she works for, and the task to be done.

Before hiring a lawyer to work for you on an hourly basis, get a written estimate from him or her as to the cost of the work, including the lawyer's hourly rate, how many hours will probably be needed, and how much money will be spent on such things as court costs, filing fees, deposition expenses, travel expenses, and investigation. Note that if your case involves a lawsuit against another person ("litigation"), the lawyer may be unable to quote you a fee as to how much the whole thing will cost. If the other party is sue happy and wants to challenge each and every little thing in court, there's nothing your lawyer can do about it. This is especially true in divorce cases that turn nasty, in which one side is determined to "bleed the other spouse dry."

Flat Fees

For certain types of routine legal work, the lawyer may charge you a single, "flat" fee. A simple will, for instance, may cost you $125 to $150. A divorce where the couple was married for less than a year or two, didn't acquire much in the way of property, and have no children may cost $1,500, plus court costs and expenses. The defense of a first-time charge of drunk driving may cost $750 up to trial and then a certain amount for each day of trial.

Before agreeing to have legal work done for a flat fee, first find out just how "flat" that fee is. Does it include court costs and lawyer's expenses (discussed below)? It usually doesn't, so your flat fee may be increased by several hundred or thousands of dollars more, depending on the complexity of your case. Before you authorize the lawyer to start working for you, have him or her itemize—in writing—*all* costs, expenses, and other charges in addition to the lawyer's fee.

Retainer Fees

A retainer fee is money you pay when you hire, or "retain," a lawyer. There are several types of retainer fees. One is a yearly fee paid by a client (usually a large corporation or a wealthy individual) to ensure that the lawyer will be there if and when the client needs legal advice. The average person doesn't keep a lawyer on retainer from year to year. If you've found a good family lawyer, you generally will enjoy the same benefits as if the lawyer were on retainer. Another type of retainer is actually a flat fee: The lawyer estimates how much time he or she will have to spend on your legal problem and calls this a retainer.

The type of retainer you're most likely to encounter is one that is really a down payment for legal services. If you hire a lawyer to represent you in a divorce case, for example, the lawyer might ask for a $1,000 retainer up front. This retainer is credited toward the legal services the lawyer performs for you. So if the entire cost of the divorce is $1,500, you will owe the lawyer $500 (plus outstanding costs and expenses, discussed below).

Contingent Fees

In some types of cases—especially personal injury cases—the lawyer who represents the injured victim takes a percentage of the money the client receives from either an out-of-court settlement or a jury's (or less common, a judge's) award. This is a "contingent fee," the contingency being that the lawyer must win the case for you before he or she gets anything. The amount the lawyer receives generally ranges from 25 percent to 40 percent—33.33 percent being used the most—depending on the nature and difficulty of the case and the expertise of the lawyer.

Many contingent-fee agreements provide that the size of the fee the lawyer receives depends on when the case is resolved. For example, the agreement may provide that if the case is settled out of court before the lawyer files a complaint, the lawyer gets 25 percent of the settlement. If the case is settled after the complaint is filed but before a trial date is set, the lawyer's fee is 33.33 percent of the gross settlement proceeds. And if the case settles after that or goes to trial, the lawyer gets 40 percent of the gross settlement or judgment.

Suppose a jury awards you $50,000, but the defendant, who is uninsured, declares bankruptcy, and you only collect $20,000. The contingent-fee agreement provides for your lawyer to receive 40 percent of the award. Is the lawyer's share figured on the jury's award or on the money the defendant actually paid? It's figured on the money actually paid; the lawyer would get 40 percent of $20,000, rather than 40 percent of the whole $50,000.

Contingent-fee agreements are not appropriate in all cases. In fact, overall they are probably more the exception than the rule. For instance, the lawyer who probates a deceased person's will cannot ask for a contingent fee, since there is really no contingency to achieve (fees in probate cases usually are set by law). However, an attorney representing a party in a will contest may be able to take the case on a contingency fee basis, and take a percentage of whatever he wins for his or her client. Criminal cases are handled on an hourly or flat-fee basis. It is unethical for an attorney to make all or part of his or her fee contingent on getting a verdict of not guilty or of saving his or her client from doing any jail time. Contingent fee agreements are generally not permitted in most divorce cases. A lawyer can't, for example, promise to charge you only if he or she manages to get you custody of your children. But if everything else has been worked out and all that remains is the property division, some states permit the lawyer to base his or her fee on a percentage of the value of the property he or she wins for you.

Statutory Limits on Fees

At one time, lawyers who had been in practice for a while wanted to protect their fees from being undercut by their less established colleagues and pushed for the enactment of *minimum fee schedules*. They argued that minimum charges were needed to preserve the integrity of the legal profession and that this would encourage lawyers to give competent advice and spend a fair amount of time on each case. The American Bar Association was all in favor of this proposal, stating: "The establishment of suggested or recommended fee schedules by bar associations is a thoroughly laudable activity. The evils of fee cutting ought to be apparent to all members of the Bar." But the only "evil" was that established members of the bar might lose some business to newer lawyers who charged less for the same work. In 1975, the United States Supreme Court held that minimum fee schedules were illegal because they violated the Sherman Antitrust Act.

Today, many states have laws that restrict the *maximum* fee a lawyer can charge in certain cases. For example, in personal injury suits against the United States government, a federal statute limits the lawyer for the injured party to no more than 25 percent of the settlement or award. The fee an attorney can charge for probating a will is set by statute in most states. (Of course, the attorney can attempt to get a higher fee by claiming he or she had to do "extraordinary" work on the case.) Many states now have limits on the fee the victim's lawyer can receive in medical malpractice cases (see chapter 11).

Costs and Expenses

In addition to the lawyer's fees, there may be a number of related costs and expenses that you will have to pay. For instance, if the lawyer files a lawsuit on your behalf, the court's filing fee must be paid, and it costs to have the marshal or a process server serve the defendant with the summons and complaint (see chapter 22). There are other expenses as well, including the cost to investigate the case, depose the other party, often travel expenses, and perhaps the cost of having an expert or two evaluate the case and possibly testify at trial.

Regardless of the type of fee arrangement you have with your lawyer, you are responsible for the reasonable costs and expenses in addition to the lawyer's fee. This should be spelled out in the written fee agreement your lawyer has you sign when you retain him or her. Make sure that the agreement calls for the lawyer to submit an itemized list of costs and expenses you are being charged for, and proof of the costs and expenses if you request it.

Let's say that you're injured in an auto accident. You want to sue the driver who injured you, but you don't have the money for the court's filing fee or for other expenses. Can your lawyer pay those for you? Yes. A lawyer usually can advance money on behalf of the client to pay the costs and expenses necessary to litigate the case.

Now let's assume that your lawyer spends $3,500 in costs and expenses to prosecute your case, but you lose. Do you have to reimburse your lawyer for the costs and expenses he or she advanced on your behalf, even though the lawyer told you at the beginning that there would be no fee if you lost the case? Yes. Although you don't owe the lawyer anything for legal services rendered, you are still responsible for all costs and expenses advanced by the lawyer on your behalf—but only to the extent that those costs and expenses are reasonable. For example, the lawyer can't bill you for the expenses of a three-day trip out of town to interview a witness if the interview could have just as easily been conducted over the telephone. Or if the trip was necessary but should have taken only, say, an afternoon, the lawyer can ask you to reimburse him or her for only one night's lodging, not three.

Let's say that your case settles for $100,000 and the contingent fee contract calls for your lawyer to get a third of that. Your lawyer advanced $7,500 in costs and expenses on your behalf. Is your lawyer's fee based on the full $100,000, or on $92,500 (the settlement amount minus the $7,500 in advance costs and expenses)? That depends on what the contingent fee agreement states. Most of the time, the contingent agreement will provide that the lawyer's fee is based on the *gross* amount of the settlement, here the full $100,000, and the costs and expenses are deducted from your share. So the settlement would break down like this:

AMOUNT OF SETTLEMENT	$ 100,000.00
Lawyer's 33.33 percent	$ 33,333.33
Costs and Expenses Advanced by Lawyer	$ 7,500.00
NET TO LAWYER	$ 40,833.33
NET TO CLIENT	$ 59,166.67

Now let's look at the difference if the costs and expenses are deducted from the award before the lawyer's fee is calculated:

AMOUNT OF SETTLEMENT	$100,000.00
Costs and Expenses Advanced by Lawyer	$ 7,500.00
Net Award	$ 92,500.00
Lawyer's 33.33 Percent	$ 30,830.25
Plus Costs and Expenses Advanced by Lawyer	$ 7,500.00
NET TO LAWYER	$ 38,330.25
NET TO CLIENT	$ 61,669.75

You receive $59,116.67 when the costs and expenses are deducted from your share alone, and $61,669.75 when they are deducted from the entire award, a difference of approximately $2,500. The higher the costs and expenses, the larger this discrepancy. Before signing a contingent-fee agreement, read it carefully to determine how costs and expenses are deducted. Ask the lawyer to explain it in simple terms if you don't understand it. And if the agreement calls for the costs and expenses to be deducted from your share, try to negotiate for them to be deducted from the gross settlement or award before the lawyer takes his or her fee.

Loans to Clients for Living Expenses

Suppose you've been injured in an automobile accident that was the other driver's fault, and you can't work for a long time. Or suppose you're retired and rely mainly on your investment income to provide you an income, but an investment company defrauded you out of your retirement savings. You hire a lawyer who files a lawsuit on your behalf, but in the meantime you can't even afford the bare necessities of life. Can your lawyer lend you money for things such as food, clothing, shelter, and medical bills until your case is resolved? In most states, no; a lawyer can advance money on behalf of the client only for the costs and expenses of litigation, not for living expenses.

A client who can't pay for the basic necessities of life may be under considerable pressure to settle his or her case quickly—often for an amount that is clearly inadequate for the degree of injuries suffered. The Supreme Court of Louisiana noted this when it observed, "If an impoverished person is unable to secure subsistence from some source during disability, he may be deprived of the only effective means by which he can wait out the necessary delays that result from litigation to enforce his cause of action. He may, for reasons of economic necessity and physical need, be forced to settle his claim for an inadequate amount." A few states therefore permit attorneys to lend their clients money for minimal living expenses in some cases, so the clients won't be forced into fast but unfair settlements.

PROBLEMS WITH YOUR LAWYER

A CLIENT'S UNHAPPINESS WITH his or her lawyer can cover a wide range of grievances, everything from the lawyer's failure to return telephone calls as quickly as the client would like to the lawyer's getting a fat settlement check for the client, then forging the client's name to it and telling the client the case was lost.

When a problem arises between you and your lawyer, you should first discuss it candidly with him or her. If the lawyer isn't returning your phone calls, write a letter explaining your grievances with the lawyer and send it by certified mail, return receipt requested. (If it's a serious matter, such as your lawyer absconding with your settlement check, you should contact the district attorney's office immediately.) Perhaps it is nothing more than a mere misunderstanding and an explanation from the lawyer will ease your fears. Or the lawyer may have put your file aside during a busy period, and a word or two from you will prompt him or her to be more diligent with your case in the future.

One thing you must realize is that your lawyer is, after all, in business. He or she has other clients to talk to, other court hearings to attend, other briefs or wills to prepare, and so on. But if you feel your lawyer has been remiss in preparing your case or advising you of progress, call or write your lawyer and say that you are beginning to worry. If this doesn't solve the problem, then more drastic action (discussed below) is called for.

When the dispute involves the amount of money you owe the lawyer or how your fee agreement should be interpreted and you can't work things out with your lawyer, send your lawyer a letter stating the nature of the dispute and requesting to have the dispute arbitrated. Many states have a voluntary informal—and often free—arbitration system that gives you a way to resolve fee disputes quickly. The dispute usually is heard by another lawyer in his or her office, and you and your lawyer each explain your respective positions. The arbitrator's decision generally is not final. If you don't like it, you can have the issue decided in court.

Some problems arise through business dealings between the lawyer and client outside of the lawyer-client relationship. For instance, a lawyer and a client might invest money together in real estate or another business venture, which then goes sour. Is it proper for a lawyer to have such business dealings with clients? There is nothing unethical about it per se. But a lawyer must deal with the client in the utmost good faith, much more so than when the lawyer is dealing with someone who is not a client. And a lawyer must never use his or her knowledge of the client's situation to take advantage of the client. For instance, suppose Mary is close to filing bankruptcy. Her lawyer tells her that she can avoid bankruptcy by selling her car and using that money to pay off her bills. The lawyer then offers to buy Mary's car (worth $35,000) for $15,000—the amount Mary needs to get out of her financial woes—and Mary, desperate, agrees. This would be unethical for the lawyer, since the price the lawyer is paying for the car is clearly far too low. But the transaction probably would be fine if the lawyer paid the fair market value for the car.

What are your options if the lawyer doesn't adequately reassure you after a frank discussion of the problem—or refuses to discuss the problem at all. You can fire the lawyer and hire a new one. If you suspect the lawyer of having done something unethical, you can report him or her to the state bar association; if you suspect the attorney of fraud, theft, or another crime, you should contact the district attorney, or, when appropriate, you can sue the lawyer for malpractice. Each of these is considered below.

Firing Your Lawyer

Just as you have the right to change doctors at any time, so, too, can you fire your lawyer at any time, with or without a reason. But, as when you leave your doctor, you are still responsible for all outstanding fees owed to the lawyer.

Suppose you have a contingent-fee arrangement with your lawyer by which he or she gets one-third of the recovery. Because of problems between you and your lawyer, you take your case to a new lawyer before it is over, who also takes the case on a contingent-fee basis, also for one-third. When your case finally ends and you receive some money, do you have to pay each lawyer a third, so you end up with only a third of the proceeds? Generally not; your first lawyer is entitled only to a reasonable amount of the fee for the work done for you up to the time you discharged him or her. This amount is based on the lawyer's standard hourly fee, the number of hours the lawyer put in on your case, and how much that work helped your case.

Contacting the State Bar Association or District Attorney

If you suspect your lawyer of unethical or illegal conduct, and the lawyer will not give you a straight answer or adequate information for his or her actions, you should call the state bar association (if the number isn't in your telephone book, call your county bar association for it) to see how and where to file a complaint. When appropriate, the lawyer's conduct also should be reported to the district attorney's office. For instance, if you think your lawyer is misusing or stealing your funds, and despite your numerous requests, the lawyer does not provide you with an itemized statement and proof (receipts, canceled checks, and the like) showing how and where the money was spent, you should file a complaint with the state bar association. Another time to contact the state bar association is when an attorney is incompetent or shows a clear lack of diligence in your case—if, for instance, the lawyer doesn't prepare your case properly, shows up for a court hearing drunk and unable to represent you properly, or doesn't take the time to research the law. You also should contact the district attorney's office if you feel the lawyer is committing fraud, theft, or any other crime.

Suing Your Lawyer for Malpractice

When you suffer damages because of a lawyer's suspected incompetence or unethical doings, think about contacting another lawyer to see if you have grounds for a legal malpractice suit against your first lawyer. Like doctors (see chapter 11), lawyers must use sufficient care and due diligence in representing and advising their clients. If a lawyer is negligent, he or she is liable to the client for the damages the client suffers because of the lawyer's carelessness. An obvious example of legal malpractice would be if an attorney failed to file a complaint on time, so it is barred by the statute of limitations. (But to win your legal malpractice suit against your first lawyer, you must first prove that you probably would have won the underlying case if it had been filed on time.) Deliberately misusing a client's funds is also grounds for a malpractice suit against the lawyer—if, for instance, the lawyer settled your case without your permission, forged your name on the settlement check from the defendant, cashed it, and kept it, all the while telling you no progress was being made on your case.

How difficult is it to find a lawyer willing to sue another lawyer for malpractice? Not very. Many lawyers who handle personal injury cases will represent clients in lawsuits against lawyers for malpractice. Some lawyers even specialize in suing other lawyers for professional negligence.

TWENTY-FIVE

Laws, the Courts, and You

mOST OF THIS BOOK has concentrated on handling specific situations involving you and the law. This chapter takes a different approach and provides an overview of the whole legal system and how it affects you in a broader sense. How do laws regulate our daily lives? What are laws, and where do they come from? How are the court systems organized? What is your role in the judicial system, especially when you're called for jury duty? Reading this chapter certainly isn't critical to understanding your rights as we've discussed them throughout this book. But like the last piece that completes a puzzle, the following material brings everything together to give you the whole picture.

LAWS

How Laws Affect Our Daily Lives

What are laws, and why are they so important to us? Laws are the rules of society by which we all must live and abide. Laws both restrict and protect us. They tell us what we can and can't do to others and what others can and can't do to us. Our daily conduct is regulated three ways: by contracts, by criminal law, and by civil law.

When you make a contract (see chapter 17), you voluntarily agree to do (or not do) something that you are not otherwise obligated to do. For instance, let's say that you buy a new car, put 10 percent down, and finance the rest through a bank. The loan agreement between you and the bank is a contract that requires you to do something you otherwise wouldn't have to do—make monthly payments to the bank according to the terms of the agreement. The loan agreement will require you to do other things as well, such as keeping the car adequately insured and in good repair. It also will prohibit you from doing certain things—selling the car without the bank's permission, for instance. All of these restrictions on your conduct are imposed by the contract you made with the bank.

Now let's say that you've had too much to drink and get behind the wheel of your car. A police officer sees your car weaving from side to side and pulls you over. You flunk the field sobriety test. The police officer arrests you for drunk driving and takes you back to the station, where you are given a breath test. The results of the test show that your blood alcohol level is over the legal limit. You subsequently are prosecuted for drunk driving, convicted, and punished accordingly. Nothing in your contract with the bank specifically forbids you from driving while drunk. But the criminal law makes it illegal for you to do so.

Finally, let's say one of your tires goes flat. Your friend Trevor offers to help you change it. You place a jack under the bumper and raise the car, but while Trevor is taking the tire off, the car slips off the jack because you didn't follow the instructions, and Trevor is injured seriously. Nothing in your contract with the bank covers this, and it's not a crime not to follow the instructions. Still, a reasonably careful person would read and follow the instructions—which is exactly what the law of torts (chapter 10), a branch of civil law, requires you to do. Since you didn't, you must pay Trevor for the injuries he has suffered because of your negligence.

SOURCES OF AMERICAN LAW

Where does the law come from? Here are the main sources of law in the United States:

* United States Constitution
* federal statutes and regulations
* state constitutions
* state statutes and regulations
* county and city ordinances
* the common law
* case law

The Constitution

The prime source of law in the United States is the Constitution and its twenty-seven amendments. Most of our fundamental individual rights are found there: the rights to free expression and freedom of religion; the right to a fair and impartial trial by one's peers; and the guarantees of equal protection and due process of the law; to name a few. No law is valid and enforceable if it is contrary to the provisions of the United States Constitution. Each state also has its own constitution, patterned generally after the federal one. But the federal and state constitutions are only the starting points for our laws. Most of our laws are found elsewhere—in statutes, local ordinances, and the common law, for example.

Statutes

"Statutes" are laws passed by Congress or state legislative bodies and signed into law by the president or governor, as the case may be. Statutes enacted by Congress are found in the United States Codes; individual states have their own code books (or "books of statutes") for state laws. A statute becomes the law if the legislative body that passed it had the power to do so and followed the correct parliamentary procedures, and if the statute does not violate any constitutional guarantees. How long does a statute remain on the books? Unless the statute by its own terms ends on a given date, it lasts until the legislative body that enacted it revokes it or until a judge rules that it is unconstitutional. A judge cannot modify or revoke a statute; only the legislature can do that. A judge can, however, interpret a statute when the parties to a lawsuit dispute its meaning. In interpreting a statute, the judge will look at the legislative history of the law to determine the legislature's intent in passing it. This review can include reading the legislative debates recorded in the *Congressional Record* (or its state equivalent).

Regulations

A government, whether the United States government or your state government, creates various administrative agencies to implement the laws its legislature passes. Each agency usually is given the power to make regulations to achieve its goals. These regulations, if it is within the agency's power to make them, have the effect of law. For example, an air quality management district may pass regulations concerning permissible emission standards for factories. A factory that doesn't comply with those regulations can be fined or even shut down.

Local Ordinances

Laws passed by counties and cities are "ordinances." They are similar to statutes passed by Congress or state legislatures, but their effect extends only to the county's or city's border, as the case may be. Zoning laws are the most familiar example of local ordinances.

Common Law

The "common law" system originated in England around the beginning of the twelfth century, when there were few "precedents" in the law and few, if any, statutes to rely upon. Judges decided disputes based on the acceptable social customs of the time. If there wasn't a custom, the judge used wisdom and common sense to make a ruling that was fair and just. Once made, the ruling became the law for all similar disputes—a "precedent" (discussed below). All states except Louisiana adopted the English common law and have expanded on it to one extent or another. Louisiana, for historical reasons, has a "civil code" system based on the French Napoleonic code—only the legislature, through the code, can give or take away rights, not the judges. Judges are limited to interpreting the code. If the code doesn't cover a dispute, the party who claims to have been wronged can't recover damages.

Case Law

"Case law" is the American equivalent of the English common law. If two parties come before a judge, one claiming to have been wronged by the other, and none of the above types of law covers the situation, the judge will exercise his or her wisdom and common sense and decide whether to permit or deny recovery. The judge's decision is called "case law" because it is the law of the case—that is, the particular lawsuit.

THE ROLE OF PRECEDENTS IN THE LAW

YOU'VE PROBABLY HEARD OF the law's reverence for "precedents," the principle of following the law as declared in a previous case. Under the doctrine of *stare decisis* (literally, "to follow decisions"), if a dispute involves a legal question that has earlier been decided in court in another case, the judge simply follows the rule previously laid down. Why this emphasis on precedents? Because it gives stability and continuity to the law. If the law were changing every day on the same point, or if each judge were free to make his or her own rule of law in every case, we would never know what to do. One day, something might be allowed; then the following day, it could be prohibited. Because the law adheres to precedents, we have an idea of what is expected of us from day to day.

But if judges unwaveringly followed earlier decisions, they would simply be enshrining the laws of earlier times. The eminent United States Supreme Court jurist Oliver Wendell Holmes Jr., once remarked of precedents: "It is revolting to have no better reason for a rule of law than it is as laid down in the time of Henry IV. It is still more revolting if the grounds upon which it was laid down have vanished long since, and the rule simply persists from blind imitation to the past." Because laws must change with the times, precedents are not ironclad, and judges need not always follow outdated laws. But even when a law is clearly out-of-date and sorely in need of change, there are still some limitations on a judge's ability to change it. As noted earlier, a judge can't modify or limit a law passed by a legislature (a statute) unless it is unconstitutional, in which case the judge must declare it null and void. Judge-made law (common law and case law) can be changed more easily, but there are still restrictions. A judge of a lower court (discussed below) is bound to follow an earlier ruling of a higher court, even if that ruling was made over one hundred years ago and is clearly out of step with modern times. For instance, a superior or district court judge cannot overturn a previous decision of an appellate court, nor can an appellate court change a law made by that state's supreme court, regardless of how obsolete and unfair that law has become.

Since it is the highest court in the land, only the United States Supreme Court can change a law that it makes. How often does the Supreme Court reverse itself? Not very often. And when it does, the reversal usually involves a practice that the Supreme Court upheld during the first century of this country's existence but that should now be banned because of the changes in society. Consider this example: At one time, the Supreme Court ruled that it was constitutional for a school district to provide separate schools for blacks and other minorities, so long as the schools afforded an "equal" education. But in the 1954 case of *Brown v. Board of Education*, the Supreme Court held that racial segregation in public elementary schools was unconstitutional, because it violated the fourteenth amendment guarantee of equal protection under the law. Declaring, "separate educational facilities are inherently unequal," the Supreme Court reversed a string of previous decisions permitting separate treatment of minorities.

Reversals by the United States Supreme Court of its previous decisions generally occur after one or two of the justices, who are appointed for life, die or retire from the bench, and the president (with the advice and consent of the Senate) selects new justices who have opposing philosophies from the retired or deceased justices. For example, suppose the Supreme Court has a general split of 5–4, with the majority voting liberal most of the time. If one or two of them die or retire and the president is a conservative, supported by a conservative Senate, the president will appoint new justices who share his or her conservative views and will be confirmed by the Senate. Then, instead of a 5–4 split in favor of a liberal majority, there will now be a 5–4 or even a 6–3 split in favor of a conservative majority.

ARE THERE TOO MANY LAWS?

To GET AN IDEA of how many laws there are, just visit any good law library. There you will find several floors filled with rows upon rows of bookcases bursting at the seams with books containing statutes, cases, treatises on the law, law reviews, regulations, and more. Some people claim that we have far more laws than we need and that we are being "lawed" or regulated to death. Things would be much simpler, they say, if only we had the same number of laws that we had, say, a hundred years ago.

How valid are these complaints? It is true that we have many more laws than ever before. And every day new laws are being added. But the number of laws simply reflects how complex our society has become. The more advanced the society, the more rules there will be to regulate conduct. That is the nature of the beast. Technological breakthroughs have led to many laws and regulations that have contributed to a safer society, particularly in the area of consumer protection. Other laws are necessary to protect interests that didn't even exist fifty years ago. For instance, before computers were invented we didn't need laws that dealt with hacking, piracy, computer viruses, the Internet, and so forth. Similarly, ten years ago we didn't need laws regulating the cloning of animals, even human beings. So long as society continues to grow in new directions, the law will grow with it to cover our rights and obligations in new situations.

WHERE TO FIND THE LAW

WHEN YOU HAVE A PROBLEM and want to find out what the law is on the issue, where can you look? Your nearby public library contains some law books: city and county ordinances, for instance, and possibly a set of your state's code books as well. General public libraries usually have some self-help books written for the layperson that may cover your area of concern. A public law library usually is located in or near the main county courthouse. Law libraries also are found in law schools.

How practical is it for you, a nonlawyer, to research the law effectively? Realistically speaking, outside of finding local ordinances, zoning regulations, and the like, not very practical at all. Finding the law that applies to your case can be an arduous task. Law students receive in-depth instruction on how to use a law library, and it still takes them several months before they are able to use the law library effectively and efficiently. You certainly can't expect to find your way around a law library in only an hour or two. There's much more to it than just knowing which section contains which books. And even if you manage to figure out where the books with the law applicable to your case are, you'll ordinarily have a tough time making heads or tails out of the information. Legal decisions and law books are written in legalese, an obscure language all its own, with myriad citations and references that seem designed to confound a layperson. It's like reading the schematic drawings and technical information for a computer: Once you have the drawings and specifications, you're not going to make much sense of them if you don't have a computer technology background.

HOW THE COURTS ARE STRUCTURED

THERE ARE TWO SEPARATE judicial systems in America—the federal system (which includes a separate system of military justice) and the state systems. Some legal matters are handled only in federal courts, because the Constitution gives Congress the exclusive power to regulate certain areas. Bankruptcy and copyright and patent infringements are examples of cases that can be brought solely in the federal court system. Other matters are handled only in state courts: divorces and probates, for instance, and most personal injury cases. Occasionally, the two systems overlap, giving you the choice of which court system to sue in.

The Federal Court System

The federal court system consists of three levels. The lowest level is composed of the United States district courts, bankruptcy courts, tax court, the court of claims, and the court of international trade (formerly Customs Court). It is in these courts that cases actually are tried. Which court a particular case is filed in depends on the nature of the dispute. Most cases in the federal court system are filed in a United States district court. The other courts handle specific types of cases. If you want to file for bankruptcy, you must file in bankruptcy court. Disputes involving federal taxes are handled in tax court. Certain types of cases against the United States come under the jurisdiction of the court of claims, while the court of international trade resolves disputes involving customs tariffs.

If you are not satisfied with the results of the trial, you have the right to appeal your case to a higher court. In the federal court system, the second level of courts consists of the intermediate appellate courts: the United States Circuit Courts of Appeal and the Court of Customs and Patent Appeals. A panel of justices (usually three) will review the transcripts of your trial, the evidence presented there, and the appellate briefs filed by your attorney and your opponent's attorney. Unlike a trial, an appeal does not involve the presentation of new witnesses or evidence in court; if something is not in the trial court's record, the appellate justices will not consider it. The parties' lawyers usually have the option of making an oral presentation to the panel of appellate justices, which is usually limited to thirty minutes for each side.

Suppose you lose your case in the district court, and the circuit court of appeals upholds ("affirms") the lower court's decision. What is your next step? You can ask the United States Supreme Court to hear your appeal. Most of the time, however, unlike the intermediate appellate courts, which *must* consider your appeal, the Supreme Court ordinarily is not required to hear your appeal. In most instances, the Supreme Court has the power, or discretion, to decide which cases it hears. Your attorney must ask the Supreme Court for permission to appeal the case to it by filing a "petition for writ of certiorari." The United States Supreme Court receives thousands of these petitions each year and approves less than two hundred. The Supreme

Court ordinarily accepts only cases that will affect many more people than just the parties to the dispute.

The United States Supreme Court has the final say on most legal matters. If, for example, the Supreme Court rules that a particular law passed by Congress violates the Constitution, the Congress cannot pass another bill stating that the Supreme Court's decision is wrong and that the law is constitutional. Once the Supreme Court declares a law unconstitutional, there are only two ways to change that decision: by amending the Constitution (a long and difficult process that has been successful only twenty-seven times since the Constitution was written in 1787) or by a later decision of the Supreme Court declaring the law constitutional (in other words, by the Supreme Court reversing its earlier decision). Sometimes Congress can rewrite the law and remove the unconstitutional provisions.

Congress has the power to determine the number of judges on the Supreme Court, but since 1869 the number has remained steady at nine. To become a Supreme Court justice, the person must be appointed by the president, with the advice and consent of the Senate. The Constitution provides that all federal judges "shall hold their Offices during good Behaviour." Once confirmed, a justice can be removed only by impeachment for and conviction of treason, bribery, and other serious crimes.

THE MILITARY JUSTICE SYSTEM

THE FEDERAL JUDICIAL SYSTEM also includes a special system to deal with military offenses committed by servicemen and servicewomen. These offenses are spelled out in the Uniform Code of Military Justice. Many of the offenses involve acts that are detrimental to the military, such as falling asleep or being drunk during guard duty, refusing to obey orders, assaulting a superior officer, desertion, and "acts against good order and discipline." Offenses that are crimes under state law (robbery, murder, rape, and assault and battery, for example) usually can be tried in civilian courts as well.

When a person in the military is charged with an offense under the Uniform Code of Military Justice, a court-martial is ordered by the commanding officer. (Unlike a civilian court, a court-martial is temporary and lasts only as long as it takes to dispose of the case; the court-martial is then dissolved.) The accused is offered a military lawyer to defend him or her, but can choose instead to hire a civilian lawyer at his or her own expense. The jury in a court-martial is composed of military officers; if the accused is an enlisted man or woman, he or she has the right to ask for enlisted persons on the jury.

If the service member is convicted, he or she can appeal the decision of the court-martial. The first appeal is to the service member's commanding officer. If that fails, the next appeal is to the Military Court of Criminal Appeals or to the judge advocate general. After that, the service member can appeal the case to the United States Court for the Armed Forces. For most service members, this is the final stop. However, about 10 percent can ask the United States Supreme Court to hear their case.

STATE COURT SYSTEMS

Most states have a tripartite court system similar to the federal system: the lowest level of courts, where cases are tried; a second level consisting of the intermediate appellate courts; and the third level made up of a state supreme court. Delaware, Maine, Montana, Rhode Island, South Dakota, Vermont, and Wyoming have only two levels of courts—the trial courts and a supreme court. North Dakota had a two-tiered system but its supreme court was being so overwhelmed by all the appeals that it created a temporary court of appeals. There is also some disparity among the states regarding the names of the courts. For example, in New York, the "supreme court" is the equivalent of a superior court or district court in other states. The intermediate appellate court in New York is the "supreme court, appellate division," and its highest court is the "court of appeals."

In many states, the lowest level of courts—the trial courts—actually comprises two levels of courts. One level (called superior court, circuit court, county court, court of common pleas, or district court) handles more serious matters, such as felonies and civil cases involving more than a certain amount, such as $25,000. Frequently, there are courts designed for specific controversies, such as criminal courts, family courts (to handle divorces, adoptions, and paternity suits, for example); probate court (or surrogate court); and juvenile court. The other level (municipal court, magistrate court, justice of the peace court) handles smaller problems, such as misdemeanors and civil cases under $25,000. Some courts on this level may handle specific problems, such as small claims court, landlord-tenant disputes, and traffic court.

As in the federal system, in a state court system you can appeal your case to a higher court if you disagree with the results at the trial court level. While the intermediate appellate court generally is required to hear your case, like the U.S. Supreme Court, a state supreme court generally is free to hear only those appeals that it wants to hear. The number of justices on the state supreme courts varies from state to state, from a low of five to a high of nine. The length of service for state supreme court justices also varies from six years to life, depending upon the state. In some states, the governor appoints justices to the supreme court, subject to confirmation by the legislature or a commission on judicial appointments. In other states, the voters elect or confirm the justices.

TRIAL BY JURY IS the cornerstone of American justice. Evidence is presented to an impartial jury, who looks objectively at all the facts and makes a decision. When the jury system began in old England, only persons familiar with the dispute—in other words, witnesses—could be jurors for the case. The jurors would listen to the parties, then make a decision based on their own knowledge of the facts. This practice was abolished in the fifteenth century amid growing complaints that juries were biased (many jurors were family, friends, and neighbors of the parties), bribed, or intimidated. The rule was changed so that only persons who had no knowledge of the dispute or the parties and could therefore reach a fair and impartial decision were qualified to sit as jurors.

If you're over 18, sooner or later you're likely to be summoned for jury duty. When you receive the notice summoning you for jury duty, the first question you'll probably have is, "How can I get out of it?" Be advised that it's not nearly as easy to get excused from jury duty as it once was. So many people were being exempted that there weren't enough people left to fill the jury pool adequately. Because of that, most courts have cracked down on letting people out of jury duty. Generally, you are excused only if you are mentally or physically disabled (if you're blind, for instance, or deaf), or you are seriously ill (although if it's only a short-term illness, such as the flu, your obligation will just be postponed for a month or two), or if your business would shut down without you there. To get excused, you'll have to send a written explanation (along with a doctor's letter, if applicable) signed under penalty of perjury to the clerk's office or call the clerk—the number should be on the summons—or go to the clerk's office at the courthouse before the date when you're supposed to show up for jury duty. What happens if you simply ignore the summons? If you don't call the clerk's office or appear on the appointed date and don't have a good reason (for instance, you were in the hospital or out of the state the entire time), you could be found in contempt of court and fined or even jailed for a day or two.

The first morning of jury duty, report to the room listed on the summons. You will receive an orientation—it may be a booklet, a videotape presentation, or a speech by a court administrator—and afterward you will be directed to the jurors' lounge to wait. At some point, a panel of you and some other members of the jury pool—perhaps twenty-five or so—will be sent to a courtroom. You and eleven other members of the panel will be directed to the "jury box," the area of the courtroom where the jurors sit during the trial. The lawyers for both sides will question you to determine if they want you to decide the case. Often, the judge will do some of the preliminary questioning. It is important that you answer the lawyers' and judge's questions honestly and frankly. If you are excused, you will be sent back to the jurors' lounge to wait until you are called again. Unless you're chosen to sit on a jury, your obligation for jury duty is usually over in one or two weeks. If you're not picked as a juror the first day, many courts let you call in to see whether you will be needed the next day. If you are required to go to the courthouse every day for a week or two for jury duty to see if you'll be picked for a jury, take along a good book or the daily paper to read, as you'll probably be doing a lot of sitting around and waiting.

If you are selected for a jury, you stay in the jury box while the other jurors are picked. Once all twelve jurors are chosen, the trial begins (see chapter 22). Pay attention during the trial. Keep in mind the fact that the fates of at least two people are in your hands or one man or woman's liberty—perhaps even his or her life—is at stake. Listen carefully to what each witness says. Also look closely at how the witness acts on the stand; a witness's body language often reveals more than his or her words.

A jury trial is an adversarial contest—one person against another, much like a boxing match. The courtroom is the ring, the judge the referee. The parties' lawyers do the actual fighting, bobbing and weaving their way through the trial with strategy, objections to evidence, and the like, delivering punches with witnesses' testimony and incriminating evidence. Sometimes one lawyer delivers a knockout blow and the judge throws the case out of court. Most of the time, though, the case goes to the jury, who, like the ringside judges in a boxing match, vote for the winner. Unlike the boxing judges, however, who make their decisions independently of one another, the jurors discuss the case among themselves before reaching a verdict.

How long does the average trial last? Most trials take less than a week. Some are over in half a day, and many take only two or three days. When a trial is expected to last longer than a week, the judge usually will ask prospective jurors whether they have any commitments or problems that will prevent them from serving on the jury for an extended period of time.

Do you get paid for the time you spend on jury duty? Yes, but not very much—usually only $10 to $20 a day and mileage one way. And if you miss work because of jury duty, your employer doesn't have to make up the difference unless your employment contract or a collective bargaining agreement requires it.

Let's say that while you're sitting as a juror on a case, a question comes to your mind that neither lawyer has thought to ask the witness. Can you raise your hand and ask the question yourself? No. Generally you must leave the questioning to the lawyers and occasionally the judge. (Quite often you'll find your question is answered, if not by this witness, then by a later one.) When jurors are permitted to ask questions, the normal procedure is for the juror to put the question in writing and give it to the bailiff to hand to the judge, who will then ask it if he or she thinks it is relevant. But remember: It is up to the lawyers to prove their case, so if they omit asking what you feel is a crucial question, you can consider this in determining whether the lawyer met his burden of proving his or her case.

Suppose that you're sitting as a juror on a case, and in the hall during a lunch break you run into an attorney for one of the parties. The attorney recognizes you and asks how you think the trial is going. What should you do? Politely tell the attorney that you can't talk about the case, leave, and immediately report the encounter to the bailiff. During a trial, it is important that jurors do not discuss the case with anyone, especially the parties to the case, their lawyers, and witnesses. If you feel that anyone involved with the case is trying to influence your decision in any way, you should report it to the bailiff right away, who in turn will convey your message to the judge.

The vote you cast in the jury room should be your own, not one your fellow jurors want you to make. Don't feel pressured to change your vote simply because you are the lone holdout one way or the other. You should evaluate the positions of the other jurors and listen to their reasoning—just as they should give you the courtesy of listening to you and thoughtfully considering your points. Be as conscientious as possible in making sure that your vote is the correct one before casting it; you wouldn't expect any less from someone who was entrusted with the duty of deciding your fate.

WHILE EACH CHAPTER in this book is designed to stand alone so you can readily determine what your rights are in a given situation without having to wade through the entire 600 plus pages, the letters we received from readers of the original edition of this book has taught me that some of you will indeed read this book from cover to cover. To those of you who have made the full journey, let me say congratulations and bravo! You now know as much about the law as many lawyers do. The major difference is that we have removed the legalese that makes the law seem too daunting for the average layperson to understand.

But besides knowing the law and how to apply it to the particular factual situation you are presented with, there is another important aspect to being a lawyer: That is, keeping up with the almost daily changes in the law and notifying your clients when a law that affects them has in fact been changed, either by the judicial branch (such as the Supreme Court making a new law or overturning an old one) or by the legislative branch (when Congress passes a new law and the president signs it into law, or when a state legislature passes a bill and the governor signs it into law).

During the time Earl Warren was the chief justice of the United States Supreme Court—appointed by President Dwight D. Eisenhower in 1953 and serving as chief justice until his retirement in 1969—the Supreme Court was called liberal because it tended to favor the rights of the individual over the rights of big business. Also, the Warren Court made sure that the rights of criminal suspects were protected against bullying police officers who would use unfair tactics and force to get suspects to confess, resulting in the confessions of many innocent persons. Further, it made sure that the "wall of separation" between church and state was high and strong.

When Warren E. Burger, appointed chief justice by President Richard M. Nixon in 1969 as a no-nonsense, law-and-order justice, the Supreme Court slowly began to move to the right. That swing continued when Associate Justice William H. Rehnquist was appointed to the United States Supreme Court by President Nixon in 1972, and was handed the chief justice's mantle by President Ronald Reagan in 1986 after Chief Justice Burger retired from the high court that year. Now it may safely be said that the United States Supreme Court is conservative, one that for the most part is friendly to big business, government, police, and religion.

With the remaining liberal justices in their advancing years, it is quite likely that Republican president George W. Bush will be in office to appoint at least one or two justices to the United States Supreme Court, thereby solidifying its conservative agenda. With Republicans in power in both the House of Representatives and the Senate, it is a given that individual rights established during Chief Justice Warren's tenure will be overturned. For example, in selecting a new Supreme Court justice, President Bush and the U.S. Senate (a justice to the Supreme Court is appointed by the president with the "advice and consent" of the Senate) undoubtedly will submit him or her to a litmus test on the issue of abortion: If the candidate is antiabortion, he or she will pass the first stage; if the candidate is for a woman's right to choose, he or she will not make it over the first hurdle. *Roe v. Wade* (discussed in chapter 1) will be put in jeopardy with the substitution of one conservative justice for one liberal justice. Additionally, another conservative justice on the Supreme Court may result in a paring down of a criminal suspect's *Miranda* rights (see chapter 23), rights that have become so integral to the American criminal system. Civil rights programs may also be imperiled.

Additionally, as discussed in chapter 11, we may see a national act passed restricting an injured patient's right to sue a medical doctor for malpractice to avoid a medical malpractice "crisis," a crisis we have seen is born more out of doctors committing malpractice and insurance companies not getting a good return on their investments than the filing of frivolous lawsuits against health care providers. In a similar vein, we may see a national law passed imposing limitations on those who wish to sue the seller, distributor, or manufacturer of a dangerously defective product (chapter 12) that has harmed them.

That said, we hope we have helped to clear the murky legal waters you may find yourself in. But bear in mind the warnings at the front of this book and in the introduction about handling the problem yourself: Every legal problem is unique and no book, even one as thorough as this one, can replace the advice of a competent lawyer who knows all the relevant facts and is up-to-date on the law in his or her state.

While we have consistently advised the reader to consult a lawyer well versed in the area of law of the dispute, I cannot help but end this work with a quote from Ralph Waldo Emerson that gives a different slant on things:

> The good lawyer is not the man who has an eye to every side and angle of the contingency, and qualifies all his qualifications, but who throws himself on your part so heartily, that he can get you out of a scrape. (*Conduct of Life: Power*)

ALLEN P. WILKINSON was born on January 2, 1955, in Edmonton, Alberta, Canada, the third of what would become five children, all boys. His family moved to southern California ten years later, in the summer of 1965.

In July 1979, after graduating *cum laude* from law school, Allen took the California Bar examination and a month later found himself in San Francisco working for his legal idol, the world famous attorney Melvin Belli. Allen was originally hired by Mr. Belli to revise the latter's landmark work *Modern Trials*, geerally acknowledged as the Bible of tort (personal injury) law, trial techniques, and the use of demonstrative evidence. Allen ultimately revised it into a highly acclaimed five-volume set.

Allen worked closely with Melvin Belli, becoming his personal legal assistant. In his ten-year association with Mr. Belli, Allen worked on a number of exciting projects with Mr. Belli involving both celebrities and "common folk" from all walks of life. He had the delightful experience of working with Oscar-winning screenwriters and a Pulitzer Prize–winning playwright. Allen was coauthor with Melvin Belli of the original edition of *Everybody's Guide to the Law.*

On his own, Allen has been in heavy demand as a legal writer of and contributor to numerous professional treatises, journals, and magazines. He has also given seminars to attorneys, doctors, librarians, dentists, medical students, and other groups, and has appeared as a guest on television and radio talk shows. As a practicing lawyer, Allen has been involved in several high-profile cases that have captured national attention.

As shown by the reviews and success of the first edition of *Everybody's Guide to the Law,*

Allen has the rare ability to translate arcane "legalese" into simple, easy-to-understand English that makes his legal writing accessible to the general public.

Besides the law, Allen's varied interests include cosmology, philosophy, protecting the environment, attending the theater and comedy clubs, and ice hockey. Allen lives in southern California with his dog, Pucci, and two cats, Feynman and Gogo.

D

price
  in new car purchases, 48–49
  for real estate, 185
prior appropriation, 204
prior wills, revoking, 131
priority workers, 492–494
  aliens of extraordinary ability, 492–493
  executives and managers of multinational
    corporations, 493–494
  outstanding professors and researchers,
    493
privacy, invasion of, 274–276
Privacy Act, 477
private associations, GLBTs and, 243–244
private places, 230
privity, 303
probable cause, 271
probable grounds, 273
probate, 97–101
  avoiding, 99–102
  defined, 97–98
probation, 556, 570–571
problems with your lawyer, 584–586
products liability, 280, 297–306
  liability of a product manufacturer or seller,
    298–302
  suing for your injuries if you've been hurt by
    a defective product, 302–306
Professional Golf Association (PGA), 335
professionals
  with advanced degrees, 494
  with bachelor's degrees, 494
professors, outstanding, 493
proficiency in English, demonstrating, 504,
    507
profits, from estates, 195–196
program accessibility, 333
promissory estoppel, 387
promotions, 308
proof of service, 437
property
  disposing of all, 131–132
  dividing after a divorce, 15–16
  gift of all
    in percentages, 132–133
    to your spouse, 132
  title to, 92–94
property damage, amount to sue for in, 431
property damage insurance, 71–72
property management, durable power of
    attorney for, 107–109, 115, 231

property ownership payout arrangements,
    153–160
  deferred payment loans, 154–155
  property tax deferrals, 154
  reverse mortgages, 155–158
  sale-leasebacks and life estates, 160
  selling your home, 158–160
property settlements, 15
property tax deferrals, 154
prosecution, malicious, 511
prostitution, pandering, and pimping, 535
protection
  when buying or selling a used car, 60–62
  see also copyright protection
provocation, 251
proxy bidding, 355
public accommodations discrimination under
    ADA Title III, 334–336
  courses and examinations, 336
  where to file your claim, 336
public disclosure of private facts, 275
public figures, 277–278
public transportation discrimination under
    ADA Title II, 332–334
  public transportation defined, 334
  where and when to file complaints, 333–334
punishment, cruel and unusual, 563–571
purchase and sale agreement, 184
purchase contract, in new car purchases, 50–51
purchase price
  in new car purchases, 48–49
  for real estate, 185

Q
QMBs, see qualified Medicare beneficiaries
qualified individuals with disabilities,
    324–326
qualified Medicare beneficiaries (QMBs), 364,
    380
questioning, by police, 543–545
"quickie" divorces, 12
"quiet enjoyment," 217–218
Quinlan, Karen Ann, 110
quitclaim deed, 198

R
rabid pets, 255
race, job discrimination because of, 308–309
radio equipment insurance, 73
railroad workers, 358
rape, 532–533